I0816097

DISCOMANIA

FANTASTIC BEATS AND WHERE TO FIND THEM

ALAN JONES

Dedication

Thanks to Diego, Dario and Disco for my life in 3D

DISCOMANIA

FANTASTIC BEATS AND WHERE TO FIND THEM

First edition published by FAB Press, March 2025

FAB Press Ltd., 2 Farleigh, Ramsden Road, Godalming, Surrey, GU7 1QE, England, UK
www.fabpress.com

Written by Alan Jones
Edited by Harvey Fenton
Picture research, page design and layout by Kevin Coward
Cover design by Jason Heeley
Indexes and additional research by Francis Brewster

Acknowledgement for visual material is due to the following organisations and individuals:
A&E Indiefilms, A&M Records, Alemannia, Allied Artists, Alpha France, Altimeter Films, American International Pictures, Amiga, Amoeba Film, Anglo Amalgamated, Aquarius, Ariola, Ariston, Artoc Corporate Services, Associated British-Pathé, Atlantic, ATV Music, Aura Films, AVCO Embassy Pictures, AVL, Baby Records, Barclay Discques, BBC, BBC Films, Beam Junction, Bell, Bellaphon Records, BFI, BGP International, Big Time Company Ltd., Billboard Publications, Black Fawn Distribution, Blood Window, Blue Dolphin, Boogie Man Film Ltd., Brent Walker, Buddah Records, Butterfly Records, Canal+, Cannon Films, Capitol Records, Capstone, Caramel Films, Carrere, Casablanca Record and FilmWorks, Casell & Co, Castle Rock Entertainment, CBS, Cecchi Gori, Chrysalis, CIC, Cine 2000, Cinefantastique, Cinema Features, Cinema-Vu Productions, Cinerama Releasing, Cineriz, Cinevista, Cinevox, CNR Records, Columbia Pictures, Compass International Pictures, Constantin Film, Consul International Films, Creole Records, Crone Film, Crystal Film Productions, Daily News, Daniel Frazier, David Dagley, Davis Films, De-Lite Records, Disco Times International, Disques ibach, Dogwoof, Dollface, Durango Pictures, Electrola, Embassy Home Entertainment, EMI, Epic, Epic Productions, Eskwad, Especial Discotecas, Euro International Films, Evening News, Faber & Faber, Fantasy Records, Fidélité, Film Colony, Film Ventures International, FilmFour, Filmways Australasian Distributors, Forum magazine, Fox 2000 Pictures, Freepik.com, FrightFest, Generation International Pictures, Genesius Productions, GMG, GMHC, Gold Mind Records, Gramercy Pictures, GTO Films, Gypsy Frog Records, Hammer Films, Hand in Hand Films, Hansa Records, Harmony Records, HarperCollins Publishers, Harvest, HBO, Hero Entertainment, Heron Communications, Hickmar Productions, High Fashion Music, Hoyts Distribution, Icon Film Distribution, IIF, Imagine Entertainment, Impulse, Independent Artists, Intermedia Films, Intramovies, Island Records, Jet Records, Johnson Publications, Julie Edwards Photography, Jupiter Records, K-tel, Key Video, KGA/Inter Planetary Curb, Kino Lorber, Kismet Entertainment Group, Latent Image/Specific Films, Les Films Jacques-Leitienne, Let In Shine, LGM Cinema, Lollipop Records, London Records, Longstar, Lorimar Distribution International, M. Hoffman & Co., Machaco Films, Madeleine Films, Malligator, Marlin Records, Maroon Entertainment, MCA Records, Medusa Distribuzione, Mercury, Metro-Goldwyn-Mayer, Metronome Records, Metropol, MGM/UA, Miracle International, Miramax, Moby Dick Records, Mondial, Morrow, Motown, Mustang Entertainment, Myriad Pictures, Neon, New Line Cinema, New Realm Distributors, New World Pictures, New York magazine, Ocean Records, October Films, Orlando Records, Outplay Films, Palace Pictures, Paramount Pictures, Park Circus, Passion Pictures, Pathé, Penta Film, Penthouse Films, Philips, Photofest, Pickwick, Playbill magazine, Polydor, Polygram Filmed Entertainment, Portman Film, Prelude Records, Prestige, Private Stock Records, Pye Records, Radar Film, Rampix, Rare Earth Records, Rastar Films, Ray Stevenson, RCA, RCA Victor, Record Mirror, Redeemable Features, Remstar, Rene Chateau Video, Rizzoli Film, Robert Crumb, Rogue Pictures, Ronco, Rook Films, RSO Records, Salsoul Records, Sanrio Communications, Scarlett Editions, Seagull Records, Seven Keys Films, Shady Films, Shivers magazine, Shock Xpress, Showtime Australia, Shutterstock, Silvio Berlusconi Communications, Simcom, Sirocco, Sirus International Films, Smart Egg Pictures, Sola Media, Sony, Sophie Dulac Distribution, Starburst Publishing Ltd., Starfix magazine, Stax Records, Stefano Film, Stellor Films, Studiocanal, Sunday Mirror, T.K. Productions, Tamla Motown, Target International, TCB Film, Teen Beat, Teen Records, TF1 Films, Thames & Hudson, The Group 1 International Distribution Organization, The Little Film Company, The Pharaoh's Company Ltd., The Sun, Timpson Films, Titanus, Touchstone Pictures, Trans-American Films, Turbine Films, Twentieth Century-Fox, United Artists, Universal, Universal City Studios, Universal Pictures, Vampix, Vestron, Victor, Videomedia, Vidmark Entertainment, Virgin Films, Vogue Records, Volker Stox, Walt Disney Productions, Warner Bros., Warren Magazines, Warwick, WEA, West Eleven Films, West End Records, Westbound, Wicked Simian, Wild Bunch, World Wide Films, Yellow Rose, Z-Films, Zeitgeist Films, ZYX Music

Printed in Czech Republic

A CIP catalogue record for this book is available from the British Library

ISBN 978-1-913051-37-2

FANTASTIC BEATS AND WHERE TO FIND THEM

ALAN JONES

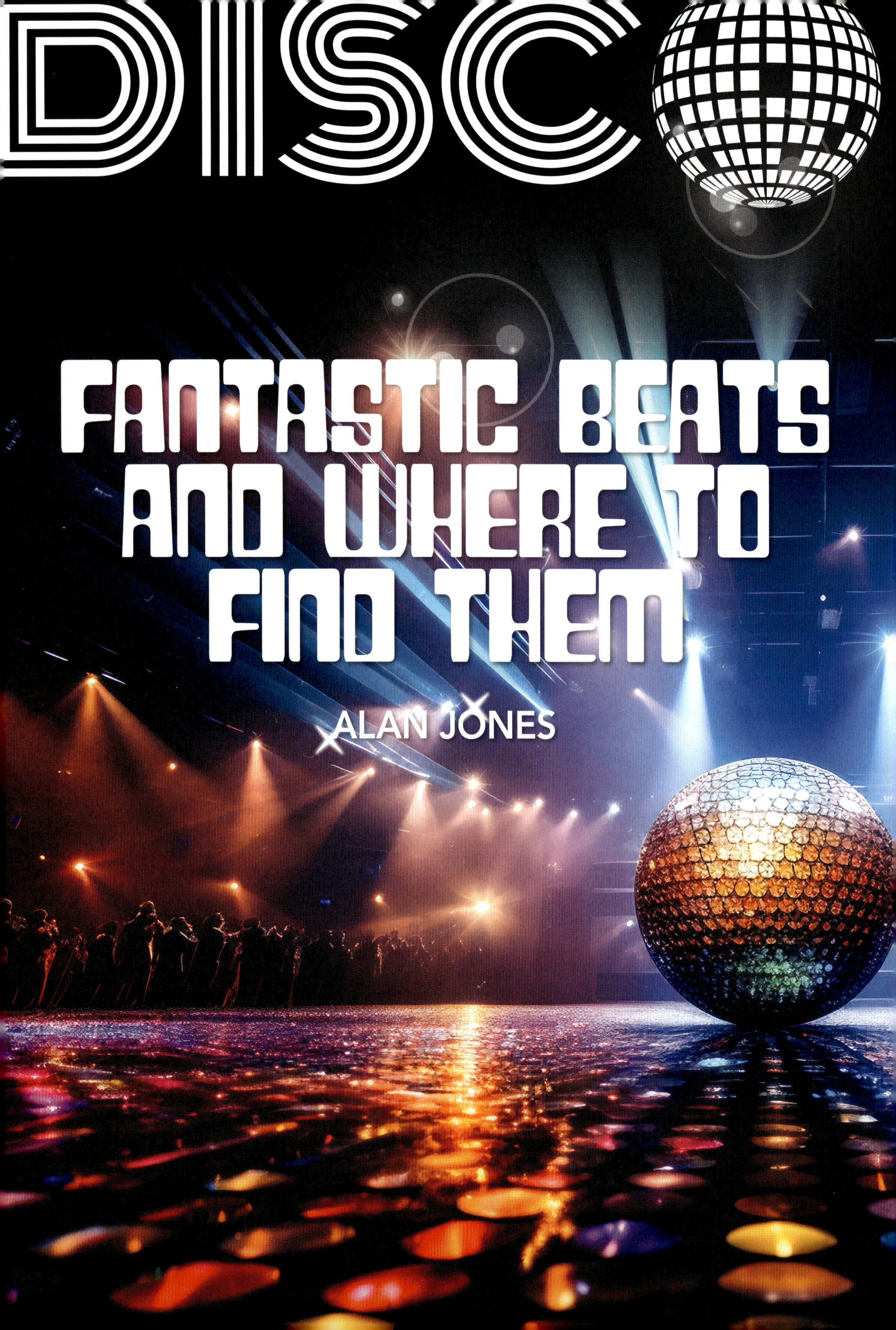
DISCO
FANTASTIC BEATS AND WHERE TO FIND THEM
ALAN JONES

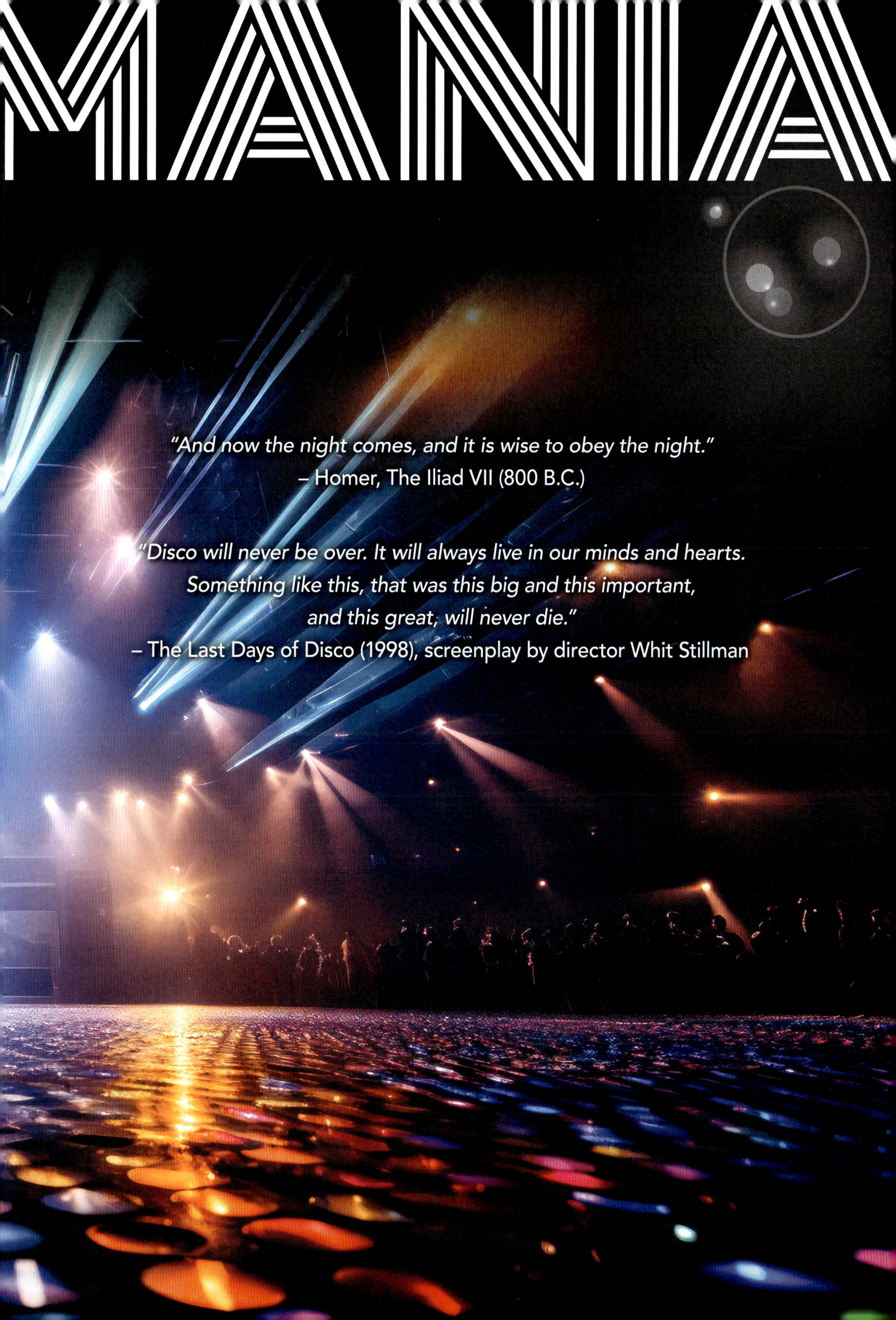
MANIA
"And now the night comes, and it is wise to obey the night."
– Homer, The Iliad VII (800 B.C.)
"Disco will never be over. It will always live in our minds and hearts. Something like this, that was this big and this important, and this great, will never die."
– The Last Days of Disco (1998), screenplay by director Whit Stillman

DISCOMANIA
The Last Days o
DISCO

FOREWORD

by Mark Moore (S'Express frontman and mega-star DJ)

How I love an Alan Jones book, almost as much as the man himself. I first met Alan when I was a bored teenager and visited the Forbidden Planet 2 shop, which had opened in St. Giles High Street, London. I swear Alan rolled his eyes on first seeing me in one of my charity-shop-bought-and-altered, post-punk, futurist looks. I would frequent the place often when bored. I vaguely remember sitting on the counter, smoking a cigarette with one of the shop assistants (a girl named Merlin) and being sternly told off by Alan. It was quite terrifying. Besides that, Alan mainly ignored me but one day I knew he was warming to my charms when he glanced up at me, sneered and slowly looked away.

At the time Alan was also writing the most wonderful horror and fantasy film reviews for 'Starburst' magazine. I took that sneer to be an offer of friendship and would pick Alan's brains about new and old movies, feeling blessed that I had access to the prophet. Basically he was trapped in the shop and couldn't get away from my endless questions – but secretly I think Alan enjoyed the fact that I was an AJ acolyte. The deal was sealed on us becoming real friends much later when I got my first hit record and moved to Maida Vale, coincidentally just around the corner from Alan. There was no escaping me now.

Music wise, Alan had got tired of Punk and had returned to his Disco roots, something which I also became obsessed with as soon as I was old enough to go clubbing – albeit a few years after Disco was declared 'dead' by the critics. Those people didn't get it and could only see the crass commercialism that lay on the surface – not the actual beauty and the glittering ritual of the nightlife world. **Saturday Night Fever** and the Bee Gees (as wonderful as they were) – along with a horde of bandwagon jumpers – changed the image of Disco into something very white, very straight and commercially omnipresent – far from its underground gay and multi-cultural roots. People chased it out of town like the Frankenstein monster. Racism and homophobia also played a part. The mass conflagration of Disco records at Disco Demolition Night in a baseball stadium in Chicago, Illinois had people burning records by black musicians who weren't even Disco artists!

However, little did those critics know that Disco would never die but would carry on in various mutated forms, along with the original sounds still being played around the world in clubs and festivals today. Not only has Disco been exonerated, it has now been given full respect as an important genre of music. The movement that began in the underground gay/black/Hispanic/mixed clubs of the 1970s continues to spread joy, not only for the Queer youth of now but for people of all ages and sexual persuasions.

Meanwhile in Maida Vale, not only can I harass Alan about Punk, horror movies, cult films and Dario Argento but I can also go round Alan's house and have him play me wonderful Disco tunes that I've never heard before. Sometimes he'll even let me take a few tunes home. My dream is that one day I will finally get to see the entirety of his rare vinyl collection stashed away in his home, in a secret locked room. This new book by Alan already has my head spinning with a mine of filmic and Disco delights – so much of which I knew nothing about. A historical delight merging chic and un-chic celluloid, grinding grooves and pounding bangers.

Thank you Alan Jones – the Oracle of Horror, Punk and Disco.

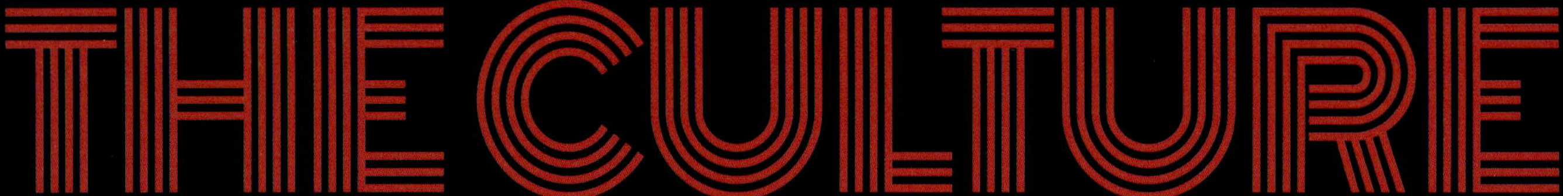

I tried to keep them apart. I really did. But Punk was inevitably subsumed by Funk in the mid 1970s for this seminal Sex Pistols original who worked in Vivienne Westwood's World's End Chelsea shop SEX. That is, until the tax inspectors arrived, Vivienne panicked, and I had to pretend to be a punter for as long as they were on the premises. I was also the one who got arrested for wearing that iconic naked cowboy dicks-almost-touching T-shirt in my most famous 1976 headline grabbing moment. And if I had a pound for every time I've seen those pictures of me, Steve Jones, Vivienne, Jordan, future Pretenders band leader Chrissie Hynde and Jones's fuck-du-jour revealingly modelling Vivienne's latest swanky modes, posed for the June 1976 pocket erotica magazine 'Forum', well, I wouldn't ever have had to work again.

As much as Punk's free spirit and rebellious nature matched my own coming-of-age in those fabulous sea-changing times, I always held on to my inner Disco Queen that surfaced in 1973 when I first heard *Love's Theme* by the Love Unlimited Orchestra at Studio One in Los Angeles. With **Pink Flamingos** (1972) star Divine. But that's a story for later. I mean I was an anarchist and all that. But I was also an in-your-face-way-out-of-the-closet homosexual too, and although many early Pistols fans – the Bromley Contingent – were gay, we found it easier to never mind each other's bollocks. I probably could have shagged my mate Sid Vicious if I'd pressed hard enough. But even at this early stage you could see No Future there.

So where else was an insatiable fashion slag going to get laid? At The Catacombs in Earl's Court or The Sombrero in High Street Kensington, the main gay clubs in pre-AIDS hedonistic London. That meant listening to such DJs as the camp one we called Pamela Motown and his constant diet of Tina Charles, Diana Ross and Thelma Houston with a pounding 4/4 beat, gorgeous Eurovision melodies and swirling violins. It came with the territory because the swooping sexual innuendo and epic tragedy contained in such classic Disco tracks as Grace Jones's *I Need a Man* (1975), Donna Summer's *I Feel Love* (1977), and Gloria Gaynor's *I Will Survive* (1978) emotionally hit the hardest. Those songs mirrored exactly the posing, ego-deifying and self-protective components of the contemporary gay psyche and lifestyle.

Much as I loved Johnny Rotten angrily barking hot-button lyrics backed by the snarling Pistols' dynamic presence, I also adored the glamour-drenched Broadway style glitz of The Salsoul Orchestra, anything on the Casablanca Records label and every Disco Diva from Penny McLean and Madleen Kane to Linda Clifford and Marlena Shaw. Nobody could understand that at the time. Music genres back then were very clearly defined and pigeonholed. You were a Hippie, a Glam Rocker, a Skinhead, a retro Mod or Rocker and you were only into what your demographic inflexibly liked. Dislikes, meaning everybody else's likes, were equally rigid. Today an eclectic musical palette is culturally responsible and socially sensible. In 1975 that distinct lack of crossover was the cause of the beginning of the end for the Pistols bass guitarist Glen Matlock when he told Rotten he'd like to play songs by The Who in their set. I found myself in the weirdest position around this time.

Championing the Pistols' ground zero sound, which many said was tuneless noise, while defending Disco's hypnotic thumping for practically the same reasons. In many ways my infamous DJ gig for the Pistols at the equally memorable El Paradise strip club event in Soho should have marked my exit from their favoured inner circle. It didn't, mainly because I was one of their first supporters, who fed them during my nightshifts at the Portobello Hotel, the watering hole of the rich and famous back then. I still remember Mick Jagger walking through the door eyeing the band lounging on the sofas with incredulity. And the cast of **Star Wars** (1977) asking me who these ruffians were! I was also one of the few who could put up with their constant bickering. There was guilt too over my banner T-shirt arrest. I had to face that courtroom totally alone and pay a £15 fine I could ill-afford despite Malcolm McLaren promising to hire a lawyer and get me off. That was prophetic in hindsight. Whenever there was trouble, Malcolm disappeared. I'd taken the fall for promoting their lifestyle so what did my Disco lifestyle matter between friends.

I tell any TV researcher or journalist wanting my input on this truly exciting time – where the attitude shifts were palpable, the paranoid heaviness surrounding us absolutely thrilling – that the Punk movement was only ever the Sex Pistols for me. They were the first, the last, my everything, the rest were mere pretenders. Except Buzzcocks, but that was because lead singer Pete Shelley was the only Punk I ever really fancied. Vivienne's clothes were another reason I remained part of this crazy world. I could always score in her designs. She used gay porno images, see-through rubber, bondage motifs, leather, zips and suggestive rips

Who knew this picture for the contact mag 'Forum' and shot in SEX would go the distance and define my Punk image from here to eternity! From left to right, Sex Pistol Steve Jones, his squeeze at the time Danielle Lewis, Alan Jones (in the original Perv T-shirt constructed with chicken bones), Pretender Chrissie Hynde, Queen of Punk Jordan and iconic designer Vivienne Westwood.

Picture credit: © David Dagley_Shutterstock

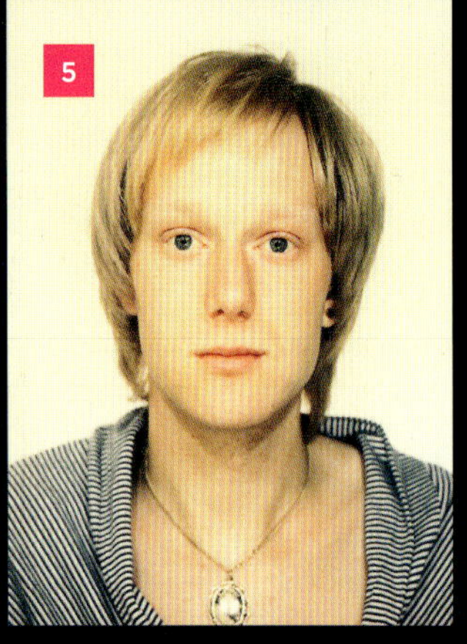

that bordered on fetish wear. Many were the times my famously bee-hived shop assistant Jordan and I had to stop elderly gentlemen masturbating in the SEX changing rooms for mistaking the basic ethos of our fashion emporium. In this respect Vivienne was way ahead of the Village People macho look that would sweep the Gay Disco world in late 1977. She's never acknowledged that though or ever been credited with it. Best to remain counterculture couture star than admit to influencing the era's most despised mass market. So when I started segueing to that Giorgio Moroder synthesized alternate universe in mirrorball reaction to the horrendous police violence ending the 'God Save the Queen' Jubilee boat party in 1977, I could still get away with wearing three seasons old Westwood evening ensembles.

I stayed friendly with the band. Glen remains my next-street neighbour after all these years and I last saw the others when Nils Stevenson, the friend I had recommended to Malcolm as the ideal Pistols manager, died suddenly. My two other famous Punk signatures were still a few years away; appearing in Julien Temple's **The Great Rock 'n' Roll Swindle** (1980) and helping director Alex Cox with his research for **Sid and Nancy** (1986) as I was close to the couple in their downward spiral.

But I wasn't sorry to turn my back on *No Feelings* (1977) for *No More Tears* (1979). Enough was enough! The initial burst of enthusiasm when everything seemed possible got more depressing by the minute walking past part-time

1. At age 4 with grandmother Mabel Weston.
2. Alan Jones in Southsea 1966.
3. Alan in Alkasura hot pants for men.
4. Alan age 8.
5. Alan in 1970.
6. Alan in LA, 1973.
7. In Bowie make-up for a Japanese magazine.
8. Alan wearing SEX rubber top at the Portobello Hotel.

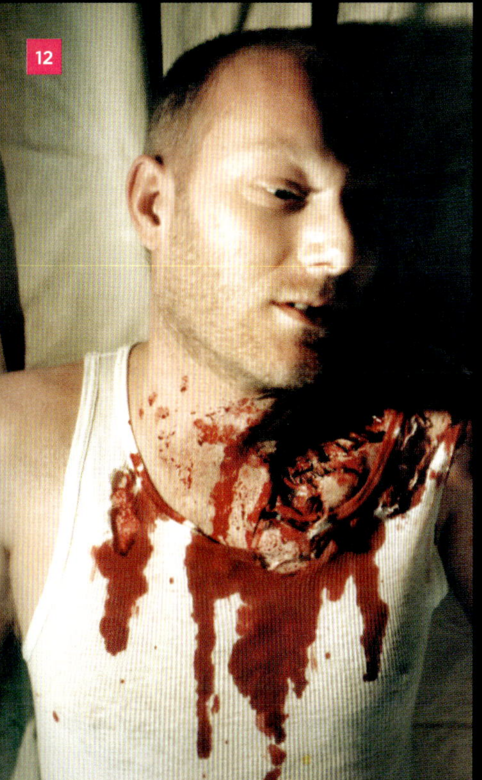

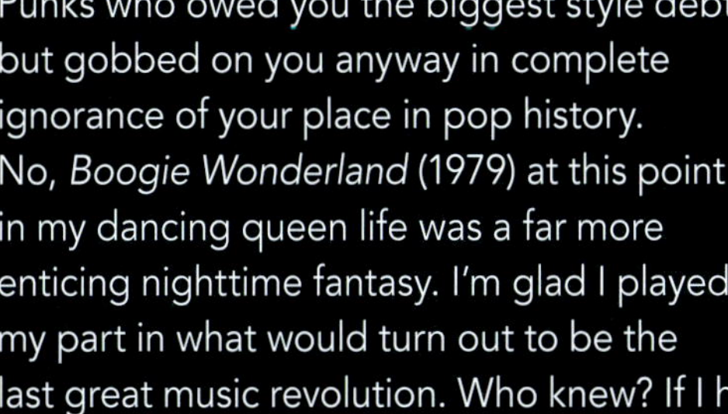

Punks who owed you the biggest style debt but gobbed on you anyway in complete ignorance of your place in pop history. No, *Boogie Wonderland* (1979) at this point in my dancing queen life was a far more enticing nighttime fantasy. I'm glad I played my part in what would turn out to be the last great music revolution. Who knew? If I had I would have taken more candid photos so I could earn all the money those one-time hangers-on still do. I did take snapshots of my massive Disco achievement, producing the Carmen Rollers roller-disco pantomime 'Cinderoller' at London's Empire Ballroom. You try getting ten stoned drag queens to skate in time to the Disco version of *Evita* (1979). But who cares about that now in political context?

I consider myself very lucky in having had one foot firmly in each music strand characterising extreme sides of the same amazing era. I'm not saying I expected that to happen. Or that I'd go on to embody and proudly uphold the memory of both contrasts. Yet Punk and Disco continue to creatively and positively impact on the music scene so I'm more than happy to do so. Any regrets about worshipping at the dual hymn altars society then so despised? Just one. I wish I could have seen Rotten's face and said "I told you so" when he finally realised *I Will Survive* would become equally important historically as *Anarchy in the U.K.* (1976).

9. Alan in Norman J. Warren's *Terror* (1978).
10. No idea what this is from but it's all about the outfit.
11. Sometime in the 90s when power suits from Milan were the thing.
12. Make-up artist Ian Brown applied this prosthetic for photos I used as my business card.
13. Roller Disco Sunday afternoons in Battersea Park circa 1981.
14. Alan at the 2001 Odyssey Disco location for *Saturday Night Fever* in Brooklyn.
15. Alan outside a Disco in Helsinki, Finland.

Steve Jones, Alan Jones (no relation!) and my great friend Nils Stevenson, for whom I got the job of managing the Sex Pistols.
(Photo courtesy of Ray Stevenson)

When I thought I was going to work for David Bowie's MainMan organisation and run his fan club.

TOGETHER BROTHERS
BARRY WHITE
LOVE UNLIMITED · THE LOVE UNLIMITED ORCHESTRA
Marvin Gaye
special disco
Got To Give It Up Pt. I+II
K.C. and the Sunshine Band
GET DOWN TONIGHT
YOU DON'T KNOW
ANITA WARD RING MY BELL
CERRONE
Love In C Minor
love and kisses
SATURDAY NIGHT FEVER
Lipstique
PATTIE BROOKS
THE SALSOUL ORCHESTRA
DONNA SUMMER
I Feel Love
TINA CHARLES
I Love To Love
MADLEEN KANE
Rough Diamond
ROXY ROLLER
VOYAGE
ANDREA TRUE CONNECTION
MORE MORE MORE
FROM HERE TO ETERNITY
GIORGIO
BACCARA
Parlez-vous français?
Amoureux
MAXI-SINGLE
SYLVESTER
You Make Me Feel (Mighty Real)
SUPER SOUND
DISCO '77
Lime
YOUR LOVE
THE RITCHIE FAMILY
BAD REPUTATION
BOYS TOWN GANG
CAN'T TAKE MY EYES OFF YOU
Singin' In The Rain
Sheila B. Devotion
LOVE ME BABY
CHARO AND THE SALSOUL ORCHESTRA
The Weather Girls
It's Raining Men
STEVIE WONDER
ANOTHER STAR
BORIS MIDNEY
EMPIRE STRIKES BACK
MARLENA SHAW
Let Me In Your Life
TOM HOOKER
FLIP OVER
RADIORAMA
DESIRES AND VAMPIRES
TARZAN BOY
BALTIMORA
AMIGA
LADY BUMP
PENNY McLEAN
KEEP ON JUMP IN'
Musique
THE HUSTLE
Van McCOY
THE SOUL CITY SYMPHONY

THE MUSIC

Long before you heard it, you could feel it – a throbbing, pounding beat that seemed to visually pulse through walls and vibrate in the air as it echoed out of brightly lit club entrances up from dingy stairwells past cloakrooms. Then you perceived that unmistakable sound, a four-on-the-floor base drum thump, thump, thump, thump, pushed through a bank of state-of-the-art speakers that grew even louder as you inescapably moved towards its increasingly eardrum-shattering source like a hypnotised moth to a scorching flame. That's when the evocative multi-coloured light shapes hit you full in the face; a giddy *demimonde* of human spirals captured by reflecting facets of spinning mirror globes. Gyrating flashes freeze-framed in strobe effects, swallowed up in a swirling galaxy of ultraviolet stars. Kaleidoscopic revolving puddles of the rainbow flitted from vivid intensity to deep shadow. Suddenly dry ice smoke effects engulfed you, obscuring the stiletto heels, trainers and platform shoes in a shroud of sparkling fog. Out of which the disembodied weaving crowd warmly beckoned you into their swaying, sweating midst and the room became a boogie wonderland pulsating with one accord. The deafening music never stopped, not for a single moment. From the second the tribal throb moved from suspended tweeters and woofers to vibrate your rib cage, it continued relentlessly until the gathering dejectedly dispersed into dawn's early light.

Selection of mix tapes 1976–86

Welcome to the world of Disco, more importantly *my* world of Disco, where the fabulous music has never stopped playing and my all-time favourite tracks take a bow. It defined a whole generation and fanatical latecomers to the 1970s pleasure-seeking party who now revere its importance. Die-hard devotees who loved the atmosphere, the fun and the thrill of the circus environment so much it became the enduring soundtrack of their lives! Who came to appreciate the double irony contained in the title of the all-time classic Disco anthem *I Will Survive* (1978) – when everyone who really should have known better said it wouldn't!

Who wouldn't have been caught dead wearing the dazzling white three-piece suit or glitter boob tube of popular polyester myth! Because the soaring melodies, harmonies and tunes were so powerful, so fantastic and so epic in emotional outline that more than forty years after **Saturday Night Fever** (1977) spawned international dance mania and a culture change on a massive scale, Disco is still here, there and everywhere.

The quickest way to get a party started? Segue from *Y.M.C.A.* (1978) by the Village People to *The Hustle* (1975) by Van McCoy and then *Le Freak* (1978) by Chic. Adverts, television and most significantly films know how to instantly summon up a feel-good ambience, and that's to turn the Disco music up loud! How many commercials have used the all-time Eurodisco cliché-turned-Tartan-Army-football anthem *Yes Sir, I Can Boogie* (1977) by Baccara to flog their product? Not to mention the countless movies and TV series putting a stereo needle drop to a nightlife classic as a quick way to evoke a precise period or atmosphere. A few examples: **Charlie's Angels** (2000) obviously featuring *Heaven Must Be Missing an Angel* (1976) by Tavares, **American Made** (2017) incorporating The Royal Philharmonic's *Hooked on Classics Parts 1 & 2* (1981) in a major montage, 'It's a Sin' (2021) using the same track and 'The Get Down' (2016) and 'Mrs. America' (2020) evoking Walter Murphy's *A Fifth of Beethoven* (1976).

Disco was a glamour-packed fantasy universe, a 'Funk Encounter' of the best kind, a reaction against the grimy and depressing reality that lay beyond the walls of your smoke-and-mirrors club cocoon. A world of sexuality and sensuality, romance and rapture, escapism and playfulness, Hollywood and hedonism – an unreal and often surreal

cosmos splashed before a background of lush vocal and orchestral manoeuvres in the dark. The Disco movement – and it definitely was a movement because the community spirit it engendered became a global calling card for many acolytes – changed the way people spent their time and money, how they dressed and lived. For after a decade of Beatlemania, Bubblegum, Flower Power and Glam Rock, music went from headtrip to hips and feet again as dancing took on a cultural magnitude not seen since the Depression era of the 1930s.

You went to the Discotheque – and French film director Roger Vadim has laid claim to coining the word – to celebrate the good things in life and to forget the bad ones. For a couple of hours a week, or day depending on how affected you were by the all-encompassing lifestyle trend, you could let it all hang out, let the lyrical dream take hold, let your body move to the pulsating rhythm and push out everything else. Everyone needed a little nightworld addiction in their lives and they found its electric heartbeat on the flashing floors.

In Disco Land, bizarre costumes and exotic masquerade mingled with haute couture and celebrity chic to create a unique fashion pack milieu that was part showbiz, part café society, part carnival, part catwalk and part Twilight Zone. Beautiful People bumped into construction workers, the Jet Set mingled with suburban secretaries on the floorshow stage where none were spectators and all were players, forsaking their normal mundane responsibilities in the pursuit of pleasure, sensation and Disco dedication. It was where celebrities came to be nobodies as they anonymously mixed with the hustling throng. It was where nobodies came to enjoy the glitterati experience for a brief moment doing their spectacular thing: a dazzling step, a sexy routine, a shimmering move.

Disco showed no ageist, sexist or racist bias as a result. Mainly because it had originated in the black, Hispanic and gay inner-city communities, during the peak Disco years every minority demographic came together in an explosion of mutual admiration and trust in the bass line. For whatever age, colour or sexual preference, everyone had one thing in common – a compelling desire to shed their inhibitions in a celebration of uninterrupted music and perpetual motion. No matter what underlying reason you had to Disco – great exercise, stress relief, fantasy trip, ego posing or social interaction – at no other time in dance history did so many participate so forcefully in a musical ethos. For Disco signalled the way ahead. For liberation and tolerance. It was a revolution, a people movement for the blissed-out and one that set a hopeful blueprint for future society.

Although nascent elements can be traced back to the Tamla Motown sound of the Swinging Sixties, Manu Dibango's Afro-Lounge stormer *Soul Makossa* in 1972 is considered the very first Disco record. There is a case for *Dance to the Music* by Sly and the Family Stone from 1968 showing the earliest signs of the lavish percussion that would typify the Disco genre though. More lush than Soul Music, easier on the ear than Hard Rock, Disco weaves together a tapestry of musical styles. From Big Band swing and Broadway jazz hands pizzazz and rhythm and blues to funkateering, via luxurious string arrangements, bold brass construction and sweetly sung chorals. And at the 125 beats-per-minute heart of this eclectic mix is the rhythm – an up-tempo, heavy, straight 4/4 time that goes directly to the feet to guide them like a metronome.

Disco proper took off in 1973 with *The Love I Lost* by Harold Melvin and the Blue Notes, the chart topping *Rock the Boat* by The Hues Corporation, *Love's Theme* by The Love Unlimited Orchestra and *Rock Your Baby* by George McCrae. Philadelphia International, Salsoul, T.K., Westend, Prelude, Solar, Lollipop and especially Casablanca were just some of the influential record labels that fuelled the largely urban American trend. Until the newly syncopated sound started firing the creative juices of European composers, intensifying the melodic movement and thematic flow of the music, and producers like Giorgio Moroder became one of the key architects of the idiom with his muse Donna Summer.

Disco as a genre was also further shaped by American studio engineer Tom Moulton, who pioneered the remixing and extending of a track, complete with break section, to cater to nightclub preferences. By popular consensus the first was *I'll Be Holding On* (1974) by Al Downing, actually an experimental 10-inch disc, before the 12-inch single format innovation became the norm as the result of Discophiles wanting the most out of their favourite songs. Moulton found further Disco immortality with Gloria Gaynor's seminal *Never Can Say Goodbye* (1975), the first continuous-mix album side ever. David Mancuso was another re-mixer who added his own pioneering twist to Disco by initiating the 'Invitation Only' parties to his own home that soon became known as The Loft, a concept that would eventually transform the entire DJ network and crystallise the club business model.

Disco showcased the most adept and professional singers around, both already famous and just starting out, while consistently changing with the times, keeping up to date with the latest trends in production techniques and giving rise to an unprecedented commercial saturation that revolutionised the entire recording industry. All achieved on the way to becoming one of the most enduring catalogues of music in pop history and all explored in this highly personal guide to the way film started using Disco music, commandeering the phenomenon to craft the most popular titles in the genre and still using it today as easy shorthand for mood and comment.

On September 13th, 1973, 'Rolling Stone' magazine published an article written by future Disco legend Vince Aletti that tried to get to grips with the burgeoning social happening being caused by this new-fangled thing called Disco music. Commenting on the rise of after hours clubs taking place in old ballrooms, converted restaurants, juice bars and aforementioned lofts, Aletti listed the records every wannabe DJ should have in their collection to get people up and strutting their stuff. Pointing out that while many of his inclusions were broken in the Discotheque environment – *Love Train* (1972) by The O'Jays, *I'll Always Love My Mama* (1973) by The Intruders and *Yes We Can Can* (1973) by The Pointer Sisters, and became huge chart hits – nothing compared to their continued popularity on the dance floor. Others, he noted, lived and died in the Disco milieu, like *Doing It to Death Parts 1 & 2* (1973) by The J.B.'s, *Composite Truth* (1972) by Mandrill, *Barrabas* (1972) by Barrabas, *Let's Do It Again* (1972) by The Fatback Band and, *Slick* and *Brother's Gonna Work It Out* from the soundtrack of The Mack (1973).

And this is where my DISCOMANIA begins….

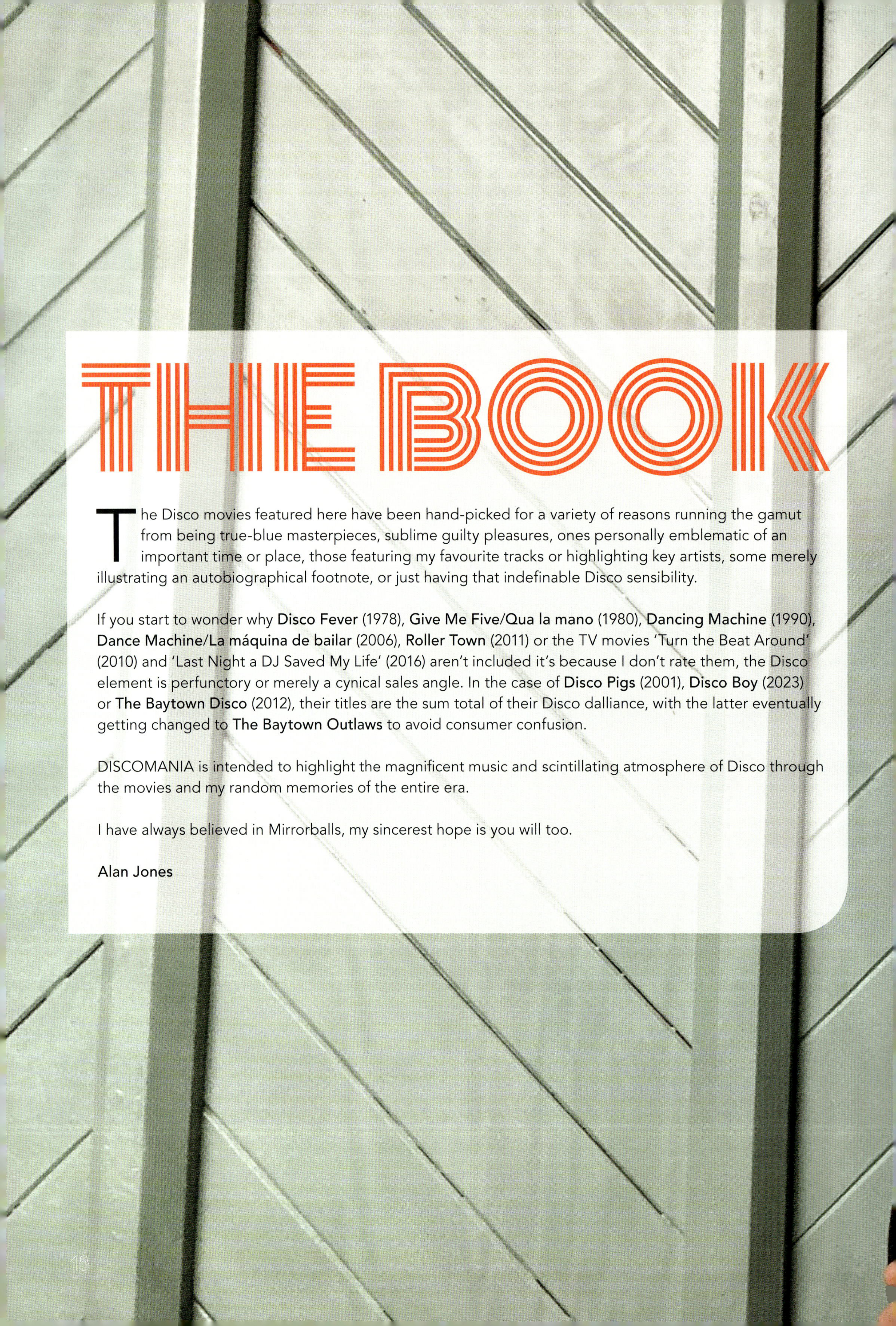

THE BOOK

The Disco movies featured here have been hand-picked for a variety of reasons running the gamut from being true-blue masterpieces, sublime guilty pleasures, ones personally emblematic of an important time or place, those featuring my favourite tracks or highlighting key artists, some merely illustrating an autobiographical footnote, or just having that indefinable Disco sensibility.

If you start to wonder why **Disco Fever** (1978), **Give Me Five/Qua la mano** (1980), **Dancing Machine** (1990), **Dance Machine/La máquina de bailar** (2006), **Roller Town** (2011) or the TV movies 'Turn the Beat Around' (2010) and 'Last Night a DJ Saved My Life' (2016) aren't included it's because I don't rate them, the Disco element is perfunctory or merely a cynical sales angle. In the case of **Disco Pigs** (2001), **Disco Boy** (2023) or **The Baytown Disco** (2012), their titles are the sum total of their Disco dalliance, with the latter eventually getting changed to **The Baytown Outlaws** to avoid consumer confusion.

DISCOMANIA is intended to highlight the magnificent music and scintillating atmosphere of Disco through the movies and my random memories of the entire era.

I have always believed in Mirrorballs, my sincerest hope is you will too.

Alan Jones

TO THE DANCEFLOOR

THE MACK (1973)

Shaft (1971) might have put Blaxploitation on the map and provided the genre with an Oscar-winning anthem by Isaac Hayes but it was a dull Hollywood crime actioner when all was said and done. No, the two defining entries of the Blaxploitation cycle are the socially conscious **Super Fly** (1972) and this Michael Campus directed exploration of the two extremes of the contemporary African-American psyche. You were either a black radical railing against US racism, or you were a dedicated follower of capitalist pimpdom with ghetto fabulous outfits to match. Enter **The Mack**, the title allegedly an Americanization of the French slang word *mec* meaning dude/bloke/guy, offering a cogent portrait of a self-made gangster and the corrupt underworld machinations trying to take him down.

That's John 'Goldie' Mickens (Max Julien, creator of **Cleopatra Jones**, 1973) who, freed from prison after serving a five-year sentence for drug possession, heads back to Oakland, California, to assemble an independent stable of prostitutes. First stop is the local pool hall where his mentor The Blind Man (Paul Harris, **Across 110th Street**, 1972) gives him invaluable pimping lessons that basically boil down to get the best looking girls, brainwash

them into indulging his every whim and then work them into the ground. With his motor-mouth best friend Slim (future comic superstar Richard Pryor) on board the soul-destroying train, Goldie makes childhood girlfriend Lulu (Carol Speed, **Abby**, 1974) his 'bottom bitch' and recruits an impressive pussy posse that makes him rich and infamous.

But his rise to the lofty heights of winning the coveted Mack of the Year Award at the 8th Players Ball is dogged by his religious mother (Juanita Moore, **Imitation of Life**, 1959) wanting him to turn his back on criminality, and his militant Black Nationalist brother Olinga (Roger E. Mosely, **Terminal Island**, 1973), shocked at his profligate lifestyle based on minority oppression. Then there's the two crooked cops Hank (Don Gordon) and Jed (William Watson) framing him for murder, and The Fat Man (George Murdock, **Willie Dynamite**, 1974), a white heroin kingpin jealous of his success, who tries to force Goldie into working for him by pushing his girls to overdose. It all ends in a bloodbath when Goldie's mother dies after a brutal assault and Olinga joins his quest for vengeance.

With street credibility at a premium (actual pimps advised on the picture, dedicated to Frank D. Ward, one who died during production) and a keen political grounding in Black Power, **The Mack** definitely earns its cool status as one of the most referenced and sampled Blaxploiters of its era. Director Campus does exactly what he did in his underrated sci-fi feature debut **Z.P.G. (Zero Population Growth)** (1972) and that's throw the audience into an alternative world where the differences are familiar enough to keep the interest piqued. Then there's the fashion show element – girls in sequined hot pants, feather boas, designer wigs and statement bling, the Macks in velvet brocade suits, extravagant furs, silk shirts, shades, alligator shoes and ivory-topped swagger sticks – and bad-ass attitude that's still prevalent today with this cult movie cited as the main inspiration.

Essentially a cobbled together mass of separately intriguing episodes, the characters and the partly improvised dialogue consistently ring true as a social commentary of the time. As does the soundtrack composed and sung by Willie Hutch, former member of

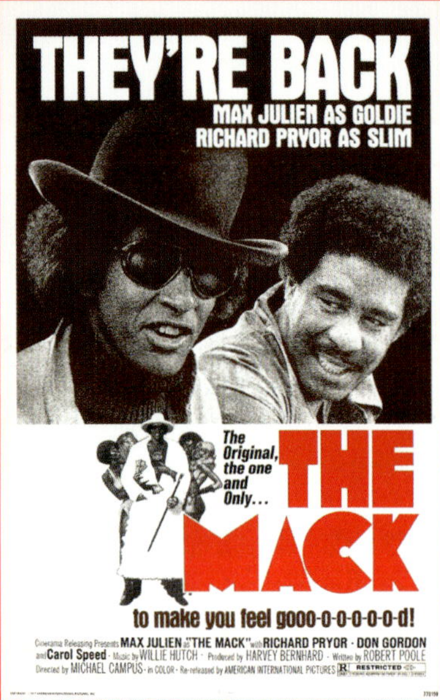

The Ambassadors do-wop group and composer of the hits *Learn How to Fly* (1968) by The 5th Dimension and lyricist on *I'll Be There* (1970) by The Jackson 5. Thanks to the latter platter, Motown head Berry Gordy signed Hutch as a staff writer, arranger, producer, and musician for his iconic label. It was when the proto Disco girl group Sisters Love were offered a cameo in the picture singing their 1970 R&B hit *Now Is the Time* at the Players Ball that their manager suggested his friend Willie Hutch compose the entire soundtrack.

With its earthy lyrics, silky southern soul style, marvellous string and horn arrangements, funky background vocals and Hutch coming across with a groove-tastic Bobby Womack meets Bill Withers vibe, the soundtrack proved to be one of the great 1970s film scores. More importantly, the hard drum and harp infested *Brother's Gonna Work It Out* and the tight, bright *Slick* cuts remained firm club favourites until official Disco charts were launched in October 1974. That's when what music stayed on the dance floor got dictated by countrywide DJs' playlists and listeners responses to the pre-release new, hot and happening becoming the most irresistible draws.

TEXAS
A SPOTLIGHT IN THIS ISSUE

Billboard

NEWSPAPER

80th YEAR

September 7, 1974

U.S. Cutouts Draw Canada's Complaints

Tape 'Hospital' Aids Retailers

Shorter Disks Bring Longer Playlists: Drew

L.A. 'LITTLE GUYS'

Dealers Organize To Battle Giants

Job Security a New Headache For Some

Aussies Next In Line for Acceptance In the States?

RANDY NEWMAN'S NEW ALBUM

ON REPRISE RECORDS AND TAPES

Disco Duck

On October 26, 1974, the leading music trade magazine 'Billboard' published the very first Disco chart based on dancers' reactions in clubs in the New York City area. Thanks to his sterling work on such seminal Disco remixes as MFSB's *Love Is the Message* (1973) and The Three Degrees' *Dirty Ol' Man* (1973) pioneer producer Tom Moulton inscribed a column accompaniment pointing out what was hot and what was not. This chart rundown then splintered into a rotation of charts from other key cities like Chicago and Los Angeles.

Subsequently, on November 16, 1974, Vince Aletti started writing his 'State of the Dance Floor' Disco File column for Record World in direct competition to 'Billboard'. This more comprehensive focus on what clubs were playing nationwide, plus Aletti's informed Disco release reviews, led 'Billboard' to create their first countrywide chart on August 28th, 1976. The National Disco Action Top 30 Chart debuted at the exact time the music was making the biggest mainstream inroads with such crossover cuts as *Cherchez la femme* by Dr. Buzzard's Original Savannah Band, *The Best Disco in Town* medley by The Ritchie Family and most prophetically *You Should Be Dancing* by the Bee Gees.

So anything pre-October 1974, including many now revered Disco classics – e.g. The Hues Corporation's *Rock the Boat* and George McCrae's *Rock Your Baby*, both hits in June 1974 – don't figure in any club-orientated recognition assessments, just the regular pop charts. And the reverse is true of such precursors to **The Mack**. While that film beat Jonathan Kaplan's **Truck Turner** (1974) to the marketplace by two weeks, the black bounty hunter crime thriller did feature the Aletti recommended 9-minute long Disco track *Pursuit of the Pimpmobile* by leading man Isaac Hayes. But while Marvin Gaye's **Trouble Man** (1972), Bobby Womack's **Across 110th Street** (1972) quartet, James Brown's raft of songs from **Black Caesar** (1973), Edwin Starr's title theme from its sequel **Hell Up in Harlem** (1973), Curtis Mayfield's **Super Fly** (1972) and **Claudine** (1974) – the latter sung by Gladys Knight and the Pips – or The Impressions' four contributions to **Three the Hard Way** (1974) proved ghetto-blaster beloved, it is hard to ascertain outside of dance-witness testimonials if they had the chops to cut it back in the earliest Discopolitan days.

The Bride of Ravenstein

Being employed at the Portobello Hotel (22 Stanley Gardens, London W11 2NG) for many years during the 1970s meant I met and hung out with countless world famous figures of that epochal era. It was a life-changing job working the midnight shift. I met them all, from pop royalty ABBA, the Eagles, the Faces, Roxy Music and Queen and celebrity writers Jean Rhys and Harlan Ellison, to movie stars Ryan O'Neal, Richard Dreyfuss, Jack Nicholson, the entire **Star Wars** (1977) cast, Jessica Harper, Paloma Picasso, Yves Saint Laurent, Elio Fiorucci, Jim Henson and his Muppet crew. There was no part of the media, fashion, music or art world I didn't have a massive in with. The Notting Hill Gate glitterati watering hole was where German actor Horst Janson lived when shooting Hammer's **Captain Kronos: Vampire Hunter** (1974), where **Race with the Devil** (1974) director Jack Starrett stayed while doing press junkets on that B-movie favourite, where Bob Fosse's **Cabaret** (1972) chorus line taught me all of Liza Minnelli's dance moves and where Maria Schneider and I connected on a more profound level when she filmed Michelangelo Antonioni's **The Passenger** (1975) just around the corner in Ladbroke Grove.

The Portobello was the place singer Carly Simon asked me into her room to listen to the first pressing of her massive global hit *You're So Vain* (1972). Where future 'The Rocky Horror Show' star Nell Campbell tap-danced on the lounge tables. Where a creative consultant on **Grease** (1978), a member of John Lennon's back-up band Elephant's Memory and a former member of the Bay City Rollers invited me into their rooms for entirely different reasons altogether! And it was where I first heard George McCrae's seismic *Rock Your Baby* way before any DJ did in the UK.

Many supermodels of the day made the Portobello their destination of choice when it came to luxury living. One of these was Apollonia Van Ravenstein, the Dutch beauty named 'The Face of 1970' who would eventually grace the covers of 'Vogue' and Andy Warhol's 'Interview'. In late 1973 Apollonia was in London to shoot **The Great Gatsby** (1974) party scenes as director Jack Clayton wanted that style of glamorous extra wallpaper. Knowing I was a Discotheque enthusiast – Disco not yet being common parlance back then – she brought over a white label vinyl disc of a new record a hip DJ friend of hers had passed on, raving about its surefire success. We literally danced to *Rock Your Baby* continuously all night long in an encapsulation of what would eventually happen worldwide.

Alan Jones attending a Chelsea wedding with best friend at the time Michael. Wearing a 'Stupid Cupid' jewelled T-shirt from Mr. Freedom and an early Alkasura design brocade and satin jacket... and Glam Rock make-up!

Alan Jones with newly wed Vanessa Yamauchi at her bridal party in the Portobello Hotel restaurant. Vanessa married Tetsu from the Faces, a band who stayed a lot at the hotel when touring. Alan is wearing an outfit created by designer Jean Seal inspired by *The Great Gatsby* (1974).

Top to bottom: More wedding party photos of Tetsu and Vanessa Yamauchi at the Portobello Hotel. Vanessa worked in the kitchen at the hotel and met The Faces bass guitarist when he was a permanent guest. The top Alan is wearing under his *Great Gatsby* onesie is a classic SEX original, a woollen, long-sleeved shirt with black leatherette gloves attached.

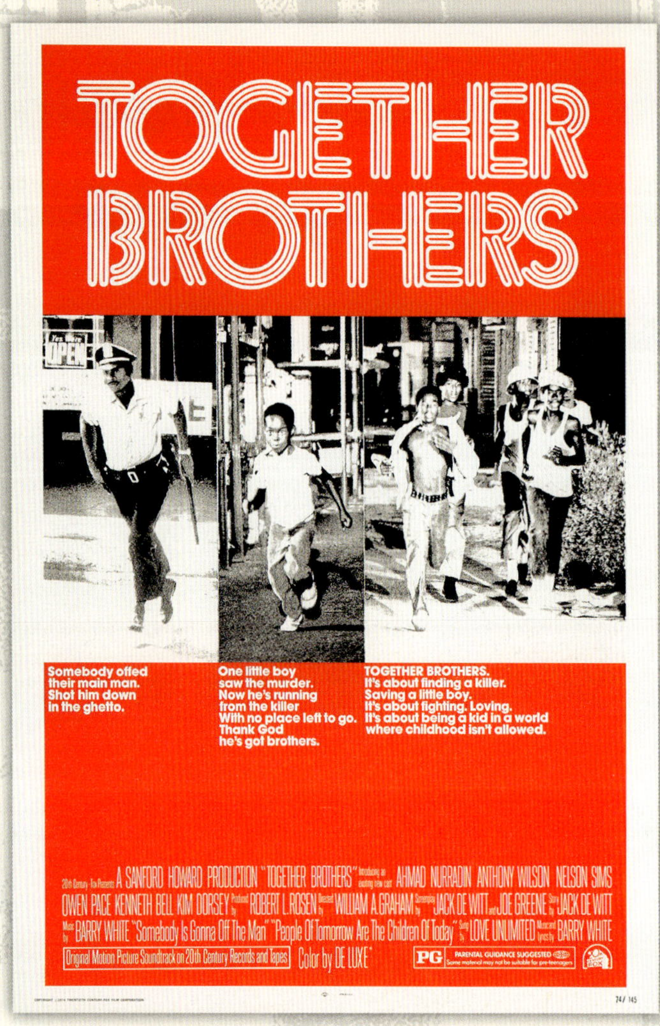

TOGETHER BROTHERS (1974)

Blaxploitation was on the way out when journeyman TV series director William A. Graham ('Batman', 1966, 'Then Came Bronson', 1969) tried to shake the moribund genre out of its **Shaft** (1971), and his own **Honky** (1971), torpor. The fact Graham was involved in the mainstream Blaxploitation TV show 'Get Christie Love!' starring Teresa Graves proved unequivocally the archetype was in serious need of a refreshment makeover. So when Graham decided to take on the **Together Brothers** project, written by Jack DeWitt (originator of the **A Man Called Horse**, 1970, franchise) and Joe Greene, he had two gimmicks up his sleeve. One was casting actual street kids as the quintet of Afro-Americans and Chicanos scouring the ghetto in search of a psycho killer. The other was hiring a soundtrack composer making chart waves of the most monumental kind.

Benevolent black patrol cop 'Mr. Kool' (Ed Bernard) is respected around the Galveston, Texas, ghetto for being fair to its diverse occupants. But when he's brutally shot to death on the mean streets the murder is witnessed by 5-year-old Tommy (Anthony Wilson), so traumatised by the event he's rendered mute. Consequently Tommy's older

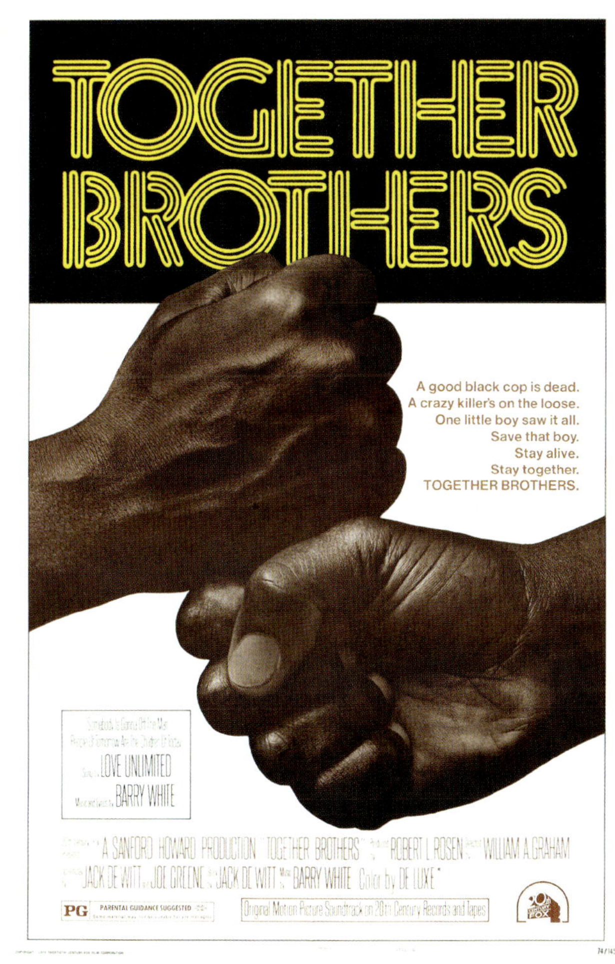

brother H.J. (Ahmed Nurradin) rounds up his gang of punks, A.P. (Nelson Sims), Mau Mau (Kenneth Bell), Monk (Owen Pace) and Gri Gri (Kim Dorsey), to gain enough clues to put the killer responsible behind bars, in this case crazy drag queen Billy Most (a brave performance indeed for the era by Lincoln Kilpatrick), before he can silence Tommy for good.

Shot on location in Galveston, Graham's amateur gamble pays off as he coaxes great, multi-dimensional performances out of the unknowns who organise the she-male manhunt, and from the real-life policemen padding out the racist extras. This docu-drama feel adds urban grit and authentic weight to what is admittedly a perfunctory and stereotypical plot in the final analysis despite some well-handled suspense during the rival gang caper at the police station.

But it's the music and songs heard blaring through the radio that put **Together Brothers** in a unique category. In a very canny move Graham nabbed composer/producer Barry White, fresh from his global Christmas No.1 chart success with *Love's Theme* (1973) by The Love Unlimited Orchestra, and accidentally created the very first movie with an anterior Disco soundtrack. For the most part Blaxploitation movies sported chunk-a-funk beats, glissando arrangements and soulful wailing by such noted R&B names as Curtis Mayfield, Isaac Hayes and Marvin Gaye. Here for the first time was a reconfiguring of those funky grooves with a string-laden backdrop, marrying slum dog atmospheres with romantic soul, orchestral bombast and pop accessibility.

Disco was still emerging from the underground at the time – the pivotal *Love's Theme* wasn't even termed a dance hit because columns devoted to commenting on the new musical genre hadn't appeared yet. However **Together Brothers** started spreading the pre-disco Disco word, ironically to a demographic which would later come to despise it. Interspersed with such Gene Page co-produced musical tracks like *The Rip, Stick Up*

and *Killer Don't Do It* played by The Love Unlimited Orchestra, were vocal versions of *Somebody Is Gonna Off the Man*, *People of Tomorrow Are the Children of Today* and the genuine hit *Honey, Please Can't Ya See*. All were classic examples of White's *basso profondo* soft soul style that announced him as one of the key originators of the burgeoning Disco sound and progenitor of a Disco baby boom.

Let the Music Play

If Cameroon saxophonist and songwriter Manu Dibango's *Soul Makossa* (1972) is by common consent the first pure Disco record, then *Love's Theme* (1973) by The Love Unlimited Orchestra must be a close second. Played in every Discotheque establishment once released in July on the *Under the Influence of… Love Unlimited* album, its climb to the No.1 chart spot around the 1973 Christmas period cemented its evergreen instrumental status. The man responsible for its soaring strings, grandiose arrangement and genuinely moving melody was Barry White. Instantly the one-time session musician and former A&R man for a variety of labels set the tone for the emergent Disco culture eager to get lost in a musical universe of romantic rapture.

White started his career at Del-Fi Records, the home of Ritchie (*La Bamba*, 1958) Valens, in the 1960s and worked with future Disco diva Viola Wills (*Gonna Get Along Without You Now*, 1979) and The Bobby Fuller Four. Other notable pre-Disco credits include co-arranging *Harlem Shuffle* (1963) for Bob & Earl, discovering Felice Taylor and arranging her Northern Soul favourite *I Feel Love Comin' On* (1967) and writing *Doin' the Banana Split* (1968) for 'The Banana Splits' TV show.

In 1969 White discovered and produced Love Unlimited, a girl group deliberately styled after The Supremes, whose mellifluous Motown-type harmonies led to the first of his many million-selling albums, *From a Girl's Point of View We Give to You… Love Unlimited* (1972). That album spawned the classic soul ballad *Walkin' in the Rain with the One I Love*, which featured White as the smitten lover answering the sexy mid-track phone call. Everyone adored his spoken cameo and White found himself with a newfound massive singing career crooning the raciest of lyrics, after creating the 40-piece strong The Love Unlimited Orchestra in 1973 as their shared backing band.

White had numerous hits, touring extensively up until his death in 2003, including *I'm Gonna Love You Just a Little More Baby* (1973), *Can't Get Enough of Your Love Babe* (1974), *Let the Music Play* (1975), *You See the Trouble with Me* (1976) and *Just the Way You Are* (1978). But only *You're My First, My Last, My Everything* (1974), *I'm Qualified to Satisfy You* (1977), *It's Ecstasy When You Lay Down Next to Me* (1977) and *Your Sweetness Is My Weakness* (1978) made the Disco grade to become bona fide club hits. The Love Unlimited Orchestra managed *Satin Soul* (1974), *My Sweet Summer Suite/Brazilian Love Song* (1976), *Theme from King Kong* (1977) and *Welcome Aboard* (1981), while Love Unlimited failed completely to garner any nightclub acceptance. No matter his erratic dance chart career overall, Barry White remains the Prince of Pillow Talk, the Doctor of Love and a true legend in the Disco Hall of Fame.

Studio One

Two of the most enduring 1970s friendships I made at the Portobello Hotel were with musicians Mark Volman and Howard Kaylan, formerly of the *Happy Together* (1967) band The Turtles, but when I knew them they'd just formed the duo Flo and Eddie and become part of Frank Zappa's Mothers of Invention. They had filmed Zappa's videotaped vanity production **200 Motels** (1971) at Pinewood Studios and were session singing with T. Rex at the time they arrived to take up an elongated hotel residence. With them they brought Lucy Offerall, an extra in Zappa's hopeless farrago, and a member of the seminal LA Girl Group, The GTOs (Girls Together Outrageously). Lucy and I got on like a house on fire, sharing our love of vintage Hollywood musicals, Roger Corman horror and showbiz scandal during many late night lobby sessions. One of our first dates together was seeing a Busby Berkeley double bill of **42nd Street** (1933) and **Dames** (1934) at The Gate, Notting Hill, a fabulous repertory venue of the day, now part of the Picturehouse chain.

When Lucy invited me over to Los Angeles I didn't hesitate to accept her offer and in August 1973 I took my first flight ever to America. Arriving at LAX I was whisked to the Hollywood Hills house of noted art dealer Nick Wilder with whom I was to stay with for the next two months. I had no idea at the time but Wilder's LA gallery was one of the most fashionable, lively and discriminating showcases for modern art in the USA. Before long I was having dinner with David Hockney and his future business manager Gregory Evans, spending time with Christopher Isherwood, writer of the semi-autobiographical novel *Goodbye to Berlin* that became **Cabaret** (1972) and his artist partner Don Bachardy, and going to gay bars and clubs with artist Peter Schlesinger, the subject of numerous Hockney canvases and the movie **A Bigger Splash** (1974).

It is no exaggeration to state that my eyes were well and truly opened by my incredible adventures through Hollyweirdness and thrilling Tinseltown in such amazing celebrity company. I attended the premieres of George Lucas' **American Graffiti** (1973) and **Jeremy** (1973), a film that would cement my future friendship with film critic Mark Kermode, and I went to a Drive-In to catch a chiller I had heard so much about, Brian De Palma's **Sisters/Blood Sisters** (1972). And one unforgettable night Miss Lucy and the other GTOs, Miss Pamela Des Barres, Miss Mercy Fontenot, Miss Cinderella/Cynthia Wells and their best friend Janet Ferguson (another **200 Motels** extra, who would move to London to head up the Casablanca Disco label's European office) took me to the hottest Hollywood hotspot at Santa Monica and Robertson Boulevard, Studio One.

It was here I was introduced to Divine, star of John Waters' **Pink Flamingos** (1972) and legendary Hollywood 'woman's' director George Cukor (**My Fair Lady**, 1964) who was more interested in meeting Lucy's latest boyfriend, Jimmy. In my early 'Too Fast to Live, Too Young to Die' couture from Malcolm McLaren and Vivienne Westwood's influential World's End emporium I cut an impressively unique figure and soon had everyone flocking to talk to me about my David Bowie connections and people wanting to take me home to show me their Marilyn Monroe etchings. But not before I was galvanised by my first hearing of the track filling the football-pitch-sized dance floor and the gap between The Pointer Sisters' *Yes We Can Can* (1973) and First Choice's *Smarty Pants* (1973): The Love Unlimited Orchestra's *Love's Theme* (1973). As I danced with a Day of the Locust frenzy alongside a There's No Business Like Show Business fray, I knew something had changed in my world. I was completely Disco Ready.

▲ My wonderful friend Lucy Offerall, member of the seminal band The GTOs. We were inseparable for three years.

Two photo booth snaps of Alan Jones wearing his Alkasura red corduroy suit.

L'ANATRA ALL'ARANCIA / DUCK IN ORANGE SAUCE (1975)

Commedia all'italiana came into its third wind during 1975 and made the often frowned upon genre one to be taken far more seriously. It was the second half of the 1950s that saw the rise of the genre instigated by **I soliti ignoti/Big Deal on Madonna Street** (1958), while the Best Screenplay Oscar for **Divorzio all'italiana/Divorce Italian Style** (1961) popularised its spaghetti sex bomb credentials and impacted on its category naming.

As the 1970s dawned sexpot actresses Sophia Loren, Edwige Fenech, Stefania Sandrelli, Barbara Bouchet, Agostina Belli *et al*, had been sashaying their way through numerous cheap and cheerful bedroom farces for years. But it was the surprise international success of Lina Wertmüller's pointedly Marxist satire **Pasqualino Settebellezze/Seven Beauties** (1975) that made Italian producers sit up again and think they too could tap into global art-house success with intellectualised picaresque sexism. So directors like Pietro Germi, Aldo Grimaldi and Sergio Martino put actors Renato Pozzetto, Paolo Villagio, Alberto Sordi, Marcello Mastroianni, Ugo Tognazzi and Johnny Dorelli through their erotic slapstick paces and minted the Christmas comedy blockbuster, a trend that continues to this very day.

L'anatra all'arancia was one such December release that was so popular – it was the third biggest film of the year – it won Monica Vitti (**Modesty Blaise**, 1966) a Best Actress prize at the David di Donatello Awards, the Italian Oscars. Directed by Luciano Salce (**Il Prof. Dott. Guido Tersilli primario della Clinica Villa Celeste convenzionata con le mutue/Medicine Italian Style**, 1969), and based on British writer and politician William Douglas-Home's stage play (he authored the massive 1955 West End/Broadway success 'The Reluctant Debutante', his elder brother was Prime Minister Sir Alec Douglas-Home), it was the usual combo of light comedy, extramarital indiscretions, philandering spouses, bedroom door slamming and racy antics featuring copious semi-nudity.

Advertising executive Livio Stefani (Ugo Tognazzi) is comfortably married to Lisa (Vitti) but having an affair with his American secretary Patty (Bouchet). After finding out about Livio's sexual duplicity, Lisa strikes up a liaison with sophisticated French Count Jean-Claude (John Richardson, **Torso**, 1973), which results in Livio inviting everyone to the Stefani summerhouse for a weekend in the country where he hopes they can sort the embarrassing situation out like proper adults. So farce, so good, but after much crude horseplay and ludicrous buffoonery, it's revealed that Livio's relationship with Patty was really an elaborate ruse to win back his wife's wandering affections.

An undistinguished melee of improbable events, made vaguely palatable by deft acting and engaging chemistry between Tognazzi and Vitti, all wrapped up in gorgeous Tuscan locations, **L'anatra all'arancia** is Disco important because it's the first time an Italian movie featured such contemporary music on its soundtrack. Pianist Armando Trovaioli/Trovajoli, writer of the huge 1951 hit *El Negro Zumbón*, and composer of a vast number of soundtracks including the peplum **Ercole al centro della Terra/Hercules in the Haunted World** (1961) and flirty **Dove vai tutta nuda?/Where Are You Going All Naked?** (1969), provided two dance cuts for the insistently tuneful soundtrack.

The instrumental *Betcha* was more in funky easy listening mode but eminently danceable nevertheless. However, it was *You Keep On Turning Me On* by Anna Maria Baratta (stage alias Suan), who had a low level 1970s career as a Patty Pravo knock-off) that earned Trovaioli (Hollywood actress Pier Angeli's widower) his

Disco stripes. From the Piper Club in Rome and Mach 2 in Florence to Altromondo Studios in Rimini and the Piranha Club on the Island of Capri, *tutti I ballerini* danced up a storm as Trovaioli harmoniously swirled around genesis Eurodisco and thumping 4/4 melodies coupled with classy orchestration as Suan mangled the English lyrics.

You Keep On Turning Me On was actually just beaten into Italian nightclubs by Franco Bixio and Vince/Vincenzo Tempera's *La Preda* from Domenico Paolella's romantic crime drama **La preda/The Prey** (1974). Often credited to veteran Italian composer Fabio Frizzi, who only conducted the orchestra, and featuring future Dario Argento super group Goblin members Fabio Pignatelli, Massimo Morante and Claudio Simonetti, the instrumental track is a complete rip-off of *Love's Theme* by The Love Unlimited Orchestra.

In fact, it's almost identical until 60 seconds in when suave arrangement just about pulls it back from copyright infringement. Did Barry White ever hear it? He would have definitely sued if he had. Because of its over-familiar sampling of the White-penned classic, *You Keep On Turning Me On* arguably wins the hotly contested race to take its place in the early Italo Disco archive.

Mondo Disco

Italy's early Disco music industry provided few worldwide hits mainly because of the language barrier and the fact the product was manically geared towards its home shores. Every once in a while a pizza platter became a global chart sensation – Raffaella Carrà's *A far l'amore comincia tu/Do It, Do It Again* (No.9 UK hit 1978), La Bionda's *One for You, One for Me* (1978), The Ring's *Savage Lover* (1979), Ryan Paris' *Dolce Vita* (No.5 UK hit 1983) – but most remained resolutely underground for the Eurovisionary Discognoscenti. As in the U.S.A., teen idols of old dusted off their 1950/60s hits and adapted them for club play, like Bobby Solo with *Una lacrima sul viso* (1978) and Tony Renis with *Quando, Quando, Quando* (1978).

Lost Horizon (1973)

The most popular homeland Disco hits were originals by established artists and included El Pasador's *Amada mia, amore mio* (1976), Lucio Battisti's instantly recognisable *Il veliero* (1976), Renato Zero's *Triangolo* (1978), (Pino) Massara's *Margherita* (1979) and Umberto Tozzi's *Tu* (1978) and *Gloria* (1979), the latter transformed into a massive global hit for Laura Branigan in 1982. Branigan would mine La Dolce Disco again for her 'Billboard' No.4 hit in 1984 – Raf's *Self Control*. Other examples: Baciotti's *Black Jack* (1977), Heather Parisi's *Disco bambina* (1979) and *Ti rockerò* (1981), Viola Valentino's *Comprami* (1980), Enzo Avallone's *Ti chiami Africa* (1980), Claudio Cecchetto's *Gioca jouer* (1981) and Lu Colombo's *Maracaibo* (1981).

But Mondo Disco waves were mainly made by such star producers as Bologna-born Celso Valli, who parlayed his work with Italian megastars Mina and Drupi into a sizeable dance career with the solo credited *Pasta & fagioli* (1977), Azoto (the 1978 *Disco Fizz* album) incorporating that unique *Mushy, Mushy, Mushy, Mushy, Mushy* chorus line, Macho (the 1979 *Roll* album) and Passengers. For the latter studio project Valli produced the Eurodisco classics *Hot Leather, He's Speedy Like Gonzales* and *Girls Cost Money* taken from the 1979 first of their four albums together. But it was with co-producer Quelli Del Castello that Valli crafted one of the biggest ever directional club hits. Staying high in the Disco charts for practically the whole of 1980, *Hills of Katmandu* by Tantra is the Disco **Lost Horizon** (1973), an entrancing 17-minute opus of melodious mysticism, choral chanting and hypnotic momentum that put clubbers into a transcendent state of nirvana. A mirrorballed haven of Shangri-la fantasy, the epic cut would be remixed by Gay Disco guru Patrick Cowley to achieve further evergreen success. Valli endures today thanks to his sterling work with Italian luminaries Andrea Bocelli and Eros Ramazzotti.

Guadaloupe-born Jacques Fred Petrus and Mirandola native Mauro Malavasi was another Disco powerhouse. Milan DJ Petrus recognised Malavasi's genius arranging talents and together they formed Goody Music Production, forging a commercial global sound for their inimitable Italian product that resulted in *I'm a Man* (1978) by Macho, *Music Man, Revenge* and *1979 (It's Dancing Time)* by Revanche (all 1979) and their greatest Eurodisco success with the Peter Jacques Band releases of *Fire Night Dance* (1978), *Counting on Love (One, Two, Three), Exotically* and *Welcome Back* (all 1979). The latter song was co-written by Luther Vandross and the future million-selling recording artist joined Petrus and Malavasi to notch up their biggest success as part of the group Change, who took *A Lover's Holiday, The Glow of Love* and *Searching* to the top of the Disco charts in 1980 and *Paradise, Hold Tight* and *Heaven of My Life* ditto in 1981.

Disco Memo

They Had The T-Shirt Off His Back

Within the proto Punk universe I'm famous for two specific things; an omnipresent photograph (see **Eyes of Laura Mars**) and a T-shirt arrest that made headline news in 'The Guardian' newspaper on August 2nd, 1975. But it was exactly a week before that date the events took place which would enshrine my fashion sense forever in the clear aspic of history. At this point in time I was merely a customer at Malcolm McLaren and Vivienne Westwood's revolutionary boutique SEX at 430 King's Road. I had frequented the place in its earliest 'Let It Rock'/'Too Fast to Live, Too Young to Die' incarnation because I lived around the corner in Chelsea for a while and my best friend owned the 'Luckies' furniture and art shop two doors along.

In the beginning 'Let It Rock' had a jukebox blaring out non-stop and Malcolm and I bonded over the inclusion of the *Some Like It Hot* (1959) EP single by Marilyn Monroe because it featured the title song never used in the classic comedy. He eventually gave it to me. We also had a shared love of such early teen idols as Buddy Holly and Eddie Cochran. So I would be visiting the shop on a regular basis and took the clothes to wear on my many jaunts to America. One even scored me a date with a chorus boy in the show 'Chicago' on Broadway 1975. I could see him staring at my outfit – the timeless 'Let It Rock' T-shirt/pegged pants combo – from the stage and during the intermission he came to talk to me in the stalls.

I knew Vivienne was expecting her new T-shirt designs on July 26th so I was there in a flash to buy two; the Cambridge Rapist side-tie and the gay nude Cowboys one. It was a hot day so I decided to wear the Cowboys on my walk into the West End. But as I got to Piccadilly Circus, I was pulled over by two policemen who took me to Vine Street cop station and started interrogating me for an hour. Why was I wearing such an obscene T-shirt? When was the last time I had seen my parents? I was completely shell-shocked and couldn't understand what was going on. I was just wearing a trendy T-shirt for heaven's sake! It turned out the police were patrolling the area for rent boys and thought I fit the bill. I was almost flattered. A few days earlier on July 22nd, the ITV channel had aired the documentary 'Johnny Go Home' about sexual predators and teenage runaways. I was simply caught in that provocative spotlight on the Dilly Boys meat rack. I was eventually charged with "Showing an obscene print in a public place" under the archaic Vagrancy Act of 1824.

Within 24 hours of my arrest SEX itself was raided for indecency and all the offending stock seized. Don't worry about a thing, soothed Malcolm, I'll be there for you in court and will pay any fine imposed. Except he wasn't and he didn't and it was then I knew every Punk was on their own in the McLaren scheme of things. It was journalist Nicholas de Jongh (future film critic for the 'Evening Standard', 1991-2009) who picked up on the story for 'The Guardian' prompting outrage from Dr. Colin Phipps, the Labour MP for Dudley West, who called my arrest "Preposterous" and couldn't understand why I was being pilloried for what was essentially a matter of taste. I always remember looking for the story in the newspaper and was shocked to see it on the front page where I'd least expected it to be. When I eventually pleaded guilty to the offence at the City of London Magistrate's Court in Victoria and got fined £15 (a fortune, I could have bought three other SEX T-shirts for that cost!), de Jongh, who was in the courtroom, gave me a hard time and said I should have contested it. Perhaps if Malcolm had actually been true to his word I might have done. But by this time I was bored by the whole thing, never realising in a million years it would become a defining moment in my whole Punk story.

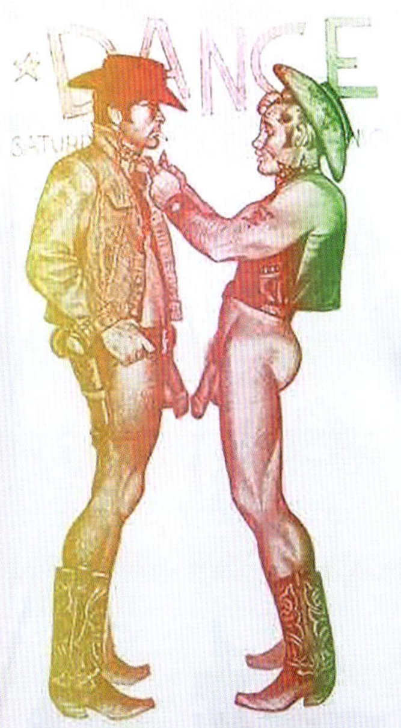

MUSTANG: THE HOUSE THAT JOE BUILT
(1976)

Or **Mustang House of Pleasure** and **Sex Ranch** to give this grubby peepshow its alternative titles. Incredibly nominated for a prestigious Golden Globe Award in the Best Documentary category – it lost to the rock and religion treatise **Youthquake!** (1976) – director Robert Guralnick's one-man and a hand-held camera fly-on-the-wall *faux* Mondo movie looks at the tawdry existence inside the Mustang Ranch in Storey County, Nevada, which in 1970 became America's first legalised brothel.

Given the green light by the very dodgy Sicilian immigrant owner Joe Conforte, and after spending months becoming part of the accepted furniture, Guralnick sleazes around the wood-panelled prison-like compound surrounded by a ten-foot wire fence to interview girls sporting such meat market names as Chi Chi, Libra and Buffy. Each has a story to tell about their dim-witted blue-collar clientele, e.g. extra bucks paid for jabbing needles into the penis, while one ugly john has a genital wash down in full camera view. Nothing shown is very pretty or even remotely erotic, despite the girls parading around in baby doll negligees and bikinis, as Guralnick mainly captures the sexual exhaustion and depressing tedium of 'The Life' as cliché pimp Conforte chomps on foot-long cigars and tackily decorates his Las Vegas mansion. Remember House Rule 11: 'No eating in the parlour'!

Unsurprisingly, only four years later Conforte fled the country to escape tax evasion charges and Guralnick moved on to twice document another exploitation industry, the fashion one, with **Portfolio** (1983) and **The Look** (1985). Responsible for the incidental music in this Best Little Whorehouse in Nevada item was Carmine Coppola, the flautist father of Francis Ford who for some inexplicable reason decided to take this low-rent job between weighty assignments for his son on **The Godfather Part II** (1974) and **Apocalypse Now** (1979). Coppola also wrote the country and western song *I've Got a Girl in Reno* sung by Giuseppe Caro, heard as Conforte gloatingly surveys his crude operation.

But elsewhere the soundtrack was tricked out with a variety of Disco acts all taken from the T.K. Productions roster. Timmy Thomas sang *Sweet Brown Sugar* (1974), Little Beaver *Party Down* (1974), Betty Wright *Where Is the Love?* (1974), George McCrae his vanguard Disco classic *Rock Your Baby* (1974), his wife Gwen McCrae *Move Me Baby* and KC and The Sunshine Band *Queen of Clubs* (1974) and *Get Down Tonight* (1975), the latter their first massive club hit. These bouncy treats help lift the mood in what is a truly miserable viewing experience.

All Day, All Night

T.K. Disco was the umbrella name used to release all the 12-inch single records from the company's affiliate labels including Alstom, Blue Candle, Marlin and Wolf. With its distinctive bamboo logo jacket design, owner Henry Stone lit the fuse on early Disco when George McCrae hit No.1 worldwide with the seminal *Rock Your*

▶ Opposite page bottom right: Because Alan used to nab every free T-shirt he could from movie distributors' offices, he can easily date most photos. This one is from Christmas 1976 because the *Rocky* T-shirt was a gift from his favourite publicist, Rosemary Goodfriend at UIP. Alan is in his friend Geoff Simm's flat just off London's Tottenham Court Road. We would gather there before we hit the West End discos.

Baby in the summer of 1974. Former jukebox operator Stone had given Atlantic Records two million-sellers with Betty Wright's *Clean Up Woman* (1971) and The Beginning of the End's *Funky Nassau Part 1* (1971), and decided to form his own shingle T.K., the initials of engineer Terry Kane who built his eight-track recording studio in Florida.

Wright's touring band included keyboardist Harry Wayne Casey, affectionately known as KC, who took his own Sunshine Band to Disco heights with *That's the Way (I Like It)* (1975), *(Shake, Shake, Shake) Shake Your Booty* (1976), *I'm Your Boogie Man* (1977) and *Boogie Shoes* (1978). On the early KC single *Blow Your Whistle* (1973) back up vocals had been provided by the husband-and-wife session singers George and Gwen McCrae. Listening to McCrae, Stone felt he would be perfect to sing a surefire hit song composed by KC and engineer-turned-Sunshine Band member Richard Finch. And the resulting *Rock Your Baby* became the cataclysmic sensation of the escalating Disco era.

Stone would continuously supply the Disco charts with 'A Lovely Bunch of Coconuts' as one of their earliest trade adverts proclaimed, including Celi Bee and The Buzzy Bunch's *Superman/One Love* (1977, the latter one of the fastest Disco tracks ever produced), *Macho (A Real, Real One)* (1978) and *Fly Me on the Wings of Love* (1978). Celi Bee/Celida Soto's Puerto Rican husband Pepe Luis also hit with his studio project Rice & Beans Orchestra, *The Blue Danube Hustle Parts 1 & 2* (1976) and *You've Got Magic* (1977). In 2006 the Rice & Beans Orchestra's scintillating *Dante's Inferno Suite* was finally released after languishing in the T.K. vaults and proved producer Soto could easily have had an extended Eurodisco-type career.

Other significant T.K. artists are T-Connection, *Disco Magic* (1976), *Do What You Wanna Do* (1977) and *On Fire* (1977), Anita Ward, the evergreen *Ring My Bell* (1979), The Ritchie Family, *Life Is Music/Lady Luck* (1976), *American Generation/I Feel Disco Good* (1978), Katmandu, *The Break* (1979), Voyage, the albums *Voyage* (1977), *Fly Away* (1978) and *Voyage 3* (1980), Amant, *If There's Love/Hazy Shades of Love* (1978), the two USA-European Connection albums *Come Into My Heart* (1978) and *USA-European Connection* (1979) and *Beautiful Bend* (1978), the last three produced by the legendary Boris Midney.

The Catacombs

Brazil by The Ritchie Family, *Summer of '42* by the Biddu Orchestra and *What a Diff'rence a Day Makes* by Esther Phillips were riding high in the Disco charts as **Mustang** escaped into redneck Drive-Ins, hovering in sporadic release for over three years. But the big story of the year concerned the lasting impact of Disco, its effect on other music and its fad status. Up until August 1975 Disco was seen as nothing more than a collection of songs geared towards club play. Suddenly the sheer proliferation of dance music and its subsequent popularity on radio transformed it into a genre – and many people weren't happy.

Cultural commentators, rock producers and mainstream DJs were worried Disco was elbowing out everything else, and what had started as an edgy underground movement was becoming over-commercialised into a fashionable range whose burgeoning recognition might signal its own end. As it turned out that wasn't going to happen for another five years at least and the playground had yet to experience the **Saturday Night Fever** (1977) club-quake. Yet it was interesting how many feared a complete Disco takeover while not accepting the reality: Disco was happening because it had a vitality, freshness and production expertise lacking on the music scene in the post Glam Rock era. Did I care? Not for one second as I had found my Disco home in London's Earls Court district at a tiny basement dive on Finborough Road. Chris Lucas was the amazing DJ at The Catacombs, which could only serve coffee as it was unlicensed, and it was in this room with dark passageways circling the far end of the dancefloor I learned to get lost in music, caught in a trap of 4/4 melody, sonic barrier sensation and close, sweaty body contact.

alan xx xx

LIPSTICK (1976)

"He wanted to kill me with it... With his cock! I hate him! I hate him, and I want him to die in jail!" So screams fledgling actress Margaux Hemmingway in her debut feature, a sordid rape melodrama executive produced by the King of 1970s Mainstream Exploitation, Dino De Laurentiis. Critically lambasted and a box-office dud, **Lipstick**, written by David Rayfiel (actress Maureen Stapleton's ex-husband and future **The Firm**, 1993, scripter), found Ernest Hemmingway's ill-fated granddaughter playing Chris McCormick, an in-demand high fashion model whose face appears on billboards all over the country advertising a new line of lipstick called, in a clue to the mundane nature of this crude **Death Wish** (1974) knock-off, 'Lipstick'.

In a major coup for the time, celebrity photographer Francesco Scavullo, who shot the infamous Burt Reynolds nude centrefold for 'Cosmopolitan' magazine, is the showcased photographer.

When younger sister Kathy (real-life kid sibling Mariel Hemmingway, cast at Margaux's suggestion, and the one who did become a terrific actress) introduces Chris to her geeky music teacher Gordon Stuart (Chris Sarandon, **Dog Day Afternoon**, 1975) at a photo-shoot, he spies her in the nude sparking off a submerged psychosis. Turning up to

Chris' apartment the next day to play one of his avant-garde compositions, he instead ties her to the bed, beats her up and sodomises her violently. Kathy walks in on the pair but assumes the kinky session is consensual until Gordon exits and Chris calls the cops.

Unfortunately assistant district attorney Carla Bondi (a clearly embarrassed Anne Bancroft, **The Graduate**, 1967, legend) fails to get a conviction at the trial because the jury believes Gordon's bogus account of the seduction that led to their rough sex lovemaking. Completely devastated by the wrongful verdict the sisters try to move on with their lives until unbalanced Gordon sets his violation sights on Kathy, a red slinky-dressed Chris blows him away with a rifle and Carla earns her salary at last when she gets her client acquitted of his murder.

Supposedly concerned with rape issues but shameless in exploiting them to the hilt, **Lipstick** features too many sloppy coincidences, redundant characters – Chris' photographer boyfriend Steve Edison (Perry King, **Mandingo**, 1975), the girls' priest brother Martin (John Bennett Perry) – is way too slow and the rape scene considered one of the ugliest ever, although now much-discussed by feminist film scholars. A startling misstep by Lamont Johnson, whose genre directing form up until this point was pretty good – **A Covenant with Death** (1967), **The Groundstar Conspiracy** (1972), **You'll Like My Mother** (1972) – it's so ludicrous at times it becomes unintentionally hilarious.

But as silly and inconsequential as Johnson's voyeuristic vigilante vision is, it features the first Disco soundtrack directly composed for a movie. French pop star/keyboardist/guitarist/producer Michel Polnareff beat both Giorgio Moroder and Alec R. Costandinos to the film score and dance floor with his playfully tuneful and uplifting theme influenced by the tinkling and melodic current Salsoul sound. As arranged by TV series composer Jimmie Haskell (**Night of the Lepus**, 1972) and David Foster, Polnareff's title instrumental climbed to No.5 in the 'Billboard' charts, while the more mental tracks *Lipstick Montage*, *The Rapist* and *Ballet* found favour with Easy Listeners and giallo lovers, the latter two tracks being experimental Disco discord of the epic kind.

Polnarevolution

With his signature blond hair, white-rimmed prescription sunglasses (because of cataract problems) and fancy black trousers, perennially eccentric Michel Polnareff wrote many popular French hits – *La poupée qui fait non* (1966), *Love Me, Please Love Me*, (1967, covered by Sandie Shaw in the UK), *Le bal des laze* (1968), *Holidays* (1972), *Lettre à France* (1977) and *Tam-Tam* (1981). The son of a dancer and a veteran Edith Piaf musician, Polnareff began his career as a Paris busker and when signed up by Barclay Records after winning a Disco Revue prize in 1965 continually courted controversy, like in 1972 flashing his bare buttocks on a promo poster. He composed the score for **Lipstick** during a self-imposed exile in America after his accountant vanished with all his money, leaving him with a massive French tax bill he didn't clear for a decade. His celebrated return to France in 1989 was cemented by the huge hit *Goodbye Marylou*, the 1990 album *Kāma-Sūtra* and deification in the astonishing Disco movie **Podium** (2004).

Disco Memo

Muppet Disco

Lipstick was released early July 1976 in London during the hottest heatwave and worst drought in the UK for 250 years. At the Portobello Hotel a group of super talented thespians had just taken up long-term residence to appear in one of the most groundbreaking and beloved television series of all time, 'The Muppet Show'. Over the next five years I spent quality time with them all – Jim Henson, Frank Oz, Jerry Nelson, David Goetz, Louise Gold – and kept in close touch – a relationship responsible for my covering the making of **The Dark Crystal** (1982) for the contemporary genre bible 'Cinefantastique' magazine. Production manager and associate producer Duncan Kenworthy was another Muppeteer who gave me *carte blanche* on many Henson hits like 'The Storyteller' (1987-88) and 'Gulliver's Travels' (1996). He would become the award-winning producer of **Four Weddings and a Funeral** (1994) and **Notting Hill** (1999), and thanks to him I was the first person in print covering the latter blockbuster for the very first issue of 'Heat' magazine.

Richard Hunt and Scooter

But the Muppeteer who became the firmest friend was Richard Hunt, primarily known for manipulating and voicing Scooter, Statler and Sweetums. It was he who invited me to visit 'The Muppet Show' being filmed at ATV Elstree, Borehamwood, on numerous occasions and it was a complete blast to meet and watch such stars as Madeline Kahn, from the Mel Brooks comedy movies, pop starlet Connie Stevens, Motown diva Diana Ross and the Broadway legend that was, and still is, Ethel Merman strut their stuff.

I was sat on my own in the front row of the studio theatre when La Merm belted out the medley of her signature hits *You're the Top/Friendship/De Lovely/Together Wherever We Go/You're Just in Love/Anything You Can Do/Mutual Admiration Society*. She was literally 10 feet away from me and it was ***the*** most memorable brush with Hollywood's Golden Era I've ever encountered. Strangely enough none of those evergreen standards made it on to her infamous *The Ethel Merman Disco Album* (1979), but I was thrilled to have met her and to have had my own private concert.

Answering the phone at the Portobello Hotel reception desk. SEX original woollen top and handcuff accessory. Can you believe the owners let Alan get away with these looks?

In the Portobello Hotel lounge. Mr Freedom satin jacket.

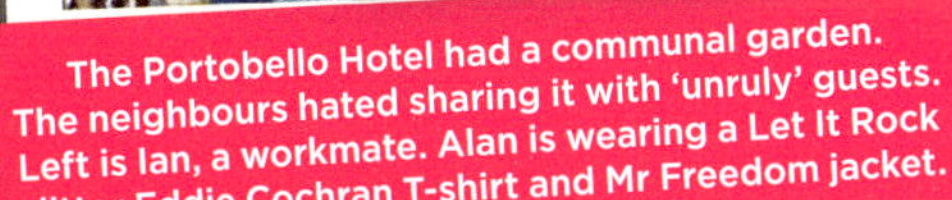

The Portobello Hotel had a communal garden. The neighbours hated sharing it with 'unruly' guests. Left is Ian, a workmate. Alan is wearing a Let It Rock glitter Eddie Cochran T-shirt and Mr Freedom jacket.

▲ Ethel Merman and friends

Another reception pose, the T-shirt is a Let It Rock classic with porno playing cards sewn on the Chuck Berry image.

CAR WASH (1976)

Director Michael Schultz's appealing comedy drama is considered the original Disco film. It is significant for being the first glimpse mainstream audiences had into what was happening on the musical, cultural and sexual fringes in those intriguing meeting places/dance spaces opening everywhere, seemingly on a daily basis. Although this hugely entertaining, unpretentious time capsule of America's Bicentennial year left critics unimpressed, it was a sizeable crowd-pleaser box-office-wise, and has left an indelible mark on pop history thanks to its Gold Record status soundtrack and title song by Rose Royce becoming a Disco evergreen.

It was while music producer Norman Whitfield was putting together his new group Total Concept Unlimited from the Watts and Inglewood districts of Los Angeles, that Schultz, fresh from the success of his debut feature **Cooley High** (1975), offered him the chance to score his next picture. At the celebrated Motown label, Whitfield had brought progressive and psychedelic funk to such hits as Edwin Starr's *War* (1970) and The Temptations' *Papa was a Rolling Stone* (1972) and wanted to branch out on his own with the octet originally Starr's touring back-up band.

Car Wash would give him the opportunity to launch his protégé outfit in the most visible way possible and so to get maximum musical inspiration Whitfield and the band visited the locations to soak up the atmosphere for the song catalogue. By this time Total Concept Unlimited had become Magic Wand, lead singer Yvonne Fair (*It Should Have Been Me*, 1976) replaced by Gwen Dickey, from the Miami girl group The Jewels, and given the stage name Rose Norwalt. After the set visit the band underwent one final name change to Rose Royce to reflect the movie's automotive theme.

Clearly influenced by the freeform, parallel story style of Robert Altman's **Nashville** (1975), the daily dramas of a cast of colourful characters all with differing personalities working at a Los Angeles car wash during a 10-hour period was the focus of Schultz's sassy and

super-smart semi-musical. Exhausted owner Leon 'Mr. B' Barrow (Sully Boyar) is considering changing bespoke hand washing to the more economical automatic version while coping with his revolutionary communist son Irwin (Richard Brestoff) always quoting Chairman Mao. All dreaming of a better life, Mr. B's screwball employees include wise ex-con Lonnie (Ivan Dixon), militant black activist Duane (Bill Duke in his film debut) who insists on being called Abdullah, distracted secretary Marsha (Melanie Mayron, **Harry and Tonto**, 1974), comic book artist T.C. (Franklin Ajaye) who wants to create black superheroes and, in a ground-breaking role for the era, flamboyant homosexual Lindy (a brilliant Antonio Fargas, 'Starsky and Hutch', 1975-79).

Driving through the Deluxe Car Wash establishment are the wigged-out Miss Beverly Hills (Lauren Jones, **Lipstick**, 1976), The Mad Bomber (Irwin Corey), The Taxi Driver (comedian George Carlin spouting his own dialogue) looking for the black prostitute who ran off without paying her fare, and fake evangelist Daddy Rich (comedy legend Richard Pryor) travelling in a huge luxury Lincoln Continental with his entourage The Wilson Sisters (The Pointer Sisters). In his 1998 autobiography 'Pryor Convictions: And Other Life Sentences', Pryor revealed he was high on cocaine for the entire time it took to shoot his minimal part. Scripted by future **The Lost Boys** (1987) director Joel Schumacher – he would reuse Lindy's most oft-quoted line "Honey, I'm more man than you'll ever be and more woman than you'll ever get" in **Flawless** (1999) – **Car Wash** is a terrific package of the funky, funny, thrilling and poignant.

Despite winning prizes and nominations at the Cannes Film Festival, the Golden Globes and a Grammy Award for Best Score Soundtrack Album, Whitfield was shocked when no Oscar acclaim came his way. *Evergreen (Love Theme from A Star Is Born)* by Barbra Streisand and Paul Williams won Best Original Song, while Jerry Goldsmith won Best Original Score for **The Omen** that year. At the time Whitfield put it down to the elderly Academy Award membership not understanding the Disco revolution that was taking place. A year later all that changed and they soon would!

Wishing on a Star

Heard three times during the movie, Rose Royce's *Car Wash* hand-clapping groove reached No.1 in the US and many other international territories, and had a 20-week stint in the 'Billboard' Disco Charts peaking at No.3. Other hits taken from the double album soundtrack were *Put Your Money Where Your Mouth Is, I Wanna Get Next to You* and *I'm Going Down.* Disco-wise the band only notched up three more dance chart hits – the double 'A'-side *Do Your Dance/It Makes You Feel Like Dancin'* (1977) and *R.R. Express* (1980) – while two slow tunes would continue their legacy beyond the dance floor – *Wishing on a Star* (1978) and *Love Don't Live Here Anymore* (1978). Re-issues of *Car Wash* would revisit the pop charts on numerous occasions (notably 1988 and 1998) and also be covered by such artists as Christina Aguilera and Missy Elliott for the movie **Shark Tale** (2004). The Pointer Sisters sang the vocals on the track *You Gotta Believe.*

Disco Memo

A Chorus Line

The stage musical phenomenon 'A Chorus Line' was having its first performance in London's West End at The Theatre Royal Drury Lane on July 22nd, 1976. After becoming the stuff of Broadway legend, and conceived by director/choreographer Michael Bennett, with songs by Marvin Hamlisch, I couldn't wait to see the milestone show about the souls, dreams and desires of serial auditioners. My best friends were all musical theatre buffs and we had booked our seats in the stalls for this first night. But what to wear to this long-awaited auspicious occasion? Vivienne Westwood had just given me the *crème de la crème* of her new SEX collection, the Anarchy Shirt, red faded, distressed stripey, graffiti plastered and complete with a swastika armband. Perfect!

Alan wearing the infamous and hugely controversial Anarchy shirt, designed by Vivienne Westwood at SEX.

Arriving at the theatre we took our prime centre seats. Suddenly, five minutes before the curtain was due to open, the theatre manager (who I found out later was one George Hoare) appeared as if from nowhere at the end of the row. He was screaming in outrage about serving in World War II, blah, blah, and never in his lifetime did he ever expect to see someone wearing Nazi regalia in his esteemed establishment. After a pretty heated argument about my right to wear what I wanted etc., I was so Punk bolshie in those days, and with much growing rumbling from the audience, I finally turned the armband around to hide the offending symbol.

My friends were mortified. The curtain had been delayed by ten minutes. Everyone stared in distaste as we left at the end – there was no interval thank goodness. And it was the first time I really became conscious of the clothes I was wearing being anything other than fashion statements. It might sound ridiculous now but it didn't even cross my mind the swastika armband would be seen as offensive by some. It didn't stop me wearing the shirt, although it did become the one item in my wardrobe to cause further street skirmishes. Something I secretly began to revel in.

BLUE SUNSHINE (1977)

One of the most infamous Disco scenes of the era appears in director Jeff (**Squirm**, 1976) Lieberman's smart chiller with a deliciously sly central concept; bad acid having a 10-year delayed reaction on former hippies causing them to become bald homicidal maniacs. Future softcore producer Zalman King ('Red Shoe Diaries') is the wrong class reunion man in the wrong bloody freak-out place who must trace the source of the dodgy LSD, named Blue Sunshine, in order to solve the chromosomal damage mystery before the police close in, thinking he murdered four partygoers.

Along with the satirical anti-drug message, Lieberman also weaves a political conspiracy cover-up plot into his deft scenario. The pusher in their Stanford University college days, 'Lost in Space' (1965-68) TV series star Mark Goddard, is running for Government office and can't let his sordid Flower Power past catch up with him.

A fun fusion of counterculture nightmare and hallucinogenic weirdness, **Blue Sunshine** ends in a Disco, Big Daddy's in the Shopper's World mall (in reality a redressed Country and Western bar), where Alicia (Deborah Winters, 'Tarantulas: The Deadly Cargo' TV movie, 1977) wonders why her date Wayne (TV veteran Ray Young) is taking so long in the bathroom facilities. Turns out he's losing his hair, going bat-shit psycho, terrorizing dancers by tossing them in the air and demolishing the Disco while Alicia cowers in the DJ booth, her face a seething mass of multi-coloured strobe light reflections.

All to the thumping sound of *Disco Blue* by The Humane Society for the Preservation of Good Music, with its minimalist funk, spacey guitar and staccato Earth, Wind & Fire style bass. *Disco Blue* had music and lyrics by

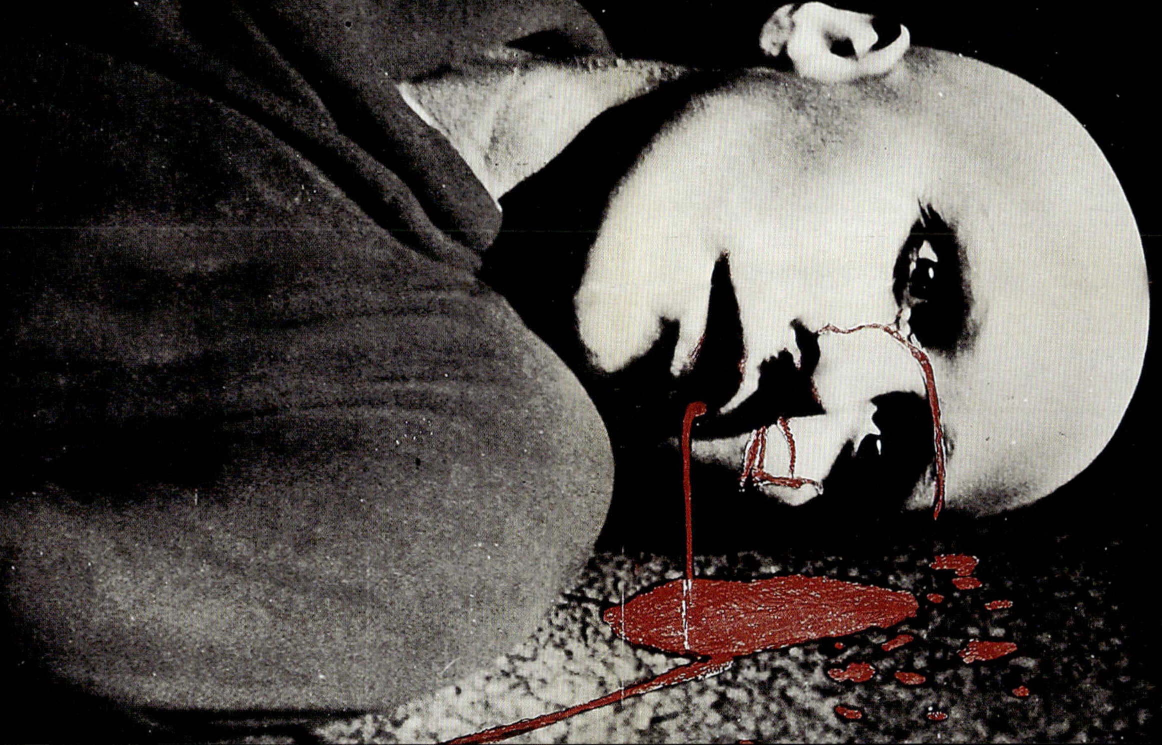

(producer) Billy Jackson, Jay Ferguson and Paul Griffin whereas Charles Gross (composer of the obscure 1975 horror **Have a Nice Weekend**) scored the bulk of the eerie gong-and-string soundtrack. Lieberman claims the choice of band name was not a reflection on his feelings towards the Disco boom gathering momentum as the movie went on release. Yet he claims many acts used the Disco Attack scene as a visual backdrop to express their contempt for the music, like the Ramones in CBGBs. No matter, it was a signature bump-and-grind prompter leading the way for the inclusion of Disco in numerous other horrors.

Splatter Disco

The 1970s as a new definition of horror infested the micro-budgeted end of the genre market during the first decade of the 21st Century and four cheap and cheesy cash-ins exemplified the trend:

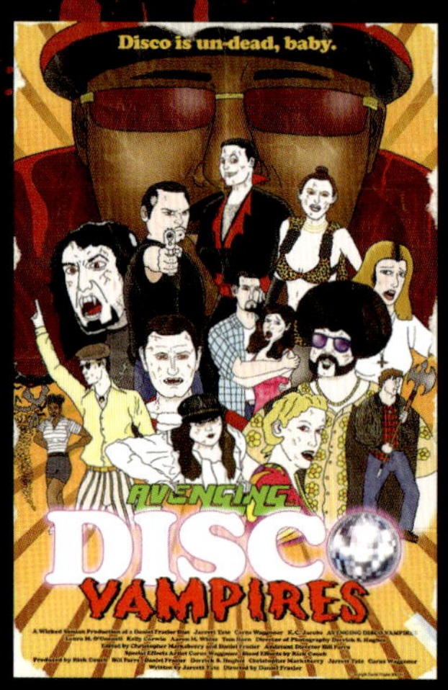

Two crooks find themselves caught up in a bloodsucker battle in Daniel Frazier's **Avenging Disco Vampires** (2001). On one side, the Disco Vampires, polyester-clad lounge lizards hiding out in a ramshackle forest Disco, The Funk Haven. On the other, The Crypts, who strive to wipe out the Master Disco Vampire, so they can lead their fang clan to the undead Promised Land. Thrown together by Frazier and his friends from Northern Kentucky University, there's a Roller Disco vampire, Hott Wheelz, and a Disco barn dance to generic filler music.

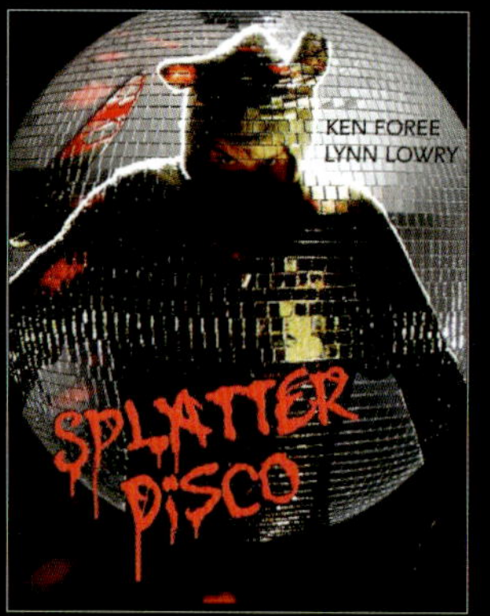

Splatter Disco (2007), originally titled 'Mondo Disco', finds the fetish nightclub Den O'Iniquity not only under attack from local narrow-minded moralisers but also by a psychopath who starts randomly picking off its employees and clientele. Boasting a game cast of genre names – Ken Foree, Lynn Lowry, Trent Haaga and Debbie Rochon – director Richard Griffin's clodhopping horror spoof is very much one of diminishing returns. With dozens of video-shot features under his belt, one-man-band Griffin seemed determined to put Providence, Rhode Island, on the trashy exploitation map as the new Tromaville. Sporting the synth-pop Disco theme *Splatter Disco* variously performed by Crutchy Larue, Mach Fox, The Hangin' Brainz and Plaid Anxiety.

The ubiquitous Griffin went back to strobe-lit sets with **The Disco Exorcist** (2011) in which the King of the dance floor has a one-night stand with a hot devil-in-disguise triggering a hellfire curse. Who you gonna call?

Why **The Disco Exorcist** of course, hopefully to put a stop to the mirrorball electrocution and cod spacey Italo Disco cuts courtesy of electro duo, Owen Thompson and Timothy Fife.

If you want to see Hitler Roller Disco, look no further than William Butler's **Gingerdead Man 3: Saturday Night Cleaver** (2011). For some inexplicable reason the Charles Band directed **The Gingerdead Man** (2006), made under his Full Moon Features banner, spawned two sequels and one crossover (**Gingerdead Man vs. Evil Bong**, 2013). Created from a mix of gingerbread spice mix and the ashes of a deceased serial killer, the deranged CGI cookie monster first terrorised a small-town bakery, a studio back-lot in **Gingerdead Man 2: Passion of the Crust** and gets whisked back to 1976 in a time machine in the third crumbly episode. To a Roller Disco going through financial problems to be exact, run by a gambling addict and her telekinetic daughter who just got crowned queen of the rink. The movie references never stop (from **Porky's**, 1981, to **The Silence of the Lambs**, 1991) and the filler Roller Disco sequences pad out the thin story and short running time. But the guy who talks in nothing but Disco song titles (e.g. "You should be dancing") is a fun device when nothing remotely familiar booms out on the soundtrack.

I Haven't Stopped Dancing Yet

If Blue Sunshine had been available during the 1970s would we have taken it? Of course! Drugs were a part of the Disco furniture and totally cool because they weren't addictive. Take as much as you like, darling, I'm not addicted and I've snorted it for years! The first 'drug' I was ever offered was 'poppers' or amyl nitrate in glass capsules you broke in a handkerchief – we really did have one in our jeans pockets back then – but I hated the old socks smell. And let's face it the high lasted all of five seconds, even when it was supposed to heighten orgasm. But as an accessory to shock the Disco newbies it was always a fun look.

Acid I didn't like at all either. I took some very strong LSD the night before the Sex Pistols gig at the Islington Screen on the Green, April 3, 1977, and was still flying when they played the next day. Siouxsie Sioux told me years later she thought I was being way too nice that night and often wondered why. The Sex Pistols' stage manager was my best friend Nils Stevenson – I got him the job – and he was convinced I was on acid when I was DJ for the boys at their infamous El Paradise gig almost exactly a year before. Not true, and I was really annoyed when that 'anecdote' made it into print.

Speed was the Punk drug of choice but I hated the strain on my nerves followed by the boring paranoia. Cocaine was a few years away yet in my universe and only appeared when the Golden Era of the Rock Video started and I found myself moving in the same circles as pioneer director Russell Mulcahy and Duran Duran. I didn't smoke but marijuana meant I did for a few years. Bad choice. I took Angel Dust once only to find myself lying on the Bang! Disco dance floor (the old Astoria cinema, Tottenham Court Road) listening in rapture to the meaningful lyrics of *Yes Sir, I Can Boogie* (1977), the reason I still adore that Eurodisco classic so much. No, my favourite drugs were the downers Mandrax, its American equivalent Quaaludes and Tuinal, all stolen from the Portobello Hotel guest stashes, and guaranteed to keep me glued to the Disco floor forever. The Tuinal Smile was endemic and the Tuinal Two-Step always was the most lethal manoeuvre you could make, especially when carrying drinks!

DISCO 9000 / FASS BLACK (1977)

Touted in TV spots as "Hollywood's First Fantastic Disco Movie", **Disco 9000** (later re-titled **Fass Black** when it was clear this tail-end Blaxploitation quickie wasn't hitting the right target audience) shows all the signs of being thrown together to cash-in on the buzz surrounding the upcoming year-end release of **Saturday Night Fever**. The daftest plot, the dumbest dialogue ("Only one bee gets this honey cone", says a Disco hottie when hit on by a lowly office clerk) delivered in monotone, and snail-paced direction by **Boss Nigger** (1974) actor D'Urville Martin (his only other helmed movie **Dolemite**, 1975) dooms this drab and tiresome affair. Even the background Disco dancers all culled from TV's premier music show 'Soul Train' look bored to death as they shuffle around the title 16-storeys-up penthouse club on Los Angeles' Sunset Strip, often tripping over the visible camera crew in the flashing rainbow lights.

Badass Fass Black (John Poole, who also played a record executive in the music biz exposé **Death Drug**, 1978) owns the record label 9000 and the popular Disco named after it. His DJ Gene Edwards (singer Johnnie Taylor in his only screen credit) is under strict instructions to just play music from the label because there's an in-Disco store where punters can buy what they hear. This would never have worked in a million years in the real Disco world but it's what writer Roland S. Jefferson (**Pacific Inferno**, 1979) considers a believable plot.

Jefferson adds more implausibility to his paper-thin scenario by having Shenandoah label head Bellamy

(Nicholas Lewis) trying to force Black into playing his East Coast product. It seems Shenandoah can't get a foothold in the Californian scene and sees Disco exposure as the only way forward to fortune. The fact that Bellamy's output is all Country and Western, even DJ Gene remarks about

the disc samples "They've got something you can pat your feet to… if you happen to be in a truck stop somewhere in the middle of Oklahoma", and would be completely the wrong music for any Disco environment doesn't seem to phase him while being blindingly obvious to everyone watching.

When Black refuses point blank to play the records or Bellamy's game, the latter puts mob moves on the club with inside help from trusted Earl Ross (Cal Wilson), first with sabotage, then random violence, escalating to sinister threats against Black's nearest and dearest, leading to a van crash tragedy. Nothing exciting to watch here really, just a low-grade formula crime melodrama badly dressed up in wrongheaded dance ambience. The sole good aspect to the entire miserable business is one-time Stax wunderkind Johnnie Taylor (*Who's Making Love*, 1968) who sings all the sub-Disco songs on the Columbia Records soundtrack, few of which are actually heard in the movie. Yet the repertoire on screen does include Taylor's boogie funk US No.1 *Disco Lady* (1976), the first single ever to be awarded a Platinum Disc for sales and also the first hit record to feature the word Disco in the title.

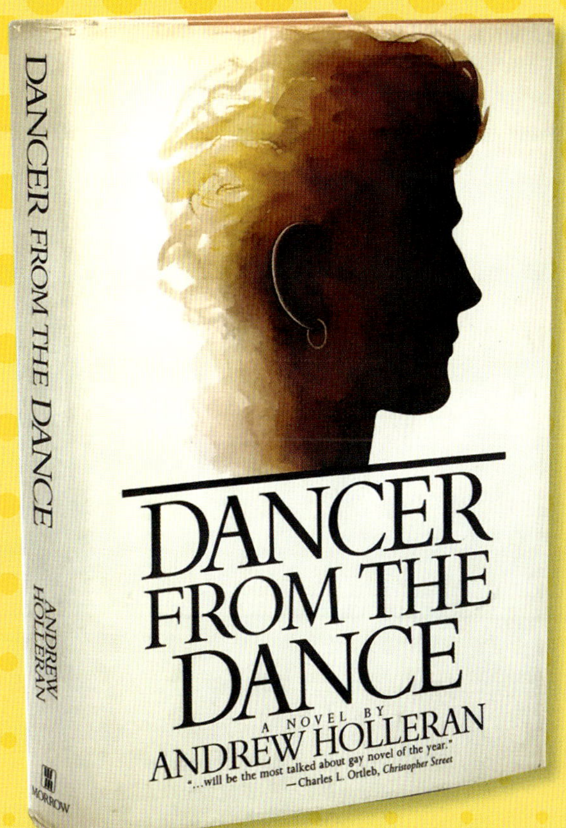

The one track heard the most often is the title soft-soul groove *Disco 9000*, which literally relates the entire plot of the film in verse. As Taylor suavely sings about "Music of the Brotherman", "People from coast to coast talkin' about it" and who is fighting over the Disco designation "King of Boogieland", audiences of the time doubtless wondered where that terrific sounding film was. Because it certainly wasn't the one on screen in front of them!

If You Could Read My Mind

The first paperback original to cover the Disco lifestyle was 'Discotheque' published in July 1977, written by 'New York Daily News' pop columnist Steven Gaines who had already ghosted Alice Cooper's autobiography. He would survive this trash-fest to write another Disco novel 'The Club' and books on The Beatles and The Beach Boys. Taking place over a three-day Fourth of July weekend in Manhattan's swankiest Disco, Elysium, soap opera and disaster movie plots swirled around cocaine addict DJ Bobby Benedetto as he interacts with the venue owner Maurice Cameron (allegedly based on Le Jardin club mastermind John Addison) and promotions man Willie Buckels. The Mob, ageing movie queens, lesbian molls, and sex pests all play a part in the sizzling narrative that supposedly lifted the lid on the mad, bad world of the Disco peppered with love, lust and ludicrousness.

It was the next year, 1978, that the definitive Disco novel was published, Andrew Holleran's 'Dancer from the Dance', revolving around gay native New Yorkers and their adventures on Fire Island. Anthony Malone is the Midwest lawyer who leaves behind his straight life to immerse himself in the gay environment of 1970s New York, and speed queen Andrew Sutherland is the social butterfly already into copious drinking, dancing, and drug use. Together they enjoy many physical pleasures and sexual explorations, but their lives lacking any spiritual depth was supposed to be the metaphor for the Disco times, especially when Andrew tries to 'marry' Anthony off to a young millionaire. Despite its rather depressing and pessimistic summation of the era, 'Dancer from the Dance' is now regarded as a key post-Stonewall gay literature classic.

The Nashville Rooms

People have often asked me when I knew the Sex Pistols were going to be big. From being a bunch of loud-mouthed tossers hanging around the SEX shop to looking like they were actually going to amount to something. I always say the gig at the Nashville Rooms on April 23, 1976. From my permanent position sitting on the speakers at the 100 Club, Oxford Street, I could see their growing charisma and accidental talent. In the Nashville the tiny staging area was attached to a pub (now The Famous Three Kings) on North End Road, West Kensington. My date for the evening was 'Melody Maker' journalist Caroline Coon who I'd convinced to attend knowing she'd find it worth reporting.

Little did I know it would lead her to cataloguing the entire Punk scene and working with The Clash! The first thing I did though when we met was make her take off the tie around her neck she'd threaded with safety pins! Suburban naff!

Looking back at the crowd everyone was there, mainly future Punk band members: Adam Ant, Tony James, David Vanian, even Sid Vicious. We were sitting in the middle of the venue and I was thrilled when Johnny Rotten snarled at the audience and roll-called his friends during the set, myself included. Naturally a fight ensued, Vivienne slapped someone and it all kicked off. But the band showed musical discipline for the first time and the atmosphere was electric.

I could see Caroline's thrilled response. The good/bad publicity began in earnest. I knew the Pistols were on their way to something. And I was delighted to be a part of their favoured inner circle.

▲ Handbill for a Nashville Rooms gig. The Sex Pistols played the venue three times during April 1976; on the 3rd, 23rd, and 29th.

Alan with his best friend Jordan and über-Sex Pistols fan Linda Ashby at the 100 Club. Note my London Leatherman studded wristband.
(Photo courtesy of Ray Stevenson)

BIG TIME (1977)

In 1976 two amateur producers, Andrew Georgias and Louis Gross, approached legendary Tamla Motown artist William 'Smokey' Robinson Jr. and pitched him a project based on a short film they had made. Fifteen other potential investors came along with the package, including his best friend and soul mate, actor Leon Isaac Kennedy. But Robinson decided to finance the whole project himself for one simple reason – he could finally follow his fellow singer/songwriters Marvin Gaye and Curtis Mayfield into the movie world and compose a full soundtrack. The middling result was the crime caper **Big Time**, a no-account addition to the last gasp of the Blaxploitation trend.

Con artist Eddie Jones (Christipher Joy, Snake in **Cleopatra Jones**, 1973) has fallen on hard times and he's in debt to vicious loan shark J.J. (Roger E. Mosely, Olinga in **The Mack**, 1973), who threatens violence if he doesn't pay up soon. Partnering with his buddy Harold (Tobar Mayo, Big Al in **Panama Red**, 1976) for yet more useless dead end grifts only makes matters worse. Then he stumbles into a mafia crime scene providing an opportunity to grab an errant suitcase full of cash. Soon Eddie has Italian mobsters after him along with the FBI, one being his undercover girlfriend Shana (Jayne Kennedy, Leon Isaac's wife).

Everything about **Big Time** is bland and safe. The racial stereotypes aren't that crude for the era, the language is dialled down, the fighting constitutes mild action at best, the jokes are unfunny and Kennedy never wears anything less than a bikini. What director Georgias seems to be aiming for is the easy-going chaos of the Sidney Poitier/ Bill Cosby crime comedies in the **Uptown Saturday Night**

(1974) and **Let's Do It Again** (1975) mode. No such luck unfortunately as it emerges more an aimless, sedated romp on life support. Even though Robinson schmoozed distributors and promoted the premiere with a short concert set before the unveiling, **Big Time** ended in a quietly settled legal dispute over credits, terrible reviews, poor box-office returns and him losing $500,000 on the bad deal.

But the interesting legacy of this mega-flop is some slick Disco funk groove that Robinson happily poured his heart and soul into as a rite of soundtrack passage. Robinson produced and wrote all the background and foreground music, with collaborators on three songs, including his elder sister, Rose Ella Jones, on the title track. *Theme from Big Time* is upbeat Disco with a sizzling Motown feel that made inroads into the 'Billboard' Dance Top 20. *J.J.'s Theme* begins like pimped up gospel before moving into easy Disco groove channels. *Hip Trip* is a top-notch mover while *So Nice to Be with You* and *If We're Gonna Act Like Lovers* are more in the classic mould Smokey developed with The Miracles. *He Is the Light of the World* is jittery gospel and *The Agony and the Ecstasy* an instrumental track drafted in from the album *A Quiet Storm* (1975). The entire effort shows Smokey Robinson at the crossroads between forsaking his elder Motown past and the new Disco sound his contemporaries were wholeheartedly embracing. And when it works, it works **Big Time**!

Dancing in the Street

Berry Gordy's Detroit, Michigan, Tamla Motown label and his incredible roster of artists played an important part in the development of Disco. Throughout the 1960s Motown had promoted nightclub culture with such classic singles as Martha and the Vandellas' *Dancing in the Street* (1964) and The Supremes' *Nathan Jones* (1971) and in the 1970s drafted many of their iconic acts into the new music idiom.

Obviously Diana Ross was tailor made for the genre,

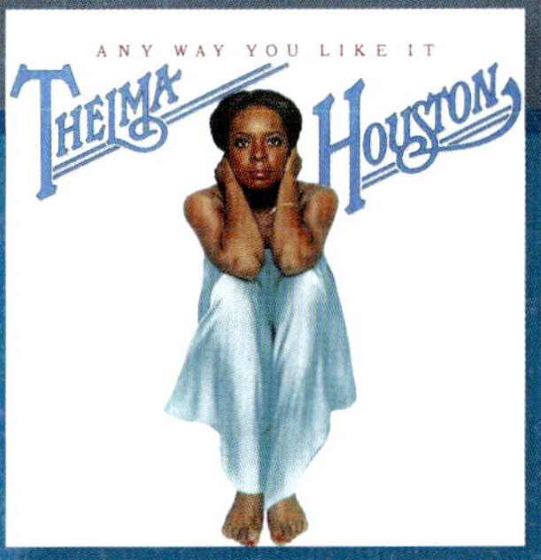

and she gave the label a multitude of No.1 Dance Chart hits, including *Love Hangover* (1976), all cuts from *The Boss* (1979) album and *Upside Down/I'm Coming Out* (1980). Her former backing group The Supremes (only Mary Wilson staying the constant in an ever-changing roster) scored three Disco hits too: *I'm Gonna Let My Heart Do the Walking* (1976), *High Energy* (1976) and *You're My Driving Wheel/Let Yourself Go/Love I Never Knew You Could Feel So Good* (1976). Wilson did have her own solo hit with *Red Hot* (1979).

The Commodores also did the Disco Chart trio before lead vocalist Lionel Richie left the group: *Fancy Dancer* (1977), *Brick House* (1977) and *Lady (You Bring Me Up)/Keep on Taking Me Higher* (1981). Thelma Houston's *Don't Leave Me This Way/Anyway You Like It* (1976) got to the pole chart position. *Overture/Love Machine* (1975) and *Spy for Brotherhood* (1977) did it for Smokey's ex backing singers The Miracles.

The Temptations did a double in 1975 with *Happy People* and *Glasshouse*, and when lead singer Eddie Kendricks went solo he hit even bigger with *He's a Friend/It's Not What You've Got/Chains* (1976), *Goin' Up in Smoke/Music Man/Born Again/Thanks for the Memories* (1976) and *Ain't No Smoke Without Fire/Whip* (1978). Bonnie Pointer left her sisters and got clubbers dancing up a storm to her two Top Ten hits *Heaven Must Have Sent You* (1979) and *I Can't Help Myself (Sugar Pie, Honey Bunch)* 1980. And The Jackson 5 got to No.1 with *Forever Came Today* (1975) before they left the label for pastures new.

Motown all-round legend Stevie Wonder's 1976 tribute to the swing jazz giants who inspired him as a child, delivered a 19-week stay in the Disco Charts with *Another Star/I Wish/Sir Duke/Isn't She Lovely*. And his ex-wife Syreeta (Wright) teamed up with Billy Preston for *Go for It* (1979). Despite cutting many of his best records during the seminal Disco years, like *What's Going On* (1971), Marvin Gaye did not make many actual Disco records. Apart from that is his epic No.1 hypno-bouncer *Got to Give It Up* (1977), which proved he could have been a Disco King supremo had he applied himself fully to the

Disco Memo

Cinefantastique (CFQ)

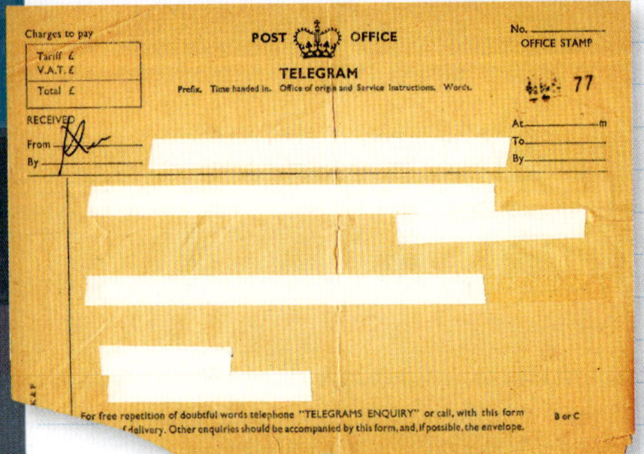
Charges to pay
Tariff £
V.A.T. £
Total £
POST OFFICE
TELEGRAM
Prefix. Time handed in. Office of origin and Service Instructions. Words.
No.
OFFICE STAMP
77
RECEIVED
From
By
At
To
By
For free repetition of doubtful words telephone "TELEGRAMS ENQUIRY" or call, with this form
delivery. Other enquiries should be accompanied by this form, and, if possible, the envelope.

There are some magical days in my life I will never, ever forget and one of those was July 20th, 1977. It was a Thursday and I found myself woken up by my front door buzzer. "Telegram [remember those?] for Mr. Jones", barked the postman and puzzled I went to collect it. I had never received a telegram before and never since. It said "Congratulations on Cinefantastique debut. Carrie On. The Gang". I knew it was from my close friend Keith Williams, a scriptwriter who would soon play a key part in the rock video revolution coming down the pike. He sent it to commemorate the fact my first feature articles had just been printed in the seminal American genre magazine 'Cinefantastique', 'CFQ' for short.

'CFQ' was edited and published out of Chicago by Frederick S. Clarke. Fred already had a London Correspondent for the magazine, Chris Knight. But my best friend from the moment I arrived in London in 1969 was Mike Childs who had got a really good job at London's premier commercial radio station Capital. He met Chris there one day when he came in to record a program about the late pop producer Joe Meek (the British Phil Spector) as they were both big fans. They kept in touch and a couple of years later Chris told Mike he was about to get married and his soon-to-be wife told him he had to stop working all hours under the sun. Knowing Mike and I read 'CFQ' he asked him if he wanted to take over his London Correspondent position. Mike said yes and he took over the role in 1976 with the **Logan's Run** (Vol.5/2) issue. But because he was rising up the producer ranks at Capital Radio, his time was limited for set reports, interviews etc., so he asked me to become more involved. I was delighted, although typing up everything was such a chore back then. Our first dual byline was in the **Carrie** (1976) (Vol 6/1) issue with feature stories on Sissy Spacek and Brian De Palma, **The People That Time Forgot** (1977) set report, and Michael Winner on **The Sentinel** (1977). Eventually Mike found it impossible to accompany me to most assignments due to his upward career trajectory, so I did it alone, took solo credit and never looked back. It was Mike's radio contacts that ensured we went to every press show and premiere, way before I could use 'CFQ' as the main calling card.

Did the magazine open doors for me? Absolutely. 'CFQ' was always considered the crème de la crème and I was asked to review movies for such other contemporary UK magazines as 'The House of Hammer' and 'Starburst' as a result. Fred did see the latter as a conflict of interest, but the landscape was so different back then, and we were paid peanuts. At first he didn't get the fact that I couldn't go to a British PR about an American magazine because they didn't care about international press as opposed to their domestic priority. Once I taught him that the way to get the best access for 'CFQ' meant also being visible on the UK front, he understood, even though it did rankle. Fred often thought I got on film sets because of the 'CFQ' name alone where it was a combo that

swung it really. I'd sometimes trade generic interviews for press packs for better access. Frédéric Albert Lévy in Paris and Jan Doense in Amsterdam had the same problem as me, I remember. In the modern era most director/horror stars I've come across mention my work on 'CFQ'. When Nicolas Winding Refn, an old friend anyway, and I decided to work on 'The Act of Seeing' book together, he bought up loads of 'CFQ' copies on eBay to read my early stuff so he would be in a happy frame of mind to let me loose on the text.

Although our friendship/business relationship was a remote one at first I grew to really like Fred. The phone would ring, he'd say "Alan Jones", I'd say "Fred Clarke" and we'd begin our lengthy conversations. Always about movies, never about anything personal or current affairs – except once when Princess Diana and Prince Charles got married and the whole of London closed down for the event. He couldn't understand why I wouldn't be able to go and conduct an interview due to local travel being impossible! We talked to each other once a month regular as clockwork. Phone charges being so outrageous back then, I'd call and tell him to call back, which he always did. I liked keeping him in the picture of what I was doing.

Unless he had specifically called the interviewee him/herself, I did all the heavy lifting when it came to making contact with whatever films were in production. I called the unit publicists, developed a relationship with them for future assignments etc. Not sure if that was the case for those on the US side. He came to London once, on Columbia's dime for **Krull** (1983), we had an awkward dinner, I asked him if he wanted to go out somewhere, he said he just wanted to read in his hotel room every night. It was only then really that I realised what an insular, insecure loner he was. And when I visited him in Oak Park, Chicago, I was shocked at how small and untidy the office was – again an insight into his psyche. All those cupboards stuffed with old 'CFQ' issues – it was only then I realised the readership probably wasn't as massive as I thought it was. Did it matter, no, we were all doing great coverage for those who counted in the industry and the genre connoisseur.

Not that I ever expected him to commit suicide but looking back I suppose the signs were there. Never met the wife or children. Fred very rarely edited anything I wrote. Sometimes he would call for clarification over certain facts, but what I wrote was pretty much the copy I read on the printed page, often including basic typos. So I owe him a massive debt of gratitude because I learnt from all my mistakes through 'CFQ', and developed my writing style as a result. I did speak to him the day before he died. I have no idea why it possessed me to do so but I told him how important he had been to my career, how grateful I was and that I would never forget it. That was the only bit of comfort I got from subsequent events – he knew what I felt about him even if he didn't realise it before.

25 years is a long time to be associated with one magazine (strangely enough my time with 'Starburst' lasted just as long, and my film critic position with 'Radio Times' continues). So naturally things evolved. I went from interviewing a stoned Sissy Spacek while lying on the bed in her hotel room for an hour to having a 10-minute round table with 15 other people with Angelina Jolie on **Lara Croft: Tomb Raider** (2001). The rise of the internet saw access reduced, control mushroom and relationships with PRs crumble over stupid storms in teacups. That's what I hate most about the business now; everything is a mega-drama over the release of one still 2 seconds before the approved time etc. Nonsense! The travelling to far-flung locations stopped too.

Gone are the days of being flown first class all-expenses paid to Buenos Aires, Argentina, for **Highlander II: The Quickening** (1991). Or Yugoslavia (now Croatia) to cover **Transylvania 6-5000** (1985) for 3 days. Or North Carolina with Clive Barker for location reporting on **Hellraiser III: Hell on Earth** (1992). Or being taken to the Venice Film Festival for Peter Jackson's **Heavenly Creatures** (1994).

It was "The Little Magazine That Could" (LA Times, March 16th, 1986) feature by Pat Broeske that first reported the blackout some studios had against the magazine in the 1980s. And I did encounter repercussions during my masthead time. There was the whole Steven Spielberg/George Lucas/John Landis/**Twilight Zone: The Movie** (1983) controversies. Once past being one of the few to cover **Star Wars** (1977) before it became the phenomenon, I never saw Lucas again. For years Landis would only tolerate me despite having covered **An American Werewolf in London** (1981) at Twickenham Film Studios. I also had a severe run in with Jeannot Szwarc after Fred inserted some 'fake news' in my **Santa Claus: The Movie** (1985) set report about reindeers being slaughtered for real for the production. I did get my own back on Spielberg though. I was covering a movie at Elstree Studio when I found a Xerox print-out left in an office machine showing the design of all the characters in **Who Framed Roger Rabbit** (1988) a full year before release. Fred printed it and all hell broke loose. I also did a great piece on **Jurassic Park** (1993) that nailed everything without getting his co-operation. Those were the days, when you'd hold your breath with each new issue just in case someone complained about what is now termed 'spoilers'.

After Fred's sudden death Mark Altman bought the franchise and everything changed. I know he did what he thought was appropriate in the circumstances, but I felt it was a mistake, and he was more concerned about his movie/TV producer career than anything else at time. **House of the Dead** (2003) aside, his credits haven't been bad. I never saw 'CFQ' as a stepping stone to anything apart from doing good writing work. I have never written a script or produced a movie because that's not what I ever wanted to do and I feel my career has flourished because of that prime focus. Looking back on my 'CFQ' career I'm amazed at what I achieved.

The weirdest interview Mike and I ever did together was the early one with Brian De Palma. He was about to leave his hotel for the airport so the PR asked him if he minded us travelling in his limo for the duration of the journey. He said fine, and in the middle of the journey, we got caught in a traffic jam. We literally sat there for 2 hours and to fill the time asked him everything this besotted fan wanted to know. That's why that interview is so good I think, and why I keep seeing it quoted. For many years after when I interviewed De Palma for other movies he would always say, 'Oh it's you, from the limo!'

I always adored covering the Muppet movies because I knew them personally anyway. The Bond movies were incredible to cover just because of the spectacular sets and hospitality, that's why Pierce Brosnan – I covered all 4 of his – will always be my favourite 007. **Little Shop of Horrors** (1986) was a dream assignment for me as I loved the musical and the original movie and to see it being filmed, with all the tape playback etc (which I'd never seen done before) was fabulous. It was great meeting Vincent Price on **The Monster Club** (1981), the one horror

actor I hadn't met up to that point. **Hellraiser** (1987) was filmed just around the corner from me in London and getting to know Clive Barker was a good thing for my future references. Dario Argento's **Opera** (1987) was the best and favourite feature I ever did for the magazine for obvious reasons.

One time a documentary crew got hold of me saying they wanted to interview me for a future DVD extra on **The Keep** (1983). The reason being they had a 20-minute 'Making of' done on set at the time for a news programme featuring me talking to Michael Mann and generally showing me going about my business. I had no idea it was being filmed and was astonished when I saw the footage – it's the only instance I know of myself being captured in the process of doing 'CFQ' work.

Because 'CFQ' was one of very few fantasy magazines back in the '70s/80s, the reach was quite incredible. At every FrightFest I have at least one person tell me how important my features were to them as they were just getting an appreciation of the genre. It doesn't make me feel old at all, but very gratified my work touched their lives. To today's director generation, Nicolas Winding Refn being an exception, 'CFQ' is something barely remembered from the mists of time although Eli Roth and Neil Marshall have brought it up on occasion. But I am so grateful for its legacy. At one point for reference purposes I started positioning 'CFQ' as the Ain't It Cool of its generation and although that website is now not-so-cool, I stick by that observation. Fred truly was a publishing pioneer and 'CFQ' was the geek culture bible before we even knew what a fanboy was. You can go back to any issue and read any feature, interview or set report on any film and it will still contain all the information you ever needed to know. It puts the current crop of mags and blogs/vlogs/podcasts/whatever to shame. Fred had a mission and he was dogged about it. He managed to find others who wanted to join him on that mission. And he created a magazine for the ages that will still be referred back to for decades to come. 'CFQ' has given me eternal life and I, with my 'sense of wonder' still as intact as it ever was, will forever be proud and so grateful.

And the day I received that life-changing telegram only got better too because that same night I was invited to attend the very first London preview of **Star Wars** (1977). The blockbuster phenomenon wasn't due to open in the UK for another six months but because of my association with the cast and crew and the fact we'd done an array of interviews for the upcoming 'CFQ' 'Making Of' double issue, we had scored some golden tickets. Taking place at the Dominion on Tottenham Court Road, to say the preview was the hottest ticket in town was yet another understatement. And, of course, George Lucas' sci-fi saga delivered on every level as everyone who saw it for the first time back then will confirm.

Not only was there a party after the laser-lit screening, there was an after-party dinner that was so celebrity packed I lost count of the Hollywood A-listers I spied. And after that I rushed on an adrenaline high to a favourite Disco, Glades (under the Charing Cross Station arches, which Heaven took over), and walked in just as the DJ started playing *Star Wars Theme* (1977) by Meco. It was as if time stood still, I couldn't believe the coincidence and it brilliantly capped one of the best days of my entire life. From that moment on I knew where my future lay. I soon put the Portobello Hotel behind me and began forging my unique career in the unknown world of genre journalism.

LOOKING FOR MR. GOODBAR (1977)

Two months before the release of **Saturday Night Fever** came this darker walk on the hedonistic Disco wild side laying the preparatory groundwork for the gritty milieu of that John Badham landmark. Fresh from her critical and popular success earlier in the year as Woody Allen's **Annie Hall**, the comedian director's muse and former girlfriend Diane Keaton starred in the controversial but commercially successful film version of Judith Rossner's bestselling 1975 airport novel 'Looking for Mr. Goodbar', inspired by the New Year's Day 1973 real-life Manhattan murder of 28-year-old promiscuous schoolteacher Roseann Quinn.

If as Annie Hall Keaton explored the kookier aspects of the free and easy single white female exploring her sexuality and lifestyle options during the heyday of Women's Lib, her role of Theresa Dunn was the murkier flipside of the gender defining sea changes occurring through every strata of 1970s society. A respected and caring physiotherapist for deaf children, Theresa is tormented by memories of a polio-stricken childhood and a rigidly Irish Catholic upbringing. Suffering severe body image issues due to scarring on her back, left by botched childhood surgery, the breakdown of a one-sided affair with a married university professor (Alan Feinstein) puts her in the "What the hell!" zone and she starts boozing, toking and cruising bars and clubs for thrilling one-night stands to find the love that has eluded her elsewhere.

Soon these celebrations of her erotic independence enter the kinky phase and become a high-risk addiction in diverse sexual ghettos represented by the three main male figures in Theresa's still-chauvinistic swinging singles scene. There's welfare worker James (William Atherton), her oppressive family's favourite match, who wins her heart by helping her get a hearing aid for a poor black girl from the projects. Then there's Tony (Richard Gere on early **American Gigolo**, 1980, form), a cocaine-fuelled hustler with mommy issues who turns her on with sadistic mind games. And finally there's Vietnam veteran ex-con Gary (Tom Berenger), a self-loathing homosexual with a

violent temper. Each is positioned as her potential killer complete with back-story psychoses before Gary steps to the fore as the prime last trick suspect in jock strap, blonde wig and feather boa, blaming a former sugar daddy for turning him into a flaming faggot.

Richard Brooks originally didn't want to direct the movie, but then the 67-year-old helmer behind **Cat on a Hot Tin Roof** (1958) and **In Cold Blood** (1967) sensed an opportunity to reprimand the Disco Generation as he had done the Rock 'n' Roll one in **Blackboard Jungle** (1955). In press junkets at the time he stated, "I became intrigued by the possibility of saying something about the lack of commitment young people seem to have today. Their infatuation with the merely sensational; their desire for instant relief and gratification; their lack of sexual joy; and their disillusionment because everything didn't turn out the way TV commercials say it should".

Many contemporary critics felt scriptwriter Brooks had done a disservice to Rossner's source material by dwelling on obvious sordid symbolism making it lighter in tone yet more heavy-handed in execution. In fact early preview performances found the under-forty crowd in hysterics at some of the supposedly harrowing scenes, which led to Brooks ordering screening rooms to be locked so reviewers couldn't walk out until the shocking finale.

But no one blamed Keaton, who received flat-out raves the second time that year for her electrifyingly explicit sexuality, pharmaceutically numb, emotionally starved and daring Madonna/whore character study of a wanton train-wreck. Keaton won the Best Actress Oscar for **Annie Hall** and many thought that decision was greatly helped by Academy voters seeing her full dramatic range on show in **Looking for Mr. Goodbar**. Tuesday Weld was also nominated as Best Supporting Actress for her role as Theresa's stewardess sister Katherine alongside another Oscar nod for William A. Fraker's atmospheric cinematography.

As with Brooks' far more searing **In Cold Blood** (1967), the suspense derives from a sickening feeling that something horrible is going to happen and everyone – including the audience – is powerless to stop it. Even if the central issues are ultimately fudged in Brooks' over-long condemnation of carnal self-destruction and the sensationalised singles scene, the Disco ambience is absolutely spot-on.

Although the book was set in Manhattan the film locale is San Francisco (but mostly shot in Chicago) and the club hits featured on the soundtrack are a super snapshot of a Disco era on the verge of going mirrorball-room ballistic. Both the Line Hustle and the New York Hustle are shown in full action as the loudspeakers blare out Donna Summer's seminal *Try Me, I Know We Can Make It* (1976), her second 'Billboard' Disco No.1, joined by *Could It Be Magic* (1976) and *Prelude to Love*, Thelma Houston's *Don't Leave Me This Way* (1976) and Diana Ross' *Love Hangover* (1976), two more Discotaneous chart toppers, the Commodores' *Machine Gun* (1974), The O'Jays' *Back Stabbers* (1972) and Boz Scaggs' *Lowdown* (1976). With its theatrical trailer composed of black-and-white photographs – **Cruising** (1980) would follow the same 'so shocking all we can show are these stills' montage template – Brooks' libidinous fascinator is a key artefact in showing the Disco movement in transgressive flux.

If you need some lovin', Some part-time huggin', Move to any beat, At Plato's Retreat!

Disco equalled Sex in the 1970s. Heterosexuals, homosexuals, bisexuals and try-sexuals were experimenting in excessively broad carnal knowledge as Fifties repression bored through emerging permissive

Steve Rubell and Ian Schrager

Sixties countercultures to explode in the Seventies as a joyful release of pent up passion. Relationship parameters changed, taboos were shattered and sexual healing occurred in every conjugation going as monogamy became passé, Mr. Right turned into Mr. Right Now and wherever Disco was played the horizontal tango happened close-by. AIDS was a decade away so sex was still great recreational fun. If you got a venereal disease, herpes or syphilis, you stopped by your local STD clinic for a few pills or shots. Nobody died. And catching crabs or scabies was seen as a badge of honour, a rite of passage.

Anything goes backrooms opened in most gay bars and clubs. In straight venues, the best example being Studio 54, rough trade happened in the balcony, the unisex toilets or the VIP basement. And if you couldn't get an invite to the Playboy Mansion in Los Angeles (written on the doorbell was "If you don't swing, don't ring") the most famous swingers' Disco in Manhattan was the members-only establishment Plato's Retreat, named after the ancient Greek free-thinker, and originally located in the rundown Kenmore Hotel on East 23rd Street between Lexington and Third Avenues. When the gay Continental Baths closed down in 1975 after violating public health warnings, Plato's Retreat co-owners Larry Levenson, a close friend of 'Screw' magazine editor Al Goldstein, and Fred J. Lincoln, porno director/actor and 'Weasel' Padowski in **The Last House on the Left** (1972), moved their hugely popular nightspot into its vacant lot, the basement of the Ansonia Hotel at 230 W. 74th Street complete with dance floor, saunas, whirlpool baths, games room, free bar and buffet and a heated swimming pool with waterfalls.

A fashionable watering hole for movie stars and porno celebrities, only straight couples were allowed through the club's hallowed doors, and once a woman left any of the play areas, her male escort had to accompany her. This was to stop any forbidden sexual activity between men although girl-on-girl action was welcomed. A No Alcohol/No Drugs/No Pressure policy was lackadaisically enforced even though the underground press adverts proclaimed "Come down and fulfil your most fantastic fantasies and stimulate your wildest dreams". Plato's Retreat relocated to 509 West 34th Street in 1980 but closed down in 1985 after becoming an anachronism in the AIDS era. It relocated to Fort Lauderdale, Florida, and renamed 321 Slammer turned gay in 2006.

Just like Studio 54, Plato's Retreat was bestowed Disco immortality thanks to American jazz funk flautist and alto saxophonist Joe Thomas, The Ebony Godfather. Written by the extraordinary combo of Andrea True Connection arranger Brad Baker, Lemon band member Gordon Grody, Meco musician Lance Quinn, José Ferrer's ex-wife Phyllis Hill and the mysterious I. Tillie (were they all incognito club members?), *Plato's Retreat* (1978) is refined Glampop Disco, wonderfully melodic, superbly orchestrated with a unique poly-rhythmic tribal chant break and featuring gorgeously warbled hooks by the ace trio of Diva Gray (Chic, Change), Jocelyn Brown (Musique, The Salsoul Orchestra, Van McCoy) and Gwen Guthrie (future *Ain't Nothing Going On But the Rent*, 1986, star). Everyone's invited, Gettin' all excited, Let's all do the freak… yeah!

Grace Jones and Andy Warhol

Disco Memo

See What The Boys In The Back Room Will Have

"Gomorrah the way it shoulda been" was how the ultimate Manhattan bathhouse, the Saint Marks Baths (6, Saint Marks Place, 8th Street and 3rd Avenue) was described by patrons. Many gay men arrived in New York on a Friday night for a Disco weekend without any place to stay. But for $11.50 per 8-hour session you could stay in one of the 156 cubicles all weekend wearing nothing but a towel. If people left the door ajar they were open to suggestion, the amber-tinted wall lamps helping the sleazy atmosphere. If the door was closed they were either busy or recovering. These facilities and cruising corridors were on the top floor of the three-storey pleasure palace. The first floor contained locker rooms, showers and a diner. The basement had a swimming pool, more showers, an enormous Jacuzzi tub, and a large, darkened orgy room. Those arriving at 10 a.m. from the local Village Discos and bars for a quickie made up the clientele for space on the giant mattress in the latter. If it was a three-day holiday weekend though, you might have had to queue on the Sunday evening.

Originally opened in 1906, for the next 50 years Saint Marks was a Turkish bath catering to local straight immigrants. Then a New York tabloid newspaper ran a headline in 1933 blaring "The pansy men of the Nation are just nuts about Turkish bathing", adding "Steam joints are the gathering places of perverts". The first gay trickle began, gathered momentum in the 1950s, but fizzled in 1975 when the slum building was considered unfit for purpose. That's when gay entrepreneurs Billy Nachman and Bruce Mailman, genius creators of incomparable Disco, The Saint, decided to invest and invent the ultimate destination bathhouse. While many bathhouses existed in the Disco '70s – The Club Baths (Disco radio station WKTU was pumped non-stop through the speakers), Man's Country, The Everard, Big Apple – and The Continental Baths practically revolutionised the industry, St. Mark's was the preferred choice for clean-living Disconnoisseurs.

THE DEEP (1977)

Jacqueline Bisset in a wet T-shirt and **Jaws** (1975) author Peter Benchley co-scripting from his own best-selling novel were enough to make this shallow sea saga a major box-office hit. It was the ninth top-grosser of the year and Columbia Pictures' No.1 release. The first production from Casablanca FilmWorks, the movie off-shoot of the biggest Disco label in the business, was directed by Peter Yates (responsible for *that* car chase in **Bullitt**, 1968) who does bring a certain amount of tension to the scenes on dry land, but once underwater fritters away every ounce of suspense by sluggishly elongating each submerged sequence into gorgeously photographed boredom.

Gail Berke (Bisset, **The Spiral Staircase**, 1975, remake) and David Sanders (Nick Nolte, just coming off his 1976 breakthrough performance in the miniseries 'Rich Man, Poor Man') are two amateur treasure-hunting divers on an adventure vacation in Bermuda. On one scuba-diving outing they inadvertently find the Goliath, a World War II cargo ship that sank with munitions and medical supplies on board, and an older Spanish galleon shipwrecked around 1714, each exposed by a recent storm. From both they recover a number of artefacts including ampoules of morphine and a gold medallion.

Soon two interested parties become curious about their finds. One is the local lighthouse keeper Romer Treece (intense Robert Shaw, adding yet more **Jaws** appeal) who knows his way around Spanish treasure history. The other is Haitian drug lord Henri 'Cloche' Bondurant (Lou Gossett Jr., starring concurrently in the 'Roots' miniseries TV event) who wants to buy the morphine stash and then starts terrorizing the couple with voodoo threats unless they comply. So Treece makes a deal with Cloche

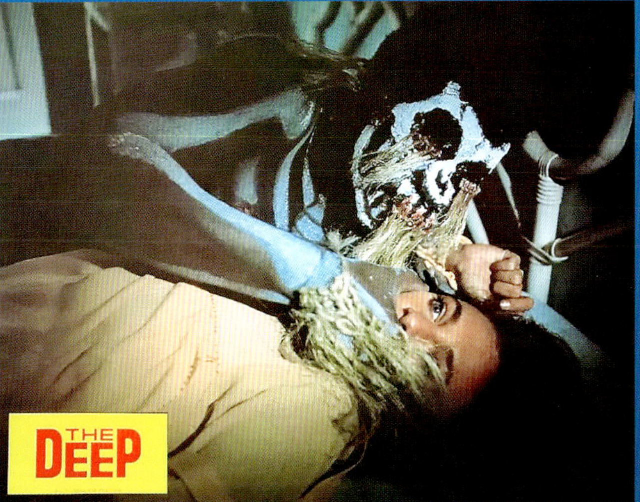

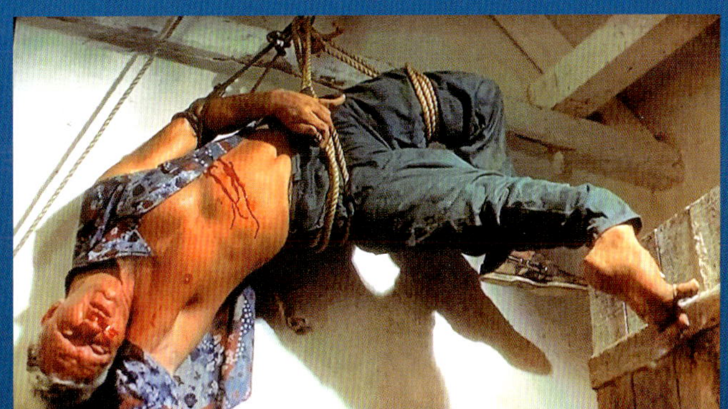

to recover the morphine for a million dollars within three days leaving them free of impediment to secretly raise the treasure trove. But once Treece has provenance that the treasure was indeed the property of Spanish noblewoman Elisabeth Farnese, he intends to destroy the Goliath and put the morphine out of villainous Cloche's reach. Cue the 'thrill-packed' climax filled with betrayal and murder as a final desperate dive causes death and destruction.

Quite why Cloche doesn't just hire freelance divers to recover the ampoules himself is just one of the many questions this implausibly waterlogged yarn poses as excitement inexorably drains away. Anyone hoping for something in the jawsome Steven Spielberg class had to make do with a haphazard shoal of bloodthirsty sharks and a halfway decent moray eel attack. Long on dumb dialogue scenes and short on narrative momentum, **The Deep** did have one major asset – Donna Summer and her No.3 dance chart hit with the catchy theme song.

Summer was riding high globally with her *I Remember Yesterday* (1977) album and Casablanca weren't going to let her brand recognition go to waste. Teaming her up with James Bond franchise composer John Barry was

a masterstroke. In one fell swoop you had a Disco Diva at the height of her powers and the Tsar of orchestral arrangements mining them for every nuance of aural moody suspense. Barry was a little late to the 007 Disco party when he uptempoed the **Moonraker** (1979) song by Shirley Bassey over the end credits. Marvin Hamlisch beat him to the dancefloor with *Bond 77* from **The Spy Who Loved Me** (1977), a Disco version of Monty Norman's famous James Bond theme. While Bill Conti just about followed in Barry's **Moonraker** footsteps with the mini Disco refrain *Gunbarrel* from **For Your Eyes Only** (1981).

Summer and Barry wrote *Theme from the Deep (Down, Deep Inside)* clearly with an eye on her talent for sexual innuendo and his flair for suave melody. While the soundtrack was notable for being pressed onto bright see-through ocean-blue vinyl, and the theme song was nominated for a Golden Globe Award, it achieved nineteen weeks of continuous Disco exposure by being double-A sided with Summer's seminal classic of the year *I Feel Love*. The other dance track on the album, *Disco Calypso* by Beckett, vanished without a trace but still retains an engaging jauntiness.

In 1999 I guested on a BBC radio talk show with Jacqueline Bisset and brought up **The Deep**. She professed to have no memory of filming it "live on-location in four oceans" (according to the final credits), ignored the fact it launched her as a Hollywood sex symbol and swore she didn't even know about the Donna Summer association. How different to producer Peter Guber's memory. According to the 1996 book 'Hit and Run: How Jon Peters and Peter Guber Took Sony for a Ride in Hollywood' (1996), Guber allegedly once said, "That T-shirt made me a rich man!"

Now is the Winter Melody of our Disco intent, made glorious Donna Summer by a "Son of My Father" (1972)

One of the world's best-selling artists of all time, she's still the undisputed Queen of Disco and the First Lady of Love. Donna Summer was born LaDonna Adrian Gaines on December 31st, 1948, found her voice in a Boston church and went to Broadway to be a star. An audition for the hit counterculture musical 'Hair' found her understudying Melba Moore (*This Is It*, 1976). Offered a role in the European touring version of the show Summer met producers Giorgio Moroder and Pete Bellotte in Munich and the rest is Disco history. She also met her first husband in Germany, Austrian actor Helmuth Sommer, the anglicised version of his surname impacting on her own when her first record cover misprinted it.

Donna Summer and Giorgio Moroder

Summer had sung background vocals on Moroder's Euro hit *Son of My Father* by Chicory Tip. Recognising her talent, Moroder then furnished Summer with the smash 1974 album *Lady of the Night* (1974), spawning two hit singles, *The Hostage* and the title track. But the album made absolutely no impact in America or the UK and Moroder knew to break both markets meant doing something really out-there and special. Inspired by the steamy Serge Gainsbourg and Jane Birkin duet *Je t'aime… moi non plus* (1969, which she would eventually Discofy in 1978), the Summer, Moroder and Bellotte trio wrote *Love to Love You Baby* (1975). When Casablanca Records head Neil Bogart heard it, he asked for a longer 17-minute version, created a game-changing, instant Disco classic and signed up Summer who would reign on dance floors until her death in 2012.

It's impossible to overstate Summer's earth-shattering place in Disco history. In her golden period she had nine No.1 Disco Chart hits – *Love to Love You Baby, Try Me, I Know We Can Make It* (1976), all cuts on the *Four Seasons of Love* album (1976), same on the *I Remember Yesterday* (1977) album, ditto with the *Once Upon a Time…* (1977) album, *Last Dance* (1978), *MacArthur Park Suite* (1978), *Hot Stuff/Bad Girls* (1979), and her duet with Barbra Streisand *No More Tears (Enough Is Enough)* (1979). Incredibly her epochal *I Feel Love* (1977) didn't hit the top spot despite it now being recognised as crucial in the development of the entire Disco form by introducing a dramatic synthesized soundscape inspired by Kraftwerk's *Autobahn* (1975). Sounding as wonderful today as it did when first released, and remixed, *I Feel Love* is the perfect Disco record and a directional milestone.

Summer's Disco star would continue through the 1980s with the Stock, Aitken and Waterman duo *This Time I Know It's for Real* (1989) and *Love's About to Change My Heart* (1989), and the 1990s with the operatic No.1 Dance Chart hit *I Will Go with You (Con te partiro)* (1999). While she looked like alienating her core gay following with misjudged comments on the AIDS crisis, something she always denied, Summer nevertheless changed the face of Disco, became the first artist ever to have three consecutive double albums reach No.1 on the 'Billboard' chart, *Live and More* (1978), *Bad Girls* (1979) and *On the Radio: Greatest Hits Volumes I & II* (1979), and the second Disco act (after Boney M.'s 'Daddy Cool' in 2006) to have a stage musical feature her back catalogue, 'Summer: The Donna Summer Musical' (2017).

The HBO documentary **Love to Love You, Donna Summer** (2023), directed by Roger Ross Williams (**Cassandro**, 2023) and Donna's daughter Brooklyn Sudano, from her marriage with Brooklyn Dreams writer/producer/singer Bruce Sudano, is a major disappointment. Barely paying lip service to the important milestones in her recording life, skipping over *Last Dance* (1978) and *No More Tears (Enough Is Enough)* (1979) with Giorgio Moroder hardly getting a look in, the reverential accent is on Summer's personal demons, inbred spirituality, her Born Again Christian period and late reconciliation with the traditional roles of wife and mother. Having a family member on the creative team clearly meant nothing too controversial would be covered. But with access to the wealth of archive media coverage, concert footage and extensive array of home movies, it's such a shame the trail-blazing music comes a fuzzy poor second. The major crime made though is wasting an ideal platform through which to reaffirm Summer's vital place in pop music history and reclaim Disco as a genre whose influence has never waned.

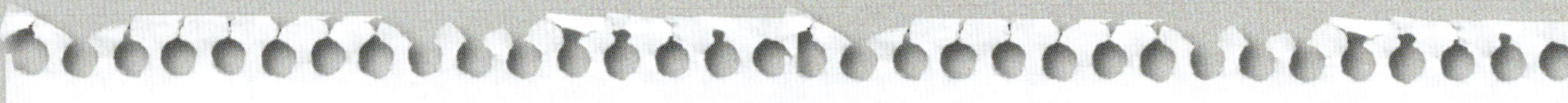

God Save The Queen

In the same month **The Deep** was released in America came the day everything changed regarding my involvement with the Punk movement, and the Sex Pistols in particular. June 7, 1977, was the date of the notorious 'alternative' celebration of Queen Elizabeth's Silver Jubilee organised by the band's new label Virgin Records, a party boat trip down the river Thames to promote the radio-banned controversial single *God Save the Queen*. It still got to No.2 though in the British Hit Parade. My date for the evening was Steve Strange, of later Visage fame, who had virtually begged to be my plus one for street cred. And the event started out well, all my friends were there, Debbie and Tracy who I worked with at SEX, artist Jamie Reid, Malcolm McLaren's fab business manager Sophie Richmond at Glitterbest, food was plentiful, Richard Branson was glad-handing the deck and the band was on great form as we sailed past the Houses of Parliament. But the police were circling as the band did their set of *Anarchy in the U.K.*, *God Save the Queen*, *No Feelings* and *Pretty Vacant*.

Then suddenly the police were pulling up alongside and without warning boarded the boat, cut the power, to which Johnny Rotten screamed *No Fun*, forced the captain to return to the docking pier and all hell broke loose as people started getting arrested for obstruction, breach of the peace, threatening behaviour and assault.

I have two vivid memories of the Boat Party and its aftermath. One was Vivienne Westwood in her signature anarchy shirt holding onto a side rail and pissing in the river. The other was Vivienne being kicked around on the floor by the police. To this day I can't understand why I wasn't targeted. I did feel removed from what was unfolding before my eyes, it felt like a movie in slow motion. I don't know what happened to Steve. But as I silently walked away from the melee I knew my time in Punk Central was coming to a close. I'd already had more than enough brushes with the law, most famously my Naked Cowboy T-shirt arrest, and although I kept in touch with everyone, especially my next-door neighbour Sid Vicious, and agreed to work on **The Great Rock 'n' Roll Swindle** (1980), I started becoming less visible on the *après*-gig scene.

BLACK JOY (1977)

Car Wash wasn't the only music-driven movie in competition at the 1977 Cannes Film Festival. But **Black Joy** adopted a similar feel-good sit-com tone to broach the pertinent issues surrounding the entire immigration system, nascent multiculturalism and the basic lot of unemployed black Britons in a vibrantly depicted South London Brixton ghetto. Often cited as the British riposte to 1970s American Blaxploitation because of its familiar urban underdog clichés, flashy fashions, action-led narrative and heightened melodrama, it succeeds best when precisely balancing emerging British black culture on a social seesaw bouncing between slice-of-life reality and fish-out-of-water irony, wall-to-wall reggae and down-to-earth Disco. Here is an ethnic minority in flux during the most crucial Disco days and as such is an important document of yet another monumental change in contemporary attitudes and authenticity.

Based on Jamal Ali's acclaimed stage play 'Dark Days and Light Nights', and directed by ex-barrister Anthony Simmons, at a cost of £150,000, **Black Joy** is the story of Ben (a continuously dazed and confused Trevor Thomas who would feature in **Inseminoid**, 1981), a just-off-the-red-eye-flight immigrant from Guyana whose country-boy naivety instantly radiates itself to everyone he meets. With his cardboard suitcase and obscure address of the relative he's supposed to be staying with written on a crumpled piece of paper, he's an easy mark bumbling around Brixton's teeming mean streets.

After first suffering the humiliation of being strip-searched at Heathrow, he loses his wallet and cash to a nine-year-old mugger, suffers further mortification

in a homeless hostel and then meets jive-talking con artist Dave (Norman Beaton) whose only source of income seems to be his girlfriend Miriam's (Floella Benjamin) greasy spoon café. It turns out the juvenile thief is Miriam's wayward son and the Pilgrim's Progress misadventures continue as Ben wins big on a horse race, making him an effortless target for assorted scum, finds a job as a dustbin man, gives his wages to a fraudulent landlord and finally gets street-wise travelling the bright lights and big city alleyways with Dave through the local gambling clubs, sex shops, brothels and Discos.

Black Joy being firmly set in the social mores of the times, prejudice, interracial relationships and abortion all make it into the over-baked melting pot screenplay co-written by Simmons and Ali. Directed by Simmons with a breakneck speed to disguise its narrative logistical shortcomings, it's an uneasy mix of the kitchen sink dourness he brought to his Judi Dench starrer **Four in the Morning** (1965) crossed with the whimsy of his Peter Sellers headlining bust, **The Optimists of Nine Elms** (1973). But many contemporary critics found its glimpse of the financial, heritage and social struggles of a barely acknowledged ethnic underclass a brutally honest and unsentimental slice of British ghetto life.

For the Disco set, this inexpensive slice of hyper cinéma-vérité proved an infectious disarmer in its nightclub sequences. The soundtrack was the last one curated by Mercury record producer Lou Reizner, best known for Rod Stewart's first two solo albums, the orchestral version of The Who's rock opera *Tommy* (1969), and Rick Wakeman's *Journey to the Centre of the Earth* (1974). Wedged between an eclectic range of 1970s chart hits – i.e. Billy Paul's *Me and Mrs. Jones* (1972), Johnny Nash's *Tears on My Pillow* (1975) – reggae album tracks – Toots and the Maytals' *Living in the Ghetto* (1976), The Heptones' *Mama Say* (1976) – cuts by African artists Manu Dibango, The Burundi Drummers and the Ipi Tombi Drummers and the title song by Jimmy Helms (co-written by Biddu), were

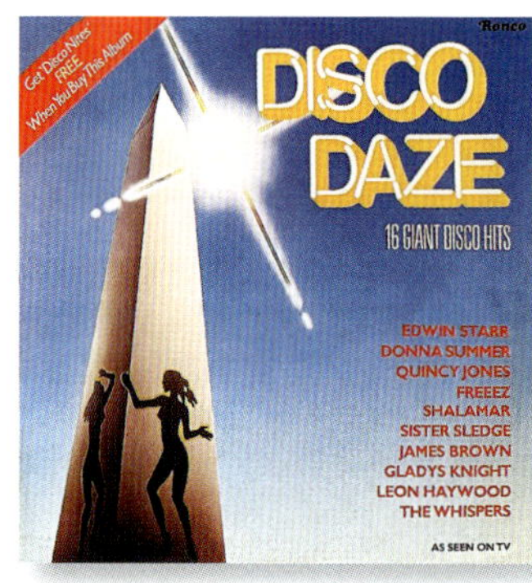

other snatches of such tried and tested Disco favourites as Harold Melvin and the Blue Notes' *Don't Leave Me This Way* (1975), the Biddu Orchestra's *Summer of '42* (1975), Shirley and Company's *Shame, Shame, Shame* (1974), George McCrae's *Rock Your Baby* (1974), Labelle's *Lady Marmalade* (1974), KC and The Sunshine Band's *That's the Way (I Like It)* (1975) and The Three Degrees' *When Will I See You Again?* (1974). Also included were such lesser-known chuggers from The O'Jays (*Darlin', Darlin' Baby (Sweet Tender Love)*, 1977), and The Real Thing (*Lightning Strikes Again*, 1977).

Bolstered by good reviews and a Cannes Palme d'Or director nomination for Simmons, **Black Joy** entered UK release in November 1977. Despite being well on the way to becoming a minor commercial success, the film had to be taken out of circulation when it was revealed that musical performing rights had not been correctly obtained. Four years later the legal wrangle was finally resolved and it went back on release. But by then it had dated so badly, especially in the wake of the burgeoning gritty Black Cinema led by the likes of **Pressure** (1975, but not released until 1977), **Babylon** (1980) and **Burning an Illusion** (1981).

Disco Ronco

Ronco was the 1970s telemarketing label created by entrepreneur Ron Popeil – remember those Tommy Vance-voiced TV commercials for such innovative products as the Chop-O-Matic and Mr. Microphone? The company launched its record arm in 1972 with the *20 Star Tracks* album and the next year topped the charts with its *That'll Be the Day* compilation of hits 'inspired' by the David Essex/Ringo Starr movie of the same name. This brand of *faux* soundtrack cash-in continued with **Black Joy, The Stud** (1978) and **The World Is Full of Married Men** (1979) and Ronco's success with such Disco laden double albums would garner it another No.1 in 1981 with *Disco Daze and Disco Nites.* While many of the songs included on the **Black Joy** soundtrack album were featured in the movie, some were just licensed filler. Yet that didn't stop it rapidly rising to chart success, achieving platinum disc status within two weeks of release.

Disco Memo

I'm Laker, Fly Me

A revolution happened in the travel business in 1977. Entrepreneur Sir Freddie Laker launched Skytrain, a low-cost, no frills airline service between London Gatwick Airport and New York City's John F. Kennedy Airport. For £37.50 one-way you could now get to Manhattan for the weekend and before long every flight was filled with clubbers desperate to experience the New York Disco scene. A popular joke at the time was, when it's midnight in Manhattan, it's 1965 in London. Which wasn't that far from the truth when even supposedly Soho sophisticates would come back home exhausted from 24-hour marathons hustling between The Loft, Tenth Floor, 12 West, Infinity, Flamingo, and, later, Paradise Garage, Le Jardin, and The Saint, telling scandalous tales of open drug use, on-site sex, and ecstatic, nonstop, all-night dancing.

I had first travelled to New York in 1975 as a guest of 'Andy Warhol's Pork' adaptor and director, Anthony J. Ingrassia. Tony took me under his wing because he had pitched me to David Bowie's publicist Cherry Vanilla (she had acted in 'Pork') and manager Tony Defries to run Bowie's fan club as part of his MainMan organisation, and thanks to him I hung out with all The Factory superstars, Wayne/Jayne County, Johnny Thunders, Patti Smith, Candy Darling, Nico, John Cale, the Ramones, 'Interview' columnist Fran Lebowitz and the New York Dolls at that banner watering-hole Max's Kansas City. Tony was the loveliest guy, an important figure in my becoming accepted in avant-garde Manhattan circles, and I was devastated when he died early in 1995 of cardiac arrest.

Because he helped Debbie Harry and company with their stagecraft and choreography, another major claim to fame was Tony putting me on the guest list for Blondie's first ever gig at CBGBs. At the after-party back at Debbie and Chris Stein's place, I saw she had a packet of **Torture Garden** (1967) seeds, the gimmick given out at Drive-Ins during its American release, pinned to her kitchen wall. Because I have collected, and still do, such freebies over the years, I asked her if I could have them and she gifted them in an instant. I loved Debbie from that moment on and was pleased to be her No.1 back stage groupie during the band's first UK tour, watching her perform from the wings.

So naturally I was on one of those first Laker flights and headed straight for 12 West, allegedly the place where producer Jacques Morali was inspired to form the Village People. Scented oxygen was pumped into the place where lessons for the Line Hustle would be taught before the club opened proper and a buffet table was stacked with fresh fruit, snacks and juices to keep the energy levels up. It was everything I ever dreamed a Disco could be and I danced myself dizzy to the classic *From Here to Eternity* (1977) by Giorgio Moroder and *Magic Bird of Fire* (1977) by The Salsoul Orchestra. The entire night is an indelible memory because I also took in other venues in the off-Christopher Street area: The Anvil (where there was a running competition to see how many beer cans participants could push up their rectum), the Mineshaft (where **Cruising** was set in 1980) and The Toilet (its tiled interiors hosed down hourly because of encouraged Golden Showers mid-dance). These NYC weekenders became an important part of my life and I revelled in the jet-set Disco marvels.

▲ Top: Left to right – Pop star Dana Gillespie, manager Tony Defries and David Bowie at the 'Pork' premiere at London's Roundhouse in 1971.

SATURDAY NIGHT FEVER (1977)

The iconic Disco movie that changed the world, sparking the mainstream dance craze, highlighting one of the most career-defining, incandescent screen performances of all time from John Travolta making him an overnight star sensation. The significance of **Saturday Night Fever** as one of the key pop cultural phenomena of the 20th Century cannot be underestimated. It did indeed become 'Discolossal' as predicted by the first US one-sheet poster featuring Travolta in that celebrated finger-pointing pose wearing that timeless white suit on that colourfully flashing dance floor. It was the grittily realistic low-budget art film costing $3.5 million, which Travolta thought was merely "**Taxi Driver** with dancing", that stayed in theatres for six months solid, made $85 million at the box-office in record time, brought 1960s trio the Bee Gees out of the pop wilderness and into the Disco charts with a vengeance and created an entire industry of Dance Contest movie rip-offs.

It began with the June 7, 1976 'New York' magazine feature 'Tribal Rites of the New Saturday Night' by music journalist Nik Cohn, who had published a history of rock 'n' roll 'Rock from the Beginning' and written the text for the classic artwork book 'Rock Dreams'. Although Cohn would eventually confess that he'd made up most of the article, at the time he said it was based on personal research carried out while exploring the suburban Disco scene in the Brooklyn area. In the introduction to the feature he stated all the events were factual, most he had participated in, and only the names had been changed. Especially that of his lead cipher Vincent, who Cohn said

▲ Above and overleaf top: James McMullan illustrations from the 'New York' magazine.

went One, and Two, and Tap, and Turn. And Tap, and Turn, and Tap.

"I was in love once. At least I thought I was," said Vincent. "I was going to get engaged."

"What happened?"

"My sister got sick and I had to stay home, waiting for the doctor. So I didn't get to the club until midnight. Bojangles, I think it was. And by then I was too late."

"How come?"

"She danced with someone else."

"Only danced?"

"Of course," said Vincent, "and after that, I could never feel the same. I couldn't even go near her. I didn't hate her, you understand. Maybe I still loved her. But I couldn't stand to touch her. Not when I knew the truth."

Around two, the band stopped playing, the Faces grew weary, and the night broke up. Outside the door, as Vincent made his exit, trailed by his lieutenants, a boy and a girl were embracing, framed in the neon glow. And Vincent stopped; he stared. No more than two yards distant, he stood quite still and studied the kiss in closest detail, dispassionate, as though observing guinea pigs.

The couple did not look up and Vincent made no comment. Down the street, Joey was honking the car horn. "God gave his only son," said John James.

"What for?" said Vincent, absentmindedly.

"Rent," replied the Double J.

It was then that something strange occurred. Across the street, in the darkness beyond a steel-mesh gate, the guard dogs still snarled and waited. Gus and Eugene stood on the curb directly outside the gate, laughing, stomping their feet. They were drunk and it was late. They felt flat, somehow dissatisfied. And suddenly they threw themselves at the steel wires, yelling.

The guard dogs went berserk. Howling, they reared back on their hind legs, and then they hurled themselves at their assailants, smashing full force into the gate. Gus and Eugene sprang backwards, safely out of reach. So the dogs caught only air. And the Faces hooted, hollered. They made barking noises, they whistled, they beckoned the dogs toward them. "Here, boys, here," they said, and the dogs hurled forward again and again, in great surging waves, half maddened with frustration.

Even from across the street, the man in the suit could hear the thud of their bodies, the clash of their teeth on the wires. Gus sat down on the sidewalk, and he laughed so much it hurt. He clasped his sides, he wiped away tears. And Eugene charged once more. He taunted, he leered, he stuck out his

JUNE 7, 1976/NEW YORK 39

he'd found hanging out at the local 2001 Odyssey Disco entrance, felt his demeanour reminded him of the old 1950s Teddy Boy attitude back in his native Ireland, so much so he wanted to place himself inside Vinnie's head to see what made him tick.

Cohn's vivid report was set against the backdrop of a crime-ridden, filthy and bankrupt New York and focused on a clique of friends known as The Faces living in the Bay Ridge area who couldn't wait for the weekend so they could dance the night away at the Disco, forgetting their mundane jobs and family problems. Vinnie was the ordinary Italo-American stud finding release and his identity on the flashing Disco floor as his spectacular and energetic dance moves shot him to local hero stardom. Vinnie may have been a composite character but the sketch used to illustrate Cohn's article was based on the unmistakable visage of Eugene Robinson, an 18-year-old high school dropout, paint store deliveryman and renowned Disco King.

The article caught the eye of visionary maverick impresario Robert Stigwood who saw the Everyman potential of the universal story given a contemporary Disco spin and he instantly bought the screen rights. Australian Stigwood arrived in London in 1957 to become one of the most famous showbiz tycoons of all time, responsible for launching the careers of super-groups the Bee Gees,

John Travolta as Vincent "Vinnie" Barbarino in *Welcome Back, Kotter* (1975).

John Travolta and Nancy Allen in *Carrie* (1976).

Cream, Blind Faith, the composer/lyricist team of Andrew Lloyd Webber and Tim Rice, and when he formed RSO Records in 1973 signed up Eric Clapton and Smokie, also producing the musical movies **Jesus Christ Superstar** (1973) and **Tommy** (1975) and, with **Can't Stop the Music** (1980) producer Allan Carr, the Mexploitation shocker **Survive!** (1977).

At the 1971 Broadway auditions for the stage 'Jesus Christ Superstar', a 17-year-old star-struck John Travolta had turned up with his slim portfolio and dance experience learned from Gene Kelly's teacher brother, Fred. He didn't get a part but Stigwood, who was in the audience that day, noted on a yellow legal pad that Travolta was one to watch. Indeed, Stigwood did keep tabs on Travolta's raw talent, through a featured role in The Andrews Sisters' Broadway hit 'Over Here!' and his subsequent TV stardom in the sit-com 'Welcome Back, Kotter'.

Eventually signed to a three-picture million-dollar contract by Stigwood, the original plan was to launch Travolta's Hollywood career with the screen version of the hit stage musical 'Grease'. Travolta had played the lead role Danny Zuko in the American touring version of the show, but because it was still playing to sell-out crowds at the Eden Theatre in Manhattan, the producers wanted to delay the film version in case it caused a drop in business, a common showbiz thought of the day. So it turned out that Brian De Palma's horror classic **Carrie** (1976) would be Travolta's film debut, while **Saturday Night Fever** was quickly put in place to be his leading man follow-up.

Working for Stigwood at RSO Records was Kevin McCormick who suddenly found himself executive producer on the movie, something he had never done before. A quick learning curve trip to Hollywood threw up the name of John G. Avildsen who had directed the critically acclaimed **Joe** (1970) and **Save the Tiger** (1973) and was just about to unleash the Sylvester Stallone phenomenon **Rocky** (1976) on an unsuspecting public.

Once hired Avildsen brought on his **Joe** scriptwriter Norman Wexler to fashion Cohn's article into a workable screenplay and it was the two-time Oscar nominee, for that and **Serpico** (1973), who brilliantly captured the gritty toughness of the concept and pushed the street lifestyle and language into controversially new mainstream areas. But Avildsen seemed to lose faith in the project and when he tried to rewrite the script against Travolta's wishes, Stigwood fired him on the very day he learned he was Oscar nominated for **Rocky**.

Reliable TV series veteran John Badham was then engaged to take control of the wayward venture. With only one feature film credit to his name, **The Bingo Long Travelling All-Stars and Motor-Kings** (1976), Badham found he had just two-and-a-half weeks to get shoot-ready for the March 11, 1977, start date. Quickly putting the actors into intensive rehearsal to ensure their camaraderie felt real and not fake, location filming was a nightmare with every single 'Welcome Back, Kotter' fan seemingly lining the Brooklyn streets to catch a glimpse of their hero. Troma Films' Lloyd Kaufman was the location manager as he was on **Rocky** and recalled the shoot was just one headache after another, especially when the Mafia turned up for their payout.

Because Travolta's character in 'Welcome Back, Kotter' was also named Vinnie (Barbarino), his **Saturday Night Fever** persona was changed to Tony Manero in the literal Disco 'Pilgrim's Progress' plot.

Belittled by his bitter, unemployed father Frank (Val Bisoglio), and constantly being unfavourably compared by his mother (Julie Bovasso) to his elder brother Frank Jr. (Martin Shakar), studying for the priesthood, Tony rules the 2001 Odyssey Disco roost at the weekends with his best buddies Bobby C (Barry Miller), Joey (Joseph Cali), Double J (Paul Pape) and Gus (Bruce Ornstein). It's when Tony dumps his regular squeeze Annette (Donna Pescow) as his partner in an upcoming Dance Contest, for uptown sophisticate Stephanie (Karen Lynne Gorney) that events take darker turns.

Frank Jr. decides to give up the priesthood, Gus is beaten up by Puerto Rican bangers, or so he thinks, Bobby agonises over being forced to marry his pregnant girlfriend and a drunk and romance-desperate Annette is gang-raped by Tony's pals. When Tony and Stephanie win the contest because the judges show clear racism towards the better Latino couple, he gives them the prize money, and confronts how empty and pathetic his whole life is.

It's when Bobby C falls to his death from the Verrazzano Bridge that Tony realises something has to change and after a long subway ride into Manhattan where he contemplates the meaning of life, turns up at Stephanie's new apartment asking to be her friend and his companion on the scary journey into the future unknown.

Although Paramount Pictures were initially scared to death of the completed movie – the studio heads were seriously worried about the urban delinquency, sexual content and vulgar language in what they had perceived a PG musical – they needn't have worried. Although it would eventually be re-edited for the teen market to maximise box-office returns, the impact the unadulterated movie had was instantaneous and it became a must-see event because of Stigwood's canny marketing strategy; the soon-to-be record-breaking soundtrack album was released a full month before the December 16, 1977, world premiere

IT IS NOW RATED PG

Because
we want everyone to see
John Travolta's performance...

Because
we want everyone to hear
the #1 group in the country, the Bee Gees...

Because
we want everyone to catch
"Saturday Night Fever."

©1977 Paramount Pictures Corporation. All Rights Reserved.

...Catch it.

PARAMOUNT PICTURES PRESENTS A ROBERT STIGWOOD PRODUCTION JOHN TRAVOLTA KAREN LYNN GORNEY "SATURDAY NIGHT FEVER" Screenplay by NORMAN WEXLER Directed by JOHN BADHAM Executive Producer KEVIN McCORMICK Produced by ROBERT STIGWOOD

PG PARENTAL GUIDANCE SUGGESTED SOME MATERIAL MAY NOT BE SUITABLE FOR CHILDREN DOLBY STEREO™ Original music written and performed by the BEE GEES. Read the Bantam Paperback. Soundtrack album available on RSO Records. A Paramount Picture.

770134

At the time of Stigwood's request the group were recording a new album at the Château d'Hérouville studios near Paris. They had already written *How Deep Is Your Love, If I Can't Have You* and *Stayin' Alive* for that project and Stigwood immediately pounced on them for what was provisionally titled 'Saturday Night'. *How Deep Is Your Love* had originally been written for Yvonne Elliman, the original Mary Magdalene in the Broadway production of 'Jesus Christ Superstar'. But when Stigwood insisted it become a Bee Gees song, they gave her *If I Can't Have You* instead. A further track, *More Than a Woman*, was recorded by both the trio and *Heaven Must Be Missing an Angel* (1976) soulsters Tavares, and to up the Bee Gees ante, their previous hits *Jive Talkin'* (1975) and *You Should Be Dancing* (1976) were also included. When they composed *Night Fever* specifically for the movie, the song impacted on the eventual release title.

in New York meaning it was already riding high on chart listings, radio airplay saturation and Disco rotation. While the double gatefold soundtrack employed such tried and tested favourites as *Disco Inferno* (1976) by The Trammps, *Open Sesame* (1976) by Kool & The Gang, *Disco Duck* (1976) by Rick Dees & His Cast of Idiots, *K-Jee* (1975) by MFSB, *Calypso Breakdown* (1976) by Ralph McDonald and *A Fifth of Beethoven* (1976) by The Walter Murphy Band as well as *Boogie Shoes* (1975) by KC and The Sunshine Band, Stigwood wanted five extra solid gold hits as crossover insurance and asked the Bee Gees to supply them. The British trio of brothers Barry, Robin and Maurice Gibb had already had a steady stream of falsetto Swinging Sixties hits since first being signed by Stigwood to his artist roster in 1967; *Massachusetts* (1967), *World* (1967) and *Words* (1968) just three of their classic ballads.

Rough demo tapes of the Bee Gees songs were used on location during filming so the actors had the right tracks

to react to. Even so, many were surprised to find them all playing slightly slower in the final master synch. Composer David Shire, already lauded for his **The Conversation** (1974) and **All the President's Men** (1976) scores, wrote the underrated incidental tracks *Manhattan Skyline*, *Barracuda Hangout*, *Salsation* and *Night on Disco Mountain* (a fabulous reworking of Mussorgsky's classical piece *Night on Bald Mountain*) and received two Grammy nominations for his sterling efforts. Because one dance sequence had been choreographed to the 1976 Boz Scaggs hit *Lowdown* but the artist's management refused clearance, Shire found he had to replicate its tempo and beat to match the moves exactly. With that one decision Scaggs missed out on royalty millions when the album became the best-selling soundtrack of all time and still remains so.

While **Saturday Night Fever** became the cultural touchstone for an entire dance-deprived generation, it was also responsible for Disco overload. For a solid six months the songs were played incessantly on every media platform and many felt it became too much, with certain radio stations actively promoting 'Bee Gee Free Zones'. It's the reason why the trio got blamed for killing Disco off after supposedly starting it in the first place, erroneous assumptions on both counts. The Bee Gees were never a Disco group to begin with despite their names now being synonymous with it. And the whole Disco Demolition Night in Chicago's Comiskey Park on July 12th, 1979, would have happened anyway in the broader backlash to Disco by rock music fans and those with racist and homophobic agendas.

Nevertheless, **Saturday Night Fever** has solo ensured the Disco era will never be forgotten and will endure well into the distant future. At the time the soon-to-be-standard songs were covered by such established Disco artists as Carol Douglas (*Night Fever*, 1978), Travolta's famous dance moves were spoofed in **Airplane!** (1980), and the Tony Manero saga was continued in the ill-conceived and clumsy sequel **Staying Alive** (1983) where our urban hero deserted the Brooklyn Discos for stardom on the Broadway stage. Doomed with clunky direction by co-writer/producer Sylvester (**Rocky**) Stallone, Travolta was embarrassingly supported by Cynthia Rhodes, Finola Hughes and Steve Inwood. Far better was the 'Saturday Night Fever' stage musical, which opened in London May 1998, and is still playing somewhere in the world. Added to the roster of evergreens were the Bee Gees' 1979 chart-topper *Tragedy* and songs specifically written for the show – *Immortality*, *First and Last*, *What Kind of Fool* and *It's my Neighbourhood*.

A Disco marvel that will never die, **Saturday Night Fever** is a forever fever. Especially as the song *Stayin' Alive* has now been appropriated by the medical profession as a guide to how CPR should be correctly administered.

Dance, Dance, Dance

Once everyone had seen **Saturday Night Fever** everyone wanted to learn to dance and the masses flocked to the clubs to experience what they saw in the movie. Whether the Hustle, the Latin Hustle, the New York Hustle or the Bus Stop, the Traffic Light, the Walk, the Foxy Trot and the Bump, dance studios had lines out the door to enrol as Disco ruled the nightlife. Those who couldn't afford lessons or turn up early at clubs for perfunctory tuition bought 'How To' LP's like the K-tel double album *Night Moves (The Professional Approach to Disco Dance Instruction)* (1979), a guide to every step needed to own the Disco floor. K-tel International, like their stable mate Ronco, sold handy consumer products via infomercials and also became a pioneer of the music compilation albums with their *Super Hits* and *Dynamic Hits* series.

One record in the two-disc tutorial contained lessons on how to do The Worm, The Freak, The Lateral Dip etc. and came with a book by trainer Deney Terrio, Travolta's choreographer and host of the US TV series 'Dance Fever' (1979-85). The other record contained a few Disco tracks you could practice to, like Sylvester's *Dance (Disco Heat)* (1978), Cerrone's *Je suis music* (1978), Mass Production's *Strollin'* (1979) and Ida Randina's *Make It a Night for Love* (1979). Perhaps K-tel's biggest contribution to Disco though were the Grammy-nominated *Hooked on Classics* (1981-83) series of classical recordings gone Disco played by the Royal Philharmonic Orchestra.

Disco dance instruction albums quickly became a cottage industry. True, there had been some pre-**Saturday Night Fever** attempts like *Disco and Soul Dances* (1976) by Rosemary 'Red' Hallum and *Learn to Hustle* (1976) from Groove Sound. But in the Travolta tsunami wake came *New York-Latin-Rope-Hustle Dance Lessons* (1978) by Jon Devlin's Dance Club ("clearly defined with over 80 photos"), *Disco Dancin'* (1978) on the Activity Records label and *Popmobility – The Disco Party Record that Helps You Keep Fit* (1977) featuring Silver Convention, Van McCoy and Tina Charles tracks. Most prolific of the lot was the *Discopedia* (1979) five-volume releases on the Pickwick label with Disco Dance Step Lessons foldout and segued cover versions of popular hits to practice to by Mirror Image.

Club Louise

LOUISE
61, POLAND ST. LONDON W.1. 01-437 1693
I warrant I am over 18 years of age
Expiry Date.......................
Signed. Membership No.
....

At the height of Disco fever it soon became impossible for the Sex Pistols and their trusted inner circle to find any peace in the club environment. At The Sombrero (Kensington High Street), Napoleon's (Bond Street), The Speakeasy (Oxford Circus) or The Roxy, formerly Chaguarama's (Neal Street, Covent Garden), you were either glared at for wearing SEX clothes or mobbed for exactly the same reason. Then someone, Siouxsie Sioux or maybe outrageous scene queen Philip Sallon whose friend was the DJ there, mentioned the lesbian Disco Louise's on Poland Street, and it soon became the preferred Punk hangout. Run by OAP Louise, the loose membership club was on two floors; you walked in from the red door entrance to a quiet bar area (it was where I cemented my friendship with Sid Vicious), and down a spiral staircase was the adequate mirrored Disco area with the DJ booth behind smoked glass.

On a good night you could rub shoulders with artist Francis Bacon, send up the solo camp waiter Tony (who had a Twix fetish, don't ask!) and get a blowjob in the toilets. The music played was an eclectic mix of Roxy Music, Marlene Dietrich and David Bowie, but the two tracks I distinctly recall being played are *Love Is in the Air* (1977) by John Paul Young and *I Get a Kick Out of You* (1974), Gary Shearston's dreamily danceable version of the Cole Porter classic. And I particularly remember the latter because of one chord change at the end and an added lyric we all thought said Christiana Steidten because that was the name of the 'Vogue' supermodel staying at the Portobello Hotel who had just become our new best friend.

THE STUD (1978)

For many living through the 1970s in Great Britain only one company summed up the era's *nouveau-riche* credentials: Brent Walker, set up by champion boxers George and Billy Walker. You couldn't get away from the company because it had multiple interests in public houses, Discos (Dolly's being one), developed the Brent Cross Shopping Centre in North London, owned the Billy's Baked Potato franchise (my favourite Disco fast food at the time) and entered the film distribution business with mainly exploitation titles like **Squirm** (1976), **The Town That Dreaded Sundown** (1976), **Futureworld** (1976), **Empire of the Ants** (1977) and **The Changeling** (1980).

Their stab at the distribution big time came courtesy of 'The Stud', the second bonk-busting, sex-and-shopping book written by newcomer novelist Jackie Collins in 1969 (her 1968 first was 'The World Is Full of Married Men'). Originally planned to go before the cameras in 1970, virtually every studio in the UK and US turned it down. Until the book sold over one million copies, Jackie's elder sister Joan Collins, looking for a comeback vehicle after spending years in the B-movie doldrums with her marriage to actor/singer Anthony Newley collapsing, said she'd star and persuaded her third husband, businessman Ron Kass, to put up the £1 million budget.

Joan plays Fontaine Khaled, the upper class, manipulative, sexually liberated, unhappily married wife of millionaire Ben Khaled (Walter Gotell, General Gogol in six Bond movies). Her insatiable appetite for younger men means she's lusting after the new manager, Tony Blake (Oliver

Tobias), of her glossily fashionable West End Disco, The Hobo (an in-joke, as Jackie's husband Oscar Lerman owned the glitterati Mayfair nightclub Tramp, where the Disco scenes were filmed). Managing to tempt Tony back to her elegant Eaton Square pad, seducing him in the lift in a permissive frenzy, Fontaine soon learns he's just as promiscuous as she is thanks to the bevy of beauties willing to bed him constantly.

Drawn further into Fontaine's decadent lifestyle and even more under her sexual control, Tony gets flown to Paris for a swimming pool orgy where her best friend Vanessa ('Crossroads' soap stalwart, Sue Lloyd) tries to ensnare him into a threesome with her bisexual husband Leonard (Mark Burns). Then it hits Tony that he's on a never-ending cycle of sex, drugs and Disco and slowly being destroyed by the very hedonism he's addicted to. Especially when he turns his attention to Fontaine's young stepdaughter Alex (Emma Jacobs), who is only using him to get back at her nymphomaniac stepmother for cheating on her father. The whole bonkers sex-crazed shebang ends up in dumping, depression and divorce.

Although Oliver Tobias had been acting since 1969, it wasn't until he answered the trade press adverts launching the hunt for "the greatest STUD of all time!" that he became internationally famous. He fitted the required bill as stated, "British, over six feet tall and between the ages of 27-30", and his only competition was apparently 1950s teen idol Adam Faith, footballer George Best, 'Starsky and Hutch' hunk Paul Michael Glaser and pop star Tom Jones. The apocryphal legend goes that Jackie took one look at his cleft-chinned face and muscular frame and insisted Tobias be signed on the spot. After seeing his name attached to the 'Monsieur Le Stud' aftershave sold in Boots the chemists, just one of the many tacky merchandise spin-offs, is it any wonder Tobias would later say the film ruined his career?

Naturally Joan Collins is utterly fabulous as the filthy rich ball-breaking man-eater spitting out choice bitchy one-liners while stripping down to the buff. Joan's nudity caused a tabloid sensation at the time mainly because few stars of her middle-aged years – she was 45 while shooting – would risk such a controversial image change. Nevertheless by the end of 1978 Joan had been voted the sexiest woman in the world, the brave shot in the arm her floundering career needed had worked (the movie grossed over £20 million globally), and she was *en route* to becoming a primetime television icon with the American super-soap 'Dynasty'.

(1978), *Native New Yorker* (1977) by Odyssey, *Sorry I'm a Lady* (1977) by Baccara, *Car Wash* (1976) by Rose Royce, *Deliverance* (1977) by Space, *Let's All Chant* (1977) by the Michael Zager Band, *The Groove Line* (1977) by Heatwave, *Cocomotion* (1977) by El Coco and *That's the Way (I Like It)* (1975) by KC and The Sunshine Band.

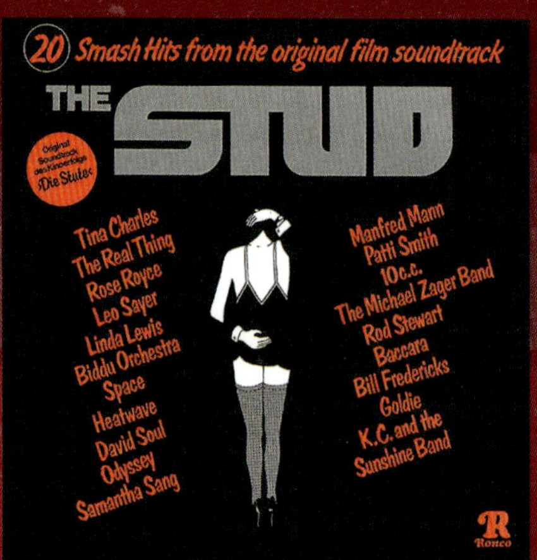

Although unmitigated softcore trash in keeping with the lame sexploitation films of the day – the supporting cast features such indicative genre heavyweights as Minah Bird, Pat Astley and Suzanne Danielle – Jackie Collins knew she'd have to update her screenplay with all the **Saturday Night Fever** (1977) style tunes and trimmings to make it feel even slightly contemporary. Odd choice director Quentin Masters – he'd only made the hippy dippy **Thumb Tripping** (1972) prior – clearly did not have his other thumb on the Disco pulse as the entire histrionic melodrama feels on demented 'Tops of the Pops' overdrive. The heavily TV-advertised Ronco album featured Disco from the movie including five Biddu compositions – *The Stud* performed by the Biddu Orchestra, *Fire Down Below* by Tina Charles, *It's Good* by Linda Lewis, *Almost* by Billy Joe Fredericks, and *Let's Go Disco* by The Real Thing (all 1978), something they later regretted doing because it primarily labelled them a Disco act – tricked out with other licensed hits like *Every 1's a Winner* by Hot Chocolate

Exodus

A key originator of the singularly strident British Disco sound, Indian-born Biddu Appaiah dropped his surname to become lauded as one of the greatest producers ever. His career began in Bangalore playing in The Trojans until creative differences with the band saw him rebranded as the Lone Trojan and heading westward to make it on the international scene. After producing a Japanese No.1 hit for The Tigers, with the song *Smile for Me* (1969) written by the Bee Gees, Biddu was asked to compose the soundtrack for **Embassy** (1972), starring Richard Roundtree, and wrote the theme song *Somebody Stop This Madness*. Singing it was Jamaican-born Carl Douglas, a hit on the Northern Soul scene with *Serving a Sentence of Life* (1968) and Biddu liked his voice so much he asked him record the single *I Want to Give You My Everything* (1974). Douglas agreed only if he could write the B-side centred on martial arts and the Bruce Lee movies that were cleaning up at the box-office. The result was *Kung Fu Fighting*, which was flipped to the A-side after becoming a Disco hit, eventually selling 12 million records worldwide and hitting the top spot in both the UK and American charts. Sadly it confined Douglas to the unenviable One Hit Wonder category as nothing else he released ever came close.

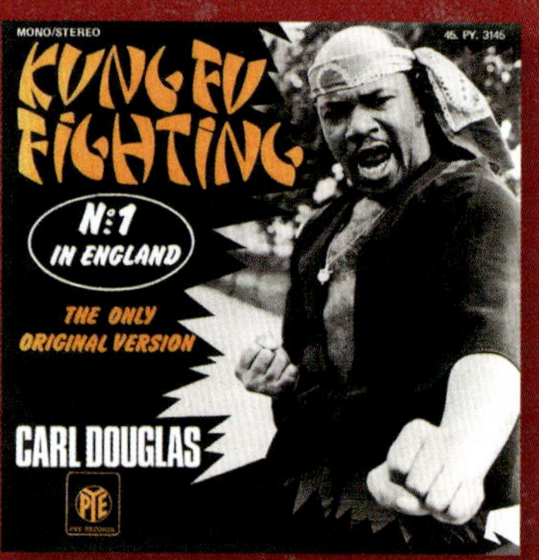

Because of a contractual problem with the accompanying *Kung Fu Fighter* album, only eight tracks featuring Douglas singing were completed. A ninth was needed so Biddu wrote the filler instrumental *Blue-Eyed Soul*. When this became a sizeable club hit (No.5 in the Disco charts), Epic Records asked for an instrumental album and the Biddu Orchestra was in

business clocking up chart hit after Disco hit: *Summer of '42* and *Exodus* from the *Blue-Eyed Soul* album (1975), *I Could Have Danced All Night/Jump for Joy* from the *Rain Forest* (1976) album, the title track also winning Biddu one of his three coveted Ivor Novello Awards, and *Funky Tropical* from the *Eastern Man* (1977) album.

After scoring **The Bitch** (1979), Biddu went back to his roots composing songs for the Bollywood movie **Qurbani/Sacrifice** (1980), especially famous for the catchy Disco song *Aap Jaisa Koi*, sung by Pakistani pop star Nazia Hassan who would then cut the full album *Disco Deewane* with him. Before he repositioned himself in Asia, Biddu also launched the Disco careers of Tina Charles and Jimmy James, and The Buggles of *Video Killed the Radio Star* (1979) fame was founded by two of his former session musicians, Trevor Horn and Geoff Downes.

Disco Memo

Who Killed Bambi?

It was during 1977 that Malcolm McLaren first mooted a film starring the Sex Pistols, which would launch them onto cinemagoers the way **A Hard Day's Night** (1964) did for The Beatles. Malcolm always promised I could play a part in whatever he concocted. So imagine my delight when he revealed he had hired American sexploitation's King Leer himself, Russ Meyer, to direct the Punk frippery. Like the band, I was a massive fan of **Beyond the Valley of the Dolls** (1970), which I would rank in my Top Ten of All-Time Great Movies. I had met Meyer anyway thanks to my great friend and Wardour Street maverick Antony Balch who was distributing his films in the UK. And I had originally encountered Balch, the director, through a passing Portobello Hotel acquaintance with Robin Askwith, the cheeky chappie star of his second terrific terror flick **Horror Hospital** (1973). His first was the truly unique **Secrets of Sex** (1970). Balch was a handsome leather boy and would really put Meyer on the British grindhouse map by energetically releasing **Supervixens** (1975), **Up!** (1976) and **Beneath the Valley of the Ultra-Vixens** (1979). I remember the **Up!** Premiere party so well; the first thing Balch said to me was "I warn you Alan, do not commandeer all of Russ's time!" I was beside myself when Balch died in 1980 because he was such a wonderful man and a great film industry loss.

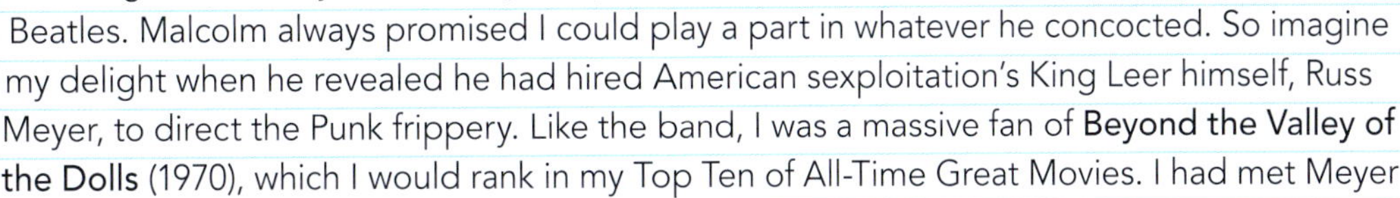

So I went along with Malcolm to the Athenaeum Hotel on Piccadilly to audition for a part in the tentatively titled 'Who Killed Bambi?' We walked into Meyer's hotel suite and Malcolm flippantly explained, "This is Alan, I want him to play one of the faggots!" His girlfriend, muse and star Kitten Natividad was with him and we sat and chatted for a while, and he told me he remembered me from the Balch screenings. I didn't believe him – all celebrities automatically say that when faced by that ubiquitous fan remark. Then he suddenly got up from the sofa and said, "Sorry guys, can you wait here for 15 minutes, I've got to go and have sex with Kitten in the bedroom?" He and Kitten exited and, for about ten minutes, Malcolm and I sat listening to "Oohs" and "Aahs" and "Russssss!" exclamations emanating from the bedroom. After the loudest and most theatrical orgasm I've ever heard, Russ came back in, minus his trousers, told me I had the part and we made our excuses and quickly left.

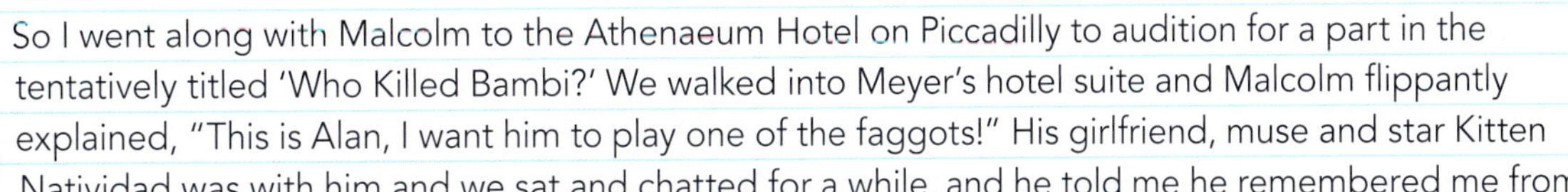

Except, of course, Malcolm fired Meyer and minimal footage was ever shot. My eventual 'performance' in a Sex Pistols film was still a year in the future. And the last time I saw Meyer was at a Scala Cinema bash for the video releases of his infamous back catalogue. My one memory from that meeting was Meyer wondering if he had enough Viagra for the evening and opening his bag to reveal at least 50 blister packs of the erectile aid! I've never auditioned for anyone else in my life and the fact I have for the late, great Russ Meyer himself will remain a monumental feather in my sporadic movie career cap.

▲ **Above left: The fantastic Antony Balch, director of *Secrets of Sex* (1970) and *Horror Hospital* (1973), and grindhouse distributor par excellence.**

▲ **Top right: Cult director Russ Meyer, the self-styled 'King Leer', and his starlet muse Kitten Natividad.**

THANK GOD IT'S FRIDAY (1978)

Six months after the **Saturday Night Fever** (1977) earthquake had upended popular culture, the next Disco watershed turned up in Casablanca FilmWorks' second production after **The Deep** (1977). **Thank God It's Friday** didn't carry any real message or dwell on the darker side of the nightclub experience. What it did, and did extremely well, was firmly place the audience in an exciting, buzzy, hip and happening Disco environment and communicated the whole joy-sharing, ecstatic attitude of the musical movement tremendously effectively. Despite revolving around a throwback concept in many instances – one glitterdust cliché follows another on the lightweight journey from the **Valley of the Dolls** (1967) to **42nd Street** (1933) – it was the nearest anyone got to an authentic you-are-there Studio 54 situation. And, of course, it featured Donna Summer, the reigning Queen of Disco, and a whole roster of beloved club cuts.

Written by (Barry) Armyan Bernstein, who would co-script and co-produce Francis Ford Coppola's exemplary musical **One from the Heart** (1981), the working title was 'Discotheque', shortened to 'Disco' in pre-production, becoming 'After Dark' for a while until someone pointed out that was a gay magazine imprint and finally settling on **Thank God It's Friday**, a phrase made popular by Jerry Healey, an Akron, Ohio, DJ on the WAKR radio station. The original director was Joe Layton, a choreographer known primarily for his Broadway work ('The Sound of Music', 1959) and TV specials starring Barbra Streisand, Diana Ross and Olivia Newton-John. But when Layton was injured in an accident a few weeks prior to production, Robert Klane (writer of the 1970 novel 'Where's Poppa?' and screenplay of the film version) was drafted in as his replacement.

Clearly influenced by **American Graffiti** (1973) and **Nashville** (1975), **TGIF**, as promo tie-ins would soon dub it, details the frenzied activities around a big dance contest taking place in The Zoo Disco (actually the four dance floor Osko's at 333 South La Cienega Boulevard, Los Angeles) and the effect those shimmering shenanigans have on a cross-section of late 1970s stereotypes. A young couple (Mark Lonow and Andrea Howard) from the suburban San Fernando Valley is wondering what all the Disco fuss is about and decides to take their first hesitant steps into the seductive world of night fever. Two fifteen-year-old girls (Valerie Landsburg and Terri Nunn, the latter becoming lead singer with *Take My Breath Away* band Berlin) who hitchhike to the club wanting to sneak in to watch the Commodores live on stage and hoping to win the prize money so they can attend a special KISS concert. There are two office girls (Debra Winger and Robin Menken) looking for Mr. Right. And then there's Nicole Sims (Summer) determined to break into stardom by crashing the live radio broadcast hosted by DJ Bobby Speed (Ray Vitte).

In true feel-good fashion everyone gets what they want in this slice-of-Disco-life that does nothing more than update all those 1950s teen exploitation stand-bys of drugs, sex, music and heartbreak with sit-com fantasy aplomb. The virtually non-stop Disco soundtrack featured an eclectic range of Casablanca and Motown artists either singing on stage or hearing their hits over the loudspeakers

TEST

including Thelma Houston's *Love Masterpiece* (1978), Giorgio Moroder's *From Here to Eternity* (1977), Village People's *In Hollywood (Everybody Is a Star)* (1977), Cameo's *Find My Way* (1975), the Commodores' *Too Hot to Trot* (1977) and Pattie Brooks' *After Dark* (1978). New songs included the Love and Kisses title track and *You're the Most Precious Thing in My Life* (1978), Paul Jabara's *Disco Queen* (1978) and *Trapped in a Stairway* (1978), and Donna Summer's Oscar-winning song *Last Dance* (1978), which went to No.3 on the 'Billboard' Hot 100 Chart, and topped the Hot Disco Action Chart even before the film had ever been seen. The tie-in album release included the Donna Summer bonus track *Je t'aime (moi non plus)* (1978) and all tracks were listed with their relevant BPM number, e.g. Santa Esmeralda's *Sevilla Nights* (1978) BPM 120.

Before release **Thank God It's Friday** was extensively test screened mainly because distributor Columbia Pictures were worried about one scene showing two men kissing. After no negative reaction, the circa $2 million production entered release to little critical favour but tripled its cost in box-office because it hit cinemas at the height of the Disco boom. Harmless, inoffensive, tacky but fun and mildly exotic for the casual Disco tourist, the energy exuded by the cast – Chick Vennera's dance number, phew! – makes it a wonderfully nostalgic time capsule of the entire era.

Casablanca Records

Only one record label embraced Disco from the start and that was Casablanca Records. Under the visionary eye of owner Neil Bogart, the label defined, refined and exploited Disco to its full potential with its roster of superstar performers and producers. Born Neil Scott Bogartz in 1943, he dropped the z in deference to his childhood movie idol, Humphrey Bogart (star of **Casablanca**, 1942), and built upon a pop promotion career at 'Cashbox' magazine, MGM Records and Cameo-Parkway Records, becoming highly regarded in the music industry for his ability to spot new trends and markets. As general manager of Buddah Records, he innovated Bubblegum music (e.g. *Yummy, Yummy, Yummy*, 1968, by Ohio Express), and signed such directional artists as Melanie. After scoring the label a massive hit with *Midnight Train to Georgia* (1973) by Gladys Knight and the Pips, he left to form his own shingle with Warner Bros, calling it Casablanca because they owned the name.

Casablanca's first so-so release was *Here's Johnny… Magic Moments from the Tonight Show* (1974) by Johnny Carson. Then a package of tracks arrived from the German-based producer Giorgio Moroder and amongst them was *Love to Love You Baby* (1975) by Donna Summer. Extended to album side length on Bogart's insistence, the Disco Orgasmo track hit the Dance Chart top spot and stayed there for 17 weeks. Because Casablanca Records had been saved from bankruptcy by this one song, Bogart saw the sense in setting his sights on further Eurodisco releases and would launch the international careers of such continental acts as producers Moroder (Munich Machine), Jacques Morali (Village People, Patrick Juvet, Phylicia Allen), Alec R. Costandinos (Love and Kisses) and Adrian Baker (Liquid Gold). Bogart would also promote the Disco careers of Cher, Lipps, Inc., Teri DeSario, D.C. LaRue, Dennis Parker, Pattie Brooks, Roberta Kelly, Ultimate and Hallelujah 2000.

With its major investments Donna Summer and Heavy Metal rockers KISS minting money, Casablanca also tapped into the funk market with the signing of George Clinton's Parliament and Cameo, and moved into movie production with Casablanca Records and FilmWorks. As Disco faded Bogart sold the company to Polygram, set up Boardwalk Records, hit the American No.1 slot with *I Love Rock 'n' Roll* (1982) by Joan Jett & the Blackhearts and died of cancer the same year. Bogart and his milestone label were pivotal in the emergence of Disco from the underground to mainstream acceptance. Even if he had only ever tub-thumped Donna Summer his name would be immortal. That he pushed Disco's innate sensuality, outrageousness, imagination and image to new levels of PR flamboyance is merely the icing on the cake.

Videomedia and Vampix

Not many people knew about my four-year stint working on-and-off for the Vampix video label for which I chose the titles to release, wrote all the copy, art-directed the covers for the slip cases and controlled the advertising. It used to make me laugh when I read retro reports on the history of the label, commenting on what a broad range of cinematic horror was encapsulated in the 22 titles that bore the distinctive Vampix logo. Had they actually done their research properly they might have realised the person who could answer all their questions about the label's history, and why exactly those specific titles were chosen, was probably sitting beside them at a hot new release screening in a Wardour Street preview theatre!

How did I end up working for a fledgling video label that suddenly found itself at the centre of the Video Nasty debate? Although my career as a horror journalist was rapidly taking off in 1978, it didn't yet pay all the bills. So I had to have other flexible employment to keep the wolf from the door and myself in Disco albums. I had just given up working for Malcolm McLaren and Vivienne Westwood at their World's End boutique SEX after the 'God Save the Queen' Boat Party fiasco when my best friend, film editor Geoff Simm came to my rescue and offered me a part-time job.

Roller Boogie 11

THE ELECTRIC JOCKEY

Geoff and I worked well together. We had established and self-published the independent 'Rollerskate Rag' fanzine for the emergent Roller Disco crowd. He was the editor and I was the music reviewer/feature writer. Geoff supplemented his income by working at The Film Stock Centre in lower Wardour Street (a Starbucks now occupies the original site). Owned by Maureen Bartlett, a former stringer for that 1960s movie magazine staple 'Photoplay', the business revolved around buying up short ends of unused celluloid from major film productions and selling them on to the lower budget end of the market to cut their costs. Many famous people used Maureen's clever and remunerative recycling service and it was how director Harry Bromley Davenport could make his first two movies, **Whispers of Fear** (1976) and **Xtro** (1982) a reality and allowed director Gabrielle Beaumont to complete **The Godsend** (1980).

Geoff had first introduced me to Maureen in 1975 and she was the reason I saw **Schizo** (1976) so far in advance of its release as Pete Walker was another of her clients. It turned out Maureen wanted to diversify into this new-fangled videotape business thing and needed someone with the knowledge of what exactly all the titles being released by the likes of the Vipco, Hokushin and Intervision companies actually were. So would I consider stocking a back-office-turned-showroom with assorted videotapes and see if they sold to the West End footfall?

A complete no-brainer offer I thought, so of course I said yes. It wasn't quite as easy as that though as back in those days JVC's VHS hadn't yet taken over as the format of choice so I also had to decide how many Sony Betamax and Phillips' Video 2000 items would be needed on the shelves too. With the former two formats retailing at circa £39.99 each and the latter around £50, it was a hefty purchase commitment and one you daren't get wrong. I must say though I used to love going to the Intervision head office/warehouse to see what sleaze they would be trying to sell to someone who knew so much more about it than they did!

By the way, all the supposed classic apocryphal stories about punters of the day are absolutely true: the furious mother of the son I'd sold a copy of **Faces of Death** (1978) to hurtling in, slamming the video down on the counter, screaming obscenities and demanding a refund; the man in the dirty raincoat caressing a copy of **Pets** (1973) and wanting the rest room location in a hurry; the respectable office worker asking me to suggest a foreign art film to expand his cinematic repertoire but ending up buying Jess Franco's **Caged Women** (1975) instead. Memories, all alone in the twilight world of Soho!

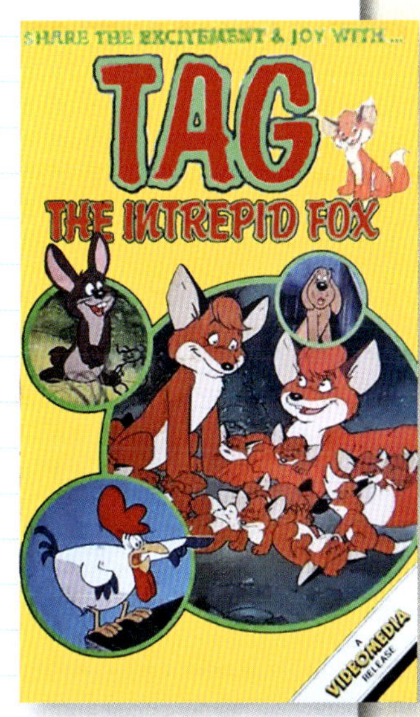

Anyway, Maureen clearly liked the return on her novelty investment and soon made the decision to enter the murky unproven world of the videotape market with a full-throttle vengeance herself. It was all part of her master plan to raise the money to put her pet film project into production. Maureen had bought the rights to author Evelyn Anthony's suspense thriller 'The Malaspiga Exit'. The novelist's 'The Tamarind Seed' had been turned into a Julie Andrews vehicle in 1974 and Maureen wanted to do the same for her best girlfriend Susannah York, then coming off the success of **Superman** (1978).

And so Videomedia was formed in 1980 to release an eclectic mix of titles like **Theodora, Queen of Byzantium** (1954), **Carthage in Flames** (1960), **Expresso Bongo** (1959), **Pocket Money** (1972), **Shout at the Devil** (1976), **The Great McGonagall** (1975) and **The Red Berets** (1969). That just goes to show how clueless the people at the top were about formulating a cohesive inventory rather than a scattershot jamboree bag of anything available. There was no vision, no curation and no thought-through selection. I had nothing to do with those titles as Maureen asked me to solely focus on marketing a series of foreign language videos, as she was convinced people wanted this new medium mainly as an instructional learning tool (!), and a series of children's animation features by producer/director Jean Image. Boring! But I always remember one cartoon Maureen picked up at Cannes about an orphaned fox titled **Vuk** (1981) by Hungarian director Attila Dargay. Obviously that title couldn't stay and so Maureen asked me to wrack my brains for a UK-friendly alternative. That took all of one nanosecond. I simply looked out the window of her office to the pub opposite and there it was – **The Intrepid Fox**! Sadly that infamous boozer is no more. Instead the site has housed numerous restaurant brands including a Bryon's hamburger joint.

One deal Maureen had done on behalf of Videomedia was with African American filmmaker Jamaa Fanaka. The UCLA student had made the post-Blaxploitation prison drama **Penitentiary** (1979) and she thought the brutal realities of incarceration were rendered with extreme believability and a welcome lack of preachiness or posturing enough to connect with an open-minded liberal audience. Which is how she sold it with a cover containing good reviews and lauding its success as a groundbreaking independent feature. It did well enough to merit the release of **Penitentiary II** (1982), but it was over an earlier Fanaka production that I really clashed with my boss. **Emma Mae** (1976) was a classic 'Country girl in the Big City' drama fitting the Blaxploitation profile more fairly and squarely due to its mid-Seventies heritage. So I felt it needed a more in-synch contemporary title like **Black Sister's Revenge** – something Maureen resisted until it sold like gangbusters at retail exhibitions under that more commercial moniker.

That wasn't the last explosive argument I had with Maureen, but it was the one that made her see me in more on-message professional terms than just a copywriter-cum-glorified salesman who also acted as her secretary typing up contracts and letters to business associates. Enter Vampix, which in this mainly sell-through based period would become the only pre-British Board of Film Censors (BBFC) certificate and rental label to solely release horror movies. Where did the product come from? Simple. Michael Klinger was the producer of **Shout at the Devil** and he loved what Videomedia had done with his tent pole title. In a former business life he had owned Compton-Cameo with future Tigon maverick Tony Tenser and both their exploitation back catalogue, either produced or bought at film markets for lower half of a double-bill playoff, became the main spine of the Vampix brand.

When I perused the list of films on offer, it was the easiest job in the world for me to cherry-pick the must-have titles. I mean here were some of my favourite horror movies of the past 25 years. Roman Polanski's classic shocker **Repulsion** (1965), Robert Hartford-Davis' cod-Hammer **The Black Torment** (1964), Riccardo Freda's necrophiliac masterpiece **The Terror of Dr. Hichcock** (1962), the super Sherlock Holmes vs. Jack the Ripper thriller **A Study in Terror** (1965), Michael Armstrong's **The Haunted House of Horror** (1969), Freddie Francis' **The Creeping Flesh** (1972) and Barbara Steele in **Cemetery of the Living Dead** (**Terror-Creatures from the Grave**) (1965). Frankly I couldn't wait to get started on designing and marketing them to a fan base I knew would be thrilled these British grindhouse greats and Euro cult chillers were finally becoming available.

Okay, the nature of the Compton-Cameo/Tigon package deal also meant handling **The Blood Beast Terror** (1967), **Curse of the Crimson Altar** (1968), **The Flesh and Blood Show** (1972), **Cauldron of Blood** (1970) and **Crypt of Horror** (1964). Not so great, but effortlessly sellable in a burgeoning industry where everything seemed to fly off the shelves. My vast personal collection of press books, stills, Front of House sets and posters became the cornerstone mainstay of the overall consistent look of the Vampix covers. Defiantly early 1980s photo montages (remember this was the far-off no computer era) or approximations of the original painted artwork were the order of the day and I spent ages hyping up the contents with purple prose and reviews (usually my own, see **The Bird with the Crystal Plumage**, 1970). That was transparently another clue to my Vampix involvement and would have been easy to divine had the 'experts' dug deeper because I often used my different reviews from separate magazines.

Other titles from the Compton-Cameo/Tigon catalogue ended up on another Videomedia subsidiary, Rampix. I can't remember who thought that name up but not bad considering the label had to peddle **Zeta One** (1969), **Permissive** (1970), **Au Pair Girls** (1972), **The Sex Thief** (1973) and **Intimate Games** (1976). The only Rampix title I put in my collection was **Monique** (1969), still one of the best examples of British sexploitation ever, to my mind. For years David Warbeck, **The Sex Thief** star and my very good friend, would send each other that videotape as a Christmas present.

I often wonder if he kept a whole cupboard full of them just to make puzzled visitors wonder if he was a complete and utter narcissist.

Other additions making up the 22 title Vampix portfolio were **Death Weekend** (1976), one of the greatest I Spit on Your Gravers with Brenda Vaccaro's stand-out performance, Norman J. Warren's wonky cannibal shocker **Prey** (1977) and Guido Zurli's dodgy **Strangler of Vienna** (1971). It was the latter slice of Euro-sleaze starring Victor Buono that caused another major argument. In my collection I only had a press book for one of its alternative titles, **Meat Is Meat** (the other being **The Mad Butcher**). But Maureen didn't want that title because it was too nasty! If only she had known what the competition were up to and what was coming down the scapegoat pike! Not that any Vampix insert is High Art but **Strangler of Vienna** remains the worst in my opinion.

At this point in my journalistic career I had struck up a professional relationship with Barry Jacobs, head honcho of Eagle Films, whose office was just around the corner in Old Compton Street (where the Soho House club now resides). Barry was the veteran British distributor of Lucio Fulci's prolific output: how do you think I saw **City of the Living Dead** (1980), **The Beyond** (1981) and **The House by the Cemetery** (1981) first, uncut and would become the primary critic to promote Fulci's latter day horror career? Hence the reason for the folding in of the latter two titles into the Vampix range. Barry also owned the rights to Mario Bava's **Black Sunday** (1960) and **Shock** (1977), Umberto Lenzi's **Eaten Alive!** (1980), Eugenio Martin's **A Candle for the Devil** (1973) and **The Bird with the Crystal Plumage**, so they were added into the mix too. I was particularly proud of **The Bird with the Crystal Plumage** cover as Barry had given me the original artwork as a present and I adapted it to fit the video box contours. I also used the same image as the cover for the very first incarnation of my book 'Dario Argento: The Man, the Myths & the Magic', then titled 'Mondo Argento'.

I can only recall one complaint about the Vampix catalogue before the company stopped trading in 1984. And that was how poorly the 3D presentation was for **The Flesh and Blood Show** release. Come on, who expected those red and green glasses to work in what was practically the dawn of the industry? Another Fun Fact: one Tigon title we turned down because its utter naffness hadn't aged well still nearly caused us all to get put in jail. Remember **Black Beauty** (1971), the horse opera based on Anna Sewell's 1877 children's classic novel starring a post-**Oliver!** (1968) Mark Lester? Well, it seems the police had got word Videomedia were considering releasing it and thought it was a porno import starring African American studs! You really couldn't make it up. Yet that was the poisonous atmosphere and scary background the entire video industry were collectively working against that gave rise to the now notorious Video Nasty scandal. And of course Videomedia and Vampix came under

Disco Memo

that harsh and ridiculous spotlight too with **The Beyond, Prey, Eaten Alive!, House by the Cemetery**, and **Tenebrae** (1982). I was out of it by this time as I had become a fully paid up member of the film journalist brigade, so I went from marketing deviant sex, lip-smacking violence, horrible torture, gory cannibalism and shocking sadism to only reporting on the ensuing misguided public debate and the draconian measures eventually taken.

I said my career with Videomedia was an on-off affair and one of the off times was due to Disco. It was some lunchtime early January 1979 and I was flipping through the new release vinyl albums in my favourite Disco import store Trax (in Greek Street, just around the corner from Videomedia Central). Suddenly the *Ultimate* (1978) album stopped me dead, with such enticingly titled tracks as *Love Is the Ultimate, Ritmo de Brasil* and *Touch Me Baby*. Up to that point I'd never heard of the group. But it was on Casablanca Records, the US label synonymous with fabulous Disco, so I figured it was worth taking a punt. I bought the album (an expensive £1.99) and walked back to the office. "What have you got there", said Maureen when I put the carrier bag under my desk. "Oh, just the latest hot Disco import", I replied matter-of-factly. "Let's have a look then", she said, reaching into the bag and taking it out.

For those who weren't around at the time, Casablanca featured some of the most outrageous no-holds-barred imagery on their album covers, courtesy of their in-house designer Gribbitt! Few can forget the stark naked girl riding a horse seemingly in the throes of beauty and the beast passion on the Love and Kisses release *How Much, How Much I Love You* (1978). And the psychedelic graphic on the first *Ultimate* album also featured a naked topless girl in blissful orgasmic ecstasy. Anyway, my (very feminist) MD looked at the album cover in shocked horror and said, "What sort of Discos do you go to?" obviously thinking in terms of Plato's Retreat-style sex clubs. Nothing I could say could convince her I was anything but Disco depraved and for the rest of the afternoon she'd look my way, nod her head in disgust, sigh and mutter. Two weeks later I was asked to take some time off, even though I would end up back there again a few months later. And although she didn't articulate the proper reason, I'm sure it was the *Ultimate* album that did it. So I'm probably the only person to have undergone a Disco Dismissal! And I couldn't be prouder.

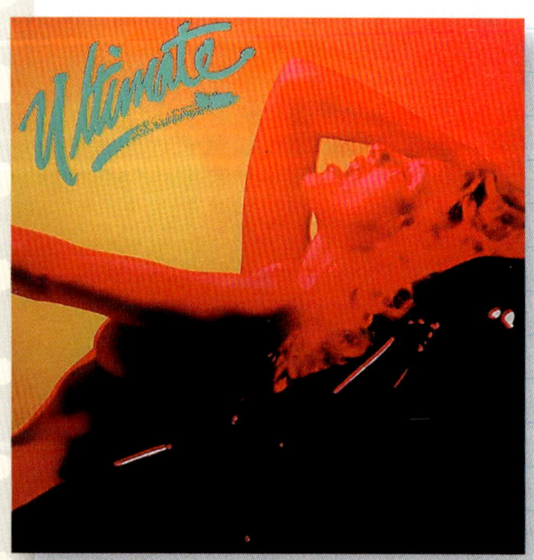

TROCADERO BLEU CITRON / TROCADERO LEMON BLUE (1978)

While not exactly in the Albert Lamorisse **Le ballon rouge/ The Red Balloon** (1956) class, and nearly three times as long, this bright and breezy French family melodrama is still a delightful celebration of the childhood experience, capturing the wonder and joys of the world as seen through innocent eyes, and the sweet pain of first love. Perhaps overly sentimental and slightly lacking in the potent whimsy department, director Michael (**Un été d'enfer**, 1984) Schock's sprightly debut feature is an agreeable outdoor Disco musical on skateboards.

Since the 1940s the gardens at Le Place du Trocadéro in Paris have been a prime roller-skating destination for those looking for sports fun in the sun. In the 1970s the area situated on the edge of the Eiffel Tower tourist attraction also became the hangout for skateboarders, the metropolitan pastime sprung out of the 1960s seaside surfing boom that became an urban craze. It's in this juvenile skater-dater milieu that writer Schock's seasoned *soufflé* is set. Annie (Anny Duperey who shot to fame in Jean-Luc Godard's **2 ou 3 choses que je sais d'elle/Two or Three Things I Know About Her...** 1967) is a single mother raising two children on a news photographer's salary. Her 10-year-old son Phil (Lionel Melet) is obsessed with skateboarding and constantly stoked to airwalk at the Trocadéro where he meets same age Caroline (Bérangère de Lagâtinerie, daughter of Swiss giallo actor Marc Porel).

After putting two straws in a Coke can so she can share his drink, Phil becomes instantly smitten by Caroline, much to the bemusement of his skateboard pack. He even dreams about saving her from the clutches of a giant ape roaming the Paris streets (this being in the wake of the 1976 Dino De Laurentiis-produced **King Kong** remake) in his superhero guise as 'The Protector'. But will his mother and her parents be supportive of their son's puppy love? More importantly can Annie persuade her local politician to defend skateboarding culture and stop the Trocadéro authorities imposing a ban?

No matter the sunny visuals on screen, it's the aural texturing here that really counts. All the rail-sliding, street coursing and zipping about on boards and skates is deliciously counterpointed by the toe-tapping Disco sounds of wunderkind composer/producer Alec R. Costandinos. The Paris transplanted Egyptian musician was riding high in the international Disco charts with his No.1 US hit album *Romeo & Juliet* (1978) and had just finished recording his *Paris Connection* (1978) collection, including dance versions of the ballad classics *Eloise, You've Lost that Loving Feeling* and *Unchained Melody*, when director

Another collaboration with arranger/conductor Raymond Taras Knehnetsky, the man responsible for French nightclub hostess Régine's Disco career, the soundtrack comprises of a sensational 16-minute *Trocadero Suite* that's vintage Costandinos, a shorter vocal version by Malaysian pop star (Dato) Shake, three easy listening fillers, *You and Me*, *Moments of Love* and *Pupuce*, and the scintillating scene-setting Disco introduction over the opening credits, *Grooves*. **Trocadéro Bleu Citron** endures as a wonderfully evocative package of the Eurodisco movement by one of its foremost architects. Shake had a double-sided single 1977 Disco release in France with *Love Is a Many-Splendored Thing*, backed by *Parce que je t'aime*, the latter an early version of the main *Romeo & Juliet* theme.

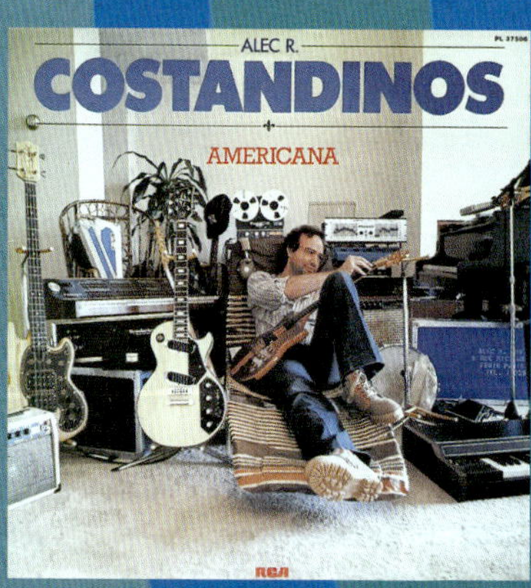

The Costandinos Phenomenon Part 1

Born Alexandre Garbis Sarkis Kouyoumdjian in Cairo, Egypt, 1944, of Armenian father/Greek mother descent, musician Alec R. Costandinos composed, published, arranged and produced some of the most memorable Eurodisco tracks of all time. Moving to Paris at the age of 22, and after recording pop fluff under just the name Alec, Costandinos helped in the development of Aphrodite's Child, featuring future superstars Vangelis and Demis Roussos. Other artists he wrote for, often under the alias Robert Rupen, include Henry Mancini, Paul Anka, Engelbert Humperdinck and French Disco Diva Dalida.

Schock asked him to provide his Gallic groove with the soaring melodies, bouncy bass-lines and thumping Disco beats for which he was becoming globally famous. Costandinos was happy to comply and the result was a wonderful compendium of contempo Disco released in France by RCA Victor and on the Casablanca Records label that nurtured the Eurodisco legend's repertoire in America.

First dipping his toes into Disco with *Crystal World* (1975) by Crystal Grass, it was his association with another French Disco powerhouse that proved to be the turning point in his monumental career. Together with Marc Cerrone, Costandinos wrote the enduring groundbreaker *Love in C Minor* (1976) that never seemed to leave Disco playlists throughout the entirety of 1977. Beginning with three girls talking about men in explicit detail – "Money ain't all he's got, look at the front of him, that ain't no banana!" – the 16-minute track is a sexually charged symphony of exciting melody, soaring strings and lush orchestration taking the listener on an utterly thrilling fantasy ride and transporting them to the far reaches of Disco heaven. If Donna Summer's *Love to Love You Baby* (1975) was the beginning of Disco Orgasmo, then the *Love in C Minor* sextravaganza is its *ménage à trois*.

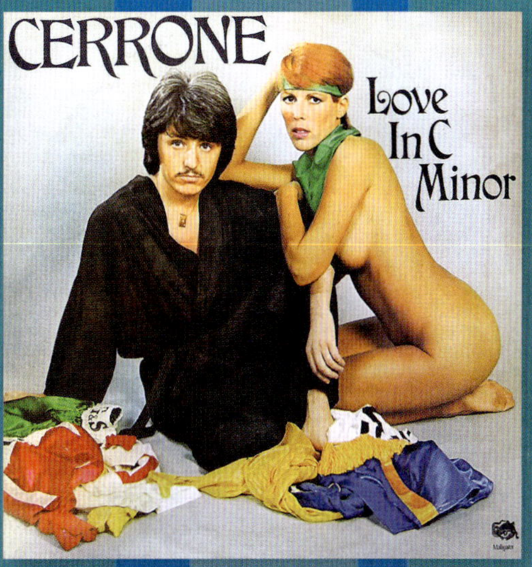

Costandinos also wrote *Midnight Lady*, featured on the *Love in C Minor* album, fleshed out with a dance remake of the 1966 Los Bravos hit *Black Is Black*, but was never given the credit for his hefty contributions to the production by self-serving solo artist Cerrone. However the music industry acclaim he received meant he could set up base at the cutting edge Trident Studios in London's Soho. And that's where he tirelessly worked nonstop for the next three years producing one ace dance album after another and in the innovative process claiming his King of the Disco Anthem designation.

Disco Memo

The Poppers

One of my closest friends throughout the entire 1970s and 1980s was singer, songwriter and keyboardist Steve Swindells. While he never attained the solo stardom he truly craved, he joined Pilot, for their *Two's a Crowd* (1978) album, and in the same year linked up with the reformed Hawkwind, renamed Hawklords, for their *25 Years On* album and tour. Steve lived in the same Notting Hill Gate house as another best friend at the time Caroline Guinness, who would marry director/producer Stephen Hopkins – **Predator 2** (1990) and the '24' TV series – and we were all inextricably and happily involved in each other's artistic lives.

So when Steve asked me one day if I'd like to join him in a studio music project, I listened intently. Steve had become friendly with producer Mickie Most, owner of RAK Records, home to the hits of Suzi Quatro, Hot Chocolate and Arrows. Most wanted a British equivalent to the Village People and asked Steve for ideas. I knew the Arrow trio's American singer/bassist Alan Merrill as they had stayed at the Portobello Hotel while filming their two TV series in 1976 and '77. Merrill's most famous composition would be *I Love Rock 'n' Roll* (1975), made a massive hit when covered by Joan Jett & the Blackhearts in 1981. A quick word with him vouched for Most's sincerity so I signed up to what was going to be pitched as leather-clad British Disco.

Steve wrote a song, *Take It to the Top*, we went into a studio to record it ("Doo Wop, Doo Wop, Let's Take It to the Top" warbled the chorus) and we spent two weeks waiting and rehearsing in front of a clothes mirror to perfect synchronised moves for our inevitable appearance on 'Top of the Pops'. And we waited, and waited. Nothing. To this day we both don't understand what happened. But if I hadn't known it before, I did then, that's showbiz. At least I came away from the experience knowing I had a good voice as everyone on the Fantasy Festival karaoke circuit can confirm.

▲ Above left: Alan Jones with his great friend Steve Swindells in Steve's Portobello Road flat. Alan is wearing a Paul Smith shirt as the designer became an acquaintance through the Roller Disco community.

BRIGADE MONDAINE (1978)

Though he is mostly unknown outside of French-speaking territories, Paris born Gérard de Villiers is one of the world's best-selling authors thanks to his S.A.S. (acronym for Son Altesse Sérénissime/ His Serene Highness) series of espionage books featuring the well-researched adventures of Austrian prince and CIA agent Malko Linge. Dubbed the Ian Fleming of France, de Villiers' first spy thriller 'S.A.S. in Istanbul' was published in 1965 and he wrote four-plus books a year until his death in 2013. It hardly seems possible that he would have any time left in his busy schedule to do anything else but he also lent his name to a hugely popular string of trashy crime novels during the 1970/80s under the umbrella title 'Brigade Mondaine'. De Villiers mostly just presented the label, frequently edited the books, only sometimes writing them himself.

Three movies sprung from this cheap *Série noire* phenomenon, the first being **Brigade mondaine/Vice Squad/Victims of Vice** directed by Jacques Scandelari and based on 'Brigade Mondaine No.1', the 1975 Michel Brice novel 'Le monstre d'Orgeval/The Monster of Orgeval' edited by de Villiers. More softcore sexploitation than *policier* procedural – Scandelari was known for delving into adult and gay erotica with **La philosophie dans le boudoir/Beyond Love and Evil** (1971) and **New York City Inferno** (1978) – the plot revolves around ace vice cops Boris Corentin (Patrice Valota) and Aimé ('Mémé') Brichot (Jean-Pol Brissart) – named Eddie in the export version – investigating the murder of a prostitute who ingested large quantities of a rare aphrodisiac drug before her death. Inquiries lead to pimp Patrick (Patrick Olivier), masquerading as a photographer, and his lesbian henchwoman Peggy (Marie-Georges Pascal) who recruit naïve girls to supposedly model for fashion magazines but dope them into becoming sex slaves for depraved aristocrats instead.

Broke shop girl Micheline (Odile Michel) is the degenerate duo's latest conquest being groomed for bondage sessions with the debauched Count de Saint-Loup (Jacques Berthier). But before the French Holmes and Watson can apprehend the Count for his kinky human sacrifices, and discover Micheline chained up in his torture cellar, witnesses Patrick and Peggy are shot dead by his besotted mistress. So Boris talks his stripper girlfriend Annie (Florence Cayrol) into becoming a decoy in their master plan to entrap the Count before he flees the country.

Underscoring this over-baked dip into call-girl sleaze, underage sex and hunky babe magnet detectives getting their man is a terrific Space Disco score by the French sensation and nightclub legend Marc Cerrone. At the time Cerrone was a fixture on every global Disco chart for his astonishing run of hit albums beginning with *Love in C Minor* (1976), progressing through *Cerrone's Paradise* and leading to the blockbuster *Cerrone 3 – Supernature*. Involvement with **Brigade mondaine** started because of his friendship with Gérard de Villiers and a yacht trip they took together while holidaying in the French Riviera resort and glitterati watering hole of Saint-Tropez. De Villiers mentioned the upcoming film adaptation and asked if Cerrone was interested in writing the music for it. Despite having no real interest in the subject matter, Cerrone agreed as a favour and headed to London's Trident Studios where he composed and recorded the soundtrack containing such fabulous cuts as *Striptease*, *Experience*, and *Générique fin* while recycling *Give Me Love* from the *Supernature* compendium.

The two other **Brigade mondaine** movies were **Brigade mondaine: La secte de Marrakech/Marrakesh Cult** (1979), directed by Eddy Matalon (**Cathy's Curse**, 1977), about a drug and prostitution ring in Morocco forming a mercenary army, and **Brigade mondaine: Vaudou aux Caraïbes/Super Witch of Love Island** (1980), directed by Philippe Monnier, concerning voodoo connected murders in the Caribbean based on a de Villiers story. Both replaced the Brichot character with actor Jacques Bouanich and also carried Cerrone soundtracks. The former featured the hi-energy Disco and soft soul shuffles *La secte de Marrakech*, *Assassinat* and *Don't Give a Damn* from the Cerrone produced 1979 Revelacion album of the same name, while the latter highlighted *Vaudou aux Caraïbes*, *Soumission* and the Disco hit *Look for Love* taken from *Cerrone IV – The Golden Touch* (1978). That was it for Cerrone on the soundtrack front until **Dancing Machine** (1990) as he turned down de Villiers' kind offer of composing **S.A.S. à San Salvador** (1983) starring Miles O'Keefe (**Ator, the Flying Eagle**, 1982) as Malko Ligne.

The Cult of Cerrone

In the pantheon of all-time-great Disco musicians, composers and producers, Marc Cerrone stands tall. A key originator of the Eurodisco sound, and winner of numerous Disco awards, Cerrone has remained at the forefront of the French music industry with over 25 solo albums released and continues to be a sell-out stadium concert attraction. *Love in C Minor* (1976) and *Cerrone's Paradise* (1977) are classic symphonies of sexual energy,

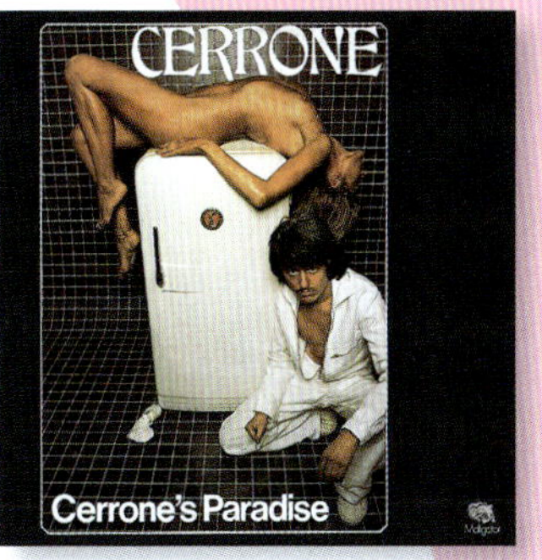

café au lait adoration, submission and desert island fantasy mixed with melodiously ecstatic dance beats while his magnum opus *Cerrone 3 – Supernature* (1977) melds glissando orchestration and rigid synthesizer sounds together for Disco perfection. Those albums along with *Cerrone IV – The Golden Touch* (1978) and *Cerrone V – Angelina* (1979) supplied clubs with an unbroken string of hits including *Midnight Lady* (1976), *Black Is Black* (1976), *Take Me* (1977), *Give Me Love* (1977), *Love Is Here* (1977), *Je suis music* (1978), *Look for Love* (1978), *Music of Life* and *Rock Me* (1979).

The youngest of three children, born in 1952 to a Parisian shoe manufacturer, Cerrone's musical talent was noted at a very early age and when his father bought him a drum kit, his fate was sealed. By the age of 18 he was musical director for the Club Méditerranée brand of vacation resorts (the reason why he had his finger on the pulse of youth trends) and by 20 had landed a lucrative contract with the French record label Barclay. Owner Eddie Barclay had seen Cerrone busking on the streets of Saint-Tropez and urged him to play a local club with a motley group of musicians under the name Kongas. Cerrone left that band after two albums, *Afro Rock* (1974), which provided the Tom Moulton remixed 1978 US hit *Anikana-O*, and *Africanism* (1977) supplying the Top 10 Disco title track plus *Gimme Some Lovin'* and *Dr. Doo-Dah*.

One of the Kongas band members was Raymond Donnez who Cerrone produced under the name Don Ray for the barnstorming Disco album *The Garden of Love* (1978), its major cuts being *Got to Have Loving*, the UK 12-inch-only *Midnight Madness* and the jazz funk preference *Standing in the Rain*. Other studio projects Cerrone produced include Revelacion who hit the US Disco Top 30 in 1978 with *House of the Rising Sun* and the Cristal double-A side *Phonic/La nuit pour nous* (1977). All these tracks have distinctively dark and sinister edges that separate them from Cerrone's own body of tuneful-to-the-max work and he set up Malligator Records to release everything to which he put his signature touch. Other Malligator artists included Italian balladeer Bobby Solo, scoring a Disco hit with the 1978 update of his 1964 smash *Una lacrima sul viso*, and poet musician Rod McKuen.

Cerrone had parlayed his early musical success into becoming a successful entrepreneur and it was his ownership of three influential record stores in Paris that sparked his breakthrough masterpiece *Love in C Minor* in conjunction with Alec R. Costandinos. Imported vinyl began identifying the daring new dance sound coming out of New York and he experimented with the 4/4 beat at London's Trident Studios. The result was a 16-minute orgasmic rush of throbbing pleasure that he couldn't sell to any French label. So he got Britain's Island Records to press 5,000 copies and sold them through his stores to hip Paris clubs. The story goes that a box of *Love in C Minor* albums were sent to America by mistake instead of unsold returns and the contents quickly found favour in Manhattan's hottest spots. Overnight Cerrone was the darling of New York Disco and Ahmet Ertegun quickly bought the property for his Atlantic Records subsidiary label Cotillion. The rest is *je ne sais quoi* Eurodisco history.

Sid and Nancy

Today I rarely talk about my friendship with Sid Vicious/John Ritchie mainly because I feel I've said all I need to about it. I've talked about him on camera for many documentaries on the Punk subject mainly because I was tired of people telling lies and painting the worst picture of what he was really like. From the moment I met Sid in SEX to the day before he left for New York on the trip he would never return from alive, I can honestly say he was a terrific guy and a wonderful friend. I know this goes against his public image, massaged by McLaren *et al* for their own ends. But I have always gone out on a limb for Sid regarding his reputation, and indeed for Nancy too.

Look, neither of them were angels, obviously, but Sid and I would always have a laugh together (I took him to the Catacombs club once!) and when he moved into Pindock Mews, Maida Vale, London, just around the corner from where I still live, we became good neighbours as well as firmer friends. We often met for coffee in Formosa Street (where you can still spy Glen Matlock, also my longtime neighbour) and I loved the fact that crescent street was the location for three films the titles of which sum Sid up perfectly – **The World Ten Times Over** (1963), **The Knack… and How to Get It** (1965) and **A Touch of Class** (1973).

Nancy warmed to me for one main reason alone – on one of my trips to New York I'd brought her back a jar of Ragu brand spaghetti sauce because she told me that was one of the things she missed the most from America. And they both came over and cooked pasta with it one night to celebrate. But there is one moment in our relationship I will never forget. My birthday was fast approaching and I had no idea Sid even knew the date. On the morning of my birthday there was a surprise ring on my door buzzer and there was Sid with a card he'd made himself, drawn in typical Jamie Reid style, with a great message. It is one of my prize possessions and one I will never, ever part with.

My one regret was not being there when the whole nightmare murder/suicide scenario was being played out that autumn in the Chelsea Hotel. I did think about going over for support, but I had only just got back from another Stateside trip, and would McLaren pay for the airline ticket? Of course not! My heartfelt memories of Sid are very personal to me and while my key role in the **Sid and Nancy** movie was still 8 years away, that's where I now tend to keep them.

April 8, 1978.
15p
RECORD MIRROR
FREE ALBUM
1
See inside for details
Cut out and keep this coupon
Why does Sid Vicious think he'll be dead in two years

SUMMER NIGHT FEVER (1978)

'NOW... the first adult DISCO 'R' movie!' blazed the tagline for this average German sex comedy directed by German TV movie, game show and mini-series veteran Sigi Rothemund (aka Siggi Götz). Er, wasn't that **Saturday Night Fever** (1977)? No matter, this ragged fun-in-the-sun romp seems to have been inspired more by the **Lemon Popsicle** (1978) franchise if dragged from the 1950s into the free wheeling Disco era with the famous and fake Eurodisco songs blaring out on annoying rotation.

Rothemund made his mark in German television directing episodes of the hit game show 'Der goldene Schuß', which when imported to Great Britain in 1967 became 'The Golden Shot' hosted by comedian Bob Monkhouse. He quickly made the move to brash comedy movies with a jet set slant such as **Bathtime in Bangkok** (1976), **3 Sexy Girls in Tirol** (1977) and **Cola, Candy, Chocolate** (1979). So it wasn't a major leap shoehorning his popular brand of virginal hopelessness and topless misadventures into a Disco-lite format and the result was **Summer Night Fever** (aka **Disco Summer**).

Peter (Stéphane Hillel, **Stop Fooling Around... Soldier!**, 1977) and Freddy (Claus Obalski, **Schulmädchen-Report. 9. Teil: Reifeprüfung vor dem Abitur/Sexy Party/When Girls Make Love**, 1975) are best friends but bored with hanging out at the Munich Discos. So they decide to hop into Freddy's yellow Volkswagon Love Bug for a lazy, hazy, crazy summer road trip to Ibiza. But Freddy is forced to take along his nerdy sister Victoria (Olivia Pascal, **Vanessa**, 1977) who keeps being mistaken as Peter's girlfriend, severely cramping his style with the clearly willing girls en route. Meanwhile, shy Freddy is bedding every woman he claps eyes on when their lemon jalopy keeps breaking down. In Monte Carlo they tangle with yachting Eurotrash and in St. Tropez, Freddy has an affair with his holidaying math teacher. It all ends on the Balearic Party Island where Peter and Victoria realise they are meant for each other. For the vital Italian

market where it played under the title **Febbre nelle notti d'estate**, Spaghetti Western icon Gianni (Sartana) Garko was featured in a cameo as Jacky.

Rothemund would return to Ibiza two years later for **Die schönen Wilden von Ibiza/Beautiful and Wild on Ibiza** (1980) with equal success despite the main characters here becoming more grating by the minute as they pass by glamorous Mediterranean locations listening to a mix of classic and quasi-faux Disco. The heavyweights included are Amanda Lear's *Follow Me* (1978), La Bionda's *One for You, One for Me* (1978) and *1-2-3-4... Gimme Some More* (1977) performed by La Bionda's alias D.D. Sound. Elsewhere on this 'Happy, Sexy Romp Through the Fun-Filled Riviera to the Smashing Sounds of the Hottest Hits of the International Disco Scene!' are Bernie Paul's soft Europop rocker *Lucky* (1978) and eight tracks by one-timers The Curtis Corporation – *Summer Night Fever, You're a Person of Importance, Disco Nights, Nobody's Perfect, Bad Woman, Baby Rock On, All Said and Done*, and *Rollin' Home to Rosie* (all 1978). When a tie-in EP was released in conjunction with the movie, *All Said and Done* was credited to Travel, and on some posters a Mona Lisa is credited as singing *Rollin' Home to Rosie* and *You're a Person of Importance*. The one bum note on the soundtrack is the inclusion of Gerry Rafferty's global Top Ten Hit *Baker Street* (1978) with its prominent eight-bar saxophone riff, the reason why **Summer Night Fever** had a subsequent limited release because of expensive copyright issues.

All the Curtis Corporation songs were composed by Gerhard Heinz who started his career as a Polydor producer and singing coach for non-German speaking Schlager stars like Connie Francis, Domenico Modugno and Rita Pavone. In 1961 he began composing soundtracks mainly for exploitation movies including **The Blonde and the Black Pussycat** (1969), **Josefine Mutzenbacher/Naughty Knickers** (1970), **Auf der Alm da gibt's koa Sünd/Bottoms Up** (1974), **Bloody Moon** (1981) and many for director Sigi Rothemund. **Summer Night Fever** is a bright, breezy and bland nudie cutie filler that is more a sunny **Schulmädchen-Report** than dance-tastic melodrama. But it's a preppy, peppy and poppy enough time-waster for those Amanda Lear fanatics who thought they knew everything about her career.

Bubbles

One of the first Disco records to be inducted into the Dance Music Hall of Fame was the stupendous *Shame* by Evelyn 'Champagne' King. Released at the explosive height of Disco music's popularity, *Shame* was written by John Henry Fitch Jr. and Reuben Cross, the former a guitarist with The Show Stoppers of the consistently re-issued *Ain't Nothing But a House Party* (1968) fame. Together the duo also wrote songs for Carol Douglas, and when Wardell Piper left the Philly-soul group First Choice, they produced her 1979 self-titled album that included the Disco hits *Super Sweet* and *Captain Boogie*.

An apocryphal discovery story but one King swears is true; she was filling in for her unwell sister as a cleaner at the Sigma Sound Studios in Philadelphia. Thinking no one was in the building she started singing Sam Cooke's *A Change Is Gonna Come* (1964) while vacuuming out offices and wiping down washrooms. But producer Theodore Life, aka T-Life, singer of *Somethin' That You Do to Me (Keeps Turning Me On)* (1981) and MFSB group member, was there, thought King's voice sounded fabulous considering she was only 15 years old and soon whisked her into the studio to record the song.

King's childhood nickname Bubbles was swapped for the more refined Champagne when the cut finally got released over a year later and became a global dance sensation. Especially when lengthened, beefed up and revitalised by mixers David Todd (a DJ at Fire Island's Ice Palace) and Al Garrison whose prowess refining all the instrumental elements allowed King's vocals to sparkle anew. *Shame* may have become King's signature song but it only got to No.8 in the 'Billboard' Disco charts; her two chart toppers were *I'm in Love* (1981) and *Love Come Down* (1982) and she remained a viable Disco star until the mid-1990s when *One More Time* (1996) by Divas of Color, featuring her as lead vocalist, became a Top Ten hit.

Based on that Diva collective template, King formed the supergroup First Ladies of Disco with her contemporaries Martha Wash from The Weather Girls, and *If My Friends Could See Me Now* (1978) superstar Linda Clifford. The group released its debut single *Show Some Love* in March 2015. In its original pressing, *Shame* is an unconventional Disco track because the standard Four-to-the-Floor drum beat is eschewed in favour of a more unusual heartbeat rhythm. But in its remixed form, it's an undisputed dancefloor classic.

EYES OF LAURA MARS (1978)

When his debut science fiction comedy feature **Dark Star** (1974) didn't become the box-office success that he hoped for, director John Carpenter went back to square one of his filmmaking career and started peddling spec scripts to various studios. The unmade 'Blood River' and **Black Moon Rising**, eventually produced in 1986 after he became a horror brand with **Halloween** (1978), were just two of many bottom draw Carpenter projects swirling around Hollywood. But one script, 'Eyes', about a trendy Manhattan photographer who develops a disturbing psychic ability to visualise gruesome ice pick murders before they occur, caught the attention of Columbia Pictures and producer Jon Peters who figured it would make a great vehicle for his current superstar girlfriend Barbra Streisand.

The **Funny Girl** (1968) eventually backed out because of the amount of violence in the script, starring in **The Main Event** (1979) instead, and singing that Paul Jabara-penned Disco theme, which reached No.13 in the 'Billboard' Dance Chart. Original **Jackson County Jail** (1976) director Michael Miller left too because of those oft quoted 'creative differences', soon followed by a disgusted Carpenter when one of the eight writers brought in to finesse the script posited the "ridiculous" idea the killer should be someone very close to the leading character. Eventually Irvin Kershner took over the helm just prior to sky rocketing his career with **The Empire Strikes Back** (1980) and Oscar-winning Faye Dunaway signed on for the lead role in a psychological thriller best described as American Giallo or Dario Argento crashing Studio 54.

Eyes of Laura Mars gets off to a cracking genre start with an unseen figure thrusting an ice pick through the right eye of a face on the cover of a book of photographs. The tome is the work of chic fashion photographer Laura Mars (Dunaway) who uses sexually ambiguous and horrific images in her spreads to grab the attention of a sensation-

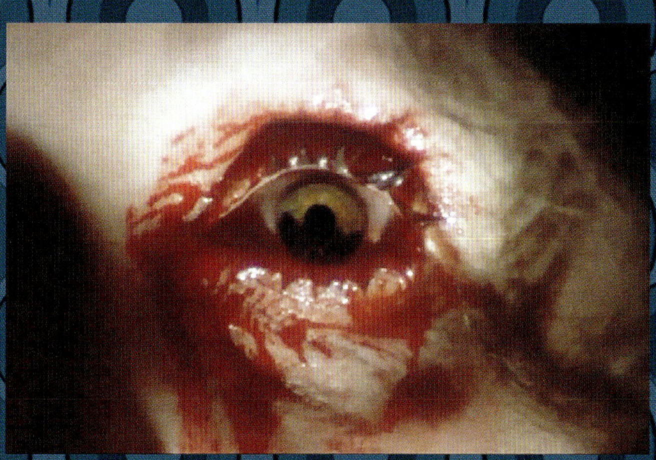

hungry, lip-smacking public (Helmut Newton and Rebecca Blake's stark photos are used as the fictional Laura's work). Fending off allegations her compositions glorify misogynist violence gets harder though when it becomes clear a deranged maniac has used her photos to pose their victims in a series of unsolved NYC murders. Weirder still is the fact Laura can witness a current spate of bloody deaths via a strange type of clairvoyance by proxy that forces her to see through the crazed eyes of the killer as they stalk their next victim.

When those victims turn out to be supermodels and close Laura associates, detective John Neville (Tommy Lee Jones, who improvised most of his dialogue) needs some convincing she's not connected to the crimes or even solely responsible. Trying to figure things out together, they become entangled romantically as the red herrings and suspects pile up in time-honoured Agatha Christie tradition. Whodunnit – her chauffeur Tommy Ludlow (Brad Dourif), her obnoxious manager Donald Phelps (Rene Auberjonois) or her nasty ex-husband Michael Reisler (Raul Julia)?

While sadly not exploring the **Peeping Tom** (1960) style ramifications of the voyeuristic conceit, and crucially never acknowledging or explaining the whole psychic link sub-plot – Laura's visions neatly depicted in terms of somewhat blurry videotape – **Eyes of Laura Mars** remains a highly polished, manipulative and glossy reflection of 1970s uptown inner-circle decadence. Dunaway cuts an appealingly vulnerable figure, Jones radiates charismatic screen presence and Kershner's measured, deliberate pacing works for the somewhat heavy-handed material, maintaining suspense throughout the moments the – very obvious – killer realises someone is tuning into their blood rage wavelength.

An astute soundtrack features part original score by **Looking for Mr. Goodbar**'s (1977) Artie Kane, part assorted Disco hits and *Love Theme from Eyes of Laura Mars (Prisoner)* by Barbra Streisand, the only song the Diva sung in a movie in which she does not appear. The well-chosen Disco cuts are *Native New Yorker* (1977) by Odyssey, *(Shake, Shake, Shake) Shake Your Booty* (1976) by KC and The Sunshine Band, *Boogie Nights* (1977) by Heatwave and the No.1 smash *Let's All Chant* (1977) by the Michael Zager Band.

FROM THE STREETS THAT BROUGHT YOU ROCKY & THE FONZ COMES A NEW ALL AMERICAN HERO...

Who is he?

Why is Donna Summer singing on his album?

Why is his album called SHUT OUT?

The multi-talented young man's name is PAUL JABARA and his debut album, SHUT OUT, is one of the hottest records to hit this season.

You can dance to it.

You can sing to it.

Entertain to it.

And make love to it.

Don't shut yourself out!

Discover

PAUL JABARA

on Casablanca Record and FilmWorks, where your questions are answered on record.

Heaven Is a Disco

After just eight previews from November 26, 1973 it closed even before its Broadway opening date, December 5th, but the musical 'Rachael Lily Rosenbloom (and Don't You Ever Forget It)' brought the songwriting talents of Paul Jabara to the public for the very first time. Produced by hotshot Robert Stigwood and Atlantic Records president Ahmet Ertegun, the show was a kitsch fiasco about a gossip columnist becoming a Hollywood star in the Barbra Streisand mould. Bette Midler turned the title role down, cabaret performer Ellen Greene nabbed it, and Jabara lost his crown as the court jester to the Stigwood empire after performing in 'Hair' and 'The Rocky Horror Show' on Broadway, and 'Jesus Christ Superstar' in the West End. But the proto Disco score – and one Jabara would return to for inspiration – was camp, clever and fun, the best description of his melody and lyrical content that would lead to Donna Summer's Oscar-winning *Last Dance* from **Thank God It's Friday** (1978) as well as her No.1 Disco duet with Streisand, *No More Tears (Enough Is Enough)* (1979).

Landing at Casablanca Records, Jabara released his debut album *Shut Out* (1977), featuring the first of three duets with Summer: the title track, *Something's Missing (In My Life)* (1978) from the *Keeping Time* album and *Never Lose Your Sense of Humor* (1979) from *The Third Album*. *Pleasure Island* was a major hit also from *Keeping Time* and *The Third Album* highlighted the brilliant *Disco Wedding* medley. While Jabara did pen songs for Midler (*No Jinx*, 1981) and Diana Ross (*Work That Body*, 1982), perhaps his greatest contribution to Gay Disco is the evergreen classic *It's Raining Men* (1982), by The Weather Girls, Sylvester's former backing singers Two Tons O' Fun, a song rejected by Summer, Streisand, Cher and Ross. Jabara's final album was *De La Noche: The True Story (A Poperetta)* featuring guest vocals from Leata Galloway, Diva Gray and Pattie Brooks. It recycled the *Ocho Rios* song from 'Rachael Lily Rosenbloom' and provided a sizeable Disco hit for Hollywood superstar Raquel Welch in 1987 with *This Girl's Back in Town*. Jabara died of AIDS complications in 1992 but left behind a rich catalogue of showbiz Disco oozing with Broadway smarts, something the 2005 workshop musical 'Last Dance' celebrated with a story about a modern teenager going back in time to spend one night in Studio 54.

Disco Memo

One-Hour Photo

I see them practically once a week. Friends and acquaintances keep me abreast of the features and newspapers they regularly appear in to illustrate. And I have more copies of them sent, texted and emailed to me than you could shake a stick at. I always joke I'd be a billionaire if I had a pound for every time I've had to explain what's going on in them. And I'm certain Chelsea freelance photographer David Dagley has made a mint from licensing them. What am I talking about? It's the infamous set of photos shot in 1976 for the June issue of the sex/contact magazine 'Forum' to illustrate their 'Buy Sexual' feature written by Len Richmond.

BUY SEXUAL

Forum's guide to London's newest, newsiest, some say nauseous sex shops. Len Richmond takes you in

SEX (430 King's Road, Chelsea) and Incognito LEATHER (267 Old Brompton Road, Earls Court) are more than mere sex-shops, they are a way of life. True, one can find enough rubber, leather, and sado-masochistic sex gear to fulfil almost any fantasy, but neither store likes to be compared with their Soho sex-shop cousins.

As the manager of SEX explains, "We're not merely here to sell sex toys and fetish clothing, but to convert, educate, and liberate. We're totally committed to what we're doing and our message is simple: We want you to live out your wildest (safe) fantasies to the hilt."

The people behind "Sex" hard at work in their Chelsea HQ. Must have sex on the behind . . .

How did Sex begin?

Vivian Westwood and her boyfriend Malcolm McLaren started Sex as a Rock n' Roll shop four years ago. "We were interested in the Teddy Boys", Vivian explains, "so we moved into the back of this shop on King's Road with a collection of 1950s records and about 40 pairs of Lurex (cloth interwoven with gold threads) trousers. We became popular with the Teds right away.

"The 1950s appealed to Malcolm and I because that was the first time the kids really had a culture of their own in which they established their own cults. Before we started the shop, I was a schoolteacher, and Malcolm was a student. He didn't like me very much then, but we've both changed a great deal and he likes me a lot now."

Vivian and Malcolm don't sell Rock n' Roll records any more. But they still sell 50s clothing, some of it altered for sexual purposes. The wall of Sex now displays an amazing variety of "hip" sex gear including rubber and leather fetish clothing; high heeled boots, rubber panties, leather bras, leather wrist and ankle restraints ("Bound to please"), rubber mini-skirts (for £12), T-shirts with a page from a porno novel written across the front (for £4), a genuine "dirty old man" raincoat (£25), and six different styles of rubber masks and hoods (£20-£50).

"I want to make rubber and leather sex stuff easily accessable to those people who feel strongly about it," says Vivian Westwood. "I usually wear a T-shirt around the shop that reads: 'Be reasonable, demand the impossible', and people are always coming up to me and asking: 'Excuse me, but what's the impossible?' They think it must be the ultimate kink, and they're missing out on something. They want to find out what it is so they can be part of the inner circle.

"To some people the ultimate is certainly wearing tight fitting black rubber gear (red is the second most popular colour). Most of our rubber masks fit entirely over the head and cause restricted breathing, which of course is part of the turn-on. A few of them lead to almost total occlusion of air, allowing only the thinest thread of breath.

21

CHRISSIE BEHYNDE

★ NOW rears a thing! This may be part of the past which Pretenders singer Chrissie Hynde would rather put firmly behind her.

★ The picture was taken around 13 years ago when the rocker was a model still struggling to find fame and fortune.

★ Chrissie, now 38 and a feminist, wore just a rubber jacket, skimpy black panties and a pair of stilettos to the opening of fashionable designer Vivienne Westwood's King's Road shop Sex. No wonder Chrissie ended up so cheeky!

In the classic pose, topless Sex Pistol Steve Jones, his rubber-clad groupie of the week Danielle, me in red jeans and chicken-bone 'Perv' T-shirt, future Pretender Chrissie Hynde in leather, salesgirl icon Jordan with her tits out and Punk couturier Vivienne Westwood in one of her signature slogan shirts, look dressed to kiss and tell. Variations on the six-some were done with our pants down, spanking each other, licking nipples, with S-E-X lipsticked on buttocks and pubic hair on display. We did it for a laugh, because Vivienne asked us to and we wanted to promote the shop. The accompanying text by Richmond was a Carry On sit-com mélange of pathetic shock and innuendo.

Do I regret the pictures? Not for a second. When I look at them now they remind me of one of the happiest times of my life. Did I feel exploited? Never. We posed, we had a laugh when they were printed, we forgot about them. Who knew they would make me more Punk famous in the future than I probably ever was at the time. The only downside in my estimation is that people still think Chrissie Hynde and I were good friends. We never were. I never liked her and that photo shoot remains the last time we ever spoke, even though one of my closest friends at the time, Anchor Records' Dave Hill, advised her to form her band the Pretenders for his newly formed Real Records label.

ALAN, JORDAN AND VOLKER STOX

In 1976 Jordan and I posed for a photoshoot at artist Volker Stox's Notting Hill studio. He would use it as inspiration for a painting titled 'The Fabulous', which is seen here for the very first time ever.

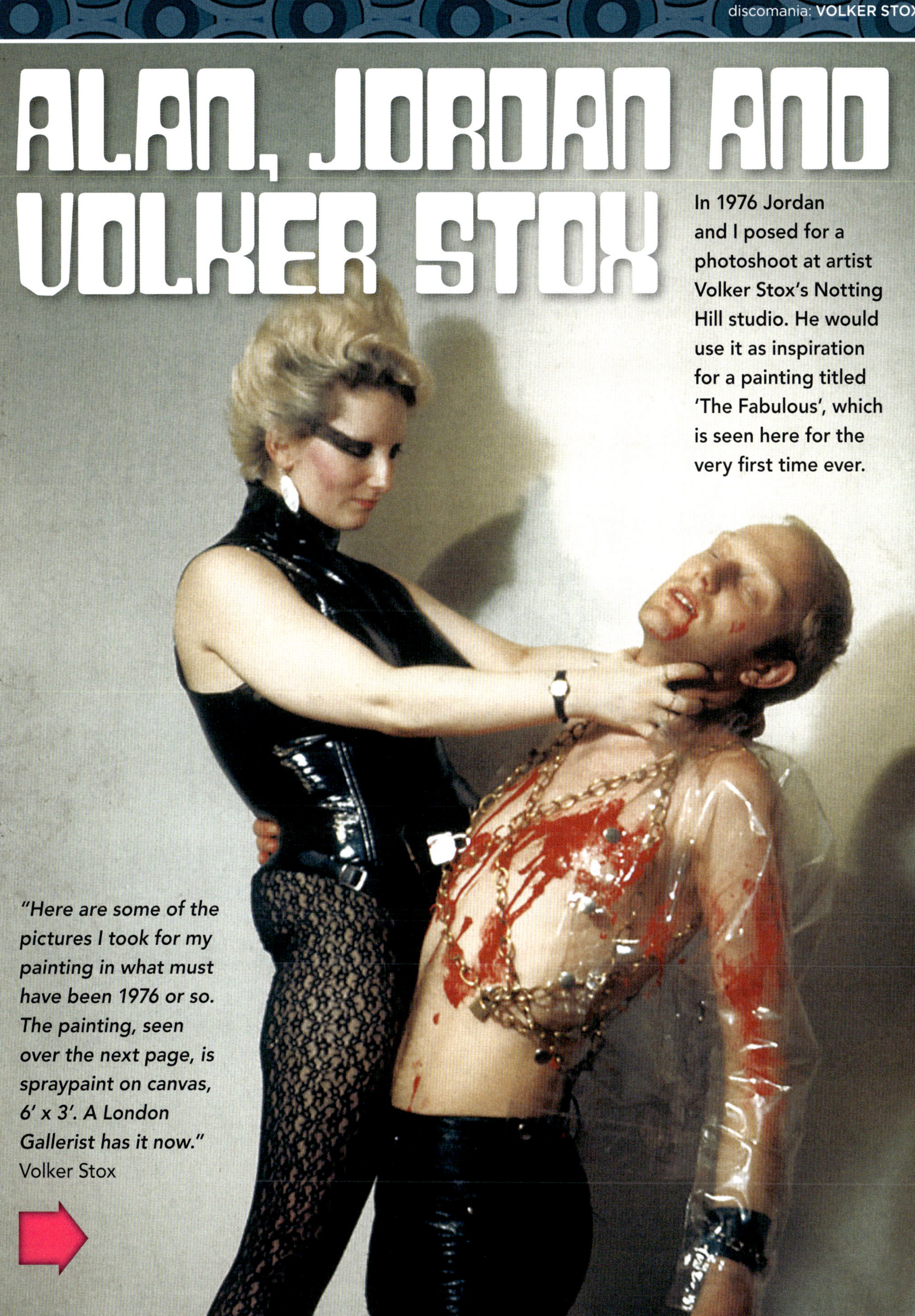

"Here are some of the pictures I took for my painting in what must have been 1976 or so. The painting, seen over the next page, is spraypaint on canvas, 6' x 3'. A London Gallerist has it now."
Volker Stox

Stox & Shares

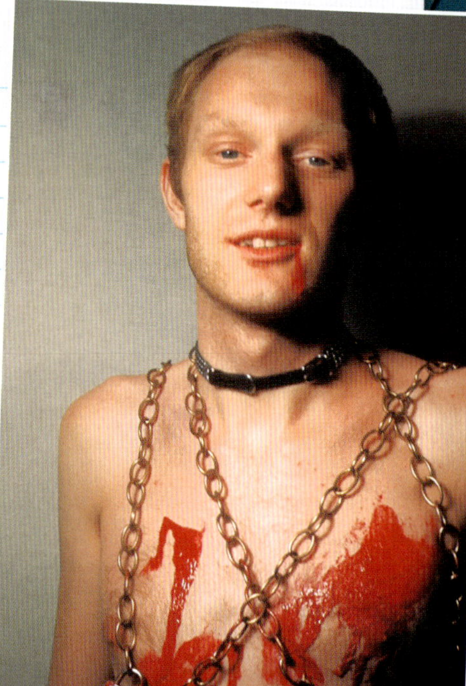

One of my fellow co-workers at The Portobello Hotel was the future acclaimed visual artist Volker Stox. Using air-brushing, spray painting, digital media and computer technology, Volker has had his vividly surreal art pieces on both paper and canvas exhibited all over the world from London and Los Angeles to Berlin and beyond. Trained as an architect – he was down to design the abandoned Pools Hotel project – he left Norman Foster Associates to start work at the Portobello because he couldn't stand the office environment there and wanted to be employed in a more creative atmosphere. Thanks to his partner John Scarlett-Davis, future rock video whiz kid director of the likes of Brother Beyond, Erasure and Aztec Camera, Volker found his niche in the Notting Hill Gate watering hole and was soon mixing with such like-minded artists as Patti Smith, Leonard Cohen, Pier Paolo Pasolini and Rainer Werner Fassbinder.

Alan Jones is wearing his beloved 'Perv' shirt designed exclusively for him by Vivienne Westwood and made out of chicken bones. The black hood is a Jean Seal original and the studded choker and wristbands are from the London Leatherman.

Volker told me much later that he was intimidated by my opinionated and confrontational character at first but warmed to me due to becoming intrigued by all my late night shift sessions with the Sex Pistols. He started hanging out with them too, got with the Punk program fast and became very excited by its wild aesthetic. So much so he asked Jordan and myself to come to his Clarendon Road, W11, studio in early 1976 and pose for a painting inspired by the movement. We both acted out scenarios wearing leather, chains, plastic, Kensington gore and SEX clothes plus studded accoutrements from The London Leatherman, the subculture brand Vivienne Westwood often passed off as her own, and the photo shoot results are shown here for the very first time.

Using these as templates Volker then painted an extraordinary 6 feet x 3 feet picture of us using a spray gun at low pressure to construct a form of pointillism. He titled it 'The Fabulous'! An exhibition was lined up in Paris by gallery owner Yuval Hanina as a showcase for the piece but he didn't like the overt Punk theme to Volker's new work and cancelled the presentation. Considering the impending Punk explosion, I hope Hanina realised the monumental mistake he made!

Volker and John would eventually become firm friends with director Derek Jarman, who would often come to their World's End house and film them dancing on his terrace with his Super 8 camera, which became part of the **B2 Tape** (1983) 30-minute short. The film also features Jordan, who had previously starred in Jarman's guerilla punk art attack **Jubilee** (1978).

THE FIFTH FLOOR (1978)

One contemporary review of this tight little exploitation horror, one of the first to feature Disco, suggested a title change to 'Psycho Disco' and dismissed it by saying it was merely a grindhouse **One Flew Over the Cuckoo's Nest** (1975). Well, what's so wrong with that? Supposedly based on a true story, but more obviously following the time-honoured cliché of the inability to differentiate madhouse patients from their medical staff, co-writer/director Howard Avedis brings a vivid luridness to the arch proceedings made more potent by a terrific cult cast including Bo Hopkins (**Tentacoli/Tentacles**, 1977), Robert Englund (the future Freddy Krueger), Julie Adams (**Creature from the Black Lagoon**, 1954), Michael Berryman (**The Hills Have Eyes**, 1977), Sharon Farrell (**Night of the Comet**, 1984), Mel Ferrer (**L'isola degli uomini pesce/Screamers**, 1979) and Patti D'Arbanville (Andy Warhol superstar and Cat Stevens' muse for his song *Lady D'Arbanville*, 1970).

But spearheading the performance roster in high method acting style, Dianne Hull turns her central role of co-ed Disco dancer Kelly McIntyre into a galvanising tour-de-force. Hull shot to the fore in her teacher Elia Kazan's **The Arrangement** (1969) and then veered between powerful studio pictures (**Aloha, Bobby and Rose**, 1975, **The Onion Field**, 1979) and exploitation fodder (**Christmas Evil**, 1980) always stepping up to the plate no matter what the subject. Here she collapses in the Disco after being poisoned with strychnine, misdiagnosed as a suicide attempt rather than the murder cover-up it actually was. Wrongly committed to the fifth floor psychiatric ward of the Cedar Springs Hospital for short-term evaluation, she soon realises stern head physician Dr. Coleman (Ferrer) couldn't care less about her 'condition', her scumbag boyfriend has no intention of helping her out of her dire situation and there is no hope of either mental or physical escape from the unwanted sexual attentions of unbalanced orderly Carl (Hopkins).

A sleazy shocker with a palpable sense of dread permeating throughout its ramped up mix of women-in-prison tropes, nasty rape, every abuse going and electro-shock therapy, Avedis had form for making the most out of this type of pulp thriller thanks to **The Teacher** (1974), **Dr. Minx** (1975) and **Scorchy** (1976). He also cameos as an occupational therapist. The fourth lowly credit for composer Alan Silvestri before he hit the soundtrack big time with **Romancing the Stone** (1984) and an impressive future blockbuster catalogue, **The Fifth Floor** featured celebrated Casablanca Records label star Pattie Brooks as the Disco singer in the opening sequence crooning *Fly Away*. Elsewhere *In So Deep*, written by Vic Thomas (composer of songs for Rhythm Heritage and T.U.M.E.), and *Spank Your Thang*, by Royal Flush members Jerline Shelton and Maurice Commander, provided the backdrop for impromptu asylum dancing.

Our Miss Brooks

If anyone could have torn the Queen of Disco crown from Donna Summer's head, it was Pattie Brooks, her one-time back-up singer and Casablanca label mate. That she didn't says much about the way the premier outfit was being run by head honcho Neil Bogart as his premium Disco brand fought for financial survival in the late 1970s. Kansas born Pattie's first break came in 1968 when she auditioned for a spotlight segment on 'The Smothers Brothers Comedy Hour'. From there she appeared in a host of other TV variety series while touring with Helen Reddy and Ann-Margret. Then in 1973 she was hired to sing *Am I Blue* in the Blaxploitation classic **Cleopatra Jones**, which actress Brenda Sykes lip-synched, that led to her running from recording studio to recording studio relentlessly session singing throughout the next decade for Diana Ross, Olivia Newton-John, Paul Jabara, D.C. LaRue, Thelma Houston, Dusty Springfield and Roberta Kelly.

It was Pattie's distinctive back-up vocals on Summer's banner *I Remember Yesterday* (1977) album that brought her to the attention of Northern Soul maven and UK DJ Simon Soussan who had moved to America to produce Shalamar's Disco Motown medley *Uptown Festival* (1977). Her solo Disco career was born with the album *Love Shook* (1977), credited to Pattie Brooks and The Simon Orchestra, featuring a *Pop Collage Medley* compromising the 1972 Hot Butter instrumental smash *Popcorn*, the Los Bravos 1966 hit *Black Is Black* (also Disco-fied by Belle Epoque and Cerrone in 1976) and the 1970 Steam evergreen *Na Na Hey Hey Kiss Him Goodbye*. This infectious assortment made it all the way to No.2 in the 'Billboard' Disco Charts along with the album's other sensational stormer *Girl Don't Make Me Wait*, a fabulous reboot of the 1968 Northern Soul classic by Timebox.

The *Our Ms. Brooks* follow-up appeared a whole fateful year later in 1978 due to its featured track *After Dark* also being included on the earlier **Thank God It's Friday** (1978) movie soundtrack. Originally the Casablanca-backed movie was titled 'After Dark' but got changed due to the fact that was also the name of a well-known gay-friendly American magazine. So while the brilliant No.1 'Billboard' classic *After Dark*, composed by Soussan and his wife Sabrina, and Pattie's biggest club hit ever, continued to fuel sales of the **Thank God It's Friday** double-disc, the release of *Our Ms. Brooks* kept getting delayed. By the time it did limp into record stores the heat had gone off the sultrily syncopated key track even though *This Is the House Where Love Died* and the medley *Come Fly with Me/Let's Do It Again* did just about scrape into the 'Billboard' Top 30.

Pattie's Disco career never recovered from that mismanagement but she did stay with Casablanca for two more lacklustre albums, *Party Girl* (1979) and *Pattie Brooks* (1980) before changing to the Mirage label for *In My World* (1983). Her last flurry on the Disco floor was *Got Tu Go Disco* from *Party Girl* produced by Bunny Sigler (Double Exposure, First Choice, Linda Clifford), the John Davis (of Monster Orchestra fame) written theme song from the flop Broadway musical supposed to do for Disco what 'Hair' did for rock.

In 1979 Pattie had branched out from Disco singing *Close Enough for Love*, the Johnny Mandel/Paul Williams theme from **Agatha** (1979) and in 1983 she sang four songs on the **Doctor Detroit** soundtrack, two in duet with star Dan Aykroyd. In recent years Rick Gianatos helped resurrect her career, recording and releasing new material on his Nu And Improved label, while her daughter Yvette Marine joined the Mary Jane Girls. Soussan formed the Harem label and persevered to score numerous Disco hits with Arpeggio (*Love and Desire*, 1978), Romance (*Dance Your Way to My Heart*, 1978), French Kiss (*Panic*, 1979), The Simon Orchestra (*I Close My Eyes and Count to Ten*, 1979) and Jessica Williams (*Queen of Fools*, 1979).

The Great Rock 'n' Roll Swindle

When Russ Meyer was fired from 'Who Killed Bambi?', Jonathan Kaplan, director of **Night Call Nurses** (1972) and **White Line Fever** (1975), took over for a while. After Malcolm McLaren had dumped him too, he asked me to suggest a British equivalent of those American superior sexploiters. Malcolm knew I was forging ahead with my genre film journalism career so I suggested Pete Walker, who was making controversial waves at the time with his Home Counties horrors **House of Whipcord** (1974), **Frightmare** (1974) and **House of Mortal Sin** (1975). Walker had also directed one of the best British adult dramas of the early '70s, **Cool It Carol** (1970), making him the ideal fit in my humble opinion.

Malcolm offered Walker the chance to salvage the Sex Pistols movie in late 1977, just after he had completed **The Comeback** (1977). For an entirely new script Walker turned to writer Michael Armstrong, director of the notorious **Mark of the Devil** (1970) and responsible for a welter of softcore exploiters including **Eskimo Nell** (1977). The result was the screenplay 'A Star Is Dead' that everyone knew would never be adhered to because the Pistols were never going to learn copious lines of dialogue. So Walker had decided the easiest option was just to film whatever chaos exploded in front of him. Then the band split up during their American tour in January 1978 and in despair Malcolm handed the poisoned chalice project over to rock video director Julien Temple. I'd never met Julien before even though he had directed a few Pistols videos and was surprised when he called up asking me to report to the Highgate terraced house set the next morning. There I had to put on a frogman's outfit and lie in a bath of (very cold) water as a half-naked extra waved a fishing line around my crotch.

We filmed for an entire day and Julien also gave me a script containing two other scenes he wanted me to appear in at the Rainbow theatre, Finsbury Park. One had Steve Jones and I sitting either side of doomed British sex queen Mary Millington in the stalls. Another had Steve pushing my face into a whirring cocktail blender in the bar upstairs. Only the former scene was filmed – at the Moulin cinema in Great Windmill Street instead of the Rainbow – with 1950s teen idol and **Konga** (1961) star Jess Conrad replacing my supposed role as Millington's boyfriend. Because he felt guilty about that, Julien gave me a wonderful 'Introducing Alan Jones' credit on the final print even though my overall contribution was absolutely minimal. Many people have asked me where I am in the film only to be disappointed when they finally find out after pausing the DVD!

I was paid £100 for my trouble and Glitterbest's Sophie Richmond told me a decade later that I and the tragic Millington were the only two people ever to see any money from the entire affair. She got £1,000 for her day's work! Two years after filming I went to a preview of the 'vandalised mockumentary' that would break British box-office records in the Rank Theatre, Wardour Street. My date for the hush-hush event was Siouxsie Sioux and is only memorable because when we went for a drink afterwards in The Ship pub across the road, two gobby blokes started hassling her for the way she looked. Amazing! It was like time had been rewound five years to when we had first met in SEX and become firm friends because I provided her with the Bernard Herrmann **Psycho** (1960) soundtrack she needed to make her screeching violin stage entrance at her first 100 Club gig.

THE WIZ (1978)

The familiar story of 'The Wonderful Wizard of Oz', L. Frank Baum's 1900 American fairytale, was retold in contemporary African-American terms in the stage musical 'The Wiz'. The idea of Ken Harper, a New York radio station programmer, who felt the time was right for a black family musical, he talked songwriter Charlie Smalls (a Hugh Masekala collaborator and composer of *Never Felt Like This Before* for John Cassavetes' **Faces**, 1968) into writing the songs and persuaded 20th Century Fox into investing $650,000 in the production. Slammed on its tryout tour, friends advised Harper to close it in Baltimore, but then costume designer Geoffrey Holder took over as director from Gilbert Moses, totally reconceptualised it and brought it to Broadway on January 5th, 1975.

The mainly white press gave it mixed notices, basing their criticisms on comparing it unfavourably to the classic 1939 movie starring Judy Garland. A closing notice was posted on opening night but Harper convinced his backer to persist with a – then – innovative television commercial campaign. Ticket sales mounted, especially among a younger demographic who had never been to Broadway before, helped by Consumer Rapport's club version of the show-stopping highlight *Ease On Down the Road* becoming a No.1 Dance chart hit two months after its Majestic Theatre premiere.

The show eventually won seven Tony Awards including Best Musical and played 1,672 performances in total. Starring in the show were many future Disco/HiNRG artists: Dorothy was played by Stephanie Mills (*Sweet Sensation/Never Knew Love Like This Before*, 1980), Glinda the Good Witch was Dee Dee Bridgewater (*Bad for Me*, 1979), Tornado was Evelyn Thomas (*High Energy*, 1984), Aunt Em was Tasha Thomas (*Shoot Me with Your Love*, 1978) and featured in the chorus was Phylicia Ayers-Allen/Rashad (*Josephine Superstar*, 1978). Incidentally Consumer Rapport, misspelt as Report on the first vinyl pressings, was a studio project featuring vocals by Frank Floyd, a pit singer in the show. Hollywood came calling once the musical was a proven and popular hit. But it wasn't Fox who decided to bankroll what would be, at $24 million, the most expensive and lavish production ever shot in New York. It was Motown Productions and Universal Pictures and they had every intention of letting Stephanie Mills reprise her lead character on screen. That was until the Queen of Motown, Diana Ross, decided she wanted the role and lobbied so intensively her ex-lover and company director Berry Gordy gave in. What swung it for Ross was her guarantee she could convince rising Motown star Michael Jackson to play the Scarecrow. However, having the 33-year-old Ross play Dorothy Gale as a 24-year-old Harlem kindergarten teacher even though the character was supposed to be 14 was far too much for original director John (**Saturday Night Fever**) Badham and he was replaced by master craftsman Sidney Lumet (**Dog Day Afternoon**, 1975,

Network, 1976) who had never helmed a musical before. Yet that lack of experience didn't show in what would sadly become a huge flop despite the nifty ideas of swapping Kansas for Harlem, the Emerald City for a surreal midtown Manhattan, the show's Glam Rock vibe for a druggy acid trip and the funky soul song arrangements with a pounding Disco beat.

Although Joel Schumacher (**The Lost Boys**, 1987) had seen the Broadway play before writing the script, none of it was incorporated into the screenplay. Whisked by a snowstorm on Thanksgiving to the Munchkin Land of Oz (the old New York World's Fair at Flushing Meadow), Dorothy and her dog Toto learn the only way to get back home is to follow the Yellow Brick Road across the Brooklyn Bridge to the World Trade Center to meet The Wiz (Richard Pryor). On the journey she meets a garbage-fashioned Scarecrow (Jackson) looking for a brain, a turn-of-the-century Coney Island automaton Tin Man (Nipsey Russell) wanting a heart, and a jungle-banished Lion who makes his living posing as a New York Public Library statue needing courage. But the quest to repair all their damaged souls is fraught with danger because Dorothy killed Evermean, the Wicked Witch of the East, who turned spray-paint vandals into their own graffiti figures, and now her equally nasty sister Evillene (Mabel King reprising her Broadway role), the Wicked Witch of the West, wants revenge. Never fear though, Glinda the Good Witch (veteran torch singer Lena Horne, Lumet's mother-in-law) is on hand to ensure Dorothy comes to understand there's no place like home.

While never as magic or as memorable as its vintage 1939 predecessor, **The Wiz**'s stellar cast all step up to the musical mark and Lumet's direction makes for some imaginative staging. However the true stars of the show are the vibrant photography of Oswald Morris, a musical maven with **Stop the World: I Want to Get Off** (1966), **Oliver!** (1968), **Goodbye, Mr. Chips** (1969), **Scrooge** (1970) and **Fiddler on the Roof** (1971) behind him, superior special make-up design from the fledgling Stan Winston, state-of-the-art special visual effects from skilled genius Albert Whitlock and especially the superb production and costume design by Tony Walton whose experience ranged from the pinnacles of **Mary Poppins** (1964) and **The Boy Friend** (1971) to **Murder on the Orient Express** (1974) and **All That Jazz** (1979). It's Walton who gives the movie its Disco sensibility what with his spectacular World Trade Center dance floor and fantastic playground backdrops. Only **Logan's Run** (1976) before it matched **The Wiz** in parallel universe Disco design.

Superstar producer Quincy Jones put the infectious soundtrack together – his studio band featured many New York jazz veterans, including Toots Thielemans, Eric Gale, Michael Brecker and Richard Tee – and augmented the original Broadway songs with a couple more written by himself, Nickolas Ashford and Valerie Simpson, and Luther Vandross. The latter wrote the fabulous, heavily Disco influenced, ecstatic anthem *A Brand New Day (Everybody Rejoice) Parts 1 & 2* sung by the entire ensemble. But it was *Ease On Down the Road* that gained a second life from Ross and Jackson's mainstream Top 40 hit, the only time they ever sang together. **The Wiz** was crucially important in the development of Michael Jackson's solo career because it marked the first time he worked with Quincy Jones, who would later produce his three mega-hit albums *Off the Wall* (1979), *Thriller* (1982) and *Bad* (1987).

Miss Broadway

One of the many Disco trends during the genre's Golden Years was taking established hit songs and making them four-to-the-floor danceable. A rich seam of inspiration came from the Great American Songbook, Broadway and West End stages as clubbers, especially show queens in the Gay Disco environment, liked nothing more than to sing along to something

they knew well. So it wasn't unusual when The Salsoul Orchestra included a version of *Ease On Down the Road* on their 1978 *Up the Yellow Brick Road* album, which charted at No.13 in the 'Billboard' Disco chart. Also included on that album were medleys from *West Side Story* and *Fiddler on the Roof*. Grace Jones gave stylish renditions of standards from 'Annie' (*Tomorrow*), 'A Chorus Line' (*What I Did for Love*) and 'A Little Night Music' (*Send in the Clowns*) on her hit 1977 album *Portfolio*. Linda Clifford nabbed *If My Friends Could See Me Now* (1978) from 'Sweet Charity', the Biddu Orchestra hi-jacked *I Could Have Danced All Night* (1975) from 'My Fair Lady' and Boris Midney superbly Disco-fied the whole of 'Evita' for Festival in 1979. Other notable versions of classic evergreens include the entire *The Ethel Merman Disco Album* (1979), Scherrie Payne's *One Night Only* (1984) from 'Dreamgirls', *The (Disco) Sound of Music* (1981) by Showstoppers '81, Murray Head's *One Night in Bangkok* (1985) from *Chess*, Johnny Mathis' smooth and velvety *Begin the Beguine* (1979) from Cole Porter's *Jubilee* and the entire *Gershwin '79* album by the Westside Strutters.

'Terror' sweeps Chicago

● THE BRITISH horror film "Terror" was released in Chicago on Friday, July 13, and grossed 190,000 dollars in its first week.
The Crown International release, which was directed by Norman J. Warren and produced by Les Young, also had a trial run at three Oklahoma City theatres, where it outgrossed all previous Crown International pictures released there.
Pictured above is James Aubrey in a scene from the film.

Disco Memo

Terror

I made my movie debut in Norman J. Warren's **Terror** (1978) and I have scriptwriter David McGillivray to thank for it. I absolutely loved Pete Walker's early nasty horror movies **House of Whipcord** (1974), **Frightmare** (1974) and **House of Mortal Sin** (1975), all written by McGillivray after landing the job through being the first person to ever interview the director. It was after watching **Frightmare** on its first run at the sorely missed London Pavilion Piccadilly Circus, I bumped into McGillivray on the street by accident. I knew what he looked like thanks to his brilliant 'The Crowded Shelf' columns in 'Films and Filming' magazine and I said, "You're David McGillivray, I love your Pete Walker movies". To this day he swears I was cruising him – not true – and it began an everlasting friendship I hold very dear to this day.

Cut to Spring 1978 and he called asking if I'd like to be an (unpaid!) extra in his friend Norman's new horror movie **Terror**, essentially a poor man's **Suspiria** (1977) that he had written, just like his **Satan's Slave** (1976) before it. It was a day out and I thought I might write about it for 'Cinefantastique' (I didn't!), so I said yes. I met McGillivray at his basement flat in Kilburn and was whisked off to the country manor location of Admiral's Walk in Pirbright, Surrey. Warren had liked the location from **Virgin Witch** (1972) and had already shot key scenes of **Satan's Slave** there. Along with my other teenage/twenty-something extras crowd I was sent to wardrobe for tuxedo and party frock fitting and we took our places in the ballroom for the sword-wrestling scene between stars Carolyn Courage and James Aubrey. All pretty easy and, in the completed film, I felt I was reasonably effective. I do like this skeleton in my closet appearing every now and again as people realise yes, that face in the crowd is indeed me! Incidentally, my dance partner was Cleo Rocos, who would eventually rise up the fame ladder to star alongside Kenny Everett on 'The Kenny Everett Television Show'.

A unit production still from *Terror* with Alan Jones in action!

▲ Above: Alan Jones with his *Terror* partner for the location shooting, Cleo Rocos, soon to become famous on 'The Kenny Everett Television Show'.

AMERICAN FEVER (1978)

Because of the game-changing success of **Saturday Night Fever** (1977), it wasn't surprising the Italian Film Industry jumped on the Disco bandwagon as they had done with every hit genre since time immemorial. In rapid succession came **Brillantina Rock/Disco Crazy** (1979), **L'anno dei gatti/I ragazzi della discoteca/The Year of the Cats** (1979), **John Travolto... da un isolito destino/The Face With Two Left Feet** (1979), **Disco delirio/Disco Music Fever** (1979) and **White Pop Jesus** (1980). In terms of overall box-office **American Fever**, released only with that English title, just made it into the Top 100 Italian movies of the year – Number 98 – garnering 21,515 ticket sales during 55 days on autumn release.

Directed in the same year he helmed **Candido Erotico**, Claudio Giorgi/Claude Miller/Claudio De Molinis co-wrote the screenplay with Italian exploitation veteran Luigi Montefiori/George Eastman (**Anthropophagus**, 1980). A pale Roman imitation of the matchless John Badham movie, with a little **Rocky** (1976) finessing here and **Shampoo** (1975) styling there, this starred Mircha Carven in the title role of Tony Ferrante. A photo novella model claiming to be the bastard son of Hollywood royalty Clark Gable, Carven's signature part was in the controversial **Lager SSadis Kastrat Kommandantur/SS Experiment Camp** (1976).

Keen on American cinema, garage mechanic Tony whiles away his tedious day shifts with dreams of Hollywood stardom. He's hoping to achieve his fame ambitions one of two ways; by dancing up a storm at the local Disco and being talent-spotted, or by his best friend Nino (Vincenzo Crocitti, **Squadra antiscippo/The Cop in Blue Jeans**, 1976) actually coming through with his promise of writing him a blockbuster action script to showcase his athletic prowess. Soon his naivety and generous character makes him an easy mark for sleazy producers who con him into doing dangerous stunts for their latest crime rip-off movie with promises of taking his acting aspirations seriously. Then he stops suicidal Lisa (Czechoslovakian actress Zora Ulla Keslerova/Zora Keřová/Zora Kéer on the verge of a substantial exploitation career taking in **Cannibal Ferox**, 1981, and **Lo squartatore di New York/The New York Ripper**) from jumping off a bridge and they team up to become the hottest dance floor duo, saving each other's damaged spirits in the process of falling in love.

Although randomly inserted when the pace flags and edited with a trowel, the Disco sequences are pretty evocative of the era and even showcase the California Hustle/Bus Stop line dance. The songs too are a Eurodisco treat with the catchy title track by Spot Light, featuring the chorus line *Ready, Steady, Go!* (the movie's shooting title), plus an instrumental version, and *A Little Bit Faster*, *Morning Sun* and *Blue Wave* by the same outfit. Elsewhere D.D. Sound warbled the Ritchie Family-style *1-2-3-4... Gimme Some More* and Cannon Ball offered the creditable shuffling Eurovision-esque anthem *Passion Flower*.

Italo Disco Primo

Closer inspection of the D.D. Sound personnel reveals the names of Sicilian brothers Michelangelo and Carmelo La Bionda who as just plain La Bionda allowed the **American Fever** producers to feature their massive worldwide

Eurodisco hit *One for You, One for Me* in return for showcasing work by their recording alias. Roughly translated as 'The Blonde', La Bionda is considered the vanguard of Italian Disco. Beginning their musical careers as songwriters, they recorded two albums of acoustic ballads between 1973 and 1975 before climbing aboard the Disco bandwagon in Munich where they recorded numerous dance tracks under the name D[isco] D[elivery] Sound. *Disco Bass*, *Burning Love* and *Café* (all 1977) made chart inroads so they threw caution to the wind and released another Disco album proper under their own name. Their profile then went international with *One for You, One for Me* (1978), successfully covered by Jonathan King in the UK, and the subtly Arabian Nights flavoured follow-up *Sandstorm* from the same *La Bionda* album. Active in every musical area, La Bionda would branch out into composing soundtracks for blockbuster movies, including Sergio Corbucci's **Poliziotto superpiù/Super Fuzz** (1980), and TV jingles and would also play their part in the careers of artists Righeria and Sabrina. Their 1979 album *Bandido*, with its haunting, trippy Space Disco feel is seen as the important bridge from Eurodisco to Italo Disco.

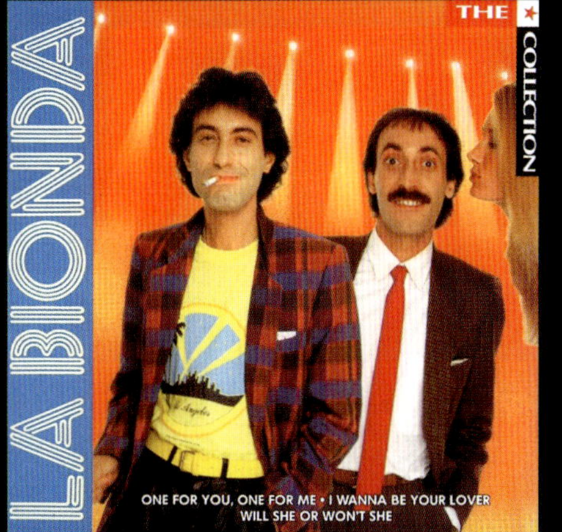

Disco Memo

Simonetti a Go Go

I was never really totally aware of Goblin super group head honcho Claudio Simonetti's Disco past until I went to his country house outside Rome to interview him for the **Dario Argento: An Eye for Horror** (2000) documentary. While setting the cameras up I found a pile of vinyl records thrown in the corner of the room in which we were filming. As I leafed through the dusty stack I was amazed by how many Disco singles and albums there were and on closer inspection how many bore his producer/writing credits. It was something Simonetti never really liked talking about even as late as 2014 when I made him an offer on behalf of Harmless Records to consider curating a CD collection of his Disco repertoire. He declined, which was a shame as he really did produce some major unsung classics.

After being part of the progressive rock band Goblin and changing the face of horror film music with Argento's **Profondo rosso/Deep Red** (1975) and **Suspiria** (1977), and George A. Romero's **Dawn of the Dead** (1978), Brazilian-born Simonetti changed tack into Disco tracks for monetary reasons and joined forces with Cannon Ball group producer Giancarlo Meo for their *Passion Flower* (1978) single. Together they founded numerous Disco studio projects like Easy Going (*Baby I Love You*, 1978, *Fear*, 1979), named after a popular Rome gay club, Trieste model Vivien Vee/Viviana Andreattini (*Give Me a Break*, 1979) and Russell Russell (*Buonasera ragazzina*, 1981) who became Easy Going's lead singer after originator Paul Micioni left.

A core member of the Italo Disco group Crazy Gang (*A Discomantic Rodeo*, 1983), Simonetti could easily flip between soundtracks (**Tenebrae**, 1982, **Demons**, 1985, **Phenomena/Creepers**, 1985, **Opera**, 1987) and easy listening club music throughout the 1980s. His *EverGreens Mix* (1988) compendium featured a 13-minute medley of everything from *Funkytown* (1979) and *Boogie Wonderland* (1979) to *Y.M.C.A.* (1978) and *Let's All Chant* (1977), and he would also remix extended dance versions of his Argento movie title themes for Italo Disco club play.

WINDS OF CHANGE (1978)

"An animated journey to a distant past" became a marketing nightmare for the Japanese merchandise company Sanrio in 1978. Internationally famous for their best-known character 'Hello Kitty', Sanrio's business model is still all about selling stationery, school supplies, gifts, animatronics, fast food and accessories branded with designs that they have made popular in Japanese 'kawaii/cute' culture. Other licenses they own include 'Peanuts' and 'Mr. Men' to show their high-end corporate ranking importance.

From 1977 to 1985, Sanrio produced movies through their Sanrio Films label and in their inaugural year scored a global hit with **The Mouse and His Child** (1977). Sanrio's next success hopeful was the originally titled 'Hoshi no Orpheus/Orpheus of the Stars', initially conceptualised as a rock **Fantasia** (1940) and designed to be the first Japanese animated movie to use the 70mm screen process just as Disney had done with their much beloved classic. Over 170 American and Japanese animators worked for three years in Sanrio's Hollywood studio under Takashi Yanase's direction to turn five fables taken from Roman poet Ovid's 8 A.D. magnum opus 'Metamorphoses' into a fabulous cartoon fantasy. The stories, Ovid's versions of popular Greek myths, were unified by a starchild character first seen as Actaeon being turned into a deer for spying on the bathing goddess Diana, then as Orpheus descending into Hades for his lover Eurydice, thirdly as Mercury struggling with the house of envy, then Perseus cutting off Gorgon Medusa's head and, lastly, as Phaeton causing havoc with Helios the Sun God's chariot of fire.

Featuring narration by impressionist Paul Frees (a Disney veteran and the voice of Boris Badenov in 'The Rocky and Bullwinkle Show') and with ill-fitting songs by Joan Baez, The Pointer Sisters and Mick Jagger never properly accompanying the on-screen action, **Metamorphoses** was distributed in America by Columbia Pictures on May 3rd, 1978. It got terrible reviews, audiences didn't understand the format – was it an anthology or one full-length tale because of the character continuity? – and tanked at the box office. But Sanrio refused to give up on their expensive property. They pulled it from release, renamed it **Winds of Change**, slightly rearranged the stories in Perseus, Actaeon, Mercury, Orpheus and Phaeton running order, shortened the 89-minute running time by seven minutes, named the starchild character Wondermaker and replaced Frees' narration with a more tongue-in-cheek and clearer one by multi-Oscar winner Peter Ustinov (the voice of Prince John in Disney's **Robin Hood**, 1973, and Manny the Rat in **The Mouse and His Child**).

However the most radical change they made was erasing the entire rock soundtrack and replacing it with a score more reflective of the dance crazy times, by Eurodisco hotshot Alec R. Costandinos. Just like he did with **Trocadéro bleu citron** (1978), the Disco pioneer provided a wonderful 18-minute 20-second narrative suite of catchy tunes, superbly orchestrated hooks and propulsive energy, plus six other tracks individually tailored to the fables themselves. *Red Hot River of Fire* was sung by back-up singer supremo turned Casablanca doyenne Pattie Brooks, while the poppier *Where Are You Going, Perseus?* and *Star Child*, the ballads *Future Legend* and *You Gave Me Dreams* were all enriched by the smoothly soulful vocals of session singer Arthur Simms. The *Creation of Man* end credit sequence music was a return to the lilting signature Costandinos instrumental.

Exactly a year after being first released as **Metamorphoses** in America, the newly re-fashioned **Winds of Change** entered theatres again and was met by similar critical shrugs and audience apathy once more. The soundtrack released by the Casablanca

Records and FilmWorks label also failed to make any inroads on the dance charts, mainly because the child-friendly movie didn't attract the anticipated adult Disco fans. Stylistically falling through the wide cracks between classic Japanese anime and Golden Age Disney zing, **Winds of Change** is a way too fluffy and long-winded fantasy for all its literary credentials with only the effervescent Costandinos factor to commend it.

The Costandinos Phenomenon Part 2

After his early pop career and launch on the world Disco stage with fellow Eurodisco genius Marc Cerrone and their cataclysmic dance bombshell *Love in C Minor* (1976), Alec R. Costandinos became the King of the Epic Disco anthem with a string of superb releases beginning with Love and Kisses. That studio group's first album was the self-titled *Love and Kisses* (1977) and featured the two chart-topping full side suites *Accidental Lover* and *I've Found Love (Now That I've Found You)*. The former was close to the spirit of *Love in C Minor*, concerning a dodgy club pick-up complete with insulting remarks, before devolving into a swirling frenzy of passion and fantasy shot through with rough-edged vocals and laser sharp strings. The latter track has Costandinos singing lead vocals on a swooping, and constantly beat-changing, declaration of love after an instantly grabby foot-tapping piano crescendo. With the chanting chorus fading in and out to keep dancers on their toes in anticipation, striking instrumental gear-changing and eccentric arrangements, it was clear with this banner release that Costandinos was experimenting with the Eurodisco format and entering exciting unchartered territory.

The best was yet to come with Love and Kisses though. In their second far more romantic release *How Much, How Much I Love You* (1978) the melodies were thrilling, the orchestration brilliant, the vocal stylization effortlessly wonderful, the string arrangements incredibly beautiful and the whole opus an outstanding and moving *tour de force*. With its lyrical rhapsodising of the most wonderful moments and beautiful seasons contained in every punch drunk love affair, and chorally repetitive to an ethereally delightful extreme, backed by the 'Beauty and the Beast' fairytale given a masterful and textured opulence, this sought-after classic is one of the most perfectly crafted Disco idylls of the entire era. The third Love and Kisses album *You Must Be Love* (1979), after the ensemble sung the title track and *You're the Most Precious Thing in My Life* for **Thank God It's Friday** (1978), tried to emulate the same delicious heady formula, but didn't quite pull it off and failed to win over dancers' hearts, minds or feet.

Many of the same session singers and musicians on the Love and Kisses albums found their way onto the *Sphinx* (1977) release that put the concept of Christian guilt into epic Disco terms. The two album sides contained one long composition. Side A focused on *Judas Iscariot* who betrayed Jesus Christ, and Side B *Simon Peter* who denied him. Expertly arranged by Don Ray and using motifs from Costandinos' roots in Arab/Egyptian music along with spoken religious quotes, the percussive pulse and relentless violin passages made these mini biblical operettas *Jesus Christ Superstar* (1970) fabulous in their own right. Powerful and harmoniously overwhelming in so many places, going to the Disco was considered the new church at the time and here was its divine soundtrack.

From one heavenly concept to another heavenly body and the unique notion *Golden Tears* (1977) by Sumeria. Clearly inspired by **The Man Who Fell to Earth** (1976), this space opera oddity finds a distraught Eva recovering from a broken relationship meeting the cosmic traveller Nezet who has been sent to Earth to experience love and death, the two things that don't exist on his own planet. Through such Disco ditties as *Dance and Leave It All Behind You* and *Why Must There Be an End/Golden Tears*, his explorations into humanity unfold with drama and delicacy in all their euphoria and melancholy throbbing with lush orchestrations and experimental touches for a starburst spectacular. Not a dance floor hit, but *Golden Tears* once more put the Discognoscenti on high alert that Costandinos was being impressively ambitious in his Disco shaped sound designs.

Credited together with his session band The Syncophonic Orchestra, the next 'Billboard' chart-topping album released by Alec R. Costandinos turned out to be his most popular, most accomplished, and a celebrated Disco landmark that instantaneously solidified his legacy. Using Trident Studio's stunning new 48-track recording innovations, *Romeo & Juliet* (1978) put the classic William Shakespeare tragedy to an accomplished Disco beat in five acts/tracks that shimmered with melody, harmony and heartfelt poignancy. Setting much of the Bard's original text to an uninterrupted flow of perfect Eurodisco, Costandinos audaciously redefined the emotional narrative with cascades of urgent voices, insistent violins, stylistic vocabulary, shattering brass constructions, countless surprises and expert danceability.

It was without doubt one of the most important releases of 1978 and marked the sea change from old school Eurodisco to the more intensely tuneful New Wave structuring combined with complex technical expertise. It was also the recording that landed him the job of composing the Perrier water jingle for American TV commercials.

After this epochal expression of his Eurodisco mindset, Costandinos composed the two soundtrack albums *Trocadéro bleu citron* (1978) and *Winds of Change* (1979), followed by another concept album, *Hunchback of Notre Dame* (1978) again under his name with The Syncophonic Orchestra. More a bitty melodramatic listening experience based on the 1831 Victor Hugo novel than anything truly crafted for the Disco environment, it inevitably stalled at No.35 in the 'Billboard' charts. The Disco version of *Eloise* from *Paris Connection* (1978) did slightly better, but *The Syncophonic Orchestra*

COLUMBIA *Symphonie Spatiale*

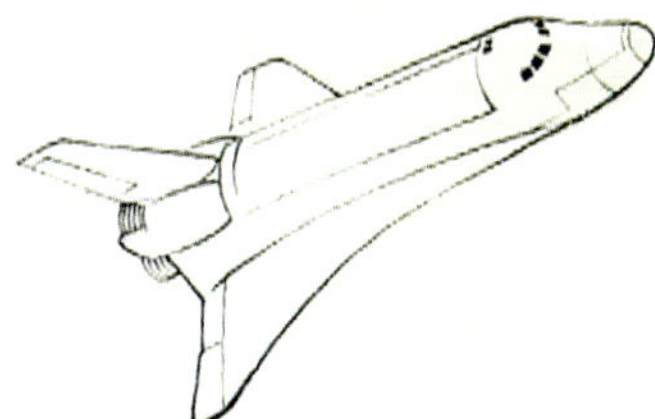

SYNCOPHONIC ORCHESTRA

featuring Alirol and Jacquet (1979) with its frantic cod classical cuts titled *Synergy*, *Benedite* and *The Rite of King Ganymede* failed to chart at all anywhere. The Syncophonic Orchestra's last brilliant solo stand was *Columbia Symphonie Spatiale* (1981), released only in France, and a Disco celebration of NASA's Space Shuttle Fleet's maiden voyage.

In 1979 Costandinos produced the comeback Tina Turner album *Love Explosion* and its failure seemed to knock his confidence so much that the rest of his output was variable to say the least. Only the *Burnin' Alive* album (1979) by Tony Rallo and the Midnite Band, spawning the British hit *Holdin' On*, and the *Universum* album by Demis Roussos made Disco inroads while *John and Arthur Simms* (1980) by the title co-writing duo, *Je m'envole* (1981) by Le Group and Costandinos' own *Americana* (1980), *Something's Cookin* (1980), *Les routes d'aeroports* (1983) and *Paese mio* all vanished in a puff of dry ice.

When promoting the stupendous Love and Kisses *How Much, How Much I Love You* album in America in April 1978, Costandinos revealed his new project was going to be a 12-album Disco interpretation of the Arabian Nights which would take two years to perfect. That awe-inspiring idea sadly never happened and Discophiles everywhere can only mourn the loss while celebrating the fact that from *Love in C Minor* through *Love and Kisses* to *Romeo & Juliet* Alec R. Costandinos provided the soundtrack to many dancers' lives as one of the most important figureheads of the entire Disco movement.

The Errand

Two years after **Terror** (1978), scriptwriter David McGillivray struck again! "Hello luvvie", he said calling me up one evening in the summer of 1979 with his signature greeting. "How do you fancy being in my new short movie? I promise I'll give you a line of dialogue this time". Once more, with a free lunch thrown into the unpaid deal, how could I refuse? So I roller-skated over at the crack of dawn that weekend to his Kilburn flat and joined a motley crew of actors, plus his director friend Nigel Finch, on a frantic drive to the location, glamorous Milton Keynes. The star was **Frightmare** (1974) victim Eddie Kalinski, who played Disco Boy in **Silver Dream Racer** (1980).

The Errand (1980) was a 30-minute slice of 'Twilight Zone' style boredom about a soldier sent on a mysterious assignment and refused help by every single person he comes across. The ho-hum reason why? Well, track it down and see for yourself! I played a patrolman and my key line was "Blue sixteen, to base", the fact I can still remember it speaks volumes about how hard I tried to sound natural and get it right. It was Nigel's film debut – he'd persevere to direct the wonderful **Stonewall** (1995) – but I scarcely recall him giving me any direction as we cruised up and down that bland Milton Keynes back road.

We did go back for a night shoot too, but everything I did during that all-nighter got cut out. The joke continued further because even my one line got dubbed! Never mind, at least my performance did get seen as, back then, cinemas often played a support item before the main feature. Remember those awful **Look At Life**, Pathé Pictorials and Global-Queensway travelogues? **The Errand** first played with **Happy Birthday to Me** (1981) and then **Outland** (1981) so all things considered I was in good horror sci-fi company – as usual.

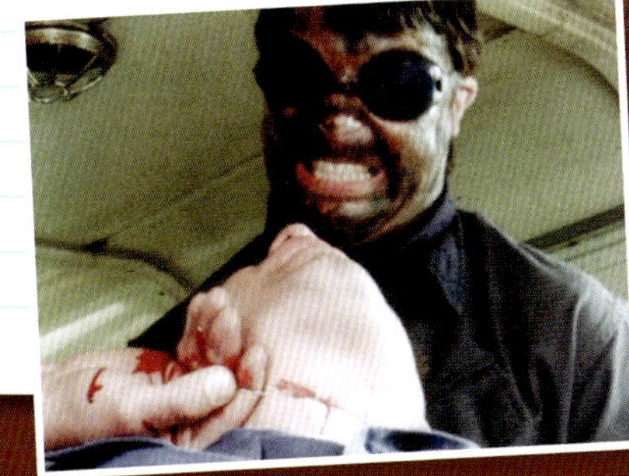

JUKEBOX / DISCO FEVER (1978)

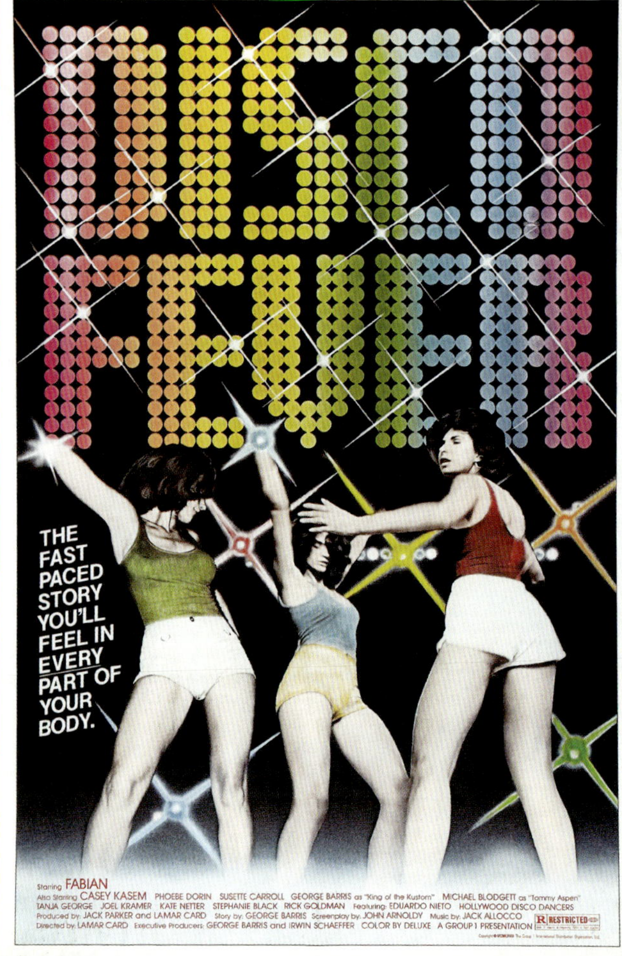

"What really goes on behind the scenes of the drug and sex crazed Disco world?" posed a tagline to this crossbreed debacle that comes on strong like the AIP youth exploiter it wanted to be but so lamely isn't. Nothing much, according to this trifling Z-movie that claims, "The beat is just right, the music is always moving through you", but fails to deliver on its promises. Directed by Lamar Card, a producer of some truly great cult items like **Nashville Girl** (1976) and **Heart Like a Wheel** (1983), not to mention **Clones** (1973) and **Terror Train** (1980), written by John Arnoldy (**Cycle Vixens**, 1978) and George Barris, builder of the Batmobile for the 1960s 'Batman' TV series, and starring faded '50s teen idol Fabian, **Disco Fever** had all the right weird credentials to surface as something better and camper than an obscure blot on the emerging Disco landscape. The main problem is its pretence at being a Disco movie when it's mainly just a throwback to the Roger Corman directed teenage flicks of the Rock 'n' Roll era.

Fabian became an accidental pop idol with eleven hit songs including *Hound Dog Man*, *Tiger* and *Turn Me Loose* (all 1959). But although he parlayed that into an interesting film career – **Five Weeks in a Balloon** (1963), **Dr. Goldfoot and the Girl Bombs** (1966), **A Bullet for Pretty Boy** (1970) – alcoholism and legal scandal meant his stock was low when he was hired to more-or-less star as himself in this misbegotten curio. He plays washed up singer Richie Desmond, still composing and wondering why Disco left his popular tunes in the dust. Nevertheless he frequents Cybil's Disco, the manager of which, Cybil Michaels (Phoebe Dorin), makes a pass at him while offering the chance of a comeback.

Urged by his manager Brian Parker (legendary radio DJ Casey Kasem) to sign the contract, Richie gets ready to debut some new material on Cybil's new venture, an airplane-turned-Disco. Unfortunately it's all been a scam on Cybil's part to lure an audience to the Disco Jet's opening and launch Disco singer Tommy Aspen (Michael Blodgett, star of **Beyond the Valley of the Dolls**, 1970) on the back of Richie being the supporting act. Further complications arise when Richie's girlfriend Jill (Kate Netter) turns out to be the ex of jealous Danny (stuntman Joel Kramer), Tommy's manager. However when Richie finally performs his set, it's a huge success and he gladly spurns Cybil yet again.

Shot under the title 'Jet Set Disco' before ending up as **Jukebox** when it became obvious audiences felt conned by the **Disco Fever** moniker, Card's kitsch novelty was filmed at Osko's in Los Angeles, the same location as **Thank God It's Friday** (1978), and in a very cramped, fairy light festooned plane fuselage making it crystal clear why flying Discos never became a thing (the nearest any Disco got to it was Club 747 in Buffalo, New York, which used actual airplane accessories for interior design). There are plenty of Disco scenes where groups of dancers perform unlikely routines, more in the Busby Berkeley style, and there's a cameo by Adolfo 'Shabba-Doo' Quinones of **Breakin'** (1984) fame.

But these are merely passing fun intervals and have nothing to do with the main action. It's up to bearded Fabian, wearing tight denim ensembles, with his hairy chest on

full display to sing the teen idol ditties written and given a soulful arrangement by Jack Allan Allocco, musical director and conductor for stars Robert Goulet and Peter Allen, and composer of the theme for the venerable 'The Young and the Restless' soap opera. *Moving On, My Turn to Fly, Carry On, Carry On, Till I Get Through to You* and *Rain Dance* are the totally forgettable featured songs.

Lipstique

Lipstique was a studio group put together by German producer Jürgen S. Korduletsch, husband of Disco Diva Claudja Barry. They only recorded one album but what an amazing album it was featuring the epic 15-minute title track *At the Discotheque*. While the musicians featured included Keith Forsey and Thor Baldursson, both Donna

Summer alumni, it was another Summer associate who made up the key vocal trio alongside Claudia Schwarz and Stefan Zauner. Roberta Kelly made friends with Summer in Germany and soon found herself recording with the top Eurodisco producers of the day. First with Pete Bellotte (*Kung Fu's Back Again (Part 1 & 2)*, an answer record to the Carl Douglas smash *Kung Fu Fighting*, both 1974), then with Michael Kunze and Sylvester Levay (she was in the original Silver Convention line-up) and most significantly with Giorgio Moroder (the super solo albums *Trouble Maker*, 1976, and *Zodiac Lady*, 1977). *At the Discotheque* is a relentlessly driving and gorgeously harmonious barnstormer, a paean to the ritual of clubbing circa 1978, and marks Roberta Kelly's glorious exit from Disco queendom before becoming her old colleague Donna Summer's personal secretary in the 1980s.

An Elephant's Memory

Sometimes a person's impact on one's life only happens after they've disappeared from it. Such was the effect American musician Chris Robison had on mine. He was another hook-up from the Portobello Hotel who took a shine to me and throughout the summer of 1976 we were practically inseparable. I even took him to see **Lipstick** (1976) at the Empire Cinema, Leicester Square, on July 10th so he could meet my friends. The tickets cost £1 each! And for the hard rocker he was, Disco was not even his third love! Chris was in the touring band for Steam once that studio project's *Na Na Hey Hey Kiss Him Goodbye* (1969) became a hit, sang back up vocals with John Lennon and Yoko Ono for the rock outfit Elephant's Memory (he co-wrote *Power Boogie*, 1972, for them) and played keyboards with the 1975 lineup of the New York Dolls, which is when he came into my life.

I had met the Dolls when they played the Rainbow Room, atop the legendary Biba department store in Kensington High Street, on November 26th, 1973. I got on best with bassist Arthur Kane when they visited Vivienne's World's End Store and the brocade-and-platform-boots emporium 'Granny Takes a Trip' just around the corner, run by the fabulous Gene Krell. The Dolls were the first inkling in Malcolm's mind of the Sex Pistols venture and were still going strong on the touring front. Chris knew everyone in the music industry. I'd mention a name and he had their phone number in his address book. One of the most memorable nights I had with him was going out to dinner with his friends actor Richard Gere (on his way to Canada to make **Days of Heaven**, 1978, if my memory serves me correctly) and singer/songwriter Peter Allen, famous at the time for his *I Go to Rio* (1976) hit and being Liza Minnelli's ex-husband. Chris would start a family with two sons thanks to a friend of Allen's who became their godfather.

Chris taught me a lot about remaining true to oneself and never apologising to anyone for anything. Other artists from his background often disguised their gay lyrics with a veneer of surreality. Like Bowie clone Jobriath, who I also knew

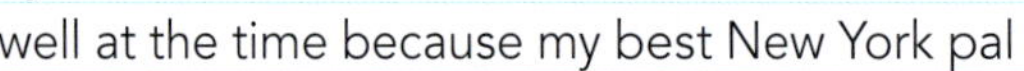

well at the time because my best New York pal Jay Reisberg was his personal assistant. Chris took a much more direct approach as his songs *Doctor! Doctor (The Shocking Tail of Jonathan Schwartz Jr)* and *Lookin' for a Boy Tonight*, from his first album *Chris Robison and His Many-Hand Band* (1973), and *I'll Be Your Man*, from *Manchild* (1974) showed only too well. Chris was as much a pioneer in the gay music world as I was in the horror journalism field and I never forgot his wise words throughout the next decades. Back then it was impossible to keep in touch once out of each other's spheres but I always kept track of his progress and am delighted he's been recognised by the gay community as a true groundbreaker.

Another band member who meant a lot to me during 1975 was Michael Montgomery, keyboardist with Back Street Crawler, and co-writer and composer of all the tracks on their debut album *The Band Plays On* (1975). Created by ex-Free guitarist Paul Kossoff, Back Street Crawler only really stayed together for a year, and Mike left to become a noted session musician. But what an exciting year that was as Mike took me everywhere with him, even groupie choosing, on their UK tour, truncated due to Kossoff's ill-health. Mike was always upbeat and optimistic about everything no matter what the circumstances – one had us both slipping and sliding over wet balconies trying to escape a particularly awful relationship drama. I was sad to hear he died of cancer in 1991, but knew categorically he lived every second of his life to the max.

▲ Bottom Left: Jay Reisberg with Jane Gould. Jay was the chaperone for Jobriath, the rock musician being groomed as a David Bowie clone by his manager Jerry Brandt. Jay's apartment in Greenwich Village became my base whenever I was in New York. Jane was the manager of the Portobello Hotel, who married horror film director Robert Fuest.

DISCO CRAZY / BRILLANTINA ROCK (1979)

In the wonderful world of Italian movie rip-offs, why settle for a single bite of the cherry when you could have two for the price of one? Obviously the thinking behind director Michele Massimo Tarantini's **Brillantina Rock**, which tried to have it both ways John Travolta style by plonking a **Grease** (Italian title **Brillantina**, 1978) motivated lead into a methodical **Saturday Night Fever** (1977) plot. Tarantini, best known up until this point for a series of *poliziotteschi* thrillers including **Poliziotti violenti/Crimebusters** (1976) and **Napoli si rubella/A Man Called Magnum** (1977), and after for **Femmine in fuga/Women in Fury** (1984) and **Nudo e selvaggio/Massacre in Dinosaur Valley** (1985) under his alias Michael E. Lemick, didn't do himself any favours with the trite script by Alessandro Capone (**Body Count**, 1986) and one-timer Pino Pellegrino that simply followed the hackneyed Dance Competition enmity scenario with perfunctory alacrity.

To the soaring 1978 feel-good Disco anthem *Love Is in the Air* by John Paul Young, Brylcreemed Roberto/Robbie (Monty Ray Garrison) rides Lizzie, his Russian motorcycle complete with sidecar and Travolta decals on the handlebar mirrors, through Milan to join his pack of fun-loving wasters. Hanging out doing nothing during the day, they dance the night away at the local Disco, entrance usually paid for by eager-to-please dimwit Oscar (Mauro Fritella), the only one with a job and the butt of the grating non-stop insults. In typical **West Side Story** (1961) fashion Robbie's unruly mob has rivals: bad boy Rick (Domenico/Mimmo Bua, **Blue Jeans**, 1975) and his delinquents-in-black-outfits gang. The only way to settle the score is on the Disco floor where each use their best hustle moves to out-dance each other.

Things get further complicated when Robbie and Rick vie to romance the new rich chick in town, ultra-sophisticated American Cindy (Auretta Gay, **Zombi 2/Zombie Flesh-Eaters**, 1979) who arrives at the club in her *faux*-leopard skin outfits and brazen single-girl attitudes. This all proves too much for Robbie's old childhood friend Sandra (Cecilia Buonocore, 'Così per caso' TV chanteuse, a 1979 one-hit-wonder with *Matta tutta*) who harbours a secret crush on him but still uses her sexual charms to land a job. Sandra trying to seduce Robbie by taking him to a posh restaurant where the *haute-cuisine* food bemuses him is supposedly the comedy 'highlight'. Who will win the hard-to-get wealthy industrialist's daughter Cindy's affections and manage to partner her for the 'King and Queen of Rock' dance competition crown? Does Sandra ever snag her man? Do you really need to think about it that much? Jogging from one familiar cliché to the next – there's also a motorbike and car chase chicken run shoehorned in for action-man Tarantini to get his teeth into – **Disco Crazy** is predictably stupid, simplistic fluff. All the catchy incidental Disco music and Country and Western flavoured pop is written by Gianfranco Reverberi who, after a solid career writing hit songs for such Italian superstars as Adriano Celentano, Gino Paoli, Mina, Lucio Dalla and Luigi Tenco, moved into the soundtrack field, making a particular splash with the track *Nel cimitero di Tucson* from **Preparati la bara!/Django, Prepare a Coffin** (1968). That formed the basis of Gnarls Barkley's 2006 hit *Crazy*, which made UK chart history by being the first ever track to go directly to

number one based on downloads alone. Reverberi's other commendable soundtracks include Massimo Dallamano's **Le malizie di Venere/The Devil in the Flesh/Venus in Furs** (1969) and the Renato Polselli duo **Riti, magie nere e segrete orge nel trecento.../The Reincarnation of Isabel** (1971) and **Delirio caldo/Delirium** (1972).

All the actors acquit themselves well on the dance floor, gyrating insanely to the oddball mix of a strangled version of The Rolling Stones 1965 hit *(I Can't Get No) Satisfaction*, the attractive instrumental *La Papaya* and Daniel Danieli's hilariously delivered broken English rendition of *Honey for Bears*, taken from his 1978 same-titled album featuring cover versions of such standards as *Good Vibrations* (1970) and *Monday, Monday* (1966). Very much a case of forget the surroundings just watch the dance sequences, **Disco Crazy** is absolutely nothing without the swirling lights, the cheesy accented lyrics and the pulsating rhythms. Although it played in more cinemas and on more days than **American Fever** (1978) in Italy, **Disco Crazy** attracted nearly 3,000 fewer cinema-goers according to the official Bolaffi Catalogue placing it statistically at Number 102 in the 1979 box office chart.

The Piper Club

Opened in February 1965, The Piper Club at Via Tagliamento 9, Rome, changed Italian nightlife and pop culture forever. To the Eternal City what Studio 54 was to become to New York, the massive subterranean space, originally an abandoned cinema, remains a weekend dance fixture for Italian *gente di notte* and minted the term Radical Disco. Owned by record producer Alberigo Crocetta with car dealer Giancarlo Bornigia and meat importer Alessandro Diotallevi, The Piper Club was designed by Manilo Cavalli and Francesco and Giancarlo Capolei. Its extraordinary interior a clash of kinetic fiberglass, purple plastic, stainless steel, **Barbarella** (1968) futurism, reconfigurable furnishings in transparent PVC, advanced audiovisual technologies like giant luminous plastic screens, and a stage for performers, which over the years was graced by the likes of Patty Pravo, discovered in the club itself and forever dubbed the Piper Girl, Genesis, Jimi Hendrix and Pink Floyd.

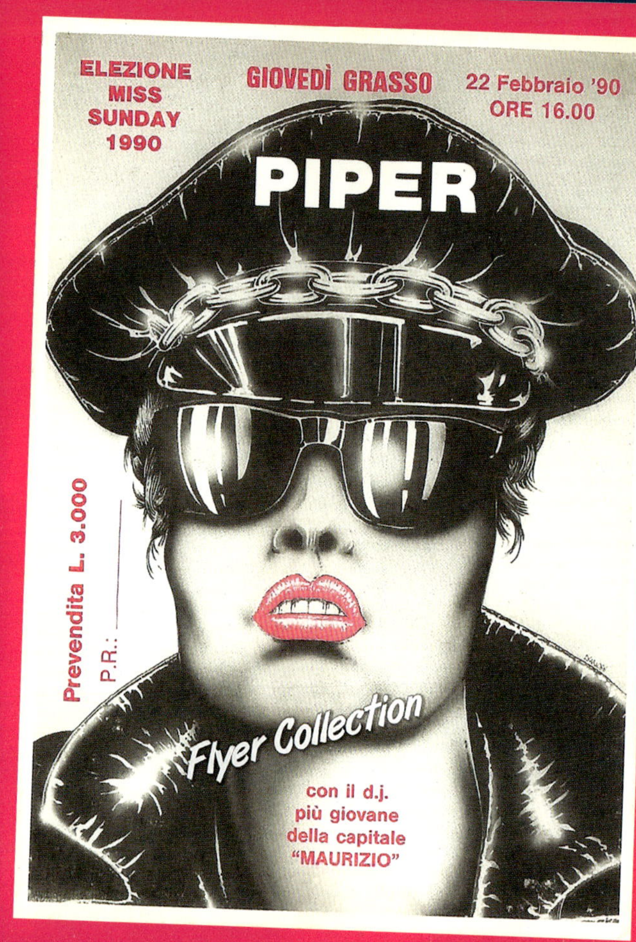

Immediately emerging as the focal point for *La dolce vita* Jet Set, with works by avant-garde artists Andy Warhol, Rotella, Schifano, Rauschenberg, Paco Rabanne and Manzoni decorating specifically designated areas, the Disco Look drastic aesthetic was so successful it became carbon copied at other venues, the term 'piper' acting as shorthand for innovative spatial architecture in unusual places like disused factories and repair shops. And as a nightclub The Piper became a phenomenon, one that left its mark across every *paninaro* generation.

The chance to seek out new sounds by a population unfamiliar with international music was transported into the Disco 1970s by the likes of revolutionary partygoers Romina Power (daughter of screen idol Tyrone), pop star Gabriella Ferri and **Performance** (1970) star Anita Pallenberg. It became the must-go place of reference, bubbling over with artistic excitement that has shaped endless trends from Pop to Glam Rock, from Soul to Disco. And what would be a typical pre-Italo Disco tracklisting from The Piper Club at the height of the dance crazy years? *Body to Body* (1979) by Gepy & Gepy, *Fly* (1978) by Tony Pacino, *I'm in Love* (1979) by Cela, *You Know the Way* (1979) by Pino Presti, *Soft Emotion* (1979) by Azoto, *Fire Night Dance* (1978) by the Peter Jacques Band, *Come to the Rainbow* (1979) by Rainbow Team, *Let's Go/ Mustang* (1979) by Sandwich, *Body, Body Love* (1977) by Billy Woost and *54* (1979) by Bob McGilpin II.

Piper Club

Piper Argento

It just so happens that the Piper Club was literally around the corner from Dario Argento's penthouse in the swanky Parioli district of Rome. The area is where the Fontana delle Rane is situated in Piazza Mincio, one of the more unforgettable locations in **Inferno** (1980), and prior to that, Mario Bava's **La ragazza che sapeva troppo/The Girl Who Knew Too Much/The Evil Eye** (1963). Obviously we're talking about the 1990s, not its Disco heyday, but Asia Argento, her half-sister Fiore, Dario's personal assistant Carla Alonzo and I would often head for The Piper Club after spending the evening at the maestro's apartment. It's where I realised cloistered Fiore had no idea how to make a cup of coffee, where I learnt a favourite pasta recipe from Dario's glamorous housekeeper – *farfalle con zucchine* – and where he would let me take whatever I wanted from his cupboard of unwanted ephemera, like his original shooting script for **Four Flies on Grey Velvet** (1971). The latter was something he came to regret when he realised the cinematic value of the items I was taking away to bolster my unique Argento collection.

WARNER BROS. presenta

JOHN SAXON · LETICIA ROMAN

LA RAGAZZA

CHE SAPEVA TROPPO

VALENTINA CORTESE

DANTE DI PAOLO

ROBERT BUCHANAN · GIANNI DI BENEDETTO · JIM DOLEN

VIRGINIA DORO · CHANA COUBERT

REGIA DI MARIO BAVA | UNA PRODUZIONE CORONET-GALATEA

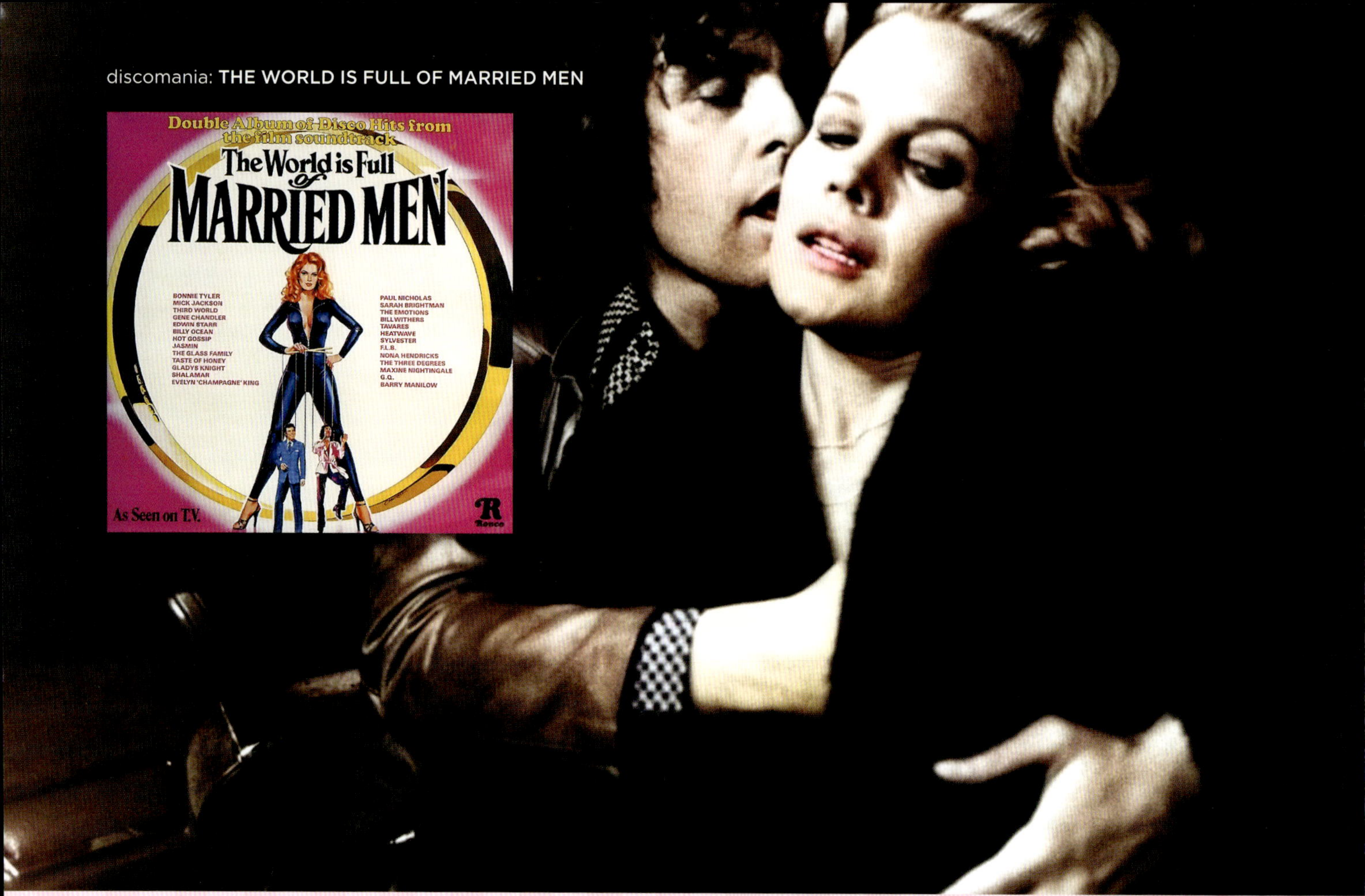

THE WORLD IS FULL OF MARRIED MEN
(1979)

In 1974, the British exploitation company New Realm (begun by British Z-movie maven Edwin J. Fancey and taken over by his children Adrienne and Malcolm) bought an erotic French movie starring Sylvia Kristel sight unseen at that year's Cannes market. Titled **Emmanuelle**, they watched in amazement as it took more than £1 million at the box-office, running at the Prince Charles cinema in central London for two years. Up until that point the company had produced and/or distributed hundreds of sex and horror flicks like Michael Winner's **Some Like It Cool** (1961), and later Wes Craven's **The Hills Have Eyes** (1977).

But when they saw how much money Brent Walker's **The Stud** (1978) was raking in, the company decided to follow the Jackie Collins/Disco formula themselves and the result was this makeshift and hysterical sexploiter based on the novelist's first book published in 1968. Warner Bros had nearly put the book's sequel 'The World Is Full of Divorced Women' (1975) into production in November that same year, but Collins, furious at what director Gerry O'Hara had changed in the upcoming **The Stud** sequel, **The Bitch** (1979), wanted as tight script control on her brainchild as possible. So her movie producer husband Oscar Lerman joined forces with the Fanceys to bankroll **The World Is Full of Married Men** and the tacky torn-marriage manual started filming at Pinewood Studios at the beginning of 1979.

Originally Collins wanted her best friend, celebrity fashion photographer Terence Donovan, to be the director. One of the architects of the 'Swinging London' creative vibe during the 1960s, Donovan shot models against stark, industrial backdrops for contrast and was dubbed 'The Orson Welles of Photography'. Donovan had made his feature film debut with **Yellow Dog** (1974), a muddled spy thriller about a Japanese cop sent to London on a secret mission, starring Robert Hardy, which virtually no one saw. And when the Fanceys advised Collins to watch it, all mention of Donovan as director was quickly dropped and Robert Young, of Hammer's **Vampire Circus** (1972) and **Keep It Up Downstairs** (1976) fame, was hired instead. American television mini-series king Anthony Franciosa

and former sex kitten Carroll Baker (**Baby Doll**, 1956, **The Carpetbaggers**, 1964, **Harlow**, 1965) play the unhappily married couple David and Linda Cooper. Advertising executive and serial philanderer David has an affair with publicity-seeking fame whore Claudia Parker (Sherrie Lee Cronn, in her only film credit) who wants to become a top model and actress. The movie had actually begun filming with Suzanne Danielle (**Carry On Emmannuelle**, 1978) playing Claudia, but after 'creative disagreements' with the producers, she was released from her contract and all her scenes were reshot.

To pay her husband back in promiscuous kind Linda hones in on rock star Gem Gemini (a very nonchalant Paul Nicholas), who sings the jingle for the soap commercial coincidentally featuring Claudia up to her nipples in oyster-shaped bath bubbles. With all this lust-sapping turmoil in his private life, David finds himself impotent and his reputation as "the last of the great shafters" in ruins as a succession of sex movie sirens of the day (Suzie Sylvie, Pat Astley, Nicola Austine, Lindy Benson) attempt to help him get it up (it's Astley and Austine who dance Disco in silhouette under the end credits).

Carroll Baker's contract stipulated her name alone would be above the film's title. But when she caught a West End screening, and spotted that both her name and Franciosa's appeared above the title, she had all prints withdrawn and fixed. It's surprising she would even bother really considering how below par the entire film is, geared around crude screaming matches in bedrooms, restaurants and driveways. With little sense or salaciousness on show, this glitzy Collins claptrap fails to deliver on every promise. Except in the Disco department. Once again the Ronco tie-in double album featured songs in the movie and other tracks licensed to fill out the vinyl running time. In the US, where the movie escaped more than got released, the album title was changed to *Dance Fever*.

The title song sung by both Bonnie Tyler and Mick Jackson is the worst kind of end-of-era Disco pap the record labels thought was still hip and happening. Likewise Jackson's *Weekend*, star Paul Nicholas' *Makin' It* and *Love Lines*, and Jasmin's *Disco Concerto* (all 1979, as are those undated below): Gene Chandler's *Get Down* (1978), Evelyn 'Champagne' King's *Shame* (1978), Hot Gossip's *Love Clone*, Barry Manilow's *Copacabana (At the Copa)* (1978), FLB's (Fat Larry Band) *Boogie Town* (1978), Shalamar's *Take That to the Bank* (1978), A Taste of Honey's *Boogie Oogie Oogie* (1978), Nona Hendricks' *Snakes Alive*, GQ's *Disco Nights*, Third World's *Now That We've Found Love* (1978), Edwin Starr's *Contact*, Maxine Nightingale's *Right Back Where We Started From* (1975), The Glass Family's *Crazy*, The Emotions' *Best of My Love* (1977), Heatwave's *Mind Blowing Decisions* (1978), Billy Ocean's *Every Woman in the World*, Sylvester's *You Make Me Feel (Mighty Real)* (1978), Tavares' *Heaven Must Be Missing an Angel* (1976) and Sarah Brightman's camp cross-dressing cut *Madam Hyde*.

I Lost My Heart To A Starship Trooper

Before she embarked on an impressive classical pop career the 18-year-old Sarah Brightman joined the gimmick Disco club with two slices of dance-lite campery.

Everyone in Europe will remember her 1978 Top Ten smash *I Lost My Heart to a Starship Trooper* backed by the dance troupe she was once a part of, Arlene Phillips' Hot Gossip. Written by Totally Tropical's Jeff Calvert and Geraint Hughes, it was a cheesy cash-in on the burgeoning sci-fi movie phenomenon with references to Darth Vader, Flash Gordon and close encounters with musical lifts from 'Also Sprach Zarathustra'. Screechy and tinny, with corny sound effects, it made no impact in any self-respecting Disco outside the Mecca dancehall circuit.

Even worse was Brightman's silver-spandex-and-sequin clone follow-up that added a comic strip twist to the sci-fi rip-offs and included riffs on Donna Summer's *I Feel Love* (1977) and The Supremes' *Stop in the Name of Love* (1965). Originally released on red vinyl, with a comic book using the song lyrics as superhero dialogue, *The Adventures of the Love Crusader* (1979) was billed as being by Sarah Brightman and The Starship Troopers in the hope the title association might help sales. It didn't, barely scraping into the Top 60 in the UK singles charts. *Madam Hyde* is a strident mishmash of creepy echoes and spooky screams and a Disco blip. An ignominious trio perhaps but Brightman's 'Cats', 'The Phantom of the Opera' and classical crossover appeal lay in her very bright future. And Donna Summer got her own back, scoring a massive Disco No.1 hit in 1999 with the Brightman/Andrea Bocelli monster duet *Time to Say Goodbye* as *I Will Go with You/Con te partirò*.

Bugatti & Musker

Featured on **The World Is Full of Married Men** soundtrack is the ballad *Woman in Love* (1978) by The Three Degrees from the album *New Dimensions* produced by Giorgio Moroder. It was written by the songwriting duo of Dominic Bugatti and Frank Musker, two people who I became very chummy with mainly because my best friend Caroline Guinness dated Dominic for a while and he and Frank threw some truly epic parties at his Queens Gate mansion house. Because they were so entrenched in the music business by then, practically every pop star I'd ever seen perform on 'Top of the Pops' would be in attendance. We also made a great crowd on the Disco round as their names got us in everywhere, especially Tramp, the Mayfair club owned by Jackie Collins' husband Oscar Lerman.

Under the name Dominic King, Bugatti had penned the two Amen Corner songs for **Scream and Scream Again** (1970) and joined forces with Musker to compose the soundtrack for **Confessions of a Pop Performer** (1975). That same year they recorded the Disco track *Take Me with You* under their own names followed by *Dancing with the Captain* (1976). They gave the latter song to Paul Nicholas who took it to No.8 in the UK charts the same year and also provided him with *Heaven on the 7th Floor* (1977). It was the B-side of *Dancing with the Captain*, *Dogs in the Yard* (1976) that would prove their most enduring song because it was highlighted on the **Fame** (1980) soundtrack. And their contributions to the **Grease 2** (1982) soundtrack have nothing to do with me liking that underrated movie so much, despite what my great friend Mark Kermode might think!

DON'T GO IN THE HOUSE (1979)

Psycho (1960) go-goes Disco in this Quentin Tarantino favourite, a notorious Video Nasty, and one put together by people with limited sexploitation pasts who clearly didn't have their finger on the slasher pulse. Director Joseph Ellison (assistant on **Pelvis**, 1977) co-wrote the script with Joe Masefield (production manager on **Lash of Lust**, 1962, and **Sin You Sinners**, 1963) and actress Ellen Hammill (Bobby Tuttle's partner in the key Disco scene). Basically the trio threw the abused psychotic mama's boy trope into a Disco Inferno and hustled up this maniac mess (written under 'The Burning' title until Miramax nabbed it for their own 1981 horror) that would have been sordid and uncomfortably sadistic if not so derivative, badly produced and poorly directed.

Donny Kohler (Dan Grimaldi) returns home from his incinerator operator job, after staring in frozen stupefaction at a fellow worker accidentally engulfed in flames, only to find his mother has died in her sleep. Because she used to punish him by holding his arms over naked flames from the kitchen gas cooker, Donny is initially thrilled by the demise of his cruel parent and literally charges around the house in jubilation and blasting out loud music. Until he hears her voice in his head whispering murderous suggestions… Quick as a flash he turns the upstairs room in his rambling house into a reinforced steel flame-proof torture room and starts hunting down girls to tie up naked and burn alive.

Don't Go in the House gained its controversial reputation due to the graphic, for its day,

depiction of the first killing, a protracted sequence piling on the vicious preparations before the fire-iron bashed victim's petrol-assisted, shrieking demise. Nothing that shocking happens again in Ellison's voyeuristic violence manual except Donny starting a charred corpse collection dressed in his mother's clothes and finally being dragged into his own private blazing hell by them when reanimated in his nightmares **Maniac** (1980) style. Grimaldi, who I called "a low-rent Dustin Hoffman" in 'Starburst' magazine at the time, didn't audition for the leading role as the producers saw him in the Off-Broadway play 'Momma's Little Angels' and offered it to him out of the blue. As the film's original soundtrack turned out to be unusable due to rickety old equipment, it had to be rerecorded and redubbed in its entirety, giving the whole grimy affair a further disembodied quality that only added to Grimaldi's gurning ineffectiveness.

But while the movie might not have been a killer, the Disco soundtrack certainly is. One scene, shot at the Palace Disco in New Jersey, finds Donny double-dating with his best friend Bobby (Robert Osth) for a relaxing night out. Dressed up in hopeless Disco duds recommended by a boutique salesman as "this is what they are all wearing" – the song playing over the shop's sound system (and over the end credits) is the fantastic *Struck by Boogie Lightning* by L'Ectrique – Donny is urged to hit the dance floor. But his date pulls his arms over the table candle, stirring up memories of his mother's punishments, and he sets her hair alight while escaping to the car park. All to the terrific strobe-lit *Dancin' Close to You* by the Daryll/Barber Band (composed by Ted Daryll) and *Late Night Surrender* performed by Jeree Palmer (composed by *Boogie Lightning* writer Bill Heller). *Late Night Surrender* is also the song which Donny dances around the house to in gay abandon when he finds his mother dead. *Straight Ahead* by The Daryll/Barber Band rounds out the song quartet while composer Richard Einhorn used his minimal electronic scoring style, with analogue synthesizers and dissonance, for the full soundtrack.

Citizen Kane

Following in the stiletto heeled footsteps of Grace Jones, Swedish-born Madleen Kane started modelling at the age of 14, won the 'Dream Girl' Pageant at 15, and transformed her high fashion career into the singing one she had always wanted. Kane had a limited vocal range and her thin, often breathy voice, could sometimes sound tinny. But her gorgeous Scandinavian looks, fabulous choice of material, superior production from Eurodisco's finest (Thor Baldursson,

Jürgen Koppers, Giorgio Moroder) and superb back-up vocals from Sue Glover and Sunny, all added up to a potent formula and for eight glorious years she hit the Disco heights with some of the best recordings of the era. It was through her Elite model work for 'Playboy' magazine that she met record producer Jean-Claude Friederich, married him and with his mentoring began her Disco career.

Kane meteorically burst onto the scene with her first album *Rough Diamond* (1978), featuring the No.3 Disco Chart double, the title track and *Touch My Heart*, full of ornate orchestration and earcatching flourishes. It was her second album *Cheri* (1979) that really made the Disco crowd sit up and take note. The A-side contained the supreme *Forbidden Love (Suite)*, 18 minutes of melodic cascades, romantic highs and lows and ebbing and flowing violins, easily putting it in the Best Disco Ever category. Staying in the Disco Charts for 16 weeks, the album also included the hit *You and I*.

Kane got ready for the 1980s by moving more into the electro synth-pop Disco sound and to the Chalet Records label owned by her husband. The *Sounds of Love* (1980) album gave her two dance hits, *Cherchez pas* and *Boogie Talk*. *Don't Wanna Lose You* (1981) provided the No.1 Disco smashes *You Can* and *Fire in My Heart* and then producers Giorgio Moroder and Pete Bellotte turned up the beat for *Playing for Time* (1982). Her last Disco chart success came with the duo *I'm No Angel* and *Ecstasy* from the *Cover Girl* (1985) album. According to her wrenching 2018 autobiography 'Rough Diamond', Kane suffered abuse through 19 years of marriage to Friederich, nearly died twice from addiction and had an equally terrible second husband. She can rest assured that even if *Cheri* had been her only musical effort, it would have earned her place in Disco immortality.

Starburst

My profile rose in the horror journalism field during this time mainly because there literally was no one else doing it. As a result of my 'London Correspondent' title on the 'Cinefantastique' masthead, I would regularly get offers of writing work. Some I embraced, like the French publication 'L'Ecran Fantastique' because I could simply get my interviews translated and no one would be any the wiser. That magazine would also allow me to attend my very first fantasy festival in Paris where I would meet Lucio Fulci, Sam Raimi and Tobe Hooper. But when it came to British magazines I knew I would have to be careful because of the clear conflict of interest.

It soon became apparent though that no British film company was interested in letting me attend advance press previews if it was for an American magazine. And in those days release dates varied so wildly between countries. Why did I need to see John 'Bud' Cardos' **Kingdom of the Spiders** (1977) with my 'CFQ' hat on when it had already been released in the USA a full year beforehand? So I accepted an offer from editor Dez Skinn to write for his brainchild 'Starburst', exploring 'Science Fantasy in Television, Cinema and Comix'. I had turned him down over 'The House of Hammer' magazine but I liked him a lot because he was enthusiastic, charming to a fault and very funny. I often used to turn up at his Wardour Street offices for an elongated chat completely oblivious to the fact he might have work to do. Anyway I made my debut in issue No.2 with a review of Ralph Bakshi's **Wizards** (1977) and if there was any doubt I'd ever be anything but honest in my future assessments perhaps this line from it will clarify, "**Wizards** fails. It's mediocre and twee and commits one of the cardinal sins of fantasy cinema – it bores".

Ultimately my 'CFQ' editor understood why I had to have a British outlet as it gave me untold access to everything being made in the studios outside London. And in due course my fantasy critical fraternity grew from being just John Brosnan and I holding court in dingy Wardour Street preview theatres like the Bijou, complete with wooden dancefloor, to include new bloods Nigel Floyd, Kim Newman and Mark Kermode. Once Alan McKenzie took over from Skinn, I was already part of the 'Starburst' furniture and became the only person he could rely on to attend every single press screening.

That was something owner Stephen Payne realised when he bought the title in 1985 and granted me the position of sole reviewer until the magazine had to stop publication in 2008 due to editorial team problems. Very few critics have been lucky to have the longevity I have enjoyed: 23 years with 'CFQ', 30 years with 'Starburst', 10 years with 'Fangoria', 30 years and still counting with 'Radio Times'. What has been so gratifying is all the people throughout the past decades coming up to me at various events saying I made a difference to their lives because of my own tastes in movies affecting theirs.

'Starburst' magazine founder Dez Skin.

One of the biggest shocks I had during my major five-nights-a-week press show phase was finding out that one of the most revered critics of my formative years actually paid other people to write their reviews for them. At first I couldn't believe it until it became crystal clear that was the truth. And it's more prevalent than you think too. One of my contemporaries used to be so drunk at previews, he used to call me up after the movie and would ask me to run through the storyline with him so he got his synopses right. At least I can say, hand on heart, I never cheated in any respect with a job I felt lucky to have.

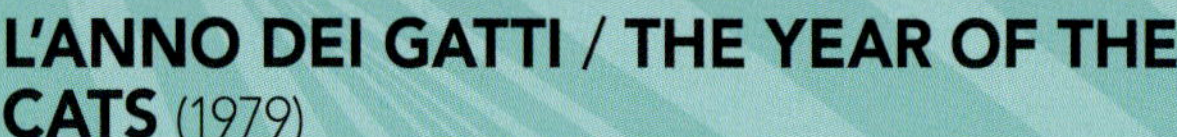

L'ANNO DEI GATTI / THE YEAR OF THE CATS (1979)

The worst-but-one performer at the Italian box office in 1979 was this whiter-shade-of-pale **Saturday Night Fever** (1977) imitation, pulled from cinemas after only nine days when just 1,448 tickets were sold in sum total. It ranked at Number 140 out of the 141 Italian movies released that year (and for the record in last place was Nello Rossati's **Una donne di notte/A Woman in the Night**). Now only famous for starring one-hit wonder Mark/Marc Boyce, an Australian discovered busking outside restaurants in the streets of Rome, which led to him securing a Sony/Epic record deal and providing a supporting role for Dario Argento acolyte and future horror director Michele Soavi (**StageFright**, 1987, **La Chiesa/The Church**, 1989, **La Setta/The Sect**, 1991, **Dellamorte Dellamore/Cemetery Man**, 1994), this Disco flop was director Amasi Damiani's follow up to the slightly more successful **Cicciolina amore mio/My Dear Cicciolina**.

First seen posing in front of a **Saturday Night Fever** poster pasted on a Roman wall, Ciro Varelli (Boyce) is the son of a tram driver with lofty dreams who works in a local bookshop. His best friend is university student Leopoldo (Claudio Sorrentino, chosen because he dubbed John Travolta's voice for Italian movie release) and together they spend their nights Disco dancing in various clubs. Finding a lost dog in the street, when he returns the pooch named Mazarin to his rightful owner, the super rich Professor Goldoni, he endears himself to the family, their maid Hyacinth and especially daughter Beatrice (Lilli Randi, in her only screen performance, you'll see why) when he turns down a cash reward. Desperate to win Beatrice's affections he bets her prime suitor Luke (wearing what can only be described as **Bugsy Malone**, 1976, cast-offs) that he'll be able to climb to the top of a live electric pylon before he can. After completing this stupidly death-defying task Ciro wins Beatrice's heart and along with Leopoldo, who finally finds his soul mate too in Rebecca, the group of fast friends head to the Disco for yet more dancing.

Containing startling full frontal nudity, Boyce in satin hot pants and loose-fitting white suit, scenes shot in hair salons, luxury villas and against eye-grazing Op Art wallpaper designs, **L'anno dei gatti** is a heavy slog through the bare **Saturday Night Fever** bones. Cynically titled after the Al Stewart song *Year of the Cat*, a massive 1976 hit in Italy, with **I ragazzi della discoteca/Disco Boys** its video retitling, the featured songs are MOR light pop and include *This Is the Year of the Cats* by Marc Boyce, co-written by Enrico Monti, the future Italo Disco maestro who married *Boys (Summertime Love)* (1987) singer Sabrina, *Sundance* by Hugh Bullen, taken from his 1978 soul funk album *Feeling*, and the mysterious *Il traliccio di Ciro/Ciro's Trellis*. The one pure Disco track is the deliciously brassy *B.B.L.S.S.T.* by Le Streghe, taken from the girl trio's 1978 album *L'iniziazione/The Initiation* produced by The Rokes band member Norman David Shapiro/Shel Shapiro and virtually a Disco version of the nursery rhyme *Ride a Cock Horse*.

Disco Morricone

Sergio Leone finally got to Studio 54 in 1977, courtesy of the Black Light Orchestra's *Once Upon a Time* album showcasing their tribute to Ennio Morricone. Produced by Canadians Dominic Sciscente and Michel Daigle, the latter the genius behind Voggue's 1981 hit duo *Dancin' the Night Away* and *Love Buzz*, the 8½ minute *Morricone* is a mash-up of two themes from Leone's **Once Upon a Time in the West** (1968), *A Man and His Harmonica* and the title theme, with a few riffs from **The Good, the Bad and the Ugly** (1966) thrown in for good measure. Wonderfully orchestrated and arranged, Morricone's landmark melodies shine through this epic contouring to the *ristretto* Disco soundscape. It was never a proper dance breakthrough though; *Touch Me, Take Me* was the only Disco hit off the sought-after album.

Strangely enough no other Morricone composition ever penetrated the Disco barrier despite a few tries. The most valiant effort came packaged as the 12-inch single *Disco '78* credited to Ennio Morricone containing *Come Maddalena*, the main theme from the religious drama **Maddalena** (1971), souped up with a 4/4 backing track. Morricone had composed two terrific Disco tracks for the incest romance **Così come sei/Stay As You Are** (1978), *Dance On* and *Spazio 1999*, but neither drew any traction away from the soundtrack apart from hip radical Italian Discos.

Disco Memo

What's Going On?

Alan Jones Roller Discoing on the Brighton promenade.

By 1979 I was into Roller Disco in a big way. My life revolved around it. Any spare moment I had I was practising under the flyover at Royal Oak underground station, skating to Battersea Park for a weekend meet-up or going to the three best Roller Discos – The Empire, Leicester Square, the Electric Ballroom, Camden and the Global Village, Charing Cross. So when the opportunity to travel to Dortmund, Germany, to Disco in one of Europe's largest roller-skating rinks arose, a group of us signed up immediately. It meant travelling by coach to Dover, making the ferry crossing to Calais, and driving another 5 hours to the venue, but none of us could wait. In fact, when the coach stopped at the Dover car park, we all strapped on our skates and did an impromptu routine right there on the smooth tarmac.

After a few minutes of us gliding, twirling and dancing, we were approached by two very large black guys. "Someone would like to say hello", they said, and we were escorted over to a black limousine with smoked glass. The window wound down and there was Marvin Gaye! The Motown superstar told us he was just about to start a European tour and how much he was enjoying our practising. Thrilled to bits, we all did our fanboy gushing, and before he drove off he handed us £50 and told us to buy ourselves drinks on board the ferry. Which is exactly what we did, toasting the legendary singer for his absolute class and warm friendliness to a bunch of excited poofs simply showing off.

By Day He was a Dull Ordinary Guy.
By Night He was a Dull Ordinary Guy...
who looked like somebody special.

The Face with 2 Left Feet

What happened to him
Shouldn't happen to a dog.

JOHN TRAVOLTO... DA UN INSOLITO DESTINO / THE FACE WITH TWO LEFT FEET (1979)

In 1974 art house director Lina Wertmüller won global praise for her bold depiction of gender relationships in **Swept Away**, or to give the multi-award winner its original Italian title **Travolti da un insolito destino nell'azzurro mare d'agosto** translated as 'Swept away by an unusual destiny in the blue sea of August'. By the end of the '70s the entire world had gone John Travolta crazy in the light of **Saturday Night Fever** (1977) and **Grease** (1978), and veteran writers Massimo Franciosa and Giovanni Simonelli – together boasting top collaborations with Luchino Visconti, Marco Ferreri, Nanni Loy, Antonio Margheriti and Lucio Fulci – with first-time writer/director Neri Parenti devised this dual parody cash-in thanks to the title language joke translating as 'John swept away by an unusual destiny'.

The trio also struck comedy gold by casting TV John Travolta lookalike Giuseppe Spezia as the lead and hiring go-to Travolta dubber Claudio Sorrentino (he would later do Mel Gibson and Bruce Willis), to voice the impersonator too. Considered the first Travoltasploitation movie, Spezia plays Hilton Hotel cook Gianni/Johnny who hangs out at the Rome neighbourhood Disco John's Fever where he's in puppy love with sexy blonde DJ Ilona (Ilona Staller, aka Cicciolina, infamous porn star, politician, pin-up and entertainer, in one of the four movies she made the same year). Shy, bespectacled, heavily moustachioed and exuding nil fashion sense, Gianni is invisible to Ilona, despite his glasses sometimes catching her eye in the Disco light reflections. Nevertheless he makes a disastrous attempt to date her and gets thrown out and barred from the club by owner Mr. Raoul (Angelo Infanti, **Emanuelle nera/Black Emanuelle**, 1975).

When the Hilton staff learns John Travolta is coming to stay for a brief Italian holiday, and one of his porter co-workers realises Gianni minus his moustache is a dead ringer for the superstar, a romantic entrapment plan is put into action. They decide to turn him into a spitting image of Travolta to fool and impress Ilona. After a local cinema trip to see **Saturday Night Fever** (where his mates all sing "Ah, ah, ah, ah" in high Bee Gees falsetto as they enter the auditorium in a conga line) they soon realise they have a major problem... Gianni can't dance! In-house hotel manicurist Deborah (Sonia Viviani, **Solamente nero/ Bloodstained Shadow**, 1978) tries her best to teach him the latest Disco moves and also convinces her *faux* gay boss Alvise/Alvin (Franco Agostini, **Perché quelle strane gocce di sangue sul corpo di Jennifer?/The Case of the Bloody Iris**, 1972) to pose as his pretend manager. Ilona is indeed impressed with the whole elaborate façade but the deception spirals out of control when the real Travolta arrives on the scene and his entourage causes mistaken identity complications.

A reasonably amusing running gag has hotel concierge Caruso (Enzo Cannavale, **La discoteca**, 1984), getting crazier and crazier as he keeps spying multiple Travoltas. Worse, John's Fever's shady owner attempts to milk the double discovery for entrance fee revenue. Gianni will have to confess to the trickery soon but will he learn the life lesson that it's better to be oneself than be in the shadow of a celebrity?

Directed by Parenti with the populist broad focus and slapstick bravado he would bring to his dazzling run of comedy hits in both the **Fantozzi** (1980-96) franchise and the hugely successful seasonal **Vacanze di Natale '95/ Christmas Holiday '95** (1995) series (**Vacanze di Natale a Cortina**, 2011, being his last to date), this **Saturday Night Fever** rip-off is an interesting profile of the Italian Disco scene before Italo Disco took over completely. Even though 'Swing Dancing' is mentioned as being the main Disco move here, the club scenes are evocative and atmospheric while the dancefloor fight between Gianni's mates and Raoul's heavies is one of the best scenes in the movie alongside Staller's poignant eleven o'clock speech concerning illusion versus reality.

No footage of **Saturday Night Fever** is glimpsed and the 'real' Travolta is seen only in flared trouser close-up, a neat joke at the expense of that film's iconic opening credits sequence. Out of the plethora of alternate titles, the most fun is **Travoltomania** and the most revealing **Teenager in Love**, clearly an effort to downplay its Disco roots and tie it to the Dion and The Belmonts 1959 hit instead. As was another alternate title, **Runaround**, after Dion's 1961 classic rocker *Runaround Sue*. After the movie sold merely 42,000 tickets in 198 days of Italian release, coming No.77 in the 1979 box office charts, Spezia only made one more brief appearance on film – director Luciano Salce's **Vieni avanti cretino/Step Forward Idiot** (1982). Perhaps people just got it confused with the much bigger hit that year, director Mauro Severino's sex comedy **Travolto dagli affetti familiari/Swept Away By Family Ties** (1978).

However, the soundtrack is an absolute winner featuring *Disco Quando* by Tony Renis, a dance update of his classic 1962 evergreen *Quando, Quando, Quando* and the spaghetti hit *Baby I Love You* (1978) by Easy Going. The surprise is how good the other original Disco tracks are. C.G. & M. Balestra (aka Fratelli Balestra) provided *Mirror* and the undisputed highlight *The Show Is Over*, the Orchestra Gianni Mazza, *Ilona Theme*, *Mascarade* and *John's Fever*, People Live, *Runaround*, Antonia, *La Bamba*, Linda Lee, *Go Away*, Nuovi Angeli, *Now*, and *Hot Cha Cha* by Bixio, Frizzi and Tempera under their Fruit of the Gum alias. The movie might not be up to much but the soundtrack really is the Disco business.

Disco Ancora

Tony Renis wasn't the only Italian teen idol to record a Disco cover of one of his own 1960s hits. Bobby Solo did the same thing with his 1964 Sanremo Song Contest entry *Una lacrima sul viso* (1978), also translated into English as *One Tear on Your Pretty Face Babe* and promoted under the heading 'New Wave Disco'. To say Solo murders the lyrics with his poor pronunciation is an understatement. Rocco Granata pulled the trick off too with *Marina*, first in 1959 and then an Italo Disco hit in 1989. Francis Thomas Avallone, or to give the **Beach Party** (1963), **The Haunted House of Horror** (1969) and **Grease** (1978) all-round entertainer his stage name, Frankie Avalon, did a great job too with *Venus*. It was a No.1 chart hit in 1959 and, given a stunning dance makeover by producer Billy Terrell, became a Gay Disco favourite again in 1975, even though Avalon remarked years later he didn't like it as much as the original.

But by far the best Disco version of a former stormer comes from Easy Listening icon Andy Williams who entered the Disco field like a rocket in 1979. Francis Lai's theme from his 1970 Oscar-winning score for the tear-jerking **Love Story** became a global hit the moment the *Moon River* (1961) crooner was given the Carl Sigman lyrics. So it was a natural to Discofy in 1979 when every other MOR artist seemed to be getting in on the dance act. Except in Andy Williams' case his *Love Story (Where Do I Begin)* wasn't just great, it was astonishingly brilliant. Produced, arranged and conducted by Bob Esty, the in-house Casablanca man responsible for many Donna Summer, Cher and Pattie Brooks hits, the track starts softly, builds slowly, reaches emotional peaks and then soars into whirling violin ecstasy with a yummy drummy backing. Over the top, definitely, but one of the best Disco stunners of all time.

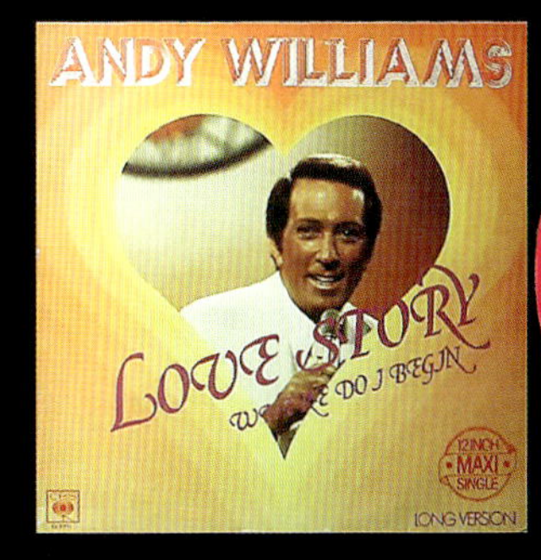

The Horror!

How did I become a horror movie fan? My journey to the delicious darkside is probably the same as everyone else's I expect. From a very early age I would be intrigued by the lurid and garish double bill film posters that appeared at the end of my Portsmouth home street on a regular basis. I can still recall the best ones: **The Gargon Terror/ Teenagers from Outer Space** (1959), **Frantic** (1958), **Confess Dr. Corda** (1958), **Circus of Horrors** (1960), **The Day of the Triffids** (1963), **Dr. Terrors House of Horrors** (1965) and the Hammer Horrors. **The Day of the Triffids** poster I managed to pry from its metal frame under the cover of darkness late one night to pin up on my bedroom wall. They all promised shock, nightmares, monsters and blood and I couldn't wait until I was 16 years old to actually be allowed to see an X certificate film.

Which I finally did at my local Essoldo, Southsea, in that desperate rite of passage unique to my generation, for I was only 15 pretending to be older. I remember with absolute clarity my nervousness as I approached the cashier to pay for my ticket, at that time 5 shillings (25p). Would she see though my dressed-up-to-look-older sweaty subterfuge? The relief when she barely glanced at me. Then the seemingly endless walk to the usher who tore my ticket in half and allowed me to enter the auditorium. The panic of where to sit quickly so I wouldn't attract any more undue attention and the constant fear I'd be tapped on the shoulder and escorted out because I'd been sussed. It still gives me the delicious shivers to this day.

The first horror movie I saw in a cinema was Mario Bava's **Blood and Black Lace/6 donne per l'assassino** (1964). What an introduction! One that would set the seal on my whole future life in film as Italian horror became my first love, something I was lucky to be able to strongly advocate through the years. My next outing to the cinema was a trip to the Classic, Commercial Road, Portsmouth, where I took my seat for a 'Sunday Only' rerelease double bill of **Circus of Horrors** and **Horrors of the Black Museum** (1959). Again I was beside myself with stunned joy. Imagine my later delight when I realised the local pub at my first London address in Maida Vale's Sutherland Avenue was The Warrington Hotel, the place **Horrors of the Black Museum** actress June Cunningham leaves before being beheaded. Then came the rerelease of **Psycho** (1960) with **War of the Worlds** (1953) and I knew I'd never be so smitten with anything else as I was with genre cinema.

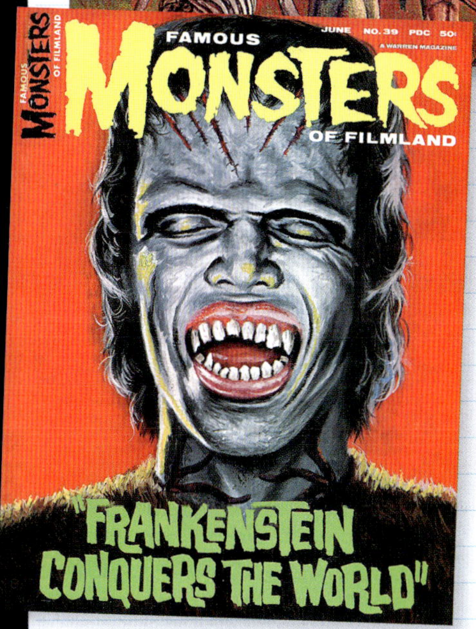

My next trip to the fleapits where I knew this type of film escaped to – and I know the correct order because I have kept a diary from **Blood and Black Lace** to this day – was **Crypt of Horror/La cripta e l'incubo** (1964), which brought me back down to earth as I really didn't think it was that great. A quick lesson in not every film living up to poster tag-line expectations! After that was **Terror-Creatures from the Grave/5 tombe per un medium** (1965), **The Castle of the Living Dead/Il castello dei morti vivi** (1964) and you can see where all this was going…

When I wasn't at the cinema with my best friend Julia Kruk, a fellow horror fanatic, now the chair and treasurer of The Dracula Society, I was combing through issues of 'Famous Monsters of Filmland' and my absolute favourite 'Castle of Frankenstein'. I can't tell you how thrilled I was to meet director Joe Dante decades later at the Trieste Science+Fiction Festival because his glowing reviews of Bava movies in that seminal magazine were a crucial building block for me. And I devoured every single horror book tie-in, especially the 'Hammer Horror Film Omnibus'.

But if I was to cite the one single moment that made me realise how important the genre was going to be in my life, it would be buying Carlos Clarens' essential textbook 'Horror Movies: An Illustrated Survey' in 1968. I read it from start to finish over one night, unfortunately the night I should have been revising for my GCSE exams. However as I have told everyone since, that book became the only education I would ever need. I hated school. They certainly weren't the best years of my life. I didn't know it then, but it's crystal clear to me in hindsight that my ambition to have something to do with horror started with Carlos Clarens and his absolutely inspiring tome.

SKATETOWN U.S.A. (1979)

The first of the Roller Disco exploitation movies to be released featured an inane storyline, long-in-the-tooth comedy shtick by TV has-beens, fantastic skating and a standout Disco soundtrack. Written by director William A. Levey (of **Blackenstein**, 1973, **Slumber Party '57**, 1976, and **The Happy Hooker Goes to Washington**, 1977, infamy), Nick Castle (The Shape in **Halloween**, 1978, co-writer of **Escape from New York**, 1981, with John Carpenter) and Lorin Dreyfuss ('Fantasy Island'), the simplistic plot has blond street skater Stan (Greg Bradford) battling bad boy Ace Johnson (Patrick Swayze in his feature debut) for the $1,000 prize money plus a moped in a roller-skating contest at the Skatetown U.S.A. Roller Disco, operated by stressed-out entrepreneur Harvey (Flip Wilson) and his stupid son Jimmy (Billy Barty). Stan's best friend Richie (Scott Baio) and his nymphomaniac sister Susan (Maureen McCormick, who would reveal decades later the shoot was Cocaine Central) wants to help out while Ace's gang do everything to sabotage the event. It all ends in a chicken run between the rivals zooming down the Santa Monica Pier on skates equipped with rockets and becoming the best of friends.

Levey ensures the cardboard antics screech to a halt whenever Bradford and Swayze strut their outstanding roller stuff because they really are brilliant and give this dire cash-in the only va-va-voom necessary. Well, them and the superb soundtrack, which is basically non-stop synchronised Disco positioned as records actually being spun by house DJ The Wizard (Denny Johnston). Dave Mason, ex-Traffic member and composer of their hit song *Hole in My Shoe* (1967), is featured as a performer in the Roller Disco, playing himself, and singing the theme song *Skatetown, I Fell in Love* and a cover version of the Traffic song *Feelin' Alright?* (1968).

The bona fide Disco hits featured are Patrick Hernandez's ubiquitous *Born to Be Alive* (1979), Earth, Wind & Fire's classic *Boogie Wonderland* (1979), The Jacksons' *Shake Your Body (Down to the Ground)* (1979), Heatwave's *Boogie Nights* (1977), McFadden & Whitehead's *Ain't No Stoppin' Us Now* (1979), John Sebastian's *Roller Girl* (1979), Marilyn McCoo and Billy Davis Jr.'s *Perfect Dancer* (1979), and GQ's *Disco Nights (Rock-Freak)* (1979). Other tracks included are a cover of Mick Jagger and Keith Richards' *Under My Thumb* (1968) by The Hounds, *Baby Hold On* (1977) by Eddie Money and *I Want You to Want Me* (1977) by Cheap Trick.

The Skatetown, U.S.A. Disco was based on Flipper's Roller Boogie Palace at Santa Monica Boulevard and La Cienega in West Hollywood where Disco on the turntables was often stopped for live band performances, and patrons included Cher, Olivia Newton-John and Gene (KISS) Simmons. The purple and blue designed building opened in 1979 and the film premiered there in October. It closed down two years later after turning into a post Punk paradise once the Roller Disco fad faded. Its allure certainly lasted longer than any memory of **Skatetown U.S.A.** that dropped the U.S.A. for overseas playoff and would often be advertised erroneously as **Skate Town**.

The Empire Ballroom Roller Disco

If it was Flipper's in Los Angeles and the Roxy in New York, the best Roller Disco in London was definitely at the Empire Ballroom in Leicester Square, the heart of the glittering West End. The deluxe establishment only opened its doors on Sundays, but from noon to 6 p.m. everybody in the Disco world turned up to strut their stuff on the adequate Disco floor. It was a wooden surface but proved perfect for the patter of polyurethane wheels. You had to be a member to enter (£2.50), but joining was free, you couldn't hire skates, you had to bring your own – which kept out the amateurs – and the bar closed at 2 p.m. The superior lighting, great sound system and comfortable furnishings meant the Empire really was the place to be and be seen.

Menswear designer Paul Smith was a regular, so too were writer Chris Fowler and 'A Chorus Line'/'Sweeney Todd' musical actor Michael Staniforth. The DJ who usually played only chart Disco could be swayed to include other lesser known tracks, especially when trying to vary the 'speed skating' session formula of Kat Mandu's *The Break* (1979), Patrick Hernandez's *Born to Be Alive* (1979) and Cher's *Hell on Wheels* (1979). The management were always very present and supportive of the skaters, often presenting bottles of champagne and other prizes to people for their birthday or just because they liked your dance routine. The atmosphere was always upbeat and fun and for many Sundays were never the same when the venue had to close for redevelopment.

The Rollerskate Rag

My first attempt at editing a magazine came in the summer of 1980 when my best friend from Videomedia, Geoff Simm, had decided he was going to set up a publication for the Roller Disco maniac. Taking our cue from my friend Mark P(erry) and his groundbreaking Punk fanzine 'Sniffin' Glue', we cobbled together 'The Rollerskate Rag' on a Roneo machine, stapled the pages together and flogged it on the Disco round for 35p. Funded – just – by sports shops, Scholl foot products and Disco adverts, it was a good, well-written read by moonlighting journalists who knew the scene inside and out. Issue 1 was illustrated with dodgy B/W photo reprints and along with my editing skills, although Geoff took the credit, I also wrote the film review column and interviewed DJs about their careers.

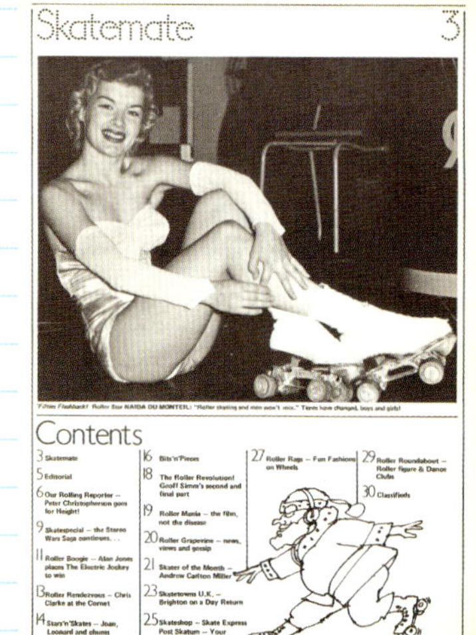

Skatemate 3

'Fifties Flashback! Roller Star NAIDA DU MONTER: "Roller skating and men won't mix." Times have changed, boys and girls!

Contents

Issue 2, December 1980, with a 5p price rise, looked far glossier and slicker all round and added 'Skater of the Month' and Roller gossip features as well as a Post Skatum letters page, mainly moaning about the poor quality printing of the first September one. As was often the case at this time, bigger and more corporate interests realised we had found a gap in the market and quickly stepped in to steal our thunder and our advertisers and writers. When 'Hot Roller' (45p) appeared looking far more professional and sporting a pull out 'Miss Roller' centrefold, Geoff and I saw the writing on the wall and shrugged it off to experience. Truthfully it was a pain to organise and we were both juggling our editing duties with properly paid work. However, it put me in good stead when I finally did decide to become a full time editor with 'Shivers' magazine in 1992, the free publication 'Film Guide' in 1996 and the New Line Cinema figurine partwork 'The Horror Collection' that fell foul of licensing laws.

DISCO DELIRIO / DISCO MUSIC FEVER (1979)

Easily the worst **Saturday Night Fever** (1977) Italian style stab, this ugly looking Disco cash-in is shamefully cynical in every forgettable aspect. Yet while it didn't do as well as **American Fever**, **Brillantina Rock** or **John Travoloto... da un isolito destino** at the Italian box-office, it certainly did better than **L'anno dei gatti**, playing for over a month in six major cities and attracting 9,020 viewers. Cobbled together by Milanese writer/director Oscar Righini/Roy, producer of the odd horror **La lunga notte di Veronique/But You Were Dead** (1966) and the Nazisploitation **Le lunghe notti della Gestapo/The Red Nights of the Gestapo** (1978); perhaps he should have titled his one and only feature 'The Long Nights in Disco Hell' because that's exactly what it feels like.

Downtown Milan, 1978, and **Saturday Night Fever** is still showing at the local cinema, as pointed out by a couple walking past a poster display on their way to dance the night away. Yes, there's an upcoming dance contest, yes, it causes friction among the group of faceless friends (Dalida Baglioni, Ada Pometti, Ambra Davi, Al Taylor, Maurizio Micheletti, Dario Bramante all singularly anonymous) and, yes, everything works out well in the end with the constantly arguing champion couple finally falling in love. The only tangent of any interest is the stupendously tacky stage show mounted as a Disco draw inspired by **Barbarella** (1968) featuring sci-fi villains, robots, satin shoulder pads and go-go girls in cages choreographed to *Araxis Space Ship* (1978) by Araxis.

Short in length but not sweet enough, the style adopted by Righini is point the camera, shoot everything as static as possible and use wipes to add the vague illusion of action. The choreography is dance floor ordinary, the performers competent enough, but the unimpressed viewer can only merely react in the same bored and listless way as the surrounding wallflowers watching the endlessly drawn out mundane Disco deeds. Beginning with a nighttime drive into central Milan with *The Day that My Heart Caught Fire* (1978) by John Paul Young pumping over the opening credits, it ends in contest bliss with his triumphant Disco anthem *Love Is in the Air* (1978). Other classic cuts heard aside from Araxis are two by Alec R. Costandinos – Paris Connection's *Eloise* (1978) and his *Romeo & Juliet* (1978) – Idris Muhammad's *S-E-X* (1978), Shotgun's *Good, Bad & Funky* (1978) and Bob McGilpin's *Superstar* (1978).

Also featured is *Rock Around the Clock* (1955) by Bill Haley & His Comets, mainly because Italian pop royalty Adriano Celentano had just had an enormous hit with the same song mixed with the **Guys and Dolls** (1955) evergreen *A Woman in Love* in an effort to appeal to the Disco set. **Disco delirio** is only of any real note today because it does feature the interiors of two popular Discos at the time – Milan's Ganesh Club and the Esplanade situated in suburban Binasco.

Stryx

Many saw the stage show mounted in **Disco delirio** as an attempt to evoke the feeling of the controversial Rai TV series 'Stryx' that could only really have happened in the Disco era. Created by songwriter Alberto Testa, director Enzo Trapani, who mentored the career of *Disco bambina* (1979) star Heather Parisi, and scriptwriter Carla Vistarini, 'Stryx' was deemed the most innovative and experimental programme ever broadcast in Italy because it broke the mould of what was considered mainstream entertainment. It was Trapani's idea to ground a dramatic music show in a world populated by demons, elves and sacrificial virgins all played out against a backdrop of strobe-lit, multi-coloured medieval castles and dry ice depictions of the underworld. Full of blasphemy, eroticism and near-nudity, 'Stryx' lasted for seven episodes, only six were ever shown, before the plug was pulled on November 19, 1978, after a storm of press protests, religious warnings and viewer complaints.

Yet in that short space of time the show featured acting as well as musical performances from such popular Eurodisco artists as Amanda Lear, Grace Jones and ringmaster Tony Renis. The theme song was *Disco Quando* (1978) by Renis, a clubbed up version of his original 1962 hit *Quando, Quando, Quando*, released only as a 7-inch single. Patty Pravo, Mia Martini and Ana Oxa made up the local star content. Divided into specific sections to illustrate a thought or sin, Dracula-caped Amanda Lear was Sexy Stryx and sang her Eurodisco hits *Follow Me* and *Gold* (both 1978), crudely gyrating on an angled glass floor surrounded by an orgiastic crowd and scampering monkeys in pantomime costumes. Fur-clad Grace Jones was Rumstryx and sang *Fame* (1978) with a live tiger on a chaise-longue after bursting out of a bottle like an Arabian Nights genie in gold Lurex. Pure Eurotrash Disco.

Disco Memo

The Danger of Disco

From Rock 'n' Roll, Beatlemania, Flower Power, Glam Rock and Punk through Rap, Acid House, Heavy Metal, Rave and Grime, every music trend has ignited fire and brimstone warnings from op-ed features in the press and do-gooders predicting the fall of civilization. Disco was no different, obviously reaching its apotheosis in the Comiskey Park Demolition Night. Out of all the doom and gloom posturing this is my favourite editorial from the New York Daily News in 1977, clearly written by someone with no experience of the developments, filed under the headline *Disco Narcissism and Society*:

★ DAILY NEWS

Sunny, upper 80s. Clear tonight. Sunny tomorrow. Details page 27

Vol. 59, No. 54 — New York, Saturday, August 27, 1977 — Price: 20 cents

"The mania which is becoming the cultural phenomenon of the 1970s is rooted in narcissism. Separated by walls of deafening music and swept up in a frenzy of bright lights, dancers do their own thing, seldom touching, never looking at each other or even speaking, 'Me, me, me, me...' endlessly. This pure self-indulgence reflects a dangerously deep-rooted philosophy in our society. It preaches that anything an individual feels like doing is 100 percent right – no matter how it affects anyone else. The attitude shows up in our soaring divorce rate, our legions of broken families and in countless books and movements keyed to self-gratification and self-esteem. There is too little room for love in the philosophy that permeates the Disco world. And that is a pity, for those who have forgotten – or never known – the joys of giving and sharing are missing the richest part of life".

▲ Disco Demolition Night took place at the Chicago White Sox baseball stadium on Thursday, 12th July 1979. The White Sox were having trouble filling their seats for games so as a publicity stunt they hired vehemently anti-Disco local rock DJ Steve Dahl to invite members of the public to hand over Disco records in exchange for 98 cent tickets to a game against local rivals the Detroit Tigers, with the promise that the records would be blown up on the field of play. Following the promised explosion fans in the stadium rioted, leading to the White Sox forfeiting the game.

ROLLER BOOGIE (1979)

Devised as a follow-up vehicle for **Grease** (1978) stars John Travolta and Olivia Newton-John by producer Irwin Yablans, who had made zillions from the surprise horror hit **Halloween** (1978), **Roller Boogie** was the second movie after **Skatetown U.S.A.** (1979) to cash in on the Disco roller-skating craze. By the time journeyman exploitation director Mark L. Lester (**Truck Stop Women**, 1974) started California shooting in Bel Air, Venice Beach and Glendale, the ones that they wanted were out and Linda Blair had been fast-tracked to the lead role in a concerted effort to navigate her way around the downward career blip that was **Exorcist II: The Heretic** (1977). Thanks to the likes of B-movies such as this – and soon **Hell Night** (1981) and **Savage Streets** (1984) – that would never happen. Peter Gallagher (**The Idolmaker**, 1980) was the Travolta substitute until good sense prevailed and an actual roller-skating champion was hired. Jim Bray had been gracing the pages of numerous skate sports magazines as eight-time US champion and was the perfect professional yin to Blair's amateurish yang on the boardwalks and rink floors.

Written by Barry Schneider (**Ruby**, 1977, **Harper Valley P.T.A.**, 1978) from a story credited to Yablans, by way of every Judy Garland/Mickey Rooney Hollywood romance going, Blair plays poor little rich girl Terry Barkley, a bored flautist whose shallow parents Lillian and Roger (Roger Corman mainstay Beverly Garland and American TV series stalwart Roger

Perry) want her to graduate to Juilliard. But fed up with her luxury Beverly Hills lifestyle all Terry wants to do is dress up in the latest Rodeo Drive leisure fashion and head down to the Venice Beach roller-skating scene with her snooty BFF Lana (Kimberly Beck, **Blackboard Massacre**, 1976) to join the crowds dancercizing on eight wheels.

There she encounters high roller Bobby James (Bray) who rents out skates and dreams of skating at the Olympics (despite the sport not even qualifying in reality) and the scarcely believable romantic sparks fly. Later at the local Roller Disco rink Jammers, Terry asks Bobby to give her skating lessons so she can enter the upcoming Roller Disco dance contest and the first of many flirty, roller raunchy misunderstandings begin. But Jammers is under threat from unscrupulous mob boss Thatcher (Mark Goddard, 'Lost in Space' 1965-68) who threatens owner Jammer Delaney (TV sit-com regular Sean McClory) with violence and arson unless he hands over the prime real estate for development into a shopping mall.

Bobby, Terry and Phones (Stoney Jackson, **The Concorde... Airport '79**, 1979) overhear this sinister plot and unwittingly tape Thatcher's menacing demands on Phones' ghetto-blaster cassette recorder. Turning to her lawyer father Roger for help, the stark reality hits Terry he's employed by Thatcher. But realising they have evidence, the wild chase through the Venice canal maze is on as they race to get the tape to the cops with the gangsters in hot pursuit. They save the day, the crooks are captured, the Roller Disco contest goes ahead and Terry and Bobby win the top prize. In a bittersweet beach coda, the star-crossed lovers say their sad goodbyes and promise to keep in touch as Terry heads off to Juilliard and Bobby to the Olympics?!?

As cash-in mindless teen fare goes **Roller Boogie** is okay up to the points where Linda Blair has to grit her teeth and actually do some wobbly on-screen skating. Saying she isn't much good is an understatement. Through a series of hilarious outdoor scenes Blair and Bray work together to form a routine for the competition, which essentially consists of her staggering towards camera cues and him holding her aloft to disguise her lack of rhythm. Despite a grabby opening slickly done salvo showing Terry getting ready in the leotard and short shorts look of the day, complete with skate mechanic checks, **Roller Boogie** has clearly been put together by people who barely understood the Roller Disco craze apart from its most superficial aspects. While Blair oozes charm, Bray remains permanently uncool as the rest of the cast exert a grim determination in both their dramatic and skating sequences.

Is it a bad movie? Not really, as the corny melodrama and camp nostalgia is in plentiful supply and it does exude scattershot fun in various dance-fighting places. And the ace Bob Esty (D.C. LaRue, Donna Summer, Paul Jabara, Brooklyn Dreams) produced soundtrack papers over many of the garishly wrong-headed cracks. Alongside his tracks composed and performed specifically for the movie – *The Roller Boogie*, *Summer Love*, *Cunga*, *Rollin' Up a Storm (The Eye of the Hurricane)*, *Love Fire* and *Lord Is it Mine* – are *Top Jammer* and *Elektronix (Roller Dancin')* by Cheeks, *All for One, One for All* and *Evil Man* by Mavis (Vegas Davis)/Michelle Aller, *We Got the Power* and *Takin' My Life in My Own Hands* by Ron Green, *Night Dancer* by Jean Shy (who sang *Roller Derby World*, 1976) and *Good Girls* by John W. Brazas. Two popular Disco classics tricked the soundtrack out further: *Hell on Wheels* (1979) by Cher and *Boogie Wonderland* (1979) by Earth, Wind & Fire.

Earth, Wind & Fire

After The Trammps' *Disco Inferno* (1976), only one other song truly encapsulates the Disco experience in user-friendly terms. And that's *Boogie Wonderland* (1979) by Earth, Wind & Fire, an American band spanning every musical genre from funk to Afro-pop, but who scored their highest profile in the Disco panorama. Formed by Chicago-born Maurice White, a member of the Ramsey

Lewis Trio and The Salty Peppers, it was while touring through the Far East he felt a more mystical route should be taken with his career. The result was Earth, Wind & Fire that would undergo frequent personnel shuffling between 8 to 10 members. Signing with Columbia Records because he was impressed with the way head honcho Clive Davis had handled Sly and the Family Stone's career, White formed his own production company Kalimba Productions, named after the mini stringed instrument giving the band their unique sound. Ramsey Lewis, The Emotions and Deniece Williams would all record for the label. And it was the girl group The Emotions (*Best of My Love*, 1977) who joined Earth, Wind & Fire for their global smash *Boogie Wonderland*, a liltingly catchy anthem that became the centrepiece of their spectacular stage shows. *Fantasy* (1977), *September* (1977), *All 'n' All* (1977) and the No.3 Disco Chart hit *Let's Groove* (1981) kept the band in the public eye to become one of the most successful recording acts of all time with 90 million sales, the winner of six Grammy Awards and induction into the Rock 'n' Roll Hall of Fame. Sadly that success did not translate into movie fame as **That's the Way of the World** (1975), a sketchy showbiz saga, and the overblown **Sgt. Pepper's Lonely Hearts Club Band** (1978) both flopped badly.

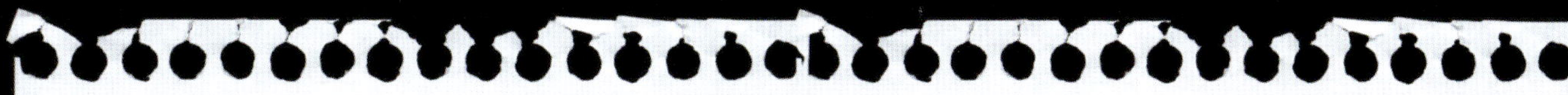

Disco Memo

Punk Books

I'm honoured that so many historians, biographers, friends and memoir writers have considered me to be so important that they sought me out to include my own thoughts on my alternative lifestyle and character-forming Punk Rock days. After Glen Matlock (with Pete Silverton) gave me a great mention in his superficial 'I Was a Teenage Sex Pistol' (Omnibus Press, 1990), the first author to really get to grips with the momentous era was author Jon Savage who wrote 'England's Dreaming: Sex Pistols and Punk Rock' (Faber and Faber, 1991). That really became the bible for all subsequent dissertations and publications on the subject. Savage's follow up tome 'The England's Dreaming Tapes' (2009) printed all the unedited highlights from our recording sessions and so many people have asked me if I really did hate Chrissie Hynde that much! When Jane Mulvagh interviewed me over two days for her biography 'Vivienne Westwood: An Unfashionable Life' (Harper Collins, 1998) I was actually in a quandary. Should I just tell her everything and be damned? Which I did – and Vivienne never spoke to me again!

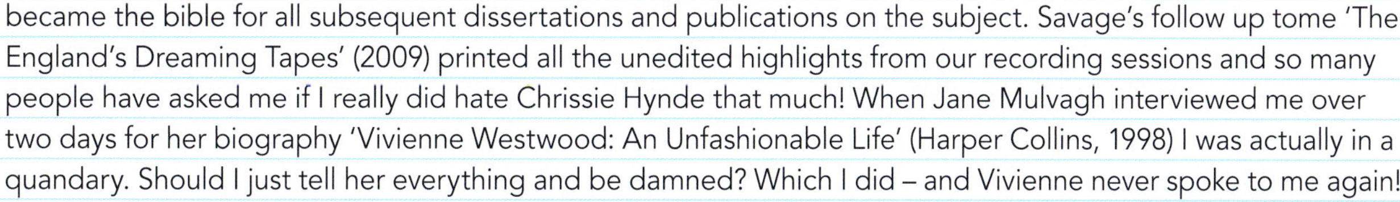

'Not Abba: The Real Story of the 1970s' (Fourth Estate, 2005) by Dave Haslam I thought gave a nice new spin to the whole subject. 'Vacant: A Diary of the Punk Years 1976-79' (Thames and Hudson, 1999) by my sorely missed mate Nils Stevenson and his photographer brother Ray, gave the fan perspective from the trenches I liked. The superb coffee table book 'Punk' (Cassell & Co, 2001) by Stephen Colegrave and Chris Sullivan put everything into order and context with lavish design and terrific photos. 'Vicious: Too Fast to Live…' (Creation Books, 2003) by Alan Parker I found an enormously moving ode to Sid. And Parker's 'Sid Vicious: No One Is Innocent' (Orion Books, 2007) wrapped up the murder suicide mysteries with a forensic eye I greatly appreciated. But my favourite of them all is the most recent, 'Defying Gravity: Jordan's Story' (Omnibus Press, 2019) by my good friend and fellow SEX worker, the late and hugely missed Jordan (Pamela Rooke), with Cathi Unsworth. I'm proudest the most of my copious inclusions in this tell-all autobiography which conveys the truth about Punk, the ethos, the fashion and the enormous fun we had throughout every single moment.

THE BITCH (1979)

Because **The Stud** (1978) made so much money on relatively little outlay for executive producers Ronald Kass and Oscar Lerman (the collective Collins' husbands), it was no surprise when this hasty sequel arrived a little over a year later. Based on Jackie Collins' contemporary bestseller, and rewritten against her wishes by director Gerry O'Hara, it continued the sexploits of hedonistic nightclub owner Fontaine Khaled (Joan Collins giving an even more mind-boggling all-fur-coat-and-no-knickers diva performance) as she faces financial difficulties. Her billionaire husband, tired of her relentless bed-hopping, has finally filed for divorce after finding that notorious sex-tape of her shagging in the lift, and The Hobo Disco is losing money because the In-Crowd have decamped to a new gay hot-spot around the West End corner. Determined not to take this reversal of fortune lying down, Fontaine heads off to Manhattan's Studio 54 to see how she can improve things for her dwindling clientele. On the airplane back from New York (the in-flight movie is **The Stud**!), she meets Italian jewel thief Nico Cantafora (bland Michael Coby, real name Antonio Cantafora, see what they did there?) and becomes implicated with world-weary Mob boss Thrush Feather (Ian Hendry) and an equally formula plot involving a stolen diamond ring hidden in her fur coat, and racehorse fixing.

Fontaine eventually loses The Hobo to Feather in this less squalid package of fast cars, fast women and fast living, meaning it's a lot less campy fun too. Considering the title, Collins doesn't have many bitchy one-liners but it is fun seeing her gyrate to the Gibson Brothers then current Disco hit *Cuba*.

Directed by genre journeyman O'Hara ('The Avengers' TV series, **The Brute**, 1977) with little oomph or flair, the scene Collins most hated filming was the one where she seduces her chauffeur Ricky (Peter Wright) wearing a black corset, suspender belt and stockings and a jauntily placed chauffeur cap. That Disco Lucretia Borgia key

image became the defining one for the film and was used to brand everything from the tie-in novel to the accompanying soundtrack. It was mainly the reason she axed any idea of a mooted third film despite Brent Walker making an absolute fortune at the box-office again, regardless of critics jeering at the press show. Of course by this time Collins had received the offer to appear as Alexis Carrington in the super-soap 'Dynasty', the signature role that would leave her low-grade 1970s movies in the dust.

The Disco element is mainly wallpaper padding in this tired exposé of unappealing decadence and lifestyles of the nouveau rich and infamous. Cherry Gillespie from the 'Top of the Pops' dance troupe Pan's People boogies on down as does the 'British John Travolta', Grant Santino, the actual reigning 1978 Disco Dance Champion. The heavily TV advertised Warwick Records soundtrack featured the usual Biddu original compositions fleshed out with recent Disco hits, although many were surprised to find some of their running times had been changed 'to ensure the highest quality reproduction' as per the gatefold sleeve disclaimer! The Biddu tunes are the title song by the Olympic Runners, *Pour Your Little Heart Out* by The Drifters, *I Feel Lucky Tonight* by Linda Lewis, *Never Say Goodbye* by The Stylistics, and *Dancing on the Edge of a Heartache* by The Hunters.

Disco filler is provided by *I Thought It Was You* (1978) by Herbie Hancock, *Turn the Music Up* (1978) by The Players Association, *Haven't Stopped Dancing Yet* by Gonzalez, *Standing in the Shadows of Love* (1978) by Deborah Washington, *Giving Up, Giving In* (1978) by The Three Degrees, *Can You Feel the Force?* by The Real Thing, *There's No Me Without You* by Len Boone, *The Lone Ranger* (1976) by Quantum Jump, *Everything Is Great* by Inner Circle and *Music, You Are* by George Chandler. In all, a lazy collection of chestnut dance fodder for lethargic Discoploitation.

Tina Charles – The British Disco Queen

London-born Tina Charles (nee Hoskins) started her recording career in 1969, accompanied by a young Elton John on three singles. She sang incognito on several of the 'Top of the Pops' cover version albums, and in 1972 also covered the Motown hit *There's No Stopping Us Now* as part of the Wild Honey trio. The 1975 Steve Harley & Cockney Rebel hit *Make Me Smile (Come Up and See Me)* featured her on backing vocals, and later that year she joined 5000 Volts (formerly Airbus), breaking through in her own right with *I'm on Fire*, a UK Top Ten hit record. The band's

follow-up hit, 1976's *Doctor Kiss-Kiss*, featured Linda Kelly on vocals, as by this time Charles had been hired by Biddu, a well-respected producer who ensured her place in the spotlight with the Disco hits *You Set My Heart on Fire* (1975), *Dance Little Lady Dance* (1976), *Dr. Love* (1976), *Rendezvous* (1977), *Love Bug/Sweets for My Sweet* (1977), and *I'll Go Where Your Music Takes Me* (1977). But Tina Charles is best remembered for the UK No.1 classic *I Love to Love (But My Baby Loves to Dance)*. A massive hit in 1976, the song was re-released in 1986, charting again in the form of a HiNRG remix.

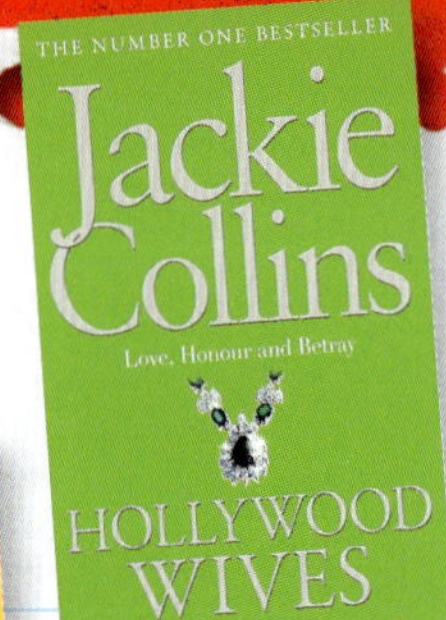

Dear Jackie

As already stated I hated school. I didn't excel in any subject. I had no intention of going to university. All I wanted to do was leave my Portsmouth hometown and live in London. I failed my English GCSE A-level, which makes me laugh when I think my future lay in a writing career. History and Economics were my passes! But I don't feel I achieved any real sense of writing style until the mid-1980s. And I hold one person responsible for that. Jackie Collins.

I had read all her bestsellers avidly and loved the film adaptations. So when 'City Limits' magazine (the alternative, more radical 'Time Out' listings publication) asked if I'd be interested in interviewing Jackie about her new novel 'Hollywood Wives', I jumped at the chance. I was scheduled as her last interview of the day at the Inn on the Park, now the Four Seasons Mayfair, and we had a terrific talk about everything, the book, the movies, her sister Joan.

As our time slot happily overran she started asking me questions. One was, what writer did I think I was? I didn't understand and she told me that for years she didn't think she was any good until she woke up one day and thought, "Fuck it, I'm going to do whatever I like". She suggested I do the same. It didn't matter what anyone thought about anything as long as you were happy in yourself. We had discussions about alliteration, which I love, over-writing, which I do, and grammar, which we both agreed we mostly ignored. "Do what you want with words and your style will evolve", was her parting sentence. And her goodbye gesture was a signed copy of the book with this written on the inside, "To Alan, Your enthusiasm makes it all worthwhile! P.S. I wish I could spell! With fondest love, Jackie. September 85".

From that moment on I never dwelt too much on what I thought might be expected from my reviews and set reports. As long as it had quality and content I went for that approach big time. Sure I made some mistakes. But as I evolved my style more work kept coming my way. From writing press releases for Warner Bros. and production notes for films to shed-loads of video covers and tie-in books. Jackie Collins was the spark that told me never to worry about what anyone else was doing, to please myself not everyone, and if I have a signature style I really do owe it to these wise words – it doesn't matter if they love or hate you as long as they never forget you.

ROLLERMANIA! (1980)

I caught this back in 1979, during a press-only screening. Never given a theatrical release in English-speaking territories, and just about managing to escape in Portugal and Mexico, director William Webb's thinly stretched-out documentary on the roots and contemporary current trends of the Roller Disco phenomenon barely made a dent on the burgeoning home video market either.

A trade advert at the time informed customers it was available on both VHS and Betamax formats and cost £29.90. More fun to watch in nostalgic hindsight than it was at the time, Webb's focus is on Venice, California – that late 1970s Mecca for eight-wheeled sun-worshippers – and "Where it's all at!" as narrator Damian Evans hypes in his laid-back L.A. drawl. Except his insipid, and mostly irrelevant, jargon-packed commentary is one of the main embarrassments in a by rote picture full of them.

Boiled down to essentials, the documentary is a hastily assembled montage of snatched sports footage mixed with newsreel clips and lengthy roller-skating routines by the famous names of the day. Featured skaters include April Allen, Jack Courtney, Natalie Dunn, Kerry Cavazzi, Fred Blood, The Body Gliders, Michael Kirkpatrick, Duke Rennie, Becky Howe, C.C. Boots, Stephanie Starr and Lynne Tyner, who was also skating consultant for the production. The footage of vintage skating from the 1930s and 1950s is of great interest but little effort goes into presenting these clips in any historical context or positioning them in the development of the sport and healthy lifestyle leisure activity over the subsequent decades.

Time and again interesting segments are raised and then quickly dispensed with, like the sequence on how to hand paint and customise your boots. What comes across the strongest are the visuals on why roller-skating and Roller Disco took off in such a big way in California, especially Venice, with its large areas of traffic-free pathways, coastal paths with smooth tarmac and glorious eternal sunshine. Perhaps the most fun are the Roller Derby clips – the women's competition especially – and for sheer nerve and guts, the bowl-riding shots demonstrate the thrills and adrenalin of the entire roller-skating experience.

In the Roller Disco scenes, the accent is very much on maximum floor space and the swirling lighting effects as the skaters limber up to do their twirling and gliding. The **Rollermania!** soundtrack is by far the best part of the entire venture. With cuts by The Jacksons, The Jones Girls and Stevie Wonder acting as filler, the heavy lifting is done by Earth, Wind & Fire's *Boogie Wonderland* (1979), Citi's *Roller Disco* (1979), Dan Hartman's *Instant Replay* (1978), Bonnie Pointer's *I Can't Help Myself (Sugar Pie, Honey Bunch)* (1979), Celi Bee and The Buzzy Bunch's *Fly Me on the Wings of Love* (1978), and The Michael Zager Band's *Life's a Party* (1978), with the latter used as the movie's anthem accompanying the most spectacular figure-skating on show.

But there was a problem in this crucial area too as Webb, sadly murdered over an inheritance spat in 2019, erroneously lets the whole music track play itself out. Meaning there's a limit to how much each sequence holds the attention before becoming repetitive. More judicious editing would have ensured **Rollermania!** didn't outstay its welcome and would probably have been more satisfying in an hour-long format rather than a feature film length. Now as a historical document though, it shows with crystal clarity why street skating and Roller Disco took off in the Sunshine State and can be filed under Past Fun Fads in the Pop Culture file.

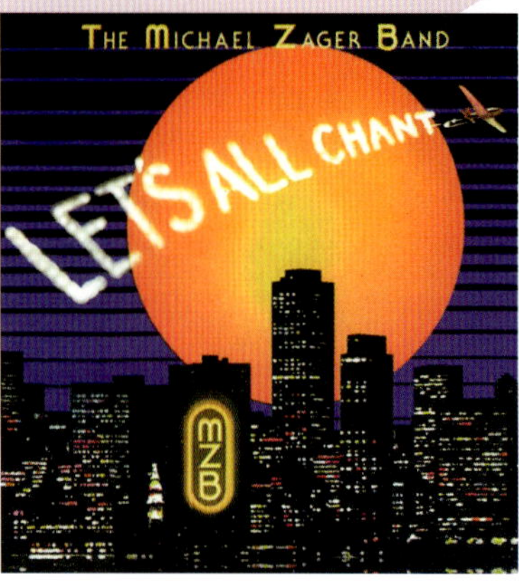

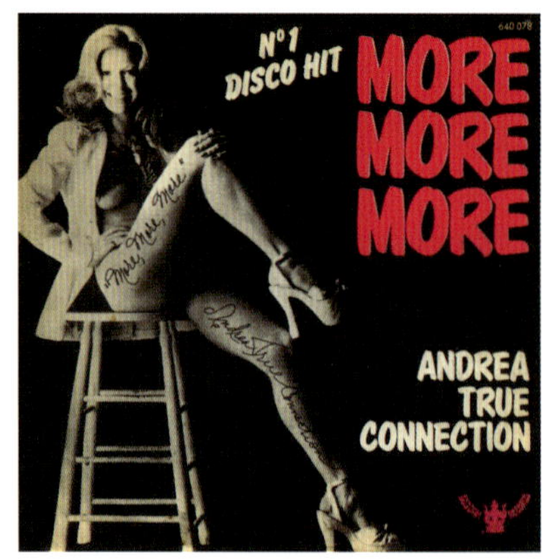

The Michael Zager Band

Hitting the No.1 spot on the 'Billboard' Disco Chart and remaining in the Top Ten for 22 weeks, *Let's All Chant* (1977) by the Michael Zager Band is the quintessential Disco anthem. Extremely catchy and melodic, with a stunning classical style chamber music break in the middle when least expected, this worldwide smash remains a key recording instantly defining the Disco era.

It was the pinnacle in the versatile career of producer, arranger, pianist and songwriter Michael Zager. Born in New Jersey and a jazz fan, he formed the pop band Ten Wheel Drive in 1968 and released four albums. With former head of A&R at A&M Records Jerry Love he produced the *Out Among 'Em* album for Love Childs Afro Cuban Blues Band in 1975, which included the cuts *Honey Bee* and *Bang Bang*. *SpanDisco* was their next release in 1977 featuring *Oye Como Va*, *The Speak Up Mambo*, *SpanDisco Band* and the medley *Spanish Harlem/Dancin' to SpanDisco*. The *Rhythm of Life* (1978) album came next containing *Black Widow Woman* and *The Moon Is the Daughter of the Devil*.

Concurrently Zager and Love formed Michael Zager's Moon Band and their debut release was *Do It with Feeling* (1976) with featured singer Robert 'Peabo' Bryson. Zager also arranged Bryson's first solo album *Peabo* (1978). By 1978 the Moon had been dropped from the band's name and they looked for a song to enter the lucrative Disco market.

Studio 54 habitué Love noted the dancers there would consistently chant "Ooh, Ooh!" to whatever track was playing to increase their participation and enjoyment.

Upon hearing this, Zager wrote *Let's All Chant* with his regular partner Alvin Fields, and Disco history was born. *Love Express* was the B-side. When the track took off like lightning those two tunes plus *Freak*, *Soul to Soul*, *Music Fever* and especially *Dancin' Disney*, a medley of *Heigh Ho*, *Whistle While You Work*, *Give a Little Whistle* and *When You Wish Upon a Star*, got hastily assembled into a *Let's All Chant* album.

With his profile rising Zager took on outside work including two porno actresses attempting to enter the Disco minefield. Marilyn (**Behind the Green Door**, 1972) Chambers' *Benihana* (1976) did nothing, but Andrea (**The Seduction of Lynn Carter**, 1974) True Connection scored big with *More, More, More* (1976), *N.Y., You Got Me Dancing* (1977) and *What's Your Name, What's Your Number*. Then he supervised Emily 'Cissy' Houston's entry into the Disco arena with the stupendous *Think it Over* (1978). Former singer with 'The Sweet Inspirations', Houston's oldest sister was Lee Warrick (the mother of Dionne and Dee Dee Warwick). Cissy also had a daughter, Whitney. And that's why future megastar Whitney Houston made her singing debut at 14 years of age on the atmospheric title track of Zager's second album *Life's a Party* (1978) with her mother.

That album was stuffed with Disco Gold. The beautiful *You Don't Know a Good Thing* followed the title track on the A-side. But it's the exceptionally haunting four-track B-side that is a Disco classic. *Love, Love, Love*, *Still Not Over*, *On and On* and *Using You* make up an emotionally draining romantic drama set to a 4/4 beat. Harmonised to soap opera perfection by ace session singers Kay Garner, Stephanie De Sykes, Chas Mills and Stevie Lange, this bittersweet Disco take on denial, rage, depression and acceptance weaponised fabulousness is an all-time Disco masterpiece.

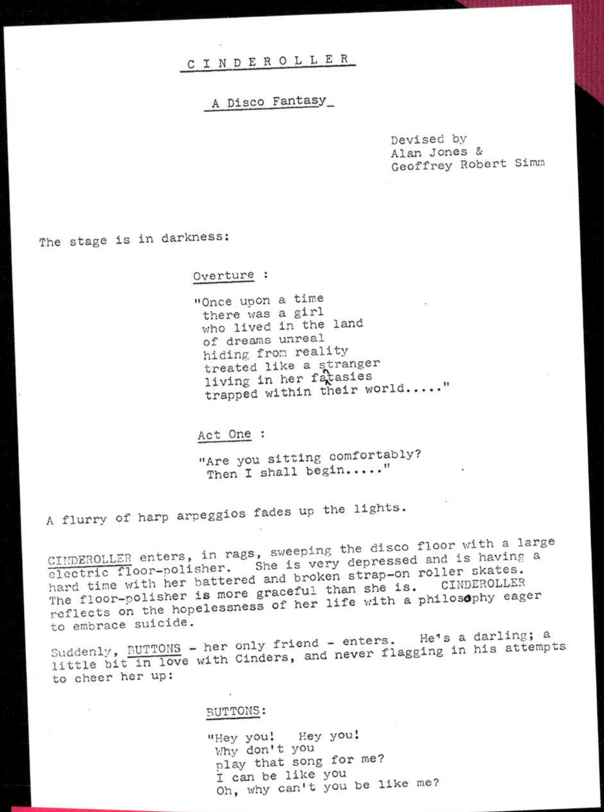

C I N D E R O L L E R

A Disco Fantasy

Devised by
Alan Jones &
Geoffrey Robert Simm

The stage is in darkness:

Overture :

"Once upon a time
there was a girl
who lived in the land
of dreams unreal
hiding from reality
treated like a stranger
living in her fatasies
trapped within their world....."

Act One :

"Are you sitting comfortably?
Then I shall begin....."

A flurry of harp arpeggios fades up the lights.

CINDEROLLER enters, in rags, sweeping the disco floor with a large electric floor-polisher. She is very depressed and is having a hard time with her battered and broken strap-on roller skates. The floor-polisher is more graceful than she is. CINDEROLLER reflects on the hopelessness of her life with a philosophy eager to embrace suicide.

Suddenly, BUTTONS - her only friend - enters. He's a darling; a little bit in love with Cinders, and never flagging in his attempts to cheer her up:

BUTTONS:

"Hey you! Hey you!
Why don't you
play that song for me?
I can be like you
Oh, why can't you be like me?

The first page of the 'Cinderoller' script, devised by Alan Jones and Geoffrey Robert Simm.

CINDEROLLER: A Disco Fantasy

In 1979 I was in the grip of Roller Disco mania! From picnics in Battersea Park to practicing in any available skateboard area or Disco, I lived my life on roller skates. And I was pretty good, so much so that when roller-blading became another big thing in the mid-1990s I was streets ahead of everyone else when I spent most weekends wheeling through Kensington Gardens, on one particular memorable afternoon being watched by Princess Diana and her bodyguards.

It was at the Empire Ballroom that my best friend Geoff Simm first came up with the idea of creating a Roller Disco Pantomime, one we would write together, based around our favourite music of the moment, using our extended family as the cast. I quickly got the Empire management on board, Geoff agreed to direct, and the date of December 9th, 1979, was chosen for the premiere of *Cinderoller: A Disco Fantasy* performed by the Carmen Rollers.

In our 30-minute Disco version of the classic fairytale, Cinderella was a suicidal scullery maid, bellhop Buttons her only friend, her three Ugly Sisters were Easy Roller (an American Indian), Steam Roller (a cowboy)

The live performance of 'Cinderoller' at the Empire Ballroom Leicester Square.

and Ritzy Roller (a leather queen), the fairy godmother was a Joan Collins pastiche (at the time Collins was appearing on skates with Leonard Rossiter in the latest Cinzano commercial directed by Alan Parker) and Prince Charming wore the tightest tights.

Frankly, the six weeks of rehearsals were a nightmare, no one took them seriously and they always devolved into devil-may-care Party Central. On the actual performance day, more than a couple of the cast had dropped acid due to nerves, journalist Chris Clarke, our Cinderoller, kept tripping up in his "thousand yards of net" ball gown creation, which we kept telling him from the start was a mistake, and yet we played to a packed house and garnered some really great reviews.

I kept hold of one review from 'Street Level' magazine: "This modern look at the traditional tale may have confused purists slightly, but this review of the interaction of sub-cultures within the ongoing class differentiation of modern society can only be described as deeply meaningful. For years skateboarders and roller skaters have been searching for the ultimate spectacle combining speed and grace. At the Empire on December 9th that goal was finally achieved". Wow! That sensational write-up was enough for us to get another encore booking at the Electric Ballroom and even some kind words from Sir Bernard Delfont, owner of the entire Empire business himself.

▲ The cast and crew of 'Cinderoller'. Alan Jones is wearing the Lonsdale sweatshirt. Geoff Simm is far right.

The original Disco track rundown sampled from gives a rough idea of the story and tone we were going for:

Once Upon a Time (1977) – Donna Summer
Disco Symphony (1979) – Lightning
Bad Girls (1979) – Donna Summer
Cat-Tails (1979) – Masquerade
Follow Me (1978) – Amanda Lear
Hell on Wheels (1979) – Cher
Love Dancin' (1979) – Marlena Shaw
Charmed by You (1979) – Caress
Embraceable You (1979) – Westside Strutters
Beat the Clock (1979) – Sparks
Suffer (1979) – Grace Jones
Tomorrow (1979) – Grace Jones
Disco Wedding (1979) – Paul Jabara
Ready for the 80's (1979) – Village People

Just for the record, also included in the sampling were *A Lover's Concerto* (1965) by The Toys, *Don't Cry for Me Argentina* (1976) by Julie Covington and cuts from the original cast recording of the stage musical 'Passion Flower Hotel' (1965) by John Barry. It was a fun project but a stressful one, something I swore I'd never do again and never did. Unless you call producing the UK's biggest and best genre event FrightFest at the Empire cinema next door in the 2000s! But this was hardcore Disco, an all-encompassing lifestyle where everyone believed they could simply dance their troubles away on a 4/4 musical high. And to tunes like these in a potently British format, it was an exhilarating experience.

Disco Memo

Alan Jones with Geoff Simm, producers and writers of 'Cinderoller'. 'To Roller-skate Is to Live' shirt worn by West End star Michael Staniforth, at that time appearing on stage in 'A Chorus Line', soon to be followed by 'Sweeney Todd'.

STEPPIN' OUT (1979)

Barely 30 minutes long, yet more people probably saw this look at London lifestyles in 1979 than the entire audience of **The Music Machine** (1979) and **The Apple** (1980) put together and then some. That's mainly because it played across the UK as the support feature to Ridley Scott's blockbuster sci-fi horror **Alien** (1979). Director Lyndall Hobbs was a firm feature on the London nightlife scene at the time frequenting the King's Road Punk watering holes. And that was because the Melbourne born TV presenter was in a relationship with Michael White, then the red-hot producer of the stage musical phenomenon 'The Rocky Horror Show' and **Monty Python and the Holy Grail** (1975), the former Richard O'Brien composed show playing at three Chelsea venues until 1979, the Royal Court Upstairs, the Classic Cinema Chelsea and the King's Road Theatre.

During their time together, White would go out every night, host dinners, schmooze investors, hobnob with the stars, and Hobbs was a very willing partner. I first met her at a party at Air Studios in Hampstead, I roller-skated in wearing a tuxedo, something doomed celebutante Paula Yates admonished me for in no uncertain terms for some unknown reason. Hobbs turned all of that knowledge into an investigation of the Disco scene unfolding in The Embassy club in Old Bond Street, the Blitz club in Covent Garden and especially the Mod Nights at Legends off Regent Street. Punk featured heavily too, a gathering of Sex Pistols acolytes outside Vivienne Westwood's famed boutique now re-christened 'Seditionaries' at Chelsea's World's End. And she hitched a ride with a coach outing to Bedfordshire to skate at Dunstable's Roller Disco, Rollerdisco.

A patchy affair all around, and edited with garden shears, but an invaluable record of the defining spirit and mood of those seminal times, even though Hobbs, soon to embark on a 7-year affair with actor Al Pacino, is not a pretty sight staggering around on roller skates. The soundtrack included cuts from two Mod bands, The Merton Parkas and Secret Affair and the Disco tracks *Disco Roller* (1979) by Cynthia Woodard (the flipside of her 12-inch single *California Dreamin'*), *Rock Around the Clock* (1979) by experimental Belgian synth-poppers Telex and *Stars* (1979) by Sylvester.

The Roxy Rollers

Featured strongly in **Steppin' Out**, and also in director Donovan Winter's short **Roller Force** (1980), were the UK's only roller-skating dance group The Roxy Rollers. For the last few years of the 1970s/80s the troupe embarked on one European tour, became smash hits at the 25th Anniversary party for 'Playboy' magazine, opened Norwich City Football Club's new grandstand, appeared on fourteen TV shows including 'Seaside Special', 'Blue Peter' and 'Arrival', spoke for the Roller Disco generation on numerous radio programmes, appeared on the Royal Variety Performance and released the single *Disco Skating* (1980).

The four-piece ensemble was formed by London Roller Disco entrepreneurs Gordon Elsbury and Ray Woolford, the geniuses behind the Jubilee Hall Roller Disco in Covent Garden, the Electric Ballroom in Camden Town and eventually the Global Village complex under the arches at Charing Cross Station. It was television director Elsbury ('Top of the Pops', 'Are You Being Served?') and still campaigning queer activist Woolford's desire to put together what would essentially be Roller Disco's answer to Hot Gossip. At the beginning it was a three-man, one-girl outfit consisting of sales-assistant-by-day Aden/Edem Ephraim, his college sister Ann, denture maker George Campbell and unemployed Dennis Fuller. The four friends used to skate together at the Global Village where they were 'discovered' by its managers.

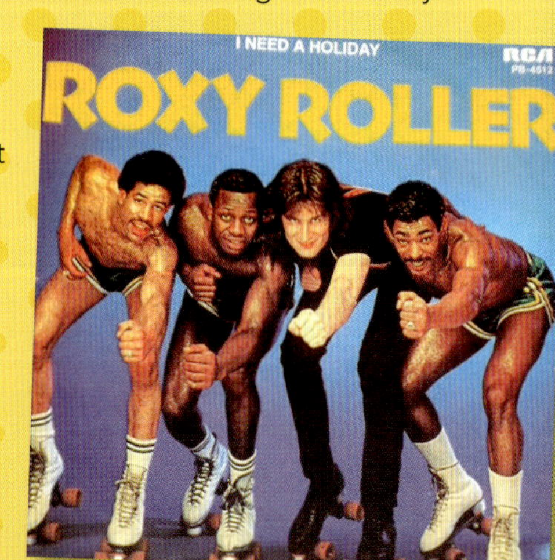

While many clubs not fitted up for Roller Disco worried about the damage to their dance floors, and others didn't think they would be a big enough draw,

The Roxy Rollers soon started pulling large crowds and broke down straight, gay and racial barriers. When one venue refused to pay their fee, both 'Stage' and 'Billboard' magazines took up their case, the result being they became fully paid up members of the Equity Union. Once the Roller Disco craze faded though, so did The Roxy Rollers. But Ephraim and Fuller moved to Germany in 1981 and as The London Boys scored a massive Eurobeat hit with their album *The Twelve Commandments of Dance* (1988), containing the terrific hit singles *Requiem*, *Harlem Desire* and *London Nights* (all 1989). Sadly the duo's story did not end well as both died in an Alpine car crash while driving to a ski resort.

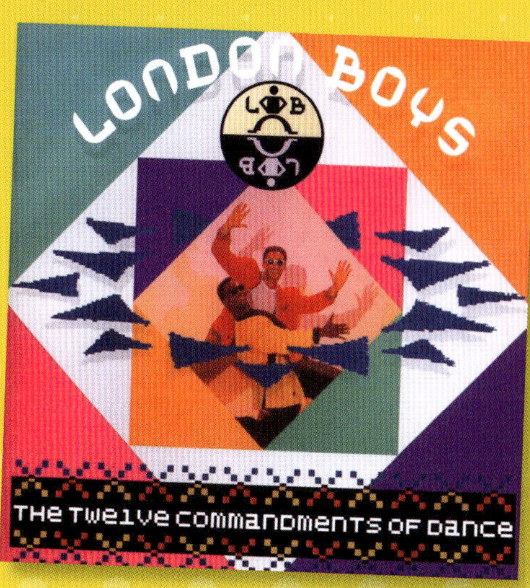

Rock video megastar Russell Mulcahy with Alan Jones at a 'Shock Around the Clock' event at the Scala Cinema.

I met my close friend and scriptwriter Keith Williams for the first time on July 10th, 1976, at a screening of **Lipstick**. By 1978 he had met an Australian filmmaker who had filmed some original footage to accompany a package on the Harry Nilsson hit *Everybody's Talkin'* (1969) for a Channel 7 pop show in Oz. Russell Mulcahy would turn making this 'film clip' into a whole new 'rock video' industry and would take Keith along with him for the mega-ride as his conceptualist of choice. Keith would eventually contribute settings, characters, storylines and concepts helping artists such as Tina Turner, Billy Joel, Donna Summer, and Bonnie Tyler create some of the most iconic music videos ever.

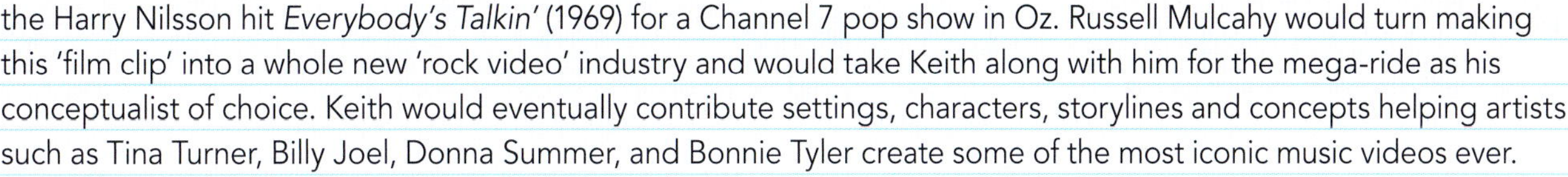

If I had any spare press show tickets for movies Keith was usually who I asked to be my plus one. For the March 1979 multi-media show of Phil Kaufman's **Invasion of the Body Snatchers** (1978) I had managed to score some extras. Keith said it would be the perfect opportunity to meet Russell, who had just arrived in London and was crashing in his Notting Hill Gate apartment. And that fateful meeting would be the start of something monumental for me also. Funnily enough, Russell fell asleep during the movie, which I always thought was funny considering the plot!

At this point in time Russell had been given a tape of a song by a new band called The Buggles and had asked Keith to come up with an idea for the accompanying video. It was Keith who thought the first image you saw should be a young girl on a beach twiddling with the knobs on a retro radio and the central conceit of *Video Killed the Radio Star* (1979) was born. That worldwide hit cemented Russell's reputation as an esteemed rock video icon, became the first music video played on the new channel MTV in 1981, and our friendship took me through the entire 1980s on a wave of celebrity access, worldwide travel, incredible opportunities and some of the most memorable experiences of my life.

From partying with Duran Duran, Christopher Lambert and Princess Stephanie of Monaco (singer of the Eurodisco hit *Irresistible*, 1986) and being on the set of so many of his landmark videos (Ultravox's *Vienna*, 1980, *The Wild Boys*, 1984) to starring in one of his lesser known ones, appearing alongside Christopher Lee for one of his movies and accompanying him to Argentina to shoot **Highlander II: The Quickening** (1991), I hitched my wagon to Russell's stratospherically rising star and stayed there. Sure we had some bumpy moments along the way, what friendship doesn't, but if ever he could include me in anything glamorous or fun, he did and I owe him a great deal of gratitude during a time of enormous life changes for me, both professionally and personally.

LOVE AT FIRST BITE (1979)

For many years the highest-grossing independent film of all time, director Stan Dragoti's unpretentious horror spoof showed suave and debonair Hollywood lounge lizard George Hamilton's flair for comedy, his leading lady Susan Saint James' precise slapstick timing and 'Laugh-In' star Arte Johnson's superior support. One of the three 1979 movies to put Dracula centre stage with Disco (alongside **Nocturna, Granddaughter of Dracula** and Carl Schenkel/ Carlo Ombra's **Graf Dracula Beisst Jetzt in Oberbayern/ Dracula Blows His Cool**) and by a country mile by far the best, Dragoti captured the feeling and atmosphere of the prime Disco years with a second to none affection and verisimilitude, perhaps because in his prolific commercials career Dragoti had conceived the famous *I Love New York* branding campaign showcasing the 1978 Disco hit by Metropolis that spent eleven weeks on the Dance charts.

Evicted from his Transylvanian castle home atop the Carpathian Mountains by Romanian communists so the Gymnastics Team can train there, Count Vladimir Dracula (Hamilton, **Once Is Not Enough**, 1975) and his faithful manservant Renfield (Johnson) head to Manhattan in pursuit of fashion model Cindy Sondheim (Saint James, 'McMillan & Wife', 1971-76), whom he believes to be the reincarnation of his one true love Mina Harker. Tracing his missing coffin to a funeral home in Harlem, Dracula eventually checks into the Plaza Hotel and his Cindy obsession becomes further fuelled when he tracks her to the Anything Goes Disco after a Central Park photo shoot.

Later whisking her around the dance floor to the 1978 Disco classic *I Love the Nightlife (Disco 'Round)* by Alicia Bridges, a night of neurotic lovemaking ensues. But when Cindy tells her ex-boyfriend and psychiatrist Dr. Jeff Rosenberg (Richard Benjamin, **The Last of Sheila**, 1973) about her experience, showing him the kinky love bites on her neck, the Van Helsing grandson realises Dracula is alive and well and haunting the top hot New York nitespots.

With Rosenberg making increasingly desperate attempts to destroy his ancient nemesis, Dracula and Cindy become more deeply involved, until the crazed monster hunter is deemed insane and thrown into Bellevue Hospital. When reports of a blood bank heist hit the newspapers though, once sceptical Lieutenant Ferguson (Dick Shawn, **The Producers**, 1967) starts to believe Rosenberg's fantastic conspiracy theories and helps him try to stake Dracula before Cindy falls irrevocably under his promise of immortal bliss.

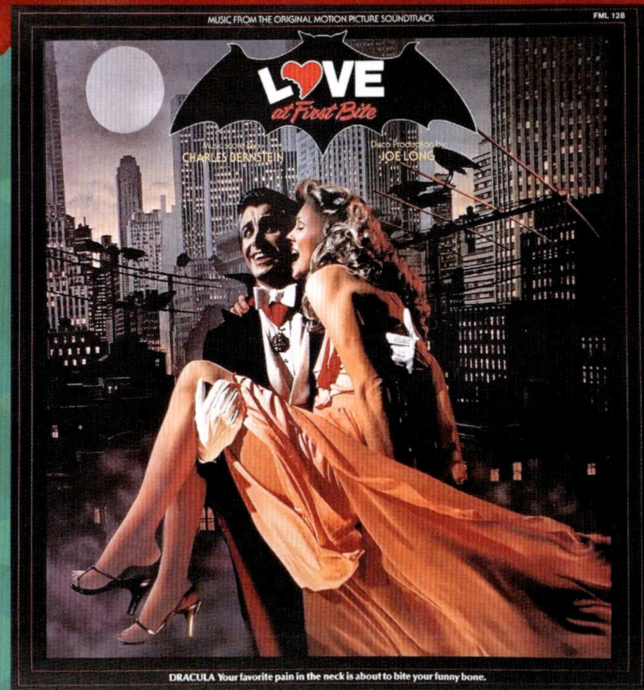

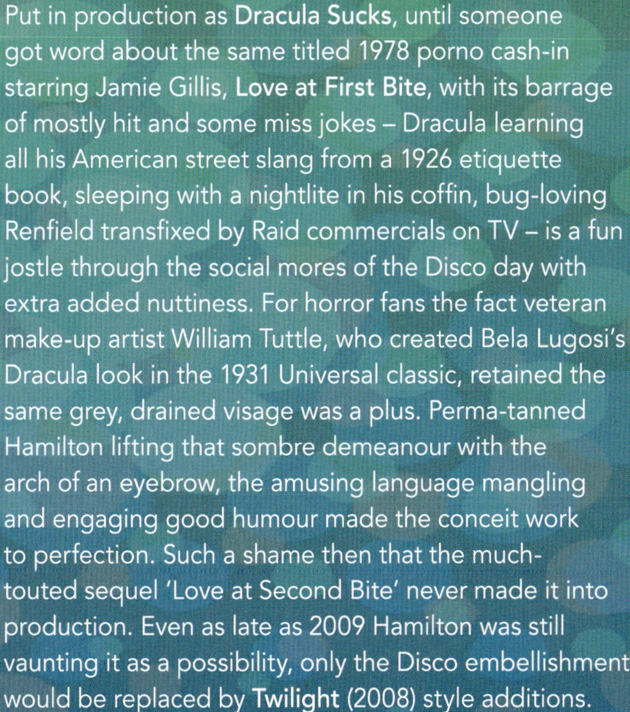

Put in production as **Dracula Sucks**, until someone got word about the same titled 1978 porno cash-in starring Jamie Gillis, **Love at First Bite**, with its barrage of mostly hit and some miss jokes – Dracula learning all his American street slang from a 1926 etiquette book, sleeping with a nightlite in his coffin, bug-loving Renfield transfixed by Raid commercials on TV – is a fun jostle through the social mores of the Disco day with extra added nuttiness. For horror fans the fact veteran make-up artist William Tuttle, who created Bela Lugosi's Dracula look in the 1931 Universal classic, retained the same grey, drained visage was a plus. Perma-tanned Hamilton lifting that sombre demeanour with the arch of an eyebrow, the amusing language mangling and engaging good humour made the conceit work to perfection. Such a shame then that the much-touted sequel 'Love at Second Bite' never made it into production. Even as late as 2009 Hamilton was still vaunting it as a possibility, only the Disco embellishment would be replaced by **Twilight** (2008) style additions.

Other than the superlative Alicia Bridges hit, the soundtrack includes *Fly By Night* stridently performed by Patricia Hodges, which got some dance floor heat in an extended 12-minute 45-second Richie Rivera remix. *Dancin' Through the Night* plays behind the Dracula/Cindy meet-cute at the Anything Goes Disco, vocals for this Richie Rivera mix are by Arpeggio's Sydney Barnes and Voyage's Sylvia Mason. Featured on the Parachute Records (a Casablanca subsidiary) soundtrack release is *Love Theme (Disco Version)*, also written by Charles Bernstein who would go on to compose **A Nightmare on Elm Street** (1984) and **Deadly Friend** (1986). "Fly by night, sleep in the daytime, fly by night, sleep all day" indeed.

Voyage

Comfortably past the stage of being viewed merely as a self-conscious trend, Disco was more confident, more laid back and much more creatively expansive than ever during the late 1970s. Especially in Europe where soul and symphony were being cleverly assimilated into the Eurodisco brand and one of the best purveyors were the French studio group Voyage who shot to international dance floor stardom with their debut album, *Voyage* (1977). The musicians who mostly powered early French Disco were a surprisingly tight-knit bunch – guitarist Slim Pezin, keyboardist Marc Chantereau, bass player Sauveur Mallia and drummer Pierre-Alain Dahan – essentially the house band of producer Roger Tokarz, founder of the seminal Tele Music label. Under such names as Arpadys, Big Jullien and His All Stars, CCPP, Disco & Co., Spatial and Co., French Funk Specialist and The Peppers, the same pool of gifted musicians floated around the French Disco scene cooking up an entire Boogie Wonderland of shimmering classics. Pezin became a fixture in the line-ups of both Don Ray and Alec R. Costandinos' productions; Sauveur played bass on most of Cerrone's studio sessions and live performances.

But most significantly and famously these four Tele Music players transformed into Voyage. Lead singer Sylvia Mason was recruited from London, where the first album was recorded at the famed Trident Studios in Soho, with back-up vocals provided by band members Chantereau, Dahan and Pezin, plus 'Birds of Paris' session singer members Stephanie De Sykes and Kay Garner. Superb melodies, phenomenal production values, immaculate orchestration and stunning arrangements made Voyage the perfect conduit for glamorous Eurodisco to reign at No.1 in America for three weeks in the 'Billboard' Disco charts and in the memory forever after. In keeping with numerous Disco concepts of the day, *Voyage* paid homage to the musical styles of different regions of the world. If you couldn't afford to travel to foreign climes in the mid-'70s, the next best thing was taking a jet set trip into global musical cultures.

Voyage hit on a new variation of such sonic continental drifting and not only made it feel fresh again but also minted a flawless Eurodisco album. The sensational send-off is the bright and breezy *From East to West*, an invitation to hitch a ride, go native and dance. *Point Zero* puts the clubber right in the heart of the jungle with a rhythmic chant of masculine voices and a dense layer of percussion in the rich Manu Dibango style. Hardly surprising as Pezin played on many Dibango albums. *Orient Express* blends Asian and Japanese melodies together with dizzying aplomb. The bagpipe-infused *Scotch Machine*, re-titled *Scots Machine* in the UK because the term 'Scotch' can cause offense in this context. The square dance *Bayou Village* seamlessly shifts into *Latin Odyssey* with its gloriously hi-tone Santa Esmeralda touches before finally landing triumphantly in the USA with *Lady America*. This standout tribute to all things Americana combined Village People-type rousing vocals, orchestral energy and a pounding beat mesmerising enough to hustle over to the stereo, start the entire album from the beginning and dance all over again.

Voyage got to the Disco top spot again with their second magnificent album *Fly Away* (1978), essentially another barnstorming globetrotting musical journey. From the hand-beaten drum based *Kechak Fantasy*, the Indian-flavoured *Eastern Trip* and the catchy *Tahiti, Tahiti* chant with Hawaiian guitar accents, through the percolating synthesizer driven *Let's Fly Away*, the *Golden Eldorado* conquistador fever dream and the Rock 'n' Soul *Gone with the Music*, it was an instant dance generator, another breathtaking take-off into the Disco heavens followed by the most carefree of flights.

The *Voyage 3* (1980) album features the 'Billboard' Disco Chart Top 20 hits *I Love You Dancer* and *Do It Again*. Lead singer Sylvia Mason was about to sign a deal with the legendary London label Stiff Records to headline the neo-Motown girl group Sylvia and the Sapphires, and *Voyage 3* reflects the subtle transformations taking place within the group and on the outside musical landscape by funking up the melody and harmony, bringing a strong rhythmic groove of electric bass and drums to the foreground. Voyage released one more album *One Step Higher* (1982) but never made the Disco charts again despite *Let's Get Started* being a classic in the old school Voyage tradition full of captivating melody, sprightly lyrics, brilliant musicality, airy sweetness and feather lightness. *Follow the Brightest Star* seemed to be blazing a new trail with its inspirational and positive anthemic lustre but marked the end of the road instead for the milestone Eurodisco project.

Disco Memo

Best of British

I could have been a British TV star if I had played my cards right and not been so scared to ask for help. In the final days of my Punk persona, I had met film, music and ITV producer Mike Mansfield whose show 'Supersonic' was popular with the kids. A camp and flamboyant figure on the Disco scene, our paths crossed many times because of the chart bands I was hanging out with – Pilot, Queen, Roxy Music, the Faces, Blondie – and one day he asked me if I'd like to front my own TV show because he was keen to branch out. Just like that. More startled by the request than anything I thought why not. So later, on December 21st, 1977, I stood on a stage in front of a huge Union Jack flag bearing the show's title 'Best of British', surrounded by an invited audience of about 200 friends and acquaintances. With no cue cards, no teleprompter and absolutely no direction from Mansfield, I was told to introduce a roster of bands. Make it up as you go along, he said.

The line-up was pretty incredible: The Damned (and the footage shot would be the only record of their 5 member line-up with Lu Edmonds and John Moss, pre Culture Club), Generation X with Tony James before he split for Sigue Sigue Sputnik, The Adverts singing *One Chord Wonder* (1977) and Rich Kids with my old SEX mate Glen Matlock, Midge Ure, pre Ultravox, and Rusty Egan, pre Visage. Not being telly savvy at the time I tried to wing it but without any assistance at all it was a lost cause. All I can really remember about that night now is the looks of pity on my friends' faces.

Mansfield eventually cut me out completely and repackaged the footage as a show titled 'Impact' that played late at night on ITV. In hindsight I think he never had any intention of using anything I did, he just needed my contacts as I knew everyone on that stage, and The Adverts were on my friend Dave Hill's Anchor Records label.

I would hone my stage skills 20 years later thanks to my freelance job at Sky Movies, but 'Best of British' was a baptism of fire I could well have lived without.

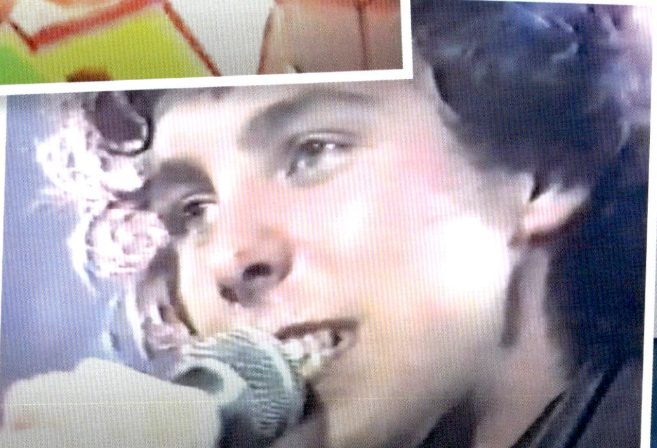

DISCO GODFATHER / THE AVENGING DISCO GODFATHER (1979)

Spurred by the success of **Saturday Night Fever** (1977), one-man Blaxploitation factory Rudy Ray Moore set his sights on flashing mirrorballs after producing and starring in the low-brow classics **Dolemite** (1975) and **The Human Tornado** (1976), based on the kung-fu fighting pimp character from his stand-up comedy routines. (Well portrayed and documented in the superb 2019 Eddie Murphy vehicle **Dolemite Is My Name**). The result is a demented cross between **Gordon's War** (1973) and **Can't Stop the Music** (1980) with Moore playing ex-cop Tucker Williams, the rapping owner and main attraction of the Blueberry Hill Disco. Called back into police action when his nephew Bucky (Julius J. Carry III) gets hooked on Angel Dust, Williams and Girl Friday Noel (Carol Speed, star of **Abby**, 1974, the Blaxploitation rip-off of **The Exorcist**, 1973) declare war on super-pusher Stinger (James H. Hawthorne) and his cronies using his nightclub to peddle the drug.

Skid-row production values meet hefty Moore's skin-tight studded Disco ensembles (in fact, the signature one-liner is "Put your weight on it") to create an off-the-rails funky fiasco packed with Roller Disco sequences, cheap psychedelic freak-outs (with zombies and skeletons), hilarious exorcisms to rid addicts of their evil spirits, a **Saturday Night Fever** album cover used as a cocaine container and jaw-droppingly awful kung-fu choreography by martial arts champion Howard Jackson. With no recognisable Disco hits the soundtrack was still acceptable filler in this solo J. Robert Wagoner directed effort. The anonymous Juice People Unlimited performed *Disco Godfather, Shermanizing/One Way Ticket to Hell* and *I Never Wanted to Say Goodbye*, the latter sung by Marquee De Marco, written by funk musicians Ernie Fields Jr. and Greg Middleton. The track *Spaced Out* is the one heard accompanying all the trippy sequences.

Stephanie De Sykes

Despite singer Sylvia Mason becoming the public face of Voyage, she had help with the gloriously sung crystal-clear vocals from a combination of backing singers collectively known as the 'Birds of Paris' because they appeared on practically every French Disco release. From Cerrone to Alec R. Costandinos and Don Ray to Voyage, the 'Birds of Paris' added their instantly recognisable signature touch of close harmonies and choral dexterity. Members of that tight-knit Disco sorority included Madeline Bell, Joanne Stone, Kay Garner, Sunny Leslie (singer of the original *Doctor's Orders* in 1974), Sue Glover, Vicki Brown (popstar Joe's wife), Katie Kissoon (who with brother Mac sang *Sugar Candy Kisses*, 1975) – and Stephanie De Sykes.

Famous in the UK for her catchy 1974 Top Ten hit *Born with a Smile on My Face* Stephanie came to session singing after realising touring Europe with a chart success was quite an expensive undertaking. "There was no such thing as rock videos back then", Stephanie told me. "So when you had a popular hit you were constantly jumping on and off trains and planes to Manchester and Barcelona. The truth was it cost a lot of money and was very inconvenient. I was never that comfortable being a solo star and performing in public anyway. Being a session singer was the perfect option; I got to sing, could drive easily to Trident Studios – the main base of Disco operations – make a good living and spend lots of time with my family. What was not to like about that arrangement?"

Stephanie's upbringing was very much a musical one: her grandfather was a silent movie pianist and her mother also played and wrote songs. "I learned the piano as a child too but my main career ambition was to go to drama school and be a theatre actress. That never really happened but I did get some acting work. My singing career started by accident. My theatrical agent was Ben Lyon, an American actor married to actress Bebe Daniels, who settled in London during World War II and became famous on British TV in the 1950s with their 'Life with the Lyons' sit-com. Whenever Ben's secretary was on holiday I'd fill in because I had taken a secretarial course. One Friday he asked me what I was doing that weekend and I told him I was singing with a semi-pro local band. 'Oh, I didn't know you could sing?' he said, which is hardly what you want to hear from your agent… But he said he'd call a friend of his who had this television show. That friend was light entertainment legend Hughie Green, the show was 'Opportunity Knocks' (the 'Britain's Got Talent' of its day), so I auditioned, got picked to appear, but didn't win. However someone at PYE Records saw the programme and contacted me asking if I read music, which I did, and that led to *Born with a Smile on My Face*. That plus singing the theme tune for 'The Golden Shot' game show and recording *We'll Find Our Day* for a wedding storyline in the top-rated soap opera 'Crossroads'".

Stephanie first came across the term Disco when she visited music publishers and other agencies. "I remember a lot of people talking about this current fad for dance music that seemed to be catching on big-time". Her first Disco job was with trail-blazing producer/arranger Alec R. Costandinos who booked her for a session with the soon-to-become equally legendary Marc Cerrone via the fixing partnership of John and Monica Watson. "I was called up and offered a job with 'some dodgy European Disco producers' along with Madeline Bell. Before I knew it I was in Trident Studios recording *Love in C Minor* and *Black Is Black* (both 1977). Then I was rushing off to another session, a Cadbury chocolate jingle or whatever. It never crossed my mind I was involved in anything special or so long lasting because it was just another job. The 'fixers' put us together in various ensembles mainly down to our availability and, I assume, how they felt we would work together for the optimum end result for the client. I'm not sure you needed a special gift to be a session singer but the ability to blend and get on with others was paramount. All the 'Birds of Paris' were so different vocally and personality wise, but we could work together in tight little enclaves and combinations on autopilot almost. As long as our voices matched the sound required, it was all that mattered".

Love in C Minor became a massive global hit and Stephanie's Disco career exploded with it. "Despite still being somewhat embarrassed by that racy spoken intro", she laughs. "But you did a good job for these people, you were professional, adaptable and enjoyed yourself. So of course they wanted to repeat that happy experience". Her sterling work with Cerrone led to numerous gigs for Costandinos including *Sphinx* (1977), *Sumeria* (1977), the first two Love and Kisses albums (1977, 1978) and her favourite, *Romeo & Juliet* (1978). Then she found herself in the Voyage line-up for producer Roger Tokarz. "He was a lovely guy and let me breastfeed my new born baby in the studio. My nanny came along to the Voyage sessions and looked after him until we had a break. *From East to West* and *Souvenirs* were memorable tracks for me because, being a bit of a wordsmith and writing songs myself (Stephanie wrote two UK Eurovision Song Contest entries, Co-Co's *The Bad Old Days*, 1978, and Prima Donna's *Love Enough for Two*, 1980), I thought the lyrical content was, well, very French, very eccentric… It was almost like, the music is so fabulous and these words will fit, so let's shove them in. In both Pop and Disco though the meaning of the lyrics is not too important".

For all the 'Birds of Paris', Trident Studios in St Anne's Court, Soho, became a second home. "I would drive in from Esher where I lived, park close to Trident in Wardour Street, walk into the tiny studio, take my coat off, listen to the music track once, stand by the microphone and sing. My recollection is I'd be arriving just as the musicians were packing up their instruments to leave. And our sessions were mainly at night – 10 p.m. to 6 a.m., with pizzas delivered from the Pizza Express in Dean Street – often the only time the studio was free because it was such a popular venue for major artists like the Bee Gees, The Rolling Stones and Genesis. Sometimes a person would play your lines on a piano rather than cue up the tape and us girls would divide ourselves into what the best way of achieving the right harmonies would be. It was all a very organic and mutually creative process. The Disco years coincided with Trident going 48-track, the first

studio to do so. Cables were everywhere linking the top studio's 24-track deck to another on the bottom floor in what I can only describe as looking like a Heath Robinson contraption. It was cutting edge technology then though, and created a much bigger sound thanks to our vocals being easily quadrupled, the reason why the Eurodisco producers loved going there. Less time was wasted that way too. The sessions were long, but we were very well paid, and we never had any problems over payment either. It was lucrative work with guaranteed earnings – everyone was delighted".

"The 'Birds of Paris' were a creative, professional and opinionated bunch. Eurodisco producers loved us because we would add to their epic musical journeys by coming up with ideas and suggestions. Something grew out of that talent pool rather than being an actual regimented system even though the producer was always in control. I remember hearing *From East to West* for the first time on the radio and thinking, Wow, that was pretty good. Then I kept hearing it being played constantly and slowly the realisation dawned that I was part of something quite major. And that feeling kept being repeated as the Disco genre took off and so much of what I was doing became so successful. I didn't realise at the time the amount of pleasure it would continue to bring to people. But now I'm proud of that fact, astonished by it in many ways, but delighted people are still enjoying it. I got to work with some truly remarkable people, got paid for the privilege and helped create some of the most discussed Disco in music history".

Disco Memo

The Embassy Club

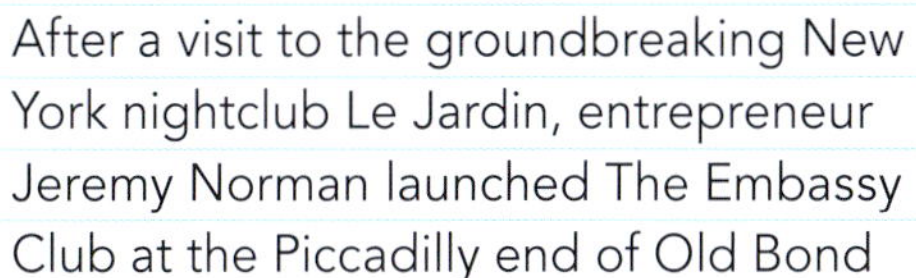

After a visit to the groundbreaking New York nightclub Le Jardin, entrepreneur Jeremy Norman launched The Embassy Club at the Piccadilly end of Old Bond Street as a London equivalent to Studio 54. Inspired by Le Jardin's omnisexual clientele and its velvet rope door policy to stop undesirables gaining entrance, The Embassy opened its doors in April 1978 and for two years ruled the Disco roost unopposed. It was my absolutely favourite club to take visiting Americans because they felt at home there as opposed to the way other British venues seemed so off-putting. Especially on a Sunday afternoon for the all-day, all-night Tea Dances that cost £4 entrance fee, but you could stay as long as you wanted, drink as much as you liked and eat likewise from the constantly groaning buffet table.

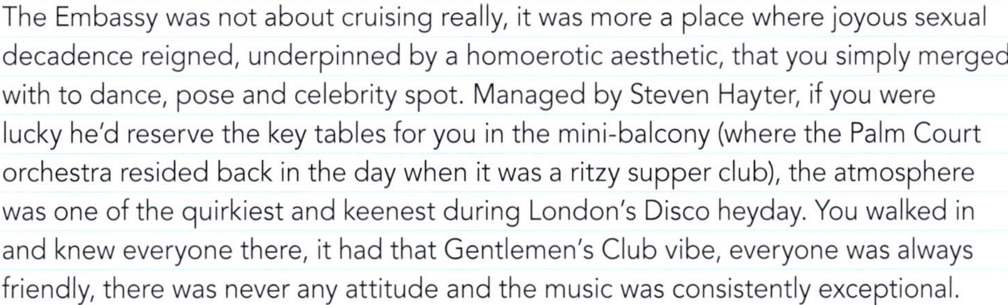

The Embassy was not about cruising really, it was more a place where joyous sexual decadence reigned, underpinned by a homoerotic aesthetic, that you simply merged with to dance, pose and celebrity spot. Managed by Steven Hayter, if you were lucky he'd reserve the key tables for you in the mini-balcony (where the Palm Court orchestra resided back in the day when it was a ritzy supper club), the atmosphere was one of the quirkiest and keenest during London's Disco heyday. You walked in and knew everyone there, it had that Gentlemen's Club vibe, everyone was always friendly, there was never any attitude and the music was consistently exceptional.

You had to step down onto the dance floor – many came a cropper stumbling about, only to be rescued by passing waiters in their skimpy shorts, the first West End venue to have that employee dress code. One might have been future New Romantic one-hit-wonder Marilyn who worked there in his lean years. But it was a special place for the Discognescenti who had no problem mixing with the drag queens, the Eurotrash aristos who nixed Annabel's across the road in Berkeley Square, the Z-list starlets thrown out of Tramp around the corner and lesbian Sloane Rangers looking beyond their Gateways Kings Road horizons. All would mingle together in this fondly remembered venue where Sylvester filmed the video for *You Make Me Feel (Mighty Real)* (1978).

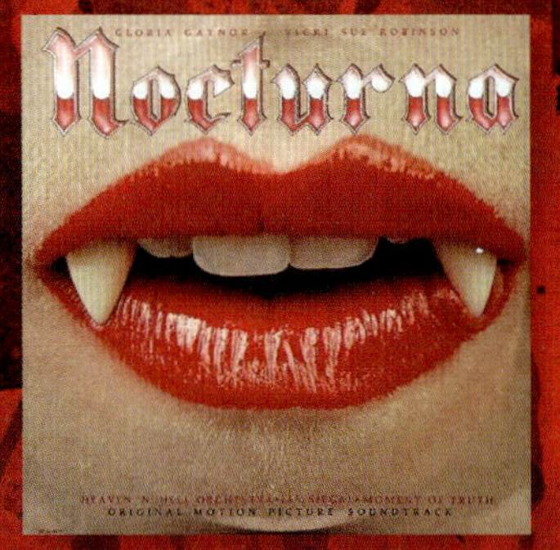

NOCTURNA, GRANDDAUGHTER OF DRACULA (1979)

One of the worst movies of 1979 contained two of the best Disco soundtrack songs of all time. Not just that both figure high in the personal bests of the artists involved, even if one of them felt that wasn't the case. Vampires were all the rage in the final year before the new 1980s decade kicked off and **Nocturna: Granddaughter of Dracula** was just one of six to feature the bloodsucking Count of Transylvanian legend. The highest profile was **Dracula** starring Frank Langella, the independent breakout hit was **Love at First Bite** with George Hamilton wearing the formal dress cape, art-house crowds were well catered for with **Nosferatu the Vampyre** played by Klaus Kinski, Germany exported **Dracula Blows His Cool** with Gianni Garko and Romania chimed in with **Vlad Tepes**, an historical account of the origins of the man who inspired Bram Stoker's literary juggernaut. Stefan Sileanu essayed that role of The Impaler.

But only **Nocturna** had an honest to God Hollywood Count Dracula in the guise of veteran horror icon John Carradine from **House of Frankenstein** (1944) and **House of Dracula** (1945). And the John Ford rep company favourite even brought along his cloak from the latter movie to save on wardrobe costs for producer, co-writer and headliner Nai Bonet. Vietnamese born Bonet began a belly-dancing career in Las Vegas at the age of 13 and was featured as an exotic dancer in such entertainments as **John Goldfarb, Please Come Home** (1965), 'The Sheik' episode of 'The Beverly Hillbillies', (1965) and the 007 spoof **The Spy with the Cold Nose** (1966). In 1966 she also released the novelty record *Jelly Belly* – the flipside was *The Seventh Veil* – and became a featured model on various exotica MOR album covers. After appearances in **The Soul of Nigger Charley** (1972), **Soul Hustler/ The Miracle Man** (1973), **The Greatest** (1977) and **Adult Fairytales** (1978), Bonet decided to take the bull by the horns and craft herself a starring vehicle because clearly no one else was going to do it for her.

Nocturna was the shoddy result. And another wonky combination of the Disco lifestyle mixed with vampire mythology where both are happening at night is the only real middleground narrative connection. Co-scripted with Harry Tampa, her director on **Adult Fairytales**

(who under the name Harry Hurwitz had made his agreeable debut with **The Projectionist**, 1970), they devised a lame comedy where down-on-his-luck Dracula (Carradine), now sporting dentures instead of fangs, turns his Transylvanian castle into a hotel-cum-Disco-complex with his werewolf concierge Theodore (Brother Theodore). But when his rebellious granddaughter Nocturna (Bonet) runs off to New York in pursuit of a rock musician (Antony Hamilton), he follows in hot pursuit. Once in the Big Apple, Nocturna meets the local children of the night, including Jugulia Vein (Yvonne De Carlo parodying her Lily Munster role) and hits the Discos where she uncovers a scam run by jive-talking pimp RH Factor (Sy Richardson) who employs sexy vampires at The Trickey Hickey massage parlour to lure lonely businessmen in to steal their money and harvest their blood.

Directed by Tampa in something of a coma, and this Dracula line of dialogue says it all – "If I'm dead... how come I still have to go wee-wee?" – Bonet raised the $350,000 budget for her vanity production from her **Halloween** (1978) producer friend Irwin Yablans, infamous sexploiter Vernon P. Becker (**Swedish Wildcats**, 1972) and allegedly William Callahan, musical child star and infamous construction business embezzler who had mob ties and was slain in a gangland killing in 1981. But as bad as this crushed velvet cloaked sleaze was it showcased two tremendous tracks, Gloria Gaynor's *Love Is Just a Heartbeat Away* and Vicki Sue Robinson's *Nighttime Fantasy*. Neither got the Disco chart action they should have, mainly because no one saw the movie, but even so Bonet knew how important the music was going to be to the finished product and spent $100,000 on that one aspect alone.

Bonet turned to record producers Norman Bergen and Reid Whitelaw to compose the music and lyrics for all the featured songs. The duo had vast producing, arranging and composing experience behind them, working with such pop luminaries as Neil Sedaka, Ricky Nelson, The Tokens, The Chiffons, Jay and The Americans and Dawn. They had already written numerous songs for the NYC Disco band Moment of Truth, whose recording of *So Much for Love* (1976) became the first 12-inch single created by the legendary Tom Moulton. The Moment of Truth appeared performing *Love at First Sight* and *I'm Hopelessly in Love with You*. Bergen and Whitelaw also wrote *Bitten by the Love Bug* and *What'cha Gonna Do* by The Heaven 'n' Hell Orchestra, and *Why Do Lovers Come Together?* for Jay Siegel, a member of The Tokens.

They roped in Disco Diva Gloria Gaynor for their composition *Love Is Just a Heartbeat Away* by getting in touch with her manager, and soon to be husband, Linwood Simon who convinced her to sing the main theme song. Gaynor hated it though, calling it a corny and badly dated affair with dreadful lyrics. I couldn't disagree more. The track is a magical delight from shimmering start to tinkling finish and a superior cascade of melody, production and finesse. Whitelaw and Bergen also got Vicki Sue Robinson to turn the beat around with the equally fabulous chug-a-lugger *Nighttime Fantasy* in which she goes the full Donna Summer and fakes an orgasm mid instrumental break.

The Disco sequences were shot at the Starship Discovery One Disco in Times Square. The three-storey watering hole opened in 1977 and was pitched as the main rival to Studio 54, the reason why the glitterati bought expensive memberships to gain admittance to its spaceship-themed interiors. Sadly the place closed down at exactly the same time **Nocturna** went on release so couldn't benefit from even that minimal promotional facet. While *Nighttime Fantasy* was Vicki Sue Robinson's last Disco gasp Stateside, she remained friends with Bonet who cast her in the supporting role of Millie in her next, and last, production **Gangsters/Hoodlums** (1980), ironically the same year Robinson returned to session singing on Irene Cara's mega-hit *Fame* (1980).

Vicki Sue Robinson

A seasoned Broadway performer, starring in 'Hair' and 'Jesus Christ Superstar' on the Great White Way, Vicki Sue Robinson attained Disco immortality for one song alone, the peak-hour energy rush of joy *Turn the Beat Around* (1976). Robinson was providing backing vocals for her friend Scott Fagan's album *Many Sunny Places* (1975) when

RCA producer Warren Schatz saw her Disco Diva potential and asked her to cut some demo discs. One became her first solo release, a remake of The Foundations' 1967 hit *Baby Now That I've Found You* (1975), which made zero impression. Nevertheless Schatz produced her debut album *Never Gonna Let You Go* thinking the title track would take off. Instead, it was *Turn the Beat Around* that would make the grade hitting the No.1 spot on the Disco charts and earning Robinson a nomination for a Best Female Pop Vocal Performance Grammy Award. *Common Thief* from the same album was her next Top Ten entry followed by the cuts *Daylight*, *Should I Stay*, *How About Me* and *I Won't Let You Go* from the *Vicki Sue Robinson* (1976) album. Her Disco version of David Gates' *Hold Tight* got to No.2 and two other tracks from the *Half and Half* (1978) album, *Trust in Me* and *Don't Try to Win Me Back Again*, made the Top 20. After *Nighttime Fantasy*, Robinson contributed *Easy to Be Hard* on the Schatz *Disco Spectacular* (1979) album of dance versions of 'Hair' songs because of the tie-in movie version's release and recorded her final album, *Movin' On* (1979). Cover versions of the Lulu theme *To Sir with Love* (1983) and Love Affair's *Everlasting Love* (1984) were Robinson's last significant chart hits in the Disco era.

Heaven

The Ultra-Disco Heaven opened in December 1979 and London was never the same again. Finally here was a gay club that wasn't hidden in the shadows down some murky back alley. It was unapologetically in your face and the equivalent to New York's legendary The Saint. Opened by The Embassy Discothequeur Jeremy Norman on the site of the former Global Village space under the arches beneath Charing Cross railway station, Derek Frost designed the interiors in Radical Disco style – raised metallic walkways led to three floors of chill-out spaces named 'Cruise Bar', 'Gaming Area' and 'Devil's Diner' – while Illusion Lighting created the spectacular crystal creations revolving inside each other sporting neon Saturn rings that snaked from one Atomic Ball construct to another. Worm lights, lasers, a huge pulsating star and proper air-conditioning were further attractions aimed at a fashionable gay clientele who were pushing the Pink Pound agenda with a 'We're here, we're Queer' alacrity.

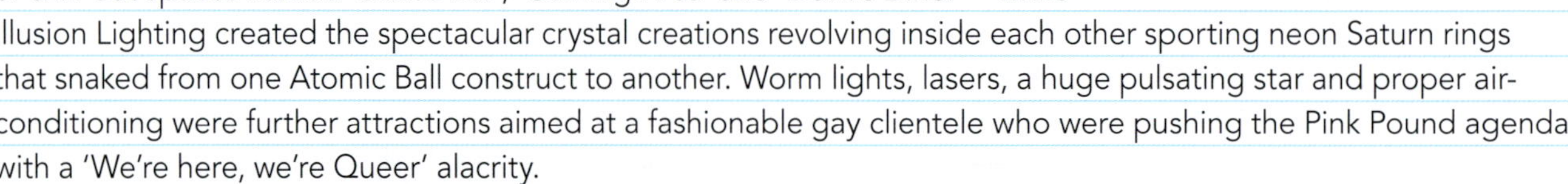

Managed by Steven Hayter, poached from The Embassy, who didn't stay too long and was replaced by David Inches, the DJ was Ian Levine, Northern Soul maverick and future instigator of the HiNRG sound. The first record he played on that cold winter night was *Vertigo/Relight My Fire* (1979) by Dan Hartman, the No.1 American Disco smash, followed by *Deputy of Love* (1979) by Don Armando's Second Avenue Rhumba Band, *Danger* (1979) by Gregg Diamond and *Night Dancer/That Old Black Magic* (1979) by Jeanne Shy. Everybody who was there that epically important night, paying their £15 membership fee, then £2 on the door, £3 for guests, realised what a gamechanger Heaven truly was. It brought gay clubbing into the UK mainstream and proved, as per Paul Jabara's wise words, *Heaven Is a Disco* (1977).

YESTERDAY'S HERO (1979)

Bestselling novelist Jackie Collins had cornered the market in sexed-up trashy soap operas glued together with a Disco beat. This was Joan's sister's third such sleazy outing for 1979 but unlike **The Bitch**, **The World Is Full of Married Men** and **The Stud** (1978), this mediocre 'The Sporting Life' meets 'Top of the Pops' combo wasn't based on any of her adultery-and-duty-free-shopping books. It was an original screenplay, if you can describe this story plainly based on the headline-grabbing life of professional footballer and tabloid superstar George Best as new in any conceivable way.

Rod Turner (Ian McShane) is the celebrity football striker stuck in a minor league due to a problem with alcohol who is persuaded to attempt a premier comeback. With 'The Saints' team, owned by wealthy pop star Clint Simon (Paul Nicholas) who wants to sign him because of childhood idolisation. Can hard line soccer manager Jake Marsh (Adam Faith) help him achieve the goals of staying sober and getting to the Cup Final against 'Leicester Forest'? Oh, and 'Three's Company' (1977-81) US sit-com star Suzanne Somers plays Disco chanteuse Cloudy Martin who eventually saves the self-destructive Roy of the Rovers from his downward spiral.

Director Neil Leifer, who would persist in the sports drama and documentary arena, can't do much with Collins' simplistic scandal sheet script. He basically jigsaws the more authentic scenes, including newsreel footage from the 1979 Football League Cup Final between Southampton and Nottingham Forest at Wembley Stadium, together with the ludicrously elongated sequences featuring Somers 'singing' her brand of Disco Muzak. Anchoring the little credibility this cut-and-paste kitsch-and-stinker has is McShane's laudable performance supplying edgy undeserved grit. Elsewhere, pop stars Nicholas and Faith tread water and, if you look closely, you'll see future **The Princess Bride** (1987) matinee idol Cary Elwes strutting his stuff as a Disco dancer.

As was the trend at the time down-market Warwick Records released the soundtrack containing all the naff Somers songs that were integrated within the plot, other background Disco titles, and some random dance and soul hits that only appeared on the vinyl. Nicholas sings the title song, Somers sings *Out of Love with Love* and they double up for *That's Not What We Came Here For, We've Got Us* and *Let's Work It Out.* The more kosher Disco tracks were a mélange of Europop, soul and funk: Anita Ward's *Ring My Bell* (1979), The Dooleys' *Wanted* (1979), T-Connection's *At Midnight* (1978), Melba Moore's *Pick Me Up, I'll Dance* (1978), Bobby Caldwell's *What You Won't Do for Love* (1978), J.A.L.N. Band's *Disco Music* (1976), Heatwave's *Razzle Dazzle* (1979), Herbie Hancock's *You Bet Your Love* (1979), Bill Withers' *Don't It Make It Better* (1978) and Peter Brown's *Dance with Me* (1977).

Liquid Gold

Talking of the Midlands, Liquid Gold was an English Disco group from Brackley, Northamptonshire, who hit the US 'Billboard' Dance Chart in 1979. Formed by Ray Knott and Ellie Hope, who met auditioning for the prog-rock Babe Ruth outfit in the early '70s, both working on the band's last album *Kid Stuff* (1976). They then recruited Wally Rothe and Syd Twynham for a new group initially named Dream Coupe. But once signed to Creole Records they changed their name to Liquid Gold and released their first single *Anyway You Do It* in 1978 . It was their next release that went the Disco distance. *My Baby's Baby* was remixed by Richie Rivera and Joe Long, and released by Parachute Records, a Casablanca offshoot, hence the heavy US promotion. Their follow-up, *Dance Yourself Dizzy* (1979), is the song most UK dancers will recognise. All of Liquid Gold's songs were produced, arranged, written, and engineered by Adrian Baker who later fronted Gidea Park, toured with The Beach Boys, and wrote the unreleased solo single *Don't Take the Night Away*, that could easily have been ear-marked for Liquid Gold who scored one last Disco hit with *What's She Got* (1983).

Alan Jones in Village People inspired moustache!

Disco Memo

I'm Coming Out

The Masquerade in London's Earls Court Square was the first gay club I ever went to. It was situated in the basement of the local launderette and consisted of two large-ish rooms. One had a minuscule mirror-walled dance floor at the end. The other was where the Alkasura label fashion queens congregated, oozing Habit Rouge cologne, and ate the tiny salad that had to be a legal provision as per the outdated late-night licensing laws. You could only serve alcohol if some food was provided in not so swinging 1971. I was taken to the Masquerade by a fellow work mate at the Great Gear Trading Company in Oxford Street and walked in to Isaac Hayes' *Theme from Shaft* (1971) playing over the speakers. Was it a big deal? Not really. I just went with the flow without any angst, self-flagellation, coming to terms with it or guilt. I know my experience is probably atypical but I never had one second thought about anything and actually embraced the lifestyle wholeheartedly. Perhaps that is why Disco is so important to me because it was emerging as a musical form just as I was surfacing into an exciting new world.

DISCO-FIEBER / DISCO FEVER (1979)

German softcore sex director Hubert Frank/Hubert F. Woisetschläger (**Zum zweiten Frühstück heiße Liebe/ Virgin Wives**, 1972, **Jagdrevier der scharfen Gemsen/ Has Anybody Seen My Pants?**, 1975) was in a quandary over his latest erotic comedy revolving around the misadventures of a claque of over-sexed (and clearly over-aged) high school students. Coming at the fag end of the naked bosom boom when that Teutonic titillation staple, the **Schulmädchen-Report** series, was faking its last orgasm due to the hardcore porno onslaught, he needed something to make his **Lemon Popsicle/Eskimo Limon** (1978) clone stand out as extra special. Casting his eyes around the pop culture landscape Deutschland Disco was big news, Boney M. and Amanda Lear the main ambassadors, so Frank hired director Klaus Überall to video various club performances of established Eurodisco acts to randomly splice into the main narrative. These 'show sequences' as per the Überall credits are shamefacedly edited into Frank's 'film sequences' with such crude bluntness giving the whole hodgepodge debacle a stunningly disembodied feel.

Yet it's one that shines a super spotlight on such performers as Boney M., Eruption and La Bionda at the height of their Disco fame. It was a canny move on future **The NeverEnding Story** (1984) franchise producer Dieter Geissler's part as this change in fashionable direction meant healthy worldwide sales under the diverse titles **Disco Dynamite**, **Teenage Fever** and **It's a Holi-Holiday**, the latter after the featured finale Boney M. hit *Hooray! Hooray! It's a Holi-Holiday* (1979). In Great Britain it was bought by blue movie pioneer David Sullivan who put his name in the title, **David Sullivan's Disco Fever**, and released it on the second half of numerous X-certificate double bills with his then-girlfriend Mary Millington's prodigious starring output **Come Play with Me** (1977), **The Playbirds** (1978), **Confessions from the David Galaxy Affair** (1979) and **Queen of the Blues** (1979).

After an opening credit sequence featuring Eruption gyrating to *Computer Love* (1977), the soundtrack segues into Boney M.'s 1978 mega-hit *Rivers of Babylon* blaring out in the Ice Palace Disco where our main characters dance themselves dizzy, indulge in naked elevator sex and are shattered in their Bavarian school the next day. Their addiction to mischief-making and complete indifference to being taught anything about 'Daphnis and Chloe' in the classroom singles them out as the rebel clique. Leather-jacketed wannabe actor/model Tommy (Tony Schneider, **White Pop Jesus**, 1980) is the serial dater in love with artist Eva (Hanna Sebek) who despite being straight-laced paints her subjects nude. Antje (Barbara May/Babsy May, **Das Mädchen mit den Feuerzeugen/Cripples Go Christmas**, 1987) lusts after Walter (Stefan Reber) who is shagging Brit (Isabelle Dumas) because he's annoyed she adores Tommy, and Charly (Peter Lengauer) is the over-weight misfit in the group desperate for any female contact, even if it is offered by a prostitute.

Thrown into the typically '70s bland and ultimately sexless haphazard mix are a horny teacher (Gisela Hahn, Jesús Franco's **El caníbal/Devil Hunter**, 1980), Eva's stern brother Tim (Michel Jacot, **Eine Armee Gretchen/She Devils of the SS**, 1973), Tommy's nonplussed father (*krimi* stalwart Ulrich Beiger) for generation gap gags – he's the one who asks "Who is John Travolta?" – belated nudie-cutie peeper action and the usual bedroom farce staples of naughty nuns, boozy convent orgies, naked roof walks of shame, swimming pool topless shenanigans and officious blonde matrons in crisp white uniforms.

An example of the toneless dubbed dialogue neatly sums up the ridiculousness of the whole inane enterprise – "She forgot to lock her bicycle again", "That's puberty for you!" – puberty being the punchline to many of the 'jokes'. Also the throwing-shapes dancing is way too energetic and hippiefied, miles away from authentic Disco, and the use of early video special effects radiates a grungy made-for-television atmosphere especially in the La Bionda sections. But on the performance level **Disco-Fieber** delivers the goods for those wondering why the chart-topping acts featured had extended music careers. Boney M.'s smash hit *Rivers of Babylon* was based on Biblical Psalms and a Rastafarian song originally recorded by the Jamaican reggae group The Melodians in 1970 and *Rasputin* (1978) accompanies a classroom boogie session. *Ribbons of Blue* (1979) sees the group dressed in black-and-white performing in a sea of dry ice, and the aforementioned *Hooray! Hooray! It's a Holi-Holiday* closes the extended hang-gliding finale where Eva crash-lands on bales of straw spelling out Tommy's ultimate love message. *Leave a Light (I'll Keep a Light in My Window)* (1979), backgrounding a silly gladiator sex fantasy, *One Way Ticket* (1979) and *Computer Love* played twice put Eruption centre stage. *One for You, One for Me* (1978) and *Baby Make Love* (1978) are the La Bionda additions while headliner Tony Schneider supplied both sides of his one and only 1979 single release, *Candy Girl* and *Do You Remember?*. Two other songs, *Funny Money Honey* (1978) and *We'll Have a Party Tonite* (1978) are performed by The Teens, Germany's belated answer to the Bay City Rollers. Despite being conceived the reverse way round, it's the perky Disco that motors this dismally vulgar sextravaganza and provides the only reason to see it.

Boney M.

Boney M. was dance dynamite during the Disco boom: their unforgettable and unbroken chain of infectiously catchy smash hits still capture the sheer exuberance and glittering fun of that hedonistic heyday. Not to mention their eccentric fashion stylings of wide-legged satin, sequin-encrusted and fur-trimmed costumes, wild hair, outlandish bejewelled headdresses and bizarre dance routines! Thanks to their expert reconfiguring of the basic tenets of the Teutonic Disco sound – bass thumps, crystal-clear production, clean sweeps of crisp strings, ethereal vocals – in the larger-than-life glitter-glam group's heyday they sold 80 million records worldwide and in 1978 their chart topping Double-A side *Rivers of Babylon/Brown Girl in the Ring* became the second best-selling UK single of all time.

It all began with German producer and composer Franz Reuther. Under his alias Frank Farian, the reluctant pop star had some success in his home country with Bubblegum material his label forced him to record that he loathed. So he wrote and produced the single *Baby, Do You Wanna Bump* (1975), taking his cue from the UK dance craze started by Kenny's *The Bump* (1974) and made Eurodisco by Penny McLean's *Lady Bump* (1975), performing every multi-tracked vocal from deep bass to the highest falsetto himself. He credited it to Boney M., coined while watching the Australian TV cop series 'Boney' and thinking "Boney? Mmm!" When the single started gaining European chart traction, he realised he needed to form an actual group for those vital television appearances. Never secure about his own looks, Farian wanted to put together a fabulous foursome to visually punch over the fun exotic image he felt the soulful chugger expressed.

Eventually, after a short trial and error period testing their chemistry together, the pop Svengali hired the perfect mix of charismatic singers and personalities to become the core members of Boney M. throughout the banner Disco years. Jamaican-born British singer Liz Mitchell was appearing in the cast of the Hamburg production of the tribal love rock musical 'Hair' when she successfully auditioned. Marcia Barrett was another Jamaican-born Brit who, as a member of The Les Humphries Singers, had become a sought after session singer and released the single *Could Be Love* (1971) in Germany. Montserrat-born Maizie Williams was chosen from a roster of models at The Katja Wolfe Agency – she assured her place telling Farian she moonlighted as a nightclub go-go dancer. And it was Williams who suggested Bobby Farrell, an exotic dancer from Aruba making a living as a DJ in Holland.

It's no secret that both Williams and Farrell's voices never appeared on the studio created tracks. Indeed Farian would be the distinctive gruff male vocalist on all the band's hits. Much to the annoyance of Mitchell and Barrett who were accomplished singers and felt they never got the proper credit they deserved. Nevertheless it was all four members who sang as one solid unit at every live gig to become one of the hottest properties on the Disco scene after releasing their second single *Daddy Cool* (1976).

Originally Hansa Records wanted the cover of Bob Marley's signature anthem *No Woman, No Cry* (1976) as the A-side of this crucial follow-up. But Farian was having none of it after testing the cut's dance floor filling impact in a local club. After giving a spectacular performance on the 'Musikladen' TV show (the German 'Top of the Pops'), the tunefully nagging refrain topped most European charts. In New York, the prestigious Paradise Garage included it on their influential club playlist ensuring Boney M.'s credentials as a credible Eurodisco breakthrough. Strangely enough Boney M.'s subsequent impact on the highly influential 'Billboard' Disco Charts was negligible. *Daddy Cool* only hit No.11, *Ma Baker* (1977) No.31 and their cover version of Tony Esposito's monster Italian hit *Kalimba da luna* (1985) No.49, the polar opposite of their complete domination of the European charts where *Sunny* (1977), a silky rendition of the 1966 Bobby Hebb hit, the bonkers socio-political *Belfast* (1977), *Painter Man* (1978) and *Gotta Go Home/El Lute* (1979) all entered the pop zeitgeist.

Perhaps Americans were suspicious of their over-the-top glamtastic image – their second album *Love for Sale* (1977) sported the infamous jock-strap-and-chains cover that was banned Stateside. Other albums *Take the Heat Off Me*, (1976), *Nightflight to Venus*, (1978), *Oceans of Fantasy* (1979), *Boonoonoonoos* (1981) and *Christmas with Boney M.* (1981) continued to supply an endless stream of Eurodisco favourites still being sung today in various original line-up conjugations. Boney M. came along at the right time for Disco fame and glory thanks to their unique look and producer Farian knowing just how much Reggae, Funk, Soul, Rock and Gospel influences to include in their amazingly rich repertoire. Their songs had a distinctively soothing tunefulness, magnificent arrangements and instantly foot-tapping beats ensuring their mega-hits got played non-stop at Discos all around the world, and especially at Christmas Discos thanks to the festive favourite *Mary's Boy Child/Oh My Lord* (1978), another classic example of essential Teutonic Eurodisco.

Alien

1979 was a good year for this fledgling journalist still trying to find his feet and navigate a film PR landscape unused to fanboy enthusiasm. A typical overture of the day would involve me calling up the unit publicist (the person who liaised set visits, photo shoots etc.) on a film in production asking if I could visit and do interviews with the director/star/writer. Invariably my request was always met with "Who are you, and why?" because they couldn't get their heads around anyone actually volunteering to cover the movie for specifically targeted publications. Most of the time they had to beg journalists to cover the title in question. That's all changed now of course but although I didn't know it at the time I was laying the foundations for what exists as the genre press today. Another shock to the system for me was how many journalists and critics had no real love of film. They had just been assigned the job by their editor and didn't care one way or the other. I think that's why I became such a fixture around Pinewood, Shepperton and Elstree studios. I knew my stuff and the talent appreciated that.

In 1979 alone I met four of my horror heroes, Christopher Lee (on the set of **Arabian Adventure**), Vincent Price (**The Monster Club**), David Cronenberg (**Scanners**) and Ray Harryhausen (**Clash of the Titans**). And I covered on location **Murder By Decree**, **Saturn 3**, **The Godsend** and **The Final Conflict**, plus attended the junkets of **The Legacy** and 'The Quatermass Conclusion' miniseries starring John Mills. Oh, and **Alien**. I have often been lucky enough to find myself in exactly the right place at the right blockbuster time and Ridley Scott's groundbreaker was a case in point. Some movies never leave you alone. **Star Wars** (1977), **Carrie** (1976), **Alien** (1979) and **An American Werewolf in London** (1981) being just four prime examples of how I'm reusing my interviews from then today and still talking about the finished product on camera, e.g. Alexandre O. Philippe's **Memory: The Origins of Alien** (2019).

THE MUSIC MACHINE (1979)

Saturday Night Fever (1977) got relocated to London's Camden Town in this low-rent knockoff from producers/directors James Kenelm-Clarke and Brian Smedley-Aston who were more comfortable in the sexploitation and horror fields with such popular items as **Exposé** (1976) and **Vampyres** (1974). Based on an outline from Ian Sharp, a documentary filmmaker at the BBC ('That's Life' and 'The Big Time', the reason why presenter of both, Esther Rantzen, appears as a competition judge), his bosses gave him a three-month sabbatical to make his feature debut with the rapidly becoming cliché tale of an unemployed working lad Gerry (Gerry Sundquist) escaping his grim reality by heading to the local Disco, The Music Machine (in reality the Camden Palace).

It's there impresario Hector Woodville (James Villiers) announces a dance competition with the aim of finding two stars to appear in a future film production. To help sharpen up his Disco skills, DJ Laurie (Clarke Peters) gives Gerry some part-time work to help pay for lessons. But his chances against favourites Candy (Mandy Perryment) and her partner Howard (David Easter) seem remote. Much to his delight Gerry gets through the first heat with friend and partner Sue (Chrissy Wickham), but her jealous boyfriend Mark (Billy McColl) issues an ultimatum; it's him or the talent contest. Enter fabulous mover Clare (pop princess, and TV's 'New Faces 1978' winner Patti Boulaye) who partners Gerry like a dream but refuses to enter the competition. Much skulduggery later – mugging, bribery, supposed change of final venue – Gerry and Clare stun the judges and leave their opposition in the dust.

Same old same old in other words and **The Music Machine** doesn't have much going for it in truth apart from location nostalgia. The Camden Town shown, and where many scenes were shot without permits – the motorcycle-in-canal sequence being the most shameless – is nothing like the current tourist trap. Costing £50,000, with £12,500 of that total coming from the Disco owners thinking it would be a cost effective advertising campaign on release, every single area of the club was used for filming. Even the production office was housed at the location to save money.

The acting is fine – Peters, Easter, Brenda Fricker and Michael Feast all went on to career longevity – but the dancing is amateur (the reason why the focus is mainly on Sundquist's face not his feet), the production values threadbare (three strings of fairy lights seem to be the Disco's illumination system) and the direction perfunctory to say the least. Contemporary reviews damned it with faint praise, The Guardian admitting, "It isn't as atrocious as it could have been", while The Observer called it "Oddly likeable". **The Music Machine** did have one major thing going for it. The original soundtrack was actually pretty good and, removed from the era where it suffered in stark contrast to the Disco rammed Top Twenty, tunefully and evocatively acquits itself well.

The producers had nothing to do with the soundtrack – it was considered a separate money making entity. Composed by a group of world-class musicians, whose CV's included recording with such luminaries as Donna Summer, Olivia Newton-John and Elton John, all the tracks were written by the moveable feast of keyboardist Trevor Bastow, guitarist Paul Keogh, drummer Harold Fisher, percussionist Frank Ricotti and bassist Les Hurdle. Standouts are The O'Jays influenced *Let Me Feel Your Heartbeat*, the tuneful stomper *Disco Dancer* (lyrics by ace session singer Madeline Bell), the driving groove *The Dilly*, the soul tripping *Get the Feel Right*, the sinuous *Move*

with the Beat, the steady *Music's My Thing*, the chugging *Ready for Love* and the atmospheric title track. Star Patti Boulaye was the featured singer on *Disco Dancer*, *Ready for Love* and *Get the Feel Right*. Standing up on its own now the film it accompanied is a nostalgic joke footnote, **The Music Machine** soundtrack is an accomplished work and deserves keen reassessment.

Orchestral Manoeuvres in the Disco

As the 1970s headed into the next decade, computer wizardry was forever changing the sound textures of Disco; acoustic instrumentation was gradually being replaced by synthesizers with knobs on and the days of forty classically trained musicians sitting in a soundproofed studio under a conductor's baton were numbered. For purists Disco was all about the Orchestra, the epic sound they made, the lushness of the strings, the perfect balance of the woodwind, brass and percussion sections. The precise tightness and tinniness of the digital technician sounded too manufactured even considering the criticisms aimed at Disco in general. Classic Disco needed the fuller, rounder soundscape and those who could produce it were masters of their art.

Vincent Montana Jr. was at the forefront of the Philadelphia sound alongside Kenneth Gamble and Leon Huff. But while he left that duo to create singular soulful compositions for Harold Melvin & the Blue Notes, The O'Jays and MFSB, the vibraphonist/arranger/composer struck gold with everyone from The Salsoul Orchestra (the stupendous *Christmas Jollies*, 1976) to his own Montana Orchestra (*A Dance Fantasy Inspired by the Motion Picture Close Encounters of the Third Kind*, 1977). Over on the West Coast Detroit session guitarist Dennis Coffey and his long-time arranger Mike Theodore scored a No.1 Disco hit with the *Devil's Gun* (1977) album by C.J. & Co. Before long Theodore was back with his own Orchestra for the dazzling albums *Cosmic Wind* (1977) and *High on Mad Mountain* (1979), the former featuring the stunning evergreen *The Bull*.

Pepe Luis Soto formed the Rice and Beans Orchestra for the hits *The Blue Danube Hustle* (1976) and *You've Got*

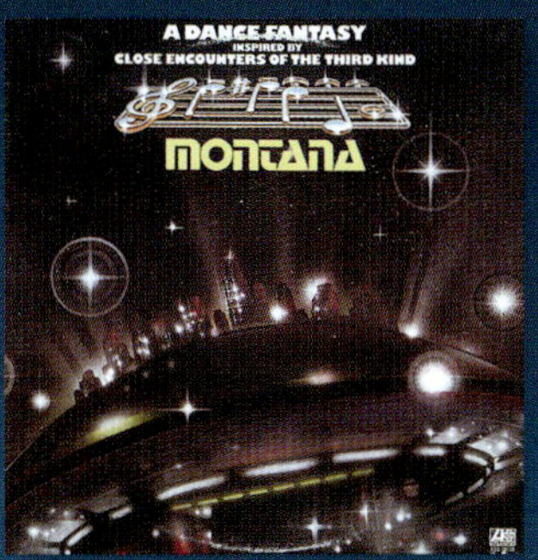

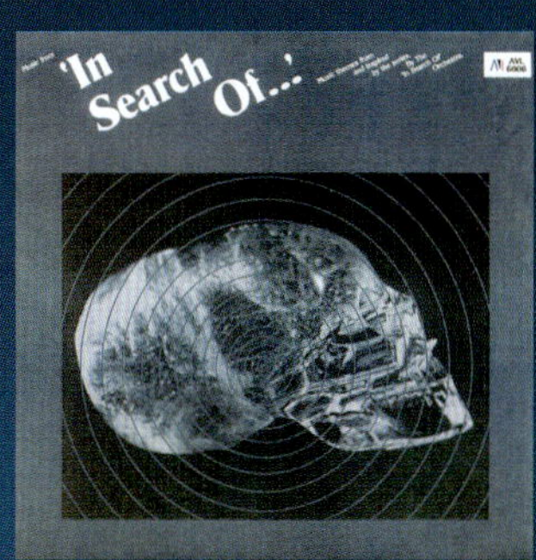

Magic (1977) but mainly to back his wife Celi Bee on her hits with The Buzzy Bunch, *Superman* (1977), *One Love* (1977) and *Fly Me on the Wings of Love* (1979). John Davis and the Monster Orchestra had a string of Top Ten Disco hits with *Night and Day* (1976), *Up Jumped the Devil* (1977), *The Magic Is You* (1977), *Ain't That Enough for You* (1978) and *Love Magic* (1979). W. Michael Lewis and Laurin Rinder put together the studio project 'In Search of' and their only effort was *In Search of… Orchestra* (1977). Former member of The Four Seasons and *Native New Yorker* (1977) producer Charlie Calello had a sizeable hit with *Sing, Sing, Sing* under the Charlie Calello Orchestra banner from the *Big Band Disco* (1979) album. And Prelude Record producers Jesse Boyce and Moses Dillard (of *Come on Dance, Dance*, 1978, by the Saturday Night Band fame) assembled the Constellation Orchestra for the memorable duo *Perfect Love Affair* (1978) and *Cosmic Melody* (1978).

France had The Paul Mauriat Orchestra (*Love Is Still Blue*, 1976), Italy The Botticelli Orchestra (*The Sounds of Today*, 1977), Canada the Black Light Orchestra (*Morricone*, 1977) and Ian Guenther and Willi Morrison's The THP Orchestra (*Theme from S.W.A.T.*, 1976). The Biddu Orchestra moreorless had the UK sewn up but there was also the underrated The Armada Orchestra, a collection of thirty-seven members of the London Symphony Orchestra who backed Ultrafunk on *Living for the City* (1974) but mainly released Disco cover versions on their album *Philly Armada* (1976). *Cochise* (1975) was the exception and they recorded exclusively for John Abbey's Contempo label, also the home of Moses Dillard and the Lovejoy Orchestra (*Theme from Lovejoy*, 1975, nothing to do with the TV series) and The Boogieman Orchestra (*(Theme from) Lady, Lady, Lady (Are You Crazy for Me?)*, 1975).

Alan Jones, Portobello Hotel manager Jane Gould and comedy superstar Spike Milligan. Alan is wearing one of the original Scum Manifesto T-shirts from SEX.

Disco Memo

That's Life

The manager of the Portobello Hotel throughout its most celebrity-packed 1970s years was Jane Gould, who would become the second wife of Robert Fuest, the brilliant genre director of **The Abominable Dr. Phibes** (1971) and **The Final Programme** (1973). For ages Jane wouldn't tell me who her boyfriend was, knowing I'd treat him to the worst fanboy worship ever. Which, of course I eventually did. Jane was the perfect example of a free-spirited Sloane Ranger and I credit her with ensuring the Portobello maintained its star-magnet appeal. She'd turn up with comedian Spike Milligan one day, the next the wonderful Dee Harrington, then Rod Stewart's partner. In fact Rod's back-up band the Faces, would be permanent fixtures at the hotel, and when Ronnie Lane's replacement Tetsu Yamauchi, married staff member Vanessa, the wedding took place at the Portobello. Guess who was the DJ?

Jane's best friend was Patricia Houlihan who worked at the BBC, produced the Esther Rantzen fronted 'That's Life' and directed 'The Big Time', the programme that discovered Sheena Easton. Thanks to her I met Norma Shepherd, one of the 'That's Life' researchers, married to **Psycho** (1960) composer Bernard Herrmann, who let me leaf through his personal papers when I was planning to write a career feature on my love of his music for the Brian De Palma duo, **Sisters** (1972) and **Obsession** (1976). His sudden death in 1975 sadly meant that couldn't happen.

It was with Jane I used to go gambling with Richard Dreyfuss, in the UK to film director John Byrum's woefully underrated **Inserts** (1975), at the Hilton Hotel Casino in Park Lane. At the time he knew **Jaws** (1975) was going to be a great film, he just didn't know how great as he would regale us non-stop about the shoot. The entire Portobello staff went on a Boxing Day excursion to see **Jaws** at the Plaza Piccadilly Circus (now a Tesco supermarket), which was the day it opened in the UK. Still one of my most memorable cinema-going experiences as the entire audience screamed and jumped in unison. It was Jane who also insisted the Portobello be closed over that Christmas holiday period so all the staff could move in and have a luxurious celebration for ourselves. Believe me, there is nothing scarier than playing Murder in the Dark in a deserted hotel! Jane always backed my SEX fashion choices too when I worked on reception, even when some Germans complained about my Anarchy shirt and swastika armband. And she would often get food sent over from Prue Leith's restaurant across the road and charge it to expenses. Such a classy lady.

My life could have taken a different turn had the crazy business idea Jane and I cooked up one day come to fruition. Her off-the-wall management of the Portobello, and the oddball staff making it the quirkiest place to stay in London, often rankled. Why should the straitlaced owners Tim and Cathy Herring (they also had Julie's restaurant in Holland Park) reap all the benefits from the way we were running the place? So we thought we should buy our own hotel and started formulating a business plan to enthuse possible financiers. We found the building, a run-down hotel in Lancaster Gate, we had the name – Pools – and we had commitments from most of the Portobello staff to move *en masse* with us. Two were kitchen staff who would also go on to bigger things. Rory Johnston became the executive producer and production supervisor for minimalist composer Philip Glass, and John Scarlett-Davis, a rock video director for the bands Erasure, The Blow Monkeys and Scritti Politti. Pools nearly happened too, thanks to Jane's connections to Pink Floyd and their desire to invest their enormous earnings into property. A very tense six months kept us on the brink of celebration until the initial excitement on everyone's side wore off. Could I have been another Ian Schrager? I'll never know, but it was a great pipe dream while it lasted.

▲ Top right: Alan Jones and Jane Gould. Alan is wearing the infamous 'Destroy' T-shirt from SEX.

▲ Above: When it seemed feasible that the staff of the Portobello Hotel could open their own boutique establishment, this was the fund-raising brochure designed by Volker Stox. Alan Jones is perched on the O wearing his 'Perv' T-shirt covered by a see-through plastic jacket.

JE TE TIENS, TU ME TIENS PAR LA BARBICHETTE / I'VE GOT YOU, YOU'VE GOT ME BY THE GOATEE (1979)

French actor, comedian, writer and composer Jean Yanne was already a Gallic national treasure because of his work with Claude Lelouch (**La femme spectacle/Night Women**, 1964), Jean-Luc Godard (**Weekend**, 1967) and Claude Chabrol (**Le boucher/The Butcher**, 1970). But when he embarked on a directing career he wanted his work to be a singular personal statement and made it an unconditional point to satirically skewer a particular issue or genre. In his debut feature **Tout le monde il est beau, tout le monde il est gentil/Everybody He Is Nice, Everybody He Is Beautiful** (1972) the subject was radio broadcasting. **Moi y'en a vouloir des sous/Me, I Want to Have Dough** (1973) targeted militant unions and skewed economic policies, **Les Chinois à Paris/Chinese in Paris** (1974) attacked communism and **Chobizenesse** (1975) lampooned society hypocrisy.

Four years later Yanne's anger at the inequality and kinks in the modern world hadn't subsided and his next film **Je te tiens, tu me tiens par la barbichette** took aim at Trash Television just as that soubriquet was about to explode globally, reaching its apotheosis with Jerry Springer and 'Big Brother'. Taking its title from a proverbial phrase lifted from the traditional fairytale of 'The Three Little Pigs' ('Not by the hair on my chinny chin chin'), its fundamental theme is based on the children's game where kids hold one another's chins and stare at each another, the one who laughs first, loses – as vividly demonstrated by cast members during the frenzied climax.

Yanne's send-up of the French television business revolves around the kidnapping of famous TV presenter Jean-Marcel Grumet (Jean-Pierre Cassel, Vincent's father) by anti-TV terrorists. Completely at a loss what to do Aurélien Brucheloir (Jacques François, French TV stalwart and in-joke), the boss of AF4, the first French premium cable channel (which didn't actually happen until Canal+ in 1984) and his financial director Miss Grief (Micheline Presle, **Peau d'âne/Donkey Skin**, 1970) call in Inspector Chodaque (Yanne) and his partner Monique Trechois (Mimi Coutelier, Yanne's second fashion model wife) to advise on the situation. However, instead of finding their man, Chodaque is trapped into becoming a contestant on a terrible children's quiz show and becomes AF4's most successful challenger. Then comes the detectives' radical idea to unmask the villains by staging a big Disco Telethon to raise the funds to pay the ransom demand. Wheeled out to plead for cash are undefeated gameshow contestant Drouillard (Jean Le Poulain, **Arsène Lupin contre Arsène Lupin**, 1962), visiting martial artist David Carradine (star of TV's 'Kung Fu'), variety show producer Mort Shuman (Jacques Brel's English lyricist), local Disco star Patrice Rengain (Michel Duchaussoy, **Traitement de choc/Doctor in the Nude**, 1973), torch singer Ladislas Anger (Etienne Chicot, **Mr. Klein**, 1976), Les Clodettes clearly at a loose end now Disco superstar Claude François had died, and genuine Disco sensations the Village People and The Ritchie Family.

The major twist comes when super-*flic* Trechois uncovers her hidden talents and turns Disco Queen singing *Boogie Lady*. It's a paper-thin scenario with most of the lampooning very hit and miss on such obvious prophecies and objectives as crooked producers, inane gameshows, money power-brokering and cynical advertising (two of the fake endorsements are for Podospray mouth deodorant and Crakpas paper). Very much a film of two halves, the first being over-the-top irreverent cipher, the second garish full-blown spectacle. But that climactic Disco show is something special to behold and features the Village People singing *Hot Cop* from their 1978 *Cruisin'* album to introduce Mimi Coutelier in a red satin hot pants ensemble giving it her all in *Boogie Lady*. Her breathy vocal inflection similar to Swedish Disco Diva Madleen Kane, Coutelier released the Henri Belolo/ Jacques Morali produced song as a single in France and Japan and clips from the film were used to promote it extensively. An instrumental version was also included on the soundtrack album.

Trust The Ritchie Family to get the best two songs in the entire movie though. Performing over the final credits with every cast member dancing on a huge sound stage dwarfed by giant mirrorballs and massive neon lights, The Ritchie Family punch over the superbly catchy half French/half English title song. And their earlier routine equally matches *La Barbichette (You Make Me Feel It)* in tunefulness, chutzpah and sheer Disco intensity. *Forever Dancing* is the Disco version of Marc-Antoine Charpentier's *Te Deum* (circa 1688) used for the opening of every Eurovision Song Contest. Sung by The Ritchie Family in pastel leotards, sequin waistcoats and silver stovepipe hats, the classic melody takes on a whole new thrilling patina in their capable hands. "Forever dancing, our love will take us to the stars" indeed!

The Ritchie Family

The Ritchie Family had massive hits in every banner Disco year and five of their irresistibly wonderful tracks made it to No.1 on the 'Billboard' Disco Charts. "Soul, rhythm, somewhere between the Philly sound and Barry White" is how independent producer/arranger Richie Rome – without the T – described his luscious evergreen *Brazil* (1975) and the female trio he put together who sang it – with the T. This chocolate box Disco revision of the Xavier Cugat 1943 hit was Philadelphia-born Rome's first link up with Parisian executive producers Henri Belolo and Jacques Morali, the duo behind the Village People, and was sung by anonymous session singers. A live group was needed to promote the *Brazil* album so the original Ritchie Family roster was formed from Cassandra Ann Wooten, Gwendolyn Oliver/Wesley (ex Honey & the Bees girl group) and Cheryl Mason Jacks/Dorman. With Rome's lush orchestrations featuring a wall of horns and ornate strings to bring the romantic Disco atmosphere potently alive, the album project also hit paydirt with *Peanut Vendor/Frenesi* (1975).

The live trio actually started work on the incredible concept album *Arabian Nights* (1976), followed by *African Queens* (1977), meaning more Top Ten hits including *In a Persian Market* (1976), *Istanbul (Not Constantinople)* (1976), *Quiet Village* (an outstanding version of the Les Baxter Easy Listening 1951 hit), *Summer Dance* and *Voodoo* (all 1977). The first release though from the live threesome was the fabulously relentless, fast-flowing *The Best Disco in Town* (1976) featuring a 7-minute medley of Disco's earliest hits. Voted Best Female Disco Group three times in a row by 'Record World' magazine, Rome departed from the production team after the *Life Is Music* (1977) album containing the poppy and peppy *Lady Luck* track.

But over the grinding years with Morali, tensions increased, Gwendolyn wanted more family time, Cheryl was asked to lose weight and Cassandra started feeling more like a puppet than a star. It was Belolo who told the girls they wanted to move the group in a different direction and in 1978 a new trio of girls came into the reinvention frame. **The Wiz** (1978) dancer Jacqui Smith-Lee, ex-telephonist Theodosia Draher and The Five Michelles recording artist Ednah Holt took over for the superb 1978 album *American Generation*, spawning the brilliant cuts *I Feel Disco Good* and *Music Man*. Vera Brown Pressley replaced Holt for the *Bad Reputation* album (1979) when the TK-Marlin label got dropped for Casablanca Records but the hits kept flowing with *Put Your Feet to the Beat* (1979) and *It's a Man's World* (1979).

Give Me a Break (1980), their featured song in the lambasted **Can't Stop the Music** (1980), was their final chart entry until Linda James took over from Draher for *I'll Do My Best (For You Baby)* (1982) from seminal Italo Disco producers Jacques Fred Petrus and Mauro Malavasi. One of the Disco decade's greatest achievements in performance, melody and hi-tone production values, for six years The Ritchie Family was held in highest regard in the fickle court of Disco and dance culture was all the better for it.

ParaDisco

SPECIAL 12" SINGLE

What is my favourite Sex Pistols memory? Easily the underground gig the band played at the El Paradise strip club in Soho's Brewer Street on Sunday April 4th, 1976. I still meet people who swear they were there even though I know they weren't, because it was such an incredible experience. Manager Malcolm McLaren had hired the place for £90 from the Maltese mafia to get an early buzz going about the boys. It was the worst dump any of us had ever seen with three broken seats stuck in the middle of the entire dank and dusty fleapit. We had to hose caked on sperm off the toilet walls and mop up urine from the cracked urinals before the band would even use it as a changing room. And with their hygiene record that was really saying something!

I took along my New Best Friend, John Paul Getty III who needed cheering up after his famous kidnapping three years before. We had just attended the Christening of his future actor son Balthazar. And I had two distinct roles that night. I took the entrance money on the door from hardcore fans and conning a few old passing geezers into thinking they would still see a raunchy stripper. I wore my newly sewn, custom-made Cambridge Rapist mask (by the criminally forgotten designer Jean Seal) in an effort to remain incognito so it would be a surprise when I turned up in my other guise as guest DJ for the evening. I'd raided Capital Radio's offices – my best friend Mike Childs worked there and allowed me monthly pilfering visits – for every 45 single and album track I thought I'd need to keep the joint jumping.

It soon became apparent I'd misjudged the crowd of ardent fans, casual on-lookers and freaked-out footfall. These were Punk's early days. It wasn't easy to determine the vibe from a youth cross-section trying to find an identity within a musical genre still grappling with its own. My club tastes, honed by endless Donna Summer nights in intimate all-male environments, cleared the scruffy dance floor. With Rotten and company glaring at me from the tiny stage I knew I had to quickly *Turn the Beat Around* (1976) in the immortal words of Vicki Sue Robinson. I didn't do it without a fight. First I played Julie Andrews singing *Thoroughly Modern Millie* (1967) in an effort to cultivate the kitsch John Waters/Kenneth Anger aesthetic. Punks had a fun sense of humour too, right? That's when Rotten lost it and literally tore the vinyl off the deck. So I played The Tubes' *White Punks on Dope* (1975) four times in a row just to get my repetitive own back. Of course that early anthem was just what the doctor ordered, not Carol Douglas' *Doctor's Orders* (1974).

EL PARADISE CLUB
BREWER ST W1
SUNDAY APRIL 4TH
7P.M-2AM

Needless to say my DJ stint was a disaster. My idea of background wallpaper for cruising was entirely different to what soon became standard conformist Punk issue. I didn't get paid anyway – Malcolm disappeared halfway through the evening with the £240 takings just as Maltese gangster Vince turned up with his glitter-haired moll. They stood at the back of their scummy venue staring stony faced at the remainder of the act making everyone really uncomfortable. A feeling made worse, thanks to Malcolm putting speed in the watered down cocktail dispenser, especially when Rotten got carried away as usual and smashed some coloured light bulbs in the tacky stage display usually reserved for the burlesque acts. Once the gig was over we all scarpered post-haste in one of the quickest escapes ever, leaving Vince screaming at the El Paradise entrance that he'd track us down and really make us pay. An absolutely thrilling, electrifying and unforgettable fast night in Soho.

1980s

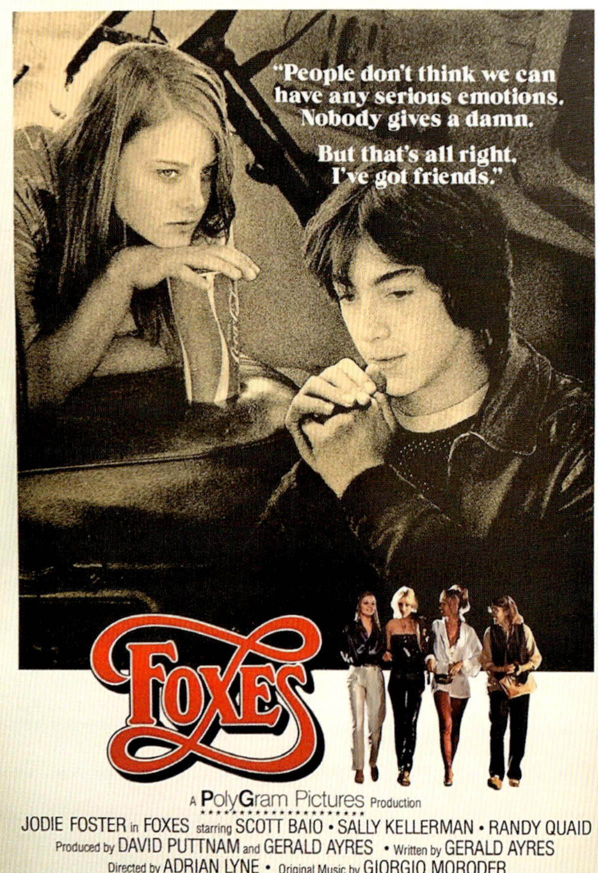

FOXES (1980)

Nothing illustrates the awkward evolution from Disco into New Music tranches better than the feature debut from commercial director veteran Adrian Lyne, way before he imprinted his name on the sexually political zeitgeist blockbusters of the next fifteen years with **Flashdance** (1983), **9½ Weeks** (1986), **Fatal Attraction** (1987), and **Indecent Proposal** (1993). Trapped between two very different colliding eras, **Foxes** is a Disco movie facing Generation X and desperately trying to say something meaningful about the transition. 'Time Out' magazine said it best when reviewing it as "An inverted **Saturday Night Fever** (1977)". Unlike the other attempt at trying to forge a new wave goodbye to Disco – Allan Moyle's dreadfully old-fashioned **Times Square** (1980) – the asphalt jungle **Foxes** looks better in hindsight as a torn teenage manual on boy trouble, drug abuse, and domestic strife.

Four San Fernando Valley girls try to become too hip too soon in this admirable, if contrived, delve into the social mores of a bored youth whose liberal parents have set a very poor example. Jeanie (Jodie Foster) is a product of a broken home (remote Sally Kellerman, concert-promoter Adam Faith) who tries to keep her blown apart life together with the help of her best friends – overweight Madge (Marilyn Kagan), compulsive liar Deirdre (Kandice Stroh) and self-destructive, promiscuous Annie (The Runaways' Cherie Currie) whose father is trying to institutionalise her. Finding a safe haven for them all becomes a priority so they can take stock, grow more mature and hopefully learn from their mistakes. But it soon becomes impossible for the quartet to remain a

cohesive unit as old sex and drug habits and juvenile frailties come rushing to the fore every time adulthood rears its head, and Annie becomes the sacrificial casualty.

Originally entitled '20th Century Foxes' until someone figured out the studio might sue, this is the second of the two movies composer Giorgio Moroder made with British producer David Puttnam – the first was **Midnight Express** (1978), which won him an Oscar for Best Original Music Score. And the soundtrack shows the same schizophrenia as the overall 'Unready for the '80s' concept. Rubbing shoulders with songs by Heavy Metal band Angel, Blues Rockers The Beckmeier Brothers, Hard Rockers Boston and singer songwriter Bob Seger are the funkylicious *Shake It* by Brooklyn Dreams, the Hot Stuffer *Bad Love* by Cher, *Greedy Man* by Munich Machine, *Fly Too High* by Janis Ian, the dissonant Disco instrumental *Valley of the Dolls* by Moroder and, what was to become the signature theme for the movie, *On the Radio* by Donna Summer that would fly high in the Disco charts for 17 weeks, far longer than the movie stayed in the cinemas.

Giorgio Moroder

The undisputed King of the Munich Eurodisco movement is Italian born Giorgio Moroder. More than anyone else in the Disco universe it was Moroder who broke down international musical barriers thanks to his teaming with Donna Summer that led to so many classic hits including the seminal *Love to Love You Baby* (1975) and the first computerised Disco cut, *I Feel Love* (1977). But he had so many other strings to his bow and was a hit-making solo artist in his own right. *Knights in White Satin*, *I Wanna Funk with You Tonight* and *Oh l'amour* scored big in 1976 and his gamechanging *From Here to Eternity* (1977) album seared itself into the memory with its blissfully electronic segued A-side. The album *E=MC²* (1979) had even further far-reaching consequences as it was the first Disco digital recording and the first 'electronic live to digital' project. Co-produced by Harold Faltermeyer (writer of the *Axel F*, 1984, theme for **Beverly Hills Cop**) who programmed the computer system to give Moroder's voice an extra falsetto bite, the *If You Weren't Afraid* cut proved a directional pointer to a whole new musical future.

Other acts Moroder escorted into the Disco charts include Roberta Kelly (the *Trouble Maker*, 1976, *Zodiac Lady*, 1977, albums), Munich Machine (*Get on the Funk Train*, 1977, *A Whiter Shade of Pale*, 1978), Sparks (*Beat the Clock*, 1979), Suzi Lane (*Harmony*, 1979), The Three Degrees (the *New Dimensions*, 1978, *Three D*, 1979, albums), Madleen Kane (*Fire in My Heart*, 1981) and Irene Cara (*Flashdance… What a Feeling*, 1983). Then there were his duets: Giorgio and Chris (*Love's in You, Love's in Me*, 1978), Freddie Mercury and Giorgio (*Love Kills*, 1984, from the rescored **Metropolis**, 1927) and Phil Oakey and Giorgio (*Together in Electric Dreams*, 1979).

After recording *Music from 'Battlestar Galactica' and Other Original Compositions* (1978) there were his original movie soundtracks for **Midnight Express** (1978) sporting the Disco hit *Chase*, **American Gigolo** (1980) featuring Blondie's *Call Me*, **Cat People** (1982) with David Bowie's *(Cat People) Putting Out the Fire*, **The NeverEnding Story** (1984) with Limahl's gorgeous theme song, **Mamba** (1985), and **The NeverEnding Story II (The Next Chapter)** (1990). Moroder went on to develop parallel careers in virtually all aspects of the music industry including the football anthem *To Be Number One*, the official song of the FIFA World Cup Italy 1990, and remains active today for being at the forefront of so many sea changes in the evolution of Disco.

TV Appearances

I've contributed to many film and television documentaries on Punk, Disco, horror ('The 100 Scariest Movie Moments', 2004, Kaufman Films) and movie stars (Jean-Claude Van Damme, Michael Caine, the 'Star Trek' cast). The most extraordinary is 'A World War II Fairy Tale: The Making of Michael Mann's The Keep' because I had no idea when I was in the studio reporting on that film I was being filmed by a local TV news crew. So director Stewart Buck intercuts between me now and then. Here's a short list of my other favourites: 'I Love the 70s' (2000, BBC) saw me talking about Punk T-shirts and my arrest plus Disco music in the summer of 1976. I appeared in two 'Behind the Music' episodes relating to **Saturday Night Fever** and '1977' (1997-2014, VH1), 'The Day Britain Turned Disco' (1999, BBC), where Tina Charles, watching from the Green Room, heard me say she wasn't a very good dancer! 'The Story of… I Will Survive' (2005, BBC) in which I was supposed to sing the Gloria Gaynor song but didn't have time to film it. 'When Disco Ruled the World' (2005, Granada) where I got to show off my vinyl collection of rare Disco albums.

With regards to Punk I've happily contributed my honest and tearful opinions to 'The Last 24 Hours of… Sid Vicious' (2005, Sky) 'My Way: The Sid Vicious Story' (2012, BBC Radio), 'Punk Britannia' (2012, BBC), 'Anarchy on Thames' (2018, Sky), Alan G. Parker's **Who Killed Nancy?** (2009), Joe Corré's **Wake Up Punk** (2021) and **I Was a Teenage Sex Pistol** (2024). The best time I had though was touring University town cinemas with director Julien Temple to answer questions on what some considered my inflammatory statements in the Sex Pistols documentary **The Filth and the Fury** (2000).

THE APPLE / STAR ROCK (1980)

Disco's supercharged hedonism not only survived the first Studio 54 era, it grew in strength and power until it conquered the universe in this infamously epic disaster that has become recognised as one of the best bad movies of all time. Originally conceived as a Hebrew stage musical about God versus the Devil by screenwriters Kobi and Iris Recht, their script ended up in the hands of Cannon Films wide-boy producers Menahem Golan and Yoram Globus, who thought it could form a new cult in **The Rocky Horror Picture Show** (1975) tradition. Their first risqué artwork for 'The BIG Science Fiction Romantic Rock Opera of The 80s' in a Cannes edition of 'Variety' featured the naked leads plugging their microphones into electrical outlets in their navels! But horrendously directed by Golan in some sort of Las Vegas glitz trance as a **Logan's Run** (1976) meets **Xanadu** (1980) confection, instead **The Apple** turned out to be a confused Faustian fable with Orwellian overtones by way of Cecil B. DeMille's biblical bluster.

But its brash production design, po-faced attitude, tasteless humour, OTT acting and completely off the wall crassness is quite something to behold and rivets all unbelieving eyeballs to the screen.

Basically the Genesis story of Adam and Eve reborn as an intergalactic Dionysian softcore sex musical – hence the

forbidden fruit title – the flash, bang walloping begins with naïve Canadian youths Alphie (George Gilmour) and Bibi (Catherine Mary Stewart) arriving in America (it was shot in Berlin) to compete in the 1994 Worldvision Song Festival. But their country folk entry is beaten to the top spot by the underhand machinations of the favoured duo, Dandi (Alan Love) and Pandi (Grace Kennedy), with the help of their management company BIM – Boogalow International Music – owned by Mr. Boogalow (an enthusiastically camp Vladek Sheybal).

Boogalow is actually in cahoots with the government to control the masses with vapid Disco Rock and signs up Alphie and Bibi to his label. But all he wants to do is split the twosome up, sideline Alphie's brand of ballad schmaltz, and transform Bibi into a Glam Rock Superstar, his pawn to take over the planet with sugar-rush pop power. Eventually temptation into the dark side of the music business is resisted, Alphie frees Bibi from Boogalow's noxious clutches and they get whisked off into outer space.

Songwriter and composer of Cheech and Chong's **Still Smokin'** (1983) and **The Corsican Brothers** (1984), George S. Clinton was the man tasked with translating the Rechts' lyrics from Hebrew to English and it was he who brought in unheard of Mary Hylan to sing Bibi's songs. Unknown to Stewart who worked for months in the recording studio until told she had to lip-synch instead. Pitched as Folk being the music of Heaven, while Disco equals Hell, the soundtrack is a superlative example of the spectacularly trite. Highlights are the camp orgy mantra *The Apple*, the dirty Disco ditty *Coming* and the collective aerobic anthem *BIM*, with *Universal Melody*, *Speed*, *Made for Me*, *Showbizness*, *How to Be a Master*, *Where Has Love Gone*, *Cry for Me*, *I Found Me*, *Creation* and *Child of Love* not too far behind in the Eurovisionary slipped Disco stakes. Much of the soundtrack (a freebie thrown at the screen in booing protest during its Montreal Film Festival world premiere) doesn't actually turn up in the movie although over time some cut scenes have been reintegrated into the release print. Packed with glitter, nuns, leather thongs, Hells Angels, silver satin, firemen, diamante, police and sequins, **The Apple** is an unusual example of trying to manufacture a cult classic, failing, but astonishingly becoming a jaw-dropping one despite itself.

Disco Eurovision

Okay, everyone knows ABBA won the 1974 Eurovision Song Contest with *Waterloo*, but the supergroup's Disco ascendancy had to wait another five years. Eurovision through the latter half of the 1970s did gamely try to reflect the contemporary Disco sound to a degree but only four acts managed to truly scale the 4/4 heights. Catherine Ferry's bouncy *Un, deux, trois* came second for France in 1976. Dschinghis Khan's full-blown Boney M. rip-off *Dschinghis Khan* came fourth for Germany in 1979. And in that same year Tommy Seebach came sixth with the hugely underrated ditty *Disco Tango* for Denmark. But coming seventh for Luxembourg in 1978 was *Parlez-vous français?* by Baccara, still the most famous Eurodisco duo ever thanks to their classic lament *Yes Sir, I Can Boogie* (1977), which became the first Spanish act to top the charts in Great Britain. The brainchild of German producer Rolf Soja (songwriter for Claude François, Hildegard Knef and Nana Mouskouri), he put singers Maria Mendiola and Mayte Mateos together, and with co-writer Frank Dostal (The Goombay Dance Band lyricist) crafted some of the finest soft Eurodisco of the decade all with the signature sound of breathy delivery, violin cadences and epic melodies. And yes, endearing mispronunciation of the English lyrics!

A selection includes *Sorry I'm a Lady* (1977), *Koochie-Koo* (1977), *Baby, Why Don't You Reach Out/Light My Fire* (1978), *My Kisses Need a Cavalier* (1978), *By 1999* (1979), *The Devil Sent You to Laredo* (1978) and *Ay, Ay Sailor* (1979). Baccara, in shifting personnel forms (Mateos never felt she got enough vocal credit), remained a nightclub force through the HiNRG '80s with the superb *Fantasy Boy* (1989), *Touch Me* (1989), *Call Me Up* (1989) and *Wind Beneath My Wings* (1993). An anonymous album *Face to Face* appeared in 2000 and then Mendiola joined Cristina Sevilla (her partner on the *Baccara 2000* remix album) for the delightful return *I Belong to Your Heart* (2017).

One-Two-Five

In the summer of 1980 Russell Mulcahy got given a track by the band 10cc, the *I'm Not in Love* (1975) legends, and was asked to come up with a hipster concept for what was essentially a nondescript chugging rock number. *One-Two-Five* – as in Beats to the Minute – was the first track on their new album *Look Hear?* (1980) and Russell decided a Roller Disco theme would be the perfect backdrop for the promo. Who did he know who was big on the Roller Disco scene? Yours truly of course! So he offered me the lead roller-skating role in the video to be shot in Carnaby Street, basically geared around a city businessman having an alternate Roller Disco personality. I did make the case for other better roller dancers in my circle playing the star part, but because Russell was comfortable with me being around, he simply cast my other suggestions as skating wallpaper.

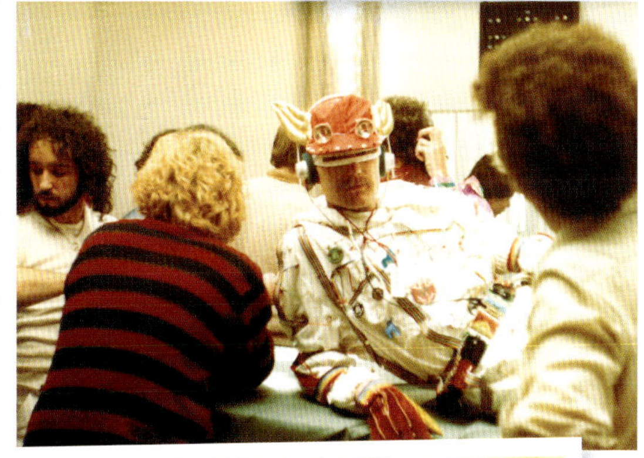

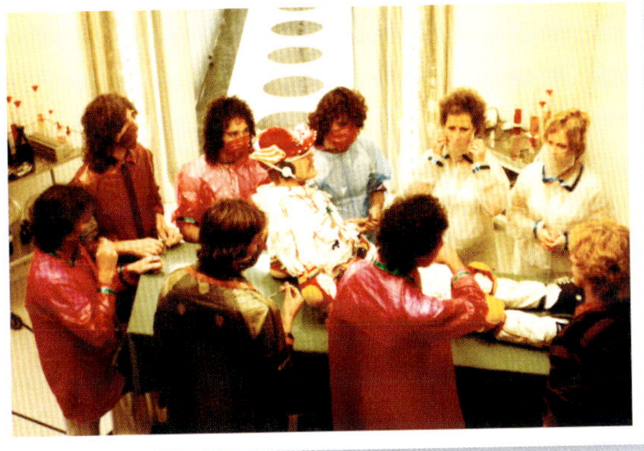

It was a relatively easy shoot even though it rained quite heavily, but I was dressed in a white boiler suit ensemble customised with the Roller Disco accoutrements of the day – whistle, winged cap, luminous skate laces, wing stirrups, flashing armbands, rainbow protective gloves and Walkman Stowaway headphones. I glided, twirled, backslid and danced for around four hours non-stop with my backing rollers in strong support. Exhausting, especially as Carnaby Street was packed with bemused tourists. Then I changed into a three-piece suit for the wraparounds. Cut, job done, and Russell was pretty good at getting something like a performance out of me. Ultimately the video was hardly seen as the single was an epic flop, but if you are lucky you can find it on YouTube somewhere. Shockingly it wasn't the last time Russell would direct me either!

▲ All pictures this page: Alan Jones in Carnaby Street and a Battersea Studio in full Roller Disco gear for the filming of the video for 10cc's 'One-Two-Five' directed by Russell Mulcahy.

CRUISING (1980)

"This film is not intended as an indictment of the homosexual world. It is set in one small segment of that world which is not meant to be representative of the whole". So said the on-screen disclaimer added to the credits of William Friedkin's ultra-controversial crime thriller when gay activists and the right-on queer brigade pointed a nail-polished finger at **The Exorcist** (1973) director's irresponsibility at equating homosexuality with psychosis and stigmatising the entire leather boy scene. Divorced from the LGBTQ+ hullabaloo surrounding the movie at the time though, **Cruising** emerges from its pre-AIDS time capsule status as an interestingly multi-faceted murder mystery in the post-giallo tradition and a snapshot of gay sub-culture moving from Disco to HiNRG and beyond.

How different the contemporary reaction was to **Cruising** considering it had come from a director hailed for the landmark gay outing **The Boys in the Band** (1970). Whereas that significant step forward for gays in film was a direct adaptation of Mart Crowley's 1968 Off-Broadway smash hit, **Cruising** was loosely based on the 1970 novel of the same name by 'The New York Times' crime reporter Gerald Walker, about a serial killer targeting Manhattan's gay community. Additional screenplay finessing by scripter Friedkin was drawn from articles written by 'Village Voice' journalist Arthur Bell detailing an actual series of unsolved murders beginning 1973 in the West Village's S&M bars and derelict piers. Ironically Bell would become Friedkin's biggest adversary in the on-going protest and heated debate that began the moment the movie started shooting on location in the Greenwich Village gay ghetto using willing extras culled from such infamous watering holes as The Eagle's Nest, The Spike, The Ramrod, The Anvil and The Cock Pit.

Friedkin's **The French Connection** (1971) producer Philip D'Antoni bought the property in the hope it would continue their partnership, but he originally turned it down through lack of interest in the subject matter. D'Antoni next offered the project to Steven Spielberg until **Nashville** (1975) producer Jerry Weintraub took it over and again tried to convince Friedkin. Two things had happened in the interim years that made Friedkin reassess its viability as a valid motion picture. He had formed a strong bond with police officer Randy Jurgensen, a bit player in **The French Connection**, who actually had gone undercover to investigate an early series of gay murders (through fellow **Cruising** actor Joe Spinell, Jurgensen would work on William Lustig's just as contentious **Maniac**, 1980). And he also learnt that Paul Bateson, who was a radiologist assistant and played one in **The Exorcist**, had confessed to some of those crimes including the murder of 'Variety' theatre critic, Addison Verrill for which he was convicted. Dubbed 'The Trashbag Killer' Bateson's modus operandi made its way into the movie due to Friedkin's consultations with him while in prison. Intrigued by all these personal connections to **Cruising**, Friedkin signed on to what would quickly become a poisoned chalice.

In a part originally offered to the more androgynous Richard Gere (who chose the thematically not too dissimilar **American Gigolo**, 1980, instead), Al Pacino bravely grabbed the central role of innocent abroad officer Steve

Burns sent deep undercover by his precinct captain (Paul Sorvino) into the sleazy back room world of Christopher Street and its surrounding S&M bars. Donning at various points the quintessential gay uniform of the period – Levi 501s, Muir cap, colour-coded hankies, aviator sunglasses, biker leather jacket – he immerses himself in the poppers, speed and Crisco sex-obsessed clubs of the Meatpacking District to track down the vicious serial killer picking up gay men, taking them to cheap no-tell hotels, tying them up and stabbing them to death after rough sex.

As his assignment grinds on, it becomes clear that Steve is becoming agitated and restless due to his own sexual identity crisis. His burgeoning close friendship with Ted Bailey (Don Scardino), the gay playwright next door having problems with jealous dancer boyfriend Gregory (James Remar), and his growing aggression towards girlfriend Nancy (Karen Allen) – if indeed she does actually exist – causes him to mistakenly identify kinky waiter Skip Lee (Jay Acovone) as the sadistic culprit. In one of the movie's most debatable scenes, which Jurgensen swears actually happened during his undercover tenure, an unexplained musclebound black man naked except for a jock strap beats Skip into confession until fingerprint evidence proves otherwise.

After much soul-searching about police brutality against a maligned minority segment of society and his near resignation, Steve follows a new lead and finally locates the probable killer, schizophrenic music graduate Stuart Richards (Richard Cox). Cruising him at the notorious Ramble area meat rack in Central Park, Steve stabs Stuart after inviting oral sex and puts him in hospital under police supervision. Crime solved? In the very ambiguous ending where Ted's mutilated body is found after that pivotal arrest, a haunted Steve gazes into a mirror while shaving as Nancy tries on his gay leather boy drag in the living room.

With the killer seen throughout the movie in various actor guises and blurred personalities, it's implied that no one will ever know who the real murderer is. And while that could be Steve going through closeted homosexual panic, that explanation might not necessarily be the case either. Friedkin at the time even said he didn't consider the murderer to be homosexual, although that was probably in response to the vitriolic waves of protest building

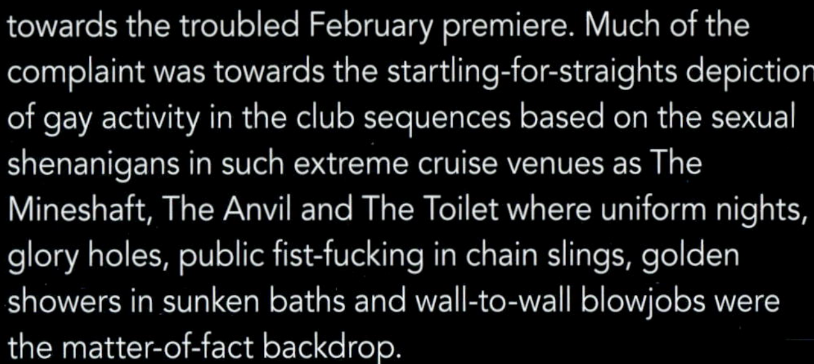

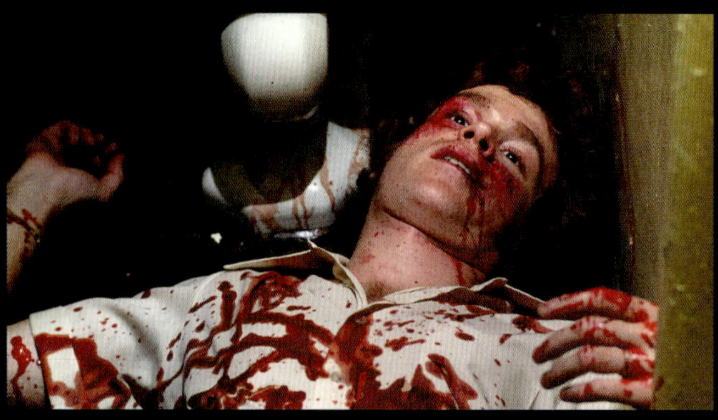

towards the troubled February premiere. Much of the complaint was towards the startling-for-straights depiction of gay activity in the club sequences based on the sexual shenanigans in such extreme cruise venues as The Mineshaft, The Anvil and The Toilet where uniform nights, glory holes, public fist-fucking in chain slings, golden showers in sunken baths and wall-to-wall blowjobs were the matter-of-fact backdrop.

This mind-boggling milieu recreated on screen so method actor Pacino could react appropriately gave a prejudicial view on just one aspect of marginal gay life according to outraged naysayers who thought its negative representation reeked of homophobic distortion. But even though Friedkin cut this reality footage to the bone for X-rated censorship and mainstream taste reasons, the whole erotically charged and seedy atmosphere sublimated was considered a trigger for reactionary bigots to vent their anti-gay hostility. (Incidentally, in 2013 James Franco and Travis Mathews released **Interior. Leather Bar** in which they appear as docu-fiction filmmakers attempting to recreate this alleged 40-minutes of deleted and lost footage.) And indeed in November 1980, outside The Ramrod, one of the key **Cruising** locations (another The Hellfire Club, dressed to represent The Mineshaft which refused Friedkin filming permission) a minister's son armed with a submachine gun mowed down two gay men.

Yet stripped of the fag-bashing furore **Cruising** is quite an entertaining crime conundrum and a fascinating glimpse into the casual sex lifestyle before disease-disaster struck. The absolute truth is that, whether a club catered for anonymous back room sex or just pure Disco dancing, gay culture has always been deliciously decadent, designer dangerous and wildly on the edge of degenerate acceptability. Many homosexuals thrived on their lifestyle's taboo trappings and underground secrecy and Friedkin's movie, despite its numerous flaws, wasn't such an inaccurate summation as the Pride do-gooders led people to believe. Gays got it just as bad from the evil lesbian **Windows** earlier the same year, the nasty poof **Deathtrap** (1982) and the screaming queen **Partners** (1982), but who talks about those today? Frankly I personally couldn't wait to see **Cruising** at the time and many pink pounders must have felt the same way because despite it being critically trashed it certainly wasn't the box-office bomb many claim as it did moderate business. Friedkin's gift for suspenseful timing and involving editorial techniques did help in that regard but, truthfully, the controversial nature of the piece would never have attracted the majority cinema-going public anyway.

The flaws were pretty monumental though and involve the unrealistic drag queen duo informants (another Jurgensen 'fact' insistence) and Pacino's convulsive dancing abilities when he takes to the floor partnering the equally awfully gyrating Acovone. But it's the complete lack of Disco on the soundtrack that is the main problem with **Cruising**. No one, absolutely no one, was dancing to LA punks the Germs (*Lion's Share*), CBGBs headliner Willy DeVille (*Heat of the Moment*) or Toronto cult band Rough Trade (*Shakedown, Breakdown*). No, the appropriate time-sensitive Disco cuts would have ranged between the bona fide chart classics of Gloria Gaynor's *I Will Survive*, the Village People's *Y.M.C.A.* and Sister Sledge's *We Are Family* to the club favourites of Destination's *Move On Up*, Saint Tropez's *One More Minute* and France Joli's *Come to Me*. Despite getting the excitingly correct seedy ambience and posing attitude spot-on, Friedkin was clearly clueless about the music of the demographic he supposedly immersed himself in before the start of shooting. Cruising for a bruising certainly, but not of the kind Friedkin initially thought.

Alan Jones in full Village People leather look.

Gay Disco

The 1970s was one long party for me. It was an era of discovery, of becoming visible for the very first time, of devil-may-care pleasure seeking and of the most memorable musical moments of my life. The Disco boom arrived on the club scene just as I did and the two of us fused together as one. I can't think of any time, event, action or sexual encounter from this time in my life without an accompanying Disco song. And I can remember as if it were yesterday being given a blowjob in the balcony of New York's legendary The Saint club, with its unique centrally controlled planetarium style light show, while singing along with Frankie Valli's *Soul/Heaven Above Me* (1981). Gay Disco was family. It was a shared understanding of everything that celebrated life, celebrated existing and celebrated the wonder of getting up from a major hustle workout the night before still with the mirrorball reflections in your eyes.

Gays, alongside Afro-Americans, Italians and Hispanics, had been one of the minority driving forces behind the early days of Disco anyway. Always looking for the next trend and the clothes to compliment it, the gay brigade has forever been conspicuously at the vanguard of every fashion development. I remember my mother looking at me aghast when I arrived home wearing the first Sony Walkman headphones. "What are you into now?", came the eye-rolling plaintive question! So Disco was in the right place at the right time for myself and an emerging gay liberation culture ready to embrace it wholeheartedly. Especially after the infamous Stonewall bar riots in New York's Greenwich Village in June 1969 had begun the process of homosexuals standing up for their love rights and the entitlement to dance together. That was echoed

in London when a handful of brave souls calling themselves the Gay Liberation Front, startled shoppers in Oxford Street by staging an unauthorised protest march demanding equal rights for Gays and Lesbians. The demonstration was firmly suppressed by the police and widely condemned in the right wing press. But the seeds were cast on that dull summer Saturday morning for the long hard struggle ahead for basic social acceptance and future Pride events.

More than that though, in hard commercial terms it was the first time canny businesses and marketing agencies woke up and smelled the poppers. They cautiously peered over the counterculture parapet to witness a completely untapped and powerful demographic emerging. It soon became crystal clear what the gay community represented in economic terms with their desirability to remain permanently on-trend and rainbow high in every aspect of their lives. Their excess disposable income and spending influence would soon impact on everything from holiday destinations and state-of-the-art electrical goods to seasonal fashion and living accommodation. Disco was one of the first businesses to recognise this new colour of money, and by targeting its music, record labels, camp divas and near-porno album covers with a Gay to Z enthusiasm, the Pink Pound became the must-have currency and irrevocably branded an entirely new focus group.

It was upon returning from Los Angeles to London after my extended period away in 1973 I noticed the amazing difference. Okay, London took a while to get to even the lower level of New York's Disco magnificence. Yet overnight it seemed Gay Disco had penetrated every area of my limited former social life. My favourite club the Catacombs in Earls Court had binned popular Tamla Motown floor-fillers in favour of *You Set My Heart on Fire* (1975) by Tina Charles and obscure 12-inchers like *(All Day and All Night) We Will Make Love* (1976) by Laurie Marshall. Other venues outside the Earls Court gay ghetto started catering to the rising queer population. Monday was Bang! at the Astoria in Charing Cross Road. Tuesday was the high class Sombrero in High Street Kensington. Wednesday was Glades by Embankment tube station. Thursday was Napoleon's in Bond Street. Friday Adam's in Leicester Square, where I first heard ABBA's *Lay All Your Love on Me* (1980) in its extended Disco mix version. Sunday afternoons were The Empire Ballroom and The Embassy Club. Every night meant a different location, but usually the same crowd – friends who only existed as such in the smoke-filled haze under the kaleidoscopic light show.

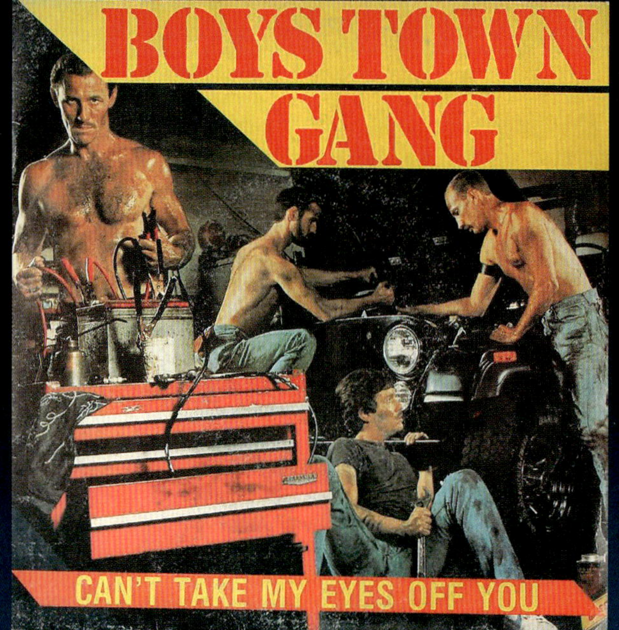

But what exactly is Gay Disco as compared to just Disco music? Is there any real definable difference? Overall the answer would be, not really, even though there could be an argument for all Disco music being Gay Disco music solely because of the hedonism it encapsulates and reinforces and the fact a lot of it is unabashedly camp to begin with. Obviously an act like the Village People is glaringly catering to the gay audience with its collection of macho man stereotypes and hanky-colour-in-which-back-pocket imagery.

From the same Jacques Morali/Henri Belolo production stable came Swiss pretty boy Patrick Juvet and his *The "Gay Paris"/French Pillow Talk* (1979) medley. So the true gay in the Gay Disco description mainly refers to the overall theme of the song (the narrative of why Disco is so fantastic in the Boys Town Gang's *Disco Kicks*, 1982), who is actually singing it (along the Diva lines of Donna Summer) or the wish-fulfilling, bluntly innuendo-laden, often just plainly overt, lyrical content pandering shamelessly to its core audience, i.e. Giorgio (Moroder)'s *I Wanna Funk with You Tonite* (1976) where the word Funk is easily misheard.

Take *Take Off (Satisfaction Guaranteed)* (1980) by Harlow for another example. The vivacious lyrics listed every gay-centric city from Los Angeles to Paris, Amsterdam to Madrid, and promoted a jet set lifestyle that sounded absolutely marvellous to those dancing along wanting to broaden their horizons. It wasn't so much in the realms of pure fantasy either as it used to be thanks to Laker Airways, meaning the Disco Mecca of New York City suddenly became an easily affordable destination. That's where the holy Disco grails were located. The glitterati spectacle that was Studio 54, the epic hustle lines at 12 West, and the legendary Continental Baths that furnished everything from steam room popper sex to chic entertainment by fag hag extraordinaire Bette Midler.

Then there were also the additional attractions of the Christopher Street West Side pier action, the anonymous sex on offer inside trucks parked in the Meat Packing District and the boys in the sand paradise that was the Fire Island cruising community, immortalised by Paul Jabara in *Pleasure Island* (1978). The Dionysian Disco revolution wasn't confined to just Manhattan either. The Boys Town Gang's ear-opening *Cruisin' the Streets* (1981) was a snapshot of after dark nightlife in the Castro district in San Francisco. "Up against the wall motherfucker, you too cunt", being the most uniquely up-front, and jolting, Disco lyrics of the entire era. Gay icons Sylvester and Patrick Cowley were San FranDisco based too, both ahead of their time musically and tragically as they were early AIDS casualties. Standing in the shadows of forbidden love you too might find *I'm a Man* (1978) by Macho, *I Need a Man* (1975) by Grace Jones and *It's Raining Men* (1982) by The Weather Girls. Sometimes the song title just said it all. Obvious perhaps, but Disco was often quite black and white in such clearly delineated straight versus gay matters. It's the reason I never heard anything by groups like Cameo or Parliament in the places I frequented and why straight guys, comfortable with their sexuality, flocked in droves to gay clubs to listen to the less funky stuff. Were any of the acts in the Gay Disco business actually gay? Not that it mattered or was rumoured. Anything could penetrate the gay market as long as the song could be sung along with, frenziedly danced to and/or was high calibre kitsch. Often the cartoon virility or OTT drag queen femininity of the most popular artists was enough to categorise them. But as a general rule who knew, who really cared?

The evolution of Gay Disco into HiNRG was more a re-branding marketing ploy than anything else. When Disco started becoming a dirty word in America (never significantly in Europe where the term is still applied), after the Disco Demolition record-burning night, dance music started being embarrassedly sectioned off into sub-genres. Like Techno, Hip-Hop, Garage, Rave, Rap, whatever, to distance it from its misunderstood status as the embodiment of trash and, yes, in-your-face gayness. All of this took place in the harsh light of the unfolding AIDS virus tragedy too. American straights had had enough, blamed gay culture for ruining Disco, and although they liked the music had to give it a name they found more acceptable.

For the gay audience nothing really changed apart from health and safety issues. Roller Disco had bridged the awkward gap between Gay Disco and HiNRG nicely thank you very much. It's ridiculous to pinpoint the 1984 smash hit Evelyn Thomas single *High Energy* as the start of something entirely new even if it did give a catchy moniker to the harder, faster beat. But Gay Disco songs had always been performed with gusto and relish throughout the past decade anyway so the finessing was more of a synth-pop technological nature. What altered most once the HiNRG scene started being recognised by an increasingly salacious media was that no report on the music was complete without references to either the sexuality of the artist or the listener. But Gay Disco had coped with that finger pointing before and emerged victorious in the sexual revolution it had helped create because it was first and foremost about community spirit.

Freak Out

Alan Jones and Mark Kermode getting ready for a Eurovision Song Contest!

What I thought would be a great opportunity turned into a big disappointment when my best friend, film critic Mark Kermode asked me and respected academic Gary Needham to join him in recording a commentary for the Limited Edition Arrow Blu-ray of **Cruising** in 2019. It's no secret Mark adores William Friedkin's movies – our first ever conversation was about the 'CFQ' special on **The Exorcist** (1973) – and he had introduced me to the director when he was guest of honour at the Strasbourg Fantasy Festival in 2018. So I was delighted to be chosen to add my strong views about the film and its cultural status. The recording was a joy and we made a great trio commenting on every facet of the film in a sometimes irreverent manner but always factual, respectful and insightful. We thought it was as urgent and as exciting as the movie deserved.

Imagine our surprise when we discovered Friedkin was less than keen. But that meant it was axed and he decided to do the commentary himself with Mark, even though his refusal to initially do so was the reason we did it in the first place. Our frank exchange of views about the film was between people who cared about it passionately and talked about it entertainingly. I remain proud of what I said about the lack of Disco, the S&M ambience and Pacino's dancing. Perhaps one day the full junked recording will be heard but as Mark has always said you're not really a part of the Friedkin universe until he's yelled at you and I must admit to a bit of pride in the fact he disliked it so much that we have now become an addition to the **Cruising** mystique.

WHITE POP JESUS (1980)

It's the Second Coming and Jesus was righteously born to boogie! Imagine Alejandro Jodorowsky directing a pious Disco **Jesus Christ Superstar** (1973) and that's roughly the unusual vibe director/screenwriter Luigi Petrini goes for in this Italian Godsploitation oddment that although crassly literal exerts a perverse fascination from stark asylum start to sincere apocalyptic ending. Petrini is little known outside of Italy but he was assistant director on the early works of Ferdinando Baldi (helmer of the Ringo Starr vehicle **Blindman**, 1970) before starting his own career with **Una storia de notte** (1964), in which sexpots Sylva Koscina and Scilla Gabel played love rivals. The only film of Petrini's to gain an international profile was **Operazione Kappa: sparate a vista/Day of Violence** (1977) but prior to that rapist hostage melodrama he had directed another lightweight spoof, **A.A.A. cercasi spia... disposta spiare per conto spie/There's a Spy in My Bed** (1976), set in the world of criminal espionage. Petrini also had lots of theatrical experience going for him because that's where he moonlighted between movie assignments.

White Pop Jesus opens in a mental asylum where a silent and enigmatic inmate sits cross-legged on the floor and thinks he's the Messiah reborn. Played by Awana-Gana (yes, the hyphen is supposed to be there), the stage name of radio/TV host and singer Antonio Costantini, and looking like a moustached axed member of the Bee Gees, the all-dressed-in-white Jesus escapes the institution by walking on water to the southern city of Taranto. There he saves beautiful Lattuga/Lettuce Pop (Stella Carnacina, star of **L'ossessa/Enter the Devil/The Eerie Midnight Horror Show**, 1974), the sister of police commissioner Vito Ragione (Gianni Magni), who also performs in the local band Playboy Smith.

Falling head over heels for her saviour, he obviously can't return her affection as he's on a mission to carry out miracles and mainly attract saintly girl disciples. Causing the neighbourhood Hells Angels to crash with prayer, food to grow for a hunger striker, a junkie to cold turkey when a giant syringe starts dancing in a cave and gun-toting nuns to turn back-up singers, the religious disorder ends at a pop concert where Judas-like acolyte Stella Young (Gisela Hahn, **Disco Fever**, 1979) betrays Jesus and gets him sent back to the asylum.

With the sanatorium standing in for Heaven, the Mafia organisation the Roman Empire, Jesus talking to the Almighty via parting clouds and a giant red metal cross appearing at the Woodstock-style finale signifying the crucifixion, there's a lot going on in **White Pop Jesus** yet much of it refuses to jell. Like the slapstick elements, best summed up by the moment Vito asks a fellow cop to get him a panther, meaning the car brand, but is delivered a roaring big cat instead and the Mafia depicted as useless bumblers in the time-honoured Italian farce way.

But the music and songs are pretty great and turn this curious Christian spiritual into a Disco must-see of biblical proportions.

Written by Italian soundtrack veterans Franco Bixio and Vince Tempera, with additional lyrics supplied by Paolo Cassella and Alberto Mandolesi (a Stelvio Cipriani collaborator), the duo were famous for their work with horror maestro Lucio Fulci, together with **Zombi 2/Zombie Flesh-Eaters** (1979) composer Fabio Frizzi. Fashioned in the Goblin supergroup mode, the trio began life as Magnetic System and implemented their writing, arranging and composing skills for singer Linda Lee among many others. This led to soundtrack work on such movies as **White Collar Blues/Fantozzi** (1975), and Fulci's **Il cav. Costante Nicosia demoniaco, ovvero: Dracula in Brianza/Dracula in the Provinces** (1975). But the trio's fully personal partnership with Fulci didn't really begin until the late-period Spaghetti Western **I quarto dell'Apocalisse/ The Four of the Apocalypse** (1975) leading to **Sette note in nero/The Psychic** (1977) and **Sella d'argento/Silver Saddle** (1978). It was their work with Fulci that put the trio on Petrini's radar and he hired them to score both **Day of Violence** (1977) and his boxing drama **Ring** (1978). By the time **White Pop Jesus** came around, Frizzi had gone solo leaving Bixio and Tempera to compose the quite stunning score themselves. Ranging between jaunty Paul Williams-style ditties, *Vivi!* sung by the mobsters, and rousing pop opera *Jesus, Jesus* by his devoted disciples, to the catchy soft Disco *Unisex* crooned by a desperate Carnacina and the full-on dance anthem *White Pop Jesus* by the ensemble (choreographed by Don Lurio, amazingly the man behind the dance moves in **Candy**, 1968, and Vera Lynn's BBC TV series, 1969-72), the songs are fitting and fun and often elevate what cheaply surrounds them to high performance art.

The national press show of **White Pop Jesus** took place at the Teatro Sistina in Rome where the director told the audience he wanted it viewed as "The **Jesus Christ Superstar** of our time". It played for eight days in Rome and Milan and then disappeared without a trace after only attracting 1,727 paying customers, ranking it fourth from the bottom of the box-office charts that year. For a key comparison Dario Argento's **Inferno** (1980) had 477,103 viewers and Petrini just beat Bruno Mattei's **La vera storia della monaca di Monza/The True Story of the Nun of Monza** (1980) by 474 people. Jesus!

Disco TV

Many television series during the 1970s sported a Disco theme tune; 'The Men' (1972-73) by Isaac Hayes, 'Charlie's Angels' (1976-81) by Allyn Ferguson, 'Baretta' (1975-78) sung by Rhythm Heritage (before Sammy Davis Jr. took over and made it more Easy Listening), 'S.W.A.T.' (1975-76) again by Rhythm Heritage and covered by The THP Orchestra in 1976, 'CHiPS' (1977-83) by John Parker and 'Angie' (1979-80), the theme song *Different Worlds* sung by Maureen McGovern, to name but a few. Many became Disco single releases in their own right by the original artists. Or in the case of *Charlie's Angels*, by The Phillip Rogers Orchestra featuring Oral Caress in 1976 and a vocal version by Donna Lynton (with lyrics by 'Crossroads' icon Jackie Trent) in 1977 and *Theme from CHiPS* (1979) by Corniche.

A few composers turned their tunes Disco for club play like *Ape Shuffle: Theme from Planet of the Apes/Escape from Tomorrow* (1974) by Lalo Schifrin, *Theme from The Incredible Hulk* (1978) by Joe Harnell, *Theme from The Love Boat* (1977) by Key Hano, *Theme from Dallas* (1985) by Paul McDouglas and *Theme from Dynasty* (1985) by Stakeout. Other more famous Disco names would apply their dance nous to TV favourites like *Theme from Star Trek* (1976) by hustle-man Van McCoy and *Kojak Theme* (1978) by John Davis & the Monster Orchestra.

The first television theme to hit the top of the 'Billboard' charts during the dawn of Disco was *TSOP* (1973) by MFSB. A classic example of the smooth Philadelphia sound it was written by the Philly powerhouse team of Kenny Gamble and Leon Huff for the popular black music showcase 'Soul Train'. In a mistake he'd always regret, series creator and host Don Cornelius refused to have the name 'Soul Train' mentioned anywhere on the single, thinking it would detrimentally impact on the show's success. He needn't have worried as the variety series ran from 1973 to 2006, the theme rearranged and rerecorded numerous times.

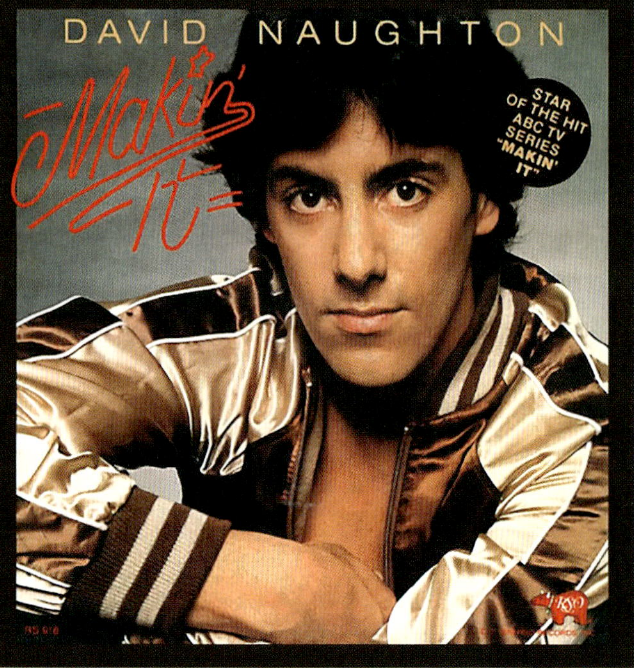

The producers of the 'Disco 77' TV show didn't make the same mistake as Cornelius. Filmed at Pete & Lenny's club in Fort Lauderdale, Florida, CBS ordered a trial four episodes featuring the greatest Disco stars of the day performing their hits. It was so successful the extended series was nationally syndicated and *Theme from Disco 77* became a Top 40 hit for Sassy, a studio project assembled by producer Ray Martinez of Amant fame. In 1978 the show changed its name to 'Disco Magic' after a 1976 track by T-Connection.

Few Disco TV themes made it to the dance floor or the Top 20 'Billboard' club charts. Those that did had an extra special something. Usually they were taken from popular sitcoms adored by the gogglebox millions. Like *Disco Lucy (I Love Lucy Theme)* (1976) by the Wilton Place Street Band, named after the Los Angeles address of producer Trevor Lawrence, *Mary Hartman, Mary Hartman* (1977) by Sounds of the Inner City mixed by Tom Moulton, and *Makin' It* (1979) by David Naughton, two years before he turned lycanthrope in **An American Werewolf in London** (1981).

Disco Memo

Inferno

A pivotal moment in my film critic career came courtesy of the 1981 Fall issue of 'Cinefantastique', Volume 11, No.2, page 45. Ken Russell's **Altered States** (1981) was the cover story and I had contributed one of the first ever interviews with director John Landis on **An American Werewolf in London** (1981), a look at the special effects of **Outland** (1981) and an interview with director John Glen on the set of the latest Bond movie **For Your Eyes Only** (1981). But in the review section, sandwiched between **Superman II** (1980) and the 1981 NBC TV movie 'Fugitive from the Empire', nestled my critique of Dario Argento's **Inferno** (1980).

Marking the first time I had ever written anything about The Italian Hitchcock, I had no idea then what that review would lead to and how Argento would become such an important figure in my life both professionally and personally. Usually the 'CFQ' reviews were written by editor Fred Clarke's coterie of trusted American freelancers. But in the case of **Inferno**, 20th Century Fox had ignominiously dumped the US release, Fred knew there would be an interest in it, and because I had seen it at the Classic Oxford Street a year before, asked me for a piece on what I still consider to be Argento's masterpiece.

It took me ages to write because I wanted to get it right and felt compelled to put across why I felt Argento was such an important figure in the world of Italian horror. I had become an instant fan of the director based on rushing to the far side of East London to see **The Gallery Murders** (as **The Bird with the Crystal Plumage** had been retitled) on a double bill with the sexploiter **Groupie Girl** (1970). I had been longing to see it based on the American posters likening it to **Psycho** (1960) and I wasn't disappointed. **The Cat O'Nine Tails** (1971) turned up at my local ABC Edgware Road on a double bill with **The Baby Maker** (1970) and its murder sequences thrilled me in a way I had never been galvanised before. **Four Flies on Grey Velvet** (1971) I had to see at the Biograph in Victoria, a notorious gay pick-up cinema, but it was worth dodging the cruisers just for that slow motion car crash. Because **Deep Red** (1975) never received a British theatrical release I saw it after attending a midnight press screening of **Suspiria** (1977) at the Paris Film Festival. Then came **Inferno**, which only compounded my everlasting love for my genre legend.

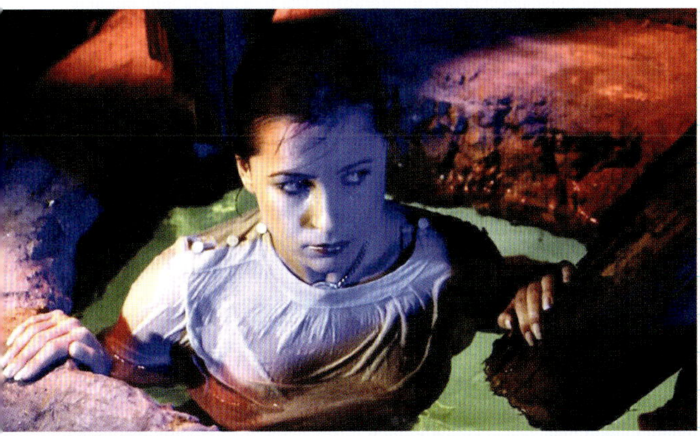

My review sported the headline "Argento's lavish occult thriller gives nonsense a good name" and within the main body I brought up everything Argento scholars still comment on today. "Magic is all around", the underwater haunted house sequence, the unexplainable dream logic, the Central Park cripple death, the Mario Bava connection, the comic book art look and the music of Keith Emerson. It's all there, the themes I ran with through every single feature, interview and book I've written since. This it where it all began and it's amazing to look back now at where my Argento admiration was destined to take me.

DISCO BUMPKINS / MO DENG TU LAO (1980)

Veteran Cantopop star George Lam Tse Cheung is the Peter Pan of the Hong Kong music industry. A popular Asian singer since the mid 1970s, he first entered the Chinese charts with souped up cover versions of such occidental hits as *Don't Go Breaking My Heart* (1976) and *Will You Still Love Me Tomorrow?* (1960). From producing his albums and designing the cover art to masterminding his own career trajectory and concert schedules, Lam is the consummate showbiz all-rounder who naturally gravitated from television specials to films. After appearing in **Money Trip/Ge shi ge fa** (1979) and **The Secret/Fung gip** (1979), Lam clearly translated his pop charms into being a personable leading man. So when the Shaw Brothers came calling with a Disco comedy script written by director Ricky Chan, Lam leapt at the chance to prove his cinematic charisma wasn't a lucky accident and load the soundtrack with his greatest hits.

After a fun animated credits sequence, the John Travolta obsessed Beethoven Jr. (Lam) is introduced along with his loopy gang of best friends Hamburger, Fen and Snoopy who all wear 'Macho Man' tank tops. The country bumpkin reference in the export title translation mainly refers to their complete uselessness and instant loser appeal. For example, one is in big trouble for getting five girls pregnant, another farts like a trooper on a bus in true **Blazing Saddles** (1974) style. But Beethoven Jr. wants to find love and happiness in the cutthroat world of TV advertising. Commercials director Selina (Ching Li) eventually hires him, but the insurance advert with denim-clad, mohawked thugs beating up the actor ends in total disaster. Then there's the car with a swastika on it and the campfire party in a junkyard that turns into a gang war – all very much business as usual in the crass, crazy world of the four **Disco Bumpkins**.

Worth seeing for the tons of footage shot inside a number of Hong Kong Discos of the era, this madcap musical is a patience-tester in almost every other area. While this barely adequate 'fun-filled' musical 'comedy' solely exists as a vehicle for Lam, whose sketchy character struggles against all odds to find happiness in both his personal and professional lives, it is a tune-packed oddity. Only the Boney M.-sounding *Alibaba* and the Village People-like stomp title song really cut the Disco mustard though in a product very much of its time and for completists only.

Disco Hong Kong

Fuelled by Asia's biggest financial boom and optimism towards the impending end of British Empire colonial rule, Hong Kong in the 1970s was a capital of hedonism as Disco ignited the city's hunger for everything new in music, fashion and culture. Pre-Disco it was the upmarket Kowloon hotel bars that catered to the Saturday night crowd. The Peninsula, where DJ Andy Bull reigned at The Scene sector of the hotel, the Sheraton, the Miramar and the Holiday Inn were packed with Beautiful People looking for action. One of the most visible movers and shakers was outrageous gay playboy Gordon Huthart who would deliberately cause camp chaos to make a point about the stupidity of homosexuality being illegal in the territory. Sick of the bouncers always kicking him out of places for indulging in sexual affray, he rented a basement in the sleazy Lan Kwai Fong area, tarted it up with Egyptian design, and in 1978 opened the club Disco Disco. DD as it was fondly referred to quickly became the place to see and be seen. And it changed free spirited attitudes overnight.

Bull left The Peninsula to become DD's resident DJ and its Studio 54 of Hong Kong reputation was sealed as celebrities crowded into the place and the ever-more-bonkers theme parties exploded. In 1979 Huthart became the local Steve Rubell after giving an interview to the 'South China Morning Post' saying, "A good Disco is like a zoo. The straighter people are, the weirder are the people that they want to watch. You can only let so many people in, so if there are too many gays, we'll let in some straights. If there are too many straights we'll let in some gays". And like Rubell he was sent to prison in 1979 for thirteen weeks after being arrested and pleading guilty to fifteen counts of buggery.

In the wake of DD's success over fifty new clubs opened including Disco Fever, Hollywood East, Today's World Disco, New York New York, New Scene Club, Club 97, Hot Gossip, Apollo 18, and Canton Disco. The club Manhattan even had a curtain the shy could dance behind. And 'Noon Disco' became a thing when teenagers turned up to party in broad daylight. Huthart would die of throat cancer in 1996 but his impact on Hong Kong's nightlife can never be discounted. If you understand Cantonese, **Night of the Living Discoheads** (2012), a superb documentary about the era is essential.

Paris Connection

The first fantasy film festival I ever attended was the one in Paris, organised by my 'L'Ecran Fantastique' editors and owners, Alain and Robert Schlockoff. Along with Phil Edwards from 'Starburst', my co-writing 'CFQ' partner Mike Childs, fantasy writer Gerard Lenne, freelancer Pierre Gires and actor Jean-Claude Romer (**Les week-ends maléfiques du Comte Zaroff/Seven Women for Satan**, 1976), I was invited on the Critics Jury of the 10th 'Festival International de Paris du film Fantastique et de Science Fiction'. The venue was the enormous Rex cinema on the Boulevard Poissonnière, just around the corner from Le Palace Disco, the Studio 54 of Paris, and was a mixture of the old and new, the classic and retro, and spotlights on particular artists in the genre.

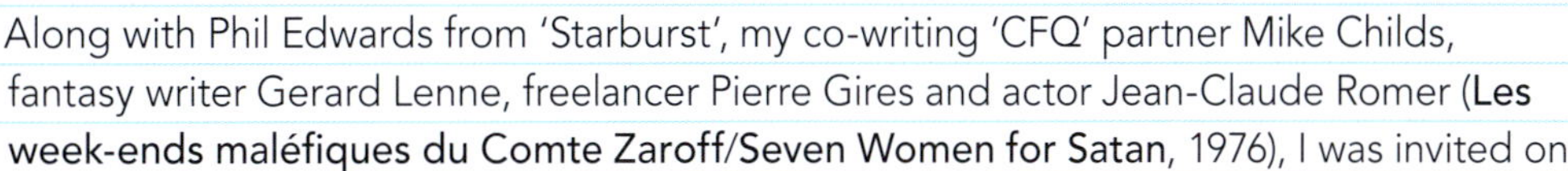

The audience was incredible. The stalls and two balconies were packed to the rafters. The jury sat in the first balcony and we soon found out what a trial that would be because the moment the short tribute to Georges Méliès started the festival off, a cascade of toilet paper came tumbling from the second balcony making an impossible to see through tissue curtain. Not just that but the louder the audience cheered and screamed, the more the projectionist turned the audio up to an ear-bleeding, deafening level. Believe me the only way to see **Deep Red** (1975) and **Shock** (1977) – in that milieu, both a total trip.

Robert Powell was on hand for **Harlequin** (1980), the film we awarded the top prize, so too was Lucio Fulci for **City of the Living Dead** (1980), which Grand Jury member Isabelle Huppert denounced when it won the Audience Award, and Lamberto Bava for **Macabre** (1980), given a special commendation. So I met Fulci, Bava and Antonio Margheriti long before Argento. Obviously I loved the experience, especially as it gave me the opportunity to catch up on uncut Italian horrors – **Contamination** (1980), **Cannibal Apocalypse** (1980) and **The Psychic** (1977) were also in the programme – I mean, what was not to like? The British were repped by **Hawk the Slayer** (1980) and **The Godsend** (1980) by the way. Say no more. It was in Paris and over the next two times I attended the event that the seeds of 'Shock Around the Clock' were first sown.

▲ Bottom left: Jury deliberation at the 10th Paris Fantasy Festival. Alan Jones far right, next to Michael Childs, my 'CFQ' co-writer and Capital Radio producer.

▲ Above right: Alan Jones with 'L'Ecran Fantastique' editor and publisher Alain Schlockoff (middle).

LA DISCOTECA DEL AMOR / LOVE DISCO (1980)

More to do with a successful film franchise in Argentina given a spurious Disco hook than anything truly hardcore dance orientated, director Adolfo Aristarain's clunky comedy crime romance was the fourth in a **Carry On**-style series of five comprising **Los éxitos del amor/Love Success** (1979), **La carpa del amor/Big Top Love** (1979), **La playa del amor/Love Beach** (1980), also helmed by Aristarain, and **Las vacaciones del amor/Holiday Love** (1981). A revolving cast of popular South American actors (Monica Gonzaga, Carlos Del Burgo, Stella Maris Lanzani) appeared in these knockabout extravaganzas primarily made to showcase the talents of local singer Cacho Castaña with cameos by assorted Latino pop stars promoting their latest releases. Think along the lines of the early British Amicus musicals **It's Trad Dad** (1962) and **Just for Fun** (1963) for the equivalent.

Here, Castaña (a tango maestro who modelled himself after Sandro, the Argentine Elvis, to extend his showbiz career) plays Luke Echeverry, owner of the Le Freak Disco where pop music pirates are surreptitiously recording the live stage acts via a carnation buttonhole microphone connected to a tape deck in the toilets. Hearing their stars' latest music on the radio before official release, Delta Records bosses are furious about this dent in future profits and hire private detective Guillaume Beaudine (Tincho Zabala) to investigate.

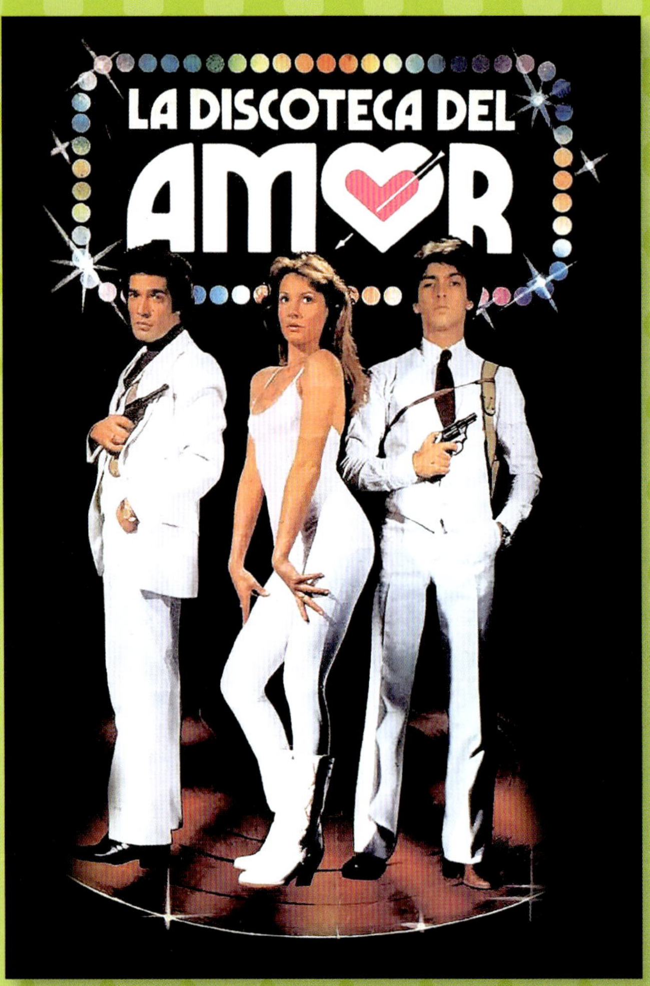

Beaudine's inquiries erroneously lead to Radio El Dorado and headline DJs Eddie Ulmer (future Argentine superstar Ricardo Darín) and Francisca (Lanzani) who co-host a show titled Love Disco. Events then escalate through a series of tacky misadventures, often tinged with surprising bursts of violence, involving a criminal cartel based in the pampas, kidnapped girls held hostage in a pig sty, a showdown in a Roller Disco and a finale where loudspeaker reverb and feedback play a crucial part.

With the villain called Lugosi (Tito Mendoza) who spends his downtime reenacting James Cagney movie scenes on a shop window mannequin parked at his dinner table, and other veiled character name checks to B-movie genius Edgar G. Ulmer (**The Black Cat**, 1934, **Detour**, 1945) and notorious director William Beaudine (**Mom and Dad**, 1945, **Billy the Kid Versus Dracula**, 1966), Buenos Aires-born Aristarain navigates through his classic movie references with a certain seedy élan.

What he doesn't do is play fair with anyone expecting a non-stop carpet of Disco promised by the title. Although the opening credits appear over a slow pan around Le Freak accompanied by *Jump* (1979) from The Ring, it's mostly ballads and torch songs that make up the soundtrack. The neat roster of featured South American pop stars includes Tormenta, Franco Simone, Ángela Carrasco, Camilo Sesto and José José. The Ring had a huge 1979 No.1 Disco hit in Mexico with the haunting screamer *Savage Lover* and *Jump* (also written by future

film soundtrack all-rounder Marcus Barone, favoured composer of David Hasselhoff) was the studio project's follow-up to that global stormer before disbanding in 1981. Cacho Castaña adds *Yo me hacia el distraido* to the Disco mix while the Giorgio Moroder and Harold Faltermeyer produced *Jump the Gun* by The Three Degrees, taken from their 1979 *Three D* album pleasantly underscores the climactic Roller Disco frenzy. This was the first credit for celebrated composer Emilio Kauderer who would endure to score the Oscar-winning **El secreto de sus ojos/The Secret in Their Eyes** (2009) also starring Darín.

The Three Degrees

Formed in 1963, the girl group trio The Three Degrees impacted on the early Disco days before becoming fully fledged Disco Queens in the 'Billboard' charts. Signed to Philadelphia International Records in 1973 under the guidance of wunderkind producers/songwriters Kenny Gamble and Leon Huff, the first song they recorded for the label was with the studio band MFSB, titled *TSOP (The Sound of Philadelphia)* (1973). But it was their first album that same year *The Three Degrees* that put them in the global pop charts with *Dirty Ol' Man*, *Year of Decision* and the everlasting monster smash, *When Will I See You Again?*

Signed to Ariola Records in 1978, they began working with producer Giorgio Moroder and their enduring Disco success was assured when their albums *New Dimensions* (1978) and *Three D* (1979) spawned the dance hits *Giving Up, Giving In*, *The Runner*, *Jump the Gun* and *Set Me Free*. While there have been a number of personnel changes and a total of fifteen women have represented the group so far, the successful Disco line-up was Fayette Pinkney, Valerie Holiday and the most visible of the three, lead vocalist Sheila Ferguson who would leave the trio to become a leading West End stage musical star.

Disco Memo

Argentina

Although I went to Buenos Aires for the first time in 1990 to cover the making of Russell Mulcahy's **Highlander II: The Quickening** (1991), what Argentina mainly means to me now is the Ventana Sur film market held every year in that country's summer in either November or December. Especially the Blood Window strand highlighting all the new genre productions made in South America. Thanks to my active part through panel discussions and meet-and-greets in encouraging the genre talent in that neck of the global woods, FrightFest has gained enormous kudos from the Latino industry and the reason why we showcase such a broad range of titles in our beloved Discovery section. Filmmakers who have become great friends include directors Demián Rugna (**Aterrados**, 2017), Valentín Javier Diment (**The Rotten Link**, 2015), Laura Casabé (**The Returned**, 2019), Ezequiel Endelman (**Crystal Eyes**, 2017), Gabriel Grieco (**Maria**, 2023) and Patricio Valadares (**Embryo**, 2020), and there's nothing quite like the group *asado* (barbecue) every time we meet up.

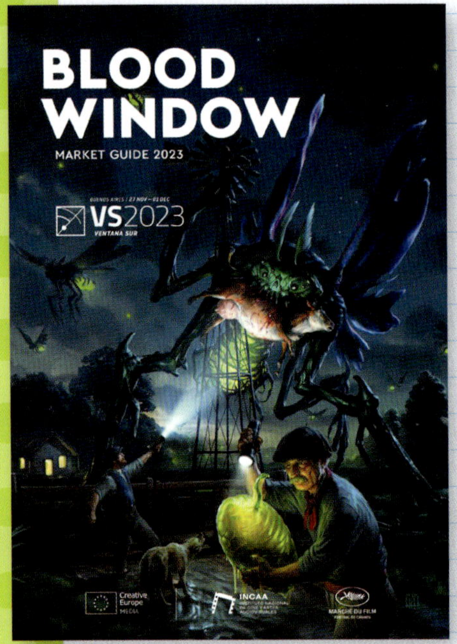

As part of the Blood Window inner circle, some years I pick a South American movie to highlight and personally promote at the Cannes Film Festival. That showcase is perhaps the only part of the whole Cannes experience I actually enjoy. I much prefer the Berlin Film Festival because it feels less arrogant and much less expensive to navigate. Film Festivals are now a part of the movie landscape and since stepping my toe in the Paris waters in 1980 I've been lucky enough to be invited on the Critic's Juries of the most world renowned: Sitges (Spain), Fantasporto (Portugal), FantaFestival (Rome), Strasbourg (France), Lund (Sweden), Neuchatel (Switzerland), RazorReel (Bruges, Belgium), Science+Fiction (Trieste, Italy), Motel X (Lisbon, Portugal), Fantastic Fest (Austin, Texas, USA) and Avoriaz (France).

For the most part I've had a great time on every Jury. I mean, they pay for everything, canapé and dine you in style, assign you personal assistants and ensure you are happy every step of the luxury way. I'm usually the luckiest person on any Jury because I've seen a great deal of the films already. Spare a thought for those oblivious members who haven't quite got their head around the fact they will have to see at least three films a day either at public screenings or on links, the latter something that has only happened in the past decade. Once you come to terms with the stark reality that it will always be everyone's second choice that wins – it initially came as a shock to me that most people didn't think my favourite picks were the best! – the Jury service demands are hardly what you call work.

My favourite Jury was my Sitges 1997 one because I spent ten days with that brilliant three-time Oscar-nominated actress Piper Laurie, star of Brian De Palma's **Carrie** (1976) and Dario Argento's **Trauma** (1993). Our closer friendship during that event meant she was happy to talk to me on camera when I contacted her three years later in Hollywood for my **An Eye for Horror** (2000) Dario documentary. But I have had two other

The Sitges Jury 1997. Bottom row left to right – Canarain film director Elio Quiroga, Oscar-nominated Hollywood star Piper Laurie, and Alan Jones.

more sobering experiences that I feel put fantasy festival Jury duties in a harsher more truthful spotlight. Once I had the grave misfortune to be part of a Jury with actor Seymour Cassel. This will be interesting, I thought, as Cassel's credits ran the gamut from those pioneering independent films of writer/director John Cassavetes to such schlock as **Death Game** (1977). But while accepting the festival in question's hospitality – and then some – he didn't attend even one film screening and at the Jury deliberation insisted we pick one of the worst films because his best friend was the star. Needless to say that didn't end well.

Another instance of the Jury process in ridiculous meltdown happened at the very last Avoriaz Fantastic Film Festival in 1993. This banner winter wonderland event took place in a lovely French ski resort and eventually transformed into the Gérardmer Film Festival. In a year featuring such terrific titles as Álex de la Iglesia's **Acción mutante** (1993) Bernard Rose's **Candyman** (1992), Richard Stanley's **Dust Devil** (1992) and Sam Raimi's **Army of Darkness** (1992), our Jury deliberations boiled down to two hotly contested Best Film titles, Peter Jackson's sublime **Braindead** (1992) and Adam Friedman's **To Sleep with a Vampire** (1993). Er, what?

The one holdout on that latter film was Marc Toullec, the editor of the popular French magazine 'Mad Movies'. I told him in no uncertain terms that if he thought I was going to vote for a lame, straight-to-video inferior remake of **Dance of the Damned** (1989) he had to have his head examined. He tried pleading the movie's case by saying **Braindead** didn't need any more awards to its name, but a clear talent like Adam Friedman could use the high profile and would lead to bigger and better things (just by the by, in 1999 Friedman directed the TV special 'When Good Pets Go Bad'!). Many frustrating hours later I walked out saying my name was going nowhere near endorsing **To Sleep with a Vampire** – and the deserving **Braindead** finally got the award. A great example of the idiocy of the Critics Jury ethos and how brain-deadening it can be. That's the main reason why I have never allowed FrightFest to give out awards, the reason we left the European Fantastic Film Festivals Federation.

PROM NIGHT (1980)

Jamie Lee Curtis inadvertently cemented her Scream Queen title with director Paul Lynch's Canuxsploitation slasher that was inspired by her **Halloween** (1978) hit. And it entered release in America two months after **Friday the 13th** (1980), the horror blockbuster Paramount Pictures chose to distribute instead. Despite getting good reviews for his wrestling drama **Blood & Guts** (1978), Liverpool-born Lynch's career was stalling and, determined to go more mainstream, he thought a Mad Doctor horror might achieve that end. But when **Halloween** producer Irwin Yablans convinced him to pick an on-trend calendar date concept instead, **Prom Night** was the successful result. Securing the $1.5 million budget was proving difficult until Curtis signed on for a big pay cheque ($30,000) and it got the green light. However none of the psycho killer thread was in the script she agreed to shoot. Had she known it would be edited into a virtual **Halloween** rip-off, Curtis now says she would have refused the role of Kim Hammond.

For it's Kim's sister Robin who is accidentally killed during a childhood game that goes wrong between four schoolfriends who swear a pact of secrecy never to tell the whole truth. Six years pass by during which Robin's death continues to haunt the Hammond family despite a mentally deranged psychopath having been caught, charged with the crime and locked away. Now it's Prom Night at Hamilton High, which holds a special significance for the Hammonds this year. Not only is it the anniversary of Robin's death,

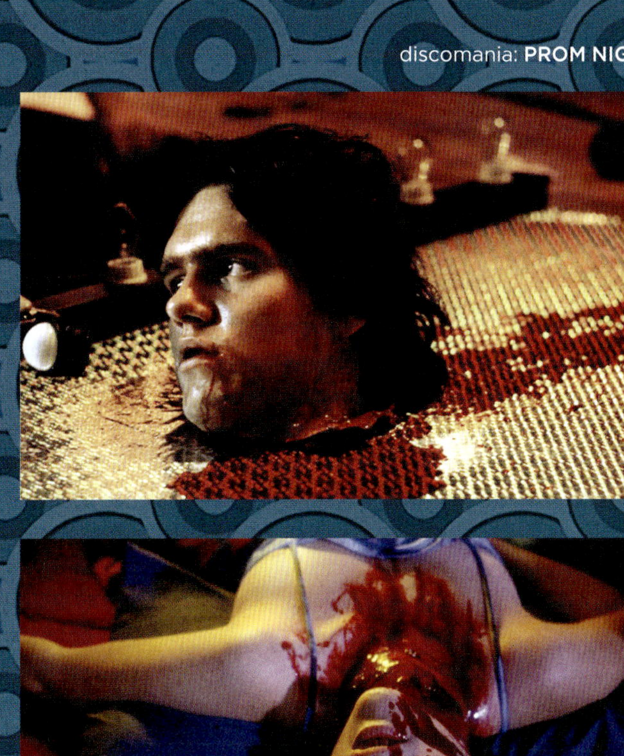

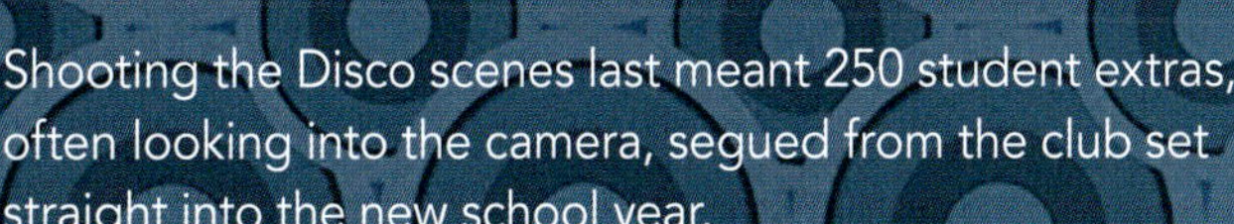

Kim's father (Leslie Nielsen just before he turned exclusively to **Airplane!**, 1980, comedy roles), the school principal will crown his popular daughter Kim and her boyfriend Nick (Casey Stevens) as Queen and King of the evening's revels. Even after phone threats and news of an asylum breakout, the Prom goes ahead in a whirl of flashing lights and deafening Disco music – the perfect environment for an axe-wielding twisted killer hell bent on revenge.

Critical reaction to Canada's highest-earning horror film of its year varied between being too violent towards women to not being gory enough, with the suspenseful campus chase and surprise identity of the maniac lifting it above the average. Many called it **Carrie** (1976) meets **Saturday Night Fever** (1977) with a growing cult responding as much to the Disco soundtrack as to the horror angle.

A month of location shooting during the late summer of 1979 took place at Don Mills Collegiate, a suburban Toronto high school, where the set designers took over the woodworking classes as their HQ. Construction manager Mark Molin got dubbed the 'Saturday Night Carpenter' because it was he who turned the school's gymnasium into a nightclub, complete with plexi-glass flooring and state-of-the-art Disco light fittings.

Shooting the Disco scenes last meant 250 student extras, often looking into the camera, segued from the club set straight into the new school year.

The best that can be said about Curtis and Stevens' Disco dance scene is they at least had a game try. And while shooting the decapitation finale, they and the extras did all dance to well known Disco hits by Gloria Gaynor, Donna Summer, France Joli and Pat Benatar. But when it came to delivering the final cut, it was clear the limited budget couldn't stretch to afford the songs they'd used. So producer Peter Simpson hired musicians Paul Zaza and Carl Zittrer to compose close copies. Classically trained pianist Zaza toured with The Fifth Dimension in the 1970s and Carl Zittrer had composed the soundtrack for director Bob Clark's seminal horror **Black Christmas** (1974). Both would become Clark's future go-to composers with **Porky's** (1981), **A Christmas Story** (1983) etc.

Within five days an entire album had been written, slathered in ersatz Disco gloss: *Fade to Black* by Gordene Simpson, *All Is Gone*, *Forever* and *Dirty Last Night* by the faceless studio group Blue Bazaar, *Prom Night* (an off-key stormer), *Changes*, *Dancing in the Moonlight*, *Love Me Till I Die*, *Prom Night (Instrumental)* and *Time to Turn Around* by Zaza and Zittrer. The latter song, obviously a complete rip-off of Patrick Hernandez's *Born to Be Alive* (1979), got the production slapped with a $10 million lawsuit, eventually settled for $50,000. Four uneven sequels followed, the only connection being Hamilton High, with the 2008 remake mainly featuring dance tracks by Kovas.

Canuck Disco

In 1979, 'Billboard' called Montreal the second-most important market in North America for Disco. Ninety radio stations across Canada were broadcasting Disco 24/7 and everyone was dancing in such famous clubs as Kébek Elektric, Régines and especially Lime Light, Montreal's Studio 54, with DJs Robert Ouimet and Gil Riberdy mixing on the double turntables and playing the backing tracks to any visiting Disco star making a personal appearance. Like the American and Eurodisco music scenes, Canada could boast many keynote producers and global stars like France Joli who hit the top Disco spot with *Come to Me* (1979), Carol Jiani and her No.4 classic *Hit 'n' Run Lover* (1981), Miquel Brown (mother of Sinitta) with *Symphony of Love* (1979) and *So Many Men, So Little Time* (1983), and Ann Joy's *Love Dance* (1980) album.

One of Canada's premier contributions to Disco society came in the logo form of a citrus fruit, Lime to be exact. The brainchild of Montreal husband and wife duo Denis and Denyse Lepage, Lime figured strongly in the Dance Charts with numerous hits including *Your Love* (1981), *Babe, We're Gonna Love Tonight* (1982), *Guilty* (1983), *Angel Eyes* (1983) and *Unexpected Lovers* (1985), all energised by Denis' distinctive voice and a persistent pulsing beat that was the best North American assimilation of the Italo Disco style sweeping through the dance industry.

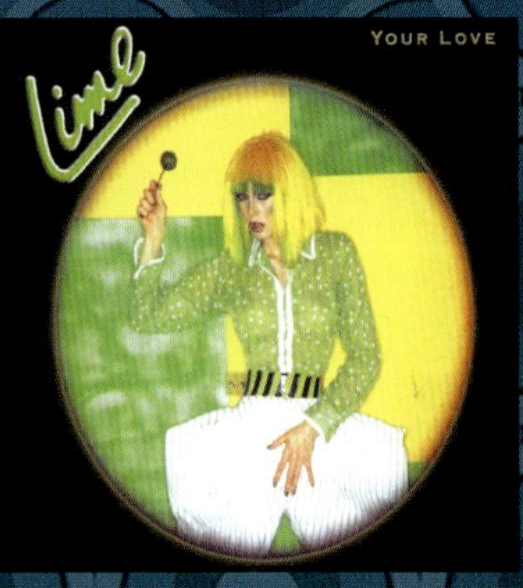

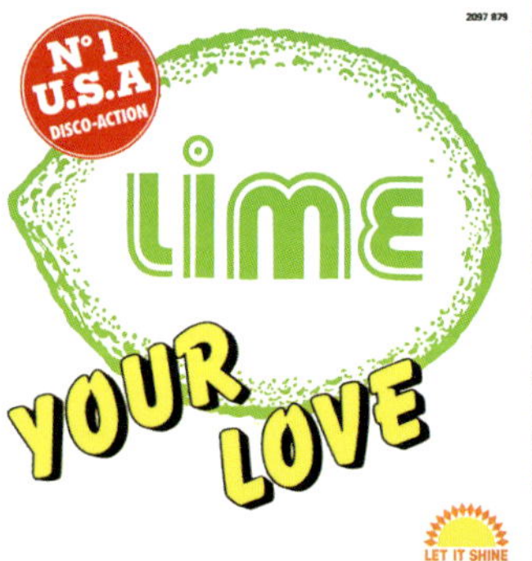

The Lepages had numerous bits on the side too, Kat Mandu's *The Break* (1979) and Voggue, a female duo composed of Chantal Condor and Angela Songui. In 1981, they released their first self-titled album containing their No.1 single, *Dancin' the Night Away*. Lushly arranged and expertly crafted, the melody shone through the crisp percussion and wall-to-wall sound effects with cool precision. Their follow-up *Love Buzz* wasn't quite as successful, nor was their second album *Take 2* (1983), so the twosome went their separate ways. Condor tried a solo career as just Chantal but it didn't work and nor did joining the trio Collage.

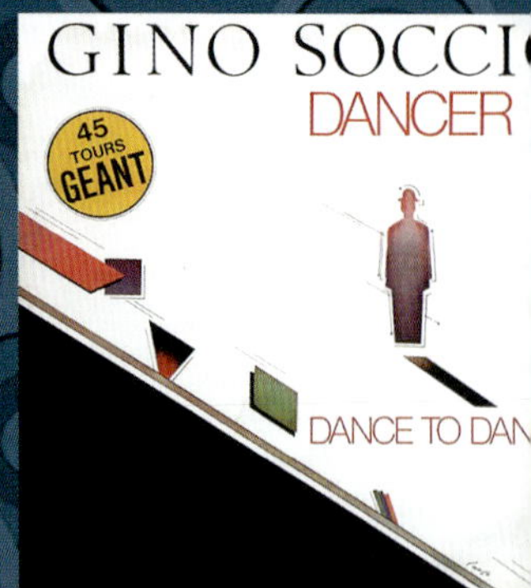

To great controversy, the bilingual singer Patsy Gallant reached the Top 10 in several countries with *From New York to L.A.* (1976), her Disco reworking, in English, of *Mon pays*, a key anthem of the Quebec independence movement. Also in 1976, Toulouse had a No.1 hit with *Lindbergh II*, their club-friendly remake of a milestone of 1960s Quebec rock originally recorded by Robert Charlebois. So too did the first best-selling album *Boule noire* by Afro-Quebecois singer George Thurston, under that title alias, who would also contribute to the signpost Disco album *La connexion noire* (1978), bringing together many of the major black figures in the Quebec Disco scene such as Alma Faye Brooks and Pierre Perpall. And Suzy Q's *Get On Up Do It Again* (1981) was the studio brainchild of George Cucuzzella (owner of the Unidisc label) who produced Nightlife Unlimited's *Disco Choo Choo* (1978).

Dancer/Dance to Dance (1979) placed Gino Soccio at the top of the 'Billboard' Disco Chart and he never looked back. Canadian by birth, but Italian by heritage, the techno Disco record producer studied piano at 8 years old and by his teenage years had begun renting electronic keyboards and synthesizers to use in his own home studio. It was then he was asked by producer Pat Deserio to play keyboards and write a tune for a studio group he was putting together with George Lagios called Kebekelektrik. That album featured the cover version of Space's Eurodisco hit *Magic Fly* (1977) and the Soccio penned *War Dance* (1978), opening the doors to his solo career. Soccio would also assemble and produce the Disco studio group Witch Queen, best known for their 1979 hit *Bang a Gong/ All Right Now*.

The Queen of Canadian Disco though was Claudja Barry who, with the backing of her producer husband Jürgen S. Korduletsch, scored one club hit after another with *Sweet Dynamite* (1977), *Dancin' Fever/Johnny, Johnny Please Come Home* (1978), *Boogie Woogie Dancin' Shoes* (1979), *Radio Action* (1981),

I Will Follow Him (1982), *Trippin' on the Moon* (1984), and with producer Bobby O[rlando] *Whisper to a Scream* (1985). During the 1980s, Canadian Disco gradually gave way to the Dance Music label represented by Candi and the Backbeat, Jane Child, Céline Dion, Eria Fachin, John James, Kon Kan, Mitsou, Simply Majestic and Spunkadelic.

Disco Memo

SEX Moments

Working for Vivienne Westwood in her World's End emporium was always a blast, sometimes a shock to the system, often dangerous and in one instance sad beyond words. How could you ever consider sitting around playing jukebox oldies and slagging off the customers a chore? Jordan and I had a good routine going whenever a bus was about to pass the shop frontage. Just outside the main door was a zebra crossing and we would delight in walking over it, stopping in the middle and putting on a vaguely obscene roadshow for the bus driver and passengers. We never stopped finding that hilarious.

BRITAIN'S BIGGEST EVENING SALE

Evening News

CITY PRICES

Pop star killed when car hits tree at 5 a.m.

MARC BOLAN DIES IN CRASH

Nor did having elderly customers come in, thinking we actually were a Sex shop and masturbating over the rubber and leather outfits in what we laughingly called the changing room, basically a flimsy curtain hiding a rickety stool! Many a red-face would charge out of the shop to our vicious taunts. Saturdays were always a problem as Teddy Boys would often try to break the windows in protest at Malcolm McLaren turning the rock'n'roll orientated store into fashionable Punk. Once I begged Vivienne to buy metal guards for the outside windows that happened less and less. Although being on the inside with insults constantly being hurled through the door was equally alarming.

Often the customers would try and pick us up and offer to pay for a bit of hanky-spanky out the back. Debbie (Juvenile) Wilson suffered the worst from that unwanted attention and at one point was hounded by a very famous Hollywood actress who begged her to become her permanent girlfriend. Debbie eventually worked in the film industry as a set decorator until her untimely death from cancer in 2011. Debbie and I were working together in the shop on September 16th, 1977, when the phone rang to tell us Marc Bolan from T. Rex had died in a car crash. For some reason the calls kept coming in from tearful fans and friends wanting to talk to us about the tragic event and to this day I can't fathom out why that was. That was the day SEX turned into a Samaritans hotline and provided a service above and beyond what we had signed up for.

▲ Above left: Vivienne Westwood filmed inside SEX by the BBC in 1977.

FAME (1980)

Inspired by the smash hit musical 'A Chorus Line', producer David De Silva hired playwright Christopher Gore to write a similar screenplay about performers chasing their showbiz dreams and having to deal with the cruel realities of the gypsy profession. Once hired to direct by MGM, Alan Parker used his blockbuster **Midnight Express** (1978) biopic collateral to insist on a rewrite to make the concept even darker in tone. He also changed the title 'Hot Lunch' to **Fame** in honour of the David Bowie 1975 album, after seeing a porno movie using the same name. The first film in Oscar history to have two songs nominated in the Best Song category – the winning title theme and *Out Here on My Own* – **Fame** quickly became the poster boy for the smoky light shaft MTV aesthetic that would soon conquer the ever-more ubiquitous visual world.

Four years in the lives of a group of teenage students attending Manhattan's High School for the Performing Arts are put under the unforgiving microscope in this hugely entertaining and gripping musical drama. Within that period are the initial audition process, three successive freshman, sophomore and junior years where they learn dance, musicianship and lighting, and finally graduation. Montgomery MacNeil (Paul McCrane) is the sensitive gay actor, Doris Finsecker (Maureen Teefy) the shy Jewish girl, Raul Garcia (Barry Miller) the wannabe stand-up comic, Bruno Martelli (Lee Curreri) the aspiring electronic keyboardist, Coco Hernandez (Irene Cara) the determined solo singer, Lisa Monroe (Laura Dean) the talented but uninterested dancer, and Leroy Johnson (Gene Anthony Ray) the street dancing genius. Their trials and tribulations as they multi-culturally interact,

Still as fresh sounding, joyous and vibrant today as it ever was, the **Fame** soundtrack is a pop culture benchmark for the ages. The film was also the first to include a visit to an audience participation late night event of **The Rocky Horror Picture Show** (1975) phenomenon so Doris could be shown coming out of her shell doing the Time Warp dance. It also put Leroy on roller skates so he could dash between classes. **Sparkle** (1976) star Irene Cara would go on to sing the equally popular Disco anthem *Flashdance… What a Feeling* (1983)

romance and grow up together are counterpointed by the symbolic heads of each department: dance teacher Miss Berg (Joanna Merlin); music teacher Mr. Shorofsky (Albert Hague), drama coach Mr. Farrell (Jim Moody) and put-upon Mrs. Sherwood (Anne Meara) who oversees her students' academic progress. Despite Parker being more interested in the frantic production numbers rather than the narrative subtleties, **Fame** is a characterful, pacy and rich view of the microcosm that was Disco New York with Afro-Americans, Puerto Ricans, homosexuals, uptown and downtown personalities honing their individual talents to make it in the cutthroat showbiz world.

Before Michael Gore was hired to write most of the songs (no relation to Christopher, but brother to *It's My Party*, 1963, Lesley who co-wrote two), Parker had asked his **Midnight Express** composer Giorgio Moroder to do the honours. Like Jeff Lynne, lead performer of the Electric Light Orchestra, his second choice, Moroder declined. Just as well. Not only did Gore contribute one of the most iconic Disco numbers of all time with the title song, (lyrics by Dean Pitchford) based on the beats of Donna Summer's *Hot Stuff* (1979) – the track danced to in the street scene because he hadn't composed it yet – he also wrote *Out Here on My Own* (lyrics by Lesley) and *Hot Lunch Jam* (ditto) all with vocals by Irene Cara, *Red Light* by Linda Clifford, and the spine-tingling anthem finale *I Sing the Body Electric* sung by the entire company. During his audition, Paul McCrane performed an original song he had written, *Is It Okay If I Call You Mine?* and once cast Parker speedily included it in the film. McCrane's other song, *Dogs in the Yard*, came courtesy of Dominic Bugatti and Frank Musker, the writers of *Woman in Love* (1978) for The Three Degrees.

from **Flashdance** (1983), but refused to reprise her Coco character in the far more successful TV series spin-off (1982-87) in order to pursue a recording career. But Gene Anthony Ray, Lee Curreri, Albert Hague and Debbie Allen did take up the series offer, spawning a media franchise encompassing stage musical adaptations and a dumbed-down 2009 remake.

Gypsy Lady

The Miss New York State titleholder in 1966 didn't need **Fame** to start her career because Linda Clifford was already a Disco star three years prior to the movie highlighting her sophisticated vocal delivery. A former member of the Jericho Jazz Singers, Clifford had an alternate career as a film actress playing minor roles in **The Boston Strangler** (1968), **Coogan's Bluff** (1968) and **Sweet Charity** (1969). But with her film career going nowhere she decided to concentrate on singing and formed her own group, Linda & The Trade Winds. Moving solo to Curtis Mayfield's Curtom Records, she released her first album, *Linda* (1977) from which *From Now On* and *You Can Do It* climbed into the Disco Top 30. The former track became famous for being played twice every hour on every major radio station in New York.

Clifford's recording of the song she loved the most in **Sweet Charity**, *If My Friends Could See Me Now* (1978) became her first Disco No.1. The track was taken from her second album, which also put *Runaway Love* and *Gypsy Lady* in the charts, followed by the Simon and Garfunkel cover *Bridge Over Troubled Water* and *Don't Give Up*, both from the 1979 album *Let Me Be Your Woman*. All the cuts from the *Here's My Love* (1979) album found erratic Disco play but then came *Red Light* from **Fame** and another notch on her No.1 belt was marked. Further No.1 smashes came courtesy of *Shoot Your Best Shot* and *It Don't Hurt No More* from the *I'm Yours* (1980) album, and *Don't Come Crying to Me* and *Let It Ride* from the *I'll Keep Loving You* (1982) album. Clifford's personal favourite song comes from that latter album, but *All the Man That I Need*, which was written by the Gore/Pitchford duo, would have its finest moment in 1990 when sung by Whitney Houston.

Disco Memo

Parker Pose-y

Alan Parker, behind the scenes on *Fame* (1980).

I didn't meet director Alan Parker until **The Commitments** (1991) when I was assigned to interview him for Sky Movies. Naturally I grabbed the chance to discuss **Fame** and while he generally towed the PR party line about his crowd-pleasing adaptation of Roddy Doyle's Soul band novel, he did say one thing about the two not-so-dissimilar movies I've always thought was interesting. Basically he said the main difference was that while his actors in **The Commitments** were grateful for the roles and were happy they had even made it through the audition process, the main leads in **Fame** expected to become famous. There was never any doubt in their minds that this was their stepping stone to the big time and vast fortunes. Parker told me he found their unshakeable driven belief quite hard to live with and it often got in the way of their performances.

▲ The cast of *The Commitments* (1991).

With the luxury of hindsight **Fame** seems to have set in stone the behaviour pattern for all future Reality TV stars. Because there is one thing I've learnt in this film journalism business game and that's the lesser the star, the bigger pain they are. I've interviewed everyone from Mel Gibson, Tom Hanks, Will Smith, Sally Field and Kevin Costner to Mel Brooks, Mike Myers, Johnny Depp, Stockard Channing and Sylvester Stallone and because they are secure in their talent they were a delight to talk to. The same cannot be said of famous-for-fifteen-minutes TV series stars who think they are bigger than the show they are in and soon find out that's not the case when it's all over. No names but I'm like a vampire slayer when it comes to them!

CAN'T STOP THE MUSIC (1980)

Through the forgiving mists of time this shamelessly dishonest Village People biopic can now be seen as a charming, effusive, idiotic snapshot of the few nano-seconds in the gay rights movement where it really did appear there was nothing but smooth sailing ahead towards acceptance and freedom. But that was before the brand of Disco the sextet sensation forged fell off a cliff, AIDS emerged and the Moral Majority annexed American politics.

Can't Stop the Music was never as bad as the scathing reviews made out. It was devised as pure entertainment in the great MGM musical tradition – it even featured stars from that Golden Era – and got criticised mainly for being the exact kind of formula fluff the Disco Sucks mob were so dead set against. I liked it then, I like it more now, and to paraphrase Gypsy Rose Lee's kid sister June Havoc, it's "Judy Garland at Carnegie Hall" with a Disco beat.

In 1978 the two things you couldn't get away from were the Village People's earworm hit *Y.M.C.A.* and the musical phenomenon **Grease**. So Allan Carr, the eccentric mink kaftan draped producer of the latter, thought a musical starring the former would be a no-brainer blockbuster. Quick as a flash he brought in his **Grease** co-writer Bronte Woodard – "A teenaged Tennessee Williams!" – to pen a screenplay under the title 'Discoland: Where the Music Never Ends!', raised the extravagant $20 million budget, hired director Nancy Walker, Rhoda's mother from the same-titled 1974-78 sitcom, making her feature debut, and cast Steve Guttenberg – "The next John Travolta!" – alongside hot **Superman** (1978) star Valerie Perrine and the Village People.

Jack Morell (Guttenberg), a thinly veiled Jacques Morali, the Village People's French producer, is a down-on-his luck New York City composer looking for that one elusive big break. So his friend Samantha (Perrine) – "The Garbo of models!" – cruises the streets of Manhattan after a "Baskin-Robbins sugar rush!" – and rounds up construction worker David (Hodo), cowboy Randy (Jones), soldier Alexander (Briley), biker leatherman Glenn (Hughes), Indian Chief Felipe (Rose) and cop Ray (Simpson) to do justice to Jack's music. Model agency magnate Sydne (Tammy Grimes in OTT drag-queen mode), Jack's mother Helen (Havoc) and muscleman Ron (Olympic decathlon champion Bruce, now Caitlyn, Jenner) all help the group, dressed up in their fantasy macho regalia, to become a world success at a gala concert in San Francisco's hip venue The Galleria.

Ray Simpson took over the cop role originally intended for Victor Willis, who quit the group as lead vocalist during pre-production because he hated the incessant gay innuendo following him around, hated the script (but then, all the Village People did) and only stuck around because he wanted his wife, Disco star Phylicia Allen/Rashad,

written into the film as his girlfriend. Altovise Davis, Mrs. Sammy Davis Jr, took over her role when he walked out, joining Carr's insisted upon ethos – a camp strata of old Hollywood and Broadway actresses, also including Barbara Rush, Leigh Taylor-Young and Marilyn Sokol.

Directed by Walker as a post-modern Busby Berkeley/ *Let's Put on a Show* breathless frolic, complete with Arlene (Hot Gossip) Phillips' choreography veering between gym bunny exercises, Esther Williams formation diving and Pan's People glitz, **Can't Stop the Music** was far too expensive, far too coy, far too much and yet not really enough. The Village People's hardcore gay audience resented it because it painted their Christopher Street heroes in heterosexual colours. Unless you were hip to the subtext (the red handkerchief in the Leatherman's left pocket meaning fist-fucking) or the double-entendre dialogue (Helen to Jack: "It's your music that's bringing all these talented boys together, they ought to get down on their knees") then the group had sold out to the female teenybopper demographic who embraced their music in the wake of *Go West* (1979) and *In the Navy* (1979). They clearly knew nothing about **New York City Inferno** (1978), the gay hardcore movie directed by Jacques Scandelari, the first film to feature officially-licensed songs by the Village People from Can't Stop Productions, *Macho Man* (1978) and *I Am What I Am* (1978), no, not that one!

Yet there is a lot to enjoy now in this camp catastrophe as the brassy showbiz knowingness and the aspic-trapped gay in-jokes sparkle with a sweet, rose-coloured innocence. When Samantha needs a pep talk, Jack says, "Anybody who could swallow two Sno-Balls and a Ding Dong shouldn't have any trouble with pride!" Despite Walker and Perrine not getting along during the shoot she's actually very endearing and when her character utters the line, "This is the '80s! You're going to see a lot of things you've never seen before", you get caught up in the moment and tend to believe it.

Capturing the Village People at the height of their fame and performance quality is no bad thing either. The essential problem though is in trying to please everyone, Carr and his blinkered company failed to please anyone with their commercial safety net.

Except the soundtrack is a 501 Disco delight with the Village People on top form on the still wonderful title song, *Liberation*, *Milkshake* (the commercial slot sporting costumes by Theoni V. Aldredge), *Magic Night* and *I Love You to Death*. The Ritchie Family chimes in with *Give Me a Break* and *Sophistication* and David London (in reality Dennis Hardy Frederiksen) sets the opening scene with *The Sound of the City* (accompanying obvious Guttenberg body double Garry Kluger roller-skating through Greenwich Village). London also sings the punchy *Samantha*, an ode to Perrine's perpetually optimistic character.

Can't Stop the Music was an instant flop the moment it opened. No one wanted to know in the declining Disco days and the critical response was devastating, ranging from "You really can't stop the music, no matter how much you want to" ('New West') to "The Village People should consider renaming themselves the Village Idiots" ('LA Magazine'). Arthur Bell, founder of the Gay Activists Alliance, and a leader in **Cruising** (1980) bashing, perhaps said it best: "It's a stupid gay movie for stupid straight people". Incredibly it became a No.1 box-office sensation in Australia and to this day is shown on the national TV station Channel 9 every December 31st at 11.15 pm to ring in the New Year. I'll drink a milkshake to that!

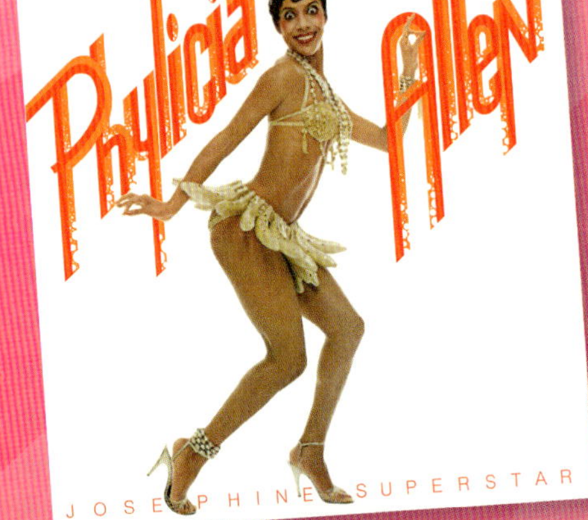

Mrs. Village People

For eight years Phylicia Rashad played Clair Huxtable in the top-rated, award-winning NBCTV sitcom 'The Cosby Show' (1984-92). But for Discophiles, under the name Phylicia Allen (she was the sister of **Fame**'s Debbie), she recorded one of the best, yet criminally little known, Casablanca concept albums.

The Broadway mainstay had met her second husband Victor Willis when they were both cast in 'The Wiz' (she played a Munchkin and a Mouse, he Uncle Henry). When Willis became lead singer with the Village People, he used his clout to get creators Jacques Morali and Henri Belolo to commit to writing and producing her solo debut album.

The result was the stupendous *Josephine Superstar* (1978) album telling the life story of Josephine Baker, the American-born Jazz Age singer and dancer who became a sensation at the Folies Bergère in Paris. With all the main songs written by Morali, Belolo and Willis, and backing vocals from the Village People and The Ritchie Family, the medleys *St. Louis/Broadway/Star of Paris* and *Two Loves Have I (J'ai deux amours)/Josephine Superstar* are sensational. *J'ai deux amours* was Baker's signature torch song from 1930. Given a showstopping beaty oomph and crystalline zippy delivery by Allen, and tremendous Village People power backing, all the tracks barely made a Disco dent in the charts. Yet *Josephine Superstar* is an unsung classic deserving of urgent rediscovery.

Disco Memo

True Andrea True

When I first moved to London in 1969 there were four cinemas in the Victoria area. The cruise-tastic Biograph, the New Victoria (now the Apollo Victoria Theatre) where every Hammer Horror double-bill opened, the Classic and the long-since demolished Metropole. The latter Rank-owned cavern was once a first-run venue for such epic roadshow attractions as **Spartacus** (1960), **Lawrence of Arabia** (1963) and **The Sand Pebbles** (1967). But it was on the fleapit skids by the time I frequented the place to see the likes of **The Fiend** (1972) and **Burnt Offerings** (1976). In fact that latter Bette Davis haunted house affair was the last film shown before it closed its doors on film screenings and converted into the Metropole Laser Theatre hosting the laugh-out-loud show 'Lovelight'. That lasted all of four months before it shuttered for another year and finally got leased by Virgin Records, re-opening in November 1978 as a concert hall called 'The Venue'.

Venue
160-162 Victoria Street
London SW1 5LB.
Tel: 834 5500
TEL: 828 9441/2/3
OVER 18s ONLY
Food, Live Music, Dancing.
Licensed til 3.00 a.m.
Thursday 12th March — AIRTO MOREIRA & HIS BAND — £4.50
Late night — GERRY ANDERSON CELEBRATION PARTY — £2.00
Friday 13th March — FISCHER Z — £3.00
Saturday 14th March — ALBERTO Y LOS TRIOS PARANOIS — £3.50
Sunday 15th March — FREEEZ — £3.00
Monday 16th March — DAVE CASH'S GOOD TIME MUSIC NIGHT featuring THE GREASE BAND + THE TONY KELLY BAND — £3.50
Tuesday 17th March — HUMAN SEXUAL RESPONSE — £2.00
Wednesday 18th March — JOHN OTWAY & THE BAND BEHIND THE CURTAIN — £3.50
Thurs 19th March — COLIN NEWMAN + Dopt S — £3.00
Late night celebrity DISCO

It was there, in the group's dying chart days, I saw the Andrea True Connection sing their Disco hits *More, More, More* (1976), *Party Line* (1976), *N.Y., You Got Me Dancing* (1977), *What's Your Name, What's Your Number* (1977) and other cuts from her two albums. It was without doubt the saddest gig I have ever witnessed and I was at the infamous Connie Francis concert at The London Palladium when she couldn't sing, broke down in tears, collapsed on stage and stormed off through the stalls after ten minutes. The ex-porno queen's gig wasn't quite that dramatic, but it was clear the sparse audience were there to drink and catcall rather than listen and dance.

I thought she was in fine voice actually, a few years later she had throat surgery meaning she would never sing again, so I feel quite privileged to have seen her perform some of the more sensual songs in the entire Disco canon. I did spy her bravely sitting at the bar after the set so I told her how much I enjoyed it. At first she obviously thought I was joking until she realised I knew my stuff and was a big fan. The only time that ever happened to me again was when I was sat two rows away from Amanda Lear on an airplane from Paris and chatted to her about her career. The Venue lasted six years, razed to the ground to make way for the glass high rises and brand outlets that are now part of the bland Victoria skyline.

XANADU (1980)

Two months after **Can't Stop the Music** was released and flopped came **Xanadu**, the second of the year's mainstream Disco disasters. Both films would endure dreadful reviews to go through the kitsch camp prism to find devoted fans, and both acted as the key inspirations for the formation of the Razzie Awards, the anti-Oscars that ridicule the worst movies of the year. Indeed, the Golden Raspberry Awards co-founder Mo Murphy summed it up best – "The key to **Xanadu** is, it was enjoyable in a way that was not intended. It was a failure as a film but not necessarily as entertainment". Even so it was still the Village People classic that won the Razzies Worst Film Award in 1980 and not this bright and breezy fragile fantasy with lo-fi special effects and anachronistic Disco taking place in a fluffy heaven and on roller skates in Venice Beach.

Initially designed as a low-budget Roller Disco cash-in, the imminent releases of **Skatetown U.S.A.** (1979) and **Roller Boogie** (1979) scuppered that route, coupled with the fact that Olivia Newton-John was showing interest in the project. Her Hollywood star in the stratospheric ascendant after the blockbuster **Grease** (1978), Newton-John saw the scant 40-page treatment as the perfect vehicle to reunite her with John Travolta. As it turned out, Travolta was waiting for an even worse script before agreeing to team up again – the 1983 dog **Two of a Kind**. So after turning down Mel Gibson as her co-star, choosing Michael Beck (**The Warriors**, 1979) instead, and bagging the last big-screen appearance of legendary dancer/actor/director Gene Kelly, Universal Pictures backed the loose remake of Rita Hayworth's wispy **Down to Earth** (1947) to the eventual tune of $20 million.

An aberration in the career of director Robert Greenwald, more well known for his issue-driven dramas and documentaries ('The Burning Bed', 1984, 'Uncovered: The War on Iraq', 2004), Newton-John plays Kira, an ancient Greek muse, reincarnated from a mural, who falls in love with Sonny Malone (Beck) a frustrated mortal artist, resigned to painting album covers instead of future big-selling gallery masterpieces. Their affair, forbidden by the Gods, acts as the catalyst for Sonny to befriend rich but washed-up Big Band clarinettist Danny McGuire (Kelly), planning to open up a Roller Disco where the 1940s meets the '80s. If the plot seems flimsy that's because the script never progressed beyond the initial slimline 40 pages and was being made up during shooting.

Hence the total mish-mash of gaudy electric mayhem, one over-blown musical number after another, animated sequences (by Don Bluth, the 'Dragon's Lair' videogame, **All Dogs Go To Heaven**, 1989), Rock 'n' Roll glitz, a *faux* '40s dream sequence, a Fiorucci fashion show staged

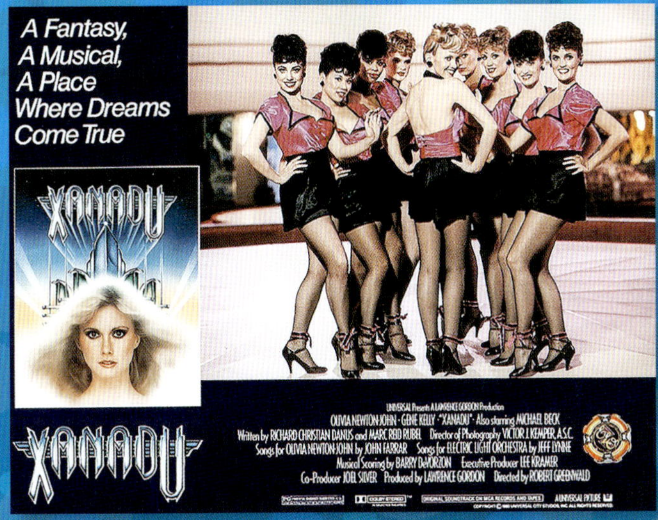

inside a pinball machine and wonky tributes to Kelly's illustrious past (**Singin' in the Rain**, 1952, on skates). In his biography 'The Films of Gene Kelly, Song and Dance Man', Kelly's only quote about **Xanadu** is this one-line dismissal, "The concept was marvellous, but it just didn't come off". Capping it all is a climactic Battle of the Bands production number featuring neo-Punks The Tubes. **Xanadu** is at the same time far too much yet way too little as visually arresting, if superficial, razzle-dazzle outdoes everything else in sight.

The picture might have bombed at the box-office but Universal's music subsidiary MCA Records found themselves with a double-platinum global smash soundtrack, peaking at No.4 on the 'Billboard' charts, launching four singles – *Xanadu, All Over the World, Suddenly, I'm Alive* – that all charted on the Top 20, plus a fifth that hit the No.1 spot, Newton-John's *Magic*. The problem with **Xanadu** is while it's a Disco movie in trappings and sensibility, the music, a collage of every other style, isn't Disco at all, being split between Newton-John soppy ballads and Electric Light Orchestra's brand of power-pop. None of the songs made the 'Billboard' Dance charts or signalled any clear way forward in the perceived post-Disco meltdown.

ELO was co-producer Joel Silver's suggestion and he would go on to work with Mel Gibson on **Lethal Weapon** (1987). The supergroup was at their commercial peak with the *Discovery* (1979) album featuring the hit *Don't Bring Me Down*, but none of the **Xanadu** songs were specifically written for the film apart from the title track. It was Newton-John who brought in songwriter John Farrar, composer of her **Grease** smash *You're the One That I Want* (1978). He contributed *Suddenly* (her duet with Cliff Richard), *Dancin'*, *Suspended in Time* and *Whenever You're Away from Me* (her duet with Kelly), plus *Magic*. Then unknown choreographer Kenny Ortega (who would work with Madonna and Michael Jackson, and direct 'High School Musical', 2006), hired The Tubes to add the out-of-synch quirkiness to the very rich day-glo mix.

However, 'A place where nobody dared to go' soon became a nostalgic cult touchstone mainly due to the 2003 Off-Broadway gay musical 'Zanna, Don't', titled after 'Esquire' magazine's famous movie review, and the critically-acclaimed 2007 Broadway parody reimagining 'Xanadu' using the original songs and including Newton-John's 1975 No.1 *Have You Ever Been Mellow* and ELO's *Strange Magic* (1975) and *Evil Woman* (1975). Newton-John's film career never really recovered from **Xanadu**, even though it certainly wasn't as bad as her embarrassing British debut in the sci-fi claptrap **Toomorrow** (1970). Stylish without having any real style and Disco without having any of the music that was going underground and back to the people who loved it without question, **Xanadu** has truly now become a stately pleasure-dome decree.

Salsoul Rainbow

Informed by the Big Band sound of Xavier Cugat, Mambo Kings percussion and an urban street savvy, a new Disco sound emerged with Joe Bataan's instrumental cover of Gil Scott-Heron's *The Bottle* (1975) from his *Afrofilipino* album. Recorded in one take, the track did so well for Mericana Records – started in 1972 by brothers Joe, Ken and Stan Cayre to cater for the Latin market – they

decided to start a purely Disco arm – and Salsoul Records was born. Defined by a rainbow logo, Salsoul offered Philadelphia style, highly orchestrated arrangements with huge string sections and soulful vocals. Modelled after Philadelphia's MFSB, and often using the same musicians, The Salsoul Orchestra was assembled by Vincent Montana Jr. who wrote their most popular tracks and ushered them into the Disco charts with a long list of hits. *You're Just the Right Size* (1975), *Chicago Bus Stop (Ooh, I Love It)* (1975), *Tangerine* (1975), an update of the Johnny Mercer 1941 standard, *Nice 'n' Naasty* (1976), *Salsoul 3001* (1976), Richard Strauss' 'Also sprach Zarathustra' goes Disco, *Magic Bird of Fire* (1977), inspired by Igor Stravinsky's theme for his ballet 'The Firebird', all cuts from the *Up the Yellow Brick Road* (1978) Broadway musical medley album, *Street Sense* (1979), *How High* (1979) and the two enormously fun singalong *Christmas Jollies* (1976, 1981) albums.

The Salsoul Orchestra also featured heavily on the two fantastic albums by Latin entertainer Charo, who had married Xavier Cugat in 1966. The Spanish firebrand had become a US TV guest star fixture in 'Laugh-In' and 'The Love Boat' series, and in **The Concorde… Airport '79** by turning her lack of English into a charm offensive. The *Cuchi-Cuchi* (1977) album, titled after her signature catchphrase, contained the evergreen lilting shuffler *Dance a Little Bit Closer* and her second album *Olé Olé* gave her Disco hits with the title track, issued as a 12-inch single on hot pink vinyl, and *Stay with Me*.

The Philly girl group First Choice had already scored mainstream success with *Armed and Extremely Dangerous* (1973) and *Smarty Pants* (1973), and had invaded the Disco charts with *First Choice Theme/Ain't He Bad/Are You Ready for Me?* (1976) and *Gotta Get Away from You Baby* (1976). But under Salsoul's guidance, on the Gold Mind subsidiary label, they hit even bigger with *Doctor Love* (1977), a chart returning perennial in 1984 and 1999, *Hold Your Horses* (1978), and *Let No Man Put Asunder* (1983).

The undisputed Queen of Salsoul was Chicago-born Loleatta Holloway who began singing with her mother in The Holloway Community Singers gospel group, and when famed Philly producer Norman Harris heard her sing, he recommended Salsoul sign her up immediately. Harris was also part of Moment of Truth who had Salsoul hits with *So Much for Love* (1976) and *Lovin' You Is Killin' Me* (1977). It was the best deal the label ever made as Holloway's colossal voice minted one hit after another: *Dreamin'/Ripped Off* (1976), *Hit and Run* (1977), *Queen of the Night* (1978), the No.1 *Love Sensation* (1980), and *Seconds* (1982). Composer Dan Hartman had written *Love Sensation* and Holloway returned the favour by adding energetic force to his No.1 smash *Vertigo/Relight My Fire* (1979).

Salsoul were instrumental in more ways than one in turning European holiday hits into Disco gold. With Tom Moulton's remix of *El Bimbo* (1975) by the French duo Bimbo Jet taking the charts by storm, Salsoul also looked to the Continent for possible crossovers. *King of Clubs/El caravanero* (1977) by the Chocolat's was one from Belgium and another was *Love Is Still Blue* by The Paul Mauriat Orchestra from France. But their biggest hit came from Argentina with (Bebu) Silvetti's gorgeous *Spring Rain* (1977). With its irresistible piano intro, string cascades and haunting melody, Silvetti's Disco confection became a global Salsoul smash.

Left to right: David Warbeck, Lucio Fulci, Catriona MacColl, during the making of *The Beyond* (1981).

Disco Memo

Dancing Death

"How do you spell filmmaking? For Lucio Fulci it's V-I-O-L-E-N-C-E!" screamed the headline on my and Mike Childs' interview with the gore maestro in 'Cinefantastique', summer 1981. We had talked to Fulci at the Paris Fantasy Festival in 1980 where we saw **City of the Living Dead/Paura nella città dei morti viventi** (1980) and became the first duo to interview him for an English language magazine. I didn't like the experience at all. Fulci was late to the interview, had been out gambling all night, and clearly hadn't tidied himself up. Perhaps he didn't think we were that important! Yet that interview has dogged me for decades because his quote "Violence is Italian Art" is the one everyone has used ever since. While I respected much of his work – I do think his giallo trio **Perversion Story/Una sull'altra** (1969), **A Lizard in a Woman's Skin/Una lucertola con la pelle di donna** (1971) and **Don't Torture a Duckling/Non si sevizia un paperino** (1972) are masterpieces – I never liked him as a person.

I have also been credited as bringing his name to an international audience with my groundbreaking 'Starburst' reviews of his latterday zombie movies. But I never warmed to him in the way I did Dario Argento. Of course, their rivalry until their pre-production collaboration on **The Wax Mask/M.D.C. – Maschera di cera** (1997) meant I had to keep my distance in so many ways. Argento would never let me speak Fulci's name when it looked like he might be becoming more famous globally. Even though my close friend and his star of **The Black Cat/Gatto nero** (1981) and **The Beyond/...E tu vivrai nel terrore! L'aldilà** (1981) David Warbeck would often try and get us back together, by pretending I was meeting his notorious agent Giuseppe Perrone instead, and in one instance got us both into a mafia orgy, one of the scariest situations I've ever been in.

The same happened with American actor Grady Thomas Clarkson, who I had met on the Italian set of Terry Gilliam's **The Adventures of Baron Munchausen** (1988) and starred in Fulci's **Demonia** (1990). He tried to lure me to De Paolis Studios in Rome where he had to film reshoots and thought we should all have lunch together! I steadfastly remained in Argento's corner all the way, and perhaps Fulci resented that. Look, I'm pleased I brought his work to a wider and more appreciative audience, but once past **Manhattan Baby** (1982) I was over my sneaking regard for the director who saw extreme horror as his last rodeo and flogged it to death.

Dario Argento and Lucio Fulci become friends again at the Fantafestival di Roma 1995.

PAUL RAYMOND'S EROTICA (1981)

In the 1970s, Paul Raymond (born Geoffrey Anthony Quinn) was Britain's most successful porn impresario and sex industry entrepreneur who ended up owning most of the prime real estate in London's Soho. He opened one of the UK's first striptease nightclubs and his publishing empire was responsible for launching the softcore magazine sensation 'Men Only', swiftly joined by 'Escort', 'Club International' and 'Mayfair'. After producing sexy cult stage shows usually starring his Z-list celebrity mistress Fiona Richmond (**Hardcore**, 1977, **Let's Get Laid**, 1978) like 'Women Behind Bars' (1977) with Divine, and the Marilyn Chambers one-woman show 'Sex Surrogate'

(1979), Raymond decided, in an uncharacteristic lack of sound judgement, to enter the fading Disco fray with this limp Strip-O-Rama set to low grade bump-and-grind.

It was mainly the idea of his daughter, Debbie Raymond, who fancied herself as a Disco chanteuse and decided to get her father to finance this misbegotten career move. So to whom did she turn to realise her dream? Only Brian Smedley-Aston, the producer of **The Music Machine** (1979), who felt it should also signal his feature debut as director. Smedley-Aston was well known in exploitation circles for producing **Vampyres** (1974), **The Wildcats of St. Trinian's** (1980) and the two aforementioned Richmond affairs plus her cult horror **Exposé** (1976).

But his suitability for this particularly inane docu-drama was well and truly exposed within the first few minutes of the sleazy fiasco.

Legendary French porn queen Brigitte Lahaie, star of Jean Rollin's **Les raisins de la mort/The Grapes of Death** (1978) and **Fascination** (1979), plays a photo-journalist sent from Paris to London to snap a magazine spread of Paul Raymond's famous Revue Bar situated at Soho's Brewer Street. Beginning with a sex romp in a Rolls-Royce car and ending with a lesbian fantasy, this extraordinarily down market *faux* Mondo mélange takes in unisex saunas (look closely and you might see the first on-screen erection in British film history), Raymond relaxing at his country club, a nude Disco in a refrigerated truck in Smithfield meat market and footage of bored punters (actually Raymond Publications staff) watching simulated sex shows in the Revue Bar theatre. So beguiled by what she's witnessed, Brigitte decides to jettison her photo career and become a stripper too!

As an assortment of jaded glamour models bare their flesh, Debbie Raymond warbles the ultra-forgettable Disco ditties *You and I*, *I'm on Fire* and *Warm*, while the tie-in soundtrack of '20 Sensual Disco Greats' included Odyssey's *Use It Up and Wear It Out* (1980), Quincy Jones' *Ai No Corrida* (1981), UK Players' *Everybody Get Up* (1980), Voggue's *Dancin' the Night Away* (1981), Wish's *Nice and Soft* (1981), Al Hudson & The Partners' *You Can Do It* (1979), Thelma Houston's *If You Feel It* (1981), Jane Birkin and Serge Gainsbourg's *Je t'aime… moi non plus* (1969) sticking out like a sore appendage, Donna Summer's *I Feel Love* (1977), Denise La Salle's *I'm So Hot* (1980), Candido's *Jingo* (1979), Imagination's *Body Talk* (1981), The Brothers Johnson's *The Real Thing* (1981), Bob Saker's *Tonight* (1981), Shalamar's *Make That Move* (1980) and Dr. Hook's *Sexy Eyes* (1979).

Also featured on the soundtrack was *Flesh* by my good friend Kara Noble, one-time Capital Radio weather girl and Heart Radio DJ who became a pariah in 1999 after selling topless photographs of Sophie Rhys-Jones, the Countess of Wessex, to The Sun newspaper causing a national scandal. **Paul Raymond's Erotica** became a moderate success on video, especially in Europe where more explicit sex scenes were inserted. But when Debbie died of a heroin overdose in 1992, Raymond became a recluse and refused to license any rerelease in order not to tarnish her memory. None of this was covered by director Michael Winterbottom in his shallow **The Look of Love** (2013) biopic about the King of Soho, played by Steve Coogan, and featuring Imogen Poots as Debbie.

Extraordinarily, while **Paul Raymond's Erotica** doesn't hit the Disco mark, it is considered by some to be the best Brigitte Lahaie distraction. Literally the star's first movie after eschewing her X-rated diversions and turning into a celebrated radio agony aunt, it was released in France on video by sleaze historian René Chateau who, in the French dubbing, got Lahaie to say she was being sent by him to discover the Raymond scene for fake co-producer credentials. In author Guillaume Le Disez's book on Lahaie's career 'Brigitte Lahaie, Les films de culte', Henri Gigoux, the director of the documentary **Brigitte Lahaie: Mes scènes les plus chaudes de l'âge d'or du X** (2000), goes on record saying it is her most arousing film, Chateau agreeing it captured her at the height of her beauty.

A Tom Moulton Mix

Known for so many things – from regional radio promoter to photographic and catwalk model – Native New Yorker Tom Moulton is most famous for being the founder and creator of the 12-inch disc and the extended Disco Mixes that made the music industry monetise their vinyl sales into the stratosphere. Disillusioned with the dishonesty and corruption of the music business, it wasn't until he was invited to the gay New York resort of Fire Island and the nightclub a colleague owned there called The Sandpiper that he saw the future. Less than impressed by the way the three-minute 7-inch singles were being presented in quick, clumsy overlaps, he was determined to solve the problem even though he never was and never would be a DJ.

Working with his extensive soul music collection, Tom assembled a 45-minute reel-to-reel tape designed to keep the dancers glued to the floor in the groove and not confused by any discernible tempo changeover. He re-edited tunes to prolong certain sections, looped in others, and made the shifts in songs disappear. Armed with this rudimentary Discomix, it was back to The Sandpiper where his tape went down a storm and the route to the 12-inch single began. Because he still retained his music industry contacts, Tom pitched his remix concept to important movers and shakers. The first to bite were Red Coach Records who agreed to let him mix *It Really Hurts Me Girl* (1973) by The Carstairs, a huge Northern Soul hit in the UK.

Then came *Do It ('Til You're Satisfied)* (1974) by B.T. Express, which Tom extended to over 5 minutes. The band hated it until it turned into a hit and suddenly the desirability of bearing the credit 'A Tom Moulton Mix' became the fashion. Responsible for the first continuous-mix album side, Gloria Gaynor's No.1 Disco smash *Never Can Say Goodbye* (1974), as his artist roster expanded he invented the 12-inch single and 'Disco Break' by accident.

The first song cut in that pioneering format was *I'll Be Holding On* (1974) by Al Downing but that was only ever on acetate for DJs to play to gain the record vital dance recognition. In the cutting room on that song they had run out of 7-inch acetates so Moulton used an album sized one instead. Because the grooves looked so tiny bunched up in the middle Tom asked for them to be spread out, which meant increasing the volume levels, and – boom! – the format was invented. *So Much for Love* (1976) by Moment of Truth was the first 12-inch to be test pressed and the first commercial crossover was *Heaven Must Be Missing an Angel* (1976) by Tavares.

The original 'Disco Break' appeared in Don Downing's *Dream World* (1973) produced by Meco Monardo, during which everything but the percussion and drums were dropped out and then brought back into play section by section over the course of 120 seconds. Everyone loved it and so the 'Disco Break' became *de rigueur*. Tom would add his production lustre to a variety of Disco acts including The Three Degrees, Grace Jones, The Trammps, First Choice, Andrea True Connection and Claudja Barry to name the tip of the iceberg. Some of his classic remixes include *Love Is the Message* (1973) by MFSB, *Love Train* (1972) by The O'Jays and *You'll Never Find Another Love Like Mine* (1976) by Lou Rawls.

Alan Jones protecting Duran Duran star Nick Rhodes at a Forbidden Planet 2 book signing.

Disco Memo

Forbidden Planet 2

Many people over the years have remembered me not just for being a writer in the beloved magazines they grew up with but also for being vividly involved with 'Forbidden Planet 2', 'The Cinema, Television and Rock Shop', at the now-no-longer standing 58 St. Giles High Street, WC2. One of my first regular stops in the West End when I moved to London was the comic book store 'Dark They Were, and Golden Eyed' situated in St. Anne's Court between Dean Street and Wardour Street. You know, the alleyway where pop star Marianne Faithfull lived in her anorexic junkie years. It was there I bought my first copies of 'Cinefantastique'. Another shopper was Nick Landau who, when the place closed down, opened up the similar emporium 'Forbidden Planet' in Denmark Street with his Titan Distributors partners Mike Luckman and Mike Lake. In a supreme irony, the 'Dark They Were' premises would actually become Trident Studios, home of Eurodisco production.

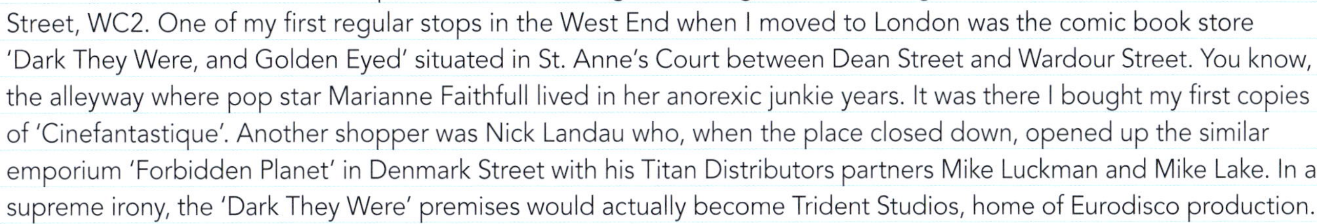

After opening a 'Forbidden Planet' store in New York in April 1981, Landau thought it would be a good idea to put all the cinema and TV-related goods, books, posters, stills and merchandise in another shop just around the corner from the original London location. He made me an offer; work as a sales assistant in 'Forbidden Planet 2' for a while to learn about the business and then I could form part of the team that would become the company's publishing arm, Titan Books. Sounded good so I agreed. Except I was kept hanging on for years and was never given the opportunity to progress one iota. In the scheme of things, would I have turned fully freelance in 1988 had Titan Books figured more in my future? I honestly don't know. What I do know is that I made sure to get exactly what I wanted out of the lop-sided deal.

That meant not giving a shit about customer service, being quite rude when any questions were asked (the part many remember all too well!) and using the staff phone for my journalist work (I'd often conduct lengthy international interviews for 'CFQ' under the desk at the back stills counter). Some people knew about my writing profile so I'd Blu Tack up Top Ten film review charts because I was seeing so many advance screenings. I nabbed new release posters from film distributors and plastered them all over the front walls. I blasted out Disco and HiNRG over the loudspeakers – regular customers Nick Rhodes (Duran Duran), Phil Oakey (The Human League) and Steve Bronski (Bronski Beat) would always comment on how great my music taste was. Honestly!

One of the part-time staff was Stefan Jaworzyn, who would become my editor for the fanzine 'Shock Xpress' and my eventual partner in celluloid crime for the legendary 'Shock Around the Clock' film festivals at the Scala and Electric cinemas. While Landau, who worked in the basement office at St. Giles High Street, put up with a hell of a lot from me – the sudden location trips abroad, diving out to see afternoon screenings at zero notice, using the back counter as my unofficial office – as the years went by I became very resentful about the whole situation. So when the announcement came that both shops would be permanently closed and relocated to New Oxford Street, and later Shaftesbury Avenue, I took the move as a sign and ended my chapter there too.

Alan Jones outside Forbidden Planet 2 circa 1985 in the old St Giles High Street, off Charing Cross Road.

My time with the company finished in July 1988, the date I went wholly freelance. I worried for a week about being able to pay the bills and then never again. To this day I refuse to go into any 'Forbidden Planet' store and have barely spoken to anyone from that time. Bitter and twisted, not really, 'Forbidden Planet 2' served its purpose in hardening my resolve never to work for anyone ever again. And I never have since.

▲ Top right: 'Doctor Who' producer John Nathan-Turner at a Forbidden Planet 2 book signing, Alan Jones lurking in the background.

DISCO DANCER (1982)

Even by Bollywood standards director Babbar Subhash's **Disco Dancer** is a gob-smacking magic carpet ride into the deliriously flighty and fanciful. A massive worldwide box-office sensation, it established star Mithun Chakraborty as the Indian Michael Jackson and a household name in Asia while its Bhangra meets Disco tunes still hold sway today. Consistently hilarious and displaying costumes that are a multi-coloured swap shop phantasmagoria, this cult cascade of kitsch is the Bollywood **Xanadu** (1980), a so bad it's so good wacky wonder.

Young Bombay slumdog Anil (Master Chhotu) and his friend Raju (Rajesh Khanna) idle around playing the drums and flute, the latter particularly good at aping electronic Disco sound effects. Invited by the local rich girl to entertain the family, her father P.N. Oberoi (Om Shivpuri) is outraged, acts abusively towards Anil and frames him for theft. Mortified with shame, Anil and his single-parent mother flee to Goa to seek a better life. Because of his nimble dance moves, elder Anil (Chakraborty) soon gets noticed and recruited by talent agent David Brown (Om Puri) to replace his current Disco King star, Sam Oberoi, (Karan Razdan) who has become a womanising, drug-addicted disgrace. Sam is of course the son of the man responsible for his shunned plight and Anil, given the stage name Jimmy, is also in love with his daughter Rita (Kim), setting the complete scene for this convoluted, but always engaging, slice of glorious musical madness.

Earnest melodrama peppered with ample fisticuffs meets Bollywood takes on Disco, especially the extravagant musical highlight, a tribute to the supreme god Krishna. Performed by Nandu Bhende, *Krishna Dharti Pe Aaja Tu* is a synth-electro-meets-laser-light Broadway production number and like all the original songs on the soundtrack was composed by Bappi Lahiri, the pioneer Disco King of India. *Goron Ki Na Kalon Ki* by Suresh Wadkar and Usha Mangeshkar is more standard Bollywood fare, *Ae Oh Aa Zara Mudke* by Kishore Kumar is monotonously bouncy loungecore, while *Auva Auva: Koi Yahan Nache* by Usha Uthup and Bappi Lahiri, appropriates the signature hook from The Buggles' No.1 hit *Video Killed the Radio Star* (1979).

On more solid MOR Disco ground is *I Am a Disco Dancer* by Vijay Benedict, which lifts its basic spelling gimmick from Ottawan's *D.I.S.C.O.* (1980). And Lahiri was clearly fond of

Ottawan as the duo's *T'es O.K. (T'es O.K., T'es Bath, T'es In)* (1980) also gets sampled in *Jimmy Jimmy Jimmy Aaja* by Parvati Khan. While many cover versions of this song exist (M.I.A., Ruki Vverh, DJ Slon and Angel-A, Kelsang Metok), it's probably most fondly remembered in the West for being featured in the Adam Sandler hairdressing comedy **You Don't Mess with the Zohan**, 2008). For the moment agent Brown first sees Anil dancing down the street in a blaze of Disco starlight, *Cerrone's Paradise* (1977) is the background music, and when he's practicing his signature moves, it's the strangely moving religious Disco mantra *Jesus Part 1 (Disco Version)* (1979) by the Dutch East Indian world music band Andy Tielman and the Tielman Brothers.

SOMEBODY PRAYED FOR THIS
A VERY SPECIAL PROMOTIONAL 12" OF
THE CELESTIAL CHOIR
A JOYOUS ANTHEM
'STAND ON THE WORD'
SUNG BY THE CHOIRS OF THE FIRST BAPTIST CHURCH OF CROWN HEIGHTS, NU YORK ON APRIL 23, 1982.
DOUBLE A-SIDE
PROMOTIONAL COPY. NOT FOR SALE
'STAND ON THE WORD' TAKEN FROM THE ALBUM SOMEBODY PRAYED FOR THIS (NR14003)
© 1982 THE FIRST BAPTIST CHURCH OF CROWN HEIGHTS INC. FOR THE U.S. MADE IN THE U.S.A ALL RIGHTS RESERVED.
THE WORD IS GOD.

Gospel Disco

Disco was church to many clubbers because it was all about coming together, singing, dancing, being uplifted and having a divine experience. So why not try and turn Saturday Night Fever into Sunday Morning Fervour? Or so many religious singers felt when Disco started becoming the main conduit of messages for their congregations. In the late 1960s church choirs would often lift choruses from familiar pop songs of the day to hook their brethren. It wasn't much of a stretch in the 1970s then for enterprising gospel artists to make Disco records with a euphoric religious message in the hope they could preach to the perverted.

Many Disco Divas came from church choirs anyway – Donna Summer, Cissy Houston etc. – so there was a business logic in investing passion longplays with the spiritual power of gospel and the hypnotic thump of Disco. The legendary Disco DJs – David Mancuso, Nicky Siano and Francis Grosso – knew Gospel Disco records

worked if they had the right remixed beat, like *Stand on the Word* (1982) by Phyliss Joubert and the Celestial Choir of First Baptist Church of Crown Heights Inc., initially pressed as a souvenir single for their congregation. Played by Messiah DJ Larry Levan at the Paradise Garage, the track took on a life of its own and made Gospel Disco a prime clubbing entity.

Keynote tracks include *One More Chance Lord* (1983) by Delores Fuller, *Jesus Is Going Away (But He's Coming Back Again)* (1979) by The Inspirational Souls, *Thank You Jesus* (1977) by The Gospel Ambassadors, *You* (1978) by Gloria Griffin, *Trouble Don't Last Always* (1981) by The Masters of Music, *Free Spirit* (1980) by Betty Griffin, *Express Yourself* (1977) by the New York Community Choir, the *First Lady* (1977) album by gospel queen Shirley Caesar and especially the Discotastic twosome *Faith Is the Key* (1984) and *What's Happening People?* (1984) by Enlightment. Add in *Hallelujah 2000* (1978) by the same titled studio project, *Silent Night, Joy to the World, O Come All Ye Faithful, Hark the Herald Angels Sing* and *The First Noel* from the *Christmas Jollies* (1976) album by The Salsoul Orchestra and everyone can sing from the same Disco hymn sheet.

Dario

1982 was a pivotal year for me. I met the one genre director I have always loved and admired above all others, continue to do so, and who took me under his wing in an unprecedented way. No other writer in my field has ever obtained the exclusive access to any director like I have had to Italian giallo maestro Dario Argento. Looking back in hindsight I now see how we helped each other. I was a young horror journalist full of vim and vigour, thrilled to be on film sets, locations and in studios watching my idols work. Nothing was too much trouble in that endeavour and I went to far-flung corners of the globe to meet and report on everything in my wide-eyed fantasy movie universe.

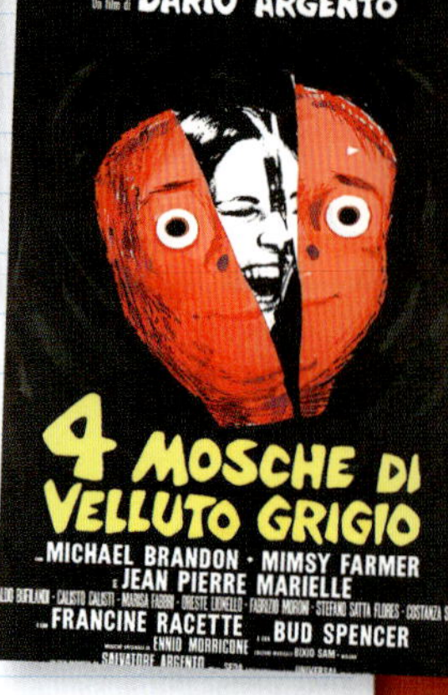

Dario Argento of course had hit the heights of acclaim with his initial Animal Trilogy, his giallo firecracker **Deep Red** (1975) and monumental masterpiece **Suspiria** (1977), then watched in dismay as **Inferno** (1980) floundered to even get released in the key territories where his name meant something, and was entering the difficult middle period of his career. That's the phase where you've made it but people think you're resting on your laurels and start being dismissive. I came along bursting with enthusiasm and worship and without really knowing it made him realise his true worth to his international legion of fans. And I have kept that up to the present day.

This is how it all happened. Maureen Bartlett, my old boss at Videomedia (the one who semi-fired me!), asked me to pop by the Wardour Street office for a talk in October 1982. My 'Cinderoller' best friend Geoff Simm was still working there. Maureen had just bought a movie for UK distribution that she was clueless about. Geoff advised her to have a chat with me because the director was a favourite of mine and I would know all about it. That movie was **Tenebrae** and she asked me to help her promote it and do the PR.

Disco Memo

I thought I had died and gone to heaven!

I saw the movie the next day, adored it, and recommended she bring Dario over for interviews and talker screenings. A couple of months later, after the Italian opening, I was in the same room as my icon – he had even brought Daria Nicolodi with him, double swoon! – and we laid out the PR strategy for his approval. It just so happened that exactly the month before I had written a career feature on Argento for the short-lived Marvel Comics magazine 'Cinema'. **Grease 2** was on the cover of the September issue No.5 if you want to track it down. My 'Starburst' editor Alan McKenzie wanted to broaden the readership of the publication, which was having a hard time finding its feet, and thought profiles of cult directors might be the way forward.

cinema profile

by alan jones

DARIO ARGENTO

So along with Argento's interview and special meet and greet events schedule, I included a copy of 'Cinema' for him to peruse overnight too. The next day he greeted me like an old friend, told me I'd nailed his work and thought my feature was fabulous. From that moment on Maureen had no problems with anything she wanted him to do – later she even got his blessing to release **The Bird with the Crystal Plumage** (1970) on video – and I had earned every penny of my retainer.

On the day I escorted them both back to the airport, Daria gave me a present I treasure to this day, a notebook inscribed with "Do You, Mr. Jones?", a lyric from *Ballad of a Thin Man* (1965) by Bob Dylan, her favourite songwriter. Argento took me aside and told me, basically, that I was the keeper of his flame in the UK. He said he wanted me to promise to keep his fans up-to-date on everything he did because I was obviously the best person to do so. Thanks to him allowing me to literally stalk him all over the world throughout the ensuing decades, I have kept that promise. And for as long as I live, I always will.

A favourite picture – Dario Argento with Alan Jones at the UK premiere of *Dark Glasses* at FrightFest 2022.

Image © Julie Edwards for #Frightfest www.julieedwardsphotography.co.uk

SOUP FOR ONE (1982)

Five years too late in the **Annie Hall** (1977) stakes to really make its mark, the debut comedy romance from writer/director Jonathan Kaufer goes for the same Manhattan locations, Woody Allen-style humour, neurotic characters, bittersweet tone and klutziness defining that epochal Oscar winner. But lacking Allen's insight or endearing self-deprecation and relying on basic sit-com mechanics more than anything innovative, **Soup for One** barely made any commercial inroads even though headlining star Saul Rubinek, a journeyman US TV series veteran, was at the time being pitched as the new Dudley Moore.

He plays shy Jewish New Yorker Allan, an obscure cable TV station employee whose dingy studio is situated underneath a Chinese laundry. Desperate for romance, Allan is looking for the perfect Miss Right, someone witty, interested in the American Civil War, Broadway theatre and who wants a meaningful relationship just like him. Completely rebuffing the wild singles scene his best friend Brian (Gerrit Graham, **Phantom of the Paradise**, 1974) indulges in, he resorts to reporting his fantasy date as a missing person to the local police so he can get an artist's impression sketch drawn up to fix exactly what he's after in his mind. Enter Maria (Marcia Strassman, Julie in 'Welcome Back, Kotter', 1975-79), an independent young woman who is mortified by Allan's interest in her. "You're short and weird," she tells him bluntly before, of course, giving him a chance no one else in their right mind would do.

None of the humour feels particularly fresh, the Single White Female gags often fall flat and the whole enterprise has an in-built staleness that dampens the charm. The moment Maria drops her diaphragm in a hurry running from Allan is the crass fairytale level Kaufer mistakes for keen emotional resonance. But the ace in Kaufer's badly shuffled pack of romantic clichés is the patchwork score by Chic superproducers, composers and musicians, guitarist Nile Rodgers and bassist Bernard Edwards.

The Disco band was becoming irrelevant by this time. After scoring No.1 Disco hits with their albums *Chic* (1977), *C'est Chic* (1978) and *Risqué* (1979) containing the classic cuts *Dance, Dance, Dance (Yowsah, Yowsah, Yowsah)*, *Everybody Dance*, *Le Freak*, *I Want Your Love*, *Good Times* and *My Forbidden Lover*, Rodgers and Edwards were embroiled in a lawsuit over *Good Times* being sampled in the Sugarhill Gang hit *Rapper's Delight* (1979). Although they emerged from the legal battle with equal copyright and a lot of money, the emerging Hip-Hop genre inevitably dented Chic's earnings as they were viewed as the 'older' generation, one still making old-fashioned 'live' music.

Even though the *Real People* (1980) album stalled in the Disco charts at No.29, Atlantic Records head Jerry Greenberg trusted Chic to figure a way through the

growing anti-Disco feeling and allowed them to fulfil their cast-iron contract of recording two more albums. He let Rodgers make the solo album *Adventures in the Land of the Good Groove* (1983) but in return gave them the **Soup for One** soundtrack assignment.

The *Soup for One* theme song is something of a departure for Chic in both tight melody and production yet it had the longevity to be sampled by French dance act Modjo for *Lady (Hear Me Tonight)* (2000), a No.1 hit in most of Europe. Besides three previously released tracks, Chic's *I Want Your Love*, Sister Sledge's *Let's Go on Vacation* from the *Love Somebody Today* (1980) album, and *Jump, Jump* from Debbie Harry's *KooKoo* (1981), another six songs and instrumentals were specifically written or adapted for the movie: *Why* by Carly Simon, a surprise hit in Europe, and No.10 in the UK (it didn't feature in the final cut of the movie though), *Dream Girl* by Teddy Pendergrass, performed by him in a nightclub cameo, *Tavern on the Green* by Nile Rodgers, an instrumental version of *Open Up* from the *Real People* album and veteran Chic vocalist Fonzi Thornton's *I Work for a Livin'* and *Riding*, two songs originally planned for his unreleased solo album *Frostbite*. Proof that not everything Rodgers and Edwards touched turned into musical gold at this pivotal time, both **Soup for One** and its accompanying soundtrack, plus *Adventures in the Land of the Good Groove* were all commercial flops. Being eclectic was what the powerhouse Disco duo was clearly not meant to be.

C'est Chic

It wasn't all bad news for Nile Rodgers and Bernard Edwards. In 1980 they had lent their signature sound to Diana Ross for her *Diana* album and scored two No.1 Disco hits with *Upside Down* and *I'm Coming Out*. When Chic split up, Rodgers continued producing several major albums and singles for such artists as David Bowie, Duran Duran and Madonna, refining their sound and elevating it to the award-winning celebrated status they still hold as dance legends.

But one of the criminally unsung albums produced by the Chic duo was *King of the World* (1980) by the French group Sheila B. Devotion. Born Annie Chancel, the pop chanteuse adopted the name of her first French release, a cover version of Tommy Roe's *Sheila* (1962). Numerous hits followed – the Cher cover *Bang, Bang* (1966), *Les femmes* (1977) – and wanting to broaden her international appeal she turned Disco. Accompanied by three male dancers – Black Devotion – she enjoyed a 'Billboard' Disco hit with a dance cover of the Hollywood musical standard *Singin' in the Rain* (1978).

Having tasted large-scale success her record label Carrere decided to team up Sheila with two of the hottest producers on the scene for her next release. The result was the *King of the World* album featuring the global smash *Spacer*, the rock video directed by Russell Mulcahy, and Black Devotion credited as just B. Devotion to avoid any racial issues. Five million single sales later, *Spacer* would become reused in movies and remixed into the 21st Century to find a constantly regenerating new wave of fans.

Down and Out in Beverly Hills

One of my early Disco Seventies close friends in Hollywood was a guy named David D who, until camp socialite Philip Sallon in the mid-Punk Seventies, was the most outrageous person I'd ever met. David would think nothing of going to the supermarket in drag and he was the greatest companion for a night out at Studio One. The crush of his life was David Cassidy whose role in 'The Partridge Family' (1970-74) sitcom had catapulted the fresh-faced teen idol to pop stardom fame with the songs *Cherish* (1972) and *How Can I Be Sure* (1972). He called me up really excitedly one night to tell me a PA friend of a movie extra friend had given him the address of Cassidy's house in the swanky Beverly Hills district. Did I want to go with him on the visit? What, just turn up on his doorstep, I quizzed? Sure, came the reply, let's see if he's in. Okay. What could possibly go wrong?

So later that evening off we went to the address David had written down and rang the entry buzzer. No reply. David tried roughly six times without any luck. Let's climb over the wall and explore, he said, he's not in so let's have a good nose around. Sounded like a good idea at the time, so over the wall we went and crept around the manicured lawns and spacious garden. We ended up at the front door and emboldened by our shared sense of adventure, David banged really loudly to see if there really was anyone at home. Still no reply. So he got down on his knees and started sucking the doorknob, the only way at that moment he could get close to the object of his devotion.

Suddenly the door was flung open and there stood Motown Goddess Diana Ross. The address David had been given was the wrong one! "I've called the police", she screamed at the top of her voice. And indeed she had. We couldn't escape in time and got carted off in a flashing car to the Beverly Hills Police Station on North Rexford Drive. How very future George Michael! Where we spent a night in a cell and caused much merriment amongst the force. We could hear them laughing as they kept repeating the story to anyone who would listen. The next day we were issued with writs saying we were both forever 'Banned in Beverly Hills'. To this day I'm still not sure if it was a real thing or just a joke. Needless to say I have been back there many times and never had any more trouble.

LIQUID SKY (1982)

Director Slava Tsukerman's post-Disco arch pose was apparently meant to be a criticism of a declining western civilization during its apex of maximum pretentiousness. And his fluorescent backlit nightmare certainly hit the mood of the times with its pre-MTV catalogue of eye-catching images smeared in a dirty, funny, perverse, crazy, Punk, New Romantic fashion consciousness. A surreal if sordid catwalk on the wild side of New York's chic drug culture, its mannered sci-fi theatrics, over-indulgent style and haughtily nihilistic attitude eventually caught on with art-house hipsters, after playing first-run poorly in Los Angeles, making **Liquid Sky** the most successful independent film during its 1983 global roll-out, grossing $1.7 million worldwide on a budget outlay of $500,000 provided by Robert Field, a Pennsylvania real estate developer.

A Soviet émigré documentarian and filmmaker living in New York City since 1976, Tsukerman originally envisioned entering the US feature film business with a sci-fi project titled 'Sweet 16' that Andy Warhol had agreed to appear in. Financing proved difficult even though he made many industry connections during the abandoned pre-production phase. One of those was actress Anne Carlisle, on the verge of having a Hollywood moment with Larry Cohen's **Blind Alley** (1984) and the Madonna vehicle **Desperately Seeking Susan** (1985) both awaiting release. Talking to Tsukerman in depth after becoming firm friends, Carlisle mentioned a true past-life experience they, with Tsukerman's producer wife Nina V. Kerova, then fashioned into the off-the-wall screenplay for **Liquid Sky**, a title derived from the slang for heroin.

Along with a number of 'Sweet 16' ideas, Tsukerman also folded in themes he'd already covered in his best-known work to that date, **Night of Decision** (1972). That Montreal Film Festival award winner dealt with free will and determinism, subject matters that caused it to be banned in the Soviet Union, the reason why Tsukerman and Kerova left their home country and emigrated to Jerusalem where they dabbled in Israeli television before heading Stateside. It was also Tsukerman's idea that a UFO host would find the New Wave avant-garde scene attractive, stemming from his own alien status in New York, and his interest in cutting-edge drug decadence as street theatre at the time.

Deeply dippy nightclubbers Margaret and Jimmy (both played by Carlisle) are celebrated fashion geniuses, designing outré drug-inspired fantasy clothes for other *faux*-Disco habitués. When a Frisbee-sized UFO lands on the roof of Margaret's Manhattan penthouse (Carlisle's own apartment, she moved out once filming was completed) and its miniature gelatinous alien visitor starts looking for an other-worldly substitute to the sexual and snorted thrills the demi-monde indulges in, it isn't long before the junkie glitterati are succumbing to the addicted

spacebeast draining their brain fluids at the height of casual sex orgasm and dope-induced highs. Margaret soon cottons on to the deathly vaporisation technique and starts using the alien's cravings to get rid of all the losers in her life. Until, of course, it comes to the time when the parasitic piper must be paid…

Occasionally adopting the crystal-shard, cranium-injecting creature's point of view, allowing for high-contrast visuals in lurid reds, purples and greens to portray intense bliss, the arresting melee of vulgar verbal distraction and visual über-camp makes for a deliberate close encounter of the acid kind. With another Russian émigré Yuri Neyman on board as both director of photography and special effects technician, and Tsukerman partly performing the discordant electronic soundtrack using the Firelight Computer Musical Instrument located at New York's Public Access Synthesizer Studio, **Liquid Sky** emerges today as a hugely entertaining put-on, a poseur's delight commenting on the impact of cultural malaise. Not that Tsukerman really understood it either; at contemporary press conferences Tsukerman often likened it to a mix of **Barry Lyndon** (1975) and **Raging Bull** (1980).

Why **Liquid Sky** is ultra Disco important comes down to the background music heard in the club where the addled nightlifers show off their erratic choreographed shapes. While Tsukerman was the composer and a lyricist for the track *Me and My Rhythm Box*, he turned to yet another Russian émigré for further finessing with an excerpt from his epoch-making album *Beautiful Bend* (1978). And that person remains the greatest producer and composer of the entire Disco era – Boris Midney.

Boris Midney

My besotted love of Boris Midney hasn't abated since I first heard the *Come Into My Heart* (1978) album by USA-European Connection at The Embassy Club. Sure, I adore Giorgio Moroder, Alec R. Costandinos and Cerrone, but there is only one Disco God for me and that's Midney. There really hasn't been a week since Midney stormed onto the Disco scene that I haven't listened to a track he composed, arranged, produced, sound designed, played on or engineered. As uniquely directional and fresh sounding today as they were the first time they were heard, every eagerly anticipated Midney album left dancers and reviewers clutching for superlatives because he minted a new marriage between music and technology that yielded successively breathtaking results.

The stunningly beautiful melodies he composed, with his engagingly odd and unique lyrics delivered in eccentric but always sophisticated style, coupled with the sparse, ethereal space effects he created in between became instantly recognisable to his legion of admirers. His clean-cut, daring technique and orchestral integrity oozed from every silky groove unafraid of experimenting on the surreal edges of dance culture. Because of these highly original aural sensations and cosmic vibrations, Midney took Disco on a journey to the far-out side of the mirrorball and created a series of musical fantasy masterpieces in a body of work that is second to none in the entire genre. Notoriously reclusive, I was lucky to interview him at length for the *Disco Recharge* retrospective of his entire catalogue for Harmless Records, and what follows are the unedited transcripts put in one place for the very first time. It's so rare to be given the opportunity to tell one of your absolute idols how much their work has meant to you. Like Argento in the movie world I was able to do that with Midney in the musical one and I will be forever grateful.

Boris Midney was born in Russia, "In Moscow, a block away from the Kremlin, the parks and squares were my 'playground'. Both of my parents were professional musicians; my mother was an opera singer and my father was an orchestra conductor. So my obsession with rhythm started early". Midney played most of the instruments on all his Disco albums, including saxophone, clarinet, keyboards, drums and percussion, and he learnt his skills thanks to being classically trained at the Moscow Tchaikovsky Conservatory, the second oldest in the Soviet Union, home to Sergei Rachmaninoff, and the Gnessin Academy. "No jazz music or saxophone permitted, though I managed", he laughs. Midney also studied photography at the Moscow House of Photography. "By invitation only, I was on the Working Professional Master Programme". This additional talent is the reason why Midney shot the cover art for most of his Disco album projects.

Growing up in the USSR during his teenage years proved a disheartening experience: "I had written the soundtrack for a Russian programme entitled 'Staircase', which won Best Score at the Monte Carlo Television Festival. No one told me, I learned about winning from the foreign press. I simply refused to accept the Soviet doctrine of 'sitting' put in the country – I just had to see the world. So I defected. I was part of a music ensemble on a cultural exchange tour in Japan. The night after completing the tour I took off for the American Embassy in Tokyo". Building a whole new life in America proved relatively straightforward. "Perhaps that was my naivety though. Being pretty young, it appeared fairly easy. Upon arrival at the airport from Tokyo, I was greeted by Helen Keane, at the time the manager of American jazz pianist Bill Evans. Apparently she had heard about me, and the jazz group I led in Russia, from an article in 'Downbeat' magazine. Complete news to me of course. Helen turned out to be a 'no-nonsense' active woman who got me signed up with ABC/Impulse Records".

The main result of that signing was the group Russian Jazz Quartet. "Fellow Russian Igor Beruk was on bass guitar, Roger Kellaway on piano, Grady Tate on drums and me on alto sax. We recorded at the Rudy Van Gelder Studios. I joined the Musician's Union and started playing the jazz club circuit. People were curious about my background and defection and would come to see and talk to me. I guess I was a bit of a novelty. Then it became widely known that I could read music and I started getting other industry jobs". (Russian Jazz Quartet's Kellaway would be Oscar nominated for Best Adaptation Score in 1976 for **A Star Is Born**, Tate moved on to drumming in Quincy Jones' band and Van Gelder is regarded as one of the most important engineers in music history due to his work with Miles Davis, Thelonious Monk and Sonny Rollins).

It was once said that Midney never recorded under his own name in a studio he didn't build himself. "Almost true. My first recordings happened to be at Mercury in NYC. I loved the sound and set up there and made it my aim to duplicate and improve it. I soon found out that acoustic designers and musicians were totally unaware of one another. I wanted to 'synch' both in a 'sweet' environment and a 'perfect' recording studio. That took years of learning – and unlearning – but I eventually got my 'sound'. The first studio built from scratch – concrete blocks and all – was at Princeton, New Jersey. We surprisingly didn't make too many mistakes. There I recorded University choral groups and local bands until I started composing for the NBC network".

As a progressive Big Band jazz arranger, Midney's works included scores for the popular Merv Griffin and Johnny Carson talk shows. Eventually he established himself as the symphonic orchestra composer for NBC TV idents and in-house projects such as their Bi-Centennial celebration. Then Midney created the ALPHA International Studio in Philadelphia. "I hooked up with co-producer Peter Pelullo because of his affiliation with a construction company and we ended up building two studios under one roof. Took about a year but they turned out pretty nice".

Disco Memo

Being at the heart of the hot and happening Philly Sound meant Midney became keenly aware of the rise of Disco but his move into the genre was more down to one sole factor. "I had an obsession with funk. In my view the list of people who actually understood rhythm, and subsequently, funk is surprisingly short – James Brown, Tina Turner, Ben E. King, Sly and the Family Stone… then it gets foggy".

Informed by his classical jazz roots, free-form variations on a theme, experimental scat vocals, and further influenced by Philly and funk, Midney decided to try his hand at turning the beat around and transforming it into a new style of Disco sound. "I didn't plunge into Disco, I slid, I'm a skier you see! When I started writing this kind of music I was not even aware it was called Disco, it was just fun and funky to me. I had this fixed idea of joining jazz, classical and pop into one with an artistic sincerity. An individuality of one's music, isn't that always the key principle?"

It was at this important juncture Midney had the idea of combining pop rhythms with more orthodox sounds. "The idea of pop meets classical had been brewing inside me for years. It was in the Princeton studio I started experimenting with strings over funk. But it wasn't until I built ALPHA that my Disco foundation truly began. There was no true Disco at the time, just a flavour – R&B with an orchestra – but there was Eurodance pop like Silver Convention. I heard their tracks first hand in Bob Reno's office at Mercury Records and loved the unique string sound. That confirmed I was on the right track in the combination of different musical styles".

Kenny Everett

After hearing *Come Into My Heart* and being bowled over by it, I rushed to my favourite Disco import emporium in Soho (Trax Records, Greek Street) and asked for the USA-European Connection album. "Not out yet" came the reply, "Try in a few weeks when T.K. Records release it". But I just couldn't wait that long and called up my Capital Radio producer best friend Mike Childs who often let me go into his Euston Tower head offices to raid the New Release cupboards. But I didn't find the USA-European Connection album – until I scanned the out-of-bounds desk of famed DJ Kenny Everett. Recklessly, before anyone had noticed, it was whisked into my bag, on my turntable at home, blaring out and I was closely studying the album cover credits. And there was the name Boris Midney, who was listed not just as composer and producer but also arranger, conductor, engineer, photographer, keyboardist and horn player – the complete package. Interestingly enough Everett had written a note-to-self in ballpoint on the inner sleeve which said, "Huge in the US, the continuously segueing sides may be too much of a good thing".

Midney recalls how the *Come Into My Heart* album was put together: "I made this tape in my studio in Philadelphia at odd times, mostly at night. I sat at the piano and played it all the way through. Of course there were a lot of objections like, 'You can't have one track on the album, too long, gotta separate them, nobody will listen… etc'. I was looking to somehow connect the Euro Sound with the US Funk and R&B one. While commuting from Princeton to Philadelphia, on the highway there was a large sign saying 'Connection to 95', and that's how I got the USA-European Connection concept and project title. Every new style of music starts with a beat and this drummer I was working with at the time had 'that beat'. I was clearly developing a sound, I just wasn't aware of creating Disco.

The subsequent Disco craze was nothing short of a revolution against established and cliché pop that allowed composers and producers to experiment with new and 'off-the-wall' sounds, truly the basis for any new movement. Later my lawyer Sandy Ross said, 'You're crazy, what kind of name is USA-European Connection? Make it shorter or it will never sell. That's when I knew I was on the right track".

The key lyric in *Come Into My Heart/Good Loving*, the album's A-side, sets the tone perfectly: "High winds of feeling tear me apart". For the dancer is immediately caught up in the surge of undulating music as wave upon wave of lilting melody, wild percussion, peripatetic strings and shrieking violins, pounding reverbs, conga breaks and orchestral ingenuity hit you between the ears with a distinctly emotional force. All that sumptuous pummelling continues in the *Love's Coming/Baby Love* B-side with tuned discordance made to sound sweetly harmonious as the 'sensuous vocals' (by Leza Holmes, Renne Johnson and Sharon Williams) go slo-mo only to be uplifted by angelic harps, echo chamber beauty and string enchantment.

David Mancuso

While some thought Midney was a lunatic recording stuff that was clearly unmarketable to their ears, many loved what he was doing. "I guess I was determined. I was doing something I really liked and deeply enjoyed. So when the master tape was finished, a friend of mine from New York told me he knew David Mancuso, the DJ and owner of the downtown New York 'underground' club The Loft and arranged for it to be premiered there. The place was crowded, full of balloons, and it went on at midnight. One by one people cleared the dance floor because they wanted to listen as it contained such a different sound. I saw this as something of a disaster that the clubbers' non-reaction was due to the recording/mix not being up to par. Without saying thank you or goodbye to Mancuso, I drove back to Philly and totally remixed it. Something that was completely unnecessary as I got a call the next night saying Mancuso had played it again a number of times and people couldn't get enough. After that it was put on regular rotation at The Loft and things started to happen very quickly. Promoters called and I was introduced to Henry Stone at T.K. Records who came up with an offer to release it on their Marlin label".

The result was a 'Billboard' Hot Dance Disco Chart No.1 that remained on every DJs playlist for the next 21 weeks. Naturally Stone asked Midney for a second USA-European Connection album follow-up. "But I didn't have anything. By then I was at my Eras Studio on Manhattan's East 54th Street, thus named for the 'Beginning of a new era' for me… and so it was". Artists Midney worked with at Eras away from his own dance universe included Theo Vaness, Evelyn 'Champagne' King, Instant Funk, Foreigner, The Ritchie Family and The Rolling Stones. "I engineered sessions for The Rolling Stones sometimes helping out by playing saxophone and keyboards. It was lots of fun. Mick Jagger's favourite resting nook was under the piano in the piano booth. I played some tricks on Mick with straight 4/4 bass drum beats and of course he loved it. But not for any price would he consider changing the band's style. I guess to them it was set in 'Stone'". A Rolling Stones Disco album produced by Boris Midney, wow, what a missed opportunity!

"One night I went to my favourite restaurant that specialised in fried, boiled and grilled ducks but my dinner didn't taste exactly right. I went back to the studio and got terrible double vision and severe nausea. I sat at the piano hoping it would pass. My engineer Dmitri Zbrizer was still there and I said 'Let's record something'. He rolled the tape and I was in and out of consciousness playing non-stop until Dmitri yelled 'How the hell do you know what you are playing' and the tape ran out. I had no sheet music only a click track in my headphones but the second USA-European Connection album was done, with just the vocals and arrangements added the following week. I learned about my father's death during the *Come Into My Heart* recording and I had food poisoning on the second album and could barely play a note on the piano. But those dual feelings of euphoria and a total reality disconnect provided the inspiration. Any kind of good music doesn't result from sheer happiness or satisfaction, there has to be some drama, discord and sadness. Melancholy is the most beautiful of human emotions and that quality is definitely invested in both USA-European Connection albums".

Sparer, crisper and more precise than the first album, the second self-titled USA-European Connection release from November 1979 featured the equally haunting *I'd Like to Get Closer/Do Me Good* and *Join the Dance/There's a Way Into My Heart*. Vocals this time provided by Chequita Jackson and Kevin Owens, a duo who would continually be employed to convey the delicious brand of Midney Magic. Each is a grandiose symphony of musical quality, focused individuality and artistic refinement that was entirely unique for the Disco era yet still retained the ability to sweep you onto the dance floor for a rapturously blissful workout.

Beautiful Bend (1978) was the second of Midney's solo album projects on the Marlin label to soar to No.1 on the dance charts and remain in the 'Billboard' Hot Dance Disco Top Ten for 14 straight weeks. An incredible achievement for the period, *Make That Feeling Come Again!* by Beautiful Bend was an astonishing recording all round. A captivating kaleidoscope of sounds so inventive and distinctive it proved overwhelming to many die-hard clubbers when sneak previewed again by ace DJ Dave Mancuso at The Loft two months prior to being officially released. With vocals credited to Xo-Xo, Midney played keyboards and saxophone while long-time associate Bruce Weeden took on bass guitar duties with Philly staple Larry Washington on congas. With its burbling synthesizer, angelic siren calls, swirling violins, heavenly echoes and haunting beat, Midney's musical roots, Philly funk and European flavourings invest every moment with a freedom of Disco spirit and total confidence in his innovative ALPHA sound.

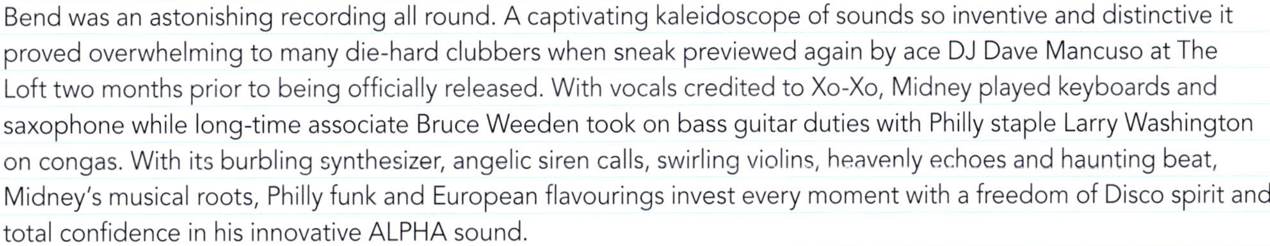

The deliciously bouncy *That's the Meaning* mixed with the rolling momentum of *Boogie Motion* and the choral ecstasy of the title track segueing effortlessly into the discordant tunefulness of *Ah-Do It* is a master class of technique and musicality. The hypnotic result is an exemplary probe into luscious melody and dazzling harmony driven by sound effects that do exactly what the studio assembly's name hints at. Each song is beautifully bent out of shape and then back again into jubilant form by Midney's miraculous artistry. Vince Aletti said it best. Disco's first and greatest chronicler wrote on July 22, 1978, "Beautiful Bend is ample confirmation of an exciting talent and should prove to be one of Disco's most durable records". Decades later, how right he was.

After completing the *Beautiful Bend* album, Midney moved his entire base of recording operations to Eras where the *Caress* album became a reality, released by RFC Records, a Warner Bros. affiliate label, in 1979. Equally as startlingly individual, *Caress* once more proved Midney was on the proto-trance front-line. Uninterrupted spans of rhythmic sound accentuated by curving string sections, walls of tinkling sliding scales and densely layered orchestration,

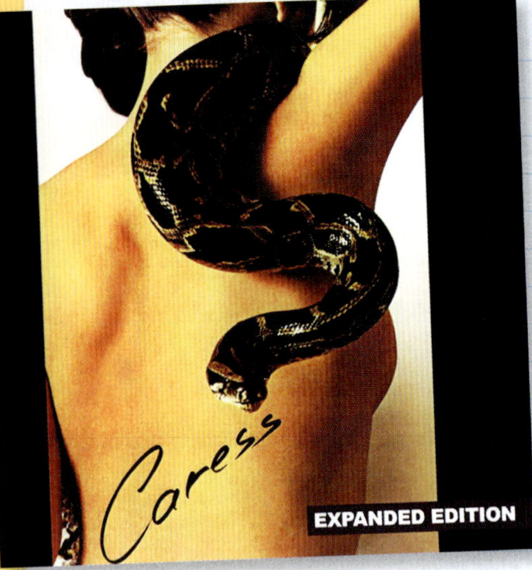

Caress is arguably the ultimate in Designer Disco. It begins with the breathlessly sung *Catch the Rhythm*, which then sinuously snakes into the jazz-infused *Charmed By You*. The unbelievably catchy *You Got It Too Uptight* is then teamed with the hyper-jittery brilliance of *Love Spell*. With vocals by Midney regulars Chequita Jackson and Kevin Owens, and his patented crisp 'Mi Sound' lifting this masterpiece to new heights of Disco amazement, shakes and shivers of delight were guaranteed. Nobody in Disco Dreamland was doing it better at the time.

One of the more endearing trends during the Disco peak was the rise of the concept album based on famous literary works. Just for starters there was *Romeo & Juliet* (1978) by Alec R. Costandinos and the Syncophonic Orchestra and *Wuthering Heights* (1979) by Ferrara. But when Midney took that fashionable route he was more on trend and relevant than anybody else by filtering his eclectic musical influences through the narrative fable for a never-ending story cascade of melody, harmony and thrilling innovation. Midney considers *Pinocchio* (1979) by Masquerade a pinnacle in his illustrious career because he's proudest of its melodic content. "Technically *Pinocchio* flows. To English composer Frederick Delius a sense of flow was the only thing that mattered. Music had flow or it didn't. If it had, it was good music. If it didn't, it was bad. So to me *Pinocchio* flows".

To be entirely accurate though the title of the Masquerade album should have been 'Buratino'. For that was Midney's true source of inspiration for his superlative Disco fairytale. Buratino is the main character in the 1936 book 'The Golden Key, or the Adventures of Buratino' by Aleksey Nikolayevich Tolstoy. Based on the 1883 novel 'The Adventures of Pinocchio' by Carlo Collodi, Buratino's name is derived from the Italian 'burattino', meaning wooden puppet or doll. According to Tolstoy, he had read 'The Adventures of Pinocchio' as a child, but having lost the book, started re-imagining it years later in an attempt to come up with a series of bedtime stories for his own children. The result turned out to be so original and beloved by the writer's family he decided to publish it. The Buratino tale quickly became hugely popular among children in the Soviet Union, and remains so to this day, having been made into several films. "I've always been fascinated by the Pinocchio story as written by Tolstoy, not Collodi… to me it had more magic, though I admire the original Italian version".

«Это я, Буратино», — сказала кукла, прыгнула на пол и давай плясать и прыгать.

12

«Ой, ой, ой, как есть хочется!» — сказал Буратино.

Тогда Карло надел куртку и пошёл на улицу, чтобы купить что-нибудь поесть.

13

Like Pinocchio, Buratino is a long-nosed wooden puppet. According to Tolstoy's fable, he is carved from a log by Papa Carlo and suddenly comes to life, his extended nose due to his creator's sloppy woodworking. On his way to school, Buratino is distracted by posters for a local puppet theatre show, befriends the inmates and becomes the focus of evil puppet-master Karabas Barabas after he learns that Papa Carlo's home contains a secret door for which he has been searching.

A golden key that Karabas once possessed opens this door and the story continues as Buratino hunts for it with his loyal friend Duremar while trying to avoid crooks Alice the Fox and Basilio the Cat who are after Buratino's five gold coins treasure. That Tolstoy story, augmented by the more famous European version, provided the basis for Midney's magical musical fantasia. Beginning with *Wooden-Wooden Puppet*, *I'm Attached to You*, *Cat-Tails* and *L.O.V.E./R.S.V.P.*, Midney's mellifluous melodies and haunting harmonies continue through *Don't Leave Me Hanging*, *The Land of Miracles* and *Open the Secret Door*. All the tracks are master classes in lyrical inventiveness and sparkling orchestral manoeuvres combined in mini arias of astral beauty that paint a funky Eurodisco pantomime of exemplary artistry and sonic sophistication. Midney's unique body of work appeared on numerous labels during the Disco era – T.K. Records' Marlin, Warner Bros.' RFC Records, RSO Records, Polydor's Tropique as well as Prelude. Did he have a preference as to the best label he ever worked with? "The one that paid on time!"

For two key album releases in 1979 and 1980 Midney changed tack. Rather than compose his own material he chose to interpret the work of others. The results were *Evita* by Festival and *The Empire Strikes Back* credited to his solo moniker. Both were commissioned by **Saturday Night Fever** (1977) producer Robert Stigwood and both were released on the Australian entertainment entrepreneur and impresario's RSO Records label. Doing Disco versions of popular songs and medleys from Broadway shows was not unusual during this banner period. However 'Evita' wasn't just any old show. After their triumph with 'Jesus Christ Superstar' composer Andrew Lloyd Webber and lyricist Tim Rice wrote another all-sung-through musical about an influential world figure. Eva Peron was the first lady of Argentina who rose from poverty to wield enormous power through her husband, President Juan Peron. Called a saint by some and a dictator by others, Eva, affectionately nicknamed Evita by the working classes who absolutely adored her, died of cancer in 1952 aged 33. In 1973 Rice heard a radio documentary about her extraordinary rags to riches life and started researching her story as the basis for a musical. Lloyd Webber though was reluctant to work on a show about such a controversial figure. However Rice continued his investigation into Evita's history, even taking a trip to Buenos Aries to scout the facts for himself. Lloyd Webber was finally won over to Rice's cause when 'Jeeves', his musical collaboration with Alan Ayckbourn, proved unsuccessful.

As they had done with 'Jesus Christ Superstar' and 'Joseph and the Amazing Technicolour Dreamcoat', the composer and lyricist presented the 'Evita' score as a concept record album before the show was expensively brought to the stage by veteran Broadway director Harold Prince. Julie Covington sang the title role and the album became a No.1 seller all over Europe. *Don't Cry for Me Argentina* (1976), Evita's farewell to her country and the best-known song from the show, was also a chart topping hit single. But Covington didn't want to star in the West End version opening June 21, 1978 so Elaine Paige got the role instead. It made Paige a household name and was one of the decade's biggest successes, running for 2,900 performances.

Because *Don't Cry for Me Argentina* had not been a hit single in America, Stigwood wanted to cover as many markets as possible for publicity crossover and promotion when the show opened on Broadway in 1979 with Patti Lupone headlining. Disco was the music of the moment, Boris Midney its biggest and most renowned purveyor, so Stigwood invited him over to London to see the West End show and asked him to tailor a dance version for the club scene.

Eva Peron

"The genre was very new then and virtually untapped. Robert gave me complete freedom to experiment. Rice and Lloyd Webber were not particularly ecstatic…" In fact, in Lloyd-Webber's 2018 autobiography 'Unmasked: A Memoir', the composer dismisses the work completely.

Yet Midney moulded choice selections from the 'Evita' songbook so expertly to the Disco medium, it became a separate work of musical art in itself and the Festival version the pioneering producer's magnum opus. A primer in how to adapt such baggage-laden material to an alternative musical genre, *Evita* tweaks the original arrangements and lyrical content into an audaciously multi-tasking Disco entertainment that engages, uplifts and spellbinds with spectacular sound and visionary lyrical drama. Beginning with a long piano intro that echoes and reverberates in the most hauntingly exciting manner, the South American journey starts with the street atmospheric *Buenos Aires*, moves into the Latino jaunty *I'd Be Surprisingly Good for You* and swoops forward with a driving momentum to *Don't Cry for Me Argentina* and its electrifying tango break. Then it soars with a truly adventurous take on *High, Flying Adored*, reaches Disco nirvana with the stupendously orchestrated *Rainbow High*, touches the heart with a violin drenched *She's a Diamond*, before ending with a Midney original, the flaming flamenco fantasy *Eva's Theme: Lady Woman*. My favourite Disco album of all time, Midney's *Evita* is a stunning achievement, insinuating his sparse and ethereal signature sound with showbiz jazz hands and Broadway pizzazz. Keen Midney-ites noticed that the bank of lights photo on the American album cover, shot by the great man himself, is the same one used on the back cover of *Come Into My Heart* by USA-European Connection in an abridged form.

There were two big stories in 1977. **Saturday Night Fever** opened in December of that year and caused a Disco frenzy of epic proportions. But seven months earlier a science fiction space opera had also changed pop culture. George Lucas' **Star Wars** revolutionised the blockbuster movie industry and also put Meco Monardo in the Disco frontline thanks to his dance version of the John Williams composed main theme. Disco versions of every released space epic then became the norm and when the **Star Wars** sequel **The Empire Strikes Back** premiered in 1980, Midney was asked to weave his magic dance spell over key soundtrack selections. RSO Records published the Williams score and because *Evita* had done so well (30 straight weeks in the 'Billboard' Disco charts), Stigwood commissioned Midney's enviable commercial talents once more.

The Empire Strikes Back album contained *Yoda's Theme*, *The Imperial March (Darth Vader's Theme)*, *Han Solo and the Princess (Love Theme)* and *Star Wars (Main Theme)*. Everything and more one had come to expect from a classy Midney production, all the tracks sport a heady jazz funk vibe and quirky intergalactic sound effects summoning the memory of Telstar and Apollo 11 to infinity and beyond. The unusually laid back and sigh-tastic sounding *Han Solo and the Princess (Love Theme)* is a chillax pleasure and a clear pointer towards his developing and emerging styles in the Trance, Hip Hop and Drum & Bass arenas. It's also interesting to compare Midney's *Star Wars (Main Theme)* with Meco's 1977 version; the former is heavier and more sophisticated while the latter is pop gimmickry on steroids, way too flowery and eager to please. Clearly Midney loved this album too. It was the first one to feature a photo portrait of the usually publicity shy iconic artist on the back cover, sitting awkwardly on the Eras Recording Studio console in signature pose.

"This is a test, this is only a test" might have meant an Emergency Broadcast in the USA. But to everyone outside America in Discoland *This Is a Test* was the opening track to the divine Mr. M's next album, *Companion*, his most rarefied dance offering to date and one strongly hinting that he was once again about to take the dancer on a mind-bending trip into the furthest reaches of club speaker systems. This return to self-penned material was a sensual rollercoaster of ethereal instrumental snatches set against bizarre clusters of airy melody, scintillatingly shot through with sparkling vocals by Charmaine and Midney regular Kevin Owens. Released by the French Barclay record label in 1981, *Companion* highlighted *This Is a Test*, *Living Up to Love (Companion)*, *Step On Out*, *There's a Way* (a stripped-back re-orchestrated version of *There's a Way Into My Heart* from the second USA-European Connection album) and *I Feel Delight*, authoritative cuts of quintessential Midney brilliance and another ample showcase of his free musical association expertise.

How did Midney choose the names for his studio projects such as Caress, Masquerade, Festival, Companion, and indeed his 1982 work Double Discovery? "Photography is my other love apart from music, the reason why I shot all my Disco era album covers. In most cases the names sprung from the photos and were often an allusion of the subject matter". An extraordinary example of the all-encompassing Midney cosmos in full Disco action is *Can He Find Another One?* by Double Discovery. Poptastic in every fabulous sense, it features one of Midney's loveliest and catchiest melodies, co-written by Katharine Meyer, his *Companion* collaborator, and Jim Burgess, one of the finest DJs and re-mixers who ruled in the NYC clubs Infinity, 12 West, The Saint and Studio 54. The *West Side* cut is the lilting instrumental version. *Thanks for Loving Me* has a flamboyant Broadway torch song quality about it, albeit with that incandescent Midney touch and spirited jazzy delivery.

Further proof that Midney could deliver something totally left field was provided by *D-D-D-Dance* that, like The Who's *My Generation* (1965) before it, stuttered for a musical genre that was transforming and splintering into new urban sound environments. There was also a startling proclamation on the 1983 vinyl 12" version that stated the song was "From the show 'Pushkin – The Black Russian'". *Living Up to Love* and *Step On Out* from *Companion* also made it to the *Double Discovery* album, as they both would again on a

1983 Double-A side 12" sporting the USA-European Connection name.

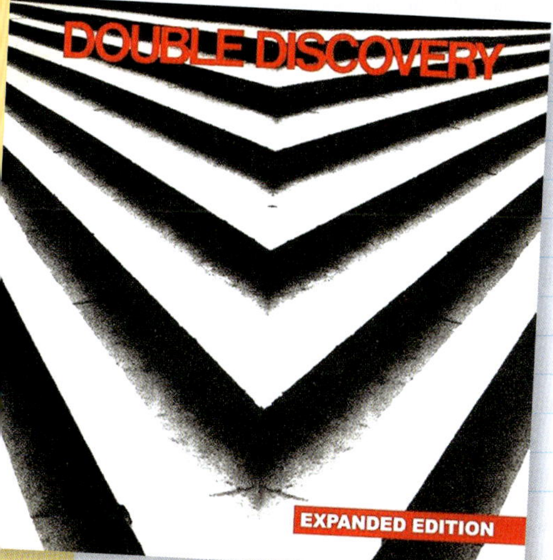

Double Discovery was well named. Midney's work endures because it went beyond the dance floor and proved equally listenable in the home environment where one could actually discover the depth of his dazzling artistry anew. Did Midney expect his Disco reputation would have such longevity in a genre considered instantly disposable? "If a genre is represented by originality – good music in good taste – then it will continue to be discovered by new generations. I suppose it is wholly understandable that I am less known for the advances I made following the Disco era – in Techno, Trance, Hardcore and Drum and Bass for instance – as these styles are more territorial and not necessarily as mainstream as Disco was".

"The biggest mistake people make about me is that I was idle in the post-Disco years whereas the complete opposite was true. 'Dance' is inherently part of me. The core of what people responded to in my Disco music had a lot to do with the melodies and the string parts – the classical elements, and it's exactly what I'm still into today. The format might be different, but the essence remains the same. In the end I had to get rid of Eras because its popularity with artists caused some major distraction. It was continuously booked up with no room for my own projects. So I went private and started producing a variety of underground stuff like *I Will Stand By You* (1996) by Petroleum Jell and my own *Trancetter* (1999) album. The love in all my work remains the orchestral sound that includes innovative arranging. And please note that arranging is an art as it is conceived not added. It has always been in my nature to understand in detail every style and genre of music. Disco was in that diversity and I'm more than happy it was".

Midney-ites couldn't believe their luck when the OZ Record label released a totally new album on CD in 1999 titled *Black Russian*. Because the 12" single of *D-D-D-Dance* proclaimed the song was taken from the show 'Pushkin – The Black Russian', it was assumed the four tracks it contained were also part of that unproduced entertainment. Midney denies all knowledge of such a venture. "*Black Russian* was a project in the early development stage. It was never finished, not properly mixed nor mastered, that ended up being released. It could be re-recorded in a different style with new arrangements… if the right party came along".

Even so, the life of Alexander Pushkin, the black Russian of the title, would seem to lend itself to the lavish Broadway musical treatment. Born of Ethiopian descent in 1799, Pushkin was the great-grandson of Abraham Hannibal, an African general and friend of Peter the Great. 'Boris Godunov', 'Eugene Onegin', 'The Captive of the Caucasus' and 'The Captain's Daughter' are his most famous novels. Notoriously touchy about his honour, Pushkin fought a total of twenty-nine duels, and was fatally wounded at the age of 37 in such an encounter with a French officer who had attempted to seduce his wife Natalya.

Midney's challenge was to adapt Pushkin's poetry and prose with a multiple mix of musical traditions and orchestral styles that made for interesting listening. *A Child Is Born* covers Pushkin's early years in the lushly melodious, classic Midney Disco style, while *Now Is the Time* and *Pushkin's Theme* get down and funky, and *Every Kind of People* hits with some interesting instrumental breaks floating between its minuet and minaret confection. Vocals for this highly unusual item were supplied by the usual combo of Midney regulars and the technical support personnel comprised of veterans Ray Volpe, Dmitri Zbrizer and Brad Johnson. "The vocalists brought a great deal of personality through their performances. Sensuality and understanding of funk was a very important criterion. My engineers, mixers and technicians were all wonderful personalities. All trained by me they became an important part of all our productions".

Midney never really met any of his Disco contemporaries. "Briefly Giorgio Moroder in my attorney's office but we had no verbal exchange. He appeared to be a nice guy. Other than that, they all have my respect". So what is the one lasting memory Midney has about the dance music era he conquered so strikingly? "Jim Burgess was like a god to me in the DJ world (Burgess ruled Manhattan's dance floors, his most successful and best-known production being Alicia Bridges' *I Love the Nightlife*, 1978). He was very musical… very snobbish… and I still had to stay in line at 1 a.m. to get into his clubs to listen to my mixes! One day I got a call asking me to dinner at his New York apartment. I was kind of hesitant. I'm not really the social type. I always felt content and protected in my recording studio behind concrete walls with my crew. But when a god calls you have no choice. We met at his place. He had arranged a nice table outside in a small garden and as he brought some wine to the table I noticed his hands were shaking. 'What's wrong Jim?' I asked. 'I'm so fucking nervous', he replied. 'Nervous?', I exclaimed, 'You are a god Jim, you don't get nervous'. And he said, 'But Boris I thought you were God!'"

FLASHDANCE (1983)

Solidifying the Hollywood mega-reputations of executive producers Peter Guber and Jon Peters, heralding the arrival of Young Turk producers Don Simpson and Jerry Bruckheimer's slick aesthetic, co-writer (with Tom Hedley) Joe Eszterhas's overly sexualised screenplays and director Adrian Lyne's shallow visual approach, **Flashdance** is by popular consensus the first movie to become a smash blockbuster thanks to the just minted MTV generation. Indeed, the now iconic imagery was borrowed wholesale from what was becoming easily accessible 24/7 on the new music channel and being created by the likes of wunderkind rock video pioneers Russell Mulcahy, David Mallet, Brian Grant and Scott Millaney. And with the videos for both the theme song *Flashdance… What a Feeling* (1983) by Irene Cara and featured highlight *Maniac* (1983) by Michael Sembello receiving heavy rotation airing, how could this post-Disco fairytale be anything but a profound pop culture sensation?

Former teen model Jennifer Beals plays 18-year-old Alex Owens, a Pittsburgh steel mill welder by day and an exotic go-go dancer by night at Mawby's bar-and-grill cabaret. But her real ambition lies in joining the local Ballet Conservatory, although she has no formal training. When Alex isn't being romanced by her boss Nick Hurley (Michael Nouri), avoiding working as a stripper at the Zanzibar club, being mentored by ex-ballerina Hanna Long (Lilia Skala) and uttering such choice lines as "Did you know that the smallest penis ever measured was 1.1 inches?"), she's looking out for her friends Jeanie (Sunny Johnson) who wants to be a figure-skater and her boyfriend Richie (Kyle T. Heffner) hoping to become a stand-up comic. When Nick uses his connections with the arts council to get Alex a Conservatory audition, she refuses at first before seeing karmic sense and passing with flying colours.

Based loosely on the life story of Maureen Marder (paid the paltry rights sum of $2,300), Beals' breakout movie eventually grossed over $150 million. That concept, welded together with numerous other tawdry Tinseltown rags-to-riches fables, made it cheesy to a fault, but Lyne nevertheless captures the superficial post-Disco zeitgeist where communications and music were going through key sea changes. So many over-directed scenes cause major eye-rolling; from the heavy-handed jazzercise workout, complete with cuts to Alex's salivating pet dog, to her running a stocking-clad foot up into Nick's crotch at a dinner date where she eats lobster in an arousing way. One does have to wonder what first director choice, suspense stylist Brian De Palma, would have done with the same potentially feminist material.

While it was Beals' idea to wear the off-the-shoulder torn T-shirt that started a hot fashion trend, it was Marine Jahan who body doubled for her dancing scenes. Alex's gasp-inducing leap through the air in the audition was done by gymnast Sharon Shapiro, the break dancing by

Crazy Legs, but none of this was revealed too early during initial release in order not to shatter the appealing illusion of Alex as an all-round loyal, confident, stubborn and sexually liberated modern woman. Critically lambasted it might have been, yet audiences lapped it up ensuring its place as a cinematic and cultural touchstone.

Much like the case with **Saturday Night Fever** (1977), the **Flashdance** soundtrack became its own separate entity, fuelling the want-to-see factor being continuously played on Disco turntables all over the world. Mega legend Giorgio Moroder produced the title song originally intended for Joe Esposito, notable for his work with Brooklyn Dreams and Donna Summer, but the producers insisted on a female vocal. Irene Cara was hot from **Fame** (1980), had sung that theme song too, so she re-wrote Moroder and his collaborator Keith Forsey's lyrics to reflect her own personality more whilst she was on her way to the recording studio. Esposito did get to sing the other Moroder/Forsey composition *Lady, Lady, Lady*.

Other Moroder produced or written tracks included *Love Theme from Flashdance* by Helen St. John, *Romeo* by Donna Summer and *Seduce Me Tonight* by Cycle 5. Laura Branigan sings two songs: *Imagination* and her massive hit *Gloria* (1982). *I'll Be Here Where the Heart Is* performed by Kim Carnes, *Manhunt* by Karen Kamon, *He's a Dream* by Shandi, *It's Just Begun* (1972) by The Jimmy Castor Bunch and *I Love Rock 'n' Roll* (1981) by Joan Jett & the Blackhearts round out the other musical contributions. But nothing beat *Flashdance… What a Feeling* in the annals of Dance music history, because it won an Academy Award for best original song, hit the No.1 spot on the 'Billboard' Hot 100, also No.1 on the 'Billboard' Disco charts and is ranked at No.26 on the 'Billboard' All Time Top 100. A 'Flashdance 2' was mooted for a while with Russell Mulcahy supposedly attached as director based on the fact his rock videos on MTV proved to have the highest rotation. Not true, but the same logic was applied when Mulcahy was offered **Razorback** (1984) as his feature film debut.

Shaw Thing!

Like Cissy Houston, Marlena Shaw's career began in the 1960s when she signed to the legendary Chess label. After an early life as plain old Marlina Burgess, steeped in jazz and gospel music thanks to her trumpet-playing uncle Jimmy Burgess, her singing career really took off in 1966 when she landed a gig with the Playboy Club chain in Chicago. It was through these engagements Marlena was noticed by Chess, who released her first two albums on their subsidiary Cadet label. She moved to Bluenote in 1972 and had the honour of recording that label's first 12-inch single *It's Better Than Walkin' Out*. A tentative Disco baby step happened with *Pictures and Memories* (1977) from her *Sweet Beginnings* album. But her deserved Disco tsunami happened when she joined the *Star Wars Theme* (1977) dream team of producers Meco Monardo and Tony Bongiovi for the 1979 album *Take a Bite*.

This dynamite Disco classic offered the sublime *Suite Seventeen*, which kicked off with the 1965 Frank Sinatra evergreen *It Was a Very Good Year* coupled with Shaw's own composition *I'm a Foster Child*, then interpolated that hybrid song with the sensational *Love Dancin'*, the Isaac Hayes composed *I Thank You* and a gloriously storming cover of the 1973 Diana Ross classic *Touch Me in the Morning*. A sensationally haunting medley sung by a vocalist at the height of her powers ("Music is a feast… so sit at my table and…") *Take a Bite* is one of the top Disco albums of all time. Shaw's last Disco entry came with *Never Give Up on You* from the *Let Me in Your Life* (1982) album.

Starfix

My French translator for the features I filed for 'L'Ecran Fantastique' was Frédéric Albert Lévy and in late 1982 he asked if I would like to write for a new magazine project he was involved with. 'Starfix' was created by film student Christophe Gans and 'Heavy Metal' magazine writer Doug Headline, mainly as a promotional arm for the Scherzo Video company. That directive soon faded away though as 'Starfix' became a cult bestseller and yet another brilliant addition to my growing CV. It only lasted for a glorious seven years from January 1983 to December 1990. But just like 'Cinefantastique' fostered the talents of **Sleepwalkers** (1992) director Mick Garris and writer Stephen Rebello ('Alfred Hitchcock and the Making of Psycho', 'Dolls! Dolls! Dolls! Deep Inside **Valley of the Dolls**'), 'Starfix' put Gans front and centre of the new French fantasy wave when he directed **Brotherhood of the Wolf** (2001), along with writer François Cognard, producer of **Amer** (2009) and **Painless** (2012), and future TV host Guilaine Chenu.

The editorial statement of the magazine was written in its tagline: "The magazine of adventure, fantasy and science fiction cinema and video". The whole ethos of 'Starfix' was a Punk one – it deliberately lionised movies with limited mainstream appeal or ones highlighting the state of the art special effects and new visual languages being explored by such hungry whippersnappers as David Cronenberg, Michael Mann and Peter Weir. I loved being a part of it and naturally contributed interviews with Russell Mulcahy, James Cameron and Dario Argento, you get the drift. In no time at all I had another international outlet, an even higher profile, and it was one of the reasons I was invited to be on the Critics Jury at France's most prestigious fantasy film festival of the day, Avoriaz, in 1993.

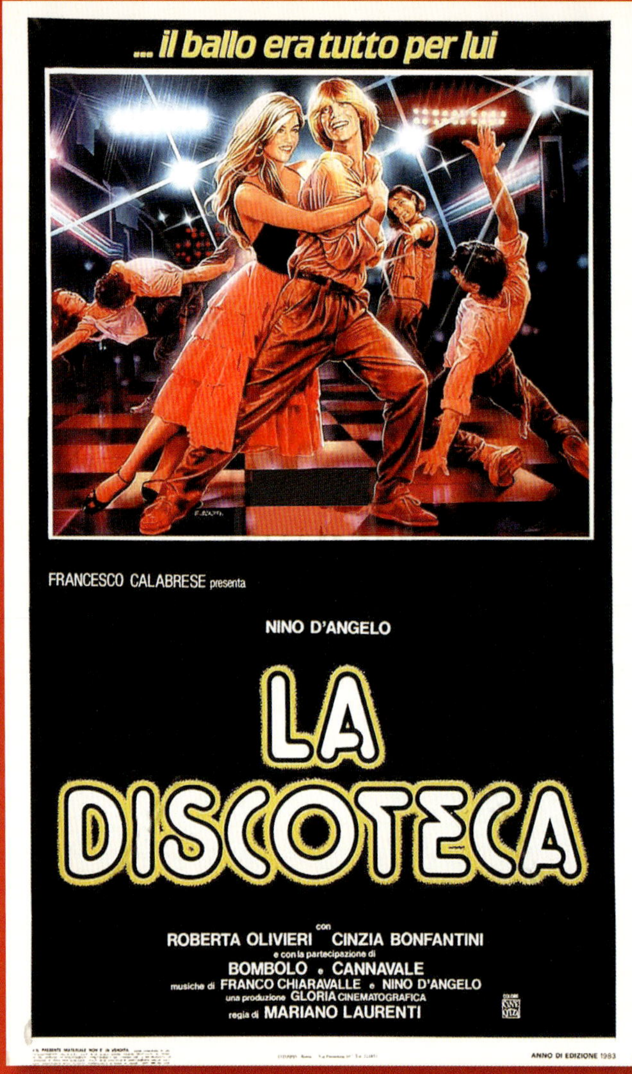

LA DISCOTECA / THE DISCO (1984)

Before the Italian *musicarelli* genre, and the movie considered to have started it all, Lucio Fulci's **Ragazzi del Juke-Box** (1959), there was the *sceneggiata napoletana* that rose to popularity after the First World War. Basically a musical soap opera where romantic melodrama was interspersed with traditional Neapolitan songs, the form found favour first on stage and grew in wider recognition when adapted for the cinema without the limiting encumbrance of local dialect. Especially during the 1970s when the genre's central themes of passion, jealousy, betrayal, treachery, honour, vengeance and petty crime could be explored to the fullest. Many Naples-born artists felt duty bound to carry on the tradition and one such all-round performer was Nino D'Angelo, who went from being a wedding singer to actor in the *sceneggiata napoletana* and eventually a chart-topping pop star.

His first album *A storia mia ('O scippio)* (1976) was received well and he built a solid entertainment career from its base. Naturally the cinema soon called and his first movie was **Celebrità** (1981) but it was his fifth starring vehicle **Un jeans e una maglietta/Jeans and a T-Shirt** (1983) that solidified his burgeoning fame. The accompanying soundtrack album sold over one million copies and the film beat **Flashdance** (1983) at the Italian box-office. So the director Mariano Laurenti, well known for his sex comedies (e.g. **L'insegnante va in collegio/The Schoolteacher Goes to Boys' High**, 1978, starring Edwige Fenech) thought a quick follow-up should be shot as soon as possible. The dismal result was **La discoteca**, written by exploitation maestro Piero Regnoli (**Lust for a Vampire/I vampiri**, 1957, **Incubo sulla città contaminata/Nightmare City**, 1980), who certainly didn't stint on the passion, jealousy, betrayal, treachery or honour topics even if the promised Disco element gets criminally sidelined.

Nino Maritozzi (D'Angelo) is a young pizza chef who lives in Positano and spends most of his time with girlfriend Maria (Roberta Olivieri, also in **Un jeans e una maglietta**). So he's torn when offered a job for the winter season at the Thoni 3000 hotel in the ritzy Stelvio Pass ski resort, Northern Italy. But Maria urges Nino to seize the opportunity, promising she'll still be there for him in the spring. Accompanied by his loser layabout friend Bombolo (a character actor so popular they used his actual name), it turns out the authoritarian hotel manager Ghitler (Enzo Cannavale, the projectionist in **Cinema Paradiso**, 1988) – see what they did there? – is a dead ringer for his boss back home. Ghitler is also the lame comic relief, being a schizophrenic and consistently bursting into tears when hearing a Neapolitan song. Through him Nino meets the hotel owner's daughter Romy (Cinzia Bonfantini) who fancies him rotten. Meanwhile back in Positano, Nino's friend Carlo is trying to seduce Maria by lying about Nino two-timing her. Amidst mistaken identities, misunderstandings, emotional torment and bedroom farce, the star-crossed lovers are finally reunited.

Oh, and Nino sings five self-penned songs while dodgy dance footage filler surrounds him. And when he's Disco dancing, an obvious body double is shot at inventive angles so you never see his face. For a movie titled **The Disco** it's a shame there's little Disco action, just simple soap opera histrionics – the moments Nino tries phoning Maria only to run into obstacles placed in his path by Carlo get old very quickly. For the record the D'Angelo songs aren't really Disco of any description except for the toe-tapping *Bimba*; the others are more in the sentimental ballad tradition and include *A discoteca*, *E' troppo tardi*, *Sotto 'e stelle* and *Pronto si tu?...* Director Laurenti has been quoted as saying the first screening in Naples caused riots and the police had to be called in to calm the over-excited crowds down. Whether that was because they were so desperate to get out he didn't say.

Porno Disco

It wasn't just female porno stars Andrea True and Marilyn Chambers who made the Disco grade. New Yorker Dennis Posa under the alias Wade Nichols was one of the few actors who made the transition from XXX-rated movies to the mainstream. Beginning his career in such gay adult films as **Boynapped** (1975), Nichols did do straight porn as well and ended up playing Detective Derek Mallory on the long-running American daytime soap opera 'The Edge of Night'. In 1979 he attracted the attention of the Village People creator/producer Jacques Morali, quickly became his lover, and recorded the Casablanca Records Disco album *Like an Eagle* under another alias, Dennis Parker. The title track, a thinly veiled paean to the delights of cruising – "hunting nightly in the city" go the lyrics – naturally became a sizeable gay club hit due in no small measure to soaring choruses of tuneful wails. Oh, and the fact Parker wore a skin-tight silver Lurex stage outfit when he promoted the single release on 'The Merv Griffin Show'! Coupled in the Disco charts with the similar orientated *New York By Night*, Parker paid cheeky tribute to his own porno career singing about 42nd Street sleaze-pits where sex was on offer in the auditoriums and where Christopher Street back room bars offered "a galaxy of pleasure and pain". Parker's end was a sad one; he committed suicide in 1985 after suffering AIDS complications.

AIDS

Two of my closest friends died from AIDS complications and never a week went past since the epidemic officially began on June 5th, 1981, that I didn't lose another acquaintance or person I knew from a distance. The Disco floor emptied but not in a good way. It's hard today to put into words the devastating effect the disease had on my generation even in the light of the Covid-19 pandemic and its depiction in the hit Channel 4 TV series 'It's a Sin'. Back in the early 1980s it supposedly only affected the gay population, and it felt like everyone else couldn't have cared less. Until someone they knew died too and then the magnitude of the problem hit home.

The moment the headline stories from America became too scary to ignore, I adopted the 'safe sex' mantra and took a test. Then you had to wait two weeks for the results and I know I'm not alone in saying that fortnight felt like the longest and most gruelling self-torturing period of my life. The moment I found out I was negative I called up everyone I knew who had tested positive and apologised profusely to them. I didn't understand how I had been spared or why?

From that moment on I made a pact to live my life to the fullest, not just for myself, but for all the people I had loved and lost and would have adored sharing the same memories I was forging. Over the next decade I attended more funerals than anyone should do in their lifetime. And I have never taken anything for granted ever since. Disco became even more important at this juncture and this dreadful period taught me to tell everyone I truly loved that I loved them at every opportunity I could. Because there might come a time you can't and you never knew when that time was going to be.

JOCKS: ANGELI IN DISCOTECA / JOCKS: ANGELS IN THE DISCOTHEQUE / MUSIC FEVER / DISCO FEVER (1984)

Every summer trendy Italians and smart tourists head to the beach resort of Rimini on the Adriatic Riviera to dance at the Altromondo Studios club on the Via Flaminia. Rated as the 44th best Disco in the world (No.2 in Italy) with a massive 4,000+ capacity and ability to attract star acts and headlining DJs from all over the world, Altromondo Studios is still as popular today as it ever was in the Disco heyday. Opened in July 1967 by Gilberto Amati as Club dell'Altromondo, it was the first Discotheque in Europe to introduce the concept of live concert performances – Hustle royalty Van McCoy one of the many floorshow attractions to appear there. But in 1984, with mainstream Disco waning and its more gay ghetto HiNRG offshoot taking hold, the new owners of Altromondo Studios, management gurus/record producers Guerrino Galli and Piero Bevitori thought they should be doing more in the PR department to advertise their huge investment.

So they asked producer Pino Buricchi (**L'ultimo treno della notte/Late Night Trains/Night Train Murders**, 1975) and director Riccardo Sesani (assistant director on **Il medaglione insanguinato/The Cursed Medallion/The Night Child**, 1975) to concoct a promotional musical movie set around Altromondo Studios (and other Rimini watering holes like the Tiffany and Geo clubs) featuring acts in their management portfolio to promote their dance establishment and the all-encompassing 24/7 lifestyle. By sheer lucky accident the two B-movie grindhousers created the first movie to highlight the burgeoning Italo Disco scene that had been established in 1982 by the German ZYX label as the descriptive international marketing tool for the global consumption of the contemporary spaghetti sound.

The movie itself was a plot-basic, hilariously awful wash-out starring as the supposedly brilliant Dijei the very camp Russel(l) Russel(l), a singer/dancer/choreographer from New York who bookended his one-hit-wonder **Jocks** career with the albums *Russell Russell* (1981) featuring the single *Buonasera ragazzina*, produced by Goblin maestro Claudio Simonetti, and *Afrodixia* (1986). Playing the macho and exceptional light technician Hifi, Russel's co-star is Tom Hooker, an American singer/songwriter who had built his career in Italy as a solo artist after the single *Flip Over* (1981) and participating in the popular homegrown talent discovery event, the

Sanremo Festival. Hooker would get the non-holds-barred documentary treatment in **Dons of Disco** (2019).

Essentially, **Jocks** concerns the interracial frenemies Dijei and Hifi joining forces after meeting on the road to open up their own Disco and stage the biggest Italian dance party of the century. Sharing sleeping arrangements in the back of Hifi's massive 'America Videodiscoteca' truck, complete with mirrorballs, hammocks and Manhattan skyline poster, when they're not punching each other incessantly, the mismatched duo stop in clearly out-of-season Rimini where Hifi has been hired to install lighting rigs for a new nightclub. There they start looking for backers for their brainstorm music event but the first local businessman they approach gets arrested for fraud outside the bank where he's supposed to withdraw the funds. Their next mark is a veteran opera singer (Giuliana Calandra, **Deep Red**, 1975) who leans on her rich ageing beau (Armando Brancia, **Amarcord**, 1973) for the cash after dreaming of making a comeback.

Further complications arise when **Flashdance** (1983) type rehearsals begin, they save homeless dancer Kim (Patricia Moore), also the opera singer's aunt, from being harassed by a motorbike gang and Hifi falls in love with her when she too moves into the truck. Said Emilia-Romagna Hells Angels branch also tear down all the posters advertising the headlining stars of the upcoming show, The Creatures, and kidnap Dijei just as the mega-Disco event is about to begin. But when the 30-minute revue, 'The Other World Show', based on The Creatures' genuine live act, does start (after real footage of queues forming to get into Altromondo Studios unspools) it's quite something – an elaborate space fantasy in the 'Stryx' TV show mode with robots, Gods, monsters, lasers, neon lights and all sorts of cosmic glitz dazzling the spectator. The final credits read 'Thermodynamic Construction and Special Effects by Pierino Galli', obviously a relation to the club owner. Anyway the show is a hit, the public goes wild and Dijei and Hifi are on the road to success.

The Creatures provide the tracks *Maybe One Day* (1983), *Believe In Yourself* (1983), *Starting from Here* (1983), *Digital Rebel* (1983), *Inspiration* (1983) and the classical Disco climax of *Aida* (1983), a BPM'd Giuseppe Verdi mash-up. The Creatures were musicians Mario Flores and Maurizio Sangineto who released seven albums between 1982 and 1991 and also wrote the incidental soundtrack music as Mario Flores and Sangy. Other tracks featured are *Breaking Breaking* by Bata Drum, *Queen of Witches* (1983) by Kano, *Let's All Dance* (1983) by Band of Jocks, *Fantasize* and *Turn the Music On* (both 1983) by Orlando Johnson and Trance, *Shame* (1983) by Stephany, *Rolling On* and *Run for Cover* (both 1983) by The Mike Lester Band and *Love Attack* by Tom Hooker. Directed by Sesani in a moribund 'The Monkees' madcap style, and played at hysterical fever pitch, with sidelines into Sony Walkman demonstrations, leg-warmer frenzy, Disco maintenance, Rimini travelogue and the DJ character literally swishing everywhere, **Jocks** is '80s excess all areas, a spectacular starcrash and burn kitsch extravaganza.

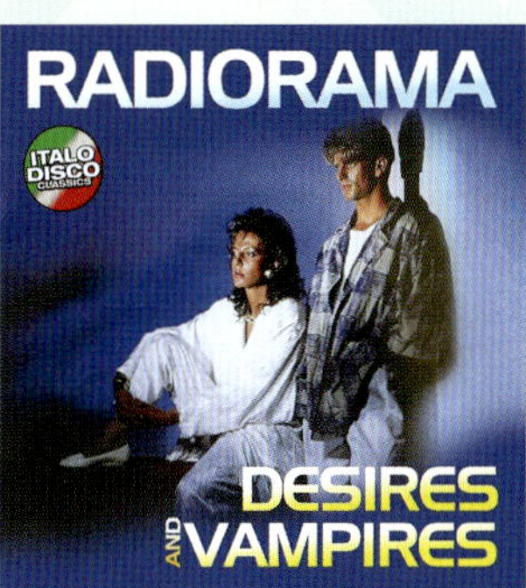

Italo Disco

During the late 1970s/early-'80s a brand of electronic dance music began evolving throughout the boot of Italy. With its insanely romantic, melodic hook-lines, distinct futuristic sounds created using synthesizers, drum machines and vocoders and most importantly lyrics in English, the genre was labelled Italo Disco. The term was merely a marketing ploy, mainly coined by the German record label ZYX Music, to enliven and sex up the club music scene. But it soon caught on internationally and would eventually encompass a whole wealth of old and new talent under the one umbrella name. It also led 'Stereo Review' magazine to write at the time "Disco didn't die, it just moved to Italy".

When Milan and Verona based producers, drenched in Giorgio Moroder and Kraftwerk influences, began crafting this poppy futuristic Disco tangent with melancholy metronome melodies and weird electronic sounds utilising unorthodox production techniques, they pounced on early mass-produced studio kit to blend their edgy experimental music with an accessible classic pop sensibility. Producers and singers worked in cramped studios almost on factory-like assembly lines, cranking out what they hoped would make the local *paninaro* kids want to get up and dance. Every Italo Disco production was meant to create illusions of raw passion, luxury wealth and fantasy romance. But because money was tight many Italian musicians released records under a dizzying variety of aliases so any promotional budget could go on brand names like Radiorama (*Desires and Vampires* album, 1986) where the vocal personnel could easily be changed rather than invest in expensive single artists. This strategy may

have been cost-effective but it's the reason why it can be so difficult to pinpoint who did what in the confusion of producer aliases, band pseudonyms and revolving behind-the-scenes talent.

Nevertheless Italo Disco provided nightclubs wanting to fight-off the onslaught of HiNRG and its gay connotations with a number of popular hits. In 1983 veteran Mondo Disco producer La Bionda devised the *Do It Again/Billie Jean* medley for Clubhouse. In 1986 Tantra maestro Celso Valli arranged the American mainstream crossover *I Love My Radio* by Taffy, an ultra-catchy 'Billboard' dance chart No.6. Verona-born singer (Ivana) Spagna said *Call Me* (1988) after being part of the duo Fun Fun singing *Colour My Love* (1984). Then there was Sabrina whose sexy, sunny *Boys (Summertime Love)* stormed the European charts during 1988 mainly due to its accompanying music video showing the one-time beauty queen wrestling with her barely-there bikini top.

Arguably the most memorable of all Italo Disco tracks comes with the dreaded 'One Hit Wonder' label internationally. But in Italy Baltimora released three albums and more single hits than just their global monster *Tarzan Boy* (1985). Written by Maurizio Bassi (future Eros Ramazzotti associate) and Naimy Hackett (Klein & MBO, *Dirty Talk*, 1982), Bassi also sang the song while Londonderry, Northern Ireland, born Jimmy McShane (who died of AIDS in 1995) lip-synched as the more press friendly figurehead front. It worked. *Tarzan Boy* is one of the few Italo Disco tracks to travel widely, hit the mainstream thanks to its lyrical and electronic simplicity, and enter pop culture consciousness by being included on such soundtracks as **Teenage Mutant Ninja Turtles III** (1993) and **Beverly Hills Ninja** (1997).

Discomagic Records was the largest Italo Disco record label in Italy during the musical genre's heyday. Based in Milan, it spawned a large number of sub-labels during the early 1980s to the early 1990s (including Fuck! Records and Cocaine Records), and set the standards for an entire variety of Eurodance music. Run by Severo Lombardoni from 1982 until 1997, Radiorama genius Mauro Farina then took over control of operations, although only the Dance World Attack sub-label survived and ZYX Music then bought the entire catalogue including the work of key artists Lee Marrow, Albert One, Kasso, Aleph and Black Box.

Way too many individual tracks to mention but some of the best Italo Disco offerings are the whole *I Like Chopin* (1983) album by Gazebo, *How Old Are You* (1984) by Miko Mission, *Tonight* (1985) by Ken Laszlo, *Midnight Girl* (1988) by Italian Boys, *I Want an Illusion* (1986) by Squash Gang, *Little Russian* (1987) by Mr. Zivago, *My World* (1989) by Sophie, *I.C. Love Affair* (1983) by Gaznevada, *Around My Dream* (1987) by Silver/Silvio Pozzoli, *Activate My Heart* (1986) by Meccano, *Love* (1988) by Gypsy & Queen, *So Close to Heaven* (1989) by Chip Chip, and *Feel the Drive* (1983) by Doctor's Cat.

Considered one of the early pioneers of Italo Disco, Kano (named after the Nigerian city) was a neo-Disco music project formed in 1979 by Italian-based producers Luciano Ninzatti, Stefano Pulga and Matteo Bonsanto. The Kano sound was synthesized Disco funk and the band had the most hits on the 'Billboard' charts of any other Italo Disco attraction. *I'm Ready, Holly Dolly, It's a War, Ahija* (all 1980), *Can't Hold Back (Your Loving), Baby Not Tonight* and *Don't Try to Stop Me* (all 1981) put Kano in the US Disco Top Ten and the term Italo Disco on the lips of everyone who heard them.

From David Warbeck's modelling portfolio.

Disco Memo

David Warbeck

I first met Eurotrash movie star David Warbeck when he, like me, auditioned for 'Who Killed Bambi?' We met on the stairs of Russ Meyer's hotel within minutes of each other having an audience with King Leer and I instantly recognised him from **Trog** (1970), **Twins of Evil** (1972), **Craze** (1974) and those famous 'And all because the lady loves…' Cadbury's Milk Tray TV commercials. David had form with Meyer of course from **Slaves/Blacksnake** (1973) so I figured he was a shoo-in for the role of the managing director of the Sex Pistols record company. His character's office was going to be at the top of the Centre Point building at the junction between Oxford Street and Tottenham Court Road. His major scene had the Pistols bursting into the boardroom in a rage over the dodgy deal they'd just signed, throwing him over his desk, pulling his trousers down, ripping his pants off and all taking turns in anally raping him. Then they were supposed to throw him through the window to his death, impaled on a fountain, in the street far below. David would have been so up for that but again, like me, once Meyer got axed by Malcolm McLaren our censor-busting scenes were history.

It wasn't long before David would figure in my life in a way neither of us had anticipated. After years of scraping the bottom of the acting barrel with the likes of **My Lover, My Son** (1970) and **Journey to Murder** (1971), he went to Italy to play a role in Sergio Leone's **A Fistful of Dynamite/Giù la testa** (1971) and his galvanising scenes with star James Coburn, memorably underscored by Ennio Morricone's incredibly moving theme *Sean, Sean* in that masterwork, put him on every Italian agents' radar and he soon became the go-to James Bond-in-waiting action hero. Our paths crossed again when he starred in **The Black Cat/Gatto nero** (1981) and **The Beyond/…E tu vivrai nel terrore! L'aldilà** (1981) for director Lucio Fulci. Those films and other roles for directors Antonio Margheriti, Tonino Ricci, Alberto De Martino and Fabrizio De Angelis made him a cult Euro star, a title he loved and lived up to every moment of his short life.

David Warbeck, Vivienne Chandler and James Coburn in *A Fistful of Dynamite* (1971).

Through Eagle Films, owned by Wardour Street royalty Barry Jacobs, I asked David for a career interview for 'Cinema' magazine. **The Last Hunter/L'ultimo cacciatore** was about to be released in the UK and I thought it would be a good time to position his rising Continental profile with the readers. That interview made us the best of friends going forward and nearly caused both of us to be sued by Russ Meyer. David always was full of juicy anecdotes and I printed one about Meyer's ex-wife Edy Williams, star of **Beyond the Valley of the Dolls** (1970), and the director hit the roof basically saying that if Edy read it she could ask for more alimony. Neither of us, nor Marvel Comics, could understand why he couldn't see the funny side of it until we realised Meyer's complete lack of irony was the stumbling block. The matter never got to court but it was touch-and-go for a time and happily cemented our relationship as up-for-anything good time mates.

David Warbeck with Catriona MacColl in *The Beyond* (1981).

We shared so many (mis)adventures during the 1980s 'La Dolce Vita' redux period in Rome where he revelled in his celebrity and I always tried to engineer being in the Eternal City at the same time he was filming so we could get up to mischief. Our extracurricular exploits, often with his Italian

Disco Memo

Alan Jones's own note on the photo says it all, the premiere was *Fatal Frames* (1996).

agent Giuseppe Perrone and his partner Howard Ross, did raise a few local eyebrows as we attended low rent premieres and paparazzi parties. Nor was it just confined to Rome. Back in London David had ploughed all his earnings – and he was still being highly paid as a model – into renovating an old convent in ritzy Belsize Park. Decorated in a style one can only call Bordello Victoriana, the place became non-stop Party Central. Much to the chagrin of the neighbours convinced he was actually running a house of ill repute. The times I was there when the police came calling, saying someone had complained about the noise!

David's New Year parties were legendary. He insisted all the men wear kilts and Scottish national dress, and all the women be as glamorous as possible. He'd hire Fay Presto, Queen of Close-Up magic, to dazzle us with clever illusions, strippers of both sexes to add extra raunch and his guest lists were always a mix of C-listers, celebrity thespians and royalty. I never missed one. Out of all the bawdy anecdotes David would tell about his co-stars, Dagmar Lassander, filming mishaps, Fulci, Janet Agren and Mimsy Farmer, my favourite was the one about Joan Crawford. The fading Hollywood legend had a reputation for trying to sleep with every male cast member she ever worked with. When she made her final screen appearance in **Trog** it was clear she fancied David and would keep inviting him into her trailer for cocktails. One day, bored on location, he accepted her offer and spent the whole time avoiding her advances as she chased him around the tiny caravan. Because it was parked on an incline, the vehicle suddenly hurtled down the slope, crashed into a tree, the door flew open and out tumbled David and Joan on top of each other. I always laughed when he told that story to an always rapt crowd and it fills me with sadness knowing I'll never hear him recite his banner party piece again.

HEAVENLY BODIES (1984)

Hollywood superstar Jane Fonda had a lot to answer for in the early 1980s. Her workout videos, tie-in books and fitness regimes became big business and a pop culture punchline. Everyone jumped on the bandwagon from Olivia Newton-John's chart-topping hit *Physical* (1981) to celebrity cash-ins by flamboyant fitness guru Richard Simmons, 'Dynasty' and 'Melrose Place' star Heather Locklear, and Cher. **Heavenly Bodies** tried putting all that aerobic energy into narrative form with Disco motoring the exercises. Packed with such Canadian horror names as Cynthia Dale (Patty from **Prom Night**, 1980), Richard Rebiere (**Happy Birthday to Me**, 1981, **Visiting Hours**, 1982), Walter George Alton (Alberto De Martino's **The Pumaman/L'uomo puma**, 1980), Stuart Stone (**Blue Monkey**, 1987), and marking the only film as director by character actor Lawrence Dane (**Scanners**, 1981, **Of Unknown Origin**, 1983), the main financial backing came from Playboy Enterprises, hence the minimal nudity but maximum jiggling around in skintight spandex with matching legwarmers.

Putting the viewer in absolutely no doubt what the inspiration for this Exerciseploitation item is from the very start – Samantha Blair (Dale) stares longingly at a poster of Jennifer Beals in **Flashdance** (1983) – Dane whisks through the usual tropes of dance rivalries to a competition climax. Single mother Samantha has quit her 9-to-5 secretarial post to open up her own aerobics studio, 'Heavenly Bodies', in an abandoned warehouse. Before you can warble "What a feeling", a montage hurtles through lightning scenes establishing the studio becoming the hottest place for exercise in town.

Membership soars and her aspiration of buying the warehouse lease looks more than a jazzercise dream.

Asked to train some professional footballers, Samantha takes the fancy of one of the team, Steve (Rebiere) who does everything to make her fall in love with him. Then the local TV station, wanting to use the fitness craze to boost ratings, holds open auditions for the host of a new show. Because the director is a friend of Jack Pearson (Alton), owner of the biggest health club brand, it looks like his girlfriend Debbie (Laura Henry) will nepotistically land the assignment. But when the producer chooses Samantha instead, bitter Debbie gets her lease terminated until both decide on the ownership being settled by a winner-takes-all Workout Marathon. Spoiler alert: Samantha out-twirls everyone, Steve gets his woman and truckloads of ladies in leotards gyrate into the credits.

With most of the pre-Zumba routines shot in boring real time, backed by a pleasing 1980s synthpop/Disco soundtrack, Dane's not entirely worthless elongated rock video is a fun time capsule enlivened by Dale's gung-ho performance. She's obviously enjoying herself and that's communicated through the silver screen. She, Rebiere and the class group sweat to Bonnie Pointer's Disco hit *The Beast in Me* and Dale goes the full Jennifer Beals in Pointer's *Heaven* (1984). Elsewhere Sparks' *Breaking Out of Prison* (1984), Cheryl Lynn's *At Last You're Mine* (1984), Boys Brigade's *Into the Flow* (1984), Joe Lamont's *Love Always Wins* (1984), Marc Tanner's *Look What You've Done to Me* (1984), Gary Wright's *Breakthrough* (1984), and Dwight Twilley's *Keep on Working* (1984) score the treadmill. Many people hold the movie and the music high in their affections and that might be because the end credits feature a full screen advertisement for it being readily available. How could they resist?

Silver Convention

One of the first Disco groups to break out of the German ghetto and take their light, sparsely produced, choppy message global, garnering 17 gold discs in the process, was Silver Convention. Produced by Michael Kunze and Sylvester Levay, the trio was formed by the duo needing female session singers for some Disco instrumental tracks they thought might be commercial. Levay's nickname was Silver and the name Silver Bird Convention was first mooted before the simpler version was settled on to brand their first and immediately massive Eurodisco hit *Save Me* (1975). More anonymous backing singers were used for the title cash-in album that spawned the further hits *I Like It* (1975), *Tiger Baby* (1975) and *Fly, Robin, Fly* (1975), originally recorded as *Run, Rabbit, Run* until someone pointed out the title could be mistaken as the British music hall standard. The latter became Silver Convention's biggest-selling record ever, a million copies in Germany alone, and the track that scored them a 'Billboard' Disco Chart No.1.

It was in the light of their burgeoning Disco success that an actual line-up was put together to send on the road for promotional purposes. Linda G. Thompson (replaced by Rhonda Heath in 1977), Penny McLean and Ramona Wulf were the able recruits and *Get Up and Boogie (That's Right)* (1976), *No, No, Joe/San Francisco Hustle* (1976) and *Spend the Night with Me/Mission to Venus* (1978) kept their profile strong in worldwide Discos even though their heavily orchestrated sound never varied from spacey, ecstatic, sweetly ephemeral vocals bouncing off the tightest of productions. McLean had her own solo Disco hit in 1975 with *Lady Bump*, a raucous shrieker that would become better known as part of The Ritchie Family's classic medley *The Best Disco in Town* (1976). Thompson would also make minor dance waves with her solo offering *Ooh What a Night (Part 1 & 2)* (1975). Their last Disco hits were with *Spend the Night with Me* (1978) and *Mission to Venus* (1978) but *Dancin' in the Aisle* (1976), *Everbody's Talking 'Bout Love* (1976), *Telegram* (1977) and *Love in a Sleeper* (1978) are just as ace too.

The Hungarian born Levay would endure well past his Disco sell-by-date composing the music for the movies **Where the Boys Are '84** (1984), **Creator** (1985), **Cobra** (1986) and **Mannequin** (1987) plus the 'Airwolf' (1984-86) TV series and Wes Craven's TV movie 'Invitation to Hell'. Together with his Prague-born lyricist Kunze, who used the pseudonym Stephan Prager on his Silver Convention credits and adapted 'Cats' and 'Evita' for the German market, Levay also composed the popular European stage musicals 'Elizabeth', 'Mozart!', 'Rebecca' and 'Marie Antoinette'.

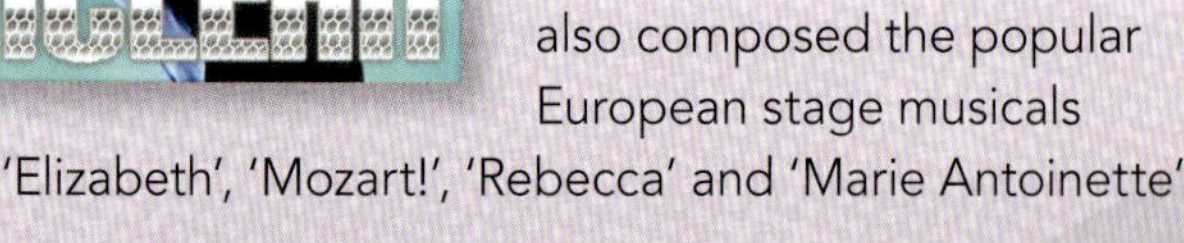

Raquel

The only time I have ever been lost for words when meeting a famous star was when I interviewed Raquel Welch. Like so many fantasy movie fans of my generation, the first celebrity poster I ever put on my bedroom wall was the famous picture of Raquel in that fur bikini from Hammer's **One Million Years B.C.** (1966). For years the actual pink day-glo quad poster was the Holy Grail for my extensive collection. What was it about her? She was exquisitely beautiful, yes. She had a unique persona too. She also appeared in some terrific movies like **Fantastic Voyage** (1966), **100 Rifles** (1969), **Myra Breckinridge** (1970) – sorry, I love it – **The Three Musketeers** (1973), the very first preview screening I ever attended, **The Last of Sheila** (1973) – the best American appropriation of the giallo idiom ever made – and **The Wild Party** (1975). And her Curtwel production company was responsible for financing Michael Reeves' superb **The Sorcerers** (1967). I mean, what's not to like?

For too many years I would argue that Raquel was a wonderful actor to anyone who would listen when it was unfashionable to do so and many dismissed her as mere window dressing. But those who truly followed her career as I did could see her development into a performer of substance. Anyone who saw her on Broadway in the Fred Ebb and John Kander musical 'Woman of the Year' in 1981 would attest to that. After her tenure in that show she would release the Disco hit *This Girl's Back in Town* (1987) and become a successful business entrepreneur.

In 1984 she jumped on the exercise bandwagon with her book 'The Raquel Welch Total Beauty and Fitness Program' and it was for the UK launch of this publication I signed up to interview her. For moral support, and as it turned out actual support when I nearly fainted, I took along my friend Frances Lynn, gossip columnist for the David Bailey/Patrick Lichfield owned socialite newspaper 'Ritz'. Raquel was every bit as Hollywood glamorous as I imagined she would be, I was so bowled over by meeting her I fell into that awful default position of saying "Miss Welch, I'm your biggest fan", which I had never done before nor since. I could see the smile on her face freeze for a few seconds as I tried to regain my composure and how I got through the rest of the interview I'll never know. But I added another personal idol to my list who I have told how much they meant to me and have lived with that memory instead of my bumbling fanboy one.

VOYAGE OF THE ROCK ALIENS (1984)

Although it tries way too hard for the cult success that has consistently eluded it throughout the ensuing decades, this low-grade spoof of 1950s sci-fi poverty row filler blended with the 1960s' **Beach Party** (1963) vogue is a very silly but fun minor entry in the guilty pleasure genre. Its inclusion here is for one specific reason only, of which more later. Starting life as 'Attack of the Aliens', an original spec script by writer James Guidotti, once Interplanetary Pictures had optioned it and director James Fargo and star Pia Zadora had climbed on board, it was turned into an ersatz MTV-style musical affair and went into production as 'Attack of the Rock 'n' Roll Aliens'.

Previously an assistant director for Clint Eastwood and several early Steven Spielberg films, Fargo made his directorial debut with the Dirty Harry film **The Enforcer** (1976), followed by the Eastwood comedy hit **Every Which Way But Loose** (1979). This box-office disaster moreorless ended that meteoric career. Pia Zadora was the Kim Kardashian of her day. After making her teenage debut in the infamous clunker **Santa Claus Conquers the Martians** (1964), she eventually married multi-millionaire businessman Meshulam Riklis who actively promoted her acting career with little success as she won back-to-back Razzie Awards as Worst Actress in both **Butterfly** (1982) and **The Lonely Lady** (1983). Zadora would gain some cool by being featured in John Waters' **Hairspray** (1988), but it would be for several popular albums of American Songbook standards, often backed by a symphony orchestra, that would gain her most critical plaudits.

Quite simply a Martian Beach Party for the nuclear age, student Dee Dee (Zadora, named in homage to Annette Funicello) attends Heidi High School in the town of Speelburgh! It's Dee Dee's dream to sing with the Rockabilly band The Pack led by her boyfriend Frankie (a pre-**Nightbreed**, 1990, Craig Sheffer, named in homage to Frankie Avalon), but he's not convinced. So when some visiting aliens transported by a guitar-shaped spaceship emerge from a telephone box with a talking fire hydrant as their guide, she grabs the chance to join their electro-pop outfit. Falling for their leader Absid (Tom Nolan), Dee Dee soon learns that she'll have to give up all human emotion and sexual feeling if she is to run away to his home planet, a price far too great to pay even in exchange for intergalactic fame and a cosmic singing career.

Fargo directs all the slapstick rock video shenanigans, culminating in a battle of the bands at the Big Cotillion Dance, with an unsubtle slickness and brassy verve even though the joke eventually wears as thin as the budget. Delights along the way include **Rosemary's**

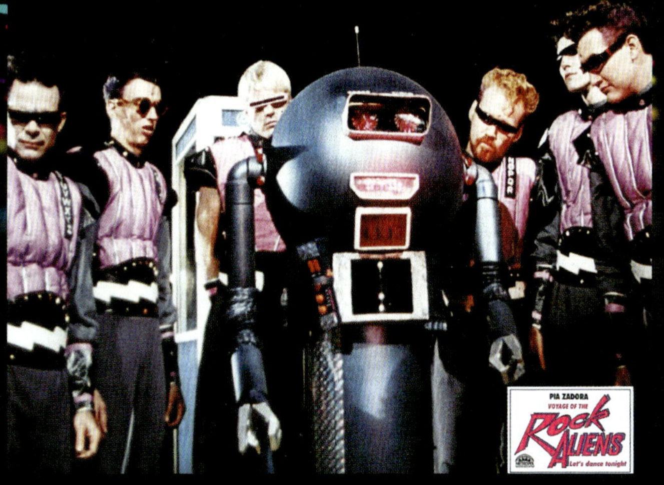

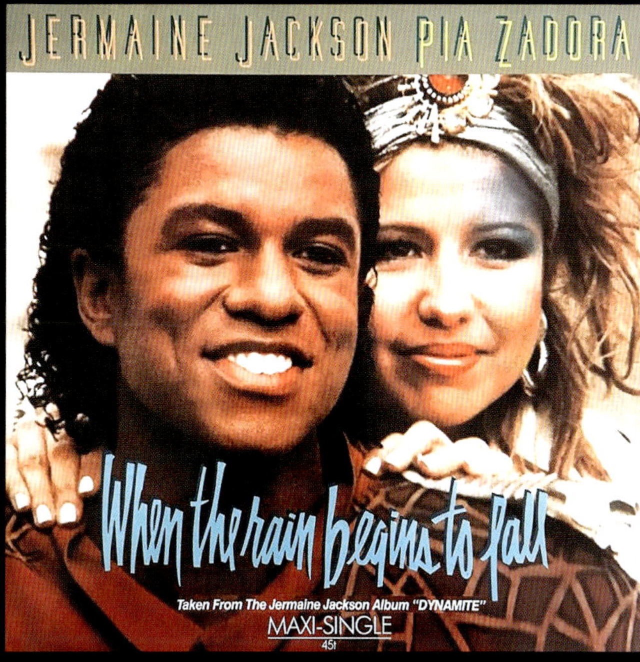

Baby (1968) star Ruth Gordon as a gun-toting, UFO-obsessed sheriff, **The Hills Have Eyes** (1977) horror icon Michael Berryman typecast as a chainsaw-wielding escaped mental patient, a mutant tentacle monster and the climactic nod to 1950s exploitation where Absid zaps Earth to clear it of all pollution.

"Prepare for a musical invasion…" tag-lined the promotional posters. But despite the boast that **Voyage of the Rock Aliens** would have an Easter 1985 release in 1,000 cinemas, it barely played anywhere. When it did, it had a new opening scene than the one envisioned by director Fargo. Seven months before that Spring date Jermaine Jackson and Pia Zadora had a sizeable European dance hit with the infectiously Tinkertoy duet *When the Rain Begins to Fall.* So the rock video for the song was edited into the opening credits as playing on a television screen to make it look like Absid and his extraterrestrial band were watching, the reason they chose Earth as their musical target. Unlike the bland songs featured in the main body of the movie and sometimes solely on the soundtrack release, like *Combine Man*, *21st Century*, *Openhearted*, *New Orleans* (produced by Disco whizkid Dan Hartman) and *Trouble Maker*, *When the Rain Begins to Fall* wasn't written for it and really had no business being there.

Yet that song is the one saving grace of the entire starshipped enterprise. *When the Rain Begins to Fall* is one of my all-time favourite Disco synth songs ever. The fourth eldest Jackson brother and pop princess Zadora are clearly straining their voices singing the relentlessly galloping lyrics, and Zadora is often out of tune too. But the fantastically echoing, power tricksy production by Jack White and the yearning melancholy chorus catches me every time and always makes me tear up. Written by

Michael Bradley, former lead singer with Paul Revere & the Raiders, Peggy March (who as Little Peggy March rose to international fame at age 15 with her 1963 No.1 hit *I Will Follow Him*), and Steve Wittmack, the song is pure pop magic and if I was ever to be on 'Desert Island Discs' this would be one of the records on my list. In some territories the film was retitled **When the Rains Begin to Fall** to cash-in on the song's popularity, a marketing ruse that still failed to bring it to receptive audiences who waited three years for the same story to be better realised in **Earth Girls Are Easy** (1988).

The First DJ

Before the names Nicky Siano, David Mancuso, Larry Levan, Richie Kaczor, Jim Burgess etc. became Disco legends and responsible for breaking some of the most iconic tunes of the era, there was Slim Hyatt, the man credited for being the first ever DJ. It was Olivier Coquelin who opened the first discotheque in New York, Le Club, on New Year's Eve, 1960. However, the members-only venue still had a big band for the dance music. Until late-night stragglers were kept on the dance floor once the live music had stopped by the bandleader's African American butler, Hyatt, who put some records on a turntable to keep people partying. Soon the band's performances had further diminished and this cheaper form of musical appreciation became the norm. Hyatt's reputation was such he was headhunted over to Shepheard's where the Disco was accused of putting musicians out of business due to 'canned music' being played. The American Federation of Musicians claimed it was unfair practice and that records should be alternated with live performance. But as costs were calculated, the writing was on the wall, and the DJ became the equivalent of a human jukebox.

Sid and Nancy 2

In 1984 I interviewed director Alex Cox about his cosmic cult caper **Repo Man** for 'Starburst'. I had loved the movie and our time together made for a solid question and answer session. The inevitable final query came up – what are you working on next? 'Oh, a biopic about Sid Vicious and Nancy Spungen', came the totally surprising reply. Before I knew it I had sprung at him like a cobra, poked him in the shoulder and literally shouted, 'Look you, Sid was a great friend, I'll be furious if you betray his memory, I knew the real person and you had better do it properly'. Taken aback, Cox asked me if we could meet up another day where, this time, he would interview me about my Punk life with Sid and Nancy.

Later that week we did exactly that and I told him everything he wanted to know from my unique perspective. When I saw the movie at an early preview in 1986 I was pleased to see he had given me a great credit for helping him get his facts straight. He even told me one of the characters was an amalgam of shop assistant Michael Collins and I, although I took that with a pinch of salt. Did I like the movie? Sort of. Obviously being actually a part of the reality he dramatised made it quite difficult for me to judge. I did think Gary Oldman was pretty good as Sid and I told him so at the beach party thrown for the Cannes premiere. Chloe Webb was too brassy as Nancy though. Oldman has since disowned it and the Sex Pistols hated it and it was probably way too soon to do them justice. Now armed with all the salient facts that have since come to light, perhaps someone should try again.

Alan Jones with director Alex Cox after he helped him research *Sid & Nancy* (1986).

1990s

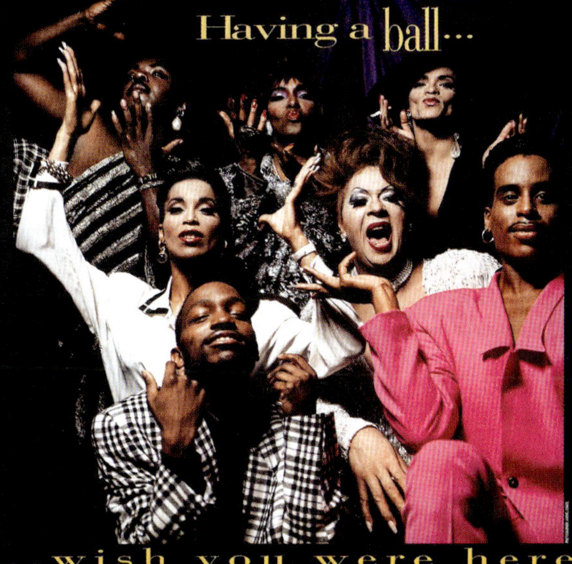

PRESTIGE PRESENTS · A JENNIE LIVINGSTON FILM · PARIS IS BURNING
STARRING DORIAN COREY · PEPPER LABEIJA · VENUS XTRAVAGANZA · OCTAVIA ST. LAURENT · WILLI NINJA · ANJI XTRAVAGANZA
FREDDIE PENDAVIS · JUNIOR LABEIJA · CO-PRODUCED BY BARRY SWIMAR · EDITED BY JONATHAN OPPENHEIM
CINEMATOGRAPHY BY PAUL GIBSON · PRODUCED AND DIRECTED BY JENNIE LIVINGSTON · A PRODUCTION OF OFF WHITE PRODUCTIONS, INC.
Partially supported by grants from THE NEW YORK STATE COUNCIL ON THE ARTS · THE NATIONAL ENDOWMENT FOR THE ARTS · ART MATTERS, INC.
THE JEROME FOUNDATION · THE NEW YORK FOUNDATION FOR THE ARTS · THE PAUL ROBESON FUND · THE EDELMAN FAMILY FUND
PRESTIGE

PARIS IS BURNING (1990)

Touted as one of the greatest independent films ever made, the commendable shadow cast by Jennie Livingston's superlative and renowned documentary has been longlasting for its cultural significance. For what began as an exercise in capturing a specific moment of late 1980s excess became a devastating ode to gender, race, class and sexual reinvention. This gritty and glitzy guide to overcoming adversity with audacity led to mainstream appropriation of the 'voguing' dance craze spearheaded by Madonna with *Vogue* (1990) and Malcolm McLaren's *Deep in Vogue* (1989), 'Ru Paul's Drag Race' reality show phenomenon and the game-changing TV series 'Pose' (2018-2021), which defines the same celebratory scene and sense of transitional time as this brilliant mix of high-spirited hilarity and colour-blind pathos.

Texas-born lesbian feminist Livingston, an ACT UP and AIDS activist, wanted to record what was going on in the poor, gay and disenfranchised Manhattan ghettos for posterity when she happened upon a group of Black and Latino queens throwing 'category shade' while 'voguing' in Washington Square. Further investigation led her to the Harlem ball scene at the title nightclub where she entered an alternate universe of top queen Legends, setting up Houses for their marginal Children to call home. These makeshift families took on the Legend's surname as theirs, like Dorian Corey, Pepper LaBeija, Willi Ninja, Octavia Saint Laurent and Venus Xtravaganza. What all the Houses had in common was a sense of style, pipe dreams of wealth and stardom, and a burning desire to imitate the society that looked down on them.

Combining footage shot at several balls and interviews with the fringe dwelling, drag, transsexual and totally unique participants, a whole subculture is revealed with its own rigid hierarchy, jargon ('reading', 'shade', realness' 'mopping') and strict rules of decorum. The balls are essentially the fabulous queer version of street gang fighting amongst the viciously aggressive Houses. Part surreal performance art, part ritual and part competition for the massive 'category' trophies, the Disco catwalk is a camp flurry of wigs, false eyelashes, satin and showgirl sequins. Don't think for one moment the drag is all Hollywood, fashion magazine, advert or 'Dynasty' glamour inspired. Heightened archetypal male attire was also worn for such categories as 'The Gay Basher Who Beat You Up on the Way Here Tonight', three-piece business suits and military regalia.

In the post-Warholian, existential gender fluid alternate universe of **Paris Is Burning**, the reality may be squalid as the fates of most of the dispossessed youth taking refuge in their own narcissism depicted was ultimately not pretty. But for a brief shining moment they were the glittering beating heart of the LGBTQ+ revolution and underground Disco movement. It's their witty and profound self-awareness and desire for their name in lights no matter how small or the cost, which elevates Livingston's unsentimental and unflinching examination into a rapturous masterpiece and a Disco must-see.

'The Best Disco Music for a Seminal Documentary' category would be won by this soundtrack, one as eclectic and diverse as the people in it: *Never, Never Gonna Give Ya Up* (1973) by Barry White, *Move Your Body* (1986) by DJ Marshall Jefferson, the two-time dance charting *Love Hangover* (1976) by Diana Ross, *Deep in Vogue* (1989) by Malcolm McLaren, obviously *Got to Be Real* (1978) by Cheryl Lynn, the very meaningful *Love Is the Message* (1973) by MFSB, the super slinky *Another Man* (1984) by Barbara Mason, *Let No Man Put Asunder* (1983) by First Choice, *I'll House You* (1988) by Jungle Brothers and the Disco Chart No.1, *Who's Zoomin' Who* (1985) by Aretha Franklin.

Disco Labels

Casablanca, T.K., Philadelphia International and Salsoul may have arguably been the most recognisable Disco labels. But there was also Butterfly, SAM, Vanguard and West End snapping at their 12-inch heels. Prelude Records was one of the smallest labels but it had a really big impact on the Disco charts by releasing a diverse number of dance classics. Owned by Marvin Schlachter, former Chess president, Scepter/Wand vice president and US PYE manager, when the latter closed down its American operation he began Prelude and engaged the services of hot DJ François Kevorkian to create 12-inch remixes for the label.

For ten years, between 1976 and 1986, Prelude defined the New York Disco scene with an amazing catalogue of releases including Musique's No.1 *Keep on Jumpin'/In the Bush* (1978), Jumbo's *Turn On to Love* (1977), 'D' Train's No.1 *You're the One for Me* (1981), Unlimited Touch's *I Hear Music in the Streets* (1980), Sharon Redd's No.1 *Redd Hot* (1982) and *Can You Handle It?* (1981), Inner Life's *I'm Caught Up* (1979), with Jocelyn Brown on vocals, Hi-Gloss' *You'll Never Know* (1981), featuring Luther Vandross, Saturday Night Band's *Come On Dance, Dance/Touch Me on My Hot Spot* (1978), Constellation Orchestra's *Perfect Love Affair/Cosmic Melody* (1978), Lemon's *Chance to Dance/A-Freak-A/Hot Bodies* (1979), Theo Vaness' *Bad Bad Boy* (1979) and their biggest breakout artist globally, France Joli with the everlasting No.1 *Come to Me* (1979) and *The Heart to Break the Heart* (1980).

Disco Memo

Buddy G

SHOCK XPRESS

INSIDE:

Spring 1987

Issue 6 60p

CLIVE BARKER
ANTHONY PERKINS
BORIS KARLOFF

One of my greatest friendships happened because of 'Shock Xpress', the fanzine launched in July 1985 by publisher Stephen Jones and edited by Dave Reeder. After two issues Stefan Jaworzyn took over the editing reins and gave it the anti-establishment voice that still resonates to this today. The first editorial explained it all: "It might be wondered why a group of horror film fanatics (sorry, horror film critics) should hack out stuff for a small magazine that they could get paid for. The answer is simply this: despite the plethora of fantasy film titles on the shelves of the specialist shops, there doesn't really seem a place for the kind of movies we want to talk about". I loved being able to write about niche subjects my other magazines would have raised eyebrows over, like John Waters, horror porno and transvestite exploitation. Alongside myself contributors to what was created as the UK equivalent to Bill Landis' US landmark 'Sleazoid Express' included Anne Billson, Ramsey Campbell, Nigel Floyd, Barry Forshaw, Craig Ledbetter, Kim Newman, Phil Nutman, Julian Petley and Steve Puchalski.

The fanzine had turned glossier by the winter 1987 issue, in which I reviewed the arrival of Buddy Giovinazzo's **Combat Shock** (1986) on Troma Video. I gave it the biggest thumbs up in my rave review, basically saying it was a work of pure brilliance. The next issue wasn't published until Spring 1988, and imagine my total surprise when the Xpress Mail column opened on a letter from Giovinazzo himself saying how much my review meant to him, how it captured exactly what he was trying to do and how thrilled he was that someone finally understood its meaning. I was gobsmacked but it began a long correspondence between us, leading to the inclusion of his vampire short **Jonathan of the Night** in the 'Shock Around the Clock' 1988 line-up, until we finally met in New York where we discovered we had exactly the same birth date.

From that moment on we were soul mates and I met Buddy everywhere, at Manhattan 'Fangoria' conventions, when he moved to Los Angeles we'd hang-out when I was in town for press junkets, and at FrightFest when **The Theatre Bizarre** (2011) and **A Night of Nightmares** (2012) were programmed. And when he relocated to Berlin to forge a career as one of Germany's top TV series directors ('Der Kriminalist', 2008, 'SOKO Leipzig', 2014), we saw even more of each other thanks to my working on **Resident Evil** (2002), **Equilibrium** (2002), **V for Vendetta** (2005) and **Gunpowder Milkshake** (2021), and attending many Berlin Film Festivals throughout the years.

In a terrific turn of events, director Tony Scott optioned his organised crime book 'Potsdamer Platz' (2004) and like every other filmmaker I've known Buddy has a slew of pet projects in his bottom drawer he'd love to make. One of those he wrote back in 1990 for me to play a part in. The enticingly titled '123 Depravity Street' was a new take on 'The Boy Who Cried Wolf' parable. A teenager comes out of drug rehab and moves into a new neighbourhood. Down the block live a married couple everyone considers upstanding pillars of society. But they're really religious freaks into necrophilia and all sorts of disgusting perversion. They don't hide anything from him because they know no one will believe an ex-junkie. Then they force him to join in with their sordid fun and games. I was to play a crazy orgy member where just-caught fish were the aphrodisiac! Originally optioned by **Street Trash** (1987) producer Roy Frumkes, I hope Buddy can finally realise his '123 Depravity Street' dream just so I can tackle the role with gusto.

Buddy Giovinazzo, director of *Combat Shock* (1986).

▲ Top left: Stefan Jaworzyn and Alan Jones, the two brains behind the legendary 'Shock Around the Clock' events at the Scala Cinema.

THE SPIRIT OF '76 (1990)

Escaping more than properly released by Columbia Pictures, barely seen by anyone at the time and underrated by those lucky enough to catch it, director/co-writer Lucas Reiner's guilty pleasure takes a blissfully silly concept and engagingly spins it into comedy gold with clear love and affection. Shot in 25 days on a transparently obvious low budget, Reiner (younger son of veteran comedian Carl, brother of **Stand By Me**, 1986, director Rob, who both play cameos) makes every constraint work in the movie's favour by summoning up a free-for-all attitude and devil-may-care imagination towards the homemade props, the cheesy special effects and the up-for-it cast. Take a well deserved bow such Seventies icons as teen idols David Cassidy and Leif Garrett (the pop Disco classic *I Was Made for Dancin'*, 1978), stoner comedian Tommy Chong, surrealist rockers Devo and cult figures Julie Brown (**Earth Girls Are Easy**, 1988) and The Kipper Kids (performance artists Brian Routh and Martin von Haselberg, Bette Midler's husband).

In 2176, the world has been devastated by an ozone hole in the stratosphere and all historical records in the desolate wasteland once known as the USA have been destroyed by a magnetic storm. So a crack team of scientists is tasked to travel back in time to 1776 and discover what was written in the American Constitution in order to found their unpredictable future on the same solid principles. But Adam-11 (Cassidy), Chanel-6 (Olivia d'Abo) and Heinz-57 (Geoff Hoyle, **Popeye**, 1980) suffer a computer glitch that means they end up in 1976 instead rather than at the Declaration of Independence. Attempting to navigate this alien past, the fish-out-of-water trio meet California potheads Chris Johnson and Tommy Sears (Jeff and Steve McDonald from the '70s influenced electro-rock band Redd Kross), unmistakably channelling Bill and Ted, who become their guides through a dazzling parade of contemporary fads, social events, gossip and fashions. Streaking, eight-track tapes, Smile badges, gas station lines, mood rings, space food, EST, lava lamps, platform shoes, polyester flares and Disco all get a well-observed and clever lampooning. But nerdy villain Rodney Snodgrass (Liam O'Brien) threatens the temporal tourists' steep learning curve by insisting they are part of his alien conspiracy theory and does everything in his power to thwart their attempts in obtaining the important artefacts and a copy of the Constitution needed to fulfil their mission.

The Spirit of '76 was a multi-showbiz royal family affair. Not only were the Reiners involved, so were producer/co-writer Roman Coppola (**CQ**, 2001, director) and costume designer Sofia Coppola (**Lost in Translation**, 2003, **The Bling Ring**, 2013, **Priscilla**, 2023, director), son and daughter of Francis Ford Coppola. Co-producer Susie Landau was the daughter of **Ed Wood** (1993) Oscar winner Martin Landau and 'Space 1999' headliner Barbara Bain (who also makes an appearance). Shelby Chong, Tommy's daughter, and Moon Zappa, Frank's ditto, played minor cameos too.

Titled **I visitatori del sabato sera/Saturday Night Visitors** in Italy, the soundtrack carries the same overall feel-good appeal as the movie. *Love's Theme* (1973) by the Love Unlimited Orchestra, *The Hustle* (1975) by Van McCoy & The Soul City Symphony, *Kung Fu Fighting* (1974) by Carl Douglas and *Rock the Boat* (1973) by The Hues Corporation cover the early Disco basics for instant recognition and keen charge. Key additions are Vicki Sue Robinson's Disco stunner *Turn the Beat Around* (1976) and The Sylvers' *Boogie Fever* (1975), with two cuts appropriated from **Saturday Night Fever** (1977) as cultural acknowledgement, *Disco Inferno* (1976) by The Trammps and *A Fifth of Beethoven* (1976) by Walter Murphy & The Big Apple Band. *Saturday Night* (1975) by the Bay City Rollers adds further texturing and while not Disco *per se* fits right into the upbeat mood and sharply honed enthusiasm infecting every part of this minor gem.

Van McCoy and The Hustle

One of the most famous Disco tunes ever is *The Hustle*, a track that instantly summons up mirrorball memories without any effort, the reason so many movies and TV series have used it as pop culture shorthand. Written, produced and recorded by Van (Allen Clinton) McCoy for inclusion on his 1975 instrumental album *Disco Baby* with his hand-picked orchestra The Soul City Symphony, it became a smash dance hit going to the top of both the 'Billboard' pop and R&B charts, to No.3 on the Disco chart also winning a Grammy Award.

Born January 6, 1940, in Washington D.C., McCoy learned to play piano as a child and by 12 was writing songs and performing in amateur talent shows with his violin maestro older brother Norman Jr. In 1956 they recorded the novelty dance record *The Birdland* as The Starlighters, which led to McCoy composing a string of 1960s hits: *Maybe Tonight* (1964) for The Shirelles, *Getting Mighty Crowded* (1964) for Betty Everett, *Baby I'm Yours* (1965) for Barbara Lewis, *When You're Young and in Love* (1967) for Ruby & the Romantics, and *I Get the Sweetest Feeling* (1968) for Jackie Wilson.

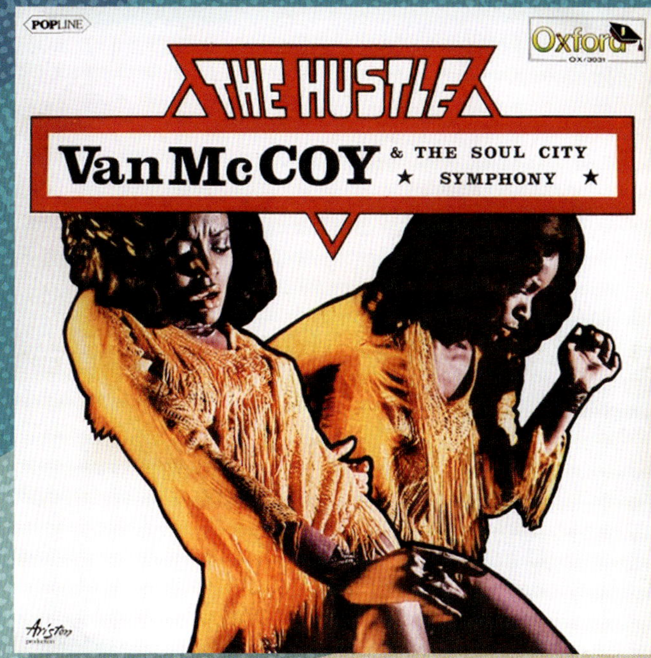

After putting together the duo Peaches & Herb, writing *Right on the Tip of my Tongue* (1971) for Brenda & the Tabulations and arranging several massive hits for The Stylistics, McCoy joined forces with songwriter/producer Charles Kipps and released his second solo LP on the Buddah label, *Soul Improvisations* (1972). Neither that nor its follow-up *Love Is the Answer* (1974) were a success so extra special attention had to be paid to the next release. Just as he was putting the finishing touches to the album that would become *Disco Baby*, DJ friend David Todd told McCoy about a new dance craze sweeping the South Bronx Latino clubs. Todd advised McCoy to hustle on over to the Adam's Apple Disco on Manhattan's East Side to see what all the fuss was about, but being too busy in the studio he sent Kipps instead.

What Kipps witnessed that fateful night was clubbers dancing to choreographed and regimented steps. Free-style moves were out and line dancing and communication were back in! Revellers arrived at the club well before opening time too to practice their steps and hand motions. Kipps spotted two secretaries from their company on the dance floor and asked them to demonstrate the dance for McCoy back in the office. As the apocryphal story goes, McCoy watched their precise display, a melody and arrangement instantly came to mind, and an eleventh song was written within the hour for the impending album. The moment Avco Records executives heard *The Hustle* infusing R&B with a Latin beat, it was rush-released as a single and transformed global Disco floors overnight. Everyone wanted to take hustle lessons, Discos mounted early evening dance classes for the uninitiated, the single sold 10 million copies to become one of the bestselling Disco hits of all time and the *Disco Baby* album sold 8 million more worldwide.

In record time the Hustle became the most discussed and written about dance since The Twist, with newspapers like 'The New York Times' printing features on the fad with footwork diagrams so you could learn it in your own home. Think pieces running the gamut between the mental communications required to keep in step and its profound socio-political effect became the order of the day. Pop culturists warned about how the Hustle could bring back the Depression era dance marathons or waxed lyrical about the small promotional contests with cash prizes on offer springing up. And so the seed for **Saturday Night Fever** (1977) was planted... Sadly McCoy only had four more years in the Disco spotlight before dying of a heart attack in 1979. In that short time he composed TV jingles, appeared opposite Hollywood sex goddess Mae West in her cult turkey **Sextette** (1978) and recorded many other hustle-influenced Disco favourites – *Change with the Times* (1975), *Rhythms of the World* (1976), *Soul Cha Cha* (1976), *Jet Setting* (1976), and *Theme from Star Trek* (1976). Every new kind of music needs a dance to define it. McCoy didn't invent the Hustle. He simply wrote the epochal tune that took it out of the Latino ghetto into the dance universe to be feted as the Chubby Checker of Disco.

The Ghastly Girls

Evening News

EXTRA ONLY 10p

FRIDAY 24 JULY 1987 | No. 30,702 | TONIGHT'S WEATHER: FINE & WARM

GHASTLY!

The floor-show shocker as the Ghastly Girls taunt caged men

Werewolf man is locked up after crazed attack

By GUY KER

A CRAZED "werewolf" who terrorised a seaside police station was under lock and key, today in a remote mental hospital.

The 43-year-old builder went berserk after he drove into the Southend station yard with a prostitute shortly after midnight.

As an officer approached him, he bared his teeth like fangs and snarled like a rabid dog.

Crouching on all fours with his fists clenched into claws, he leapt on the terrified officer and mauled him about the face and neck.

A battle then raged as eight policemen stuggled to save their colleague from being strangled.

The man, whose identity is being kept secret to protect his family, suffers a one-in-50-million condition.

It is called lycanthropy, and victims believe they are werewolves and develop super-human strength.

During the terrifying battle to control the man policemen were hurled through the air.

A doctor administered a triple dose of sedatives to calm him down.

The first injection had no effect but a second, double-dose finally calmed him down.

A statement on his condition was expected later today.

Southend police say the man had a similar attack three years ago and are in little doubt about his condition.

Strutting sex girls are London's answer to Beastie Boys

By STEPHEN WARR

BRITAIN'S most outrageous girl rock group shocked London night clubbers last night with a 20-minute orgy of foul language and simulated sex.

Aiming to out-beastie the notorious Beastie Boys, the Ghastly Girls hurled insults at male fans as they fought on stage and ripped at each other's fish-net stockings.

The four girls then threw tampons and condoms to stunned fans at a packed Hippodrome as they strutted to the music.

They pulled three eager men from the audience and simulated sex with them before dragging them off to their dressing rooms.

The nauseating antics were watched by a group of caged men who grabbed and groped the girls at every opportunity.

Two members of the group, Bidet La Douche and Viki Snatch cavorted together, taunting the men while Scarlett and Lil pranced around.

Later when I tried to interview the girls, they unbuttoned my jeans, stripped off my shirt and offered me a session of steamy sex.

But I was saved when they started spraying each other with wine and food.

The show shocked the young audience.

"I've never seen anything like it before," said one girl from Wood Green. "I came here to dance but – they were revolting."

A boy from Stratford said: "No girl should behave like that. They pretend to hate men but were happy to be mauled by them.

"I tried to grab one but she shook me off."

Night clubbin' – your hottest guide to London's night life – is on Page 16

Simon McMarn, 21, from Chiswick, said: "I've seen worse – but only on videos and things like that. I'd come and see them again."

For the Ghastly Girls it was just a beginning.

"We're going to screw London by storm, Lil shouted.

"The Beasties have buggered off but we're here to stay. Just watch out."

Our man Stephen Warr bares up to the girls

BROOKES

I'M AFRAID THE BACTERIA'S OFF SIR

TV and RADIO: pages 2 & 3, WEATHER: page 9, SHORT STORY: page 20, SPORT: pages 29-31, DIARY: back page

I was on the front page of the newspapers again on July 24th, 1987. Under the screaming headline 'Ghastly!', there I was in a photograph grinning at two girls, Bidet La Douche and Vicki Snatch, simulating S&M sex on the stage at the Hippodrome venue Leicester Square. My friend Caroline Guinness had decided to manage the post-Punk girl group The Ghastly Girls and talked me into helping out with their act. Caroline was a bit late in the outrage-means-controversy-means-press-attention stakes but I thought it would be a laugh, having no idea the London 'Evening News' would even notice let alone slap us on Page One.

Essentially the girls' set (the other two members were Lil and Scarlett) consisted of songs so crap I can't even remember their titles, hurling insults at the audience, swearing non-stop, pulling men out of the audience to humiliate and generally being as obnoxious as possible. Meanwhile I had corralled some of my more handsome Disco mates, put them with me in a cage behind to taunt everyone in sight and throw condoms and tampons I'd bought from Boots up the road into the baying crowd.

The 'Evening News' went berserk: "strutting sex girls are London's answer to Beastie Boys"; "a 20-minute orgy of foul language"; "the nauseating antics were watched by caged men who grabbed and groped at every opportunity"; "the floor show shocked the audience"... Wordsmith Stephen Barr even complained about being stripped, offered steamy sex and sprayed with wine and food. He should have been so lucky! The night was a massive PR success, and we had a great time planning it, but no one ever heard of The Ghastly Girls again. Wonder why?

YOUNG SOUL REBELS (1991)

What exactly is director Isaac Julien's Cannes Critics Best Feature prizewinner? Is it a murder mystery, a gay romance, a drama documentary highlighting London's underground society in 1977, a musical about soul, Punk, Disco? Whatever it is, at no point does CBE-awarded (in 2017) Julien's ill-conceived shambles make you care. Considered worthy in its day more for its politically correct racial and sexual messages than anything truly ambitious – the acting is terrible, the narrative a clunky mess, the direction slow and dutiful – but its delve into contemporary diverse Disco culture does manage to hold the attention. Just.

Set during the week of Queen Elizabeth II's Silver Jubilee, Julien's jamboree bag of Punk versus Funk focuses on lifelong black friends, straight Chris (Valentine Nonyela) and gay Caz (Mo Sesay), who are DJs on the pirate radio station Soul Patrol broadcasting its world music message from an East London garage. The story picks up a little speed when their friend TJ (Shyro Chung) is murdered cruising the local park and Chris realises a ghetto blaster found by his little sister near the scene of the crime contains a recording of the killer's voice. Not that his identity is really a secret…

Anyway, the duo do a regular live DJ gig at The Crypt, a mixed-music gay club, where punks pogo to X-Ray Spex and become bored wallflowers the moment the Disco starts. It's here Caz hooks up with Sid Vicious lookalike Billibud (Jason Durr, future 'Heartbeat' and 'Casualty' TV star), who delights in stealing Vivienne Westwood T-shirts, and the boyfriends start rehearsing for the anti-monarchy 'Stuff the Jubilee' concert that ends the picture. With the park venue besieged by rioting black-clad saboteurs, skinheads and punks and the stage set ablaze, the killer's identity is revealed in time to get his just desserts.

Primarily exploring the social issues of the day, with the token murder taking a fuzzy back seat, this muddled look at the roots of Punk, reggae devotion and the sexual politics of dance culture is a wasted opportunity. But its soundtrack is filled with the eclectic music its characters are promoting, and is great fun to listen to, even when it has no connection whatsoever to the plot. *Let's Get It Together* by El Coco (1976), *I'll Play the Fool* (1976) by Dr. Buzzard's Original Savannah Band, *You Make Me Feel (Mighty Real)* (1978) by Sylvester, *Message in*

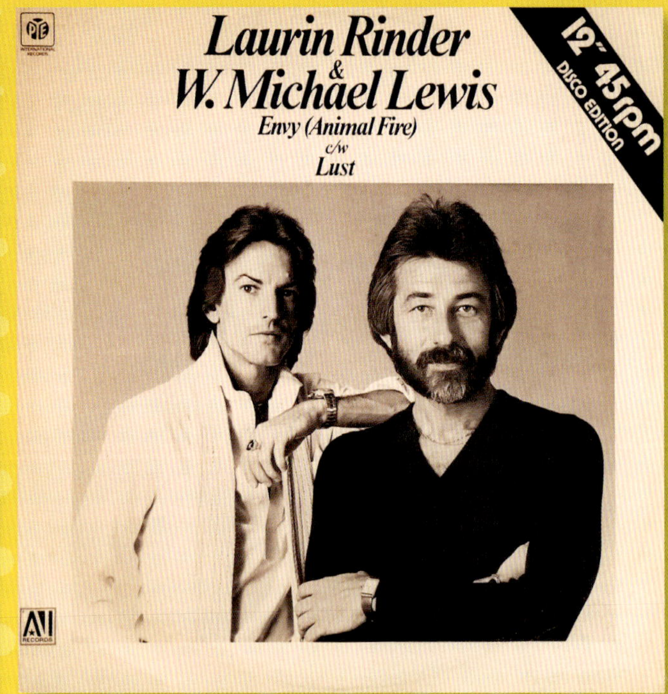

Our Music (1976) by The O'Jays, *P. Funk (Wants to Get Funked Up)* (1976) by Parliament, *One Nation Under a Groove* by Funkadelic, *I Like It* (1977) by The Players Association, *Let the Music Play* (1978) by Charles Earland, *Say You Will* (1978) by Eddie Henderson, *Me & My Baby Brother* (1975) by War, *Don't Let it Go to Your Head* (1978) by Jean Carne, *Running Away* (1977) by Roy Ayers Ubiquity, and *Rock Creek Park* (1975) and *Time Is Movin'* by The Blackbyrds make for a truly wide-ranging and emblematic mixture. Reggae artists The Heptones, Sly and The Revolutionaries and Junior Murvin get their look in too, along with the X-Ray Spex classic *Oh Bondage! Up Yours!* (1977), and Mica Paris sings the soft soul title song.

Rinder and Lewis

El Coco was one of the many aliases used throughout the Disco era by producers Laurin Rinder and W(illiam) Michael Lewis. Mainly attached to the AVI label (American Variety International), home of Liberace, Lewis first met Rinder in 1971 when the latter auditioned to be in his new band Joshua, a reincarnation of The Standells. But with Disco taking off, AVI president Ray Harris told the duo to head for the Studio One club in Hollywood and take copious notes. This baptism by fire led to the creation of *Brazil* (1975) and their first full-length Disco effort *Mondo Disco* (1975), both credited to El Coco. While the latter platter didn't really take off in the US, it became a big hit in Europe so AVI demanded a follow-up.

Inspired by the sounds of Barry White and Van McCoy, El Coco's third album *Let's Get It Together* (1976) landed in the 'Billboard' Disco Top Ten, as did *Cocomotion* (1977) and *Dancing in Paradise* (1978). Their next far funkier studio project was Le Pamplemousse (grapefruit in French!), which made the Disco Top 20 with *Get Your Boom, Boom (Around the Room)* (1977), and No.5 with *Le Spank* (1977), based on the groove of White's *It's Ecstasy When You Lay Down Next to Me* (1977). Other Rinder and Lewis pseudonyms would be Discognosis, Sweet Potato Pie, In Search of... Orchestra, The Rinlew All-Stars and the excellent Belle De Jour. But they signed their own names to the *Seven Deadly Sins* (1978) and *Warriors* (1979) albums, the latter featuring the Top 20 Disco hit covers *Willie and the Hand Jive* and *Love Potion #9*.

But Rinder and Lewis' most commercial venture was with the studio project Tuxedo Junction and their Glenn Miller goes Disco concept that stretched to the two albums *Tuxedo Junction* (1978) and *Tuxedo Junction II – Take the A Train* (1979). Big band wartime standards, Broadway torch songs and Duke Ellington schmoozers came alive for the new dance generation with *Chattanooga Choo Choo, Rainy Night in Rio*, both No.5 Disco hits, *Moonlight Serenade* (1978), *Toot Toot Tootsie Goodbye* (1979), *That Old Black Magic* (1979) and *Stardust* (1979). Using some of the original musicians from many of the vintage Miller recordings, the seasoned professionals even fixed the complicated arrangements because they knew what worked best.

Opera

After first meeting Dario Argento for the **Tenebrae** (1982) UK release, things moved very quickly indeed. We kept in touch via letters, Christmas cards and through his fantastic personal assistant Carla Alonzo. I'd gone to the American Film Market in Hollywood in 1985 to see the first screening of **Phenomena** (1985), basically consisting of me virtually alone in a vast Beverly Center Shopping Mall cinema auditorium. I got invited to the world premiere of **Demons** (1985) in Rome where I reacquainted myself with Lamberto Bava. Met Asia Argento for the first time when Daria Nicolodi invited me over for dinner. Struck up a friendship with Dario's sometime assistant director Michele Soavi through his documentary **Dario Argento's World of Horror** (1985), and **StageFright** (1987). And then I landed *the* dream assignment in June 1987 – a week on location in Rome following the making of **Opera** (1987).

What a week that was. It was mainly night shoots, and everyone knows how awful they are from a mental time clock perspective. Rome was sweltering and my hotel had no air conditioning. Dario wasn't in the best frame of mind either as his father Salvatore had just died the month before and I learnt very quickly to judge his moods for those all-important nuts-and-bolts conversations. And star Cristina Marsillach was an absolute bitch. I am still clueless as to what her problem was with me, Dario, the world, and Simone Scafidi's bland Argento documentary **Panico** (2023) doesn't clear it up either. But I loved every single second of being there. I was on an actual Argento giallo shoot, how much much better could life get? Urbano Barberini (playing Inspector *Alan* Santini!) was terrific and kept asking me to work out with him. Coralina Cataldi-Tassoni treated me like family. Daria was a delight and made sure I was always entertained. I was amazed by the way Dario directed and still am. And watching the movie come to life before my eyes was incredible. Especially when I witnessed the climactic Opera basement fire sequence and surreptitiously stole the Music Room sign as a memento. Years later when Dario found that out he demanded I give it back to him. I never did.

My entire set report and retrospective on Dario's career was published in the March 1988 special double issue of 'Cinefantastique', three months after I'd seen the film in Rome at two advance previews and once at a public showing with Clive Barker, who was in town to promote **Hellraiser** (1987). Appreciation for that 14-page marathon report was swift and positive and actually took me aback. It was then I realised the true global reach of Dario's work and put the idea of a future book in my mind. These fond memories are the reason I've always rated **Opera** as one of Dario's best works, something I only finally convinced him about when we had dinner together on the **Mother of Tears** (2007) Turin location 20 years later.

Alan Jones and Dario Argento, another favourite photo by Julie Edwards.

CARLITO'S WAY (1993)

One film that should take pride of place in the upper echelons of the gangster genre is director Brian De Palma's undervalued focus on a criminal underworld turning away from its time-honoured codes of conduct towards a more dog-eat-dog environment. Few films actually made in the seminal Disco era can match the flamboyant elegance, suspenseful undertow or nervous energy of this absolutely first rate production. Starring a blistering Al Pacino in his second mobster movie for De Palma after **Scarface** (1983) and a memorably sleazy Sean Penn as his friend and ultimate nemesis, **Carlito's Way** is based on two books – 'Carlito's Way', but mainly 'After Hours' – by real-life Judge Edwin Torres, whom Pacino had met while preparing **Serpico** (1973).

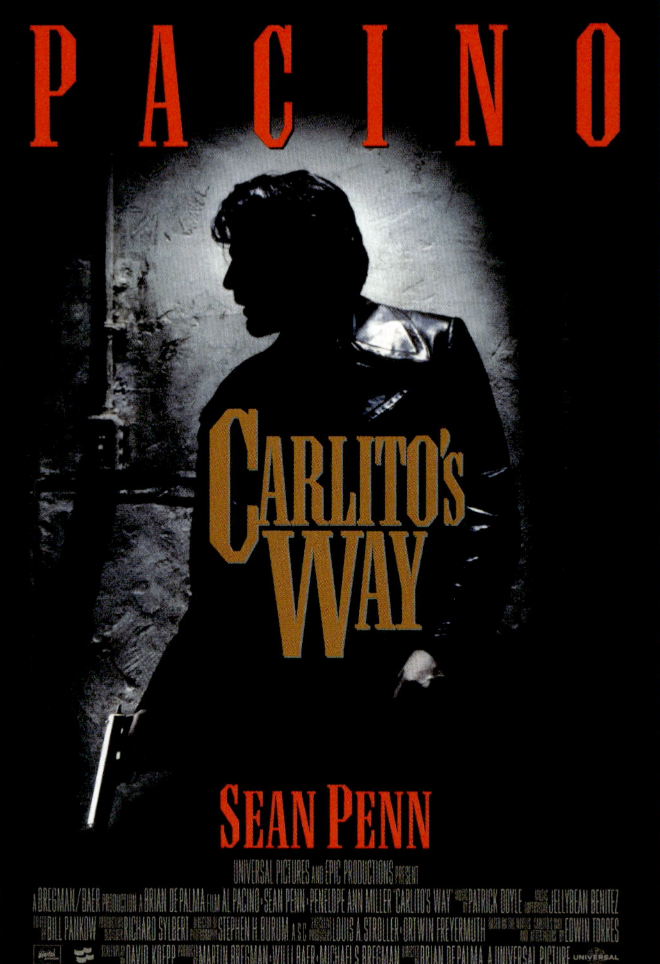

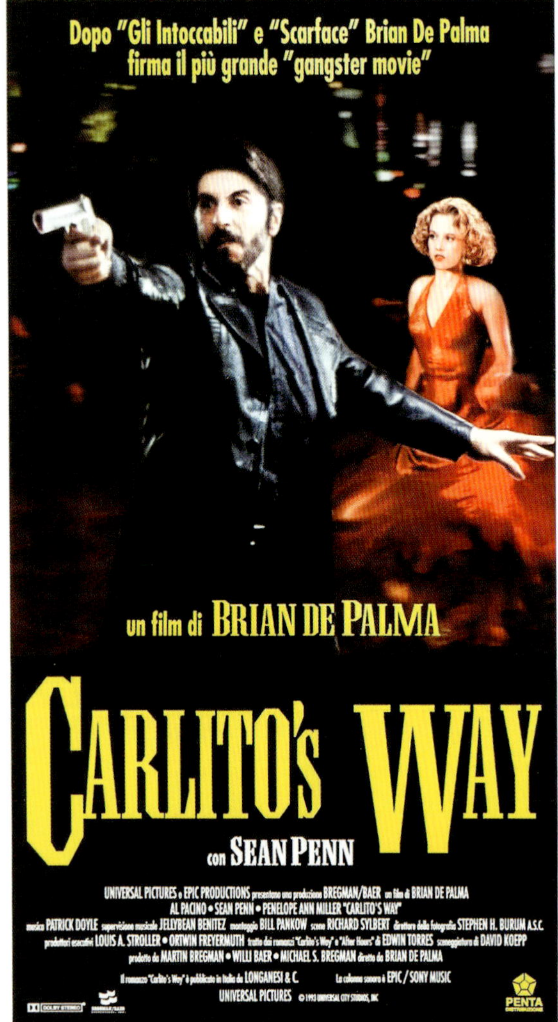

Twenty years later author Torres took Pacino to Spanish Harlem to help research his lead character.

It's 1975 and Puerto Rican drug dealer Carlito Brigante (Pacino), dubbed "the J.P. Morgan of the smack business", has just scraped his way out of a 30-year prison sentence, after serving only five, thanks to his conniving coke-head lawyer Kleinfeld (Penn, in young Art Garfunkel guise). Determined to go straight and raise enough money to open a car rental business in the Bahamas, Kleinfeld offers him a stake in a Manhattan Disco going bust. But despite Carlito moaning about clubland being just "Platforms, cocaine and dances I don't dance", he agrees to run the El Paraiso club, and after renewing the relationship with his go-go stripper girlfriend Gail (Penelope Ann Miller), things start looking up. However, old habits die hard, Kleinfeld's naïve and deadly machinations inexorably pull Carlito back into violence and mistrust, and a deadly endgame begins.

A great story told in De Palma's signature operatic style, it often calls to mind his past glories **The Fury** (1978) with regard the incendiary domestic drama, **Dressed to Kill** (1980), the elevator murder, **Body Double** (1984), the peeping into Gail's ballet class, and **The Untouchables** (1987), the superbly choreographed shoot-out sequence at Grand Central Station. Not to mention all the Disco scenes looking prom-tastic **Carrie** (1976). The El Paraiso

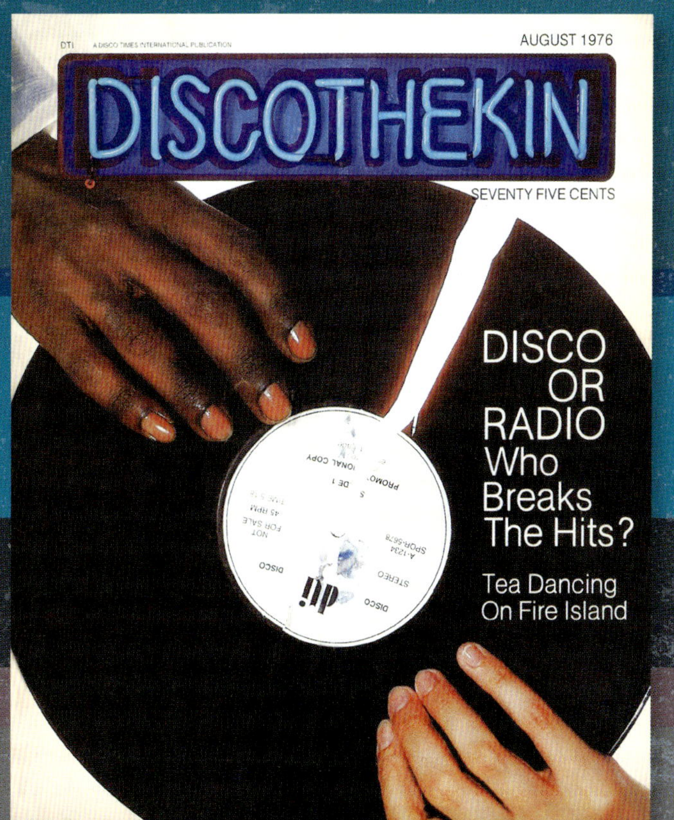

was a two-storey set built at the Kaufman Astoria Studios in Queens and designed by Richard Sylbert in the style of a 1930s ocean liner. The chrome, steel and frosted glass interiors were deliberately made spacious to allow De Palma's continually roving camera access to all areas ensuring a densely layered canvas moving with confident, compulsive energy. Some filming took place at the famed Manhattan club, the Copacabana, while dancer extras were talent spotted from a wide array of Discos and bussed to the Queens set.

Exciting action, extreme violence and intense emotions pulsate through this rogue's gallery morality play where doing the loyal or right thing becomes a Sophie's choice. Pacino has danced his way through a few films in his career although none of it as crazily off-centre as his **Cruising** (1980) gig. Genuine rhythm is shown in his most famous dance sequence from **Scent of Woman** (1992) and Courtney Galiano, his partner in **Stand Up Guys** (2012), has gone on record to say he never stepped on her toes once. Even Dennis Dugan, director of the 'Dunkaccino' commercial for Dunkin' Donuts, praised Pacino's dance work after filming for 12 hours non-stop.

Disco-wise the music is spot on, every track is heard within the context of the El Paraiso confines and the Hustle is ably demonstrated: *Fly Robin Fly* (1975) by Silver Convention, *Back Stabbers* (1972) by The O'Jays, *You Should Be Dancing* (1976) by the Bee Gees, *Got to Be Real* (1978) by Cheryl Lynn, *That's the Way (I Like It)* (1975) and *(Shake, Shake, Shake) Shake Your Booty* (1976) by KC and The Sunshine Band, *Rock the Boat* (1974) by The Hues Corporation, *Do It ('Til You're Satisfied)* (1974) by B.T. Express, *TSOP – The Sound of Philadelphia* (1974) by MFSB featuring The Three Degrees, and *Lady Marmalade* (1974) by Labelle. Four cover versions are also featured: Sylvia's *Pillow Talk* (1973) by Sinoa, The O'Jays' *I Love Music* (1975) by Rozalla, and The Trammps' *Disco Inferno* (1976) and George McCrae's *Rock Your Baby* (1974), both by Ed Terry.

The Best Discos In Town

In 1978 America's 'Discothekin' magazine listed the best Discos according to their readers. Voted Best Nationwide was Studio 54. Best Regional was Studio One in Los Angeles, The Limelight in Florida and namesake The Limelight in Montreal. Best for Style was New York New York. Best Gay Disco was The Loft in New York. Best Women's was Sahara in New York. Best Latin, Black and Rock were Les Nuages, Pippin and Ashley's, all New York City. In 1977, 'Billboard' picked Sharon Lee as the Top Female DJ for her sets at Miami's Scaramouche Disco. And apart from Studio 54, the other most exclusive, hard-to-get-into Discos were considered Zorine's in Chicago, Doubles, in the Sherry Netherlands Hotel basement in Manhattan, The Daisy in Hollywood, El Privado in Los Angeles and Tramp in London.

While dancing was always the uppermost activity in Discos, in the early years in the UK, the music would often grind to a halt for a drag queen display. The trend to feature live performers in Discos really only began in 1977 when Bette Midler took to the stage at the Copacabana in New York and attracted sell-out crowds. Crown Heights Affair and the Andrea True Connection followed suit in Manhattan's Starship Discovery 1. B.T. Express did a turn at Chicago's Happy Medium, and Silver Convention and Tuxedo Junction appeared at The City in San Francisco. Amanda Lear made it to the Camden Palace in London and Grace Jones got carried into Maunkberry's, in Jermyn Street, London on a leopardskin couch by loinclothed musclemen, both events I attended and both were amazing.

Shivers

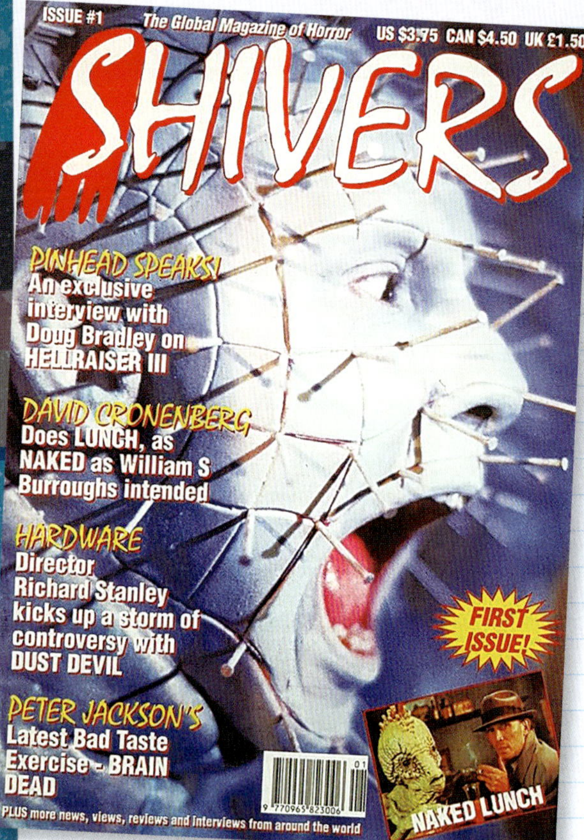

'Shivers', 'The Global Magazine of Horror' debuted in June 1992. Visual Imagination Ltd, owned by Stephen Payne, had taken over 'Starburst' in December 1985 and given me free rein over the film review column. He liked what I did and while Payne and the people he brought in were more on the 'Star Trek'/'Doctor Who' side of the genre, he knew he needed me for my all-round horror knowledge. So when Payne asked me to edit his new brainchild 'Shivers' I agreed to give it a go. At the time I was writing for so many publications and newspapers anyway – 'GQ', 'Femme Fatales', 'The Independent', 'What's On' as well as my permanent outlets – I thought it would be great to finally put my firm stamp on something well and truly my own.

Hence the coverage of Peter Jackson, David Cronenberg, Joe D'Amato, Frank Henenlotter, Clive Barker, Robert Englund and of course Dario Argento. I wheeled in friends David McGillivray to answer readers' questions, Mark Kermode to help out on the feature front, and my 'Vox' magazine editor Bob McCabe for video reviews. I was most proud of the three-part retrospective I asked Mark Ashworth to write on the career of Sergio Martino (**All the Colors of the Dark**, 1972, **Torso**, 1973), plus his 'Heroine Addict' retro on Italian Giallo Girls, and also Kim Newman's overview of Christmas-based horrors. None of those subjects had ever really been done properly before and the feedback was great.

Unfortunately Payne thought my approach was way too niche – where were the articles on Hammer, Christopher Lee and Peter Cushing? Done to death was my reply. And so after a year I was retired as editor and David Miller took over to go more mainstream with Frankenstein and 'The X-Files'. Lovely guy David, I bore him no ill will at all but I did love it when he used to get letters saying since I left the magazine had gone to hell! Obviously I still wrote for it right up until the last issue in May 2008, which is when Visual Imagination folded due to an unforeseen bereavement. But I still look back at 'Shivers' with a proud fondness because I stayed true to my ideals in the light of people saying to me, who wants to read an interview with Peter Jackson on **Heavenly Creatures** (1994)? I rest my case.

Alan Jones with horror icon Robert Englund, Freddy Krueger himself!

THE ADVENTURES OF PRISCILLA, QUEEN OF THE DESERT (1994)

Two Australian films appeared in 1994, both geared around social outcasts and outsiders looking for acceptance, both reaching the dizzying heights of exhilaration and the depths of downbeat despair, and both featuring ABBA hits on their soundtracks. But unlike P.J. Hogan's **Muriel's Wedding** – wonderful in its own wickedly mocking, subversive way – it was Stephan Elliott's hilariously poignant breakout that had its Disco sensibility completely present and resplendently correct.

Probably that was the reason why it became such a cult icon and was turned into a very successful dancing-in-the-aisles stage musical and choreographed party event. If you asked him on the publicity tour what his inspiration was to make **Priscilla**, Elliott would always joke he did it to bring screen musicals back from the grave into which **Xanadu** (1980) had put them. The reality was far starker though and came from a trip he made with his boyfriend into the Australian Outback and how he felt dangerously menaced in a bogan (redneck) bar when relentlessly baited as gay.

Tick (Hugo Weaving) works in a Sydney gay bar as a drag queen under the name Mitzi del Bra alongside Adam

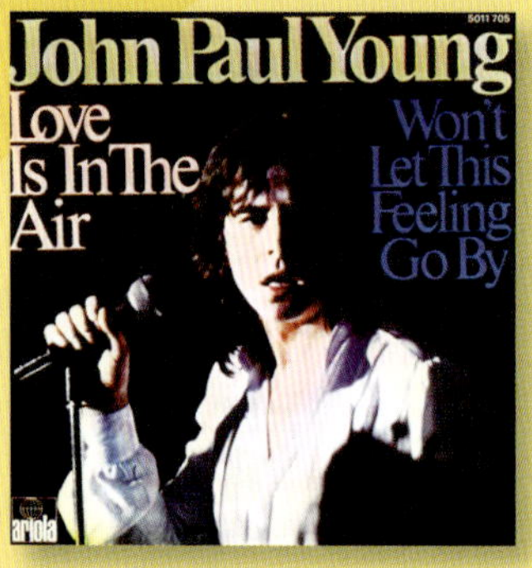

(Guy Pearce), alias Felicia Jollygoodfellow. Turns out, Tick was once married and has a son who is now asking to see him. So together with transsexual Bernadette Bassenger (Terence Stamp in a superbly shaded performance), they head off to the casino resort his ex-wife runs in Alice Springs, on a bus dubbed Priscilla, Queen of the Desert. When the bus breaks down along the way they face homophobia and gay bashing until elderly mechanic Bob Spart (Bill Hunter) helps them out, dumps his Asian mail order bride, a dab hand with cabaret ping-pong ball tricks, and joins them on their road trip towards more discrimination, hesitant recognition, new normal family values and unexpected romance.

A warmly human story told with wit, wisdom, bitchiness and panache, Elliott's hugely entertaining, enormously touching and big-hearted escapade is full of utterly divine moments. Like the hilarity of Mitzi miming to the cheesiest song ever, Charlene's *I've Never Been to Me* (1982); the joyous rush felt when Priscilla hits the road to the Village People's *Go West* (1979); when Felicia walks into a Coober Pedy video store in full drag and asks the clerk whether he has 'The Texas Chain Saw Mascara'; or when the trio don their Oscar-winning outfits to mime to Gloria Gaynor's classic *I Will Survive* (1978) to an audience of bemused aborigines. *I Love the Nightlife (Disco Round)* (1978) by Alicia Bridges, *Shake Your Groove Thing* (1978) by Peaches & Herb, and *Mamma Mia* (1975) by ABBA also underline the brilliance of Elliott's direction and meticulous sense of time and place as he gazes into the macho minefield of the Australian psyche.

Proving that showmanship was still alive and well and manifesting itself in Australia, look no further than this line in the final credits. "Shown in Dragarama at select theatres" was a suggestion to some cinemas to lower a mirrorball and cue the coloured lighting so audiences could get up and dance along to Ce Ce Peniston's *Finally* (1991). And many did just that to celebrate the release of an outrageously camp Disco and Australian classic.

Oz Disco

The Bee Gees, Olivia Newton-John and John Paul Young are probably the only three names people know when it comes to talking about Australian Disco in the 1970s. Young's 1978 chart-topper *Love Is in the Air*, which gained a second level of popularity after being featured in **Strictly Ballroom** (1992), is a rare example of a successful attempt at Disco from an Australian artist of the Golden Era. It was another hit for the producing team of Harry Vanda (Johannes Hendrikus Jacob van den Berg) and George Young (producer of AC/DC, the band fronted by his brothers Angus and Malcolm). The former Dutch Australian musician was the lead guitarist of The Easybeats and they both penned many of that band's recordings including their 1965 global smash *Friday on My Mind*. As Vanda and Young they had a major international success with their own studio project Flash and the Pan, achieving many hits round the world, particularly in Europe where they had numerous chart topping records. Grace Jones had a hit with a cover of their *Walking in the Rain* (1981).

The biggest Australian single of the 1970s was *Eagle Rock* (1971) by Daddy Cool, heard in the Outback horror **Wolf Creek** (2005). But despite that band's Boney M. sounding name, like so many others they eschewed dance music, and there were very few 'Made in Oz' Disco hits. Apart from Marcia Hines' *You* (1977), which Rita Coolidge covered in 1978, that has an ecstatic Shirley and Company feel. The star of the Australian touring versions of 'Hair' and 'Jesus Christ Superstar' had dance form for singing a soul version of James Taylor's *Fire and Rain* in 1975. Christie Allen's *Goosebumps* (1979), co-written by B.A. Roberston and Terry Britten, arrived late in the Disco day and had more of a Newton-John vibe.

Considered the best Australian soul album of the 1970s is *Moving Along* (1977) by Renée Geyer. And from that soft Disco album came *Heading in the Right Direction*, *Stares and Whispers* and best of all *Be There in the Morning* (1977). Formerly with the Melbourne band Nova Express, who covered *(Take Another Little) Piece of my Heart* (1975), Miss Linda George had an Oz-only hit with *Mama's*

Little Girl (1974), very much in the similar jazz-fusion mode. Once past a series of other covers, George eventually went into session work after her successful solo career.

Pussyfoot consisted of Melbourne musician, songwriter and producer Mick Flinn, former member of The Mixtures, and vocalist Donna Jones. Flinn remained behind the scenes though as Jones was marketed as a solo artist. In 1976 they recorded the Banned-By-The-BBC suggestive Disco ditty *The Way That You Do It* that became an overnight sensation in Australia. After entering 'A Song for Europe' in 1980 as a five member combo with *I Want to Be Me* and coming fourth in the voting, an old Pussyfoot song *Dancer Dance* was revamped, remixed and reached number three on the British Disco charts in 1982. Donna Jones and Mick Flinn joined The New Seekers who still tour singing that group's signature 1971 hit *I'd Like to Teach the World to Sing (In Perfect Harmony)*.

Disco Memo

Before Sunrise

I've had so many great experiences covering film shoots on location in such faraway places as Buenos Aires, Argentina, (**Highlander II: The Quickening**, 1991) and Chernobyl in the Ukraine (**Return of the Living Dead: Rave to the Grave** and **ROTLD: Necropolis**, both 2005). But my favourite unit publicity job came in the summer of 1994 when I was asked to handle all the press and set visits for what would turn out to be a surprise romantic masterpiece, Richard Linklater's **Before Sunrise** (1995). Naturally I had loved **Slacker** (1990) and **Dazed and Confused** (1993) and couldn't wait to start work on what turned out to be one of those primo magical experiences. The cast and crew were a total delight (not always the case believe me!) and Linklater was class personified.

But he and his producer Anne Walker-McBay really had a strange opinion of me at first. The film was shot in Vienna, Austria, and I arrived at the airport to be met by a car that took me to what I can only describe as the ritziest hotel in town. I was shown to my three-room suite and introduced to my personal butler! Taken aback a bit, I thought, wow this is great as my valet served me chilled lemonade and canapes. However, after a night of never feeling comfortable or at ease with this person literally hovering over me at all times (how do those royals cope?), I called the production office and asked to be moved. Where is everyone else staying, I asked. The Holiday Inn, came the startling reply. So why aren't I staying there? Oh, because you are English we thought you'd be used to servants!!!! I was stunned, moved into the Holiday Inn and, after laughing about this very peculiar circumstance, spent all my evenings throughout my stay hanging out with Julie Delpy, who I had the great pleasure of working with again in **An American Werewolf in Paris** (1997) in Luxembourg. I can still see us giggling by that famous Giant Ferris Wheel in the Prater…

▲ Top left: James Bond and Harry Potter special effects maestro John Richardson, director Russell Mulchay and Alan Jones on the *Highlander II: The Quickening* (1991) set in Argentina.

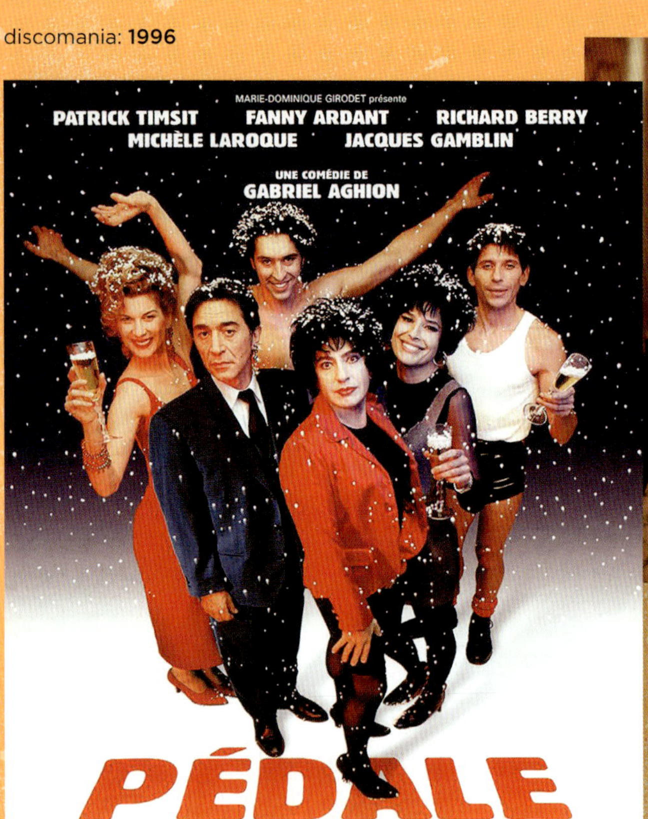

WHAT A DRAG! / PÉDALE DOUCE (1996)

A month before **The Birdcage** (1996) was released in France, along came this spoiler attraction that turned into one of the year's biggest box-office hits winning three César Awards (the Gallic Oscar) including Best Actress for Fanny Ardant. Cut from the same spangly drag as the many variations on the 'La Cage aux Folles' formula, **Pédale douce** was co-written and directed by Egyptian-born Gabriel Aghion (in Alexandria, in fact, hence the inclusion of Claude François' *Alexandrie Alexandra*, 1978), known for his comedy drama forte. Indeed, in 2001 he would direct **Absolument fabuleux**, the French feature version of the hit British TV series 'Absolutely Fabulous'. Aghion's co-writer was star Patrick Timsit, who would turn up in **Dalida** (2016), the Disco subject of which contributed the three songs *Salma ya Salama* (1977), *Je suis toutes les femmes* (1980), and her signature anthem *Bambino* (1956).

But it's another French Disco icon, Mylene Farmer and her massive hit *Sans contrefaçon* (1987), who starts – and ends – the show in fun style. By day Adrien Aymar (Timsit) works as an executive in a big Paris bank but by night he becomes the queen of Chez Éva, a gay restaurant/bar/backroom/Disco run by his best friend, unsurprisingly named Éva (Ardant). When his boss Alexandre Agut (Richard Berry) invites him to dinner at his home to discuss a new German contract, not wanting to come out of the closet, Adrien asks Éva to pose as his wife. During the fraught meal Alexandre becomes captivated by Éva despite being married to Marie (Michèle Laroque). It's only a matter of time before Alexandre turns up at Chez Éva and the manic deceptions, mistaken identities, gay rumours and farcical mayhem begins.

Light as a cream puff and just as narratively substantial, no old fashioned flouncing stereotype is left undisturbed in this conservative combo of drag queenery, gay hysteria, macho humour, vulgar slapstick, toxic masculinity and backroom behaviour with sobering strays into AIDS awareness and quiet self-obsessed contemplation. With male strippers, leather outfits, whips and chains, outrageous costumes and that emblematic "c'est la vie" French attitude in abundance, **Pédale douce** exists in a grudgingly accepting universe symptomatic of so many gay fantasies of its ilk, a naïve vision of a perfectly tolerant world. Looking very dated compared to other 1990s entries, what gives it a major lift is the terrific soundtrack, an object lesson in how to musically engineer the necessary feel-good factor.

Each having a solid impact on the carefree mood, there's *Y.M.C.A.* (1978) by the Village People, *I Love*

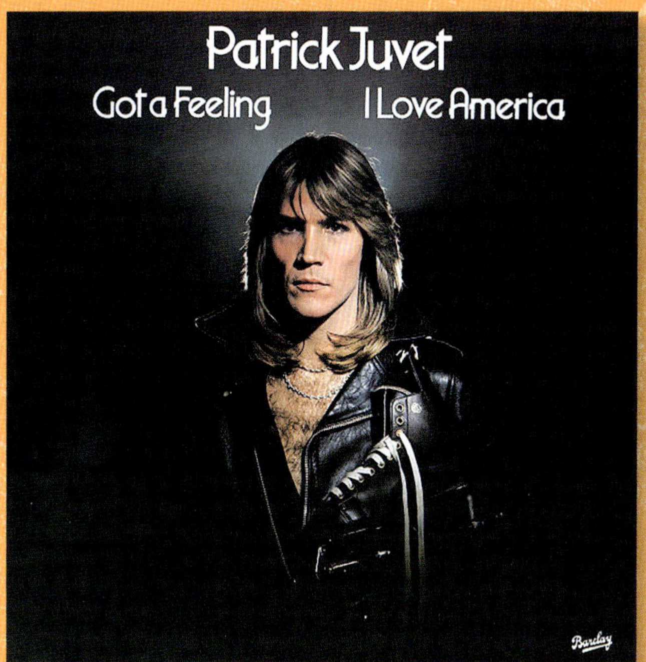

America (1978) by Patrick Juvet, accompanying a magical snowstorm sequence, the *Rivers of Babylon/Sunny/Daddy Cool/Ma Baker/Rasputin* Megamix (1992) by Boney M., the instrumental *Schöneberg* (1993) by Marmion, *C'est la vie* (1989) by Marc Lavoine, *Club Rules* (1994) by Namby Pamby, and a Disco version of Zizi Jeanmaire's 1962 smash hit single *Mon trucs en plumes* (1995), the Hollywood dancer immortalised in Peter Sarstedt's *Where Do You Go To (My Lovely)?* (1969). Formidable! Aghion would visit the blueprint again in **Pédale dure** (2004) concerning surrogate gay adoption.

Patrick Juvet

Purveyor of some of the classiest Disco ever was Swiss-born Patrick Juvet. One of the many artists taken under the wing of Village People producer Jacques Morali, bisexual Juvet began a modelling career in Germany before meeting French music doyen Eddie Barclay who launched his singing career with the Jacques Brel-style single *Romantiques par mort* (1971). After writing *Le lundi au soleil* (1972) for Claude François, he represented Switzerland at the 1973 Eurovision Song Contest with *Je vais me marier, Marie*, placing No.12. In 1977, Juvet collaborated with French composer and musician extraordinaire Jean-Michel Jarre (*Oxygène*, 1976) on the album *Paris By Night*, featuring the hit song, *Où sont les femmes?*

With English lyrics by the Village People's lead singer Vic Willis that song became *Where Is my Woman*, one of four tracks on Juvet's blistering Casablanca Records debut *I Love America* (1978). That track, the title one and *I Got a Feeling* hit the 'Billboard' Disco Top 5 and had a four-month staying power. It was Juvet's next album that entered the classic Disco category. Musically accomplished, melodically out of this world and orchestrated with Disco finesse, *Lady Night* (1979) sported another four killer tracks: the swooning title song, *Swiss Kiss*, *Viva California* and the sublime medley *The 'Gay Paris'/French Pillow Talk*. In the same year Juvet composed the part-Disco soundtrack for director David Hamilton's softcore, soft-focus romance **Laura**, featuring musicians Marc Chantereau and Slim Pezin of Voyage fame and Space session bassist Jannick Top.

Nostromo

In the summer of 1995 I was offered another dream unit publicity assignment. Would I travel to Cartagena, Colombia, and work for a month on the Italian produced TV series 'Nostromo' starring Claudia Cardinale, Albert Finney, Colin Firth, Brian Dennehy, Serena Scott Thomas, Joaquim de Almeida and Claudio Amendola to name just a few of the starry cast? Before you could say "Andiamo" I was on a plane to Venezuela, in a limousine to Bolivar, Colombia, and working in some of the most sweltering and difficult conditions ever. Based on the classic Joseph Conrad novel 'Heart of Darkness', the expensively mounted costume drama was the brainchild of producer Fernando Ghia (**The Mission**, 1986) who had been intrigued by director David Lean's obsession with the book when working with him on **Lady Caroline Lamb** (1972). When Lean died in 1991, Ghia decided to forge ahead with his friend's pet project and **Anne of the Thousand Days** (1969) writer John Hale's four-episode screenplay was the result.

The script was absolutely brilliant but the miniseries by veteran TV director Alastair Reid that aired in 1996/97 was a great disappointment for so many reasons. Without putting too fine a point on it, the freely available local cocaine was $3 a gram! But I have so many fantastic memories from the gorgeous locations, the same ones where director Gillo Pontecorvo shot **Queimada/Burn!** (1969). One night we all went out to dinner with Claudia Cardinale and I ended up dancing on a table with her to the massive South American Disco hit of the day *Ritmo de la noche* (1994) by Chocolate Featuring Chico & The Gypsies. 'Nostromo' was also the production where Colin Firth met his wife Livia Giuggioli and that was nice to witness. Ghia would often let us use his private yacht at the weekends too and we'd travel to tiny deserted islands for picnics in the Caribbean Sea. Amazing!

Playing General Montero in the cast was Salvatore Basile who had been Ruggero Deodato's assistant director on the infamous **Cannibal Holocaust** (1980), shot in the same area. He and his wife regaled me with one shock story after another about that movie. Incredible! The one person I hated on the film was Albert Finney. When he found out I never touched alcohol, he made it his mission to try and tempt or trick me into drinking the whiskey he had a huge stash of in his hotel room. He would often just sit and stare at me with those piercing eyes. To say this got old pretty fast is an understatement. I mean, surely he had better things to do? Like be sober enough to learn his lines! I'd really admired him up until then and had often seen him in our favourite greasy spoon on Shaftesbury Avenue, Valoti, when working up the road at Forbidden Planet 2. The old adage is so often true; never meet your idols. Finney was the only fly in the 'Nostromo' ointment though because it really was an indelible experience.

Alan Jones loved working with Italian superstar Claudio Amendola on 'Nostromo'. He was famous at the time for *La Reine Margot* (1994) with Asia Argento.

▲ Top right: Alan Jones's nemesis Albert Finney, with co-star Claudia Cardinale, in 'Nostromo'.

THE BIRDCAGE (1996)

The third mainstream cross-dressing movie in as many years to put across the message of gay tolerance (the other two were **The Adventures of Priscilla, Queen of the Desert**, 1994, and **To Wong Foo, Thanks for Everything! Julie Newmar**, 1995), director Mike Nichols amiably repurposed the breakout French drag farce 'La Cage aux Folles' (1978), which spawned a successful 1978 Gallic movie adaptation and two sequels in 1980 and 1985. He was originally going to direct the 1983 Broadway musical version but **Can't Stop the Music** (1980) producer Allan Carr fired him after employing composer Jerry ('Hello, Dolly!') Herman. Shifting the location from Saint-Tropez (New Orleans in his musical treatment) to Miami's South Beach and getting his longtime writing partner Elaine May to elevate the gags from insultingly unsubtle to less so, **The Birdcage** – originally developed as 'Birds of a Feather' and then 'The Queen of Basin Street' – works because of the central performances by Robin Williams and Nathan Lane who spark off each other like steel marshmallows.

Lane is Albert, the star attraction at the top transvestite nightclub The Birdcage. His partner of 20 years is Armand Goldman (Williams) and they have a son, Val (Dan Futterman), the product of an inquisitive one-night-stand with power executive Katherine Archer (Christine Baranski) before he met Albert. When Val becomes engaged to Barbara (Calista Flockhart), the 18-year-old daughter of conservative Senator Keeley (Gene Hackman), cofounder of the Coalition of Moral Order, naturally he wants to meet his parents. So Val pleads for Albert to play it straight for one night only to seal the marriage deal. But Albert can't resist the challenge of dragging up as his mother in concerned housewife mode meaning camp chaos all round.

It had always been a funny set up through its previous incarnations and the timed-to-perfection performances really make the comedy and sentiment work once more. Nichols actually hired PBS producer Rick McKay to film global transvestites in action and this 'Drag for Dummies' footage was used to train Lane for his Starina alterego, making his outlandishness somewhat more humanised. Everyone gets in on the Disco dressing-up act, including Dianne Wiest as the Senator's wife and Hank Azaria as Agador, the effeminate houseboy in cha-cha heels, who camps it up like Danny La Rue on steroids. Stereotypical, yes, exaggerated, of course, but often hilarious when Lane is trying to walk like John Wayne or Williams is barking out such dance directions as, "Fosse, Fosse, Fosse, Martha Graham, Martha Graham, Martha Graham, Madonna, Madonna, Madonna".

The boa-wrapped preaching about equality, love, and acceptance begins from frame one when Sister Sledge's *We Are Family* (1979), sung by the The Goldman Girls, features as the opening number. Other Disco touchstones include Labelle's *Lady Marmalade* (1974), Donna Summer's *She Works Hard for the Money* (1983) and Gloria Estefan and The Miami Sound Machine's *Conga* (1985). The two songs it weirdly doesn't feature are Discofied versions of the showstoppers from the Broadway hit. Gloria Gaynor turned *I Am What I Am* (1983) into another chart-busting Gay Disco anthem alongside her *I Will Survive* (1978). La Cage also recorded a cover version. And the show also provided a club hit for the stridently produced title song by La Jetée.

ZE ZE Top

What was the hippest Disco label? Jump in the cab pictured on the yellow record sleeves and head on over to ZE Records. Formed by British-born Michael Zilkha (his father was the owner of Mothercare) and Punk publisher Michel Esteban, ZE (from their surname initials) sprung out of Velvet Underground founder John Cale introducing them after he produced the French new wave band Marie et les Garçons for his SPY Records label with Esteban. (Fun Fact: I knew the Velvet's John Cale and Nico well and invited them to my 23rd Birthday Party where we danced all night to the Gloria Gaynor album *Never Can Say Goodbye*, 1975).

ZE Records' ethos was to release new music under the labels Mutant Disco or No Wave and they quickly signed up the likes of James White and the Blacks, Was (Not Was), Lydia Lunch, Lizzy Mercier Descloux, The Waitresses, Bill Laswell's Material, and Richard Strange. The Disco-No-Disco contingent was led by Dr. Buzzard's Original Savannah Band creator August Darnell's latest retro fling, Kid Creole and the Coconuts (*Annie I'm Not Your Daddy*, 1982), Don Armando's Second Avenue Rhumba Band (the No.1 hit *Deputy of Love/I'm an Indian Too*, 1979), Coati Mundi (*Que Pasa/Me No Pop I*, 1981), Aural Exciters (*Spooks in Space*, 1979), Ron Rogers (*Don't Play with My Emotions*, 1982), Gichy Dan's Beachwood #9 (*On a Day Like Today*, 1979) and the fabulous Cristina.

Cristina was Zilkha's wife, they met when both worked freelance for the 'Village Voice' paper, and he persuaded her to record *Disco Clone* (1978), written by Ronald Melrose, an ex-Harvard classmate. Produced by John Cale and featuring an uncredited Kevin Kline on vocals, this steamy robot fantasy led to two scintillating albums, *Cristina* (1980), containing the tracks *La poupée qui fait non*, a cover of the 1966 Michel Polnareff hit, and the two August Darnell compositions *Jungle Love* and *Blame It on Disco*, plus *Sleep It Off* (1984) featuring the brilliantly titled *Don't Mutilate My Mink*. But Cristina's best recording is the one ZE found themselves in legal hot water over with veteran Brill Building songwriters Jerry Leiber and Mike Stoller. Her 12-inch aggressively pitched version of the 1969 Peggy Lee classic *Is That All There Is?* (1980) is punchy Disco divertissement of the highest calibre.

Fruit Machine

In the olden pre-email, pre-texting days, I only ever received three actual written letters from people thanking me for my coverage of their movies. Not that you do it for that of course. The first to do so was director Michael Winner who liked my 'CFQ' set report on **Scream for Help** (1984). The second was Diane Ladd (Laura Dern's mother) after our Sky Movies show celebrating the **Rambling Rose** (1991) premiere attended by Princess Diana. What an event that was! And the third was Wes Craven who loved my on-stage interview with him about **The People Under the Stairs** (1992) at the Dylan Dog Film Festival in Milan so much, he sent me a note with a promo sweatshirt for his 'Nightmare Café' TV series. But what's it like when friends and acquaintances hate your reviews of their work? It has happened on numerous occasions but I've never swerved from writing what I truly feel about a movie, either good or bad. It's why I'm still reviewing today because people know I always speak the truth no matter what the consequences.

When I gave Russell Mulcahy's **Highlander II: The Quickening** (1991) a terrible 'Starburst' review, he was really angry as he had paid for my first class trip to Argentina to cover its making. My comeback was he got value for money from all the coverage and, frankly, even he knew it wasn't very good. One of the funniest altercations I've ever had was with Mariano Baino on his boring Russian-shot horror **Dark Waters** (1993). I hated it and refused to give it houseroom in any publication I wrote for. "No one cares what you think", he said. I agreed, it was only my opinion, others should always make up their own minds, a mantra I have stuck to right up until the present FrightFest day. If you can't retain your own personal integrity, what's the point? Directors, stars, whoever, if they can't take criticism, and I certainly can, then get out of the business.

None of this sitting on the fence either with such non-committal phrases as "Good just isn't the word", "Well, you've gone and done it again", "How remarkable" or "It's so fresh, so different", that I have often heard when people are lost over what to say to someone they know. The worst instance of someone taking umbrage at what I wrote are Miramax over Richard Stanley's **Dust Devil** (1992) that nearly ended up in court. But the only time I felt really threatened was when I wrote a no-stars review for the gay coming-of-age crime drama **The Fruit Machine** (1988). Someone from the production had gotten hold of my telephone number and kept calling saying why I should have given Philip Saville's Vestron release a better write-up and I had better watch my step at my next preview screening. I had to report it in the end but what a peculiar movie to get so upset about. I think the only good words I had for it were because Divine's two 1988 HiNRG hits *I'm So Beautiful* and *You Think You're a Man* featured on the soundtrack.

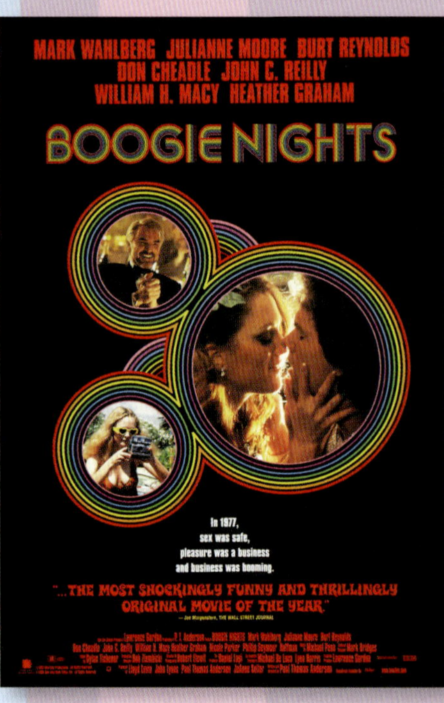

BOOGIE NIGHTS (1997)

Pornography, drugs and Disco are the driving forces of director Paul Thomas Anderson's potent parable of the hedonistic 1970s. Spanning the height of the Disco era this unvarnished unzipping of the adult movie industry is pure dynamite in its forensic focus on people searching for a family, holding on to their dignity even while in what many perceived as the gutter, and grasping at any slim chance of love and affection. A visually stunning and poignant exploration into sexually diverse flesh peddling and the cynical fiends behind it, this keynote '90s masterpiece is a stunningly surreal take on the naked American Dream that is as startling as it is entertaining.

Veteran hardcore producer/director Jack Horner (superb Burt Reynolds in an Oscar-nominated performance) discovers well-endowed busboy Eddie Adams (Mark Wahlberg) working in a club to make ends meet. Quickly Eddie is transformed into porn icon Dirk Diggler (obviously inspired by the John Holmes persona) and star of hardcore hits featuring Horner's girlfriend Amber Waves (Julianne Moore, also Oscar-nominated) and their protégée Rollergirl (Heather Graham), who won't do anything minus her roller skates.

As Eddie's X-rated fame rises, he and his close-knit extended family, including fellow studs Reed (John C. Reilly) and Buck (Don Cheadle), and technician Little Bill (William H. Macy) live and party well. Then the 1980s happen, the cocaine flows way too easily, Eddie's talent becomes toxic, the skinflick industry heads to cheap videotape and the drug-related rock bottom screeches into view.

An hilarious and harrowing rags-to-riches-to-rags-again saga outlining a group of misfits trying to forge something approaching normal out of the crudest materials, **Boogie Nights** is a swingers' fantasy decked out in shoddy polyester leisure suits, Wahlberg's prosthetic penis and a full-blown Disco attitude. Beginning with a brilliant extended Steadicam shot through a nightclub as all the main players come into the spotlight, the Hustle

is demonstrated halfway through Diggler's meteoric success story and the Disco hits never stop.

Included in the hefty 155-minute running time are *Best of My Love* (1977) by The Emotions, *Sunny* (1977) by Boney M., *Fly, Robin, Fly* (1975) by Silver Convention, *You Sexy Thing* (1975) by Hot Chocolate, *I Want to Be Free* (1974) by Ohio Players, *Boogie Shoes* (1978) by KC and The Sunshine Band, *Machine Gun* (1974) by the Commodores, *J.P. Walk* by Sound Experience, *Got to Give It Up* (1977) by Marvin Gaye, *Ain't No Stoppin' Us Now* (1979) by McFadden and Whitehead, *Do Your Thing* (1969) by The Watts 103rd Street Rhythm Band, *Disco Fever* (1977) by Roger Webb, *Jungle Fever* (1970) by Chakachas, and *Compared to What* (1969) by Roberta Flack.

The one song not heard is the UK No.2 chart hit *Boogie Nights* (1977) by Heatwave. When Anderson tried to license the rights the group's lead singer Johnnie Wilder refused to deal. A devout born again Christian after a 1979 car crash left him paraplegic, even though he would still continue working with the band in the studio and on tour, Wilder would not endorse a movie about pornography no matter what the cost to the band's bank balance.

Domenico Disco

Twenty years prior to the day **Boogie Nights** premiered at the Toronto Film Festival, Meco's *Star Wars and Other Galactic Funk* (1977) album was exploding in Discos all over the world. Born Domenico Monardo, the record producer had seen the George Lucas movie on its opening day in May and returned for a further four viewings. Realising that soundtrack composer John Williams had used classical thematic leitmotifs for the main characters he had the idea to turn those melodies into Disco. The result was a certified platinum hit for the Casablanca Records subsidiary Millennium and the template for other Disco versions of popular sci-fi fantasy blockbusters.

The adept trombonist was not a pop music fan until he heard Petula Clark's monster smash *Downtown* (1964) and then studied arranging, eventually putting his talents to work on the Tommy James and The Shondells' hit *Crystal Blue Persuasion* (1969). Meco's major career breakthrough came when he co-produced, with regular partner Tony Bongiovi and Jay Ellis, Gloria Gaynor's seminal Disco album *Never Can Say Goodbye* (1975). Another terrific Meco, Bongiovi, Ellis and Harold Wheeler production was *A Disco Symphony* (1977) by Camouflage featuring Mysti, a pounding suite of original songs mixed with *MacArthur Park* (1968), *I Hear a Symphony* (1966) and George Gershwin's *Rhapsody in Blue* (1924). Donna Summer's version of *MacArthur Park* (1978) later produced by Giorgio Moroder is clearly heavily influenced by this Meco arrangement.

Meco's next album *Encounters of Every Kind* (1978) included the Disco arranged *Theme from Close Encounters (Inspired by the Soundtrack of Close Encounters of the Third Kind)* from which also came the singles *Topsy* and *Meco's Theme. Themes from The Wizard of Oz* (1978) was undoubtedly Meco's masterpiece, a superior slice of Disco whimsy geared around the classic 1939 Judy Garland fantasy. It was diminishing Disco returns from then on as *Moondancer* (1979), *Superman and Other Galactic Heroes* (1979), *Music from Star Trek and The Black Hole* (1980), *Plays Music from The Empire Strikes Back* (1980), *Christmas in the Stars: Star Wars Christmas Album* (1980), and *The Raiders March* (1981) all failed to chart.

By the time of *Impressions of An American Werewolf in London* (1981), *Pop Goes the Movies* (1982) and *Ewok Celebration* (1983), it was clear the Disco movie theme fad was over and Meco retired to Florida. Until the last gasp *Music Inspired by Star Wars* belated vanity project surprisingly appeared in 2005.

The Cinema Bookshop

Fred Zentner

If you couldn't find what you were looking for at the 'Dark They Were, and Golden Eyed' emporium in St. Anne's Court, it was only a ten-minute walk to the other epicentre of film fandom in early 1970s London. The Cinema Bookshop at 13 Great Russell Street, WC1, was a dusty hole in the wall but it was crammed with everything you ever wanted. The enigmatic Fred Zentner ran the place and he was like the father figure you always wanted who would tell you what was happening on the London movie scene. Customers would commandeer his attention for ages discussing the latest Claude Chabrol art-house release at the Academy Cinema around the corner in Oxford Street, his vintage posters or collection of reprint stills he sold quite flagrantly. Copyright? What's that?

Fred was a pattern cutter for Swinging Sixties fashion designer icon Mary Quant until he gave the rag trade up to focus on his first love, books. He rented a shelf in the Atlantis bookshop on Great Russell Street and acted as a finder for people looking for those hard to locate items. So successful did he become that the Atlantis owners got quite annoyed, literally forcing him to open up his own establishment in an old wine shop further up the street. Not having any money to redecorate, Fred kept the old wine shelves, the reason why they were so deep and never ideal for display.

One of the people he found rare books for was horror star Peter Cushing who loved the subject of miniature paintings. On the day Fred opened his shop, he found a cardboard box on the doorstep. Inside was a whole stack of portrait photographs signed by the Hammer icon and a note wishing him every success in his new endeavour. Fred never forgot that act of kindness and thanks to his trading with that legendary Hollywood Boulevard institution, the Larry Edmunds bookshop, began importing everything the genre fan could ever want – at a hefty price.

From 'Films and Filming' (the gay 'Photoplay' that invariably featured semi-naked male stars on its covers) and 'Films Illustrated' (edited by David Castell, who I would eventually work with at Sky Movies) to 'Cinefantastique' and 'Photon' magazines, you could find it at Fred's. I still have my first American edition copy of the 'Film Fantasy Scrapbook' by Ray Harryhausen from 1972 because Fred had written in pencil on the inside the price of £7, astronomical for its day. But more than a shop, it was a place to meet up with friends for a chat. Fred knew his customer base and it's one of the reasons I copied this strategy for Forbidden Planet 2. By then we were friendly business rivals, yet I was really sorry when the place closed in July 2005 as I felt a part of my formative film youth had gone forever.

THAT'S THE WAY I LIKE IT (1998)

Singapore was not immune to the all-encompassing power of Disco. In the wake of **Saturday Night Fever** (1977), Discos sprouted everywhere throughout the South Malaysian Republic drawing the young, hipster and happening to the dance floor to boogie the monsoon nights away. One convert to the new dance craze was 16-year-old Glen Goei who began his broad-ranging professional career in the arts playing the male opera singer Song Liling in the 1989 West End production of the Tony award-winning play 'M. Butterfly' starring opposite Sir Anthony Hopkins' besotted French diplomat. This led to Goei becoming the Artistic Director of Mu-Lan Arts in London from 1990 to 1998, the first Asian theatre company to be established in the UK, whereupon he returned to his native Singapore to pursue his other goals in film, musicals, arena shows, World Expos, dance, music and architectural design.

Goei mortgaged his London apartment to make his first feature film based on personal experiences motivating him at the height of Singapore Disco madness so others could feel the magic of those exhilarating days. In the process he wrote and directed one of the best **Saturday Night Fever** clones of all, an amusing, sentimental, touching and affectionately nostalgic combo of the Travolta blockbuster, **Strictly Ballroom** (1992), **The Purple Rose of Cairo** (1985) and **Enter the Dragon** (1973) that became the first Singapore movie to achieve a worldwide release.

It's 1977 and Bruce Lee fan Hock (Adrian Pang) is working in the Oriental Emporium supermarket with no prospects, no romantic interest and a miserable home life. Depressed, he pops into his local cinema to see the current box-office sensation 'Forever Fever' (the original title in Singapore), a copycat **Saturday Night Fever** affair (starring John Travolta lookalike Dominic Pace). Fired with enthusiasm he decides his life needs a similar radical change to the one on screen affecting Italian-American youth if he's going to amount to anything. So he enrols at the Bonnie and Clyde Dance Studio to learn the Hustle, the Bump and the Bus Stop. There he teams up with barmaid Mei (Medaline Tan) and together they start practicing for the upcoming dance contest at the Galaxy Disco. First prize is $5,000, with which Hock intends to buy a new motorcycle.

If ever his mood drops, Hock heads back to the cinema to see 'Forever Fever' again for extra motivation where his polyestered Guardian Angel Pace steps out of the screen to give him advice on love, fashion, style and dance moves.

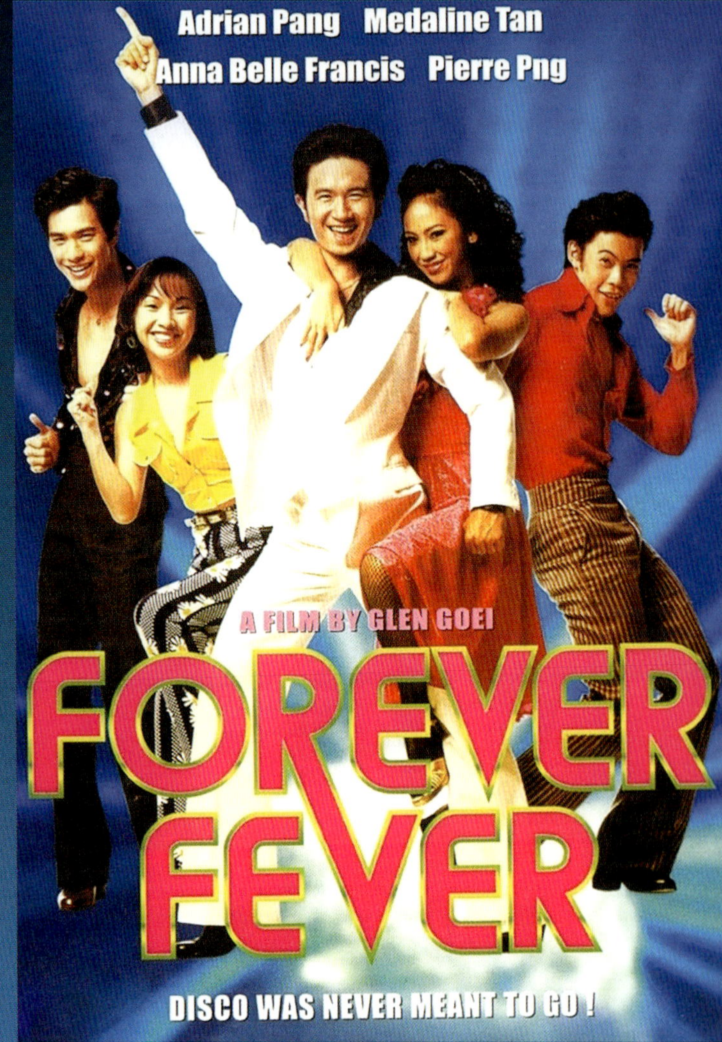

But talented hustler Julie (local Singapore DJ Anna Belle Francis) has her eyes on the fast-improving Hock and lures him away from Mei for the big night. Something her jealous ex-boyfriend Richard (Pierre Png) is determined to put a stop to by having Hock savagely assaulted to sabotage their championship prospects. Battered and bruised on the Galaxy floor, Hock realises he's in love with Mei, beats up Richard, wins the contest, and gives the prize money to his alienated brother Leslie (Caleb Goh) to pay for his sex-change operation.

Sometimes a virtual frame-by-frame replica of John Badham's game-changer (the heated family dinner table exchanges being the most significant), Goei's startlingly crass East meets West affair is nevertheless a crowd-pleaser that's one of the few dance-orientated movies to successfully portray the wonderment and thrill of the actual Disco experience. Discophiles cherish it for that palpable atmosphere alone. Filmed under the shooting title 'Don't Call Me John Travolta', the appealing fantasy sequences, the transgender dilemma (a nifty twist on the priest sub-plot) and the martial arts vibe (Hock's Disco mantra is "Don't think, feel", lifted from **Enter the Dragon**, and the final kung fu battle is pure **The Big Boss/Fists of Fury**, 1971) add pleasing nuances to the familiar bases. While Goei's debut feature is very ragged around the edges, it's charmingly so and its trans-cultural sharpness only helps punch the fluffy imitation games across for extra entertainment value.

Expertly choreographed by Zaki Ahmad, all the dance routines are accompanied by variable cover versions of Disco classics by risen or rising local Malaysian artists all executive produced by Ruzita Zaki and Zul Othman. Dan Hartman's 1978 *Instant Replay* and the Bee Gees' 1978 *Stayin' Alive* are sung by innovative veterans October Cherries, Carl Douglas' 1974 *Kung Fu Fighting* and The Real Thing's 1976 *You to Me Are Everything* by producer Zul, with an additional 1998 remix of the latter by Esam, The Jacksons' 1979 *Shake Your Body* by Kevin Verghese, the Bee Gees' 1976 *You Should Be Dancing* and 1975 *Jive Talkin'* by Jai, KC & The Sunshine Band's 1975 *That's the Way (I Like It)* by Najip Ali, the Bee Gees' 1978 *Stayin' Alive* and The Hues Corporation's 1973 *Rock the Boat* by John Klass, the Bee Gees' 1977 *How Deep Is Your Love* by Chris Vadham and Chic's 1978 *Le Freak* by Pabby Love.

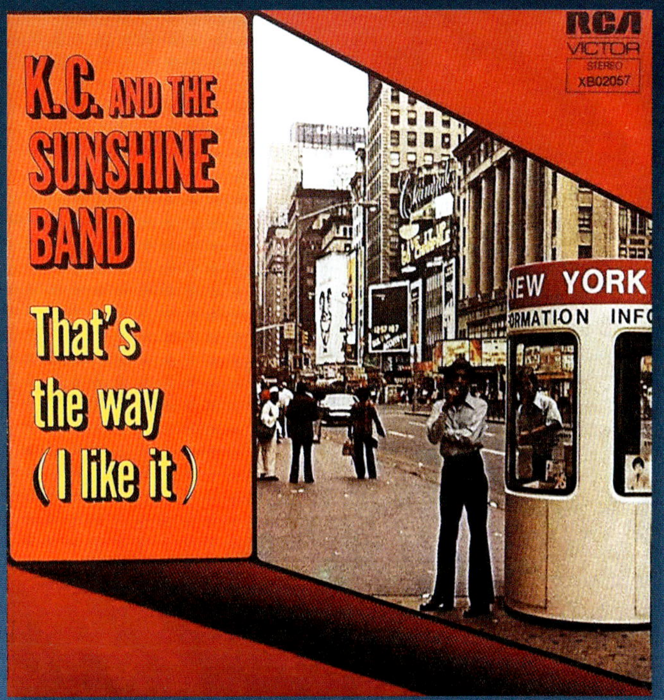

The one original track is *Elektrik-Sequinned Soul* (1998), a cheesy Muzak medley of Disco riffs by Stoned Revivals. Chris Vadham also sings Harry Nilsson's 1968 classic *Everybody's Talkin'*, the sonic backdrop to Hock's motorbike fantasies. Goei paid a budgetary disproportionate fortune for the copyright fees to re-record the selected songs but as MOR as all the musical tracks turned out it was this crucial element that allowed Miramax head honcho Harvey Weinstein to connect with the movie when he viewed it at a market screening. Re-edited and re-dubbed for worldwide distribution, **That's the Way I Like It** made a healthy profit for all concerned after initial Pacific Rim takings didn't even come close in allowing it to break even. And the ersatz soundtrack is what contributes another adorable layer of fuzzy fairytale to its guilty pleasure panache.

Got You Covered

Disco classics have been continually covered ever since the Golden Era faded, KC and The Sunshine Band's *That's the Way I Like It* by Dead or Alive to mention the obvious one in context here. But at the height of the movement many songs and instrumentals did double duty for a variety of reasons. Canny American producers wanting to beat popular Eurodisco to the US marketplace by rush releasing their own versions meant Sunny's early 1974 UK Top 10 hit *Doctor's Orders* got pimped up later that year for Carol Douglas who scored a 'Billboard' Disco No.2 and Space's French-produced sensation *Magic Fly* (1977) got more easily contoured for nightclubs the same year by Kebekelektrik. Not all of this jumping on the Eurodisco bandwagon worked of course; The Heart and Soul Orchestra backed the wrong horse completely when they took on the Cerrone *Love in C Minor* powerhouse in 1976; so did Rick Summer with his version of Patrick Hernandez's 1979 No.1 *Born to Be Alive.*

Early Disco Queen Carol Douglas actually tried to revive her stunning post-1976 *Midnight Love Affair Suite* success with three 'why?' covers – ABBA's 1976 *Dancing Queen* (1977), the Bee Gees' 1977 *Night Fever* (1978), and The Three Degrees' 1979 *My Simple Heart* (1981). All way too poppy Yacht Disco. Other examples of this genre would be Henry Mancini and His Concert Orchestra's 1975 cover of Van McCoy's 1974 Top 20 Disco hit *African Symphony*, the Graffiti Orchestra's concurrent version of Meco's 1977 *Star Wars Theme* smash and likewise (Vince) Montana's version of Meco's 1977 *Theme from Close Encounters of the Third Kind.*

Some classic songs just never die though and are constantly ripe for reinterpretation, like the three dance versions of *House of the Rising Sun* by Hot R.S. (1977), Santa Esmeralda, and Revelacion (both 1978), *Don't Leave Me This Way* by Harold Melvin & the Blue Notes (1975) and Thelma Houston (1976), *Je t'aime* by Saint Tropez and Donna Summer (both 1977), *96 Tears* by Thelma Houston and Garland Jeffreys (both 1981). Especially those from the Motown catalogue it seemed: *Ain't No Mountain High Enough* by Boys Town Gang and Inner Life (both 1981), *I Heard It Through the Grapevine* by P'zzazz (1980), Diana Ross' 1976 *Love Hangover* by The Players Association (1977), *Reach Out I'll Be There* by Gloria Gaynor (1975) and J.T. Connection (1979), *Standing in the Shadows of Love* by Deborah Washington and Fever (both 1978), and *You Keep Me Hangin' On* by David Matthews with Whirlwind, and Roni Hill (both 1976).

▲ Alan Jones with his director Russell Mulcahy on *Talos the Mummy/Tale of the Mummy* (1998).

▲ Above: Alan Jones in full Egyptian King regalia; the costume was made up of clothes from the *Cleopatra* (1963) wardrobe.

Disco Memo

Pharaoh Enough?

Did you know I starred in a movie with Christopher Lee, Honor Blackman, Gerard Butler and Shelley Duvall? It happened quite by accident and all stemmed yet again from my good friends scriptwriter Keith Williams and director Russell Mulcahy. Russell had broken his leg in a skiing accident during Christmas 1995 and was confined to a wheelchair. To stop him driving everyone crazy, Keith suggested they write a nasty horror script together based around his love of Hammer's **The Mummy** (1959), and 'Talos the Mummy' was the outcome. After the usual financing hurdles, the movie finally went into production at the Carousel Picture Company in Luxembourg and I turned up in September 1997 to file a few set reports. By the way, the Europop song of the moment was *Barbie Girl* (1997) by Aqua and we heard it non-stop everywhere.

So there I was with my trusty tape recorder in hand when Russell sidled up to me and said he needed my help. Someone had pointed out that the crucial

▲ Above: Alan Jones with his best friend, writer/rock video conceptualist Keith Williams.

Disco Memo

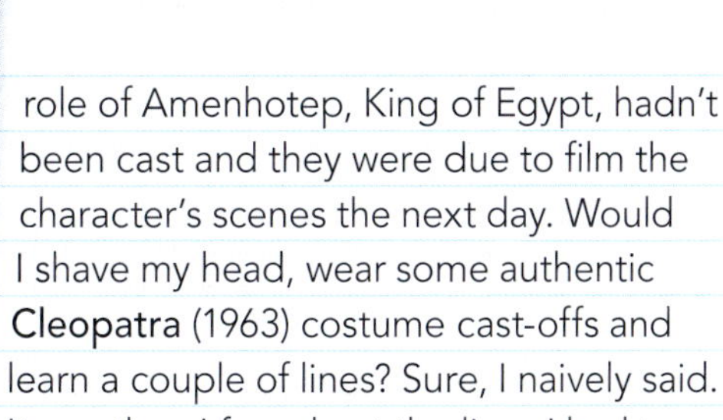

Alan Jones with Shelley Duvall, star of *The Shining* (1980).

role of Amenhotep, King of Egypt, hadn't been cast and they were due to film the character's scenes the next day. Would I shave my head, wear some authentic **Cleopatra** (1963) costume cast-offs and learn a couple of lines? Sure, I naively said. It was then I found out the lines I had to memorise were in Egyptian! I was up all night trying to phonetically cram such dialogue as "Ne se chemet, nen pari fa mahiwat ne djet". The next day I was terrified as Russell barked out directions while my co-stars Lee, Duvall, Butler, Jack Davenport, Sean Pertwee, Lysette Anthony and Jason Scott Lee looked on. Eek!

Alan Jones with his *Talos* co-star Louise Lombard and co-scripter John Esposito.

Alan Jones with director Russell Mulcahy, filming in Luxembourg.

I did look Nile-tastic in my royal regalia though, but in the end it didn't matter as my scenes were all cut from the final print that emerged under the title **Tale of the Mummy** (1998).

But what another bunch of fantastic movie memories thanks to Russell and Keith. Driving into the country with Duvall for a picnic and hearing everything about **The Shining** (1980). Hanging out with Lee before he became more pompous post-**The Lord of the Rings** (2001) and **Star Wars** (2002) franchises. Avoiding the sexual advances of one of the cast members, which Lee unknowingly rescued me from! Good times.

▲ Above: Jack Davenport, Honor Blackman and Jason Scott Lee in *Talos*.

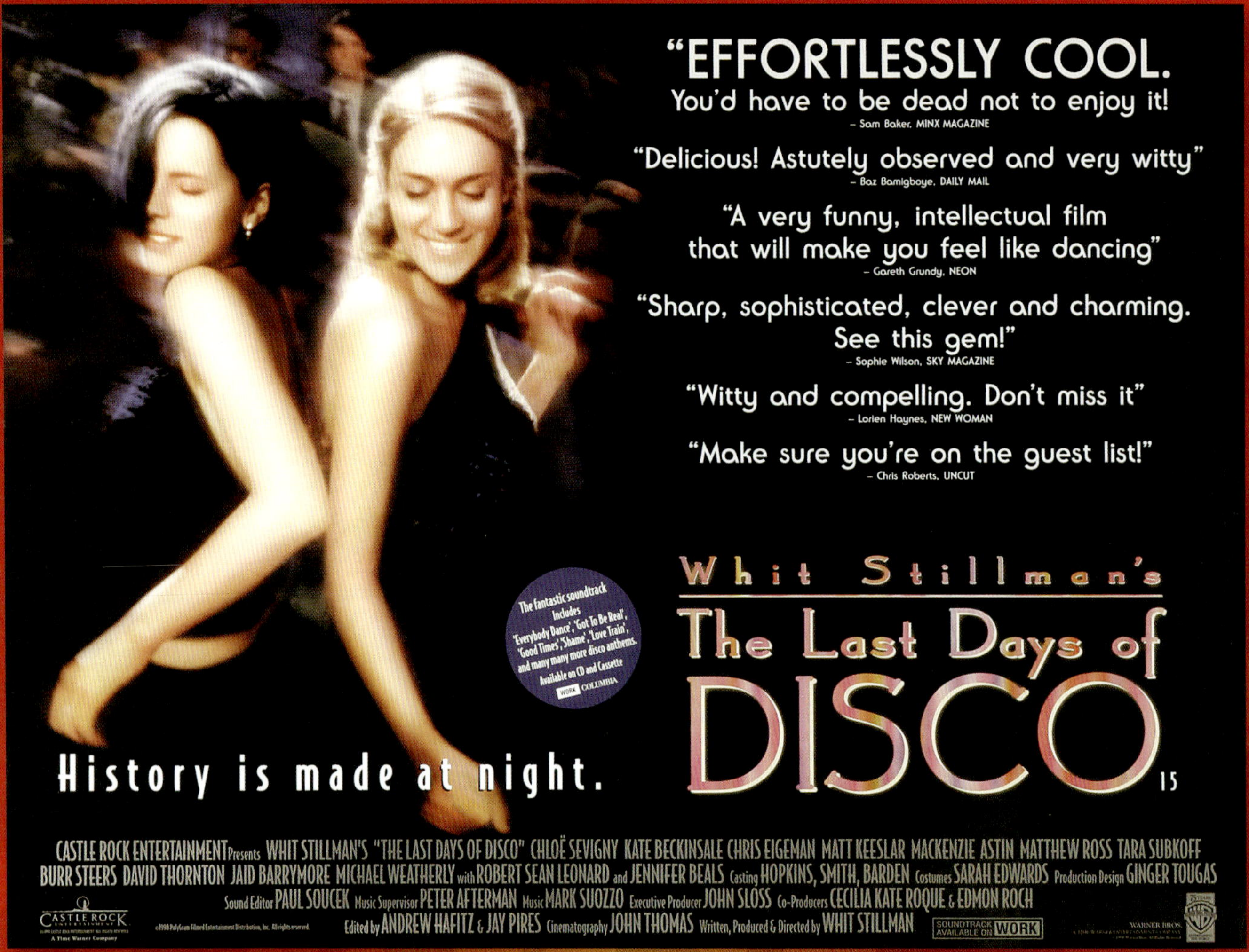

"EFFORTLESSLY COOL.
You'd have to be dead not to enjoy it!
– Sam Baker, MINX MAGAZINE

"Delicious! Astutely observed and very witty"
– Baz Bamigboye, DAILY MAIL

"A very funny, intellectual film that will make you feel like dancing"
– Gareth Grundy, NEON

"Sharp, sophisticated, clever and charming. See this gem!"
– Sophie Wilson, SKY MAGAZINE

"Witty and compelling. Don't miss it"
– Lorien Haynes, NEW WOMAN

"Make sure you're on the guest list!"
– Chris Roberts, UNCUT

The fantastic soundtrack Includes 'Everybody Dance', 'Got To Be Real', 'Good Times', 'Shame', 'Love Train', and many many more disco anthems. Available on CD and Cassette
WORK COLUMBIA

Whit Stillman's
The Last Days of DISCO 15

History is made at night.

CASTLE ROCK ENTERTAINMENT Presents WHIT STILLMAN'S "THE LAST DAYS OF DISCO" CHLOË SEVIGNY KATE BECKINSALE CHRIS EIGEMAN MATT KEESLAR MACKENZIE ASTIN MATTHEW ROSS TARA SUBKOFF BURR STEERS DAVID THORNTON JAID BARRYMORE MICHAEL WEATHERLY with ROBERT SEAN LEONARD and JENNIFER BEALS Casting HOPKINS, SMITH, BARDEN Costumes SARAH EDWARDS Production Design GINGER TOUGAS Sound Editor PAUL SOUCEK Music Supervisor PETER AFTERMAN Music MARK SUOZZO Executive Producer JOHN SLOSS Co-Producers CECILIA KATE ROQUE & EDMON ROCH Edited by ANDREW HAFITZ & JAY PIRES Cinematography JOHN THOMAS Written, Produced & Directed by WHIT STILLMAN

CASTLE ROCK ENTERTAINMENT A Time Warner Company

©1998 PolyGram Filmed Entertainment Distribution, Inc. All rights reserved.

SOUNDTRACK AVAILABLE ON WORK

WARNER BROS.

THE LAST DAYS OF DISCO (1998)

Completing unique director Whit Stillman's trio of brittle urban romantic comedies, in the timeline scheme of things fitting between **Metropolitan** (1990) and **Barcelona** (1994), this glacial glance at how the '80s Yuppie ethos emerged during Disco's twilight years is a canny and scintillating depiction of the etiquette and atmosphere of the era. Conceived by the writer/director after filming the Eurodisco scenes in **Barcelona** (featuring *Boogie Oogie Oogie*, 1978, by A Taste of Honey and *You've Got What It Takes (To Please Your Woman)*, 1976, by Silver Convention), Stillman based his script on personal experiences in Manhattan Discos including Studio 54. His surname perfectly describing his creative approach, Stillman's keen sense of group dynamics coupled with his ear for mannered comedy gives the rock steady nonchalance of the piece a fresh tempo. Suffused with great ensemble performances and a slayer soundtrack, Stillman's strobe-lit still life marvellously conveys the hedonism and bitchy camaraderie of the Night Fever milieu with loads of love and affection.

Alice (Chloë Sevigny) and Charlotte (Kate Beckinsale) are two college friends who work in publishing and room together in Manhattan. Every Saturday night they hit the most exclusive Disco in town and "ferociously pair off" with their Harvard contemporaries, Jimmy (Mackenzie Astin), Tom (Robert Sean Leonard) and Josh (Matt Keeslar), under the watchful eye of the coke-sniffing maître d' Des (Chris Eigeman). It's when Josh, a rising star at the District Attorney's office hints of a raid on the premises due to Des stashing bags of skimmed cash in the basement, that the social mores, moral perspectives and conflicting attitudes come to a crescendo, signalling the end of the first era of the Disco movement.

Loaded with Stillman's trademark sophistication and wit, it's a painfully funny look at the Disco lifestyle highlighting sexual identity, promiscuity and dysfunction while indulging in scalpel-sharp comments on a vast array of topics from Disney's **Lady and the Tramp** (1955), using venereal disease as a dating device, the stark truths only your best friend will tell you, and a pertinent oration on why Disco will never die (part of which is prefaced in this book).

Sevigny plays 'nice' in a marvellously understated performance while Beckinsale lights up the dance floor display capturing her superficial and unsure character with an amazingly deft artfulness. This was Beckinsale's first American feature film and she could not have had a better calling card. Keeslar makes the most impact from the handsome Ivy League contingent. What **The Last Days of Disco** does that few others get right is in the conveying of the anxious excitement of entering such a glitzy establishment (the Disco location here being an old Jersey City cinema being renovated). The fretting over getting past the velvet ropes at the entrance, the thrill of hearing the muted Disco beat from the cloakroom area, the initial flirty cruise through the elegantly posing crowd, checking out the unisex talent, edging your way to the flashing dance floor and finally letting the cascade of Disco take you on a magic carpet ride – all superbly put across. And what a wonderful selection of Disco hits too. *Doctor's Orders* (1974) by Carol Douglas starts the movie in hyperdrive and it continues on an all-time high with *I Love the Nightlife (Disco Round)* (1978) by Alicia Bridges, plus a cover version by India and Nuyorican Soul, *I'm Coming Out* (1980) by Diana Ross, *Got to Be Real* (1978) by Cheryl Lynn, *Good Times* (1979) and *Everybody Dance* (1977) by Chic, *He's the Greatest Dancer* (1978) by Sister Sledge, *Shame* (1977) and *I Don't Know if It's Right* (1977) by Evelyn 'Champagne' King, *The Love I Lost* (1973) by Harold Melvin & the Blue Notes, *Let's All Chant* (1977) by the Michael Zager Band, *Got to Have Loving* (1978) by Don Ray and *Knock on Wood* (1979) by Amii Stewart.

Part wistful, part sardonic, part self-conscious but always entertaining, two instances where Stillman uses the music to underline those key facets come with *More, More, More (Part 1)* (1976) by Andrea True Connection wonderfully underscoring a hesitant seduction scene between Sevigny and Leonard as they slink into his bedroom. And the ending where everyone on the New York subway system suddenly bursts out dancing to *Love Train* (1972) by The O'Jays will leave a smile on the face and reduce any self-respecting Disco fan to tears. One of the best Disco movies ever made.

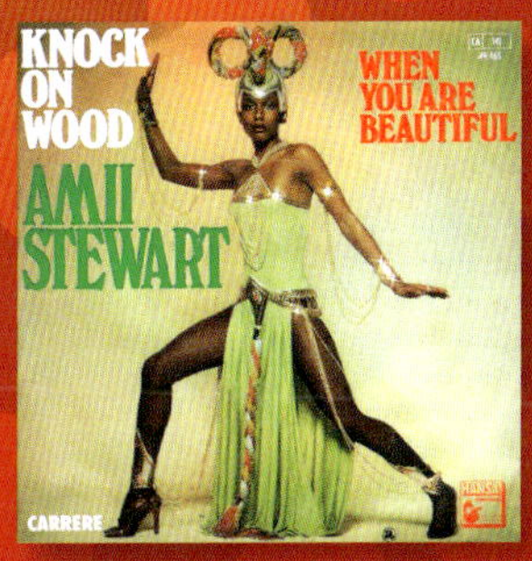

Amii Stewart

Disco is filled with great one-hit wonders: Anita Ward's *Ring My Bell* (1979), Shirley and Company's *Shame Shame Shame* (1974), Alicia Bridges' *I Love the Nightlife (Disco*

Round) (1978), Ryan Paris' *Dolce Vita* (1983) and A Taste of Honey's *Boogie Oogie Oogie* (1978) to name the tip of the niceberg. Amii Stewart's *Knock on Wood* (1979) falls into that category too, but unlike the majority of artists who hit once and ran fast, she relocated to Italy to have a second successful all-round career.

Amy Paulette Stewart (she changed the spelling of her Christian name for Equity reasons) first came to the forefront by appearing in the Broadway and West End versions of the musical 'Bubbling Brown Sugar'. Quickly signed to Ariola records, her Disco cover of Eddie Floyd's 1966 hit *Knock on Wood* topped the charts in many countries and earned her a platinum record and Grammy nomination. But that really was it even though her creditable follow-up was yet another cover, this time The Doors' 1967 classic *Light My Fire* incorporating *137 Disco Heaven* (1979).

Leaving her flamboyant feather and glitter costumes behind, the stepsister of Miquel Brown and aunt to Brown's daughter Sinitta, recorded the soft Disco hit *Friends* (1984) and then made Italy her home. There she reinvented her singing career with the wonderful *Pearls – Amii Stewart Sings Ennio Morricone* (1990) album and in 2003 toured with the musical especially written for her, 'Lady Day', based on the songs of Billie Holiday.

Disco Memo

SKY

For the whole of the 1990s I worked for Sky Movies and interviewed on camera practically every single star and director who had a film released in that time span. It was an incredibly important part of my development from mere journalist to all-round broadcaster because I learnt so much about timing and presentation that I would eventually bring to the FrightFest table and my BAFTA/Academy Award Q&As. Every week I was interviewing at least three big names and every other weekend I was on a junket jaunt either to New York and Los Angeles, sometimes Paris or to assorted European film festivals. **The Last Days of Disco** is particularly resonant because I attended the New York premiere, then the London one and then escorted director Whit Stillman to his Spanish premiere at the Sitges Festival. Every time *Doctor's Orders* played you could feel the pleasure vibe go off the scale.

You name the celebrity and I asked them pertinent questions. Highlights I recall vividly are Mel Brooks making me laugh so much I could hardly function, the four bodyguards surrounding Steven Seagal being really scary, a sick John Goodman throwing up in a bucket after every answer, Stockard Channing saying she thought I was too harsh a critic (mind you that was after cajoling her to sing a chorus of *Look at Me I'm Sandra Dee* from **Grease**, 1978), asking Guy Pearce what his favourite frock was from **The Adventures of Priscilla, Queen of the Desert** (1994), Chevy Chase needing to know up front what interview I wanted, funny or serious, and being caught red-handed by Jean-Claude Van Damme looking through his underwear drawer in his hotel room.

What was also interesting about my time at Sky was how many future stars I got to talk to for their very first time, like Thandie Newton for **Flirting** (1991) and Stephen Moyer for **Prince Valiant** (1997). On the flipside of that I got to meet so many past Hollywood legends like Maureen O'Hara because of **Only the Lonely** (1991), MGM musicals mainstay Louis Jourdan thanks to being on the Loch Ness location for **Year of the Comet** (1992) and his **Gigi** (1958) co-star Leslie Caron for **Funny Bones** (1995). My two co-workers at Sky were Julia Wrigley and David Cox, who I had met at Forbidden Planet 2, and when they moved to Film 4 my tenure was over, especially once esteemed BBC film critic Barry Norman moved in. But then they were instrumental in Film 4 sponsoring FrightFest when we needed to expand… the circle of cinema life is indeed a mysterious thing.

▲ Above, clockwise from bottom left: Stephen Moyer, Mel Brooks, and Thandie Newton.

54 (1998)

The story was Cliché City and its decadence barely scandalous but writer/director Mark Christopher's snapshot of the Disco era filtered through the fabulous glamour of the world's most famous nightclub is strong on ambience, vividly capturing the Studio 54 atmosphere and lovingly drenched in a superb array of classic Disco numbers. Christopher directed the acclaimed short **Dead Boys Club** (1992) about a pair of magical shoes transporting a man back to the pre-AIDS time of his deceased gay uncle, and spent the next five years researching Studio 54 at its 1979 fashionable height. Yet while a noble attempt to put the notorious watering hole in cultural context, the plot is formula **Saturday Night Fever** (1977) meets **Boogie Nights** (1997).

Completely naïve and wearing the wrong Bridge & Tunnel clothes, fish-out-of-water Shane O'Shea (an invested Ryan Phillippe), a character allegedly based on actual 54 bar man Tieg Thomas, leaves his drab New Jersey existence and heads to Manhattan in order to gain admission into the most exclusive Disco in the world. Club owner Steve Rubell (Mike Myers giving a multi-layered performance), lets Shane cross the velvet ropes when he strips off in the line, thus beginning his fast rise from amateur busboy to hunky bartender and posturing 'Andy Warhol's Interview' magazine centrefold. Mirroring Mark Wahlberg's Eddie Adams character in **Boogie Nights**, the club and its eclectic employees become his surrogate home and extended family as he gets sucked into the Anything Goes glitzy lifestyle, mixes with the upper class Park Avenue set and becomes romantically involved with soap star Julie Black (Neve Campbell).

The action takes place over ten nights, each illustrating a major narrative thread as the Disco evolves from celestial

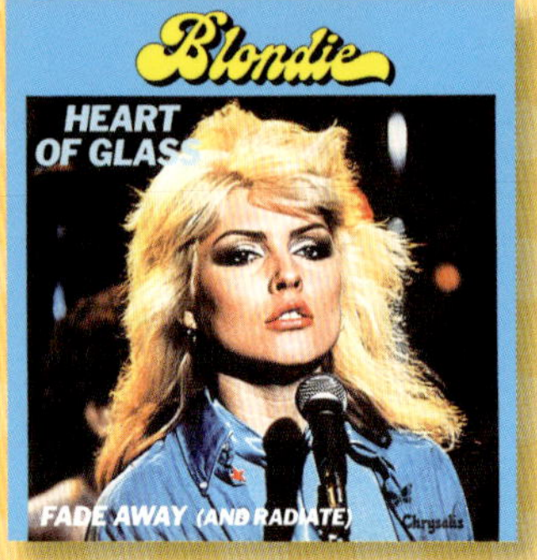

dream paradise to a lost one awash with drug overdoses, tax investigations, Rubell's subsequent imprisonment and Shane's rehabilitation as a New York University business student. Rich texturing comes from the crazed patrons depicted covered in gold, naked or having farm animal props, Salma Hayek playing cloakroom attendant Anita Randazzo aspiring to be a Disco singer, Ellen Albertini Dow as famed senior citizen club habituée Disco Dottie, designer Elio Fiorucci playing himself and Disco Diva Thelma Houston crooning a Christmas classic in her own persona.

Shot deliberately in a populuxe 1970s way by Alexander Gruszynski (**Tremors**, 1990) to evoke the excessive period use of lasers, Mylar discs, fake snow, glitter, reflective bubbles and mobile lighting devices, **54** splendidly elicits the feeling of stepping back in time. Christopher's whipped cream cabaret is deliciously fastened to the Disco era like the broken zipper on a pair of satin hotpants, and the continual party aspect of Studio 54 is adeptly conveyed even when the clunky melodramatics sashay centre stage into the dirty martini spotlight.

While Miramax Films gave Christopher's first cut a positive response, two Long Island previews gave them cause for concern. Audiences complained that none of the characters were likable, and found the edgy gay content, in particular, the kiss between Shane and Greg Randazzo (Breckin Meyer, Phillippe's best friend in real life), uncomfortable viewing. So Miramax head honcho Harvey Weinstein ordered a major edit and reshoots meaning one third hit the cutting room floor, the last half hour changing tone, Campbell's love interest role beefed up, a new ending added and the entire heart of the film – sex, drugs and bisexual anti-hero – being completely lost in the panicked mix. Producer Dolly Hall would thereafter continually refer to this wide release version as '55'.

Indeed, this compromised **54** was considered something of a faulty smoke machine when originally released, with many complaining it lacked insight and played it far too safe. Still miffed after a decade, Christopher assembled a bootleg Director's Cut in 2008, with forty-five minutes of never before seen footage, and unofficially screened it at New York's Outfest. This version reinstated Shane's prolific promiscuity and bisexuality, especially in the core love triangle between him, Anita and Greg.

Seven years after receiving positive reviews for that amended version, Christopher officially launched a reshuffled 105-minute long **54: The Director's Cut** at the 65th Berlin Film Festival. It featured over 30 minutes of footage from the original shoot never seen in any previous cut (culled from VHS dailies due to be destroyed) and deleted all but a few seconds of the studio-dictated reshot footage. Another major addition was rewriting the opening voice-over with a clearer perspective and getting the 40-year-old Phillippe to re-record it as looking back at his callow teenage years. What this version basically did was reinstate Shane's innocence and his addiction to hedonism while positioning the club environment as a Utopian microcosm where race, gender and sexual preferences made no difference. Finally, Christopher's love letter to the Eighth Wonder of the Disco World made sense.

In all versions of Christopher's labour of love charting his own development from Iowa farmboy to world-weary roué, the soundtrack is an absolute scorcher with many of the cast shown dancing along to the actual songs. For starters: *Keep on Dancin'* (1978) by Gary's Gang, *The Boss* (1979) by Diana Ross, *Dance, Dance, Dance (Yowsah, Yowsah, Yowsah)* (1979) by Chic, *Vertigo/Relight My Fire* (1978) by Dan Hartman, *You Make Me Feel (Mighty Real)* (1978) by Sylvester, *Move On Up* (1979) by Destination, *Love Machine (Part 1)* (1975) by The Miracles, *Contact* (1978) by Edwin Starr, *Let's Start the Dance* (1978) by Bohannon, *I Got My Mind Made Up* (1978) by Instant Funk, *Young Hearts Run Free* (1976) by Candi Staton, *Native New Yorker* (1977) by Odyssey, *Que sera mi vida* (1979) by the Gibson Brothers, and *Wishing on a Star* (1977) by Rose Royce.

But there's more: *Haven't Stopped Dancing Yet* (1977) by Gonzalez, *Heaven Must Have Sent You* (1979) by Bonnie Pointer, *Loving Is Really My Game* (1977) by Brainstorm, *Disco Nights (Rock-Freak)* (1979) by GQ, *Found a Cure* (1979) by Ashford and Simpson, *Don't Leave Me This Way* (1976) by Thelma Houston, *Come to Me* (1979) by France Joli, *Take Your Time (Do It Right)* (1980) by The S.O.S. Band, *Don't Let Me Be Misunderstood* (1977) by Santa Esmeralda, *Spank* (1978) by Jimmy 'Bo' Horne, *Galaxy* (1977) by War, *I Need a Man* (1975) by Grace Jones, *Heart of Glass* (1978) by Blondie, *Cherchez la femme/Se si bon* (1976) by Dr. Buzzard's Original Savannah Band and *Fly, Robin, Fly* (1975) by Silver Convention.

As if that Disco hit-packed soundtrack wasn't enough, three original tracks were recorded in a marketing effort to appeal to the young demographic who really didn't know or care what Studio 54 was. The 54 All-Stars sang the theme song *Studio 54*, Stars on 54 (Ultra Naté, Amber and Jocelyn Enriquez) reworked Gordon Lightfoot's 1971 breakthrough success *If You Could Read My Mind*, a 1980 No.2 Disco hit for Viola Wills, and Mary Griffin did the same with *Knock on Wood*, Amii Stewart's 1979 No.5 dance classic. In all a superior package of Disco brilliance, a remarkable distillation of songs representing the era, and probably the best 2-Disc soundtrack released since **Saturday Night Fever**.

Studio 54

It was a Mecca of magic, madness and magnificence. Camelot for both the glitterati and the paparazzi, and for three years it was the most talked-about, written-about and shocked-about venue in the entire universe. Situated at 254 West 54th Street, between 7th and 8th Avenues, Studio 54 was the only Disco that truly mattered. Everyone wanted to go because they read about it in the news and saw the photos of the endless stream of celebrities parading past its velvet-roped entrance. They heard about the drug-fuelled orgies in the darkened off-limits areas and the no-expense-spared theme parties for the **Grease**

Steve Rubell and Ian Schrager outside the door of Studio 54.
(Picture credit: Photofest)

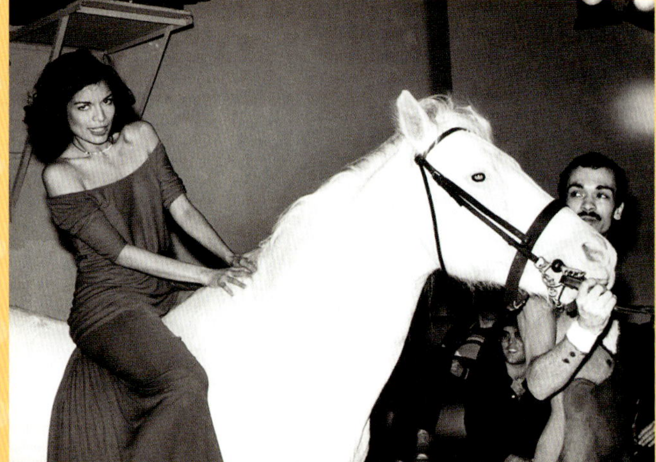

(1978) premiere, Folies Bergère and Rio carnival nights, and outrageous Disco launches for Grace Jones.

Studio 54 was Shangri-la for the hipster, star-spotter, voyeur and poser. Never before, and never again, would the superstar famous mix with the great unwashed in such harmonious accord at the altar of the mighty Disco sound. Because once inside, after catwalking through the burgundy carpeted lobby lined with 20-foot tall fig trees, the world was your oyster, time stood still and the throb of Disco became your magic carpet ride to everlasting night fever.

It all began with tennis pro Steve Rubell, who eschewed the business courses at Syracuse University to borrow $13,000 from his bewildered parents to open up a Steak Loft Restaurant in Rockfield Centre, Long Island. His partner in the venture was University pal and real estate agent Ian Schrager. By 1974 they had a four-eaterie franchise, but Rubell saw the Disco trend coming down the pike and turned their Douglaston, Queens, branch into a nightclub. The Enchanted Garden didn't last too long as noisy customers and annoyed neighbours forced the venue to close. But Rubell had definitely caught the Disco bug.

Over the bridge in Manhattan events were taking place that would impact on Rubell's razzle-dazzle future. German socialite Uva Harden, ex-husband of future **Never Say Never Again** (1983) Bond Girl Barbara Carrera, was looking for a site to open up a state-of-the-art Disco and thought the West 54th address was perfect. Built in 1927 and opened during the Great Depression as the San Carlo Opera House, it was converted into the Casino de Paris theatre restaurant in the late 1930s and finally turned into a CBS TV studio the following decade. 'What's My Line?' and 'Captain Kangaroo' just two of the shows filmed there in what was then dubbed Studio 53 because of its alternate entrance on 53rd Street.

When CBS relocated to Hollywood, Harden leased the derelict building in 1976 and Disco renovations began. When his financing collapsed, Harden turned to his party promoter friend Carmen D'Alessio for advice, who suggested he speak to Rubell with whom she had worked at The Enchanted Garden. In the ensuing negotiations Harden was paid off and Rubell and Schrager raised the $4 million capital investment by splitting it three ways with their silent partner, discount retailer Jack Dushey.

Within six weeks Studio 54 was conceived as the most exclusive and glamorous nightclub in dance history. The spacious Disco design incorporated fluttering fabric flames, floating aluminium strips, neon wheels, giant strobes, towers of multi-coloured lights that could rise

and fall on cue. Blizzards of plastic snow and balloons would descend on the jam-packed dancefloor and most notoriously of all, the Man in the Moon figure lowered at key junctures to sniff up the flashing white contents of a silver spoon. Such risk-taking and flouting convention would lead to Rubell's downfall but at the time this daring strategy was thrilling.

On the chilly evening of April 26th, 1977, the doors opened on the most anticipated club ever, Bianca Jagger posing on a white horse at her birthday bash just the first of many photo ops guaranteed to make Studio 54 the place to go and be seen. However it wasn't easy to get in thanks to the much-hated selective door policy. Waving your $10 entrance fee didn't mean a thing if doormen Marc Benecke or Al Corley (future 'Dynasty' star and HiNRG singer of *Square Rooms*, 1984) didn't think you were famous, beautiful or outrageous enough to enter the hallowed halls. Rubell called it "Tossing the salad" because he didn't want any one particular group – gay, black, straight, drag queen, model or senior – to dominate the dance floor.

If you were Andy Warhol, Halston, Liza Minnelli or Truman Capote nothing stood in your way. If you were part of the self-styled Fantasy Folk, like 78-year-old Disco Sally, transvestite Potassa or skating starlet Rollerena, step right up. But if you were one of Rubell's "Grey People" you had to line up and take your chances for he knew the more desperate people were, the more attractive the club would become, and the outside was as much theatre as the inside. Bad decisions were often made though; Cher was turned away one night, so too were Nile Rodgers and Bernard Edwards, but they turned their experience into the mega-hit *Le Freak* (1978). The whole nightmare scenario was preserved on vinyl as *Dario, Can You Get Me Into Studio 54* (1979) by Dana & Gene, written by August Darnell, also recorded by his Kid Creole and the Coconuts. And in adverts too when the club entered the clothing market: "Now everyone can get into Studio 54… jeans"!

Once inside the club it was partytime on steroids, or cocaine, Quaaludes, acid… whatever. Rubell would give you anything you wanted to make sure the night went with a bang. And talking of sex, it happened everywhere, in the VIP basement, the darkened balcony, the unisex toilet cubicles, and if you fancied one of the staff, well, they were encouraged to be accommodating. Studio 54 became a bacchanalian Fellini Discoland expressly designed to make its clientele forget the depressing reality outside. Everyone knew it couldn't last; everything was far too wonderful, far too extreme and far too illegal.

The first inkling of impending disaster came with the puzzling fact that Studio 54 didn't have a permanent liquor licence. Every day Rubell applied for a 24-hour cabaret licence in order to serve alcohol, a flagrant abuse of the law in itself. So the authorities put the place under the closest of scrutinies in case the owners slipped up.

They didn't have to wait too long. Rubell gave an interview to 'New York' magazine quoted as saying "The profits are astronomical, only the Mafia does better!" This blatant arrogance, plus a skimming tip-off from a disgruntled ex-employee, attracted the attention of IRS criminal investigator Frank Frattolillio who got a search warrant and raided the premises on the morning of December 14th, 1978. Double sets of accounting books and hidden stashes of cash were found. Not even their infamously clever lawyer Roy Cohn could save the duo when it became clear a third of the takings were being skimmed off, meaning only $8,000 in tax had been paid for the whole of 1977. Schrager didn't help matters either by turning up with cocaine in his briefcase for the rummage around.

After plea-bargaining to income tax evasion on two counts, both men were given three-and-a-half-year prison sentences. On February 1st, 1980 Rubell and Schrager were jailed at the Metropolitan Correctional Centre – after a fabulous Going-Away-To-Prison party at Studio 54 the night before, of course. Business continued as usual at the club for a while until the licence expired and it closed down for fifteen months. In severe financial straits, Rubell negotiated a $5 million deal with hotel owner Mark Fleischman who became the new owner with Rubell and Schrager retained as consultants. Released after less than a year for informing on other Disco entrepreneurs' under-the-counter deals – especially Maurice Brahms, owner of New York New York – the less than dynamic duo found it hard back in the Disco landscape now blighted by the Comiskey Park demonstration, the first signs of AIDS and the hedonism of the 1970s being considered passé.

Initially crowds came to the new Studio 54 out of curiosity, but being able to get in easily missed the mystique point, the stars stopped coming and mounting lawsuits closed the place for good to eventually become a noted theatre space. Rubell and Schrager tried to recreate the atmosphere at the Palladium, which opened in 1985, but it never caught on. With Fleischman's help Schrager became a global boutique hotel owner and Rubell died of AIDS complications on July 25th, 1989 at the age of 45. His gravestone bears the inscription 'The Quintessential New Yorker' and everyone who attended his funeral had to pass through velvet ropes. Their Disco brainchild is now a pop culture touchstone for the 1970s that has become a glorious badge of dishonour if you were ever lucky enough to be allowed to dance there.

The Choice

I brought Greg Day into the FrightFest fold as our PR man in 2002 because I trusted him implicitly and he had become one of my best friends. We first met in the early 1980s when he was working in the publicity department at Columbia Pictures after dabbling in acting ('Grange Hill') and playwriting ('Bust', 1986). Greg loves to tell everyone that he was warned about me visiting Columbia's Wardour Street offices and told to lock all merchandise cupboards when I was due to arrive! Hey, how else do you think I built up my extensive tie-in freebie collection! Before he wound up heading the publicity departments of Channel 4 and Channel 5, Greg worked for the boutique PR agency Zakiya and Associates (run by owner Zakiya Powell, the company promoted the cult classic **Withnail & I**, 1988). And indeed it was in 1988 that Greg offered me a set visit to cover an independent horror film in production, which turned into a weird adventure so extraordinary and unusual, it bonded us together forever.

The title of the film was 'The Choice'. Don't bother trying to track it down because it was never completed even though writer/director Robert Paget tried desperately to do so. Paget was a veteran journeyman US sit-com actor ('My Favorite Martian', 'The Many Loves of Dobie Gillis') who had directed the virtually unknown **Fluff** (1974) starring Sirpa Lane, a year before the Finnish star appeared in Walerian Borowczyk's contentious **The Beast** (1975). Nevertheless he had convinced actor Peter Ensor (**The Spy Who Loved Me**, 1977, **A View to a Kill**, 1985) to produce

Disco Memo

'The Choice', a genetic engineering-cum-Frankenstein screenplay, to be shot during the summer in Gstaad, that alpine Swiss playground for Hollywood stars and Eurotrash royalty alike. Who wouldn't want a free trip to that upscale resort, with luxury hotel accommodation thrown in too?

The other attraction was the cast: horror star Ferdy Mayne (**The Fearless Vampire Killers**, 1967, **The Vampire Lovers**, 1970, **The Vampire Happening**, 1971) was the sinister Professor Kleist, Oliver Tobias (**The Stud**, 1978) the rich and ruthless lover Jeff Harris, '40s matinee star Moira Lister was a mysterious Black Widow and Deborah Shelton was Jeff's girlfriend Deb, sucked into a web of reproductive terrorism. Shelton, fresh from playing Mandy Winger in the supersoap 'Dallas', and more importantly from my perspective, Gloria in Brian De Palma's superlative **Body Double** (1984), arrived on the picturesque yet very disorganised mountain location with her then husband Shuki Levy, composer of the theme tunes for such children's cartoon favourites as 'Inspector Gadget', 'Dragon Quest' and 'He-Man and the Masters of the Universe'. She was so friendly, adorable and happy to answer all my questions about her career. In return Greg and I decided to take part in her morning aerobic exercise classes. What an exhausting mistake that was! But at least I can say I've been taught breath-control by the star of one of my favourite shockers!

A worse mistake was Paget's insistence we join the main cast and crew to look at the rushes filmed the previous days. Now, this is something no director should ever do just in case the talent with more clout than they have demands their scenes be reshot because, say, one of their hairs is out of place. I have seen that happen before and fully understand why most actors are banned from seeing anything until the first assembly. Anyway, 'The Choice' rushes were terrible – and triple-take endless. Look, watching rushes is a total bore anyway, but it was clear to everyone in that hired local cinema, the film was in dire trouble.

In fact one of investors was so mortified he committed suicide soon after by jumping out of his Geneva apartment building. That dreadful turn of events resulted in everyone in the cast and crew being held hostage in the hotel because no one had been given a return flight ticket back to their homes. Far worse, the hotel management, realising the group booking bills were unlikely to be paid, banned everyone from eating anything other than veal at every meal. So late one night a very disgruntled and rebellious crew broke into the hotel restaurant, emptying all the meat from the kitchen deep freezers into the heated swimming pool. The staff woke up the next morning to find rancid sides of beef stinking out the spa area and the manager stormed into Greg's room demanding he call the police. Soon afterwards the hotel realised they would have to take the losses on the chin and everyone eventually drifted away from the depressing fiasco.

Unfortunately for Greg, 'The Choice' meant he ended up in hospital on crutches for a few weeks too. He had found out that the best way to engender any publicity in Switzerland was to get a celebrity to plant a tree in a televised ceremony. Moira Lister was shortlisted as the star and the cast and crew were bussed to the middle of a forest for the event. However, the forest was on a steep incline, and one of the short-of-stature cast fell over, rolled down the hill, and when Greg tried to catch him, lost his balance and sprained his ankle. We laugh about it now of course.

There is a trailer for 'The Choice' you can find online, assembled by Paget to try and attract completion financing at the 1989 Cannes Film Festival. One look will reveal why that was never going to happen. There were a few upsides to this doomed set visit – the morning alpine walks with Greg were lovely, the initial crew camaraderie was easy going and fun – but I've never before or since been in such a bizarre situation as this one. Astonishingly, three months after our return, Greg did get paid for the assignment, but by whom exactly we never found out.

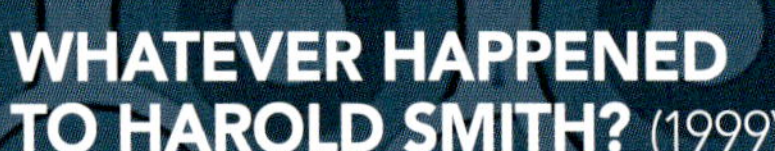

WHATEVER HAPPENED TO HAROLD SMITH? (1999)

From **Bill & Ted's Bogus Journey** (1991) director Peter Hewitt comes one unholy mess of Seventies pop culture trivia looking for a better movie to make it all shine. An unsuccessful attempt at merging a coming-of-age working class romance with dreamy Disco fantasy and supernatural mystery, this leaden comedy features few upbeat moments throughout a disjointed narrative that fails to connect the entertainment dots. Clearly Ealing comedy whimsy was the best-case scenario aimed at; a pity then it falls squarely into the kitchen-sink **Carry On** misfire category.

It's winter 1977 and **Saturday Night Fever** (1977) is all the rage in the dreary Northern steel town of Sheffield. Disco loving legal clerk Vince Smith (Michael Legge) is 18 years old, practices his John Travolta dance moves in his bedroom and secretly lusts after co-worker Joanna Robinson (Laura Fraser, 'Breaking Bad', 2013). Living at home with his tarty nightlife-loving mother Irene (pop star Lulu, **To Sir, with Love**, 1968) and eccentric father Harold (British national treasure Tom Courtenay), Vince's life completely changes when during the Christmas holidays it's revealed his dad shares current sensation Uri Geller's spoon-bending paranormal abilities and as a child exploded a turtle.

When Harold makes headlines for a psychic party piece at an old folks' home accidentally causing pacemakers to suddenly stop working, he's arrested and interrogated

about the suspicious deaths. Vince's law firm is appointed as Harold's defense counsel to prove his kinetic mental powers are genuine, meaning he's forced to work alongside Joanna who is rebelling against her overbearing lecturer father Dr. Peter Robinson (Stephen Fry). To that end Joanna has immersed herself in the Punk movement, look and ethos. So to give himself a fair crack at romance out goes Vince's love of the Bee Gees' *Night Fever* (1977), Tina Charles' *I Love to Love* (1976), Heatwave's *Boogie Nights* (1977), Maxine Nightingale's *Right Back Where We Started From* (1975), and The Real Thing's *You to Me Are Everything* (1976), and in comes the Sex Pistols, The Clash and Buzzcocks.

Although providing a showcase for many bright future talents – Charlie Hunnam, James Corden, Matthew Rhys – and highlighting a puzzling array of British TV celebrities – broadcasters Angela Rippon, Alan Whicker, John Craven and Keith Chegwin – Hewitt's period detail is all over the place and each Disco/Punk/fantasy story thread grates on the other to distracting effect, minimising whatever satirical punch was originally contained in Ben Steiner's threadbare screenplay. Did Steiner ever go clubbing or pogoing? If he did, none of his research has made it into the finished product. Whatever happened to **Whatever Happened to Harold Smith?** indeed?

Feels Like... Kelly Marie

From the summer of 1980 through to… well, now, there wasn't a club, party or Disco that wasn't playing the stridently hook-laden dance juggernaut *Feels Like I'm in Love* by Kelly Marie. Born Jaqueline McKinnon in Paisley, Scotland, Kelly Marie appeared on the British talent show 'Opportunity Knocks', caught the eye of the PYE Records label and recorded the single *Who's That Lady with My Man* (1976), a Top 5 hit in France. It was the follow-up single *Run to Me* (1977) that shifted her musically into the Disco arena and gave her a No.27 position in the 'Billboard' dance charts. Her next upbeat release *Make Love to Me* (1978) was covered by superstar Helen Reddy, which scuppered any further dent in the Disco market.

But just as Kelly Marie thought she would simply have to make do with a mid-range career and modest fame in Europe, along came the game-changing break of a lifetime. Ray Dorset, the lead singer and founder of Mungo Jerry, the *In the Summertime* (1970) band, had written a song with Elvis Presley in mind. But because Kelly was on the same label as Mungo Jerry, it was she who got to sing *Feels Like I'm in Love* and the rest is Disco history, even though that history did take time to unfold. Released in 1979, the song first took off in South Africa, but looked like it was going to tank in Britain until buzz began to build up slowly due to increasing dance floor reaction. Soon it was atop the British pop charts and, dualled with *Loving Just for Fun* (1980) in a Bobby 'DJ' Guttadaro remix, became a Top Ten Disco hit in America. Nothing Kelly Marie did after that instantly accessible mega-hit came close (she tackled the Patrick Hernandez hit *Born to Be Alive* in 1986), but she has made a longterm cabaret career out of it, still singing her signature smash to this very day.

Mark Kermode

I feel like I've known Mark Kermode forever. Introduced to me by fellow film critic Nigel Floyd at a press show in the mid-1980s we became firm friends instantly through our shared love of the horror genre. Mark has deservedly become a film industry national treasure thanks to his forensic attention to movie detail and constant work ethic that even has me in awe. I'm grateful he credits me with showing him the press show ropes and giving him career advice, but he would have learnt all that by himself in time. And boy, have we had some wild times together. Like our shared interview with **Bonnie and Clyde** (1967) star Michael J. Pollard when he was in London shooting **Split Second** (1992) with Kim Cattrall and Rutger Hauer. Pollard was so stoned we could hardly make sense of anything he said. Bombing around Milan with Wes Craven, Brian Yuzna and Robert Englund at the incredible Dylan Dog Film Festivals was a blast too. Mark also proved himself a true friend in a very personal time of need and I will never forget his sacrifices for me.

We have done many interviews and on-stage discussions together and the one story we consistently tell that sums up the total lunacy of our close friendship is this one. Remember **Repossessed** (1990), the lame-brained parody of Mark's favourite film with Linda Blair once again possessed by Satan and Leslie Nielsen as the exorcist? Well, I bet Mark that I would be the first to see it and constantly hounded the UK distributor to be let into the first screening. Mark had also done the same and by the time the evening of the multi-media show arrived I made sure I was first in line to nab a seat in the front row. Mark had no other option than to sit behind me, meaning the images reached my eyes first. So I won! He never lets me forget either us sitting together at the first screening of **The Godfather III** (1990). When the movie finished he leant over to me and asked what I thought of it. Off the top of my head came "An aria of savage beauty", and to this day that's the phrase we always utter after any similar entertainment.

Alan Jones with his best friend Mark Kermode.

SUMMER OF SAM (1999)

David Richard Berkowitz was first dubbed The .44 Caliber Killer but eventually became known under the more infamous Son of Sam moniker for committing numerous shootings in the New York City area throughout 1976-77. Eluding the biggest manhunt in the history of the NYPD, Berkowitz left letters at the scenes of his crimes mocking the investigation, and also sent one to the 'Daily News' outlining his aberrant behaviour. When finally caught he pleaded guilty to eight attacks but claimed to have been obeying the orders of a demon manifested in the form of his neighbour Sam's pet dog (here voiced by John Turturro). In prison serving eight consecutive life sentences, he later admitted the possession story was a hoax in order to be declared mentally incompetent for trial.

Director Spike Lee's gripping and provocative joint is less about Berkowitz (Michael Badalucco), than the community he terrorised, Throggs Neck, an Italian-American neighbourhood in the Bronx. Originally written by actors Michael Imperioli (Christopher Moltisanti in 'The Sopranos') and Victor Colicchio (Pepe his porn-de-plume) as a direct account of the serial killer's exploits, families of the victims objected to possible glorification of his crimes, so Lee changed the narrative focus, making it more a harder-edged Disco version of **West Side Story** (1961). Proving a refreshing change of pace for the **Do the Right Thing** (1989) director who did exactly the right thing here, **Summer of Sam** is a darkly complex study in how a macho culture creates a breeding ground for lynch-mob hysteria.

With young women and their boyfriends being brutally murdered at random by the deranged killer and a pall of paranoia seizing the sweltering city, the key Throggs Neck residents are introduced. Serial adulterer, hairdresser Vinny (John Leguizamo), his waitress wife Dionna (Mira Sorvino), gay for pay Punk dancer Richie (Adrien Brody) and his date Ruby (Jennifer Esposito). When Vinny almost becomes a victim while cheating on Dionna, the equally promiscuous Richie looks like he has a sexually deviant target on his back. The cops failing to identify the socially devious killer at every turn, Detective Lou Petrocelli (Anthony LaPaglia) enlists the help of local Mafia chief Luigi (Ben Gazzara) to find someone, anyone, to blame.

Lee (who pops up as a news reporter) expertly nails the look and mood of the perfectly captured period. Terrific performances stud the *faux* Martin Scorsese mean streets atmosphere with the polyester, knit shirt and bellbottom fashions on full display, the drug lifestyle depicted in a non-judgemental way, the laissez-faire attitude to permissive

sex well captured, the lining up to get into the Discos appropriately portrayed, and the neon wash once inside the clubs sparkles. No question, **Summer of Sam** is a notable crime thriller and a fascinating change of pace for Lee.

Adding to that mesmeric quality is a non-stop soundtrack packed with memorable musical touchstones of the day and an era-representative slew of Disco hits: *Boogie Nights* (1977) by Heatwave, *Let No Man Put Asunder* (1977) by First Choice, *There But for the Grace of God Go I* (1979) by Machine, *Running Away* (1977) by Roy Ayers, *Best of My Love* (1977) by The Emotions, *Dance with Me* (1977) by Peter Brown, *La vie en rose* (1977) by Grace Jones, *It's Ecstasy When You Lay Down Next to Me* (1977) by Barry White, *Everybody Dance* (1977) by Chic, *Galaxy* (1977) by War, *Love Is the Message* (1973) by MFSB, *Let's All Chant* (1977) by the Michael Zager Band, *Don't Leave Me This Way* (1976) by Thelma Houston, and the inevitable *Dancing Queen* (1976) by ABBA. One of the best uses of the tracks is *Got to Give It Up* (1977) by Marvin Gaye as Vinny and Dionna gyrate on the dance floor at the Virgo Disco.

Change

A studio project from absolutely nowhere stormed the dance floors and stayed atop the 'Billboard' Disco charts for a straight nine weeks with their debut album in 1980. *The Glow of Love* by Change created a catchy, smooth and polished sound that was part Chic, part pop funk, all club-tastic, and the perfect example of the USA-European connection in magical action. Change was initially formed in 1979 as a studio band with a revolving cast of musicians, led by Guadeloupe-born businessman and executive producer Jacques Fred Petrus. Together with his closest companion, Italian-born Mauro Malavasi, Petrus had been producing music since 1978 under their company name Goody Music Production. The duo had already been responsible for such Disco hits as *I'm a Man* (1978) by Macho, *Fire Night Dance* (1978) by Peter Jacques Band and *Music Man* (1979) by Revanche.

The main force behind Change though was Italian Davide Romani, who had joined GMP in 1977 as a self-taught bass player, and fellow countryman Paolo Gianolio, a solid classical guitarist. With the majority of songwriting and production carried out by Malavasi, Romani, Gianolio, Tanyayette (Zinc) Willoughby, Wayne (Hi-Gloss) Garfield and Paul Slade (co-writer of Grace Jones' *I Need a Man*, 1975) the studio band's dual Italian and American identity was a result of a unique production system. The music, excepting the vocals, was written and recorded by the Italian and American collaborators in Fonoprint Studios, Bologna, Italy, with house engineer Maurizio Biancani. The backing tracks were then taken to the USA where GMP had a small Manhattan publishing office and there vocals were added by American performers before being mixed into final versions at New York's Power Station by engineer Bill Scheniman (of Eartha Kitt's *I Love Men*, 1984, fame) and Media Sound by Michael (Animal Nightlife) Brauer.

And the two main vocalists used on the band's debut album were none other than future megastar Luther Vandross and perennial soul diva Jocelyn Brown under her married name Jocelyn Shaw.

A Lover's Holiday, *Searching* and the album title track couldn't be shifted from the Disco No.1 slot during the months of March and April 1980 and the album won seven Grammy Awards as a result of its musicality and craftsmanship. With its carpet of groovy guitars, smooth melody, jazz riffs, classic handclaps and ultra-modern sound, *A Lover's Holiday* was by far the biggest hit taken from the album. *Searching* nearly didn't make it to first base but its replacement *Starlette* was eventually sidelined for another Petrus/ Malavasi studio concept, the B.B. & Q. Band. *The Glow of Love* proved to be one of the most popular covered and sampled Disco tracks of all time with over 40 licensed versions to date.

Change's second album *Miracles* (1981) was released to similar No.1 victory. But Vandross only featured on backing vocals due to solo success beckoning despite *Hold Tight* being expressly written for him. Taking his place was James 'Crabs' Robinson, a Lonnie Liston Smith collaborator, who owed his place in the new line-up to his uncanny ability to perform in a similar Vandross vocal style. Robinson shared vocals with Deborah Cooper (from The Fatback Band and later with C&C Music Factory), Jocelyn Brown's replacement. Blessed by a visit to Romani's studio by Change's patron saint Nile Rodgers, *Paradise*, *Hold Tight* and *Heaven of My Life* combined were another huge hit because the whole album was playful, spiritual, speedy and packed with addictive refrains that exhibited distinct musical maturity. It proved impossible to resist then and is now considered a platinum-plated highlight in the heavenly winds of musical Change.

Alan Jones, a teenage hippie in Portsmouth!

Dressed to Kill

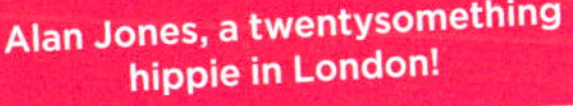
Alan Jones, a twentysomething hippie in London!

When I moved to London in 1969 I was still wearing suburban hippie chic – huge plastic medallions, Flower Power bells, leather fringe waistcoats, scarlet-lined cloaks, crushed velvet flares and 'Surf City' T-shirts. But once I started working for the souvenir emporium 'The Great Gear Trading Company' – the flagship store was in Carnaby Street, but I was in the Oxford Street Branch – I had to dress the trendy sales assistant part to flog tat like those 'Your Country Needs You' Lord Kitchener ashtrays and scented joss sticks. Luckily in the alleyway next to the shop was the base of operations and warehouse for Alkasura, the clothing empire run by designer John Lloyd. John's main outlet was at 304 Kings Road and I was literally one of the first people to wear his outrageous clothes including the red corduroy leisure suit printed with tiny toys, blue velvet hotpants for men and his masterpiece, the giant cherry motif on pink satin jacket that he designed for Rod Stewart; I got the second one off the production line.

Alan Jones in his Alkasura suit in Notting Hill Gate.

Alan Jones in David Bowie make-up for a Japanese magazine shoot.

Alan Jones in Hyde Park wearing Mr Freedom, just before The Rolling Stones concert.

Alan Jones relaxing in the Portobello Hotel lounge wearing the Scum Manifesto SEX T-shirt.

John died in the mid 1970s in very tragic circumstances – he thought he was possessed by the devil, poured petrol over himself and burnt to death. But his outré Glam Rock designs were the stepping stone to Vivienne Westwood's and Malcolm McLaren's 'Let It Rock' label and he is rarely given the credit for that. Especially when you realise future Sex Pistols Steve Jones and Paul Cook, and The Clash's Mick Jones were valued customers alongside Marc Bolan and Todd Rundgren.

Alan Jones, on the left, at the David Bowie Ziggy Stardust concert at the Royal Festival Hall in 1972. I was always being mistaken for Mick Ronson in my pink cherry jacket, only Rod Stewart and I had one from Luckies in the King's Road.

Alan Jones in his Cambridge Rapist SEX T-shirt outside his flat in Portobello Road.

Another relatively unsung fashion icon was larger-than-life Tommy Roberts, who first created the 'Kleptomania' boutique in the King's Road but turned it far more successfully into the 'Mr Freedom' brand, named after the 1969 William Klein directed film. For a while I lived next door to his Kensington Church Street branch and lapped up his platform boots, logo T-shirts sporting such pop culture images as Walt Disney characters and Roy Lichtenstein-style 'Pow' and 'Zap' cutouts. I even bought some of his crazy furniture, and a *faux* acid green tortoiseshell set of drawers still has pride of place in my London home. It was his 430 Kings Road branch that became 'Paradise Garage', with Vivienne and Malcolm selling old records in the back room, which the proto Punk duo then took over as leaseholders to open 'Let It Rock'.

Apart from my 'Let It Rock', 'Too Fast to Live, Too Young to Die', SEX and 'Seditionaries' apparel, the only other clothes shop I really had any time for during the 1970s was Swanky Modes, opened by Willie Walters, Melanie Herberfield and Judy Dewsbury in Camden Town. Esme Young (now famous for her judge role on 'The Great British Sewing Bee') was one of their designers. My favourite ever purchase was a pair of multi-coloured glitter brothel creepers, which I wore to death, often paired with Vivienne's bondage trousers, still the sexiest outfit she ever designed. Another great Vivienne design was the pink see-through nylon T-shirt. Before putting it on I would streak stage blood over my torso so it looked like I'd been whipped the night before. A very arresting look on the high street!

Out of all the clothes I wore at that time I have only kept two items. Mainly because they fell apart or in the case of my 'Perv' shirt, the chicken bones spelling that out disintegrated. I still have the 'Fuck Your Mother' Tom of Finland graphic design shirt because people still can't believe I'd walk down the road wearing a fist-fucking image. For many years afterwards I'd wear it to '70s themed parties just to cause a stir. And the 'Holidays in the Sun' British flag handkerchief that reminds me of Steve Jones so much because he wore one knotted on his head for ages. Steve Strange tried to buy them off me once for quite a lot of money but I refused because I did want to keep some mementos from that incredible part of my life.

MYSTERY MEN (1999)

Before all the DC and Marvel Comics cinematic metaverse takeovers, there was this pre-**Guardians of the Galaxy** (2014) slab of Dark Horse originated wacky, witty and ridiculous fun, stuffed to the giddy gills with Disco. It didn't tickle everyone's funny-bone, it was hardly a resounding box office success, only making a little over $33 million worldwide against a $68 million budget, and it was far too long for its own good. But former commercials director Kinka Usher's feature debut is a fun snigger-fest with lots of laugh out loud moments, mainly through gazing in admiration at the zany and artful production design. If you can imagine a superhero spoof as done by the Farrelly Brothers – a not too spurious parallel since Ben Stiller headlined this over-polished gem and starred in **There's Something About Mary** (1998) – then you've got a handle on more or less what to expect from a worthwhile diversion.

All is not well in Champion City. Resident superhero Captain Amazing (Greg Kinnear) has been twiddling his muscular thumbs ever since the incarceration of his arch nemesis Casanova Frankenstein (Geoffrey Rush) and is missing not many frontpage headlines his exploits have engendered, turning him into such a media-friendly handsome hero. So through a legal loophole he secures the release of Frankenstein in order to have a worthwhile super-villain adversary to fight visibly through the streets once more. Unfortunately Frankenstein evilly turns the tables and manages to imprison him in his menacing Disco-equipped castle. Captain Amazing's capture has been witnessed by Furious (Stiller), a wannabe superhero with the yet-to-be seen power of rage fuelling his supposed super-strength.

Herman' Reubens on comic form literally blowing the support cast away. Stiller is perfect as the goofy leader of the Dark Horse created comic pack and even his bumbling romantic interludes with waitress Monica (Claire Forlani) don't dispel the accumulative offbeat weirdness of the keenly bizarre notion, even if it does often become exactly what it is snappily satirising.

Added amusement comes from the cool special effects – Garofalo's skull-resin bowling ball bouncing every which way and loose – the lavish look giving Champion City an epic Tim Burton quality and the numerous quality Disco references thanks to Frankenstein's flared-trouser henchmen led by **Saturday Night Fever** (1977) reject Eddie Izzard. Especially as the soundtrack includes the Bee Gees' *Night Fever* (1977), The Trammps' *Disco Inferno* (1976), KC and The Sunshine Band's *That's the Way (I Like It)* (1975), A Taste of Honey's *Boogie Oogie Oogie* (1978), Anita Ward's *Ring My Bell* (1979), Chic's *Le Freak* (1978), Wild Cherry's *Play That Funky Music* (1976) and Walter Murphy & The Big Apple Band's *A Fifth of Beethoven* (1976).

You see, Champion City is packed with such would-be Batmans, Robins and Wonder Women with even more peculiar powers and it's from this wacky talent pool that Furious recruits a not-so Fantastic Seven to take on Frankenstein and halt his nefarious domination plans. Along with his two good friends, the equally inept garden tool-brandisher Shoveler (William H. Macy) and the fork-throwing Blue Raja (Hank Azaria), the eventual line-up is completed by The Bowler (Janeane Garofalo), using a ten-pin bowling ball possessed by her dead father to knock down the enemy, The Sphinx (Wes Studi), who dazzles the foe with mind-boggling swami riddles, the Invisible Boy (Kel Mitchell) who has never disappeared in his life, and The Spleen (Paul Reubens) whose deadly flatulence makes all in smell distance instantly pass out.

How this incompetent Justice League of America-type team eventually take full command of their dotty gifts, win the respect of their families and friends who think they're crazed losers, finally defeat Frankenstein and become tabloid sensations themselves makes for an amiably funky, appealingly nutty and fond send-up of previous comic book fantasies. If some of the lampoons are rather obvious – Amazing's disguise as a glasses-wearing civilian, for example – they are still done with a great amount of hip style from a wonderfully deadpan cast who milk each gag, no matter how middling, for all it's worth.

Out of the stellar brand X-Men, Azaria is hilarious as the mummy's boy sporting a fake British accent, Garofalo steals every scene she's in with her marvellous line of droll putdowns, and how great it is to see Paul 'Pee-wee

Ring My Bell

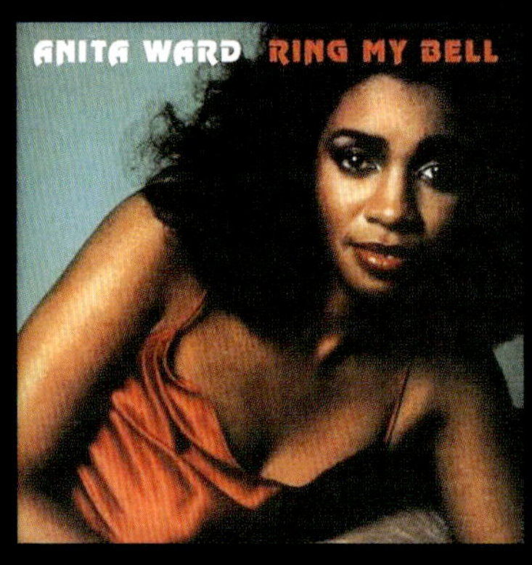

It spent nineteen weeks in the Disco charts and reached the No.1 slot. But Anita Ward's *Ring My Bell* is another of those One Hit Disco Wonders that still resonates today. The song's simplicity was the reason it chimed big in clubland; who couldn't sing along with its catchy, infectious lyric? Spotted in a college production of the stage hit 'Godspell', Ward was managed by teacher Chuck Holmes, who dabbled in the music business. One connection he had was with singer/songwriter Frederick Knight whose independent label Juana was issued through T.K. Records and he asked Ward to demo a song written with Stacy Lattislaw in mind. Mixed by Richie Rivera, Ward brought a lilting falsetto charm to *Ring My Bell* ensuring its Disco longevity. The album *Sweet Surrender* followed later in 1979 and the *Bell* derivative *Don't Drop My Love* managed to climb to No.26 in the Disco charts, but Ward's overnight success soon faded into becoming a fixture on touring Disco nostalgia tours.

2000s

MOULIN ROUGE! (2001)

"Sparkling like nothing we've seen since **The Wiz** (1978) or **Xanadu** (1980)" effused one contemporary review of the third crowdpleaser in maverick Australian director Baz Luhrmann's 'Red Curtain' trilogy after **Strictly Ballroom** (1992) and **Romeo + Juliet** (1996). Excessively over the top in every effervescent way – from its dazzling design and clashing use of songs and music drawn from every historical genre, to its incredible energy and luminescent performances – Luhrmann's pop pastiche is a bejewelled *tour de force* of driving glitz and gutsy glamour. Imagine a rock video 'La bohème' set in Studio 54 using every trick in the visual book directed by Hollywood genius Busby Berkeley and that's the impact of this glitterdust blow in the face achievement using a heady Disco landscape to weaponise its fabulousness.

Poor Parisien writer Christian (Ewan McGregor) falls for consumptive courtesan Satine (Nicole Kidman), the headlining chanteuse at the bohemian Moulin Rouge nightclub. She however is romancing The Duke (Richard Roxburgh) who has promised to fund her next show

'Spectacular Spectacular' and make her a star in return for hot nights of passion. The plot has about as much depth as an underbaked *tarte tatin* but that's not what this heart-piercing extravaganza is about. It's the ultra bold style and sequined sheen Luhrmann brings to the glorious chaos that miraculously guides it over every possible pitfall. And its delirious celebration of a century of pop culture – quoting French silent film fantasist Georges Méliès as much as the golden MGM musical era – is creatively deranged risk-taking on the highest of electrifying wires.

It's the flamboyant dance routines that are the sole point of existence, set as they are in a vast Discoland of lighting, special effects and pulsating music. Superbly performed, choreographed and edited to dizzying degrees are sound bites from Rodgers and Hammerstein classics, Madonna hits, Marilyn Monroe evergreens, Dolly Parton blockbusters and Labelle's *Lady Marmalade* (1974) performed by Christina Aguilera, Lil' Kim, Mya, and Pink, DeBarge's *Rhythm of the Night* (1985) by Valeria, and both KISS' *I Was Made for Lovin' You* (1978) and Harold Melvin & the Blue Notes' *Don't Leave Me This Way* (1975) formed as part of the *Elephant Love Medley* sung by the superb ensemble. Just a wonderful fraction of the treasure trove of delights contained in a staggeringly beautiful and bravura fairytale that remains Baz Luhrmann's best movie and his unfettered ode to the Disco spirit in all its many conjugations. Unfortunately the movie spawned a watered down, re-jigged and partially rescored 2019 Broadway and West End theatrical hit that was geared more towards raucous Hen Parties than fans of the film.

Queen of the Night

Barmaid and cloakroom attendant Régine/Rachelle Zylberberg had an idea in 1950s Paris that would transform the city's nightlife and make her the darling of the international jet set. Sick of hearing the same jukebox songs being played over and over again at the famous Whisky-à-Go-Go club, she installed two record turntables so continuous music could be an option. It was the start of a career as a nightclub owner for the flame-haired Disco doyenne who would become known as just Régine and would see her credited as creating La Discothèque. From her first club in Paris's Latin Quarter, Chez Régine, established in 1957, her empire would eventually stretch to more than 20 establishments entertaining the world's rich, famous, fashion pack and royalty. Dancing was her passion: "If you can't dance, you can't make love," she was quoted as saying and she famously taught the Duke of Windsor to do The Twist.

It was Régine who pre-empted Studio 54 in many ways, especially when she put a false 'Full' sign outside the club doors to sometimes create the illusion of success. Only London failed to fall for Régine's charms.

Her two attempts to open clubs in the city crashed. "The English have no style," she claimed, but the truth is, she wouldn't even consider letting the hoi polloi in and that was her big mistake. She became a singer and occasional actor, her best being **The Seven-Percent Solution** (1976) where she sang Stephen Sondheim's brilliant *The Madame's Song (I Never Do Anything Twice)*, and she listlessly covered Gloria Gaynor's anthem for the ages *I Will Survive* as *Je survivrai* in 1979. In 1978 she had tried the Grace Jones languid approach to the Irving Berlin 1934 classic *Cheek to Cheek* from the album *Régine*, to little Disco effect. In the post Golden Age Disco era she launched her own signature fragrance to balance the losses her clubs were making and began her first concert tour in 2015 after claiming to have written 300 songs. When she died in 2022, many obituaries cited the reason for her club success was because she had to make up for the parties she never had growing up due to a traumatic childhood being Jewish during the Nazi occupation of France.

CFQ R.I.P.

An end of an era shockingly happened on October 19th, 2000. For that was the day my 'Cinefantastique' editor Frederick S. Clarke committed suicide at the age of 51 after suffering from clinical depression. I had no idea about his medical condition. To me he was always the same bouncy Fred who would call me from his Chicago office in Oak Park once a week to see what I was working on and what I had coming up for the next few issues. Only two days prior to him crossing the state line into Iowa to take his life, I had called to give him updates on **Sleepless**, the Dario Argento giallo I had just covered on location in Turin. For some reason I told him how important he had been to my career, how I would always consider him my mentor and be eternally grateful. To this day I don't know why I chose that exact moment to tell him but in the light of what happened I take some comfort in the fact that I did open my heart.

He was a strange man make no mistake. I did travel to suburban Oak Park once to see the 'CFQ' set up and was taken aback by how dinky and untidy the office was. He did come over to London once for a James Bond junket and I asked him where he wanted to go, what sights he wanted to see and what restaurants he wanted to visit. But all he wanted to do was sit in his hotel and order room service. I just thought that was him being typically Middle-American boring. Although I did continue to write for the magazine when Mark Altman bought it, transformed it into 'Geek Monthly', then sold it on to Fourth Castle Micromedia who gave it an online presence, it was never the same. But I owe everything to Fred and 'CFQ' and I will never forget it.

GLITTER (2001)

A Star Is Corn! Movie history is littered with vanity productions from pop stars hoping to translate chart success into film careers. Remember Neil Diamond in **The Jazz Singer** (1980), Rick Springfield in **Hard to Hold** (1984) and Vanilla Ice in **Cool As Ice** (1991)? **Glitter** has to be one of the worst going, even considering those dismal comparisons. Touted as being Mariah Carey's film debut – it wasn't, **The Bachelor** (1999) was – it's something of a conundrum that anyone would think this poor, bland showbiz saga was in any way the right career move for the *All I Want for Christmas* (1994) diva with the eye-grazing rider demands.

Most would have realised how derivative the material was and nipped it in the bud before any further embarrassment. But then, if all the apocryphal stories are accurate, no one in her entourage was strong enough to tell Carey the unvarnished truth. For **Glitter** is like a traffic accident you can't tear your eyes away from because it consistently crashes and burns as it staggers from one hopeless cliché to the next without any irony or intentional camp value.

Fussily directed by actor Vondie Curtis-Hall (at the time he was a featured player in 'ER'), this semi-biopic charts the rise (not the fall, heaven forfend) of Billie Frank (Carey) as she goes from girl group ensemble to providing the vocal tracks for a talentless singer. Realising how versatile her octave range is, Billie gets turned into a top-selling solo artist by her DJ boyfriend Julian 'Dice' Black (Max Beesley) and superstardom beckons. When it becomes obvious that Dice is in over his head on the managerial capability front, their devotion, creativity and love for each other are sorely tested as the trite and violent conclusion looms large.

It is plain Carey cannot cope with the acting demands. Watching her struggle to run the emotional gamut beyond A and B isn't pretty. Nor does the soapy script help. "You must have a movie", says a producer at a promotional party. "But I don't know the first thing about acting", laments Billie. Never a truer word… Why do so many bad movies always commit the cardinal sin of putting words into reviewer's mouths? Then there's the toe-curlingly dreadful flashbacks to Billie's childhood life touring the Harlem jazz clubs with her alcoholic mother (Valarie

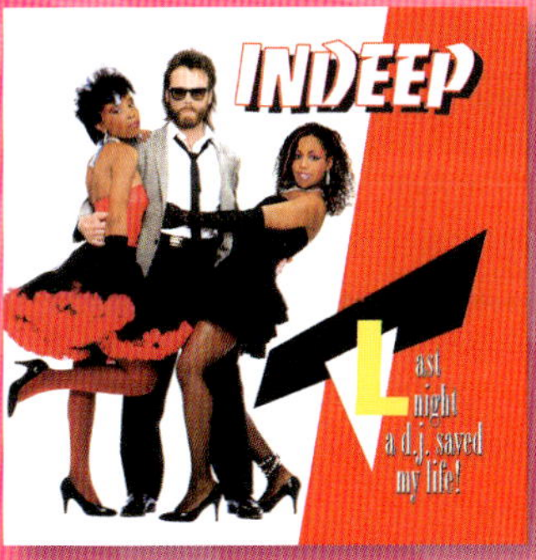

Pettiford) before being put into care with only a kitten to keep her company. Sounds a trashy delight but apart from a few moments of unintentional hilarity, it's a vapid and yawn-inducing bore. Spare a thought for her supporting cast though who try to salvage their dignity when it's clear they are all fighting a losing battle with shoddy and tarnished merchandise.

But 'All That Glitters', as per the movie's original title, does have some gold Disco nuggets tucked away on its soundtrack of struggling Carey hits like *Loverboy* in tandem with Cameo. *Babe We're Gonna Love Tonight* (1982) by Canadian sensation Lime, *Heart of Glass* (1978) by Blondie, *Last Night a DJ Saved My Life* (1982) by Indeep, plus a Carey cover version, *The Message* (1982) by Grandmaster Flash & The Furious Five, *Never Too Much* (1981) by Luther Vandross and the soft Disco swooner *Tell Me If You Still Care* (1983) by The S.O.S. Band.

Luther Vandross

What an amazing Disco career Luther Vandross had even before he became a 25-million selling singer/ songwriter and multi Grammy Award winner thanks to his mainstream breakout with the *Never Too Much* (1981) album and standards like *Here and Now* and *Power of Love*. Vandross did it all before a stroke claimed his life in 2005: founded the first Patti LaBelle fan club, wrote A *Brand New Day (Everybody Rejoice)* (1975) for 'The Wiz' Broadway musical and sang back-up vocals to Bette Midler, Roberta Flack, Chaka Khan, Diana Ross, Donna Summer, Barbra Streisand, David Bowie, Sister Sledge and Chic.

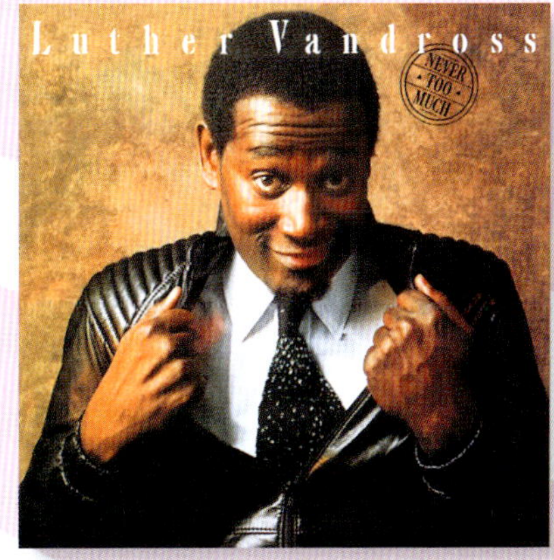

He was lead vocalist on a variety of Disco studio projects including *Hot Butterfly* for Gregg Diamond's *Bionic Boogie* (1977). On the Quincy Jones album *Sounds... and Stuff Like That!* (1978) Vandross appeared most notably on *I'm Gonna Miss You in the Morning* along with Patti Austin and *Takin' It to the Streets* with Gwen Guthrie. He also sang with the studio bands Hi-Gloss, Roundtree, Mascara, The B.B. & Q. Band, Charme and Soirée; for the latter he contributed backgrounds along with Jocelyn Brown and Sharon Redd on a scintillating 1979 album of Motown and Bacharach and David Disco covers. But it was The B.B. & Q. Band producer Jacques Fred Petrus who would change his fortunes forever with the group Change and the album *The Glow of Love* (1980).

Disco Memo

Wide Scream

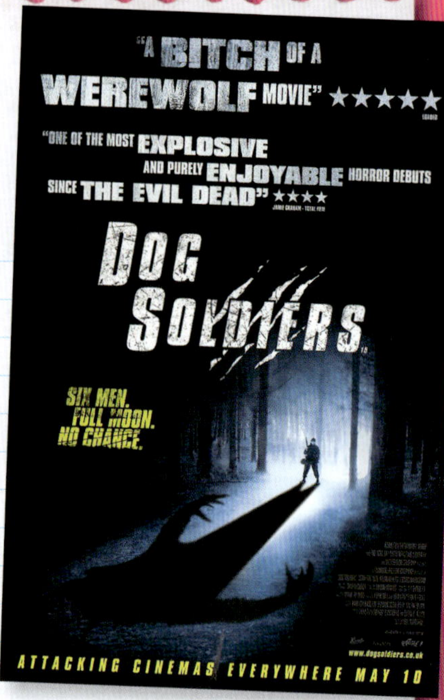

In October 2000, when I realised my cushy Sky Movies gig was over, my great cameraman friend Rel Pinto and I decided to form the company Wide Scream Ltd, and entered the Electronic Press Kit business. EPKs are interviews with the cast and crew of a film while in production, which are then edited together with clips from the final print for TV news filler purposes. Now they usually make up the DVD Extras package. We did well. There was Don Boyd's **My Kingdom** (2001), a Liverpool-set modern-day version of 'King Lear' starring Richard Harris and Lynn Redgrave. It meant I could talk Disco versions with Harris, the originator of *MacArthur Park* (1968) and tell Redgrave that I lived on the same street where she filmed **Georgy Girl** (1966).

Neil Marshall's wonderful werewolf classic **Dog Soldiers** (2002) followed, cementing an enduring relationship with the director and its star Sean Pertwee. One of the nicest movies to work on was Lewis Gilbert's **Before You Go** (2002) with Julie Walters and Tom Wilkinson. Walters marched in to our first interview saying, "Ask me anything, but don't call me a National Treasure!" Needless to say we both fell instantly in love with her. John Hannah was also in the picture and he was coming off the massive success of **The Mummy** (1999) franchise. "Don't ask him about any sequels", said his personal PR. And the first thing Hannah mentioned was **The Mummy Returns** (2001)! Personal PRs are the bane of the film industry, yet another barrier to navigate, but merely the makers of stupid rules to justify their positions and salary.

We will never forget Metin Hüseyin's **Anita & Me** (2002) starring Max Beesley, Sanjeev Bhaskar, Meera Syal and Lynn Redgrave. For we were filming B-roll (background material) on September 11th, and all shooting stopped when news about the Twin Towers hit that terrible morning. Redgrave was beside herself because of her family back in New York and that entire day now plays out in my memory as a truly surreal movie art reflecting real life moment. Our last EPK was done on location in the deserts of Morocco for Louis-Pascal Couvelaire's **Sweat/Sueurs** (2002), a French heist thriller starring Jean-Hugues Anglade, Joaquim de Almeida and Cyrille Thouvenin. It was our last because the producer Samuel Hadida, who I thought was a friend due to my 'Starfix' days, refused to pay us for our hard work and having to pay local bribes. Hadida essentially bankrupted Wide Scream and I never forgave him for it, making sure I bad-mouthed and embarrassed him at every opportunity thereafter.

BET ON MY DISCO / HAE-JEOK, DISCOWANG DOEDA (2002)

South Korea entered the Disco nostalgia wave with this hopelessly inane comedy romance featuring gangsters, wannabe criminals, Kung-Fu amateurs and dance contest fever. Signifying the feature debut of director Kim Dong-won who would unsurprisingly only make one other film afterwards – the sentimental drama **Drifting Away** (2009) – **Hae-jeok, Disco King**, to give this its other export title, is a self-consciously old-fashioned affair wallowing in the coarsest of humour mainly to do with the staggeringly stupid ineptitude of the leading characters.

Set in the early 1980s, three high school students, Hae-jeok (Lee Jung-jin), Bong-pal (Im Chang-jung) and Seok-gi (Yang Dong-geun), spend most of their time arguing about nothing as they hang out in their primitive village neighbourhood practicing their Bruce Lee moves. One day, after yet more brainless infighting, Hae-jeok meets Bong-ja (Han Chae-young) and falls in love with her at first sight, not knowing she's Bong-pal's sister. When her father has a terrible accident, Bong-ja is forced to work in the local Disco run by an ex-mambo king, which morally outrages the trio. So the boss makes Hae-jeok an unexpected proposal: if he wants to free Bong-ja from her imposed servitude he must win an upcoming Disco dance contest. With only one week remaining, Hae-jeok must take a crash course in Disco to save his heart's desire.

It's bubblegum nonsense done in the brashest and most obvious of broadstrokes with few surprises along the familiar route towards the taken-for-granted happy ending. If the trio dressing up in frilly fashions doesn't raise laughs, perhaps the mincing around on the dance floor will, seems to be the anything goes approach taken by Kim Dong-won who has absolutely no clue about the era he's trying to spoof. Only one scene points towards the sophistication it could have achieved – Hae-jeok practicing specialised moves in an underwater workout filled with a balletic grace sorely missing from the rest of the dire Disco antics. Another problem is actor Lee Jung-jin essaying being a dreadful dancer to begin with but actually showing no marked improvement, making his win completely unjustified.

Two genuine Disco tracks are used during the dance contest: *Boogie Shoes* (1978) by KC and The Sunshine Band and the lesser known No.11 'Billboard' Dance Chart hit *Designer Music* (1981) by Lipps, Inc., the *Funkytown* (1980) mob. Elsewhere, treacly MOR is provided by Yang Dong-geun, aka YDG, K Pop star, rapper, songwriter, record producer and breakdancer, who sings *Song from the Snow* during the fantasy snowstorm finale backdropped by a heart-shaped moon.

K-Disco

Neon Boogie and Moog Funk arrived late in the Disco day in South Korea mainly because of dance music being looked down on by the military dictatorship of Park Chung-hee from 1963 until his assassination in 1979.

But Bunny Girls put their heads above the parapet in 1978 with the album *Yes Sir, I Can Boogie*, the title track nothing to do with the 1977 Baccara hit, even though the duo's logo featured an identical red rose design to their Spanish counterpart. Another track was *Love You Till I Die*, another Baccara title, another totally different song. Bunny Girls lasted a full decade and their latter songs are in the best Italo Disco style, especially *Que Sera Sera* (1989), which, guess what, is nothing to do with the Doris Day 1956 standard either. Other K-Disco acts include Kim Nam-mi and her *Disco Star* (1980) album, the Lee Eun-ha album (1985) and the super Space Disco sounds of Ha Jin-i (1982). The Seoul Sisters made waves in 1987 with their *Best Album* and Kim Wan-sun was touted as the Korean Madonna when she entered the Disco field with her self-titled 1986 album.

FrightFest

Alan Jones commemorating the very first FrightFest at the Prince Charles Cinema.

None of us expected FrightFest to take off in the way it did. I always saw it as a confluence of factors: the video revolution meaning access to everything, genre interest growing because of the internet, and finding family with like-minded aficionados. It was because he had attended 'Shock Around the Clock' that Paul McEvoy, owner of the now defunct The Cinema Store in Covent Garden, asked me to help him set up a similar endeavour that slotted in between Montreal's Fantasia in July and Sitges in October. In fact, we wanted to keep the 'Shock Around the Clock' title, but even though I had coined it – see the **Scala!!!** (2023) documentary – 'Shock Xpress' publisher Stephen Jones insisted he owned it. I couldn't be bothered arguing with him and am so glad now as we needed to forge a completely separate identity.

After 'Shock Around the Clock', I had organised 'Fantasm' at the National Film Theatre, with my 'Time Out' film critic friend Nigel Floyd. We mounted retrospectives on Mario Bava, Dario Argento and John Carpenter, with the latter two in attendance, showcasing everything from early David Cronenberg shorts to Clive Barker premieres and a whole range of new genre releases from Alejandro Amenábar's **Thesis** (1996) and Gabriele Salvatores' **Nirvana** (1997) to Pupi Avati's **The Arcane Enchanter** (1996) and Ray Brady's **Boy Meets Girl** (1994). After a few years I soon realised the NFT was not the right place for a horror fantasy season because of its rarefied auteur atmosphere and the too right-on argumentative staff not quite understanding what we were trying to do.

Disco Memo

The FrightFest team, left to right: Ian Rattray, Paul McEvoy, Alan Jones and Greg Day.

So that's why Paul, his Cannes friend film booker Ian Rattray and I joined forces for the first FrightFest at the Prince Charles Cinema, Leicester Square, August 25-27th, 2000. It started slowly, my movie PR friend Greg Day joined us in 2002 to take over that part of the business when I couldn't deal with the incessant calls to interview Kylie Minogue about **Cut** (2000) in our first edition. Soon we gained more followers, more sponsorship, the event became an instant hot ticket annual sell-out, we moved to venues all over the Square, and one year even to Shepherd's Bush when every central London cinema was undergoing renovations, and proved a word-of-mouth platform for so many great movies that wouldn't have seen the light of day otherwise.

FrightFest was and always will be 'for the fans by the fans' and the growing camaraderie and community spirit that has grown up over the years is one of the best aspects of the entire process. I have always made a point of being available throughout every event to talk to everyone, those fans of my writing career who always say, "I used to read your reviews when I was at school!", and made sure the talent mix and mingle too. I'm constantly asked what my favourite memories are of the past decades and I always say introducing **Pan's Labyrinth** (2006) on stage with director Guillermo del Toro and producer Alfonso Cuarón, and beating every other festival in showing Pascal Laugier's **Martyrs** (2008), which I firmly believe is one of the greatest horror movies ever made.

▲ Inset right: Alan Jones with future Oscar-winning director Guillermo del Toro at FrightFest.

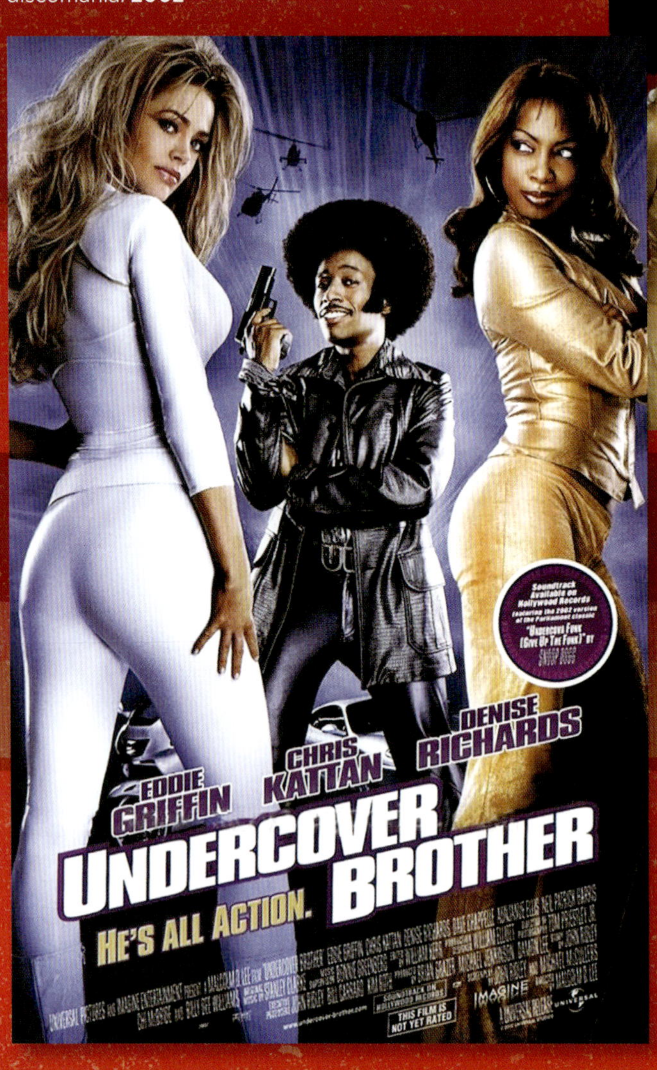

UNDERCOVER BROTHER (2002)

The first major feature to be adapted from an internet cartoon (by John Ridley), director Malcolm D. Lee's consistently genial if relentlessly hit-and-miss send-up is unmistakeably inspired by the spy spoof mayhem of **Austin Powers, International Man of Mystery** (1997). Indeed the screenplay is by Michael McCullers who wrote the two Austin Powers sequels. His attempt to poke fun at the white perception of black culture while celebrating the glories of the era ushered in by **Shaft** (1971) gets adroit attention by comedian Eddie Griffin, 'Saturday Night Live' cast member Chris Kattan and stand-up Dave Chappelle as well as Neil Patrick Harris, Billy Dee Williams and a cameo by James Brown who contributes four of his greatest hits to the soundtrack. **Undercover Brother** is definitely the sum of its Get Smartass parts, but when those parts work they really do zing.

The B.R.O.T.H.E.R.H.O.O.D. is a Top Secret agency that has been set up to protect the African-American nation and their culture from sliding into redundancy. Their archenemy is The Man, a faceless white despot intent on unleashing a psycho-hallucinogenic chemical weapon to brainwash the entire black population into mindless zombies. So The B.R.O.T.H.E.R.H.O.O.D. chief (Chi McBride), his assistants, Sistah Girl (Aunjanue Ellis), Conspiracy Brother (Chappelle), Smart Brother (Gary Anthony Williams) and intern Lance (Harris), call on Undercover Brother (Griffin) to foil The Man's plan using war hero General Warren Boutwell (Billy Dee Williams) to distribute the lethal drug via his fried chicken GFC outlets. With his leather-clad style, funky Afro, smooth way with the ladies, Bruce Lee film buffery and outrageous arsenal of gadgets and disguises, Undercover Brother moves into slick action. Until he meets The Man's secret weapon, Penelope Snow (Denise Richards), aka the White She-Devil, whose mission is to cast a spell on Undercover Brother and create a superfluous milquetoast honky.

Undercover Brother works best in the more tactless moments where he's falling under Snow's enchantment. Suddenly the stereotypical black man of a hundred **Super Fly** (1972) knock-offs turns into a faithful fine dining liberal in checkered golfing trousers minding his four-letter language. For once the racial identity caricature is turned on its head to great comic effect. Politically incorrect for sure, the one-liners are hilarious – "You mess with the 'fro, then you gotta go!", "Once you go black, you don't go back" – and the escapist silliness often slides into utter stupidity. But as cleverly slanted, agreeable nonsense goes there's a lot worse one-jokers out there, **Black Dynamite** (2009) anyone?

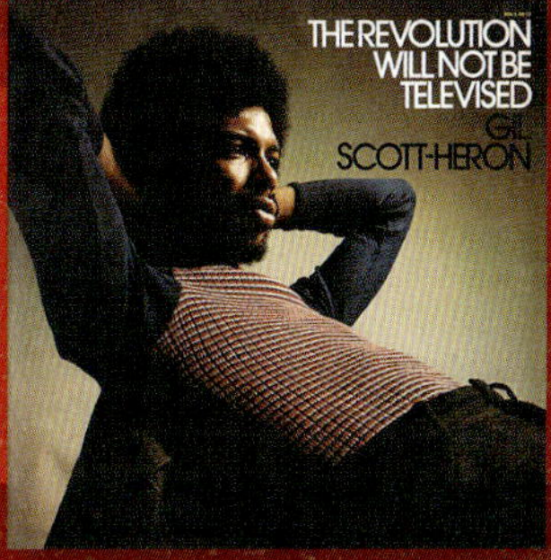

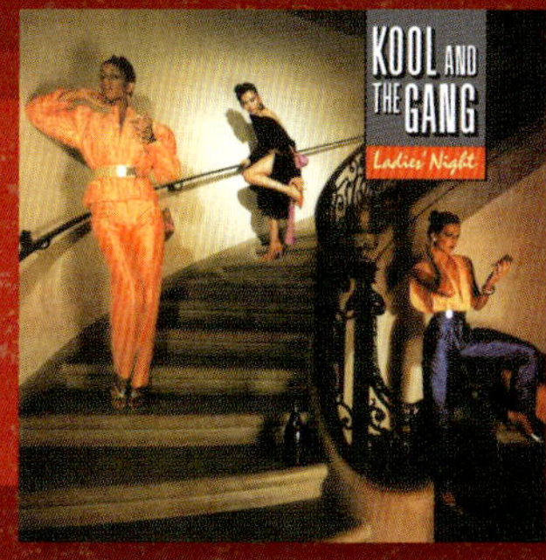

The Disco selections on the over-stuffed soundtrack are *Pick Up the Pieces* (1974) by the Average White Band, *Tear the Roof Off the Sucker (Give Up the Funk)* (1976) by Parliament, *Close the Door* (1978) by Teddy Pendergrass, *The Revolution Will Not Be Televised* (1974) by Gil Scott-Heron, *She's a Bad Mama Jama (She's Built, She's Stacked)* (1980) by Carl Carlton, *Brick House* (1976) by the Commodores, *Jungle Boogie* (1973) and *Ladies' Night* (1979) by Kool & The Gang, *Love Train* (1972) by The O'Jays, *Play That Funky Music (White Boy)* (1976) by Wild Cherry, *Got to Be Real* (1978) by Cheryl Lynn, and *Car Wash* (1976) by Rose Royce. The music in the belated Netflix sequel **Undercover Brother 2** (2019) starring Michael Jai White was all composed by jazz-fusion pioneer Stanley Clarke.

Disco Circus

Foxes (1980) and **Flashdance** (1983) had led producer Keith Forsey to (co-) writing songs for a myriad of other movies, **Ghostbusters** (1984), **Beverly Hills Cop** (1984), **The NeverEnding Story** (1984) and **The Breakfast Club** (1985). Fitting really as the British drummer first became known for his work with The Spectrum, the group supplying the end title theme for Gerry Anderson's Supermarionation puppet series 'Captain Scarlet'. But in the golden Disco era, he became a long-time associate of pioneer producer Giorgio Moroder (playing on Moroder's breakthrough hit *Son of My Father*, 1972, by Chicory Tip) and can be heard on several landmark Donna Summer albums for which he co-wrote key songs. He also formed TRAX with Moroder's co-producer Pete Bellotte, their album *Watch Out!* (1977), an underrated gem, and played drums for Sparks, Munich Machine, Boney M. and the New York based studio project Disco Circus.

The brainchild of German producer Jürgen S. Korduletsch (Claudja Barry's husband) for his Lollipop Records label in 1978, Disco Circus hit with a cover version of Iron Butterfly's legendary 1968 rock anthem *In-A-Gadda-Da-Vida*, so titled apparently because composer/singer Doug Ingle was so drunk and high when he told fellow band member Ron Bushy to write down the title 'In the Garden of Eden' it became lost in garbled mistranslation.

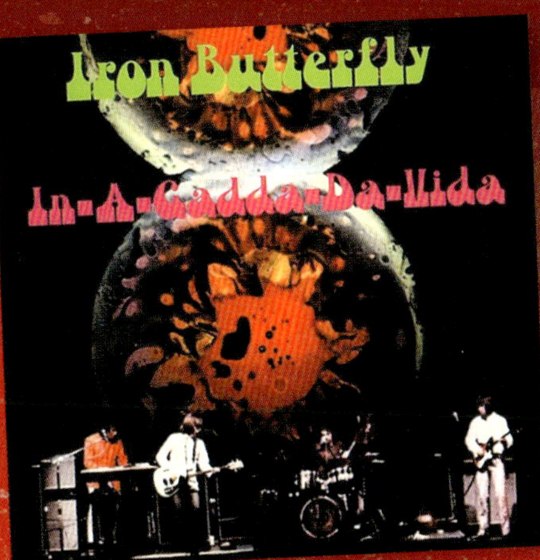

Ten years later Korduletsch was looking for suitable material to take the Munich electronic sound onto yet more dance floors and thought of the Iron Butterfly song, one often seen as the first move from psychedelia into Heavy Metal. So what better vehicle to move Disco into electronica? Beefed up by Forsey and Munich Machine's Mats Bjoerklund with extra lyrics, *In-A-Gadda-Da-Vida/Garden of Eden* helped create a musical progression in the vibrant 1970s Disco landscape. The duo also contributed the vibrantly echoing Disco hit *Over and Over* to the album, featuring vocals from Roberta Kelly.

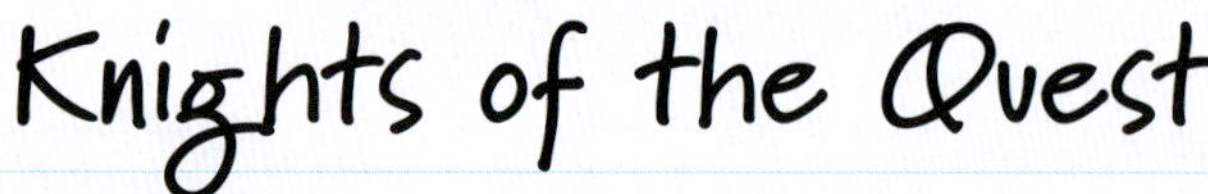

Knights of the Quest

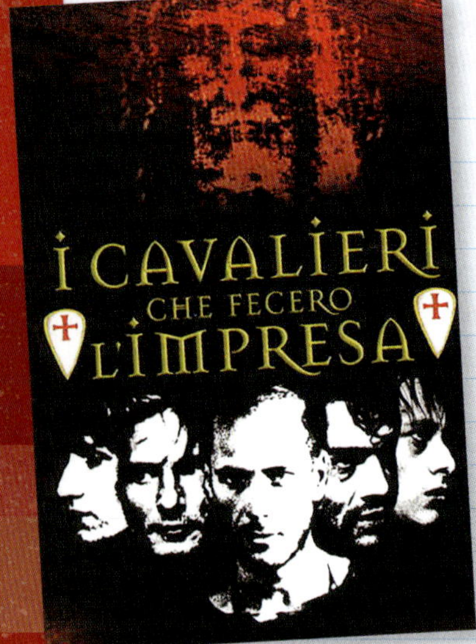

I've covered many movie shoots in Italy away from the entire Dario Argento oeuvre, Michele Soavi's **Dellamorte Dellamore/Cemetery Man** (1994) being one memorable occasion, others being the Federico Zampaglione directed duo **Tulpa** (2012) and **The Well** (2023). One of the most rewarding was being on location with director Pupi Avati for his medieval adventure **The Knights of the Quest/I cavalieri che fecero l'impresa** (2001) starring Edward Furlong, Raoul Bova and Thomas Kretschmann. Anyone who has seen Avati's masterpiece **The House with the Laughing Windows/ La casa dalle finestre che ridono** (1976) will need no introduction to his unique work including **Zeder** (1983) and **Il signor Diavolo** (2019). I had asked him to attend 'Fantasm' with **The Arcane Enchanter** (1996) but he was in the middle of shooting one of his most popular hits, **Festival** (1997) at the time.

I had been invited to the Barletta Castle location in South East Italy thanks to my great friend Mark Ashworth who had moved to Italy and become an esteemed dialogue coach. Mark was another 'Forbidden Planet 2' customer made good and I had employed him as my translator when filming the Rome sections of the Argento documentary **An Eye for Horror** (2000), which I asked my other best friend Mark Kermode to narrate. Mark A eventually became a go-to translator for the brilliant director Giuseppe Tornatore.

Barletta Castle was where Avati's friend Pier Paolo Pasolini had directed **The Gospel According to St. Matthew** (1964) so I had a wonderful time on the movie. Avati gave me a fantastic career interview, and it was great to tick him off my Italian Horror Greats list. I had tried to interview Riccardo Freda once at the Sitges Fantasy Festival. The moment I told him I loved **The Terror of Dr. Hichcock/L'orribile segreto del Dr. Hichcock** (1962) he told me to fuck off and walked out. Oh well, you can't win them all! Kretschmann and I went back a long way, and I already had dealings with the fantastic Bova thanks to my connections to popular comedy director Carlo Vanzina.

There was one fly in the ointment. **Terminator 2** (1991) star Furlong was an absolute nightmare, but I've had my fair share of celebrities behaving badly so I ignored him. That's always the best thing to do in my experience, something I learnt dealing with Dudley Moore on **Santa Claus: The Movie** (1985) and Jeremy Irons on **Dungeons and Dragons** (2000). No one was as rude as Sean Connery on **Highlander II: The Quickening** (1991) though when people got in his eyeline while on set. I was glad I stole his pass for the Talking Heads concert in Buenos Aires, even though the bouncer patrolling the VIP seating area instantly saw through my disguise!

PARTY MONSTER (2003)

Rich Kid James St. James (Seth Green) was already a celebrity party animal when star-struck suburban wannabe Michael Alig (Macaulay Culkin) knocked on his Manhattan door, asking "I want you to teach me how to be fabulous". Together the outrageous duo turned early 1990s New York nightlife into an orgy of sex and drugs fuelled by Disco dance music, kinky cos-playing and petulant attitude to spare. A definitive force in underground culture in the late 1980s, the real Club Kids were the key social influencers of their day, a youth cult of fashionistas and bizarre behaviourists on a perpetual promotion quest who made their entire self-styled living on party organisation, rent-a-crowd flash mobs and paid guest appearances on talk shows and at society events. Their drag-to-bitches history was chronicled by St. James in his best-selling book 'Disco Bloodbath', which co-directors/writers Fenton Bailey and Randy Barbato adapted first into an eye-opening, award-winning documentary titled **Party Monster: The Shockumentary** (1998) and then this equally potent and sizzling dramatic edition.

Everything ran smoothly in the demonic duo's Limelight-based Disco universe – except the soiree arranged in a truck driven around town by an acid-crazed drag queen – until the vehemently anti-drug Alig experimented to see what all the fuss and attraction was about. Alig's subsequent fall into the paranoid addiction abyss ended in the 1996 conspiracy to murder his lover and dealer Andre 'Angel' Melendez (Wilson Cruz) with his

roommate Robert D. 'Freeze' Riggs (Justin Hagan). Alig was eventually imprisoned for 17 years, convicted of first-degree manslaughter. A sordid true-life tale of fashion victim martyrdom and fame whore glamour told in thought-provoking and hilarious mode, and one perfectly encapsulating the Living Large deranged times of hardened New York in the mid 1990s.

How the boys minted their alternate lifestyles and seduced others into their glittering excesses explodes with vibrant electric design, shocking gay humour, non-judgemental compassion and poignant truth. Yet this handbags-at-dawn holocaust has much more on offer than incandescent BPM sparkle and OTT camp. Because it's graced by the most startling performances from Green (Scott Evil in the **Austin Powers** franchise) and Culkin, the latter **Home Alone** (1990) star marking his return to the big screen after a nine-year gap.

As remarkable and image shattering as Culkin's satin chaps and feather boa wearing precise reading of Alig is (he spent time with the real Alig in prison to ensure that verisimilitude), **Party Monster** unquestionably belongs to Green who's a scene-stealing revelation as the disinherited dancing queen swept away by a colossal tide of sequin-encrusted extremes into the starkest of brutalities. From his uproarious instructions on how to network a crowded Disco to Voguing along to Stacey Q's Disco hit *Two of Hearts* (1986), Green gives the most unexpected performance of his career. With its soundtrack of electro synth pop including *Give Me Tonight* (1984) by Shannon, *New York, New York* (1983) by Nina Hagen, *You're My Disco* (2000), *Kiss Me* (1985) by Stephen Tin Tin Duffy, and *Take Me to the Club* (2003) by Mannequin, **Party Monster** gets its Disco ambience and culture twinkle exactly right.

Bobby O

Bobby Orlando, one-time amateur boxer turned undisputed King of the Manhattan HiNRG sound, was born Robert Philip Orlando in Westchester New York. Bobby O, as he soon became known in the golden Disco years, played guitar in local teenage Glam Rock bands before teaching himself to play keyboards. His glittering recording career began when he produced *Dancin'*

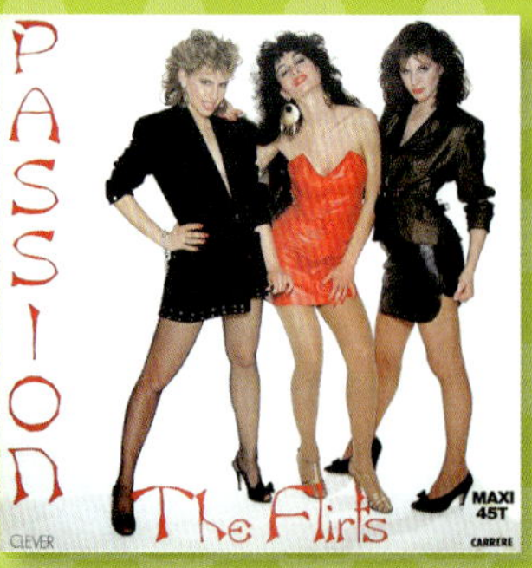

(1979) by Tod Foster, which led to the creation of the 'O' Record label, the showcase for such renowned acts as Claudja Barry, Roni Griffith, The Flirts, Divine, Oh Romeo, Malibu, Girly, Eric, Free Enterprise, Gomez Presley, Band of South, Bonnie Forman, Barbie & the Kens and Waterfront Home. Orlando had even signed British fans of his productions, the Pet Shop Boys, early on in their career, with the first recorded version of *West End Girls* (1984).

Roni Griffith was one of the original Coconuts in Kid Creole and the Coconuts and signed with Orlando when making the decision to go solo. The result was four Disco chart hits: *Mondo Man* (1980), *I Want Your Lovin'* (1981), *Desire* (1981) and the No.2 platinum hit *(The Best Part of) Breakin' Up* (1982). The Flirts was arguably Orlando's biggest act to set the dance floors ablaze with shimmer and sizzle. *Passion* (1982), *Calling All Boys* (1982), *Boy Crazy* (1982), *Jukebox (Don't Put Another Dime)* (1982), *Helpless (You Took My Love)* (1984), *Dancing Madly Backwards* (1985) and the No.1 Disco hit *You & Me* (1985) were massive for the white female trio whose line-up changed from album to album. Orlando also recorded under his Bobby O alias, two of the best being his frenzied HiNRG version of the Elvis Presley 1969 hit *Suspicious Minds* (1988) and *Whisper to a Scream* (1985) with Claudja Barry.

Disco Memo

NWR

I first met **Pusher** (1996) wunderkind director Nicolas Winding Refn when I asked him to attend the UK premiere of **Fear X** (2003) at FrightFest. We were staying in the same hotel during the festival and got to know each other well, especially when I found out he had a poster of **The Texas Chain Saw Massacre** (1974) framed on his kitchen wall in his apartment in Copenhagen. We stayed in touch through our mutual friends at his distributor Vertigo and his insatiable desire to know everything about my 'CFQ' career and sleazy times in 1970s New York. Then he arrived in the UK to direct an episode of the long-running 'Agatha Christie's Marple' TV series, 'Nemesis', which he literally filmed in the church opposite my London apartment, so I was pretty much an on-set fixture. When I look at the cast he assembled for that pure money-earner on his part – Dan Stevens, Lee Ingleby, Amanda Burton, Anne Reid, Ruth Wilson – it's amazing how many have now become established stars.

It was on the shoot that something happened to cement our friendship forever. I was with him in his car when his driver crashed on Battersea Bridge leaving us all injured with whiplash and shaken up badly. Medics call it 'Trauma Bond'. From that moment on I became part of his trusted inner circle. On **Bronson** (2008) he asked me to direct star Tom Hardy for a shower orgy scene that didn't make the final cut. On **Valhalla Rising** I stayed with him on location in Scotland through some very frosty cast readings. Nicolas also insisted I be his moderator for the DVD commentaries on all three films.

So when he said we should combine our talents again to produce 'The Act of Seeing' (2015) book I was delighted. Using his exploitation poster collection and my knowledge of the genre, we put together the book in his Copenhagen production office, Space Rocket Nation. We then went on a global tour to publicise it – Austin in Texas, Sitges in Spain, Lyons in France – and it turned out brilliantly. Nicolas' rising profile means we don't see each other now as much as we used to but he remains a good friend and I'm very proud of the work we did together.

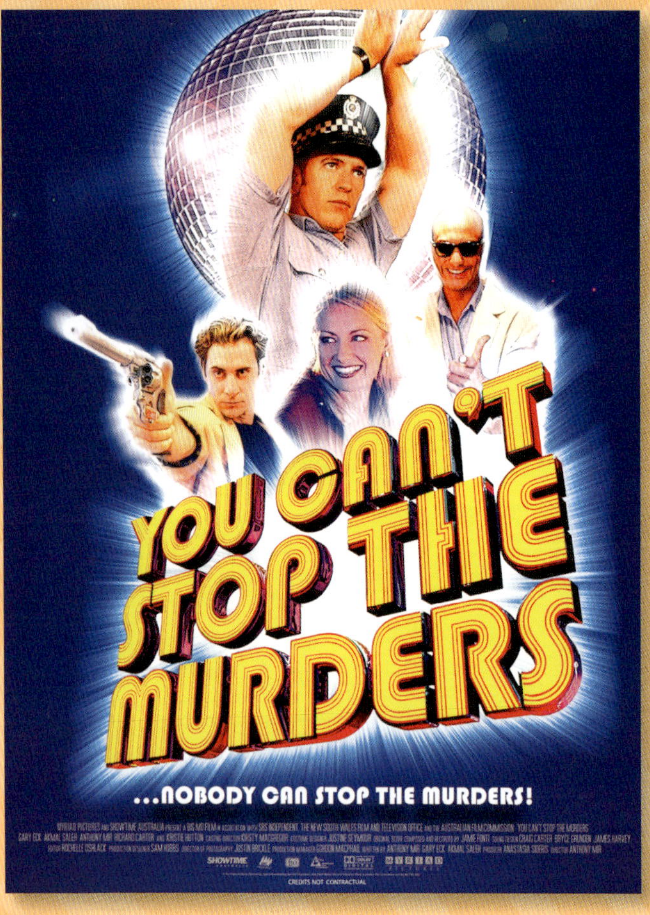

YOU CAN'T STOP THE MURDERS (2003)

...Nobody can stop the murders! If any country was going to make a low-budget comedy punning the title of the Village People ersatz biopic **Can't Stop the Music** it was bound to be Australia. The Nancy Walker directed gays-in-aspic reproduction might have been a box-office disaster everywhere else in the world but in the Land of Oz it was a No.1 hit. Go figure? Written by and starring Gary Eck (who would write/co-direct **Happy Feet Two**, 2011), Akmal Saleh and Anthony Mir, three stand-up comedians who had worked together for over ten years, and featuring the cream of Aussie comics in many featured roles – Jimeoin, Bob Franklin, The Umbilical Brothers, Kitty Flanagan, Garry Who, Haskel Daniel, Richard Carter, The Dickster, Rash Ryder, Kenny Graham, Sandman – **You Can't Stop the Murders** is a more hit than miss fun affair. But while rough around the edges it's held together by director Mir who does nothing more than let the absurdity of the quirky concept unfold with droll campery and lashings of endearing charm.

In the tiny backwoods town of West Village (population: 350), a serial killer is on the loose, and he's obsessed with the iconic Disco group the Village People, famous for their 1978 anthem *Y.M.C.A.* First a biker is decapitated, then a construction worker is murdered, followed by a cowboy, an American Indian and finally a sailor. By the time the slow-witted local constables Gary Raymond (Eck) and Akmal (Saleh) work out the grisly Disco connection, they realise the last in the pop group's line-up was a policeman. And that can only mean one thing – one of them is the next target. So flash, trigger-happy detective Tony (Mir) is drafted in from Sydney to help them find the killer using his best 'Miami Vice' style tactics.

With plenty of silly subplots, ludicrous red herrings, a love triangle and a gay champion line-dancer, the humour ranges between obvious one-liners and homages to **Strictly Ballroom** (1992) to a barrage of Village People references and surreal wannabe ideas

spouted by movie-crazy Akmal as they wait in the patrol car for speeding motorists to pass by. This is where the clear comedy-sketch/double act basics show through the scattershot middleground narrative. However, the gags built on the finer points of smalltown life and its weird inhabitants are neatly contained and resoundingly hit the spot. And kudos must go to the writing trio for not predictably dwelling too heavy-handedly on the gay aspects of the premise.

Anyone expecting wall-to-wall Disco hits on the soundtrack will be sorely disappointed. Obviously the meagre budget could not afford the hefty license fees for any of the Village People's back catalogue, controlled by surviving producer/writer Henri Belolo. Instead, three songs from top Australian singer/songwriter Peter Allen are featured. While Melissa Manchester had a 1978 hit with *Don't Cry Out Loud* (1976), it's Allen's version showcased here, along with *I Go to Rio* (1976), which Gary Eck line-dances to at the climax. Allen's biggest success was with *I Honestly Love You* (1974), written with Jeff Barry, a major hit for Olivia Newton-John, and sung here by Rebecca Mir.

Mir also sings a version of the Bette Midler theme song *The Rose* (1979) from her same titled movie, while the tracks *Cuando Vuelvan (Song)* (1998) and *Pop (For Jack Maittlen)* (1998) both by the Australian outfit Tigramuna add an infectious Latino Jazzy flavour. The only true blue Disco hit featured is *You to Me Are Everything* (1976) by The Real Thing, while the original composition *Everything We Do* by Asli Ozdogan adds peppy mirrorball zing over the final credits. Retitled **Super Disco Killer** in Spain and **Village Police** in France, this Cherry Ripe flavoured pop tart is goofy, ridiculous and irresistible and deserves a lot more respect for its infectious Disco vibe.

The Best Bette

Disco deliberately aimed at the specific gay demographic didn't necessarily click. Cher's *Take Me Home* (1979) did, Ethel Merman's *The Ethel Merman Disco Album* (1979) spectacularly refused to. Someone who knew that fact better than anybody else was the sublime Diva of every single show business strand, Bette Midler. Over four decades The Divine Miss M conquered Broadway, Hollywood, the Grammys, Las Vegas, the Emmys and every gay boy's heart. It was in the summer of 1970 that Midler, after appearing in the Broadway musicals 'Fiddler on the Roof' and 'Salvation', began performing at the Continental Baths, located in the basement of Manhattan's Ansonia Hotel, with her piano accompanist Barry Manilow.

My Knight in Black Leather.

With Alan Bates in *The Rose* (1979).

Thanks to its dance floor, cabaret lounge, sauna rooms and 45-foot "Olympia blue" swimming pool, the place became a gay Mecca and Midler its star attraction. Completely embracing her core following, Bette released many gay-friendly albums and entered the Disco landscape first in 1976 with *Strangers in the Night* (1976), a languid version of the Frank Sinatra staple, taken from her *Songs from the New Depression* album. When that failed to chart, Midler waited three years to take on Disco again with a four-pronged attack from her *Thighs and Whispers* album. *Married Men*, *Hurricane* and *Hang On in There Baby*, an up-tempo rendition of the Johnny Bristol 1974 hit, are par-for-the-course, sensual easy listeners.

But the uproarious pounder *My Knight in Black Leather* saw Midler in typical "hungry, tired and looking for love" drag queen mode cruising Ronardo's 'Boom Boom Room' on South Street for hot action. One-time Dusty Springfield and Bee Gees producer Arif Mardin augmented Midler's camp sensibility brilliantly, especially in the long shopping list of leather gear that punctuates the main chorus, while background vocals featured Luther Vandross. Fabulously catchy, hilariously horny, wonderfully OTT and perfectly capturing Midler at the height of her 'homo promo' fame, this sleaze on steroids cut typifies the Gay Disco genre. There was a lot more to come over the next two decades too, with her 1995 'Billboard' Dance Chart No.2 *To Deserve You* deserving the most recognition.

Kim Newman

I've lost count of how many commentaries I've done since they became a fixture on every DVD/Blu-ray release. But I will only do them if I feel I have something positive to contribute, either knowing the director/star or loving the movie itself. Filling up over 90 minutes of soundtrack discussing every aspect of a production isn't easy either. That's why I've loved doing so many with my great friend Kim Newman, 'Empire' magazine's national treasure. You go into a sound proofed booth with your notes – always best to have something down on paper, even if you don't use them they're a security blanket – and you enter the zone where nothing else but facts and anecdotes reign for however long the running time is. Alone and with Kim we've received great reviews justifying how worthwhile the hard work and micro research is.

Here's a short list of the commentaries I've really enjoyed: Nicolas Winding Refn's **Fear X** (2003), **Bronson** (2008) and **Valhalla Rising** (2009), Alejandro Jodorowsky's **Santa Sangre** (1989), Tom Shankland's **WΔZ** (2008), Andrew Birkin's **The Cement Garden** (1993) and Dario Argento's **The Bird with the Crystal Plumage** (1970), **The Cat O'Nine Tails** (1971), and **Trauma** (1993) with Mark Kermode, **The Card Player** (2004), **The Stendhal Syndrome** (1996), **Opera** (1987), **Tenebrae** (1982) and **Suspiria** (1977). Other giallo commentaries include Massimo Dallamano's **What Have You Done to Solange?** (1972), Duccio Tessari's **The Bloodstained Butterfly** (1971), Emilio Miraglia's **The Red Queen Kills Seven Times** (1972) and one of my all-time favourites, Giulio Questi's **Death Laid an Egg** (1968).

My starriest commentary was the one I moderated with Oscar-winning actress Helen Mirren for Tinto Brass' **Caligula** (1979). What a class act she was, allowing me to ask her anything and everything I wanted. The most fraught commentary was for Tony Maylam's **The Burning** (1981) because he didn't get what we were doing. He was embarrassed about making the movie in the first place and every question I asked was met with either stony silence or "Why do you want to know about that?" and "I can't see why you are consistently raking all of this up". He missed the point completely and saw it more as an attack on his credibility as a filmmaker. I couldn't wait for those endless 91 minutes to be over.

You can see me adding my views during a lot of Talking Head interviews too, on **Heavenly Creatures** (1994), **Combat Shock** (1986), **Climax** (2018) talking Disco, **The Wax Mask** (1997), **StageFright** (1987), **The Keep** (1983), **Four Flies on Grey Velvet** (1971), **The Five Days of Milan** (1973), **Opera** (1987), **The Church** (1989), **The Sect** (1991), **Video Nasties: Moral Panic, Censorship & Videotape** (2010), **Video Nasties: Draconian Days** (2014) and the **A Nightmare on Elm Street** (1984) Blu-ray collection, to name the tip of a very large iceberg.

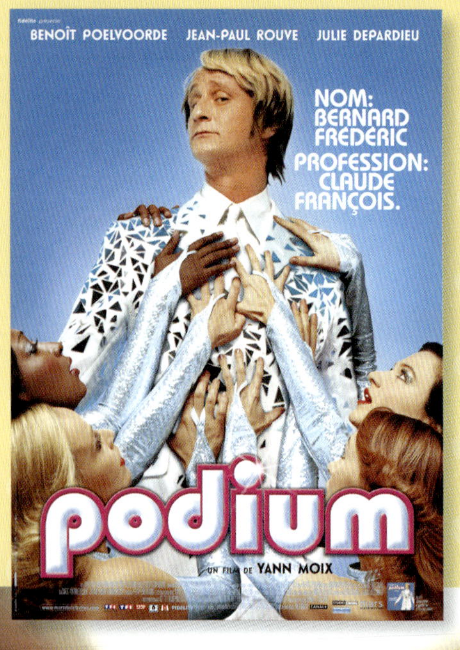

PODIUM (2004)

One of the biggest French-language box-office hits of all time is this absolutely wonderful tribute to the blond, diamante encrusted, crushed velvet Disco Divo that was the Gallic pop phenomenon Claude François. The French Elvis, who began his career singing cover versions of popular American hits like *If I Had a Hammer* (1963), had numerous dance smashes during the 1970s after he accidentally electrocuted himself in the bath in 1978. Known by the nickname CloClo to his legions of fans, *Alexandrie Alexandra* (1977), *Magnolias for Ever* (1977), *Disco Meteo* (1977) and *Laisse une chance à notre amour* (1977, co-written with Biddu) were just four of his signature dancefloor fillers.

Of course, François is best known outside France for writing the French lyrics to the Jacques Revaux composition *Comme d'habitude* (1967), which Paul Anka rewrote as *My Way* for Frank Sinatra. François was a household name in France for his lavish television specials drenched in kitsch spectacle and glittering schmaltz, featuring his own incredible outré choreography expertly mirrored by his equally famous and sequin-bedecked backing dancers, Les Clodettes.

All this and a whole lot more finds its way into director Yann Moix's hilarious, witty, affectionate delight in which dull bank clerk Bernard Frédéric (the brilliant Belgian comedian Benoît Poelvoorde) is acknowledged as the best Claude François tribute act working the nostalgia nightclub circuit. Although he promises his wife he'll stop tinsel tonsiling around and hang up his sparkling wardrobe, when a TV programme offers a €100,000 prize for the best François lookalike, the showbiz lure proves irresistible and soon he's auditioning (and bedding) wannabe Clodettes and acting like the petulant star.

Egged on by his best friend Couscous (Jean-Paul Rouve), himself an uproarious dead ringer for Michel Polnareff (the composer of the Disco soundtrack **Lipstick**, 1976), Bernard sings every famous François song, plus *Chanson populaire* (1973), *Cette année-là* (1976, the cover version of The Four Seasons' hit *December 1963 (Oh, What a Night)*), and *C'est comme ça que l'on s'est aimé* (1977). But in the enormously touching and moving finale, Bernard blows his chance of winning the competition by crooning his wife's favourite Julien Clerc song *Ma preference* (1978) instead of a François classic. Also featured on the soundtrack is Sheila & B. Devotion's *Spacer* (1979). Titled after the name of the François fanzine, **Podium** is a visually perfect recreation of the doomed singer's ethos, precisely summed up by the amazing opening credit sequence that gets its Disco sensibility exactly right while offering up so much more than a knowing saturation in the era's camp excess and glam spectacle. Nor was this the last word in French François Fever either as a bare eight years later came the biopic **Cloclo/My Way** (2012). But **Podium** really is as good as effective Disco movies get.

Disco Français 1

Daniel Bangalter is now better known as the father of Daft Punk's Thomas Bangalter. But during the Golden Era of French Disco he had numerous hits with the Gibson Brothers, Ottawan, Chocolat's, Amii Stewart and Sheila & B. Devotion. The Gibson Brothers (Chris, Patrick and Alex) might have been born on Martinique in the West Indies, but they migrated to France to record their first single in 1976. Thanks to producer/writer Daniel Vangarde (Bangalter's alias) they scored three big Disco chart successes with *Cuba* (1979), *Ooh What a Life* (1979) and *Que sera mi vida* (1979). Ottawan comprised of singers Patrick Jean-Baptiste and Annette Etilce and had massive Eurodisco hits with the catchy *D.I.S.C.O.* (1980) and its flipside, *Hands Up*.

Bangalter also made up the studio group Who's Who, who jumped aboard the Roller Disco craze with the same titled 1980 album. The opening track *Palace Palace* can only be referring to one place and that's Le Palace, the Parisian Studio 54, situated at the crossing of the Rue du Faubourg-Montmartre and the Boulevard Poissonnière, where Amanda Lear reigned supreme. Tapping into the two fads of the day, Roller Disco and non-stop whistling on the dance floor (a phallic silver disco whistle featuring erotically on the Maxi 45 colour sleeve), Bangalter clearly was a patron of the place because the entire Who's Who album is simple, funky and sleek Disco with a distinct flash of the flamboyant and foreign.

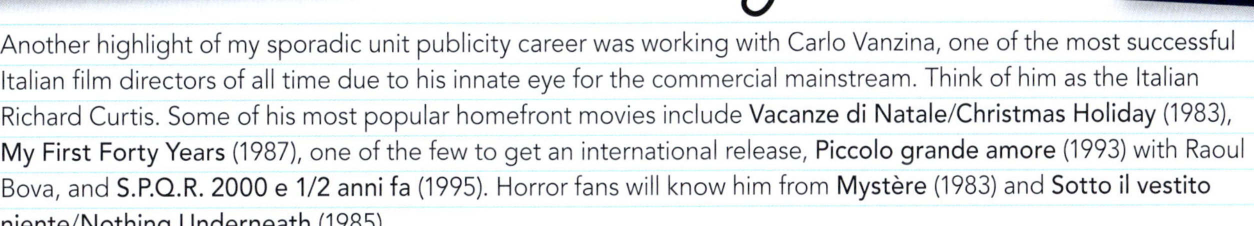

Another highlight of my sporadic unit publicity career was working with Carlo Vanzina, one of the most successful Italian film directors of all time due to his innate eye for the commercial mainstream. Think of him as the Italian Richard Curtis. Some of his most popular homefront movies include **Vacanze di Natale/Christmas Holiday** (1983), **My First Forty Years** (1987), one of the few to get an international release, **Piccolo grande amore** (1993) with Raoul Bova, and **S.P.Q.R. 2000 e 1/2 anni fa** (1995). Horror fans will know him from **Mystère** (1983) and **Sotto il vestito niente/Nothing Underneath** (1985).

Which is precisely the reason why I said yes to the job. Well, that and the fact he was the son of Steno (director of the **Totò** movies and the 1959 fave **Tempi duri per i vampiri/Uncle Was a Vampire**). **South Kensington** (2001) was devised as a shameless rip-off of **Notting Hill** (1999) with Rupert Everett and model Elle Macpherson standing in for Hugh Grant and Julia Roberts. Other cast members included Sienna Miller and the top Italian comedian of the moment Enrico Brignano, thanks to the TV sitcom 'Un medico in famiglia/A Doctor in the Family'.

Mark Ashworth was the dialogue coach so it did indeed feel like a family because of my history with Everett on **Dellamorte Dellamore/Cemetery Man** (1994) and the fact that Vanzina and Dario Argento were old friends. It was a fun picture to work on despite Macpherson being difficult – she was coming off being in the TV sit-com phenomenon 'Friends' and didn't we all know it – and Brignano being just so jokey OTT all the time. But it was precisely because of this film that I landed another dream assignment, being part of the annual Cinema Made in Italy UK Festival, held every February at the Cine Lumiere. In South Kensington! Even though I had worked on **Before Sunrise** (1995), the 'Nostromo' (1996) miniseries and wrote more non-genre reviews for the likes of 'Film Review' and 'Radio Times', I was still pigeonholed as 'The Horror Man' by people who should have known better. And it was **South Kensington** that gave me that all-round credibility. At last!

ROLL BOUNCE (2005)

Three years after spoofing the Blaxploitation era with **Undercover Brother** (2002), director Malcolm D. Lee whisked back to the 1970s again for this sociological journal of disaffected youth at the Roller Disco. However his nostalgia time machine malfunctions here because **Roll Bounce** might have all the correct pop culture references in place and polyester clothes in the wardrobe department, but it looks too pristine, comes across as too knowing and the slang dialogue feels way too up-to-date. Basically it's just not that well done and feels faked at every toe jump, triple Salchow and Lutz. Never for one moment do you feel it's 1978 although the superficial details are fun up to a certain point and the soft-rock, funk and Disco soundtrack (some artists and songs shared with **Undercover Brother**) does serious wonders for the spotty narrative.

But not since **Roller Boogie** (1979) has the roller-skating lifestyle looked so seductive in this flimsy paint-by-numbers coming-of-age chronicle. Xavier 'X' Smith (Shad Moss/ex-Lil' Bow Wow) hangs out with his smart-mouth posse at the local roller-skating rink where he's the Southside skate champion. However the place is suddenly closed down and they have to head to the glitzy Sweetwater Rink on the Northside of town where X's unrefined skills are no competition for the venue's reigning celebrity, Sweetness (Wesley Jonathan). Challenged to a skate-off by their high and mighty rivals, X deals with extra layers of stress when his beloved mother dies, the vacuum created by his uncaring absent father Curtis (Chi McBride) and the romantic overtures of hot-to-trot Naomi (Meagan Good).

With much screentime devoted to affectionately ticking off the brand names, fads, personalities and cultural touchstones of the era – Atari, **Star Wars** (1977), old Pepsi-Cola cans, the 'What's Happening!!' sit-com, Lite Brite, 'The Mod Squad', 'Happy Days', NBA star George 'Ice Man' Gervin – the racial and economic tensions central to the rink battle come a very poor second and only serve

as the weakest of plot crutches. Both sides of this familiar and formulaic African-American tween angst tale fail to jell. And it all gets in the way of the impressive skating, the only real reason to see the one-dimensional drama play out.

Filmed at the massive Lynwood Skate Center in Lynwood, Illinois, the movie's true star is cinematographer James Muro who showed his prowess directing **Street Trash** (1987) and became the Steadicam operator of choice for James Cameron. Muro's low-level camerawork is exquisite, capturing every footwork manoeuvre and roller trick with a floating rhythm and grace. Obviously this narrow focus, close-up technique has a double purpose in hiding the fact that Bow Wow and company can do few of the cool moves. Never mind, the deft collision between acrobatic highlights and smooth gliding in the fast lanes of the vast Disco space sells this roller trip down memory lane.

Backed by a serious funk and Disco soundtrack, the sounds of the mid-1970s and beyond keep the bounce buoyant with *Flashlight* (1977) by Parliament, *Bounce, Rock, Skate, Roll* (1979) by Vaughan Mason and Crew, *Emotion* (1977) by Samantha Sang, *Can You Feel the Force?* (1978) by The Real Thing, *Love to Love You Baby* (1975) by Donna Summer, *I'll Keep Lovin' You* (1977) and *Kung Fu Fighting* (1975) by Carl Douglas, *Rock the Boat* (1973) by The Hues Corporation, *I'm Your Boogie Man* (1977) by KC and The Sunshine Band, *Boogie Fever* (1975) by Sylvers, *Pick Up the Pieces* (1974) by the Average White Band, *Le Freak* (1978) by Chic, *Hollywood Swingin'* (2004) by Kool & The Gang featuring Jamiroquai, *Fire* (1974) by Ohio Players, *He's the Greatest Dancer* (1978) by Sister Sledge, and a cover version of A Taste of Honey's 1978 Roller Disco favourite *Boogie Oogie Oogie* (1978) by Brooke Valentine featuring Fabolous and Yo-Yo.

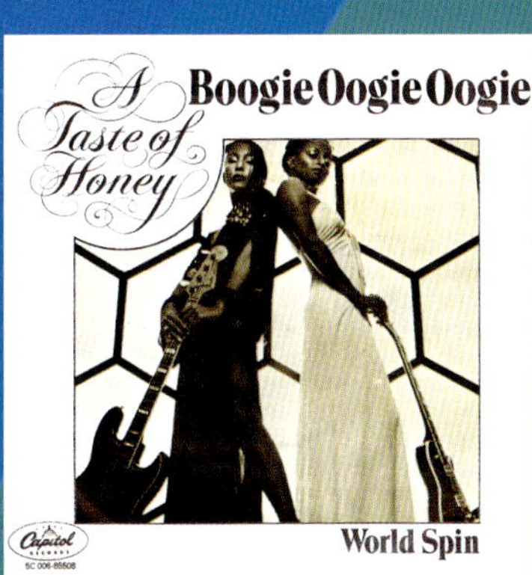

AWB

One of the best sounding – and selling – funk bands in the world was the Average White Band, a Scottish R&B group who had a series of soul and Disco hits in the 1970s. Bassist Alan Gorrie and lead guitarist Onnie McIntyre had both been members of the band Forever More before teaming up with saxophonist Malcolm Duncan, keyboardist Roger Ball and drummer Robbie McIntosh (from Brian Auger's Oblivion Express) to form AWB. McIntosh died of a drug overdose in 1974 and was replaced by fellow Oblivion Express friend Steve Ferrone.

Signed to Atlantic Records by boss Jerry Wexler when a performance at a party impressed him, their first Disco chart hit was *Pick Up the Pieces* (1974), which featured The Dundee Horns from the 1972 Johnny Nash reggae hit *I Can See Clearly Now*. With Arif Mardin (producer of the Bee Gees, Bette Midler and Diana Ross) the AWB reached gold and platinum status with their 1970s output, and their double album *Person to Person*, recorded during their 1975 American tour, remains among the best selling live funk albums ever. Their 1980 Disco hit *Let's Go Round Again* continued to market their unique but predominantly white funk sound to the black community without ever losing the core soul lover's respect.

Disco Memo

Shaun of the Dead

After appearing in a few B-movies, I finally made the hipster grade when I agreed to play a background zombie in Edgar Wright's cult classic **Shaun of the Dead** (2004). My shambling-by-telephone-box performance outside the Duke of Albany pub (39 Monson Road, London SE14) is now my most recognised movie cameo and I've lost count of how many interviews the subject has come up in. I had given Edgar a great review for his debut film **A Fistful of Fingers** (1995) and was delighted when a quote from it was printed on the poster. So when Working Title, the production company behind Edgar's romzomcom starring Simon Pegg and Nick Frost, asked me to be part of the Living Dead contingent, I didn't hesitate to say yes. For here was my chance to finally learn what it was like to go through an extensive make-up session like every major horror actor I'd ever interviewed about how awful it was.

An old library in New Cross Gate is where I had to report for my make-up application as a Prime Zombie. In my trailer were my 'Total Film' colleague Jamie Graham, also roped in to cover the shoot and be a free extra, and a young Jack Tarling, future producer of **God's Own Country** (2017) who would eventually employ me to work on the publicity of **Await Further Instructions** (2018). After customising and distressing my own khaki vest and jeans with a shirt from the wardrobe department, the hour-long makeover consisted of scabs, scar and white powder applications, with drawn mascara veins lining my face. Stage blood was thrown all over me too. And then came the worst of it – opaque contact lenses that became so irritating and tortuous to wear, I was assigned my own location nurse to administer eye-drops every thirty minutes.

Taken to the location by assigned crew (we always had to be accompanied because earlier extras had wandered off causing shocked panic on the local high street), Edgar placed me by the red telephone box with a half-eaten corpse inside. The torn flesh was effective shards of watermelon. His direction to me was "Move slowly towards the actors in ravenous hunger". After six takes he said I was convincing but all I really did was open my mouth and stare blankly. Who knew that warm June day of filming would become a potent footnote in my cameo career. What was my one overriding memory of the whole experience? Two weeks after playing my role I was in Toronto covering the making of Zack Snyder's **Dawn of the Dead** (2004) remake. And not one person in the cast or crew believed me about **Shaun of the Dead**, thinking it was my British sense of humour sending them up. Clearly Edgar definitely had the last laugh there.

POLTERGAY (2006)

Immediate Disco Alert! *No No No No* (1979) by S[heila]. B. Devotion backdrops the peekaboo credits for this supernaturally lowbrow French farce that builds towards a funky phantom finale after a rickety start. Men are dancing in L'Ambigu, a cellar Disco in the outskirts of Paris, when – *catastrophe!* – they are all electrocuted thanks to a faulty foam machine. That was in 1979 and now, 27 years later, hunky construction worker Marc (Clovis Cornillac) and archaeologist Emma (Julie Depardieu) Modena are moving into the bargain-priced dilapidated house built above the club, in the hopes of starting a family.

Soon Marc is woken up by loud music at 1.55 a.m. on the dot, flying penis logos keep being painted on the walls and his jeans are always found perfectly ironed in the wardrobe. It turns out that five gay victims of the fire are spiritually trapped in the basement thanks to the house being built on an old Templar shrine. Only he can see the ghosts at first, causing marital strife, and the belief he's in a homosexual panic over being in the closet. But after hiring an exorcist, he gets to know the camp ghouls, who decide to help him reclaim his straight life in return for Disco absolution.

It takes time for director Eric Lavaine's scrappy slapstick poltergeist riff to find its feet, but when it does, the toilet humour subsides, the well-earned laughs multiply, the sharp comments hit their target and the emotional core resonates. Only in a French movie would you find the leading man actually sexually experimenting to ascertain his true path. Cornillac is brilliant in the gay bar sequence, completely misunderstanding every pick-up cliché. The five Disco bunnies are deliberately stereotypical – the closet heterosexual, the bickering couple, the broken-hearted lover, the OTT queen – just so the point of their sobering road trip jaunt into Gay Paree can be starkly contrasted to the more liberated attitudes of the day. The jokes are sometimes crass – ghostly buttocks protruding from the wall, the Village People costume party. But then along comes the Cyrano de Bergerac romance by proxy subplot and the quite brilliant dinner table scene where Marc tells his family he might be gay, and his grandmother reveals her lesbian past over the tiramisu.

In Disco terms the actual dance hits are limited to Boney M.'s *Rasputin* (1978), which is repeated so many times you will be yelling along with Marc to "Change the goddam song!",

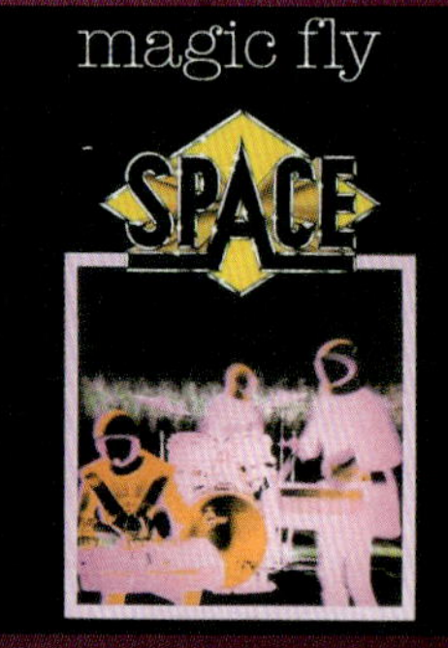

and *Born to Be Alive* (1979) by Patrick Hernandez, also sung in a smoochy rendition by star Depardieu. Most of the other dance and interstitial beats are originals by Moto & The Supermen Lovers (songwriters Guillaume Atlan and Grégory Louis): *Sensual Healing, Miami 2006, Shower Thrill and Pool Vision, Paris 1.55 AM, Under Pressure, Heartbreaker, Mea Culpa (The Supermen Lovers Remix), De Sorgues, Working Is Wonderful (La Tristesse de Joséphine), Who Cares?, Magic Pool*, and *Hermanos Dias. After Pressure* by Blackstrass, *Do It for Me* by Jennifer, *On est bien* by director Eric Lavaine, *Beata viscera* by Quattro Stagioni, *Touch-O-Drome* by Dark Love, and *Rasputin Kitchen* by Les Fantômes round out the potholed soundtrack.

Disco Français 2

Magic Fly (1977) by Space was one of those Summer Hits imported back from Eurodiscoland to take over the worldwide charts. In Britain it reached No.2 in the 'Top of the Pops' rundown, while Kebekelektrik took their identical cover version to No.9 in the 'Billboard' Disco charts. The tune was originally composed by electronica pioneer Didier Marouani as a theme for a French television programme, hosted by celebrity astrologist Elizabeth Tessier. Although well known as a singer in France – he'd toured with Johnny Hallyday and Gallic Disco sensation Claude François – Marouani's true ambitions lay in experimenting with synthesizer and keyboard techniques to create new cosmic sounds in the *Oxygène* (1976, by Jean-Michel Jarre) mode. The astrology show gave him wide latitude to compose that type of melody with futuristic sci-fi and space connotations and the result was the magnetically echoing *Magic Fly*, which ironically was never actually used in the programme.

Producer Jean-Philippe Iliesco then put Marouani with three session musicians – Jannick Top, Joe Hammer and Roland Romanelli – to form the band Space and create a full album when the infectious hi-tech track became an instant dance-floor hit. *Carry On, Turn Me On* and *Tango in Space* from the *Magic Fly* album reached No.5 in the Disco charts. The second album *Deliverance* (1977) featured lead vocals by noted session singer Madeline Bell to create other memorable Space odysseys like the fabulous title track with its synthesizer melodies augmented by a full choral chant and the sublime *Prison*. The third album, *Just Blue* (1978) put both *Save Your Love for Me* and *My Love Is Music* in the Disco charts. The band broke up soon after when Iliesco refused to let Marouani do live stage performances because he felt their sound couldn't be replicated well enough away from the studio and would hurt the brand.

James Ferman

Disco Memo

In the Bush

If you're a die-hard horror fan censorship still remains a hot-button issue. From when I first started watching X-certificate movies to the present day, where bland PG-13 rated horror seems to be the required form, I have been vociferous in condemning any kind of censorship not allowing adults to make up their own minds on what content to watch. From appearing on television panels during the stupid waste-of-time Video Nasty era to argue freedom of choice, to the moment FrightFest fell foul of the Westminster City Council for programming **A Serbian Film** (2010), based on one person complaining about it being listed in the programme, incidentally, I never stopped slagging off the BBFC despite some of the nicest people I know working there.

A turning point for me in the whole debate came on May 12th, 1976, at BAFTA in Piccadilly, when James Ferman (director of the BBFC 1975-1999) laid out his new order stall in no uncertain terms in front of an audience of invited film industry workers. Keith Williams was a member of BAFTA and used to take me to all these special events. During the course of his two-hour lecture about the evils of sex, horror and exploitation films, he showed before-and-after cut scenes and amended trailers from a diverse range of titles, all listed here for the very first time: the suggestive clipumentary **Ain't Misbehavin'** (1974), the western **Breakheart Pass** (1975), the Mondo shocker castration in **Zumbalah/Savage Man, Savage Beast** (1975), a whole reel of Michael Armstrong's torture history lesson **Mark of the Devil** (1970), the shower scene from **The Crimes of the Black Cat/Sette scialli di seta gialla** (1972), the Patty Hearst-based drama **Abduction** (1975), **The Rape** (1970), the cigarette scene from **Emmanuelle** (1974), **Hot Nights in Bangkok** (1975), **The House of Bamboo Dolls** (1973), the skin-flaying from **Rebel Nun/Flavia, la monaca musulmana** (1974), **The Texas Chain Saw Massacre** (1974), **Violent City/Roma violenta** (1975), **Framed** (1975) and various nunchuck scenes from Hong Kong martial arts titles. The trailers shown were **Boss Nigger** (1974), **The French Connection** (1971), **To the Devil a Daughter** (1976) and the aforementioned **Savage Man, Savage Beast**.

The effect all these out of context sequences had, a virtual 'That's Exploitation' catalogue, was a shock value build-up that left everyone reeling and practically only us two left in the auditorium. It was targeted theatre of the most shameless kind and put in stark relief Ferman's entitled attitude and his assumed almost divine right to protect us from this filth and atrocity. I did everything I could from that moment on to point out the ridiculousness of one man virtually telling the entire British population what was right or wrong according to his tastes. And don't get me started on Mary Whitehouse! This eventually led to a lot of my contemporaries – Mark Kermode, David McGillivray, Kim Newman and the sorely missed David Prothero – creating the anti-censorship magazine 'Scapegoat' in January 1995, with 'The Dark Side' editor Allan Bryce. It only survived one issue, mainly because once we'd gotten everything off our chests there really was nowhere else to go. But I do think we did serve some purpose in the great censor debate scheme of things.

MAMMA MIA! (2008)

The continuing love for the 1974 Eurovision-winning Swedish supergroup ABBA, and by no small means for all things glitterdust, Spandex and kitsch, turned the movie version of the hit stage musical into a global phenomenon and one of the highest grossers of all time in the U.K. Very much a musical in the classic tradition, the stage version which world premiered in London's West End on April 6th, 1999, got as many bad reviews as good, mainly because the show's creators, producer Judy Craymer, director Phyllida Lloyd and writer Catherine Johnson, went for the lowest common denominator holiday romance melodrama to hang a winning bunch of catchy ABBA hits on.

Film buffs everywhere knew from the start it was merely a rip-off of **Buona Sera, Mrs. Campbell** (1968), starring Gina Lollobrigida. But such was ABBA's gold-plated repertoire that the money, money, money-minting jukebox musical was cause for mass global celebration and a revival of Agnetha, Benny, Bjorn and Anni-Frid/Frida's fortunes, culminating in the incredible 'ABBA: Voyage' virtual reality concert event. The dancing in the aisles aspect that transferred from the theatre to the cinema turned every showing into a Wedding Disco, especially as many of the ABBA songs featured became major club hits.

The very starry cast plays it to the hilt in the apricot-glazed looking movie version, which Phyllida Lloyd directed once more in her obvious, plain style. Former singer Donna (Meryl Streep) has raised her daughter Sophie (Amanda Seyfried) alone on the remote Greek Island resort of Kalokairi. When Sophie finds her mother's diary it reveals there are three men who might be her father (Pierce Brosnan, Colin Firth, Stellan Skarsgard). About to be married to Sky (Dominic Cooper), she secretly invites all three to the wedding. How will mum and her two best friends (Julie Walters, Christine Baranski) react? And so the sunny scene is set for songs to be slyly introed, clumsy dancing to end in the crystalline blue waters and forgiveness taken a chance on.

While Streep blazes on *The Winner Takes It All* (1980) and Brosnan reveals he can't sing a note on their duet *When All Is Said and Done* (1982), a No.8 dance chart hit, the Disco aspect is well served by Seyfried and Cooper's cover of the No.1 hit *Lay All Your Love on Me* (1980), ditto *Super Trouper* (1980), and ensemble covers of *Voulez-Vous* (1979) and the classic nightclub wind-down anthem *Dancing Queen* (1976) performed by Streep, Walters and Baranski.

A decade later came the even more decayed sequel-cum-prequel **Mamma Mia! Here We Go Again** (2018) using reprises from the original movie and ABBA's less familiar album tracks. Flatly directed by Ol Parker (because **Imagine Me and You**, 2005, resided in the same marriage ballpark), the wafer-thin plot flashbacks to Donna's adventurous past, outlining its impact on Sophie's future. Occasional fun twinkles aside, this solely commercially driven venture amounted to little beyond the returning superstars (with additions Lily James, adorable as young Donna, and Cher hilarious as the grandmother) performing yet more quality Europop in sun-kissed, summer holiday surroundings. The autoDisco ambience here comes from *Angel Eyes* (1979) by Walters, Baranski and Seyfried, with an ensemble *Dancing Queen* and credit-accompanying *Super Trouper* picking up the slack. ABBA's two other Disco chart hits – *On and On and On* (1981) and *The Visitors* (1982) – still lie waiting in the wings for a promised/threatened third outing…

ABBA Land

With ABBA sweeping everything else away on Swedish shores during the latter 1970s, and forging the way to an Abbatar gig future with their extraordinary, jaw-dropping and groundbreaking ABBA: Voyage ILM created spectacular, what other Disco Dansbands were there? And why did they all wear extravagant Boney M.-style satin, sequins and Lurex? The latter question is easily answered – performers found a Scandinavian tax loophole allowing 'fantasy' outfits, i.e. ones not worn during average daily life, to be income deductible. The former a bit harder as the shadow of ABBA's global domination loomed so large. But there was bandleader Lars 'Lasse' Samuelson's *Disco-Dance-Party* (1978), Glendisco's *Live Fast, Love Hard and Die Young* (1980), Disco cover artists extraordinaire Little Mike and The Sweet Soul Music Band's *Get On Up!* (1983), The Impossibles' *Hot Pepper* (1975), the unfortunately named Schytts and their Schlager-infused *Hålligång 6* (1976) album, Caddies and their *Paint It Black* (1980) Disco cover, and Shine's *Dance-O-Matic* (1983).

The Swedish Disco Princesses title landed squarely at the feet of sisters Inga-Lill and Susanne Päivärinta, or simply Lili and Sussie. While *Candy Love* (1986) was the song that put them on the dancefloor, they scored their biggest break in 1987 with the Eurodisco derivation *Oh Mama*, complete with lyrics alluding to past club hits as in the line "Oh Mama can't you tell, If he wants my love will he ring my bell?", and followed it with *We Were Only Dancing* (1988), *What's the Colour of Love* (1990), *Boyfriend* (1990) and *Okey, Okey!*, the latter a Eurovision Song Contest hopeful in 1989.

The Last Days of Starburst

My 'Starburst' critic career came juddering to a halt in October 2008 with the last issue published under the Visual Imagination Ltd. moniker. A death of a key team member in the company caused untold problems and hardship, meaning editor Stephen Payne sold the title. After three decades of reviewing every single genre title released I greeted the news with both sadness and relief. Keeping on top of release dates, plus my FrightFest duties expanding as the festival exploded, was quite a juggling act. My last six reviews were for **The Dark Knight**, **Hellboy II: The Golden Army**, **The X Files: I Want to Believe**, **Journey to the Center of the Earth 3D**, **Hancock** and **The Ruins**. Not a bad swansong.

It became clear very early on in my tenure at 'Starburst' that Payne would publish what I wrote no matter the length. Because I was paid by word count then I droned on for pages and when I look back at some of those reviews I can't believe I managed to fill up so much space with such no-mark titles as **Zone Troopers** (1985) or **America 3000** (1986). I'm proud my reviews have stood the test of time too. I was right about **Blade Runner** (1982) being a classic when practically everyone else hated it at the time, despite what their revisionist selves say now. I did get **Howard the Duck** (1986) wrong but my excuse for liking it so much is because I saw it at a Hollywood preview in a longer cut that was never seen again. Keith Williams and Russell Mulcahy were living in Hollywood at the time and I would go and hang out with them when the blockbuster season was about to start so I could get the edge on everything release delayed in the UK.

AJ, Russell Mulcahy and Keith Williams in LA at producer Patrick Wachsberger's house.

Out of all the years I did my 'Starburst' column, there was only one month I couldn't review any new releases. I had intended to fill my March 1991, issue No.151, preview rundown with **The Silence of the Lambs**, **Misery**, **Highlander II: The Quickening** and **Edward Scissorhands**. But word got back to the distributors of each about my plans and I was put under an immediate embargo for every single one. Back in those days company press officers had monthly meetings where they'd discuss their opinions of each critic and their practices. Apparently my name used to be raised quite a lot! Anyway, due to that unforeseen circumstance I was forced for the first time ever to review three noteworthy straight-to-video releases, Tommy Lee Wallace's **Stephen King's It** (1990) miniseries, Larry Cohen's **The Ambulance** (1990) and Tobe Hooper's **I'm Dangerous Tonight** (1990). Even though that was a pretty good trio, the complaints were many, and I never did it again, embargoes be damned.

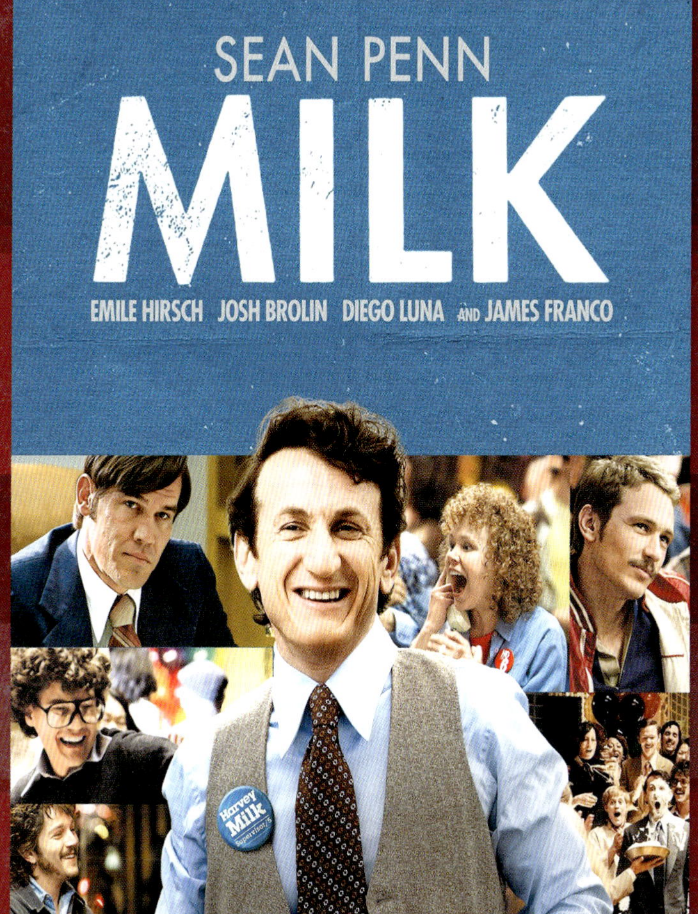

MILK (2008)

Rob Epstein's great Academy Award winning documentary **The Times of Harvey Milk** (1984) practically served as the template for Gus Van Sant's pet project about the first openly gay person elected to office in California, in 1977. Cannily scripted by Dustin Lance Black (Olympic diving champion Tom Daley's husband) and headlining a head-turning Oscar winning portrayal of the Jewish politician by a cosmetically transformed Sean Penn (again!), **Milk** became a pointedly mainstream cry of anger for homosexual rights. Something remarked on by Penn and Black at the Academy Awards due to the vocal anti-gay protesters outside the Kodak Theatre in Hollywood. "You commie, homo-loving sons of guns" was Penn's amusingly pithy acceptance speech.

For fifteen years Van Sant had unsuccessfully tried to get this subject on screen. The first attempt was an adaptation of the 1982 Randy Shilts' biography 'The Mayor of Castro Street', but in the wake of the groundbreaking, yet total flop, release of director Arthur Hiller's gay romance **Making Love** (1982), the idea was quickly shelved. However, as a more vocal gay community continued to emerge in the wake of the AIDS crisis, attitudes slowly began to change and Focus Features bit the bullet to take a chance on Van Sant adding an art-house lustre to the controversial proceedings. Any of the original casting choices – Robin Williams, Richard Gere, Daniel Day-Lewis, James Woods – would have easily made the grade but Penn's bad boy reputation and determined political viewpoint sealed the deal.

He's absolutely on point as the ugly American first seen picking up young stud Scott Smith (James Franco) on the New York subway and beginning an unlikely but enduring relationship based on understated charm and charisma as much as sexual needs. Moving to San Francisco in 1972, the couple set up a camera shop in the Castro district where Harvey became famous as a gay activist and neighbourhood fixer, boycotting products to make a pink-dollar stand. Elected as a district supervisor in 1977, his political ambitions and influence seemed to be leading to the mayoral heights.

But his jubilant grassroots campaign and fight against Proposition 6 – a suggested statewide referendum to fire gay schoolteachers – put him into direct conflict with newly elected supervisor, fireman Dan White (Oscar-winning Josh Brolin). So offended by this attack on family values, White shot and killed both Milk and Mayor George Moscone (Victor Garber) on November 27, 1978. White pleading diminished capacity was infamously dubbed the 'Twinkie Defense' – too much junk food fuelled his depression – and two years after serving a five-year prison sentence he committed suicide.

Filmed on the actual locations the events all took place and using judicious archival footage from the 1950/60s of gay harassment by police and Board of Supervisors' head Dianne Feinstein announcing the murders, Van Sant never demonises White, just illuminates the facts from both ends of the spectrum. The unfolding reality united an entire city, first in grief, then violent rage, and the beauty of the biopic comes from that balanced frankness. Although the viewer is privy to political speeches and campaign tactics, the effect is not remotely one of worthiness as San Francisco is vibrantly shown as the gay Mecca it was at the time, with its eternal sunshine climate, relaxed atmosphere, casual openness, sly banter and sensual Disco mischievousness.

Love and amyl nitrate was indeed in the air if the **Milk** soundtrack is anything to go by. A popular joke of the day went: Where's the best place to dance in America? San FranDisco! And that's certainly the diverse case here as showcased by *Rock the Boat* (1973) by The Hues Corporation, *Everyday People* (1968) by Sly and the Family Stone, *Love in C Minor* (1976) by Cerrone, *The Player* (1974) by First Choice, and by Sylvester, the San Francisco gay icon himself, *You Make Me Feel (Mighty Real)* (1978).

West Coast Disco

San Francisco remains a cultural Mecca for the trendsetter. Bohemians made their home there in the 1950s. The Summer of Love was born at the Haight-Ashbury crossroads in the Flower Power 1960s. It was gay-friendly in the 1970s before that term had even been coined, thanks in no small part to author Armistead Maupin and his 'Tales of the City' series. And it was also the birthplace of many independent Disco record labels. Moby Dick Records was perhaps the most distinguished, owned by Bill Motley and Victor Swedosh, and named after the latter's popular gay bar in the heaving Castro district. Their main claim to fame was the Boys Town Gang, formed in the Village People mould to cater to the Californian city's large gay community.

Bill Motley

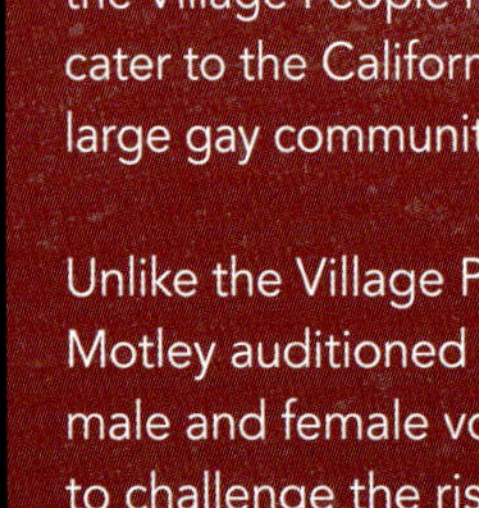

Unlike the Village People, Motley auditioned both male and female vocalists to challenge the rising local talent pool of Sylvester, Two Tons O' Fun and Patrick Cowley. Cabaret singer Cynthia Manley took lead vocals on the group's first No.5 Disco success – the Diana Ross Motown medley *Ain't No Mountain High Enough/Remember Me* (1981). But it was the cutting edge album title

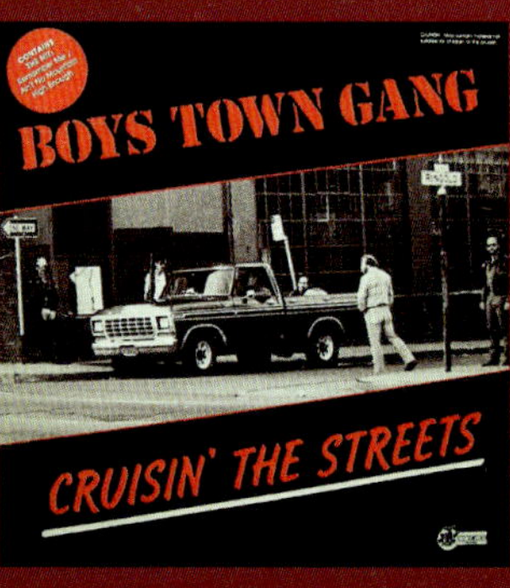

Patrick Cowley and Sylvester

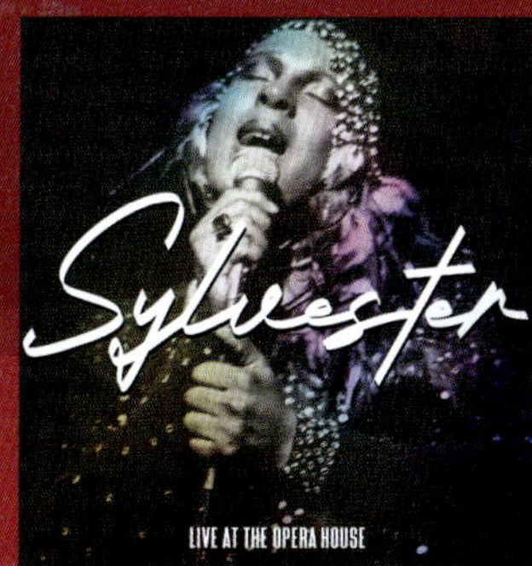

track *Cruisin' the Streets* which raised eyebrows for being a 13-minute gay porno fantasy complete with graphic sex act and peppered with startling four-letter words.

Motley wanted a less earthy voice for the next album *Disc Charge* (1981) and chose Jackson Moore for the stunning tracks *Disco Kicks* and *You're the One*, both reaching No.6 on the Disco chart. But the Disco perennial from that album remains the cover version of the Frankie Valli 1967 standard *Can't Take My Eyes Off You*. Considered the last great Disco record because very few releases after it used an orchestral backing (computer keyboards being the Latest Big Thing), it's an upbeat, classic construction of driving beat, melody and hook lines capturing a celebratory snapshot of the entire era. It was Moore (she later teamed up with Jimmy Ruffin for the HiNRG hit *I'm Gonna Love You Forever*, 1984) with back-up singers Tom Morely and Bruce Carlton who exhaustively toured the world when the track became a massive global hit.

Moby Dick also released Patrick Cowley's protégé (Frank) Loverde's *Die Hard Lover* (1982), Peter Griffin's *Step By Step* (1981), Yvonne Elliman's *Love Pains* (1982), the thrilling Lisa's *Rocket to Your Heart* (1983) and powerhouse Italian producer Celso Valli's Passengers output. Producers Ian Guenther and Willi Morrison also provided the exceptionally driving dark slice of comic book electronica *The Ultimate Warlord* (1979) by The Immortals.

Written by Muff Murfin, the producer of *The Ultimate Warlord*, Technique's ABBA-esque *Can We Try Again?* (1983) was produced by celebrity DJ Michael/Mike Lewis. The producer most associated with the Moby Dick label and also the Disconet remix service was a much sought after DJ on the West Coast and had residencies in the foremost Los Angeles clubs Studio One, Circus Disco and Probe, and the Trocadero Transfer and The Detour in San Francisco. While Lewis put his signature traditional Disco stamp on major cuts by the Boys Town Gang and Passengers, *Can We Try Again?* remains his signature endeavour.

For many though Sylvester is the Queen of San FranDisco. No other gay artist has been able to capture that indefinable Disco magic than the grandson of celebrated 1930s jazz singer Julia Morgan, and former member of The Cockettes, who will always be remembered for his mega-smash *You Make Me Feel (Mighty Real)* (1978). It was producer Harvey Fuqua who recognised Sylvester James' raw talent, insolent manner, non-conformist attitudes, ability to consistently shock, and gender unspecific stage presence. Together they made Sylvester a brand name on the global gay circuit especially when he teamed up with fellow gay icon Patrick Cowley and his signature sound for *Do You Wanna Funk?* (1982). One of the more unique results of their union was the hypnotic, spacey shuffler *I Need Somebody to Love Tonight* (1979), the B-side of *I (Who Have Nothing)*, a superb cover of the 1961 Italian classic by Joe Sentieri, that proved Sylvester lived to push Disco to a higher artistic plateau along with *Stars* (1979), *Can't Stop Dancing* (1979) and *Someone Like You* (1986) before becoming a 1988 AIDS casualty.

Patrick Cowley was a man ahead of his time too – both musically and tragically. In common with what Giorgio Moroder was doing in Munich, Cowley in San Francisco pioneered and hugely influenced electronic dance music, putting the Megatone Records label he owned with Marty Blecman on the Disco map. Before computers and synthesizers could punch up atmospheric effects, Cowley crafted his music the hard way, painstakingly patching his own programs by hand to create his trademark gay club sound. Like his entire body of work (including productions for his friends and Megatone stable mates Sylvester and Paul Parker, *Right on Target*, 1983, and epic remixes of *Hills of Katmandu*, 1979, and *I Feel Love*, 1977), the three-album output *Megatron Man* (1981), *Menergy* (1981) and *Mind Warp* (1982) came to define the highs of early 1980s gay culture. And the decade's lows too as Cowley was one of the very first famous people to fall victim to AIDS complications, dying November 12th, 1982.

Lucky Star

Thanks to my three-decade reign as the 'Starburst' magazine film critic, ditto for 'Film Review' and my on-going 'Radio Times' career, I have been quoted on so many UK posters – and a few international ones too – I've lost count. It was such a thrill to begin with. **The Terminator** (1984) and **Explorers** (1985) were two of my earliest and I remember so well being a headline quote on **A Nightmare on Elm Street 3: Dream Warriors** (1987), with artwork by my friend and future FrightFest/Trieste Science+Fiction Festival poster artist Graham Humphreys. That poster was the first to put my name in lights outside the sadly missed Odeon West End in Leicester Square and I remember shamelessly posing underneath it for photo opportunities as I accidentally on purpose drifted by the outside. I've always been happy to promote the underdog titles too, like Mark Romanek's little remembered **Static** (1985), because they are the films you can really help by praising. That ethos remains something I believe in regarding FrightFest inclusion too.

Only rarely have I felt embarrassed by a poster quote. In one such instance I wrote a scathing review of Steven Lisberger's sci-fi adventure **Slipstream** (1989), which upset me because producer Gary Kurtz was a good friend at the time due to our **Star Wars** (1977) connection. Would you believe it, a line was taken out of complete context – "A great performance by Mark Hamill" – and splashed above the title. I was mortified and my protestations led to the eventual Gentlemen's Agreement amongst critics and distributors not to play so fast and loose with review quotes. Eventually the US side of the film business cracked down hard on the scam and made it a legal requirement to notify whatever critic about their publicity intentions. Hard lessons were learned and since those days I have always insisted on approval for any quote used by anyone. I related all of this on camera, plus a few more pithy insights into my career in total, for the thus far unreleased documentary **No Stars** (2022) by director Daniel Rodriguez.

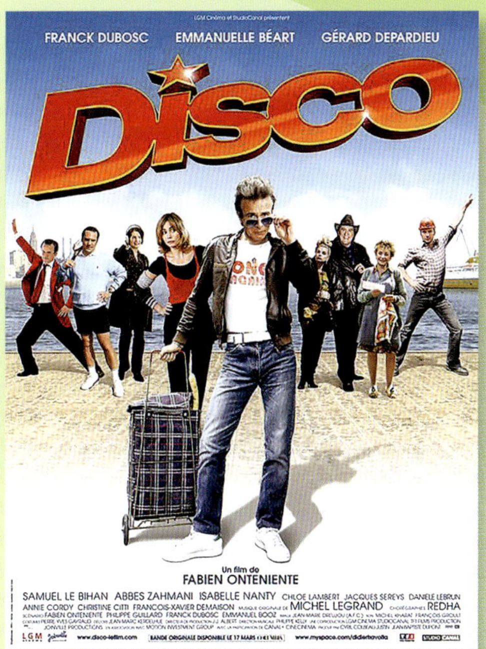

DISCO (2008)

Director Fabien Onteniente owed veteran French star Franck Dubosc a big favour. Their film **Camping** (2006), based on a sketch by the actor, had become a Gallic comedy sensation, enough to spawn two later sequels in 2010 and 2016. But in the first rush of success they both wanted to work together on something else they could really enjoy. The irresistible, charming and enormously funny result was **Disco**, in which a 40-year-old admirer of Boney M. – that is, until the drummer died! – realises that the powerful attraction of the music doesn't have to end when you reach a certain age. It's a religion and can provide everlasting lessons for love, life and family. And in relaying this message in the sweetest, loveliest and smartest way possible, **Disco** provided an instruction manual for every Disco fan, whatever the age.

Beginning just like **Saturday Night Fever** (1977) only with Didier Travolta (Dubosc), the surname his teenage nickname thanks to youthful Disco prowess, struts through the streets of Le Havre with a shopping trolley, not a paint tin. Unemployed but an eternal optimist, Didier has just learnt his estranged British wife won't let their son Brian spend the summer with him in the French port, unless he has a proper holiday plan. Enter old friend Jean-François (Gerard Depardieu) who has just taken over management of the Gin Fizz Disco determined to bring back the 1970s with a dance contest, the top prize a trip for two to Australia.

So Didier gets his old dance trio The Bee Kings back together to increase his winning chances to take Brian away for an unforgettable trip. Docker union head Walter (Samuel Le Bihan) has called a strike so has plenty of time to practice. But Darty store worker Neuneuil (Abbes Zahmani) is studying for a management position and his wife Coco (Christine Citti) would be furious if he neglected his homework. By a miracle they get through the elimination round (Neuneuil does a runner spying Coco in the audience) but Didier knows they need to work on their moves. Enter single dance teacher France (Emmanuelle Béart) whose posh family want her to get married, but not to a no account/no prospects loser like Didier. Does romance rear its head? Do The Bee Kings on scorching form win the contest? The answers are a bit more bittersweet in the typical Cinema Français tradition than expected.

Disco is wall-to-wall Disco in terms of production design (the competition venues Gin Fizz, The Pirate and the Macumba club are all Mecca Ballroom perfect), costume design (Didier's array of Bee Gees and spangly logo T-shirts and John Travolta cameo necklace), choreography (the 'Windmill of Love' gets a welcome update and look for the signature Claude François moves) and the dialogue fizzes with hilarious moments relating to every aspect of club mindset and etiquette (the argument over what music to dance their routine to – Patrick Hernandez, Boney M. or Eartha Kitt, and Jean-François supposedly owing money to Cerrone and Patrick Juvet).

Then there's the soundtrack, which works as sly comments on the visuals as well as the dance routine backing tracks: *Sunny* (1976) and *Daddy Cool* (1976) by Boney M., *Boogie Wonderland* (1979) and *September* (1977) by Earth, Wind & Fire, *Kung Fu Fighting* (1974) by Carl Douglas, *Give Me Love* (1977), *Supernature* (1977) and *Laisser toucher* (2007) by Cerrone, *From East to West* (1977) by Voyage, *I Love to Love* (1976) by Tina Charles, *Never Can Say Goodbye* (1974) by Gloria Gaynor, *Last Dance* (1978) by Donna Summer, *H.A.P.P.Y. Radio* (1979) by Edwin Starr, *It's Raining Men* (1982) by The Weather Girls, *You Make Me Feel (Mighty Real)* (1978) by Sylvester, and *Tu sais je t'aime/You Know I Love You* by Shake (1976).

Elsewhere Tina Arena sings the **Saturday Night Fever** title theme *Night Fever* while Philippe Kelly tackles the classic *How Deep Is Your Love*. Christophe Willem sings cover versions of *September* and the Dionne Warwick 1982 hit *Heartbreaker*, and the *Disco* title theme is by DJ Milan featuring Nivo.

The soundtrack is just fabulous, but the real treat is Gloria Gaynor's latterday 1992 entry *First Be a Woman* accompanying a montage of The Bee Kings getting their act together and taking it on the dance floor. From Depardieu in an afro wig, and a random pigeon too, to Dubosc dancing in his tighty-whiteys while banging out a 4/4 beat on his heart, **Disco** puts a permanent smile on the face and leaves it there long after the credits have finished rolling. A total joy and another Disco movie absolute must-see.

Disco Français 3

Okay, we know all about Cerrone, Voyage, Sheila B. Devotion, Patrick Juvet and Space. But coming a close second to those acts in hitting the Disco stratosphere was Santa Esmeralda, put together by Leroy Gomez, a Cape Cod native of Portuguese descent, who moved to Paris in the mid-1970s to become an in-demand session musician. His idea to Discofy The Animals' classic 1965 hit *Don't Let Me Be Misunderstood* along with Latin licks, Flamenco *frisson* and a driving beat broke record sales all over Europe in 1977 and reached No.4 on the 'Billboard' Disco charts. Gomez left the group to pursue a solo career with the *Gypsy Woman* (1978) album and Jimmy Goings took over, hitting Disco paydirt again with another cover of a smash by The Animals, this time 1964's *The House of the Rising Sun* (1977). After adding *Sevilla Nights* to the **Thank God it's Friday** (1978) soundtrack, the ultra-catchy *Another Cha Cha* (1979) came next but it was all over for the group by 1982.

Other global Gallic offerings came from Belle Epoque and the *Miss Broadway* (1977) album featuring the umpteenth Disco cover version of the Los Bravos 1966 hit *Black Is Black*, and the Cerrone assembled Kongas with *Africanism/Gimme Some Lovin'/Dr. Doo-Dah* (1977). Most home grown French Disco stayed at home, like *Tout petit la planete* (1978) by Plastic Bertrand (aka Roger Allen François Jouret), who never topped *Ça plane pour moi* (1977), the one on which he didn't sing – Lou Deprijck did the honours. Other determinedly French Disco acts include *Super Star* (1978) by Contessa, *Music Madness* (1980) by Beckie Bell, *Toulouse* (1976) by Toulouse, *(Love) Will Call On You* (1979) by Didier Makaga, *Casbah in Cairo* (1978) by Sabine Sauvant, *When the Sun Goes Down* (1978) by Monserate featuring Lyda Zamora, *If/My Life* (1978) by Soraya, *Hot Love in Spain* (1978) by Crystal Grass, *Queens of Space* (1978) by Akka B, *Lady Jones* (1975) by Over Drive, *Gibraltar* (1977) by Marc Chantereau, and *Un fait divers et rien de plus* (1982) by Le Club.

Three French movies provided Les Discotheques with dance material. Veteran composer Francis Lai wrote *À nous deux* (1979) for the same titled Claude Lelouch crime drama starring Catherine Deneuve. **Story of O/Histoire d'O** (1975)

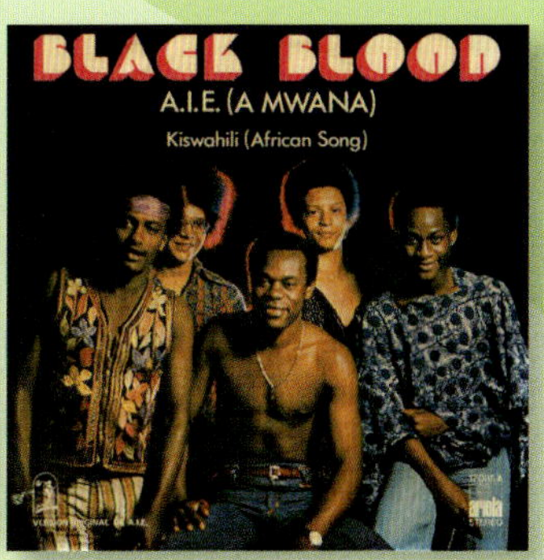

star Corinne Cléry did double duty in the controversial Just Jaeckin directed S&M romance by also singing the upbeat theme song *Je ne suis que de l'amour* written by Pierre Bachelet. And Bachelet also took the song *Hors piste* (1979) onto the Disco floor because it was featured in the comedy blockbuster **French Fried Vacation 2/Les bronzés font du ski**.

Particular note should be paid to Black Blood's early Swahili Disco hit *Aie A Mwana* (1975), which became the first British release for Bananarama in 1981. The 1977 self-titled album by Arpadys featured early Space Funk Disco – the same trio also headlined V.I.P. Connection and their amazing Disco belter *Please Love Me Again* (1975). Candy Sylver's double A-side *How Is Love/Cry Me a River* (1977) is pure Space/*Magic Fly* (1977) as is The Droids' *Star Peace* (1978) album featuring the Star Warsy *(Do You Have) The Force Parts 1 & 2* complete with R2-D2 sound effects.

Rose Laurens crooned one of the biggest gay anthems of the 1980s. *American Love* was the export version of her 1985 French hit *Quand tu pars* and became a massive global *chanson d'amour*. But the biggest Eurodisco smash the former singer with the progressive rock band Sandrose had was with *Africa* (1982), written by Jean-Michel Bériat, a Dalida colleague, and Jean-Pierre Goussaud who penned for Celine Dion. A celebration of the Dark Continent, sung in her signature velvet chocolate style, Laurens sang the original French version of *I Dreamed a Dream* from the soon-to-be 1985 musical blockbuster 'Les Miserables'.

Perhaps the best undiscovered French Disco album is by John Ozila. *Africa Goes Disco* (1978) has catchy tunes, atmospheric production values (by Gérard Hugé) and call-and-response vocals making it a hypnotic and addictive dance experience. *Hey Macumba* is a funky singalong, *Harlem Reggae* a rolling lilter, *La koumba* synth textured bliss, *Kandika* a percussion symphony and *Kon Tiki* an early rapper. Everything blends and every track is something special, the reason why it was huge all over Africa, but remains undeservedly obscure on every other continent.

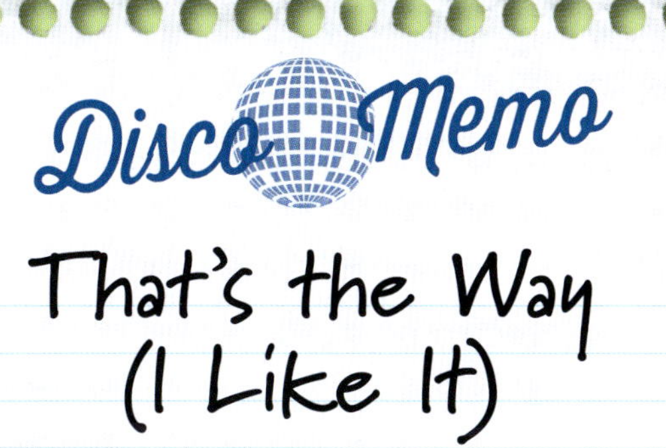

That's the Way (I Like It)

One place all horror fans rushed to see forbidden uncut movies was the National Film Theatre, an oasis for art-house sleaze back in those dark old days. Keith Williams had got quite friendly with one usherette there, Maureen Maron, and one day he asked her if she'd like to join us to see a double-bill at the ABC Edgware Road where the Hilton London Metropole Hotel now stands. On March 30th, 1977, we paid our 95p ticket and took our seats to watch **Shudder/Kiss of the Tarantula** (1976) and **Chained Women** (1973), which Maureen absolutely hated. A few weeks later I arrived at the NFT to see some long-forgotten attraction and saw Maureen collecting the tickets. As I approached her to say hello, her face dropped with a look of utter dismay. "What's wrong", I asked? "Oh, nothing", she said, "It's just that now when I see you here to watch something I know it's going to be absolutely terrible!" Many decades later that comment still makes me laugh. And so does the classic 1979 marquee at the ABC Edgware Road advertising **10 Meatballs Escape from Alcatraz!**

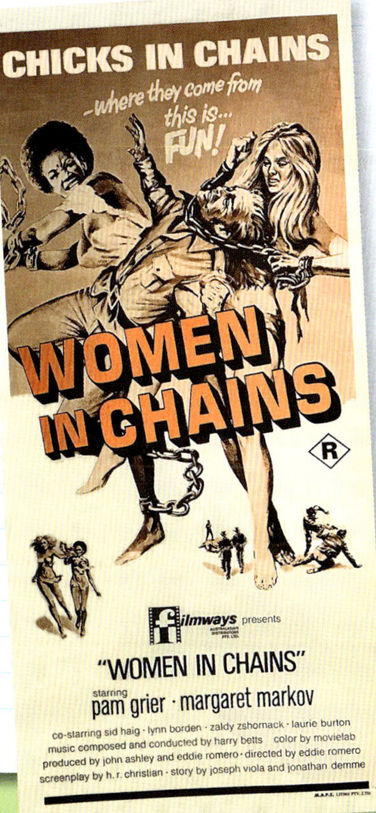

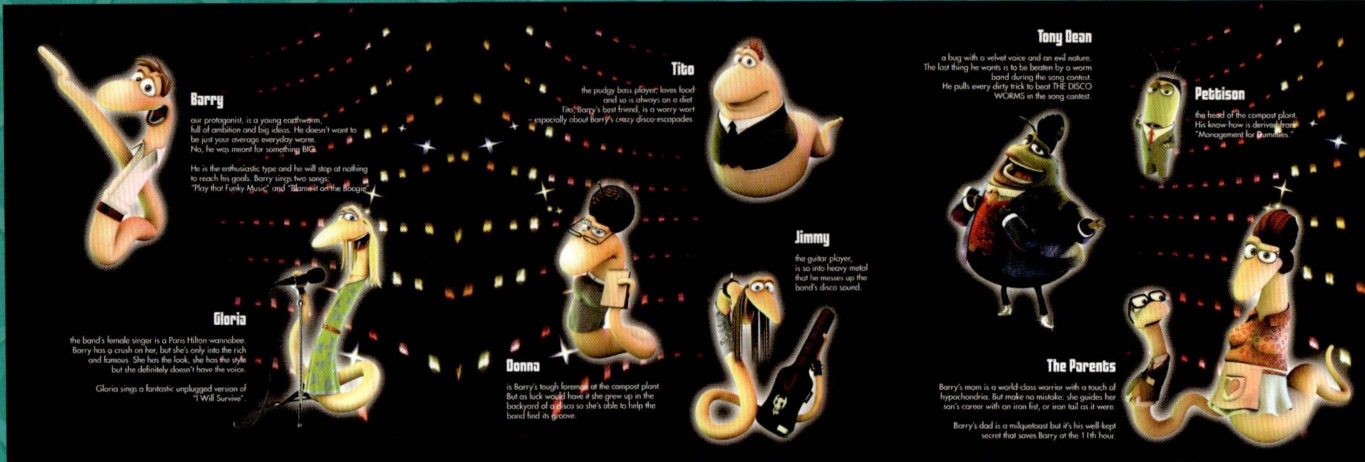

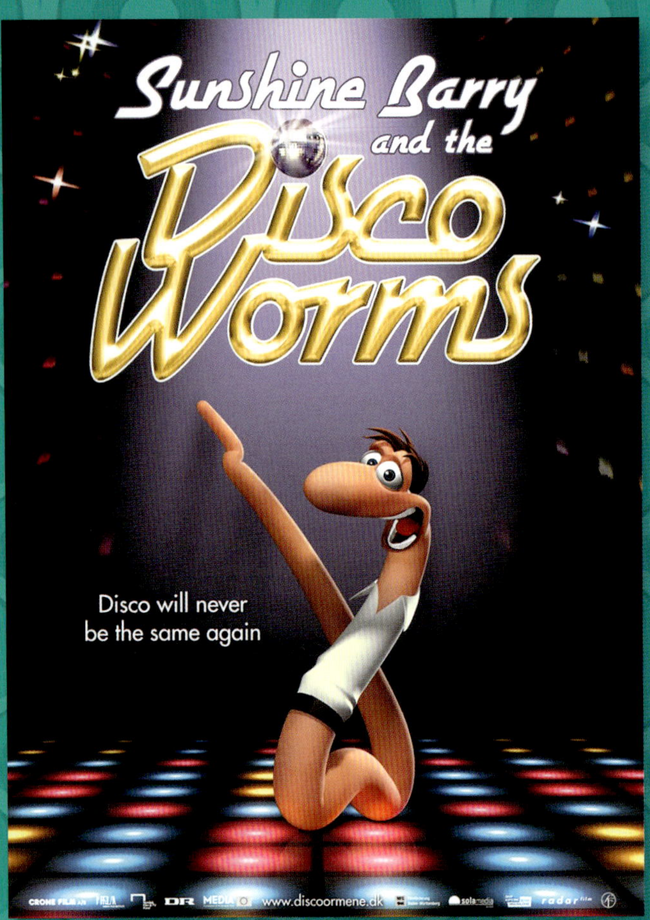

SUNSHINE BARRY AND THE DISCO WORMS / DISCO ORMENE (2008)

Director Thomas Borch Nielsen turned his love of earthworms into this animation treat for all Disco lovers. The noted Danish visual effects supervisor on Ole Bornedal's sci-fi horror **The Substitute** (2007) and **I Am Dina** (2002) often walked alone picking up his favourite breed of worms and moving them to safety. One evening he was pursuing this eco hobby while listening to his iPod. The moment Wild Cherry's *Play That Funky Music* (1976) started, he looked at the wriggling worm in his hand and had a "Eureka!" moment – a Disco Worm – and the central concept for this appealing cartoon was born.

Barry (voiced by Peter Frödin) is a young earthworm fed up with being bottom of the food chain in his own backyard, his only future prospect a mid-level management career in the compost-making industry. But then Barry gets passed down a box containing his father's dusty memorabilia and inside is an old Disco album. Immediately smitten by the boogie, the 4/4 beat enters his bloodstream, makes his body move and he's just gotta sing, gotta dance. Assembling a motley crew of friends with raw talent, including crush Gloria (Trine Dyrholm), who all need plenty of practice and finessing, Sunshine Barry and the Disco Worms are born. All they have to do is beat the evil balladeer beetle Tony Dean (Henning Jensen) in an upcoming talent contest to realise their mirrorball dreams.

Easy on the eyes, while not exactly up to Pixar standards, the animation technique sparkles with enough clean lines and vibrant colour while the comedy shtick and visual detailing are enormous fun. As with most family-orientated cartoons, there is a disguised message contained in the frantic action. Here it's that ye olde reliable Disney standby of yore, believe in yourself to succeed in your dream ambitions, coupled with class discrimination is bad but community values are good.

It's also very easy on the ears too. Plainly the budget couldn't stretch to licensing the Disco gold standards any self-respecting tribute band would sing. So Nielsen rounded up a Kool Gang of Scandinavian singers to record cover versions of iconic tracks. Martin Hedegaard

performs Earth, Wind & Fire's *Boogie Wonderland* (1979), Soundfactory featuring Mavelicious do The Trammps' *Disco Inferno* (1976), Ida Corr does Diana Ross' *Upside Down* (1980), Sophie does Baccara's *Yes Sir, I Can Boogie* (1977), Magnus Carlsson does the Village People's *Y.M.C.A.* (1978), Velvet sings Donna Summer's *Love to Love You Baby* (1975), and Lizzie takes on Chic's *Le Freak* (1978).

Featured voice talents Frödin and Dyrholm duet for The Jacksons' *Blame It on the Boogie* (1978), while the former solos on *Play That Funky Music* and the latter sings Gloria Gaynor's megabuster *I Will Survive* (1978). An absolutely charming cartoon, with every Disco element present and strobe-lit correct, it ends pitch-perfectly with Andreas Van Lunteren's version of that Morris Albert schmaltz classic, *Feelings* (1974).

Mickey Mouse Disco

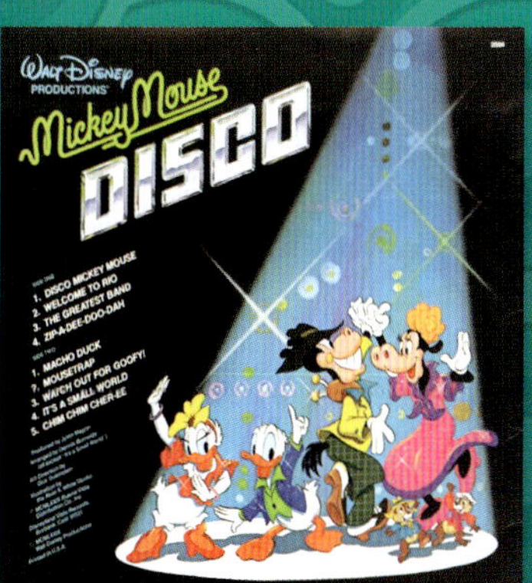

In order to update the Mickey Mouse brand, the Disney Studio hit on the idea of rereleasing extracts from some of their classic short cartoons – **Mr. Duck Steps Out** (1940), **Mickey's Birthday Party** (1942) and **The Three Caballeros** (1944) to name just three – synchronised to modern 'pop music', already released on a Disneyland album in 1975. The successful result of that experiment finally saw Disneyland Records get with the Disco programme in 1979 with another range of dance originals and reworked classics. The accompanying 7-minute compilation short proved very popular with cinema audiences when it played second bill to the likes of **Herbie Goes Bananas!** (1980).

A canny marketing tool it might have been by the Mouse House, but the surprise was how Disco Good a few of the nine songs on the album actually were, the cover art displaying Mickey and Minnie in typical **Saturday Night Fever** (1977) pose. *Disco Mickey Mouse* kicks off the foot tapping and Ritchie Family homage with keen and quite suspenseful glissandos. *The Greatest Band* is standard Kool & the Gang, while little is done with *Zip-A-Dee-Doo-Dah* (from **Song of the South**, 1946) apart from an upbeat arrangement fix. *Macho Duck* is pure Village People with Donald getting in on the vocal action. *Mousetrap* is funky filler and that annoying Sherman Brothers' earworm *It's a Small World* merely plods along on an averagely booming keel.

But the three stand-out cuts are *Welcome to Rio*, a super Mike Theodore Orchestra style South American riff by way of Santa Esmeralda and Carmen Miranda, the zippy Brass Construction-tastic instrumental version of *Chim Chim Cher-ee* from **Mary Poppins** (1964), with the definite jewel in the crown, *Watch Out for Goofy!* Written by George Charouhas and Steven Bruce Furman, the latter is a sophisticated production containing great melody and lyrical content portraying Goofy as a Disco Demolition on the dancefloor. As with most of the deft Imagineering by Disney personnel, this idea eventually grew into a successful series on The Disney Channel, in which popular songs by name artists were synchronised to classic cartoon content.

My Favourite Things

In all the many newspaper articles, documentaries and books where I have played a key Punk reminiscence role, these are my three favourite on-point quotes:

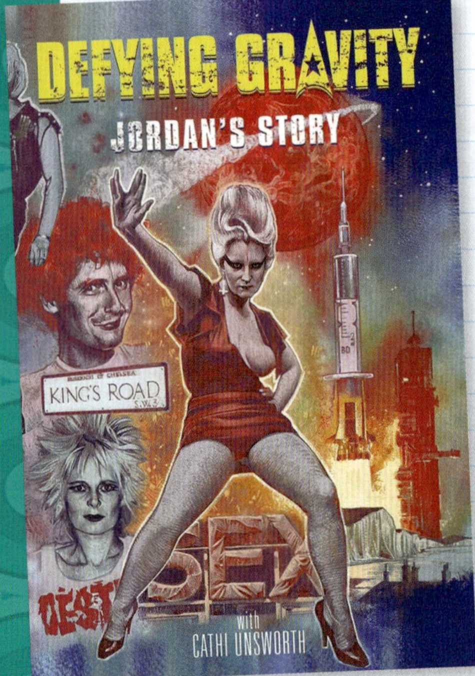

"Back then in Piccadilly, people would just lean on the railings; that was where all the rent boys were. I was only ever a rent boy for one day. I was sharing my apartment with a hooker when I worked at the Portobello on night shifts – she was using it to bring her customers home and she split the cash with me. All along Notting Hill, Queensway and Lancaster Gate was where people would trawl for prostitutes, and I was in Clanricarde Gardens, which was in the centre of all that. She got me out on the game one night… and I didn't like it. If it was a sexy man, it would have been all right, but it was an old man. It was horrible".
~ 'Defying Gravity: Jordan's Story'

"Sid was such a strong person. The one thing I really want to believe in all of this was that he really did love Nancy. I hope that's true. I'd hate to think he didn't have anything. Sid had the iconic Punk look. As much as I loved the others, Sid, on image alone, is what all Punk rests on".
~ 'Punk'

(The Pistols should have disappeared as soon as the *God Save the Queen* record came out). "It should have ended with the boat trip. They'd done it all – the clothes, the hit. They couldn't get more anarchic. And you just knew it would end in violence".
~ 'Vivienne Westwood: An Unfashionable Life'

Multimedia artist Thomas Dellert, and the Sex Pistols in 1978.

TONY MANERO (2008)

Before directing **Spencer** (2021), Oscar-nominated Natalie Portman in **Jackie** (2016), producing the Oscar-winning **A Fantastic Woman** (2017), **Gloria** (2013) and its American remake **Gloria Bell** (2018), Chile's Pablo Larraín had earned his artistic chops with this critically acclaimed prize-winner, a disturbingly Disco-nnected portrait of psychopathic existence lost in a socially, politically and culturally repressed morass of corruption and underhand American intervention. A work of intense manic genius and emotional heft – Chilean society circa 1978 is shown at a shocking dead end by contrasting General Augusto Pinochet's brutal regime and torture of the working class against the Hollywood dazzle of the similar **Saturday Night Fever** (1977) demographic looking for weekend release. In the case of the latter it was Disco, but for the crushed suppressed of the former it became casual murder.

Middle-aged lowlife thug Raúl Peralta (co-writer Alfredo Castro in an astounding turn) becomes so obsessed with John Travolta in **Saturday Night Fever**, he puts all his energy into perfecting the actor's white suit wardrobe, arrogant attitude and fluid dancing so he can win a Tony

Manero lookalike TV contest. He will even kill to realise his dream. Saving an elderly woman from teenage muggers, Raúl beats her to death to steal her television so he can sell it to buy glass to build his own flashing dancefloor and mirrorball for the local cabaret Disco in Santiago. Spending his days in the cinema watching Travolta's moves over and over, he dyes his hair black and meticulously rehearses the slick choreography with his girlfriend, her daughter and boyfriend. But when his local cinema drops showings of his favourite film for **Grease** (1978) instead, the projectionist is beaten to a pulp. And to ruin his main competitor's chances, Raúl cynically defecates on his tailored white suit.

Shot with a hand-held camera for maximum documentary impact and presented in elliptically edgy style, **Tony Manero** is a bleak, yet riveting, comment on what horrors Pinochet's reign of terror was putting Chile through while Disco reigned worldwide. The violence is shocking and clearly disturbing compensation for what Raúl lacks in every other aspect of his life, something his sick celebrity obsession will never sate. But through his passionate fixation, nihilistic Raúl is trying to find some meaning in his twisted life, even if it is more a Disco Nightmare than a Boogie Wonderland.

The only proper **Saturday Night Fever** song included on the minimal soundtrack is *You Should Be Dancing* (1976) by the Bee Gees. The song sporadically heard on the tapedeck is *Era solo un chiquillo* (2002) by José Alfredo Fuentes featuring Godwana. The other four tracks are *Te estás quedando solo* (1975), *Gigolo* (1978), *Cállate... ya no me mientas* (1978) and *Qué clase de hombre eres* (1980), all South American chart hits by Super Frecuencia Mod, the Chilean Three Degrees.

Comprising of Dolores, Patricia and Soledad García, the trio hit big with Disco contoured songs like the breathless *Duele Duele* (1976) and *Yo soy una dama* (1977), a cover version of Baccara's *Sorry I'm a Lady.* Composers of that latter ditty, Frank Dostal and Rolf Soja, also wrote the *Gigolo* featured here. Light on the tunes, but packing a unique Disco punch like no other using a dance-crazed ambience, **Tony Manero** is truly a Chilean chiller.

Eurodisco presence with *The Night* (1982), *Technovision* (1982), *El hombre lobo* (1984) and *Hitchcock Makes Me Happy* (1984), which became the soundtrack for the RTVE show 'Los sabios' the same year. Other notable Spanish Disco hits include *Spanish Disco Dance* (1979) by Touch, *Stay on the Line* (1979) by Sergio y Estibaliz (or Beans, the name their English language albums sported), and the unique Flamenco Disco camp sound of *Diki Diki* (1979) by Amina.

Talking of camp, pass the feathered cha cha heels for Jeanette's *Don't Say Goodnight to a Lady of Spain* (1978)! Jeanette was born in London as Janette Ann Dimech but moved with her family to Barcelona when she was 12. There she learnt how to play guitar and in 1971 began her solo singing career with the hit *Soy rebelde/I'm a Rebel.* Her name was spelt with an extra E on that record label and so she became Jeanette rather than Janette for the rest of her amazing career.

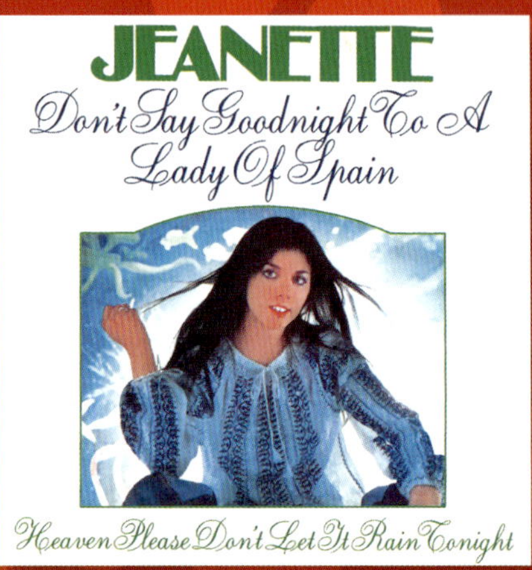

Spanish Disco

The one supposedly Spanish Disco song everyone knows is the No.1 party singalong *Y Viva Espana* (1974) by Sylvia. But it was originally written in Dutch for Belgian popstar Samantha and then made world famous by Swedish Eva Sylvia Vrethammar. Yet its catchy lyrics and pasodoble Disco beat placed it firmly in the Iberian consciousness and now everyone thinks that's where it originated. While it was Baccara who took Spanish Disco to global heights, spare a thought for that other Madrid duo Faly and Lola Chacón. As Las Deblas they made it Eurodsico big with the hilarious *You Are No Matador, Señor* (1980) from their album *Dime quien es esa*, the title track, *Soy una gata* and *Sabato noche* also scoring well. Their first album *Llorar por amor* (1976) was pitched more as Rhumba Disco but still goes down a treat. The duo dissolved when Faly took the boards for the Spanish stage version of the 'Evita' musical.

Another super duo was the Spanish techno-pop band Azul y Negro, founded by guitarist Carlos García Vaso and keyboardist Joaquín Montoya in 1981. They had a massive

Her biggest Spanish hit was with *Porque te vas/Because You're Leaving* (1974) and it was this song that brought her to the attention of German writer/producers Bernd Meinunger and Ralph Siegel who spied hidden Baccara potential and recorded *Don't Say Goodnight to a Lady of Spain* with her. Delivered lisping nymphet style it's a kitsch girlie Disco delight about sex, sun, sangria and dodgy English. Jeanette survived this obvious glitch in her career and has sold millions of records after appearing with such luminaries as Julio Iglesias and Sacha Distel.

Former Miss World Venezuela, Maria Conchita Alonso still has a prolific acting career after appearing in Hollywood fare like **The Running Man** (1987) and **Good Boy** (2020). Back in 1979 she became the Donna Summer of South America with the album *Love Maniac* credited to A'mbar. Recorded in English with a similar structure to Summer's early Casablanca releases, Side A includes a 17-minute long version of the title track while the flipside is devoted to the Disco stomper *Sweet Lover* trilogy. Local artists recording in English were a novelty in Venezuela at the time, the reason why the instantly recognisable Alonso was not pictured on the album cover, and who exactly was the singer was shrouded in PR mystery. The marketing strategy paid off and the album topped the Venezuelan charts in that September. Fuego sang *Fiesta Argentina* (1982), Carte Noire *Argentina Disco Parts 1&2* (1978), Pacific Blue *Argentina Forever* (1978), and Argentina *Baby, Don't You Break (My Heart)* (1986). But Argentine Disco proper was very much about imports and few local artists. However there was the Paul Barresi Orchestra with *Sal Soul Boogie* (1977), the Music Hall Pop Orchestra with *Moonlight Serenade* (1974), the flipside featuring an instrumental version of Barry White's *I'm Gonna Love You Just a Little More Baby* (1973), and Etta Cameron's *I'm a Woman* (1976) album featuring *Life Is Fascination* written by the Village People producer duo Henri Belolo and Jacques Morali.

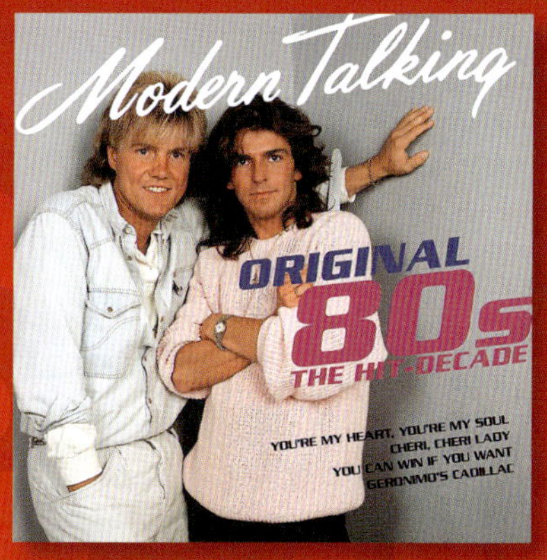

One Spanish artist went the full Eurodisco distance. Luis Rodriguez [Luis Rodríguez-Salazar] had local hits in 1979 with *Mujer, Shady Lady Baby Doll* and *Highway Queen*, and in 1980 with *Trinidad*. Then he moved to Germany and became the co-producer, arranger, mixer and engineer behind the 1980s *You're My Heart, You're My Soul* Disco sensations Modern Talking right from their first 1985 album. Other Dieter Bohlen-produced acts Rodriguez worked on are C.C. Catch, Blue System and ex-Smokie man Chris Norman, plus ex-Hot Chocolate singer Errol Brown, New Baccara, Italo Disco man Mike Mareen and Lian Ross (the alias of his wife Josephine Hiebel), singer of the wonderful *Say You'll Never* (1985) and *Fantasy* (1985).

Eeenglish!

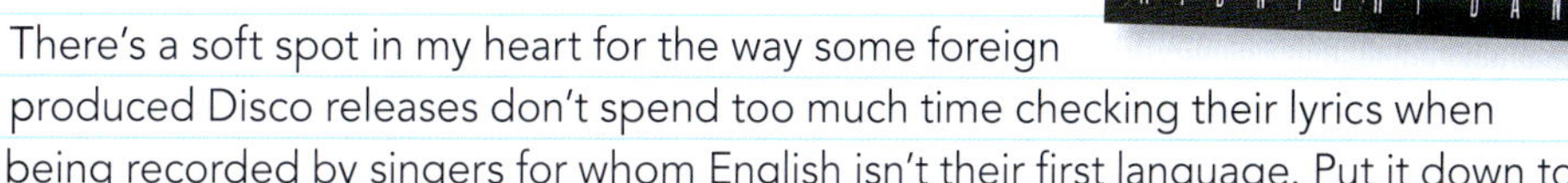

There's a soft spot in my heart for the way some foreign produced Disco releases don't spend too much time checking their lyrics when being recorded by singers for whom English isn't their first language. Put it down to either bad diction or impenetrable accents, but their Disco mistakes prove only more endearing and make the tracks so much more diverting. Take for example the classic case of Baccara who pronounce 'Boogie Woogie' as 'Boogie Voogie' in their classic *Yes Sir, I Can Boogie* (1977). But the Spanish duo had another all-time clinker in their western-themed, whip-cracking *The Devil Sent You to Laredo* (1978). Complete with honky-tonk piano and gunshots, the word 'Desperado' is mispronounced 'Desper-ay-do' solely to force it to rhyme with Laredo.

The German trio Arabesque committed the same mind-numbing mistake on their Disco single *Midnight Dancer* (1980), rhyming 'Tequila' with 'Venezeula', pronouncing it 'Venez-wheeler'. All can be forgiven there though because member Sandra Lauer left to marry *Enigma* (1990) producer Michael Cretu and forge a solo dance career with the megahits *Maria Magdalena* (1985), *In the Heat of the Night* (1985) and *Everlasting Love* (1987).

Elsewhere we're in Margarita Pracatan territory where murdered and garbled lyrics are the order of the day, like in Sabine Sauvant's *Casbah in Cairo* (1978) where 'Turkish Coffee' becomes 'Turkisssh Kavi' or Monserate's *When the Sun Goes Down* (1978) where keeping up with what's being said is a real effort. The complete opposite is the case with Luv's *You're the Greatest Lover* (1978), which is so pedantically sung the Dutch trio must have been reading off cue cards!

2010s

FUNKYTOWN (2011)

Saturday Night Fever (1977) gets given yet another deft Canadian spin in director Daniel Roby's sprawling multi-story affair where the foibles of the Disco era are paralleled to the Parti Québécois' 1980 attempt to make Quebec a sovereign state. Scripted by Steve Galluccio, who had scored with the film adaptation of his gay coming out play **Mambo Italiano** (2003), and Simon Trottier (the producer of **Martyrs**, 2008), the excesses of the 1976-80 Disco years are paraded in all their strobe-lit glory against a political backdrop of coerced cultural change. The first Québécois feature after **Bon Cop, Bad Cop** (2006) to unfold in both French and English official languages, if the format feels too **Boogie Nights** (1997) related, and the melodrama a bit too soapy, it doesn't matter that much because **Funkytown** gets its Disco flavour and atmosphere exactly right even if some of the music featured is played out of timeline.

How the non-stop glamour and decadence of colourful habitués at Starlight, Montreal's hottest nightclub and poor man's Studio 54, eventually affect their overall lives is the throbbing heart of Roby's ambitious enterprise. Local celebrity Bastien Lavalée (Patrick Huard) is at the centre of the unfolding action. Host of the popular TV show 'Disco Dance Party', he's a womanising cocaine addict with little regard to the consequences. Record producer Gilles Lefebvre (Raymond Bouchard) owns the Starlight and ensures his roster of dance artists are promoted in the club and on Bastien's show. His timid son Daniel (François Létourneau) manages the Starlight and is in love with his secretary who wants him to stop being so submissive towards his father.

Gay gossip columnist Jonathan Aaronson (Paul Doucet) fancies star dancer Tino (Justin Chatwin) who burns up the floor with his girlfriend partner Tina (Romina D'Ugo). Model Adriana (Sarah Mutch) is Bastien's mistress with Disco Queen ambitions even though she can't sing. And Nicole (Jocelyne Zucco) is Adriana's no-nonsense agent caught up in scandal when the real singer behind Adriana's records, Mimi (Genevieve Brouillette) realises the scam.

From the cynical showbiz trials and jaundiced tribulations of fame-seeking dancers to the upfront sexual ambivalence and violence driven by intolerance, **Funkytown** covers the entire Disco gamut from polyester fashions, distorted ugly reflections in the mirrorballs and snorting coke off body parts. With the ritzy characters vaguely based on key scenesters of the day, the Starlight is the stand-in for the real Quebec nightclub The Limelight and was actually filmed in and around the same building, now La Boom club and stripperama Chez Parée. Some of the uneven story strands are more interesting than others and the over-extended two-hour plus running time does

mean the nostalgia-tinged sub-plots and self-pitying often becomes tiresome. However, when it strikes the pose and elegantly swans around, it's an engaging Disco wallow.

The terrific soundtrack is a non-stop catalogue of original Disco hits and re-recorded cover versions; Boney M.'s *Daddy Cool* (1976), Carol Douglas' *Doctor's Orders* (1974), Penny McLean's *Lady Bump* (1975), Tavares' *Heaven Must Be Missing an Angel* (1976), Santa Esmeralda's *Don't Let Me Be Misunderstood* (1977) and obviously Lipps, Inc.'s *Funkytown* (1979) capture the heady heights of the Starlight and contribute to its easy charm. Covers by an assortment of Canadian pop stars include *Don't Leave Me This Way* and *Young Hearts Run Free* by Jully Black, *Hot Stuff* by Nancy Martinez, *I Love to Love* by Marilou, *Knock on Wood* by Marie-Christine Depestre, *Disco Inferno* by Andrew Leader, and *I Feel Love* by Florence K. Other songs featured are by Jean Robitaille, internationally acclaimed composer of film music, hit songs, jingles and creator of the 1976 Montreal Olympics theme song, *Je t'aime*. As **Funkytown** comes to a close, down-on-her luck Mimi sees the writing on the wall and mentors an all-girl punk band as Bastien utters "Disco sucks" while listening to Jefferson Airplane's *White Rabbit* (1969).

Grand Tour

"Come and take a trip with me. Fantasy, you can be sure…" the opening lines from the first track on producers Willi Morrison and Ian Guenther's *On Such a Winter's Day* by Grand Tour, one of the finest albums ever made during the height of the golden Disco era. After putting The THP Orchestra together, Morrison and Guenther momentarily stepped away from their sleek style of dance funk to appropriate the more elegant Eurodisco sound that was making such an impact. The result was their high-gloss, ethereally haunting and supremely melodic masterpiece by the session group Grand Tour.

While Willi Morrison and Ian Guenther would add their trademark touch to a wide range of dance acts in the Disco and early HiNRG era – *The Ultimate Warlord* (1979) by The Immortals, *Evergreen* (1984) by Hazell Dean – their earliest step outside The THP Orchestra arena came with the studio project Grand Tour. In one fell swoop it would provide ample proof of their unparalleled orchestral diversity and find them riding high in the 'Billboard' Disco Chart throughout the spring of 1978. Willi Morrison recalls, "The *Two Hot For Love* (1977) album by The THP Orchestra had been an enormous success for the Los Angeles based Butterfly Records label so they asked us to come up with another Disco concept. For some reason the first thing that came to mind was the phrase Baroque Disco, ornate in style, reminiscent of the palace of Versailles, the art of Caravaggio, the classical music of Vivaldi, Handel and Bach. But there was only one person who I knew could pull this ambitious sound off and that was Jimmie Haskell".

Veteran arranger/conductor Jimmie Haskell had worked with numerous legendary artists including Ricky Nelson, Etta James, Dusty Springfield and The Moody Blues and had won Grammy Awards for his arrangements on *Ode to Billie Joe* (1967) by Bobbie Gentry, *Bridge Over Troubled Water* (1969) by Simon & Garfunkel and *If You Leave Me Now* (1976) by Chicago. "It turned out that our engineer/mixer Mark Smith, who had moved from Toronto to LA, knew Haskell and arranged for us to meet up. What was important to me about the whole Grand Tour idea was its ethereal atmosphere and that's what Haskell brought to the project. We picked our singers that way too, by working backwards from the sound we wanted to achieve and chose LA session singers who fitted in with our overall design".

"The Eurodisco influences came through because we wanted to create a more melodic tapestry full of keen musical hooks. There's a folksy feel about it also because when I started my musical career in 1960s Glasgow I leant very much towards the work of the alternative Scottish group The Incredible String Band. Their mix of the psychedelic with folk music was formative even though I took it more in a poppy direction when I began getting serious about forging a career in the industry. Looking back, all these confluences made the Grand Tour an exceptionally fabulous combination of sound, atmosphere, instruments and vocals".

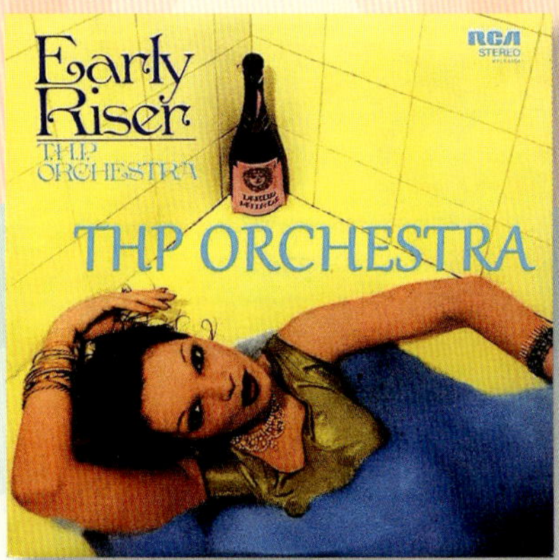

On Such a Winter's Day is anything but a typical Disco product of the time. For its gentle, low-key approach somehow manages to unlock a symphonic beauty within its delicate artistry that evokes a Disco dreamland of harmonious escape to faraway places. After all, the title of the album referred to the traditional trip of Europe undertaken by the moneyed upper class as an educational rite of passage during the Early Modern era until railways arrived in the mid 19th Century. Morrison and Guenther summon up a musical mood that is simultaneously sophisticated, deep and sublimely elegant.

And none come thrillingly cooler than the opening track *The Grand Tour* composed by Bruce Ley, Morrison's co-writer of choice. It sets the stage for an epic journey through France, Italy and beyond filled with sonic sun, rain and mystery featuring sweet, creamy vocals, an airy production to match and a supremely rich break to neatly sew up the whole heavenly dance adventure.

Let's Go Boating is a deceptively danceable cut superbly melding horns and castanets into an instrumentally rich landscape evoking the easy listening style of lounge wizard Bert Kaempfert and his *A Swingin' Safari* (1977) disciples. Written by John Shand, who wrote *The Ultimate Warlord* and Duncan Sisters' songs for Morrison and Guenther, *Let's Go Boating* is an instantly hummable exercise in Disco good taste with just enough of a hard edge to make nightclub turntable impact. "It's the track that says it all, summing up what we were trying to achieve – melodic and modern MOR with quintessential Disco appeal".

Just like the producers did on the very first album by The THP Orchestra, *Early Riser* (1976), the third and sixth track were stirringly sparse faithful cover versions of favourite tunes culled from the vast back catalogue of their collective pop memories. *Still I'm Sad* was a lesser-known 1965 song from the UK chart-toppers The Yardbirds, and *California Dreamin'* was the first hit from Mamas and the Papas, the latter 1966 song's lyrics giving the album its title quote. Both tracks summon up the palpable melancholy mood of the overall arrangement and are Morrison's preferences. "Those are the kinds of songs that just worked magically for me in the Disco format. The Bee Gees were my idols because the songs they composed for **Saturday Night Fever** (1977) were brilliant and showed their pure craft. But they weren't doing anything differently to what they were doing in the 1960s with such songs as *World* or *Massachusetts* (both 1967). It was the arrangement that changed. That was the key to all the old songs we adapted to the Disco idiom. The mathematical part of the equation was the four-on-the-floor bass drum. Everything else, like the hi-hats, the snare drum and the handclaps, just allowed you to vary the formula further".

Flight from Versailles (or *Flight to Versailles* depending on whether you read the cover or the label on the clear blue vinyl record) is the most THP Orchestra sounding track on the whole Grand Tour album. Written by Morrison, it's a winning confection of popping synthesizer, swirling strings, drawn-out sighing and scat vocals set to a quick tempo throbbing beat. Swerving through burgeoning ecstasy and tunefully textured peaks and troughs, *Flight from Versailles* is an exquisite Disco odyssey that leads into the Bruce Ley-penned *Late November*, a subtly engrossing and effective soft hustler.

"You want to know the one thing I learned very early on in my Disco career? The ultimate point of the recording experience is when you do your final mix and you sit back in your chair and say, yes, that's it, that's the perfect sound. It's the most satisfying of experiences because you know at that moment the music is ideal. I can recall that precise moment on the Grand Tour project, the exact instant I knew it would never disappear". For just like Donna Summer's 'Winter Melody' that could almost have been an influence on it seeing iconic producer Giorgio Moroder's muse was a Morrison idol, the Grand Tour album evokes an exhilarating chilly heat, perfectly captured by the Christmas card look of its album cover. One definitely for the Disconnoisseur.

Hollywood Is Just a Dream

Keith Williams had moved to Hollywood in the 1980s to capitalise on his rising Video Conceptualist career and I was a constant guest at his Glencoe Way apartment near the Hollywood and Highland crossroads. Probe was the nearest Disco and when I heard Billy Idol's *White Wedding* (1985) there one night it was like my two worlds colliding again. Keith had actually conceptualised Idol's *Dancing with Myself* (1982), the rock video directed by Tobe Hooper, despite the star taking all the credit. I always timed my visits for the American Film Market, which during its early years took place at the Beverly Center cinema complex. There I managed to score many great interviews just bumping into my favourite directors by accident. I stood next to Larry Cohen at the urinals on one memorable occasion and casually asked if I could talk to him about **The Stuff** (1985). "Sure", he said, "Just as long as you're not one of those journalist assholes with a script in his back pocket!" I liked him instantly.

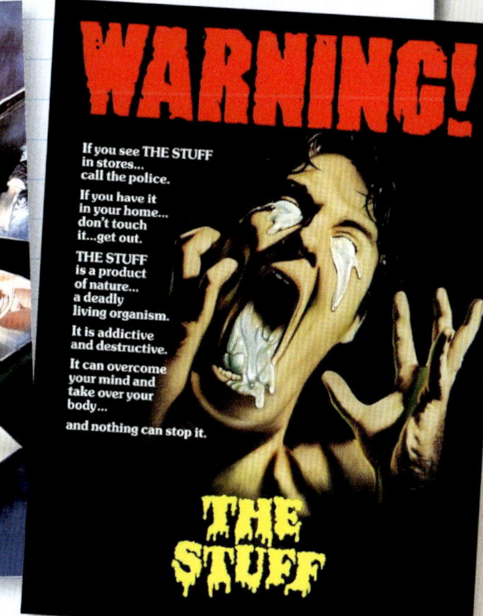

Other key AFM link-ups included Ulli Lommel, director of one of my favourite slashers **The Boogey Man** (1980), Joe Alves, director of **Jaws 3-D** (1983), who couldn't get over the fact I was prepared to take two buses to get to his house, and the director of a big 1985 horror release who made it quite clear to earn an interview I'd have to sleep with him first. I didn't, but got the interview anyway when I mentioned the indecent proposal to his studio. Keith was really on a roll throughout this period, being involved in visualising the songs for *Ghostbusters* (1984) by Ray Parker Jr. (a No.6 Disco hit), *She Works Hard for the Money* (1983) by Donna Summer (No.3), *The Fox* (1981) album by Elton John, *The Glory of Love* (1986) by Peter Cetera, *Holding Out for a Hero* (1984) by Bonnie Tyler, *Against All Odds* (1984) by Phil Collins, *Say You, Say Me* (1985) by Lionel Richie and *Twist of Fate* (1983) by Olivia Newton-John from the film **Two of a Kind** (1983). The latter proved another groundbreaking moment for the rock video industry because it was the first promo to contain footage from the actual film itself.

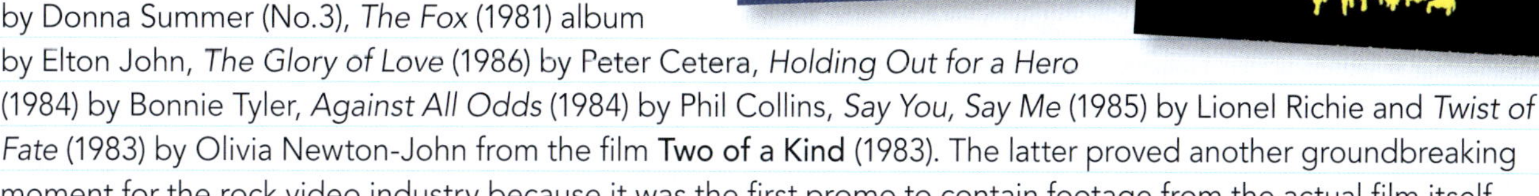

Those years in Hollywood are full of elliptical memories, especially when Russell Mulcahy was also around and we painted the town Disco. There was always some party or event to attend that come back to me as WTF flashes: at the very first **Blue Thunder** (1983) preview on the Columbia backlot Robert Wagner said hello, convinced he knew who I was; meeting **Carry On Emmannuelle** (1978) star Suzanne Danielle at **Nosferatu the Vampyre** (1979) agent/producer Michael Gruskoff's party and her telling me she was a Disco dancer in **The Stud** (1978); the orgy at *Everybody's Talkin'* (1968) singer Harry Nilsson's Beverly Hills mansion; limousining with Tina Turner; going to see **Bloody Birthday** (1981) star Julie Brown do her stand-up show in the San Fernando Valley before her proper breakout with **Earth Girls Are Easy** (1988); getting invited to one of primetime fantasy TV producer Glen A. Larson's celebrated New Year's Eve shindigs and meeting everyone from Gil Gerard to David Hasselhoff. At least I could tell the latter I loved his German Europop hits – especially *Crazy for You* (1990) – and mean it!

CLOCLO / MY WAY (2012)

The sizeable hit **Podium** (2004) proved to be at the French box-office clearly indicated there was more money to be made from beloved icon Claude François' brand name. But while **Podium** took a quirky approach to the wealth of teen-idol-turned-Disco star material, director Florent-Emilio Siri goes the straightforward route with a big scale biopic charting the pop star's 1939 birth in Egypt to his accidental electrocution by bathtub lightbulb in 1978, just as he was about to take the gamble of his life and embark on forging a global career.

Prior to this study of a showbiz manic control freak Siri's other main credit was the thrilling mafia actioner **The Nest/Nid de guêpes** (2002). So while the main narrative may be studiously graphing the poor little rich kid's rise to Gallic fame in bite-size chunks, Siri goes for the ambitious set-up big-time to add maximum interest. Most famously in the one-take sequence where François leaves his bijou apartment to be mobbed by fans, gets in his car, drives to his record company office, gets mobbed by more fans and swishes into reception with one overly attentive admirer having a nosebleed. Because François' public image was so immaculately maintained, and the private scandals so soap opera basic, Siri's only recourse is pure style. And **Cloclo**, his family nickname, simply oozes with it.

His idyllic childhood in Egypt cut short by the Suez crisis, Claude (Jérémie Renier) moves to Monaco with his family where, against his strict father's will, he becomes a drummer and works his way up to being a respected nightclub singer in the crooner tradition. Something Philips Records balks at when he tries to get signed up, until he sees the light at a Johnny Hallyday concert, starts performing cover versions of American pop hits and becomes a massive star with an all-important besotted female fan-base.

Contrasted against his frenzied drive to succeed – he even orchestrated an on-stage collapse to remain in the headlines – are problems with his gambling addict mother and the search for the perfect wife on his calculating terms. First wife Janet (Maud Jurez) leaves him for singer Gilbert Becaud, second France Gall (Joséphine Japy) dares to win the 1965 Eurovision Song Contest with *Poupée de cire, poupée de son*, causing a massive jealous hissy fit, his third Isabelle (Ana Giradot) gives him two

sons (only one is ever declared in case it ruins his boyish image), and interchangeable models and members of his Clodettes dance troupe from then on.

Once past his role in the creation of *Comme d'habitude/ My Way* (1967) – its mega-success for Frank Sinatra meaning non-stop caviar, flash motors, country houses, adoration and business ventures into his own label Disques Flèche, softcore magazines and modelling agencies – is when the Disco starts. Claude hears *I'm Your Boogie Man* (1977) by KC and The Sunshine Band at a party, rushes to the DJ booth and asks what type of music it is. "Why, Disco" he says. Fast as lighting Claude is in a London studio recording the fantastic *Magnolias for Ever* (1977) track for his same-titled album. From that quintessential French Disco treat comes *Ecoute ma chanson* and *Alexandrie, Alexandra,* sung over an end credit montage and signifying the single released on the day of his burial to become his Disco requiem. *Eve* and *Disco Meteo* from *Magnolias for Ever* are wonderful too.

Charismatic, obsessive about detail and visibly unabashed about the tackier sides of showbiz, François has remained in the blazing French spotlight ever since his tragic death. Dead ringer Renier couldn't be better whether primping in front of the mirror wearing era-perfect wigs or recreating his high-spirited recording sessions and live performances, the highlight being a bilingual rendition of *My Way* at London's Royal Albert Hall. **Cloclo** takes its time getting to the Disco nub, just as François did himself, but both the ride and destination are well worth it.

Belgica Disco

When he wasn't singing the lead vocals on Plastic Bertrand's *Ça plane pour moi* (1977), Lou Deprijck was one third of the Belgian Latin Disco band Two Man Sound, best known for their carnival medleys, *Disco Samba* (1977), *Qué tal America* (1977) and their Disco Top 20 hit *Club Tropical* (1981). Otherwise Disco Belgica was a very underground business, which barely made waves outside Brussels let alone Belgium. Take for example René Roland's *Ethero-Disco* (1979), Sweety Anderson's *Baby Won't You Turn Me On* (1978), Marianne's *Queen to the Pharaoh* (1978), Flame's *Groovin' to the Music* (1977), C.C. Band's *Crazy Dance* (1978) and *Be My Love Tonight* (1983), Quartz's *Cool & Get Up* (1979), L2's *La gomme* (1981), Bubble's *Bubblegum* (1981), La Bush's *Disco Bush* (1977), System Love's *System Love* (1978), Cora Corona's Yma Sumac sounding *Jungle Love* (1978), The Rogers' *Cosmos 81* (1981), Rendez-Vous's *My Blue Bird* (1977), and Raymond Joniaux's *All' A Bi Bi* (1978).

No doubt about it the most famous Belgian Disco single is also one of those evergreen markers of the entire era. Patrick Hernandez's *Born to Be Alive* (1979) is a landmark – just hearing the jittery beat with its 'Boingggg' echo sound effects brings back many happy memories for an entire Disco generation. It was the No.1 chart song you couldn't get away from throughout the whole of 1979 and it gained an extended life by becoming a Roller Disco speed-skating favourite too.

Patrick Hernandez and Madonna in 1979.

French singer Hernandez wrote it, Jean Vanloo produced it in a Belgian studio, and after having immediate success in France, the song spread like wildfire all over Europe and then caught on in America. After touring the world (one of his backing dancers was a very young Madonna), by the end of the 1970s Hernandez had racked up 52 gold and platinum record awards from more than 50 different countries. And it still sounds as fresh and fabulous today as it ever did, a Disco diamond shining for dance eternity.

AJ hippie look, Kew Gardens 1971.

Crowther's

SEX wasn't the first clothes store I worked in. For a while in early 1971, just prior to joining the Portobello Hotel elite staff, I became the only male sales person at the Crowther's concession in the Oxford Circus Top Shop. John Crowther was a clever retailer and made a success of his outlets in Manchester and Birmingham with 1940s style women's fashions. I found out later he was also the manager of the progressive rock band Barclay James Harvest, which is where he got the money for his business. Wanting to penetrate the 'Swinging London' market John first opened the Top Shop concessions and then a flagship store in the busiest part of Kensington High Street. I was positioned there when one of the Oxford Circus Top Shop managers saw me wearing my 'Alkasura' blue velvet hot pants outfit and said it wasn't suitable attire for his establishment. A shame as I used to steal so many 'Mr Freedom' clothes from my neighbouring concession stand – I wore them under my 'work' clothes and left through the security entrance looking fatter than I went in. The Top Shop back security entrance was only three doors down from The Speakeasy Disco where every band I knew hung out anyway so it was an easy task stripping off in the toilets there.

Roxy Music

I didn't last very long at the Kensington branch either. I was always skipping out to see my friends over at Kensington Market or into 'Che Guevara', the other directional fashion emporium everyone has forgotten about. That's where I first met designers Anthony Price, who would later style Roxy Music, and Ossie Clark who would introduce me to 'Ritz' writer Frances Lynn. Also my bitch manageress, Suzie, absolutely hated me for some reason and always kept looking for ways to discredit me. It was all very 'Are You Being Served?' without the laughs. In the end she did indeed fire me but I didn't care. The Portobello Hotel headhunted me and I never looked back. Revenge was sweet when Crowther's closed down though soon after. Suzie ended up as a waitress in a hamburger joint up the road, and I purposely made sure she served me when I went in with my superstar guest that day, Don Henley of the Eagles!

THE SECRET DISCO REVOLUTION (2012)

The true agenda of the Disco era was the freedom of gays, blacks, and women from the tyranny of straight white male-dominated rock music according to director Jamie Kastner's straightforward bullet-point documentary charting the rise and initial tapering off of the musical movement. Kastner had documentary form with **Djangomania** (2005), an incisive look at the legendary gypsy jazz guitarist Django Reinhardt, and applied the same vehicle of liberation ethos to this entry-level discussion starter pack. But by leaning heavily on author Alice Echols and her book 'Hot Stuff: Disco and the Remaking of American Culture', who over-politicises everything to an eye-rolling degree, this scattershot primer veers into dryness eschewing all the more fun aspects. Indeed, not one of the featured Talking Heads interviewed come the finale wrap-up agrees Disco even signified a revolution in the first place, sweeping away the previous 80 minutes' attempt to position the music as an intellectual Disco = Protest exercise.

Folk music fuelled the Civil Rights movement in the 1950s, Woodstock and Vietnam did the same in the 1960s and then came Disco in the 1970s. From that starting point the supposed vapid veneer of Disco is exploded as a subversive touchstone for multi-cultural acceptance. After scenes of School Discos in England, the world's largest Silent Disco and Disco ice-skating in Dubai, numerous pundits, journalists and artists take us on a Disco history lesson through Discotheque Rock transforming into a four-to-the-floor soundscape with Manu Dibango's *Soul Makossa* (1972). Then comes The Loft opening in 1974, the rise of the DJ as taste guru, radio stations freaking out about Disco setting the chart agenda instead of them, the Hustle bringing back the Nazi Swing Kids era, the ascension of Casablanca Records, **Saturday Night Fever** (1977) victory, Studio 54, the barrier-breaking Village People and the mass-record-destruction at Comiskey Park's 1979 'Disco Demolition Night'. Jarringly cut into the main thrust of the piece are specially filmed interstitials with three people wearing silver satin Disco clothes coldly and quizzically surveying each sea change.

People joining Echols in the discussion include 'Village Voice' journalist Michael Musto, Gloria Gaynor, Evelyn 'Champagne' King, Peter Shapiro (author of 'Turn the Beat Around: The Secret History of Disco'), Robert 'Kool' Bell, Larry Harris (Vice President of Casablanca Records), Thelma Houston, Martha Wash, Henri Belolo, DJ Nicky Siano, 12-inch pioneer Tom Moulton, Harry Wayne 'KC' Casey, Anita Pointer, 54 doorman Marc Benecke and Maxine Nightingale. All par for the course but where this documentary scores most points is for its range of vintage clips, newsreel and archive footage of live performances from the featured artists singing their most famous Disco songs revealing, without any layered-on political irony, the true beat revolution of the genre.

From the Burger King Disco commercial and the Village People early videos singing *San Francisco (You've Got Me)* (1977), *Y.M.C.A.* (1978), *Macho Man* (1978) and *In the Navy* (1979) to Donna Summer panting *Love to Love You Baby* (1975) and Maxine Nightingale demanding *Right Back*

Where We Started From (1975), all the Talking Head artists get their spotlight moment, as do Barry White, The Love Unlimited Orchestra, the Bee Gees and Chic. Getting a look in elsewhere on the soundtrack are *Boogie Fever* (1975) by The Sylvers, *Knock on Wood* (2012) by David Wall, Jamie Shields and Adam B. White, and *There's No Business Like Show Business* (1979) by Ethel Merman.

Where Kastner's treatise really comes unstuck is the highly embarrassing sit-down interview with the surviving Village People members. As their writer/producer Henri Belolo likens Disco Demolition Night to the Nazi book-burnings and says his lyrics were all meant to be double-entendres, original group members Felipe Rose (the Indian) and David Hodo (the construction worker) mumble through completely unfocused and conflicting statements, the latter ending the interview by admonishing the interviewer "Don't read no more books! You're reading too much". Especially those by Alice Echols!

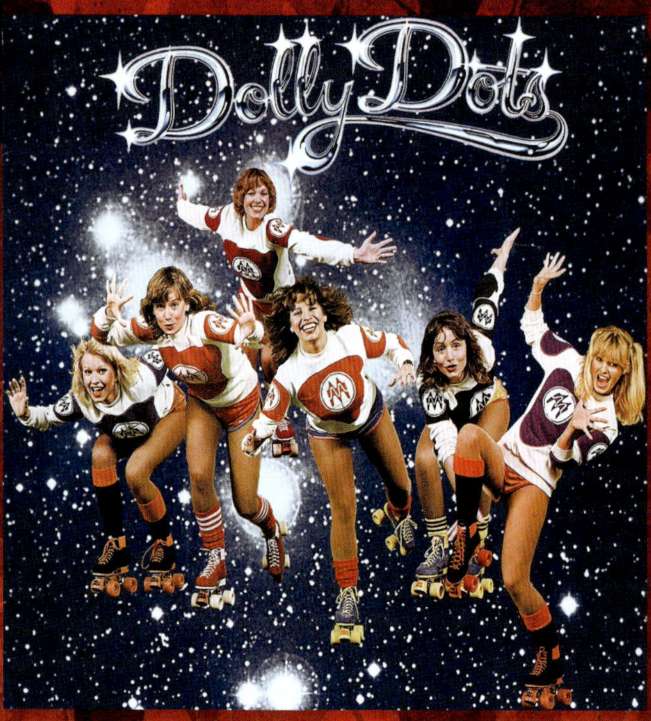

Dutch Treats

Disco lived in a windmill in old Amsterdam if The Netherlands' sound was anything to go by. Determinedly on the dance cusp of Europop, Dutch Disco is best represented by Luv', a girly trio put together by producers Hans van Hemert and Piet Souer to compete with Silver Convention. Considered Holland's best export act the threesome sold more than 7 million records worldwide, their best known songs being *U.O. Me* (1978), *You're the Greatest Lover* (1978), *Trojan Horse* (1978), *Casanova* (1979) and *Ooh, Yes I Do* (1979). They also recorded a version of Raffaella Carrà's global Disco smash *A far l'amore comincia tu* (1976) as *Don Juanita de carnaval* (1978).

Elsewhere local bands included Darlin' (note the similar apostrophe to Luv') and their fun *Chicago* (1981) with the lyric "Chic, Chic, Chicago", Bisquit's *Roller Boogie* (1981), Dolly Dots' *Rollerskating* (1979), Babe's *Boomerang* (1983), Doris D and the Pins' *Shine Up* (1981), Earth & Fire's *Weekend* (1979) featuring Jerney Kaagman, 1983 pin-up

in the first Dutch issue of 'Playboy', Saskia & Serge's *Let Me Fly/Judy* (1985), and the nostalgic funfair sound of *Holland Disco* (1978) and *Summer Disco* (1979) by The New Dutch Organ Group. One of the few groups to become a Eurodisco mainstay was Champagne with their *Rock 'n' Roll Star* (1977), *Rollerball* (1979) and *Sjooh Sjooh Sugar* (1980).

You should never underestimate the power of nostalgia and that's what Indonesian born Dutch singer Taco Ockerse figured out when he released a soft Disco version of the Irving Berlin standard *Puttin' on the Ritz* (1982).

Polydor Records first released the track in Germany but wide playing throughout the US took it to No.4 on the 'Billboard' Hot 100 as well as top of the Cashbox charts. Lightning unfortunately did not strike twice as Taco's follow-up releases, all drawn from Hollywood's golden era (*Singin' in the Rain, Over the Rainbow, Cheek to Cheek* and *Let's Face the Music and Dance*), failed to chart although his vintage American songbook album *After Eight* (1982) proved massive in Norway, Austria and Finland.

By 1980 the ritualistic 4/4 beat of dance music was being seriously challenged by more technologically based developments, as exemplified by Lipps, Inc.'s *Funkytown* (1979). And that classic track clearly impacted on one of the best slices of Eurodisco to ever come out of the Netherlands. Fantastique were round-faced Dick van Dam and blue-eyed Astrid Leuwener from Haarlem and the duo were formed by the famous Dutch producing team Cat Music who had at various stages in their careers been the bands Catapult and The Monotones. The sublimely catchy, mega-poppy and supremely camp *Mama Told Me* (1981) topped the charts in many European countries and such was this song's popularity it was used on the soundtrack of the Dutch suicide comedy **Ik ben Joep Meloen** (1981).

The next year actress/singer Connie Witteman appeared in the Dutch hit comedy movie **Boezemvriend/Bosom Friend** (1982) and turned that visibility clout into the big Eurodisco hit *Upside Down (Dizzy Does It Make Me)* under the pseudonym Vanessa. The model entered show business by accident when a demo disc she recorded for a friend landed on the desk of the Dutch Recording Company DURECO. She never looked back and by 1987 was married to her third husband, Free Record Shop boss Hans Breukhoven, had become a canny businesswoman and was making regular appearances at Gay Pride rallies in Amsterdam. 'Upside Down (Dizzy Does It Make Me)' was co-written by Piet Souer, famous for his collaborations with Luv', Eurovision stars Mouth & MacNeal, Champagne and Katie Kissoon. He also wrote the hit *Fantasy Island* for The Millionaires, covered by Tight Fit in 1982.

And hailing from Maastricht, The Chaplin Band was formed by brothers Jo and John Bartels in 1976, the year they recorded *Disco Party Continued*. While their line-up changed a great deal over the years, they consistently made it into the Dutch charts, pulling in Demis Roussos producer Gerard Stellaard for *Madmen's Discotheque* (1978) and the catchy cover version of Lucio Battisti's 1976 Italian hit *Il veliero* (1982).

La Vie en Rose

Ever since I met director Eli Roth on the global promotional tour for his debut feature **Cabin Fever** (2002), we became friends. Especially after I dubbed him one of 'The Splat Pack' in a very influential feature I wrote for 'Total Film'. If I wanted to show any of his movies at FrightFest all I had to do was ask, the reason why **Hostel** (2005), **The Last Exorcism** (2010), **Aftershock** (2012), **The Sacrament** (2013), **The Green Inferno** (2013) and **Clown** (2014) made their banner UK appearances. I was happy to repay the favour by research working and writing on his TV show 'Eli Roth's History of Horror' (2018). For a while Eli, his adorable ex-wife Lorenza Izzo, and I would be at every single fantasy film festival together, and in fact it was at the 2012 Sitges Fantasy Festival he gave me one of the biggest surprises of my life.

"Let's meet up at a bar in central Sitges later tonight", he said one evening. Always happy to spend time with him, I dutifully turned up to a back-alley Disco in Sitges Old Town and was shocked to find him sitting with Quentin Tarantino. "Surprise", he laughed. "I've wanted you two to meet for a while now". Tarantino couldn't have been nicer to me. Further shocks lay in store when he told me he was an avid reader of my 'CFQ' features and 'Starburst' reviews and actually quoted lines from my **Body Double** (1984) assessment. That's something that has never happened to me before, but how fantastic it came from him!

We chatted about everything and anything and then came a question, "Why didn't you like **Kill Bill Vol. 2** (2002) as much as the first part?" I didn't know what to say. Talk about tongue-tied and to this day I can't remember my reply. All I can recall is leaving the Disco at dawn walking on a cloud completely thrilled to death at meeting one of my cinematic heroes. Better still knowing he knew everything about me too.

Eli Roth and Quentin Tarantino

I FEEL LIKE DISCO / ICH FÜHL MICH DISCO (2013)

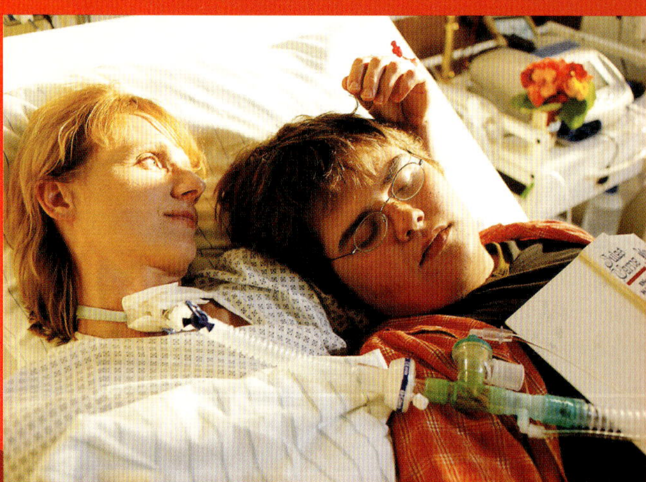

A sizeable hit on the Queer festival circuit, director Axel Ranisch's semi-autobiographical coming out saga was that rare beast, a German comedy with a big heart. Charming, touching and poignant, this minor gem charting normal life transforming into an extraordinary journey for a buttoned-down father and his overweight, sensitive son might show its low budget restraints but its resonance is high impact on every human level. Key to its success is the non-pandering to cliché, the realism striven for and brilliantly achieved and the basic life truths uncovered as it navigates through difficult emotional waters.

Fifteen-year-old Florian Herbst (an exceptional Frithjof Gawenda) lives in East Berlin with his tyrannical father Hanno (Heiko Pinkowski) and mother Monika (Christina Große). Hanno wants his pudgy, shortsighted son to be more manly while Monika adores going on flights of fantasy with Florian when dad's at work – magical interludes where they dress up in glittering Disco duds, paint on fake sideburns and dance around the flat to the upbeat music of celebrity Schlager singer Christian Steiffen (Hardy Schwetter).

But then Monika falls into a coma and father and son are forced through shared grief to compromise over their clashing attitudes coming from two entirely different angles, eras and generations. Over time Hanno starts showing real interest in his son, discovering things he was

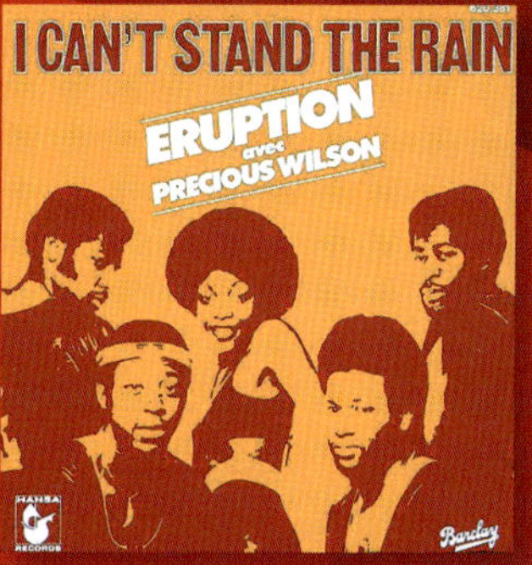

clueless about before. Then, through Hanno's job as a high diving trainer in an indoor swimming pool, Florian meets Radu (Robert Alexander Baer), a learner swimmer from Romania. And his latent romantic feelings are awakened by this gamine, acned lust object.

By turn hilariously deadpan and tear inducing, **I Feel Like Disco** is tragi-comedy gold that proves impossible not to like. One uproarious self-reflective moment has Rosa von Praunheim, director of the groundbreaking documentary **It Is Not the Homosexual Who Is Perverse, But the Society in Which He Lives** (1971), playing himself on a sex education DVD explaining the joys of anal sex to an aghast Hanno. That also goes for many of the moments between father and son, especially when Florian wants a piano for his birthday yet Hanno resists all hints to give him a clearly unsafe, refurbished motorbike instead. Such a rough-around-the-edges approach by Ranisch textures the unsentimental narrative in key knowing areas and balances the sadness with keen delight for terrific empathy.

Six Schlager songs are sung by Schwetter's lounge lizard alter ego Christian Steiffen on the soundtrack with only the kitsch title song *Ich fühl mich Disco* (2012), also performed by Frithjof Gawenda, really fitting the Disco contours. The other spoof songs adhere to the Schlager music definition of catchy, stomping Europop, with the added bonus here of each positioned as fantasy self-improvement intrusions on stark reality in **The Purple Rose of Cairo** (1985) mode. *Sexualverkehr* (2012), also performed by Gawenda and Christina Große, *Ich hab die ganze Nacht von mir geträumt* (2012) and *Eine Flasche Bier* (2012) were originally released as a CD EP while *Das geht eigentlich nicht* and *Hanno, du bist ein Supertyp* are specific to the movie.

A former member of a seven-man Elvis Presley tribute band, Schwetter invented his Steiffen persona in 2009 in the wake of Swedish model Mats Söderlund finding club infamy with his own comedy alter ego Günther and the hardcore campy, catchy album *Pleasureman* (2004). When **I Feel Like Disco** was released in Germany, Schwetter went on a cross-promotional tour with the songs heavily featured and also licensed the use of *Sexualverkehr* for the comedy crime thriller **Winterkartoffelknödel** (2014). He is still touring because, as his key line of dialogue here states, "Life is not all fries and Disco".

Deutschland Disco

It wasn't just the career of Boney M. premier German producer Frank Farian was managing in the mid 1970s. He also controlled the acts Gilla (singer Gisela Wuchinger) with *Help! Help!* (1977) and the Disco version of Amen Corner's 1968 UK Top Ten hit *Bend Me, Shape Me* (1978), and Eruption. The latter band started life as Silent Eruption in 1974 in Britain with Leslie Johnson as lead singer. But it was Precious Wilson they went on tour with in Germany, where they landed on Farian's radar. Farian produced their massive Eurodisco hit *I Can't Stand the Rain* (1978), an update of Ann Peebles' 1974 smash. Giving a 4/4 twist to the R&B original, and adding an electronic percolation to imply raindrops, Wilson invigorated the song in her uniquely rough-edged soulful way. Wilson left the band after another Disco cover version, Neil Sedaka's 1959 hit *One Way Ticket* (1979) to pursue a solo career and achieved two major hit singles in the early 1990s with revisions of Sheila & B. Devotion's *Spacer* (1979) and Donna Summer's *I Feel Love* (1977) with techno group Messiah.

The most flagrant Boney M. rip-off band was created to compete in the 1979 Eurovision Song Contest by Eurovision producer/songwriter veteran Ralph Siegel, who co-wrote the 1982 winner *Ein bißchen Frieden/A Little Peace* for Nicole. Dschinghis Khan singing their Disco tribute to the 13th Century Mongol Emperor *Dschinghis Khan/Genghis Khan* placed No.4 in their year, but the glitzed up Schlager bandits had an international hit with *Moscow* thanks to it being used as the theme tune for the 1980 Summer Olympics there. Other notable examples of

Dschinghis Khan's Disco Camp are *Rome* (1980), *Pistolero* (1981) and *What Shall We Do with the Drunken Sailor?* (1981).

Silver Convention mastermind Sylvester Levay was also a long-time member of the Ambros Seelos Big/Show Band who like top veteran German orchestra leader James Last (*I Can't Move No Mountains*, 1975) moved in Planet Disco circles when the mood took him. In 1979 Seelos scored the movie **Midnight Sounds – Six Girls in Athens** with a Disco timbre and also recorded *Gimme More* (1980). Other notable German Eurodisco players are funk rocker Supermax (*Lovemachine*, 1977), 'Hair' actress Su Kramer (*You've Got the Power Parts 1&2*, 1976), gay Diva favourite Marianne Rosenberg (*Wieder Zusammen/ Together Again*, 1976), Berlin TSOP channellers the Alfie Khan Sound Orchestra (*Illegal Toys*, 1976), East Germany's Veronika Fischer & Band (*Philodendron*, 1975), Caviar (*Come to L.A.*, 1979), produced by Leo Leandros, Vicky's father, Lilac Nation (*I Wanna Be Superman*, 1979), a local **Superman** (1978) movie tie-in, and Easy Listening auteur Berry Lipman (*Sex World*, 1975, which became the theme for the BBC TV series 'Star Maidens' and, with lyrics added, the theme for the same titled 1977 porno movie).

More from the Disco Kraut galaxy include veteran '60s pop star Udo Jürgens with *Ich Weiß Was Ich Will* (1979), Jumbo (*Turn On to Love*, 1977), the Viennese Ganymed (*It Takes Me Higher*, *Dancing in a Disco*, both 1979), Schlager superstar Christian Anders (*Running Away*, 1979, from his debut kung fu feature **Die Brut des Bösen/ Roots of Evil**), Silver Convention session vocalist Jackie Carter (*Treat Me Like a Woman*, 1976), *krimi* composer specialist the Peter Thomas Sound Orchestra (*Opium*, 1976), jazz fusioneers Peter Herbolzheimer Rhythm Combination & Brass (*Feedback Brother*, 1978), Hustle-influenced Carsten Bohn's Bandstand (*Disco Cisco*, 1978), legendary producer Giorgio Moroder's studio band Munich Machine (*Get On the Funk Train*, 1977, *A Whiter Shade of Pale*, 1978, *Party Light/Let Your Body Shine*, 1979), transsexual icon Romy Haag (*Superparadise/Hermaphrodite*, 1978), and cult Eurodisco babes Arabesque (*Hello Mr. Monkey*, 1978, *Midnight Dancer*, 1980, *High Life*, 1980).

Manfred Alois Segieth first recorded in the archetypal German boom-bang-a-bang Schlager style under the alias of Tess Teiges. But it wasn't until he changed his name again to Fancy that his singing career took off and the constant stream of Eurodisco hits began. *Slice Me Nice* started it all when it shot to the top of the German charts in 1984. Produced by Anthony Monn, the genius behind numerous Amanda Lear hits, 'Slice Me Nice' crystallised the melodic pop synth HiNRG Fancy sound that continued through other signature successes *Bolero (Hold Me in Your Arms Again)* (1985) and *Flames of Love* (1988). Fancy entered the 2000 Eurovision Song Contest for Germany with *We Can Move a Mountain*, remaining a force of nature and one of Eurodisco's triumphant constants.

Disco Memo

Femme Fatales

AJ with Rosie Perez at the Venice Film Fesitival for *Fearless* (1993).

In the summer of 1992, my 'CFQ' editor Fred Clarke launched a sister publication titled 'Femme Fatales' (without the correct extra S) focusing on the actresses in fantasy movies. It was a huge and immediate success and I found myself with yet another remunerative outlet for expanded interviews garnered on my exhaustive location travels. From Bond Girls to Hammer Heroines and established stars like Sigourney Weaver, Julia Roberts, Uma Thurman, Cameron Diaz, Michelle Yeoh, Sophie Marceau, Denise Richards, Tia Carrere – really too many to mention – the magazine was yet another major string to my high profile bow. I even managed to get Rosie Perez to pose for my 1993 Christmas card!

But the one *femme fatale* I came to respect more than any other was Angelina Jolie. I worked with her because I wrote 'The Official Film Companion' for **Lara Croft: Tomb Raider** (2001) and 'The Official Movie Souvenir Magazine' for **Lara Croft Tomb Raider: The Cradle of Life** (2003). The ultimate professional, eloquent, considerate and quite wonderful to me, Jolie was just so unlike the press image I expected, and that mainly stemmed from her not having her own personal PR exerting damage control. Or that was certainly the case back then. So every decision was made by herself alone, either good or bad. She said what she thought, didn't give a damn and I wish more megastars had her gumption. Doing the tie-in writing on those two movies was a major career highlight.

'Femme Fatales' lasted eight years after Fred's death, inspired the same-titled 2011 Cinemax TV series, and proved a nice sidebar to my career. Fred did try the same trick again with 'Imagi-Movies' launched in 1993 that was supposed to focus more on the low-budget end of the fantasy genre but it quickly became exactly the same as 'CFQ'. After nine issues it was absorbed into the main magazine as both 'CFQ' and 'Femme Fatales' took up so much of the short time Fred sadly had left.

DISCOPATH / DISCOPATHE (2013)

At first you'll be afraid, you'll be petrified… Writer/director Renaud Gauthier proclaims he's always found Disco music scary and thought the perfect murder could be carried out on the dance floor because no one would notice amidst the flashing strobe lights and dry ice. Hence the inspiration behind the Montreal-based former art director's feature debut, following a popular series of shorts, which became the first Canadian horror movie since **Prom Night** (1980) to infuse its shock with a keen Disco ambience.

Gauthier's bilingual so-so Saturday Night Cleaver affair is set in 1976, when Donna Summer is atop the charts and everyone believes there's no Love Hangover. Except Manhattan short order burger cook Duane Lewis (Jérémie Earp-Lavergne, whose prior acting credit, the TV musical series 'La Mélodie de la Terreur/The Melody of Terror', seems strangely prescient) who goes psycho when he hears the pulsating rhythm of Disco. Unable to control his maniac impulses that stem from a childhood trauma caused by his father (played by Gauthier), Duane turns the local Seventh Heaven nightclub into a blood-spattered Disco Inferno when he kills a girl who comes onto him. Filmed in outré Brian De Palma-esque style, with the victim crawling for her life beneath the transparent dance floor as everyone boogies obliviously above, this sequence is the highlight of this hit-and-miss tongue-in-cheeker that borders on boredom once the retro magic loses its lustre.

With hardboiled New York detective Paul Stephens (Ivan Freud) in hot pursuit, Duane heads to Montreal where he lays low as a janitor at a religious girl's school overseen by a strict Mother Superior headmistress and a priest with a roving eye for the young lovelies in their cute uniforms. Wearing hearing protection to block out those provocative Disco sounds, his homicidal tendencies soon surface once more when he can't resist peeping on two students who strip down to their underwear and use a

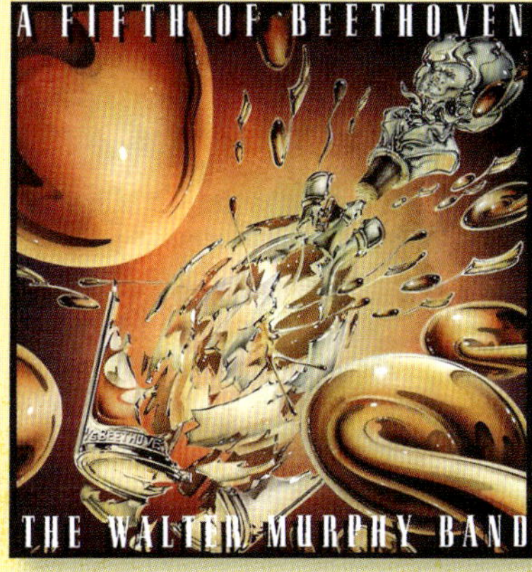

Disco backdrop for their kissing practice. And disembodied heads (one modelled on Gauthier's daughter Sibylle), cut off by vinyl record shards, start revolving on stereo turntables before he gets his comeuppance at a funeral dressed in nun drag.

As an all-too-knowing meld of **Boogie Nights** (1997) and **Henry: Portrait of a Serial Killer** (1986), **Discopath** doesn't fully work. And like Gauthier's later **Aquaslash** (2019) it's sloppy splatter seconds. But as ever, the power of Disco ensures it punches above its slasher weight with some well chosen unusual tracks augmented by composer Bruce Cameron's evocative synth score. Kicking the movie off in perfect style is *Flight 76* by The Walter Murphy Band, a great Disco version of the Nikolai Rimsky-Korsakov 1900 composition *Flight of the Bumblebee*. Although overused, once past Duane running frantically through back alleys, it makes a change to hear this cut from the former advertising jingle writer instead of that hardy perennial *A Fifth of Beethoven* endlessly recycled for easy **Saturday Night Fever** (1977) sheen.

Duane's first maniac meltdown comes courtesy of *I'm Your Boogie Man* (1977) by KC and The Sunshine Band, the Florida funksters behind the 1975 floor-filler *That's the Way (I Like It)*. Elsewhere Roni Griffith chimes in with her Bobby Orlando produced 1982 hit *Desire*, while *Ça plane pour moi* chanteur Plastic Bertrand provides the soul-chugger *Stop ou encore* (1982), and French music icon Robert Charlebois warbles *Discobol* (1976) in his inimitable Gallic style. But the key track is the one alluded to in the strapline on many of the international **Discopath** posters. *I Was Made for Lovin' You* was a stab at Disco glory by those face-painted glamsters KISS. Taken from their 1979 album *Dynasty*, significantly on the Casablanca label, it reached No.5 in the 'Billboard' Dance charts. One can only wonder if the New York hard rockers are still as embarrassed as Gauthier clearly is for mining the frightening Disco idiom for success.

If My Friends Could See Me Now!

With the ridiculous amounts of money being made by **Saturday Night Fever** (1977) and all the songs from its record-breaking soundtrack riding high in the charts, filling dance floors worldwide, it was hardly surprising so many established artists decided to jump on the Disco bandwagon after years of decrying it was ruining the music industry. KISS were certainly not the first to rush to the recording studio to cut anything with the prerequisite BPM and, of course, their label Casablanca was the market leader in the field. Bryan Adams with *Let Me Take You Dancing* (1979), Burt Bacharach with *When You Bring Your Sweet Love to Me* (1977), The Beach Boys with *Here Comes the Night* (1979) and Neil Diamond with *The Dancing Bumblebee/Bumble Boogie* (1978) represent just the tip of an enormous Disco Kitsch iceberg. But while some stars came up tuneful trumps and kept their reputations intact, others crashed and burned spectacularly. Here is a selection of both ends of that taste spectrum:

CLAUDIA CARDINALE *Sun... I Love You* (1977)
The critically acclaimed, award-winning Italian actress who worked for Mario Monicelli and Luchino Visconti before becoming an international star thanks to Federico Fellini's classic **8½** (1963) and Sergio Leone's monumental **Once Upon a Time in the West** (1968) had sung before. She crooned the soundtrack songs *Popsy Pop's Song* and *Keep Up Your Smile* for **Popsy Pop/The 21 Carat Snatch** (1970), and *Prairie Woman* and *Seduction* for **Les petroleuses/The Legend of Frenchie King** (1971). If she had any ambitions to be a singer though she certainly didn't let on but surprised everyone when Charles Rinieri (Shelia B. Devotion writer), Gilbert Di Nino (Sylvie Vartan arranger) and Leo Carrier (New Paradise Disco studio project producer) talked her into recording a few Disco tracks in France. The result was three mild cuts, *Love Affair, Private Life, Do It Claudia,* and the absolutely fabulous *Sun... I Love You*, a gorgeous slice of prime unfettered Eurodisco. Featuring a catchy chorus, lilting melody, sexy delivery, soaring violins and wonderful overall production by Jean-Luc Drion, the man behind Chocolat's exotic Carnival Disco output, this underrated release is a sheer Disco Delight. Sunsational!

RICK WAKEMAN
Rhapsody in Blue (1979)

The London-born keyboardist, songwriter, television and radio presenter, author and actor is best known for being a member of the progressive rock band Yes across five residences between 1971 and 2004, and for his solo albums released in the 1970s. In 1979 he released the double album *Rhapsodies* from which this abomination came. Translating the 1924 George Gershwin *Rhapsody in Blue* into oom-pah-pah Schlager music complete with fairground organ does the classic American composition no favours at all. Nor did it have any impact on the dance charts. Even the Royal Philharmonic Orchestra finessed their fast tempo classical music to an electronic beat concept far better with their *Hooked on Classics* albums. Gershwin got off lightly as it turned out. Wakeman's *Swan Lager* from the same collection was worse and must have had Tchaikovsky turning in his grave. Messy!

TWIGGY
Angels Never Sleep at Night (1980)

Discovered as the 'Face of 1966', teenage hairdresser's assistant Leslie Hornby from Neasden in North London became one of pop culture's most enduring icons after changing her name to Twiggy and entering the Swinging Sixties modelling world. Throughout the 1970/80s Twiggy established herself as an accomplished all-round entertainer, moving into television with her own variety series 'Twiggs', film (**The Boy Friend**, 1971, **W**, 1974), Broadway musical theatre ('My One and Only', 1983) and landing a recording career with the Mercury label, gaining a Top Twenty hit with *Here I Go Again* (1976). After collaborating with David Essex on the failed Disco track *Falling Angel* (1978), Twiggy relocated to Los Angeles where she became friends with Donna Summer. Before long Twiggy was in the studio recording *Angels Never Sleep at Night* with producer Jürgen Koppers, who had just completed the Donna/Barbra Streisand powerhouse duet *No More Tears (Enough Is Enough)* (1979), with contributions from Donna mainstay Pete Bellotte and Donna's husband, Bruce Sudano of Brooklyn Dreams. Unfortunately Twiggy's vocals never soar like that iconic dynamic duo and the stodgy result is a mishmash of Europop and progressive rock with an apologetic Disco patina. Unreleased until 2007 to tie in with Twiggy's 40 Year Showbiz Anniversary, it's easy to see why this questionable chant didn't make the grade as Disco entered its twilight years. Wonky!

ILONA STALLER / CICCIOLINA
I Was Made for Dancin' / Save the Last Dance for Me

Porn star, Radical Party politician, alleged KGB spy, artist's model and Playboy centrefold, Hungarian born Ilona Staller became all these and more after she moved to Rome in the 1970s. It was from her phone-in sex show Radio Luna that Staller derived the stage name Cicciolina, as she called her listeners *cicciolini* – little dumplings. The first woman to bare her breasts on Italian television, she parlayed all her excessive media attention into the film **Cicciolina amore mio** (1979). And this led to Staller's debut RCA album *Ilona Staller*, which showcased two songs from the movie soundtrack – *I Was Made for Dancin'*, a cover version of teen idol Leif Garrett's American Disco Top Ten smash, and *Più su sempre più su*. Plus an English/Italian Disco version of The Drifters' 1960 classic *Save the Last Dance for Me/Lascia l'ultimo ballo per me*. Despite her weak, reedy, often out of tune voice and bad English delivery, these two tracks are surprisingly potent thanks to ace Eurodisco production values by Staller's manager Riccardo Schicchi, who also shot the softcore photos gracing the original gatefold sleeve. Camptastic!

ROD MCKUEN
Amor, Amor (1978)

Bing Crosby, Julio Iglesias, Ben E. King and Luis Miguel are just a few of the artists who have recorded bestselling versions of the classic 1943 Latino evergreen *Amor, Amor*. Unfortunately when Rod McKuen shoved it out on green vinyl in 1978, all it got was a little traction in gay clubs due to its Easy Listening weirdness, sudden Big Band break and hilarious back-up vocals.

One can only wonder why the American singer/songwriter, musician and poet responsible for the superb *Jean* theme from **The Prime of Miss Jean Brodie** (1969) and the translations of Jacques Brel's *Le moribond* into *Seasons in the Sun* and *Ne me quitte pas/If You Go Away* for Terry Jacks' two 1974 chart hits didn't chose one of the many in his impressive back catalogue. Peculiar!

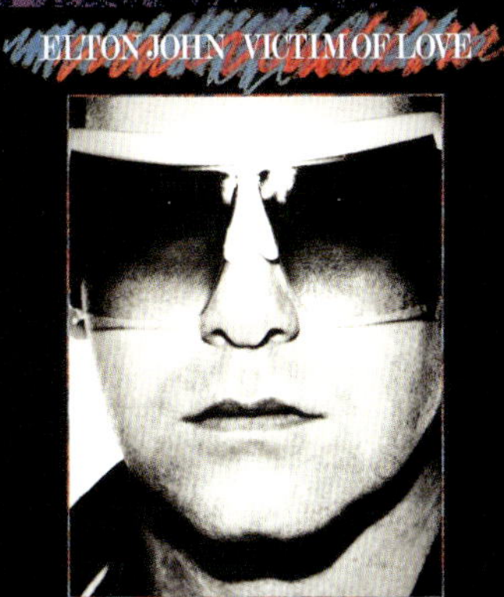

ELTON JOHN
Victim of Love (1979)
Considered by his fans as the worst album of his entire career, Sir Elton John's careen into Discoland didn't make any real chart impact either – it only got to No.55 in the crucial 'Billboard' Disco charts in the late autumn of 1979. While it's crystal clear that Elton isn't entirely comfortable in the Disco world, despite being no stranger to Studio 54, he had the good sense to surround himself with veteran dance talents in his effort to stay musically relevant. Elton was friends with producer Pete Bellotte way before he co-produced Donna Summer's string of hits and, together with arranger Thor Baldursson (Madleen Kane, Grace Jones, Munich Machine, Lipstique) and musician/producer Keith Forsey (Trax, Claudja Barry, Boney M.), put together this creditable and catchy segued seven-track effort beginning with an okay cover of Chuck Berry's *Johnny B. Goode* and ending with the pounding pleaser *Victim of Love*. Evocative!

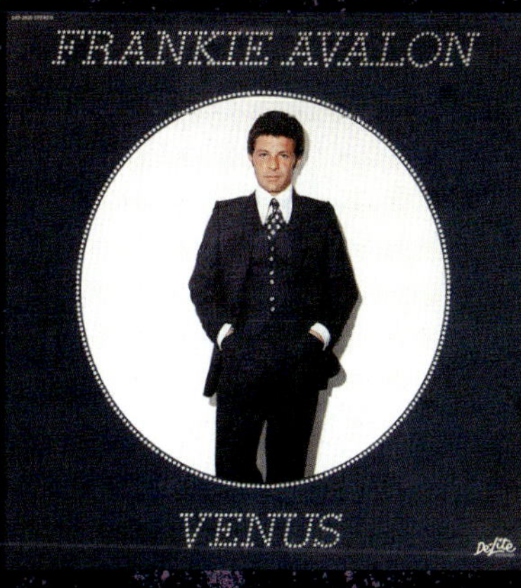

FRANKIE AVALON
Venus (1976)
1950s teen idol Frankie Avalon needed a boost to his career in 1976. With his pop chart-busting days over and his **Beach Party** (1963) franchise celebrity fizzling out with duds like **Skidoo** (1968), the one-time trumpeter turned to his past song catalogue and chose his first 1959 No.1 hit to contour to the contemporary Disco sound. With outstanding, punchy and complex arrangement by Joe Renzetti, Avalon found his Disco *Venus* embraced by mainly gay venues enough for a Top Fifty placement in the dance charts. Although Avalon at the time of his musical comeback described the remake as "All right, but I still prefer the original", it did have the desired effect. Mega-producer Allan Carr loved the cover version so much he asked Avalon to appear as Teen Angel in the blockbuster film musical **Grease** (1978). As for Renzetti, he embarked on a soundtrack career counting **Dead & Buried** (1981), **Child's Play** (1988) and **Frankenhooker** (1990) among his many subsequent composing credits. Exciting!

STEELY DAN
Glamour Profession (1980)
Gaucho was the seventh studio album by the *Do it Again* (1975) rockers and represented their penchant for perfectionism and obsessive technique. More than 42 different musicians spent over a year in the studio and overspent on their monetary advance for a project plagued by creative, personal and professional problems. Then came the battle to release the album, especially as the minimal groove and spacey feeling was hardly anyone's idea of a new direction. Case in point, *Glamour Profession*, aimed at the dance market, failed in every respect to engage clubbers while enraging the band's fan-base for being superficial fluff. Mystical!

TONY ORLANDO
Don't Let Go (1978)
Before Dawn, and his numerous hits under that name including *Tie a Yellow Ribbon Round the Ole Oak Tree* (1973), Tony Orlando (born Michael Anthony Orlando Cassavitis) had been a 1960s teen idol in the clean-cut Frankie Avalon tradition with songs in the charts like *Halfway to Paradise* (1961) and *Bless You* (1961). And just as Avalon did in the mid 1970s with the dusted off Golden Oldie *Venus* (1959), Orlando entered the Disco field with the elegantly crafted *Don't Let Go* (1978). Produced by Jerry Wexler and Barry Beckett, this nifty cover of Roy Hamilton's 1958 hit starts out slow in relaxed mode before gathering steam and wrapping a glowing arrangement around the laid-back vocals. With its pulsing drumbeat, striking horns, electrifying organ, wash of violins and subtle choral vocals, *Don't Let Go* had a cooled-down vibe that actually made it hotter as it scorched up the summer playlists. Sweltering!

DEMIS ROUSSOS
L.O.V.E. Got a Hold of Me (1978)

The kaftanned Greek pop sensation was coming off a massive string of Easy Listening hits – including *Forever and Ever* (1973), *Goodbye My Love Goodbye* (1973) and *Happy to Be on an Island in the Sun* (1975) – not to mention his water-cooler moment mention in Mike Leigh's iconic 'Abigail's Party' (1977), when he decided to hit the Disco scene head-on in 1978. But *L.O.V.E. Got a Hold of Me*, released as a 10-minute mix on a promo-only US 12-inch disc, was his first and only Disco splash (reaching No.26) mainly because his breathy, high tenor voice didn't suit the idiom and in the case of this caterwauling cut proved painful to listen to and certainly not a case of *We Shall Dance* (1971). Screechy!

JOHNNY MATHIS
Begin the Beguine / Gone, Gone, Gone (1979)

In 1978 Teddy Pendergrass, one-time lead singer of Harold Melvin & the Blue Notes, scored a solid pop hit with *Life Is a Song Worth Singing*, a soulfully funky cover of the Johnny Mathis 1973 recording. Mathis took serious note and decided to give the same sumptuous treatment to two tracks from his 1979 Columbia album *The Best Days of My Life*. The results were phenomenal for the third biggest selling artist of the 20th Century, whose countless hits include *Misty* (1960) and *When a Child Is Born* (1976). The romantic balladeer's powerhouse version of the Cole Porter standard *Begin the Beguin*, from the 1935 musical 'Jubilee', highlights orchestral quality, top class production values and lush arrangements by Gene Page from the Love Unlimited Orchestra for a truly awe-inspiring serving of Disco perfection. The flipside to that sleek touch of Disco velvet was the equally sublime *Gone, Gone, Gone*, both the finest illustrations of a veteran megastar adapting his enviable skills to the Disco schematic and creating masterpieces of effortless sophistication and melodic craft. Gone!

BRITT EKLAND
Do It to Me (Once More with Feeling) (1979)

The Swedish film, stage, and television personality who married comedian Peter Sellers always wanted to be a singer first and an actress second. She fulfilled the latter lesser ambition in such movies as **After the Fox** (1966), **Get Carter** (1971), **The Wicker Man** (1973) and achieving Bond Girl fame in **The Man with the Golden Gun** (1974). But her singing career was a complete non-starter and never would have happened at all if it hadn't been for manager Don Arden and Disco. During her much publicised tabloid romance with rock star Rod Stewart, the music entrepreneur noted the interest surrounding her over *Tonight's the Night* (1976) being all about their affair and arranged for her to record this track in her own right. On the Jet label, and credited to Nissenson, Grody and Delia, produced by Joel Diamond and arranged by Kenny Lehman, *Do It to Me (Once More with Feeling)* was dreary and draggy and its release on Ekland nude pin-up picture disc vinyl quickly vanished into the Disco disaster ether. The B-side *Private Party* was equally as dismal. Naff!

ANN-MARGRET
Love Rush (1979)

Before he became known for his collaborations with David Bowie, Alice Cooper, Madonna, Prince and Elvira, American singer, songwriter, producer, and guitarist Paul Sabu (the son of Indian-born film star Sabu, **The Thief of Bagdad**, 1940, **Cobra Woman**, 1944) joined forces with the **Kitten with a Whip** (1963) herself. The strawberry blonde actress and singer Ann-Margret had become one of the most famous sex symbols of the 1960s thanks to such hit pop ditties as *I Just Don't Understand* (1961) and a range of films from **Bye Bye Birdie** (1963), **Viva Las Vegas** (1964), and **The Pleasure Seekers** (1964) to **Murderer's Row** (1966) and her Oscar nominated role in **Carnal Knowledge** (1972). A near-fatal accident at a Lake Tahoe cabaret show in 1972 only momentarily stopped her career and she capped her late 1970s showbiz comeback with the scorching *Love Rush* that became the title of her 1980 album. Peaking at No.8 in the 'Billboard' charts, Ann-Margret tears up the hard rock infused track like no one else and the infectious melody underscored with superb production values smashes it out of the Disco park. Slinky!

ETHEL MERMAN
The Ethel Merman Disco Album (1979)
It was one of the most highly anticipated albums of 1979. Yet it turned out to be a *faux*-hipster damp squib and became the *ne plus ultra* of the entire Disco movement. The undisputed Queen of Broadway starred in thirteen musicals over four decades after becoming an overnight sensation singing *I Got Rhythm* in the 1930 George and Ira Gershwin show 'Girl Crazy'. 'Anything Goes', 'Call Me Madam', 'Annie Get Your Gun' and 'Gypsy' just four of her massive musical hits, songs from which became her cabaret repertoire for life. So when A&M Records offered The Merm as she was dubbed by co-workers the chance to BPM her famous standards it seemed the perfect synergy between Diva and Disco. But just as she told Irving Berlin when he tried to change the lyrics to a song one week before opening night, "Call me Miss Bird's Eye. It's frozen", so Emmy, Tony and Oscar winning producer/arranger Peter Matz (Noel Coward, Marlene Dietrich, Barbra Streisand, Dionne Warwick) found Merman equally intractable in the recording studio. The brassy broad refused to give an inch, sang each song exactly the way she always had, declined to sing along to the Disco track and sang the songs alone, with accompaniment and backtrack added afterwards. Hence the reason why *There's No Business Like Show Business, Everything's Coming Up Roses, I Get a Kick Out of You, Something for the Boys, Some People, Alexander's Ragtime Band, They Say It's Wonderful* (never released as part of the original package) and *I Got Rhythm* sound quite awkward, removed and plodding, lacking any real dance excitement. Fourteen songs were recorded in all, but only seven were initially released on what is now regarded as the cult Disco album of all time. And you know what? Despite being completely dismissed at the time by critics and dancers alike, it now exudes a unique kitsch appeal that has made it an acceptable addition to nostalgia playlists. Timeless!

Munchausen Syndrome

One of the longest and most exhaustive set reports I ever wrote was on Terry Gilliam's **The Adventures of Baron Munchausen** (1988) for the May 1989 issue of 'CFQ'. Columbia Pictures had sent me over to Rome where the movie was being made on fabulous sets at Cinecittà and I arrived for my week assignment at the exact moment the chaotic epic was falling apart. First hand I witnessed the bitchiness, the fights and the money problems and dutifully reported every single fact as I saw them. It turned out to be one of my most read features ever, garnering me much high profile recognition. Mainly because I managed to hit the nail on the head so precisely I have been quoted in every book on Gilliam's folly, his career and the vagaries of the film industry ever since. My new best Argento friend Michele Soavi was a second unit director on the movie, so that gave me more of a personal insight too. And as Gilliam's main Arabian Nights set was built in Stage 5, the one known as the Fellini Stage because he shot 90% of his work there, the grand maestro himself tuned up to bless the production. Rome, Gilliam and Fellini, it doesn't get much better than that.

NORTHERN SOUL (2014)

The lives of two Lancashire lads change forever after discovering the sounds of underdog American soul music. It's 1974, Wigan Casino the place to dance all night on speed, and they dream of scouring USA music store basements for enough rare grooves to become the hottest DJs on the burgeoning Northern Soul scene. One of the best British independent movies of the new millennium, **Saturday Night Fever** (1977) gets filtered through the grim up north backstreets of **Saturday Night and Sunday Morning** (1960) to capture the look, energy and working class youth culture desperate for excitement, while not shying away from its darker and drug-fuelled sides.

Originally intending to make a documentary about the underground Northern Soul movement, and being an active participant herself, photographer Elaine Constantine decided a deep-rooted rites-of-passage dramatic piece would best serve the ethos instead. Why her uplifting and pitch-perfect debut feature succeeds exceptionally, and became a UK box-office sleeper hit, is because it works both as an authentic primer in the subject matter and as a snapshot of a sea-changing era.

Set in the pokey terraced houses of fictionalised Burnsworth, rebellious schoolboy John (Elliott James Langridge) finds escape from his stifling family, authoritarian teachers and depressing factory job through the liberating power of Northern Soul music. John's rapid step into the cool crowd comes from his impulsive new mate Matt (Josh Whitehouse), called a "Northern Arsehole" at one point, who initiates him into an amphetamine-fuelled lifestyle of open-all-night clubs, gymnastic Bruce Lee dance moves and the fierce arrogance and competition on the scene. Soon hosting their own club nights, and planning their USA trip to search out rare vinyl, John lusts after mixed-race nurse Angela (Antonia Thomas), his saviour when he seemingly ODs on the Casino dancefloor.

Between superbly choreographed, twirly, wide-legged trousered dance sequences and precise recreations of small-town locations and attitudes, there's a fatal car crash, growing petty crimes and the inevitable fight between the best friends before it ends on a bittersweet note. Langridge and Whitehouse are outstanding as the ever-optimistic duo finding their haphazard way through life's wrinkles, with key cameo support from a Northern powerhouse of actors including Steve Coogan (whose

entire family seem to feature somewhere or another), Lisa Stansfield, Ricky Tomlinson and John Thomson.

Disco may have swept the country during the 1970s, but Northern Soul was its antichrist even if the often shared 4/4 beat eventually crossed over due to key DJs in the field becoming prominent dance producers. Listen to the Disco nuance in the outstanding and electrifying soundtrack complementing the ebullient style of Constantine's tonally perfect, multi-faceted gem. John enters the local youth club to Edwin Starr's Motown runner-up *Time* (1970), back at Matt's house the classic *I Really Love You* (1967) by The Tomangoes is playing with Tobi Legend's sensational *Time Will Pass You By* (1968). Edwin Starr's *Back Street* (1966) is another local youth club smash alongside the quintessential *The Night* (1972) by Frankie Valli and The Four Seasons and Shirley Ellis' *Soul Time* (1966).

John ODs to *Just Say You're Wanted (and Needed)* (1967) by 14-year-old Gwen Owens after excitedly entering the Wigan Casino to *Crying Over You* (1966) by Duke Browner, with the whole dancing crowd handclapping along. A pivotal funeral wake is orchestrated to *Exus Trek* (1966) by The Luther Ingram Orchestra with *Turning My Heartbeat Up* (1972) by The MVP's playing over the end credits featuring yet more signature dancing. Heard elsewhere on Constantine's love letter to Northern Soul are *Right Track* (1966) by Billy Butler, *This Loved Starved Heart of Mine (It's Killing Me)* (1965) by Marvin Gaye, and two essential tracks that perfectly sum up the energetic drive of the entire movement, *I'm Com'un Home in the Morn'un* (1965) by Lou Pride and *Stick By Me Baby* (1967) by The Salvadors. Few films rarely capture the palpable thrill, immediacy and allure of a clubbed-to-death dance subculture like this one does.

A brief mention must be made of **SoulBoy** (2010), about a bored teenager having a Northern Soul epiphany when he chases the girl of his dreams to the Wigan Casino. Directed by Shimmy Marcus, starring a terrifically endearing Martin Compston, and made on an even smaller budget, it's an agreeable salute to the same period with its retro heart in the right place and the one obvious track – *Tainted Love* (1965) by Gloria Jones.

Northern Soul

In 1968, after a recce to Manchester's Twisted Wheel club, Dave Godin, owner of London's Soul City Records shop, told his staff not to waste time playing current hits from the US charts to visiting northern customers, just the passionate sounds of Afro-American soul that the North of Watford demographic loved and danced to on extended weekends away from the grind of their industrial, menial and factory work. The Northern Soul moniker stuck and would soon epitomise the love affair between mostly white British working-class kids and the fast-paced dance music of urban black America.

The harbinger of what disaffected youth would soon transform into Punk, and running parallel to the Disco frenzy, at the height of Northern Soul thousands of party people would descend on venues like the Wigan Casino, the Twisted Wheel, the Golden Torch in Stoke and the Blackpool Mecca every weekend for all-night parties, driven by high-octane music usually drawn from the past decade of flop, ignored or overlooked R&B soul-strutters from such independent US labels as Mirwood and Revilot. It was the dance music of drama, heartbreak and blissful elation sung by men and women who were mainly clueless that these forgotten A and B sides would become cult items of desire among fans in Bolton and Wolverhampton.

The former Beatnik coffee bar The Twisted Wheel (now just a blue plaque on the wall of a 3-star hotel by Piccadilly Station) was the first pivotal step in Northern Soul's fledgling history. Its patrons were informed by Tamla Motown appreciation, but who also knew there was a vast seam

of undiscovered material recorded in the wake of label founder Berry Gordy's success. These punters didn't want to be told what music to dance to, they wanted to discover it themselves and it's why the movement became far more active as rabid consumers. As the BBC were starting up Radio One and broadcasting mainstream 'Top of the Pops', Twisted Wheel dancers, and those in Lord Jim's, Halifax, the Catacombs, Wolverhampton, The King Mojo, Sheffield etc., set the popular agenda spurred on by canny DJs.

Sure the scene was cultish and intense, with its own dress code, language and moves, but it was also inclusive and democratic because it owed its very existence to a seemingly alchemical combination between the working class Afro-Americans in America's rust belts and their counterparts in the industrial North of Great Britain. Just like Disco, Northern Soul was called "second rate pop" by critics but they missed the point. For it was all about sharing, unity and magnifying the collision between the self-expression of differing yet similar cultures for the biggest bang on the dance floors.

Name DJs on the circuit included Tony Jebb, Les Cockell, Alan Day, Ian Dewhirst, Martyn Ellis, Colin Curtis and Ian Levine, who all knew their job was to create an alternative to the horrendous world outside their club doors. A world of industrial unrest, power cuts, the Bay City Rollers and football hooliganism. Fans travelled from far and wide on an organised underground circuit of bus hires, car sharing and train carriage meet-ups. September 1973 saw the start of regular all-nighters at the Wigan Casino (mysteriously set ablaze in the 1980s) lasting eight years before the first wave subsided. But like Disco, if you loved Northern Soul you carried it forward through the next decades and the scene is still as vibrant as it ever was. Hence the affirmation, the 'Northern Soul at the Proms' event at the Royal Albert Hall in 2023 performed by the BBC Concert Orchestra.

DJs Ian Levine and Colin Curtis pioneered a new Northern Soul sound in 1974. Modern Soul married soulful harmony with contemporary dynamism as epitomised by The Carstairs and their seminal *It Really Hurts Me Girl* (1973) and The Montclairs's *Hung Up on Your Love* (1973). This eventually morphed into the New York Disco sound that would take Levine to London, to DJ at Heaven and eventually to produce some of the best-known HiNRG releases. Northern Soul and Disco would happily collide in *Are You Ready for This* by The Brothers, featuring George Young, taken from their terrific 1974 album *Disco Soul*, comprising mainly of instrumental versions of then current dance hits like *Doctor's Orders*, *Never Can Say Goodbye* and *Kung Fu Fighting*. All cuts were snappy and jazzy, perfectly capturing the bright and breezy mid-1970s crossover Disco atmosphere.

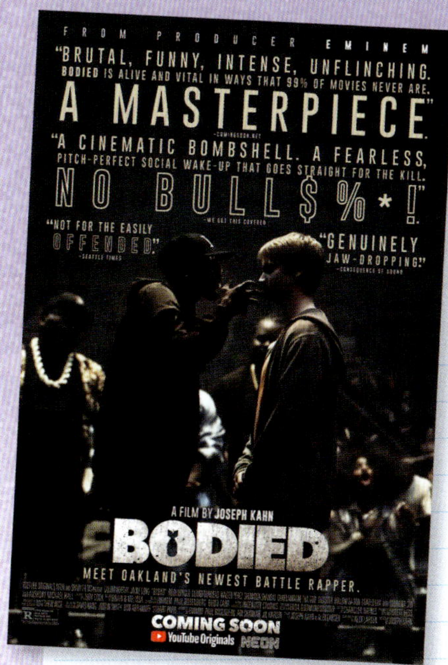

Disco Memo

Candy

Anyone who attends the banner FrightFest event in London every August Bank Holiday knows I always have a firm favourite in the line-up that I will continually talk about and big up to ensure it gets the audience it deserves. But I had no idea that my 2011 choice would lead me back into the rock video world in such a splashy way. I had picked director Joseph Kahn's self-financed **Detention** because it was such a fast and furious teen comedy slasher unlike any other I had seen. Full of post-modern playfulness and riffing on everything from **Prom Night** (1980) to **Back to the Future** (1985), it signalled a new approach and way forward for the genre. The late night Sunday screening was everything I could have hoped for and cemented a bond with the director that led to us also showing his next movie, the battle rapper **Bodied** (2017).

Of course I knew Korean-American Kahn was a Grammy-winning rock video director of renown having worked with an incredible number of superstars like Taylor Swift, Eminem, Britney Spears, Backstreet Boys, Jennifer Lopez, Lady Gaga, Kylie Minogue, George Michael and Christina Aguilera. But I was surprised when he called me up in 2012 asking if I'd like to appear in the video he was directing in London's East End for the Robbie Williams song *Candy*. Naturally I said yes – you don't turn down opportunities like that – and I had experience thanks to my Russell Mulcahy friendship. So, dressed up in road worker gear I took my place at the Old Spitalfields Market/Petticoat Lane locations so ex-Take That group member Williams could walk past dismissively following 'Skins' and **Moon** (2009) actor Kaya Scodelario into saintly dangers.

It was a fun day out. Williams was nice. Kahn is a workaholic genius. The song went to No.1 in the charts and people kept recognising me every time the video played on television. I felt like my life had come full circle, bookended by probably the two most famous rock video whizkids of all time. Incidentally, just for a laugh, I introduced Scodelario on stage at the Empire, Leicester Square as my *Candy* co-star when she promoted her leading lady role in **Crawl** (2019) on FrightFest's opening night that year.

THE MARTIAN (2015)

In space no one can see you boogie! Just as we all suspected it would, Disco keeps a stranded astronaut sane in Ridley Scott's riff on **Robinson Crusoe on Mars** (1964). A perfect example of how Disco will still be relevant in the future no matter what the naysayers' opinions, **The Martian** is an affecting survival adventure given a BPM heartbeat. Smartly scripted by Drew Goddard (**The Cabin in the Woods**, 2011), based on Andy Weir's blog-turned bestselling novel, and elegantly directed by cosmic connoisseur Scott, this day-after-tomorrow sci-fi adventure followed in the thematic wake of **Moon** (2009), **Gravity** (2013) and **Interstellar** (2014) by probing the mundane psyche more than the usual alien creature danger.

Astronaut Mark Watney (Matt Damon on top engaging form) is left behind, thought dead, on the red planet Mars when a colossal storm forces his five fellow crew members to abandon their intergalactic mission. Impaled by a broken antenna, injured Watney eventually regains consciousness and must quickly assess his situation. With only fifty days of food left and the next mission to Mars operation not due to arrive for another four years, the botanist by profession has no intention of dying alone in the vast universe. So he starts growing potatoes using his own waste as fertiliser and finds some old NASA lo-tech equipment, which eventually reconnects him back to Earth to reveal his plight.

Ultimately it comes down to the courage and willingness of Mark's devoted crewmates (Jessica Chastain, Michael Pena, Kate Mara, Sebastian Stan and Aksel Hennie) to put themselves at great risk by attempting a mutinous rescue with only an outside chance of being successful. And in any case, should five lives be put in danger for the reward of saving one?

Touching on the melancholy of Mark's dilemma and keeping the excitement levels high through his savvy invention and innovations, the only way to keep his mind active are two old school diversions left behind by a former astronaut. Videotaped episodes of the 'Happy Days' sitcom (1974-84) and a treasure trove collection of 1970s Disco hits. And so the final frontier becomes a Disco remix of wonderful chart-

topping tunes to keep the spirits high and forever in the sky. The six stormers featured are Vicki Sue Robinson's Olympus Mons energiser *Turn the Beat Around* (1976), Donna Summer's Phobos classic *Hot Stuff* (1979), The Hues Corporation's Deimas seminal *Rock the Boat* (1973), Thelma Houston's asteroid essential *Don't Leave Me This Way* (1976), The O'Jays' evocative Valles Marineris soulster *Love Train* (1972), and Gloria Gaynor's quintessential *I Will Survive* (1978), perhaps the most appropriate use of that evergreen anthem ever. Space Disco lives!

John Davis and the Monster Orchestra

As Disco gathered momentum during the mid-1970s one of the key trends was the symphonic orchestra sound. Before the rise of the computer wizard simply pressing buttons to turn pre-recorded tracks into pure electronic dance textures, seasoned musicians were gathered in a studio to play off sheet music and deliver the necessary rhythms with a skilled accuracy honed through years of session work experience. Extravagant orchestrations, augmented with swirling strings and vibrant percussion, soon became synonymous with the New York Disco sound and every major record label wanted to cash in on its full rounded style and epic delivery. One of the major maestros of the symphonic Disco beat was writer, producer, arranger, conductor, singer and ace musician John Davis who, with his celebrated Monster Orchestra, released four superb albums in the latter half of the Disco decade.

Born in Philadelphia, Pennsylvania, in 1947, alongside his (future famed trumpeter) twin brother Joe, Davis learned how to play the clarinet at an early age and then also took up the saxophone when he joined his school's jazz band. Word about his musical talent grew, so when he graduated from high school he was invited to join the US Naval Academy Band in Annapolis, Maryland. Within that organisation he started writing for various instrumental combos and had one tune published, entitled *Nightfall*. After exiting the service Davis headed back to Philly where the melding of soul music, jazzy funk and lush instrumentation were laying the foundations for quintessential early Disco as perfected by such prominent luminaries as McFadden and Whitehead, and Gamble and Huff.

"My recording career proper began at Sigma Sound when I was hired as an arranger for different Philly groups", John Davis told me. "Then I saw an advert in a local newspaper looking for a musical arranger at Omega Sound Studio, a company who recorded people for money. Artists would come through the doors, and I would write and arrange songs for them. One particular day singer William DeVaughn arrived and played *Be Thankful for What You Got* on his acoustic guitar. I thought it was a catchy tune with a great hook line. So we went into the studio with guitarist Norman Harris, drummer Earl Young, vibraphonist Vince Montana and myself on organ, made one pass on the track and recorded it. Joe Tarsia was my engineer, a role he would fill on several of my independent projects and I have to say I learned so much from him. The song was simple and very infectious".

That soul-chugger also became a million-selling 1974 hit. If The Sound of Philadelphia mavens didn't know the name John Davis beforehand, they certainly did after that major coup, and many of the musicians he used on the recording, including guitarist Bobby Eli, percussionist Larry Washington and string-man Don Renaldo, would become core Monster Orchestra band members two years later. Doors flew open for Davis in this wake. "Labels called up wanting me to work with their artists and that's how I ended up at Midland International

Records producing the hit Carol Douglas album *Midnight Love Affair* (1976). The president of Midland was Bob Reno who liked what I did with Carol and asked me to produce Touch of Class and their single *I'm in Heaven* (1976). It became a big Disco hit and led to a very successful album. It was then I got a call from Sam Weiss who told me *I'm in Heaven* was his favourite record EVER and, as flattering as that was, soon started talking business and asked if I would consider joining his label SAM Records".

It was an offer Davis couldn't refuse. Romanian-born Sam Weiss and his older brother Hy(man) had founded the Old Town Records label in 1953 and successfully promoted the doo wop sound via groups like The Earls, The Solitaires and The Capris. After co-writing *Life Is But a Dream* (1969) for Jay and The Americans, selling their catalogue to Atlantic Records in 1970 and working for a while with the legendary Stax outfit, the duo could see the dance music craze rapidly emerging and formed the SAM Records label in 1975 to highlight the burgeoning genre. Their first release was *Woman of the Ghetto* (1975) by Doris Duke but it was Weiss cannily signing up solo artist John Davis and his back-up band the Monster Orchestra that would put the fledgling label squarely in the Disco spotlight.

Why the Monster Orchestra? "Because Harry Chipetz, general manager of Sigma Sound Studio, started calling me 'the monster maker' when the records I worked on all started becoming monster hits. I eventually shortened it to 'monster' and the nickname stuck". And it was the studio's resident girl group session singers Barbara Ingram, Carla Benson and Evette Benton, known collectively as The Sweethearts of Sigma, who provided the melodious back-up vocals to the Monster Orchestra assembly of rhythm section musicians Eli, Washington, Renaldo, Charles Collins, Craig Snyder, Jimmy Young, Roland Chambers and Vince Fay.

John Davis and the Monster Orchestra's rise to quality Disco heights began with the single *Night and Day* (1976), which followed the overriding vogue of the time – giving pop standards the luxuriant Disco treatment. From The Beatles songbook and Glenn Miller's Big Band evergreens to Tamla Motown hits and Charlie Chaplin movie tunes, everything was being cleverly rearranged by smart producers to access their dance beats. "Sam asked if I was aware of the trend of doing instrumental versions of old favourites. I said I was and the result was *Night and Day*, which reached No.5 in the 'Billboard' Disco Charts and led to the first album. Cole Porter songs were chosen because when I considered the music of past eras, there wasn't a better back catalogue selection than Porter's, he truly was a genius".

Also Broadway composer and lyric sophisticate Porter had many songs popularised on stage and in movies by high calibre stars Ethel Merman, Frank Sinatra and Doris Day. Giving his album the title *Night & Day* (not AND) after the Fred Astaire break-out hit from the 1934, **The Gay Divorcee** musical, Davis added a free-for-all soul, fizz, lilt and punch to the equally massive chart-toppers of yester-year *I Get a Kick Out of You, I've Got You Under My Skin, In the Still of the Night, You Do Something to Me* and *It's De-Lovely*. (Note: some titles don't exactly mirror their original ones!) Two new songs penned by Davis and guitarist Craig Snyder were added into the mix – *I Can't Stop* and *Tell Me How You Like It* – for a contrast to the Golden Age of Hollywood nostalgia, putting the album on every DJ's turntable throughout Spring 1976.

Just under a year later the band were back in the Disco Top Ten with the 12-inch single *Up Jumped the Devil* that would become the title track from their second album released four months later in June 1977. "Because *Night & Day* did so well, when Sam called for another album I was caught in a bit of indecision. I didn't want my legacy for the band to be re-recording old standards forever so I decided to begin writing my own material. Craig and bass player Vince had become my two best friends, we came from similar backgrounds and I felt we really gelled together well in the studio. We were always free to pitch riffs and writing ideas to each other and would meet at my house to work out different grooves for songs. That way I came up the idea for *Up Jumped the Devil* as I wanted to deviate from the big orchestral material and get a little funkier. The hope was it would separate me from the many other Disco Orchestras and it worked out brilliantly".

Indeed it did. *Up Jumped the Devil* is a hard-hitting invigorator, packed full of pumping bass, spiky percussion and loaded with thrilling vocals. It's the perfect opener to an album bristling with orchestral manoeuvres like the exciting *We Can Fly*, the laid-back and cadenced *You Gotta Give It Up* and the sweetly stylish slice of fairytale funk *Once Upon a Time*. But it's the three-part medley *The Magic is You* that shines out with its insinuating glissando of melodies, attractive production finesse throughout

You're the One and the mainly instrumental delight of *Recapitulation*. "For *The Magic Is You* medley I wanted my signature Monster Orchestra sound infused with such other strong elements as a funkier bass line and memorable rock guitar licks. Stringing those three songs together meant it became one of the very first cuts released to encompass one side of a dance album without stopping the beat. It worked well and in clubs all over the world people danced their asses off to its 14-minute length".

As a renowned producer, songwriter, musician and arranger, John Davis also had a major impact on the careers of such artists as John Travolta, Grace Jones, Gary Criss, Ashford and Simpson, The Stylistics, Diana Ross, The Trammps, Arthur Prysock, Silver Convention, Charo and Donna Summer before composing themes for the television shows 'TJ Hooker', 'Dynasty', 'MacGyver' and 'Beverly Hills 90210' once the Disco boom subsided. But it wasn't over for the Monster Orchestra after *Up Jumped the Devil*, not by a long chalk, as there were still two more superb albums to come from a period Davis glowingly terms "The most magical time in Philly. The beauty of *Up Jumped the Devil* was it freed me up creatively and allowed the Monster Orchestra to become more original, more innovative, more... more! That was the really fun part of my Disco years".

"I knew my Disco music was making inroads due to a memorable incident in Bermuda. Bass player Vince Fay and I took a holiday with our wives and were checking into the hotel. When he heard our names the desk clerk jumped up and asked us if we were the guys from the Monster Orchestra. We were both so surprised and flattered to be recognised at all, let alone in another country. Needless to say we were freaked to realise our music meant so much around the world. It was a very rewarding experience for us both".

Nevertheless when SAM Records called up requesting a third Monster Orchestra album, Davis was extremely busy with numerous other artists. "When I look back now I can see I was rather overwhelmed by the demands being made on me and I guess I developed something of an attitude. That's the reason why the first track released, and subsequent album title, is *Ain't That Enough for You* (1978). I'm sure you can make the lyric correlation between my mood and creative juices at the time! It became our biggest hit ever (No.4 in the Disco Charts) and we were soon in the studio recording a tie-in album. It was Sam who suggested I put myself on the album cover for the first time. I wasn't sure because the Monster Orchestra was a group effort involving so many talented people. But Sam prevailed and to this day I'm not sure if the formal attire I'm wearing in the photograph is supposed to suggest class, the Phantom of the Opera or a vampire monster!"

Ain't That Enough for You retrenched from the funk punch, but developed its melodic flavours, choppy hustle and high style further in the additional *A Bite of the Apple*, *Disco Fever*, *I'll Be the Music*, and *Stay with Me*, all mainly composed by Davis with help from guitarist Craig Snyder and Fay. *I've Got the Hots for You*, written by Big Dee Irwin (of *Swinging on a Star*, 1963, duet fame with Little Eva) and his jazz synthesizer pioneer son David Ervin, *Whatever Happened to You and Me*, and *Kojak Theme* (an ingenious Disco version of John Cacavas' theme to the top rated TV detective series starring Telly Savalas) round out the stellar eclectic symphony, the success of which attracted the attention of Columbia Records who acquired the SAM Records label from Weiss in a very lucrative deal. "Like many Disco producers who were too busy working on the music itself, I didn't do a lot of clubbing. But Sam and I often went to Studio 54 in Manhattan to get a feel for reactions to the Monster Orchestra releases. It helped enormously when it came time to record new music because the energy and sheer joy of dancing in that Queen of Clubs was never more obvious".

News of the Columbia Records deal struck a very ominous chord in Davis though. "I couldn't have been less excited in truth. A few years earlier I produced *I Just Can't Say Goodbye* (1974) for Philly Devotions and it was storming up the Disco charts – until Columbia got hold of it, decided to 'promote' it, whereupon it promptly tumbled off. Philly Devotions were the first group in pop history to release a 12-inch single (*I Just Can't Make It*, 1975) and it was how I met up with Disco legend Tom Moulton. We became great friends and he was the only person I felt safe with to remix any of my records. I would watch Tom mix and note how he used his heart not just his ears. He was always looking for that feeling we all get when we hear a record sound and feel the way it should be. I've always credited Tom with teaching me how to listen to music differently and how the heart and soul are important ingredients in themselves. I truly owe him".

With reassurances from Sam that his Philly Devotions experiences with Columbia would not happen again, Davis entered the recording studio to cut the fourth album, *The Monster Orchestra Strikes Again.* Pushing for an even wider appeal with a creamy funk approach and spicy orchestration, the tracks *Baby I've Got It, That's What I Get,* and *When It's Right for Love* were underpinned by three now famous Disco era standards. *Love Magic* and *Holler* were twinned on a 12-inch single reaching No.5 and *Bourgie, Bourgie* became one of the most popular tracks Davis has to his name. "That was written by the very talented Nick Ashford and Val Simpson and featured on their 1977 album *Send It*, but only as an instrumental. I'll never forget Nick arriving at the studio with lyrics to the music handwritten on a crumpled piece of paper. It looked like he had honestly written them on the way there. No matter, the three of us sang them, and I loved the whole experience. It just proved to me what a genius Nick was, and he and Val are two of my favourite artists I've worked with".

Recording alongside Ashford and Simpson was the sole bright spot for Davis regarding *The Monster Orchestra Strikes Again.* "I had just won the 'Billboard Magazine Disco Orchestra of the Year' Award, *Love Magic* took off like crazy in the clubs and everything was looking great. Except history repeated itself, Columbia once more did not get behind the record and it fell off the charts. I was really disappointed by the whole affair and that was the last project Sam Weiss and I ever worked on. Although Sam was supportive of my creative decisions, he just didn't have the clout at Columbia to bring the Monster Orchestra the attention it needed to break through at the radio level".

"I started out as a musician and part of me still enjoys the playing experience. But when you undertake doing an album like the four I did with SAM, you have to reach into so many levels of yourself. Just getting the ideas for the songs was always so exciting to me because that part of the process would dictate what direction to go in. In my mind the song and arrangement were the same thing, it all formed into one and I would become driven to get everything down on paper. I could always hear the whole production in my head, which was truly a blessing. Once the arrangement was nailed I would determine the instrumentation, the singers and what part I would involve myself in. I always tried to play at least one instrument on every record I made. That was the best way to convey the musical 'feel' to the other Monster Orchestra members. It was always important to me that I felt part of the group, not just their leader". Although two further stand alone singles were released under the Monster Orchestra moniker – *Hangin' Out* (1981), *Theme from 'Dynasty'* (1983) – that was it as far as John Davis was concerned, who turned to composing the themes for those hit television shows.

"Does it surprise me how popular Disco still is all over the world today? Not really. I think it was the last time there were honest true melodies and big production in pop music. You couldn't hear a good Disco song without it infecting you and you'd always find yourself singing it while just walking down the street. I always hoped my music made people cheerful or evoked a strong emotion from them. Disco was happy, uplifting, exciting to hear. I think my music and other producers' work from the golden Disco era will always remain relevant because of their subject matter. I mostly wrote about relationships and issues of interest to the widest possible audience. And it's those topics that will continue to be popular as long as the human condition remains intact. Everyone has experienced a little *Love Magic* in their lives as well as doing everything to maintain a relationship as in *Ain't That Enough for You.* Life will always have a place for love and Disco – and that is never, ever going to change".

Sweet Dreams

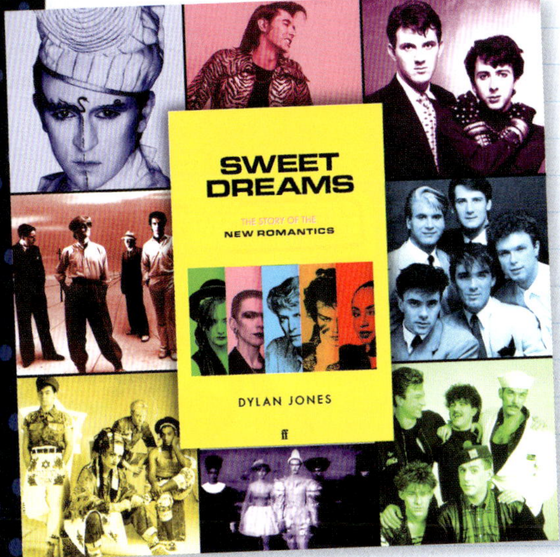

I've been name-checked in so many books about London in the 1970s, I've lost count. But even I was surprised by an entry in Dylan Jones' 'Sweet Dreams: From Club Culture to Style Culture, the Story of the New Romantics' (Faber, 2020). For one of the quotes in the 'GQ' editor's pithy history of synth-pop splendour, the Blitz kids, Browns and the aesthetic revolution that birthed the gaudily rococo fashion-conscious New Wave was from club promoter Graham Ball. It said "I remember Alan Jones who used to be a shop assistant in SEX and who was probably the first Punk. After the Boat Trip he said, 'I'm done'. He got in early and got out early".

Probably the first Punk? Hmm. Was I really? Perhaps. I was certainly unique in the individual look I worked hard to communicate and I could be nasty and vicious to a fault. It wasn't until I walked through the shop doors of Malcolm and Vivienne's 'Let It Rock' that I felt I'd found like-minded people to hang out with. But I was never into the radical politics they spouted as part of their personality, Vivienne with her Scum Manifesto and Malcolm with his Situationist rants. What being a Punk meant to me was dressing how I wanted, saying what I thought without any social filter and having the best possible time all the time. As I still live by that credo, I suppose I will forever remain a Punk. And if people want to believe I was the first of that revolutionary lifestyle, great. Who am I to say any different?

AJ in Bowie make-up for a Japanese magazine shoot.

AJ in an original Let It Rock T shirt worn in LA, 1973.

AJ in camp leather look at the Portobello Hotel.

THE GREASY STRANGLER (2016)

"Hootie Tootie Disco Cutie!" Just one of many lines to endlessly quote after seeing this puerile, ridiculous, disgusting, shocking, repulsive and absolutely fabulous original trashterpiece. Gonzo Midnight Movie philosophy returned with a massive bang in this part Z-movie spoof, part bad taste epic, all gory slasherama executive produced by the awesome holy trinity of director Ben Wheatley (**Kill List**, 2011, **Sightseers**, 2012, **High-Rise**, 2015, **Freefire**, 2016), actor Elijah Wood (**The Lord of the Rings** trilogy, 2001-3, **Cooties**, 2015, **A Girl Walks Home Alone at Night**, 2015) and Fantastic Fest/Alamo Drafthouse founder Tim League. The bastard child of John Waters, the Kuchar Brothers and Quentin Dupieux, it's a gross-out Disco delight from the warped minds of director/co-writer Jim Hosking (the 'G for Grandad' segment in **ABCs of Death 2**) and co-writer/storyboard artist Toby Harvard ('Downton Abbey') where the jokes go on for way too long – purposely, to bury themselves in the disbelieving brain – the dialogue is repeated *ad nauseam*, the costumes a sparkle-drenched scanty-panty Studio 54 fever dream and everything else is covered in oodles of grease.

Socially inept, ageing Disco enthusiast Big Ronnie (Michael St. Michaels, **The Video Dead**, 1987) and his downtrodden son Big Brayden (Sky Elobar, 'New Girl', 2015) run a scuzzy Disco Walking Tour through the back streets of Los Angeles. Basically making the facts up as they go along, in their pink hot pants ensembles they point out where the Bee Gees supposedly wrote *Night Fever* (1977), Robert 'Kool' Bell worked before he formed the Gang, and the home once shared by all members of Earth, Wind & Fire.

On one particular tour Big Brayden catches the glad eye of the voluptuous Janet (Elizabeth De Razzo, 'Eastbound & Down', 2013) and he's convinced she's the one to help him lose his virginity. But when he discusses his dating plans with Big Ronnie, a romantic rivalry is sparked, not because his smooth-talking bullshit artist father is attracted to Janet so much as he doesn't like Big Brayden's attentions shifting away from his self-centred universe. So begins a competition between father and son that runs parallel to the exploits of a sleazy maniac covered in cooking fats killing their clients and friends in gruesome ways.

As former Disco manager Big Ronnie boasts of booking Michael Jackson at the height of his *Smooth Criminal* (1988) fame and spending weekends on John Travolta's luxury yacht, he takes Janet clubbing to John and Ron's Dance Jungle where he flashes his enormous penis in a see-through glitter Disco onesie. Big Brayden can't compete in the genitalia area, but it's clear his heart is in the right place concerning Janet just as he begins to suspect the Greasy Strangler stalker is indeed Big Ronnie, who is spied going to a car wash to get rid of all the oily evidence under the watchful eye of his blind pal Big Paul (Gil Gex, **Dead on Arrival**, 2013).

With eye-watering farting sequences, eye-popping sexual clinches and eye-grazing splatter, the gutter aesthetic on show in this carnival of filth, fun and depravity is a total cohesive success of fizzy excess and palpable Disco ambience. How the actors kept straight faces throughout this once-seen-never-forgotten item is anybody's guess? Other lines worth memorising are "I could use a boogie woogie, I've got the blues", a full list of shits starting with bull and progressing to king penguin and "I'd rather be here than in New York with John Travolta". No Disco songs of any note feature in Hosking's hoot 'n' tooting hootenanny but complementing every outrageous scene in an impressive way – Big Ronnie's spot-lit dance down the street is a highlight – is lo-fi electronica synthesizing from Bristol band Fuck Buttons member Andrew Hung.

(Hosking's next outing, **An Evening with Beverly Luff Linn**, 2017, proved his love of Disco wasn't just a cynical ploy as it featured Cerrone's *Supernature* on a hotel nightclub loop and one dynamite dance sequence to F.R. David's soft EuroDisco hit *Words*, 1982.)

J-Disco

In 1968 the Japanese Sony conglomerate cut a deal with CBS Records in America to create an explosion in Nippon pop artists and in return promoted their subsidiary label Philadelphia International. Before long The O'Jays, The Three Degrees and MFSB were on the Oricon charts (aka Original Confidence, the company supplying statistics on the Japanese music industry since 1967). JVC/Nippon Victor did the same for Motown while Toshiba/EMI put Isaac Hayes, Kool & The Gang and B.T. Express on the pop music landscape.

But City Pop didn't transform into Geisha Boogie and Nippon Disco until 1974 when Japan was introduced to *The Bump* by the Commodores, which sold an unheard of 100,000 copies. A year later The Finger 5, a Jacksons clone, released *Banpu (Bump) Tengoku*, a more City Pop take on the original, but this one came with dance instructions. As its popularity spread, the Japanese appetite for the new stylings of Disco proved insatiable and the All Japan Soul Disco Organisation was formed in 1975 by a union of 40 clubs that had popped up offering the American Disco experience. Between 1973 and 1976, Japan went from eight clubs nationwide to around 600, and from that pool 30 DJs travelled to America for inspiration on how to cater Disco better to

their home market. And when Van McCoy's *The Hustle* (1975) was released, it spawned the All Japan Hustle Contest and Disco arrived bigtime.

Tokyo Discos included Byblos, Mugen, The Crazy Horse and in the Shinjuku area, Apple House. But Disco radio airplay was virtually non-existent as most DJs hung on to their tried and tested rock formulas. Until *Soul Dracula* (1975) by Hot Blood broke through big-time, offering a greater, freer and fun release from bland chart rotation, and soon full-blown Japanese product followed in its wake. The first domestically produced Japanese Disco record was *The Birth of the Dragon* (1976) by Dr. Dragon & The Oriental Express, from the most prolific producer of the genre, Satoshi 'Hustle' Honda, who would lead the way with such other hits as *Boogie Train* (1977) by The Funky Bureau, *Sex-O-Sonic* by The Love Machine, *Got to Get Ready* (1978) by Something Special, and *The Flasher* (1979) and *Charlotte* (1979) by The Eastern Gang.

The challenge facing Japanese Disco came in trying to meld the American Disco spirit with quintessential Japanese concepts and culture. Some managed it brilliantly, like the jazz-funker Terumasa Hino and *This Planet Is Ours* (1978), Cosmos' *Bourbone Suite* (1982) and Hiromi Iwasaki's *Fantasy* (1976). But the purest Disco experience came from Rie Nakahara's *Sentimental Hotel* (1978) and *Disco Lady* (1978), Kay Ishiguro's *Banana* (1982), Black Level's *Disco Action* (1976), Chakra's *Free* (1981), Yuko Asano's *Summer Champion* (1979), a cover of Sergio Mendes' *Summer Dream*, and Naoya Matsuoka and Minako Yoshida's *Lovin' Mighty Fire* (1979). Ebonee Webb was an unusual entity because the band was actually a Disco combo from Memphis, Tennessee. But one gig at the Mugen Disco changed their direction and they began Discofying past Japanese pop hits and traditional songs, like *Disco Otomisan* (1978) and *Yashow Macashow* (1979).

The biggest Japanese Disco act of all was Pink Lady, who released thirteen albums from 1976 to 1980 and branded everything from lunch boxes to fast food menus. Starting out as Cookie, formed by Mie (Mitsuyo Nemoto) and Kei (Keiko Masuda), they won 'The Star Tanjou' talent show, changed their name to the cocktail, the Pink bit giving a hint of the Japanese name for softcore movie sleaze, and their Disco career had lift-off. *Pepper Keibu* (1976), *S.O.S.* (1976), *Nagisa no Sindbad* (1977), *Wanted* (1977), *UFO* (1977, and their biggest-selling single), *Southpaw* (1978), *Monster* (1978) and two Donna Summer covers *MacArthur Park* (1980) and *Last Dance* (1980) are just a few of their mega-hits. Signed to Elektra in 1979 to record in English for the international market, the *Pink Lady* album featured more obscure covers like Tom Jones' *Love Me Tonight* (1969) and The Four Tops' *Walk Away Renee* (1967), but even an American TV show spotlighting this Japanese Baccara failed in the penetration stakes to make them a global sensation.

Disco Memo

Sadistic Mika Band

It was thanks to Malcolm McLaren that I had a thrilling brush with the Japanese music industry. But let me start from the beginning… When David Bowie released *The Rise and Fall of Ziggy Stardust and the Spiders from Mars* (1972) album, his record label RCA used the Portobello Hotel for junket purposes to promote it. That's how I first met Bowie and his wife Angie. For a while there I kept being mistaken as Mick Ronson too! Everyone flew in from all over the world to interview the biggest star on the planet at that time and Nippon TV sent in a terrific camera crew whom I got very close to. Their photographer actually took a series of fantastic portraits of me in Bowie drag complete with make-up and Ziggy Stardust symbols painted on my face that he published in Japan. I became famous for 15 minutes there and was Big in Japan before that phrase had ever been coined!

When they returned to Japan the crew's word of mouth on the hotel proved very influential. Not to mention the Bowie lustre by proxy and pretty soon a lot of other Japanese stars checked in. One was Ryuichi Sakamoto, member of the influential electro-pop band Yellow Magic Orchestra (*Bridge Over Troubled Music*, 1978) and future Oscar, BAFTA, you name it, award winner for **Merry Christmas Mr. Lawrence** (1983) and **The Last Emperor** (1987). Another was Kazuhiko Kato who with his wife Mika formed the Glam Rock outfit Sadistic Mika Band, named in parody of Yoko Ono's Plastic Ono Band. Mika and I got on like a house on fire and I had loved their self-titled debut album in English. Mika also loved my Vivienne Westwood clothes and it was through this connection that McLaren ended up with a copy of the album, which he then passed on to Bryan Ferry of Roxy Music fame.

Before you could say *Cosmic Watch* – one of the album's best songs – the Sadistic Mika Band was signed to support Roxy Music's *Siren* (1975) album tour. And in gratitude Mika gave me front row tickets for the first date at Wembley Stadium. Afterwards she told me that had been a terrible mistake. It was like I was in her face and she felt very self-conscious performing. From that moment on I asked my band friends for seats at least ten rows away from the stage in case of any future embarrassment. Nevertheless it was a terrific show, the first ever UK tour by a Japanese rock band, and the after party was truly fabulous. We kept in touch too, especially as she divorced Kato and married Chris Thomas, the English producer of the two follow up albums *Black Ships* (1974) and *Hot! Menu* (1975). And, of course, the producer of the Sex Pistols.

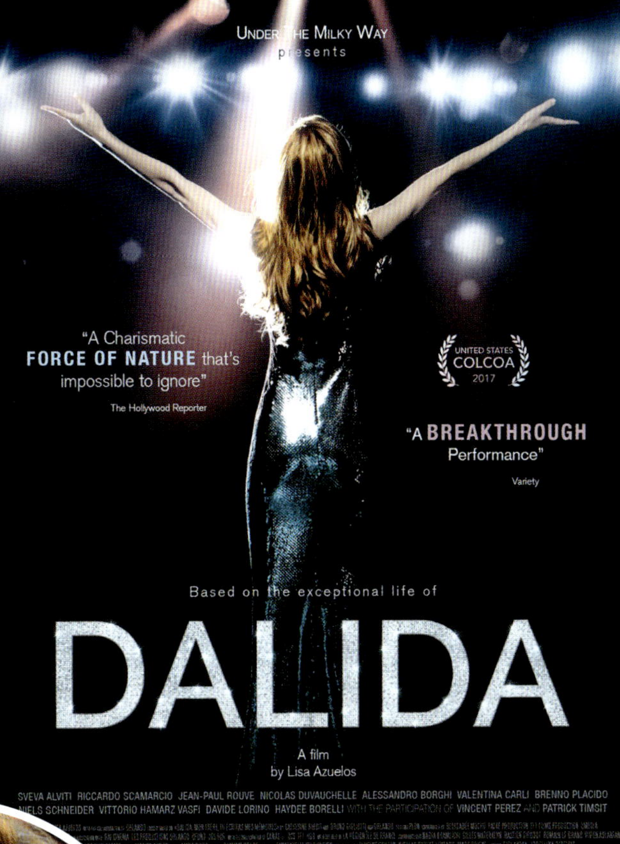

DALIDA (2016)

Her life was as tragic and tumultuous as her singing career was spectacular and memorable. And while this highly-polished biopic of the legendary Dalida searches for contemporary resonance by hinting at what it meant to be a liberated woman in the late 1950s and the emotional price she ultimately paid for being so successful in a man's world, it rarely breaks from the conventional format where bullet-point incident takes preference over any semblance of character psychology. A €15 million passion project that took director Lisa Azuelos, best-known for the coming-of-age dramedy **LOL** (2012), five years to get made, the ace in this pack of showbiz clichés and eye-opening facts is Italian model-turned-actress Sveva Alviti. She looks every inch the Dalida part and exudes the same brand of strength, vulnerability, glamour and charisma lip-synching to the all-encompassing original hit soundtrack.

Opening with Dalida's first attempt to take her own life on February 26th, 1967, in a luxury Paris hotel, one month on from the needless suicide of her lover, Italian singer Luigi Tenco (Alessandro Borghi), who killed himself when their duet *Ciao amore ciao* was eliminated from the final Sanremo Song Festival competition, Azuelos divides her bright, beguiling and breezy homage to megastardom into two distinct chapters. During her period of convalescence, we are brought up to speed with flashbacks to her unhappy childhood in Cairo, Egypt, where she was born Iolanda/Yolanda Cristina Gigliotti, and witnessed her violinist father incarcerated just for being Italian. Then after being crowned Miss Egypt, it's off to the 1956 'Number Ones of Tomorrow' variety show at the Paris Olympia, attended by Lucien Morisse (Jean-Paul Rouve), the Director of Programming at Radio 1 Europe, who married her, propelled her to chart-topping fame with the hit *Bambino* (one of French pop history's biggest ever selling singles) helped by record label owner Eddie Barclay (Vincent Perez).

After this 1967 turning point, the second portion outlines how the dead-inside Dalida picked herself up, glitter-dusted herself off and shaped her identity and public image while searching for the happiness she always found so elusive. Throughout an affair with an Italian student who got her pregnant, referred to only as Lucio (Brenno Placido), the subsequent abortion that left her

unable to conceive and a destructive relationship with Richard Chanfray (Nicolas Duvauchelle), a louche high society knobhead dubbed the Count of Saint-Germain, the only real constant in her life was her younger brother Orlando. Born Bruno (Riccardo Scamarcio), it was Orlando who skilfully managed her career and has since kept his beloved sister's memory alive and back catalogue a permanent public fixture thanks to constant reinvention, club remixes and co-writing this gift-wrapped valentine with Azuelos.

Morisse, Chanfray and her close friend Mike Brant (not depicted here) would also all commit suicide and finally Dalida succumbed to her dark depression doing so too by overdosing on barbiturates on May 3rd, 1987. Could Dalida never find contentment because she still grieved for Tenco, the man she loved so intensely? That's the question one is left with at the heartfelt climax of this melodramatic yet effective exploration of Dalida's sad, empty and tortured life that nevertheless provides a fascinating portrait of her importance as a 170 million worldwide record-selling superstar. Superior editing deftly uses television, radio and written archive material for a more authentic experience than 'Dalida' (2005), the Joyce Buñuel directed two-part TV movie starring Sabrina Ferilli.

It was Orlando who felt Dalida was ready for Disco Divadom. As vividly depicted in the movie, he listens to the classic war anthem *J'attendrai* (1938) by Rina Ketty – a song as important to the French war effort as Lale Andersen's *Lili Marleen* and Vera Lynn's *We'll Meet Again*, both 1939, were to Germany and Great Britain respectively – and bangs out a Disco beat along with it on the kitchen table. Quick as a flash it becomes the first ever fully French Disco hit and in rapid succession Dalida's stellar Disco output and mirrorballed locations flesh out the final 40 minutes of the running time. *Besame mucho* (1976), *Comme disait mistinguett* (1979), *Laissez-moi danser (Monday Tuesday)* (1979) and her two absolute masterpieces *Gigi in Paradisco* (1980) and *Mourir sur scène* (1983) give razzle-dazzle uplift and poignant texture to this elegant portrayal of glitzy love and shattering pain. The latter song, about wanting to die on stage, is fittingly played over the final credits and alongside the heartrending ballad *Pour ne pas vivre seule* (1972) represents Dalida's Edith Piaf-style classic barnstormers.

With its time-shifting, episodic structure and focus on the spotlit heartbreak and backstage compromises made to the gods of fame and fortune, **Dalida** is a Disco **La Vie en Rose** (2007), far better than **Gainsbourg: A Heroic Life/Gainsbourg (Vie héroïque)** (2010), and on a par with **Cloclo** (2012). And in the prophetic words of Shirley Bassey's 1986 English *tour de force* version of her friend's *Mourir sur scène*, Dalida's star will never die because through her established entertainment footprint she was clearly *Born to Sing Forever.*

Amanda Lear

The undisputed Queen of Eurodisco, Amanda Lear never made any impact on the US dance charts, yet the French model, actress, and TV all-rounder is still going strong and releasing new material along with endless Greatest Hits compilations.
No one really knows when she was born or where, and Lear has actively promoted the transgender rumours

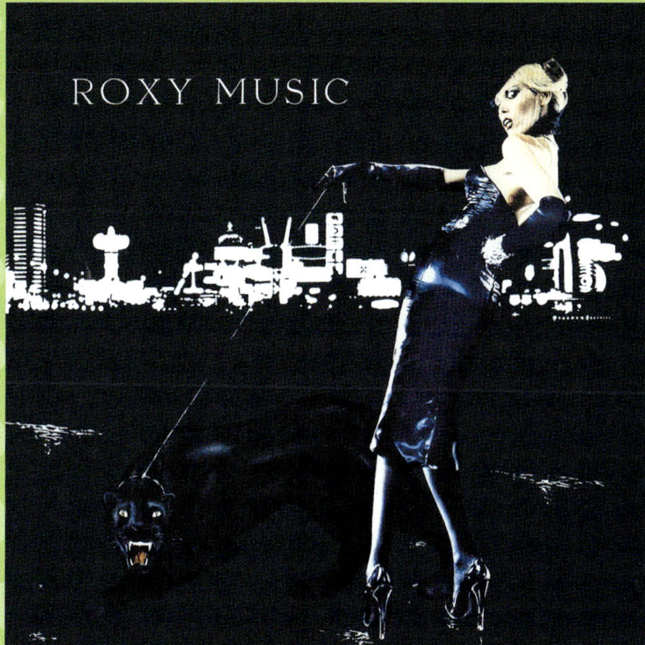

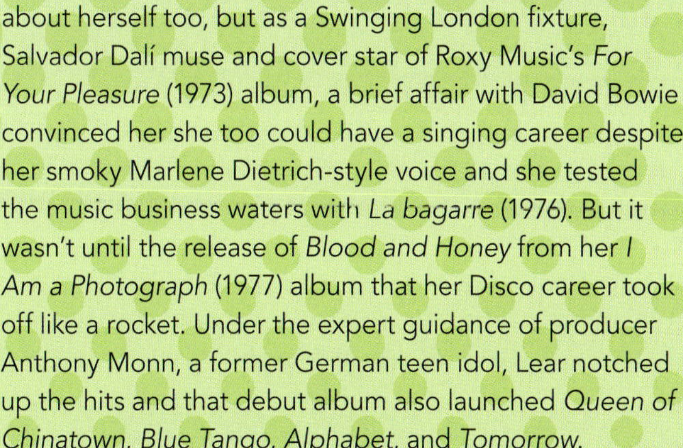

about herself too, but as a Swinging London fixture, Salvador Dalí muse and cover star of Roxy Music's *For Your Pleasure* (1973) album, a brief affair with David Bowie convinced her she too could have a singing career despite her smoky Marlene Dietrich-style voice and she tested the music business waters with *La bagarre* (1976). But it wasn't until the release of *Blood and Honey* from her *I Am a Photograph* (1977) album that her Disco career took off like a rocket. Under the expert guidance of producer Anthony Monn, a former German teen idol, Lear notched up the hits and that debut album also launched *Queen of Chinatown*, *Blue Tango*, *Alphabet*, and *Tomorrow*.

It was her second album *Sweet Revenge* (1978) that crystallised her Disco pre-eminence and was destined to become an ageless classic thanks to the Faustian-themed A-side of *Follow Me*. It remains timeless, distinguished, melodic and orchestrated Disco of the highest order. The non-stop dance hits continued with the *Never Trust a Pretty Face* (1979) album and the cuts *Fashion Pack*, *The Sphinx*, *Black Holes* and yes, as an in-joke, *Lili Marleen*. 1980 brought the *Diamonds for Breakfast* album with the standout tracks *I Need a Man*, *Oh Boy*, *Diamonds*, *Insomnia* and *Fabulous (Lover, Love Me)*. *Incognito* (1981) was a tour through the Seven Deadly Sins with *Hollywood Is Just a Dream*, *New York*, *Egal*, *Nymphomania*, and *If I Was a Boy*.

The underrated *Tam-Tam* (1983) album revealed yet more superb tunes from the Disco Diva's pen; *Bewitched*, *Magic*, *No Regrets*, *Gipsy Man*, and *Music Is*. The 12-inch single *Love Your Body* (1983) cashed in on the aerobics craze and *She Wolf* (1986) was Lear's first true HiNRG bestseller. Since then Lear has been redefining her ever-changing image with every successive release from *Fantasy* (1993), *Alter Ego* (1995) and *Love Boat* (2001) to *Kiss Me Honey Kiss Me* (2006), *Back to Black* (2010) and the cheeky *I Don't Like Disco* (2012).

The Alternative Miss World

Two days after their Marquee gig on February 12th, 1976, the Sex Pistols turned up to Andrew Logan's Valentine's Day Ball at his Butler's Wharf London warehouse thanks to Malcolm McLaren and Vivienne Westwood conning the *demimonde* sculptor and jewellery designer into thinking the band were some sort of art installation. Five chords into their exuberantly ramshackle set most of the invited fashionistas walked out, despite what filmmaker Derek Jarman captured on his Super-8 camera. I'd met Logan through my 'Ritz' journalist friend Frances Lynn who was considered one of his clique and always invited to his soirees and art openings. But Logan's *pièces de résistance* were the quite brilliant Alternative Miss World 'beauty' pageants he founded in 1972.

It wasn't the biggest of them all; that honour went to his Olympia event in 1981, but the most fun and celebrity-packed was his Big Top version on October 20, 1978. On that stellar night Jordan, Bromley Contingent members and I crowded into a circus tent erected on Clapham Common and found ourselves seated next to Virgin's Richard Branson and 'The Rocky Horror Show' creator Richard O'Brien. The caged judges included Joan Bakewell, Lionel Bart and Zandra Rhodes and the contestant parade boasted future **Love Is the Devil** (1998) film director John Maybury (as Miss Windscale Nuclear Reactor), **The Final Programme** (1973) actress Jenny Runacre (Miss Slightly Misanthropic) and future Kinky Gerlinky nightclub hostess Gerlinde von Regensburg (Miss Proposition 13). The winner was Miss Carriage, Miss Linda Carriage (Stevie Hughes). The host with the most was Divine and everyone was filmed by director Richard Gayer, with Frances doing the vox pop interviews.

A year later **The Alternative Miss World** (1979) documentary record of that memorable night received its midnight premiere at the Odeon Leicester Square on November 15th, 1979. That date was chosen because it was the same one as the actual Miss World contest. And who was the Miss World Organisation spokesperson trying but failing to block the screening? None other than the future British Prime Minister Tony Blair! While the film was draggy in the sadly alternative meaning of that word, everyone at the screening celebrated well into the night at the after party at the Empire Ballroom. The one song playing I vividly recall was *No More Tears (Enough Is Enough)* (1979) by Donna Summer and Barbra Streisand, a fitting musical cap to my own personal 1970s drawing to a close if ever there was one.

GRACE JONES
BLOODLIGHT
AND BAMI
A FILM BY SOPHIE FIENNES
Grace Jones
& FRIENDS
BROADCAST LIVE TO CINEMAS 25 OCTOBER
BOOK TICKETS AT GRACEJONESTICKETS.CO.UK
NATIONWIDE FRIDAY 27 OCTOBER

GRACE JONES: BLOODLIGHT AND BAMI (2017)

One of Gay Disco's premiere Divas, Grace Jones has been making mega-waves as a unique and innovative performer, actress and musician since she left Jamaica as a 12-year-old in the 1960s. First finding fame as an 'Elle' magazine fashion model in Paris during the early glitter rock 1970s, she became an avant-garde Disco Queen during the heady Studio 54 years with an image best described as a cross between Ziegfeld showgirl and surrealist Glamazon. From Andy Warhol confidante and 24-hour party animal to Bond villain in **A View to a Kill** (1985) and the blueprint for Madonna and Lady Gaga's ever-evolving careers, the post-modern icon transformed her Disco career into the timeless reggae house electronica hybrid that created such new wave classic hits as *Pull Up to the Bumper* (1981) and *Slave to the Rhythm* (1985).

Both of which, naturally, are heard in director Sophie Fiennes (**The Pervert's Guide to Cinema**, 2006) unusually impressionistic, annoyingly superficial but still intriguing documentary about one of pop culture's legendary and most recognisable personalities. Fiennes, sister of actor Ralph, and Jones worked on this movie memoir for twelve

years – one of the home videos of Jones' mother Marjorie singing church gospel has a 2005 banner behind her – and it's so clearly a labour of love for them both. Originally titled 'Grace Jones – The Musical of My Life', the new moniker refers in patois to the red light that illuminates when an artist is in the recording studio and 'bami' meaning the local flatbread, the substance of Jamaican daily life.

Essentially the documentary weaves Jones' public persona and private life snatches together via contrasts between her lavish stage act, filmed in Dublin, based on concepts designed by Oscar-winning designer Eiko Ishioka (**Bram Stoker's Dracula**, 1992), and ragged fly-on-the-wall travelogue reality footage. So *Slave to the Rhythm* being danced with a hulahoop is intercut with stage door fans brandishing her Disco album covers *Portfolio* (1977) and *Fame* (1978), begging for autographs. *Pull Up to the Bumper* segues into Jones setting the record straight over that infamous British chat show incident with camp host Russell Harty. *Nipple to the Bottle* (1982) showcases a startling strip to the buff in her hotel suite. And the autobiographical tracks *Williams' Bloods* and *Hurricane* (both 2008) are the prompts to explore her sadistic upbringing with her twin brother under the dominant household regime of Mas P, the man her guardian grandmother married when her parents moved away to start a new life in America.

Jones' Disco heritage is dealt with in quite a perfunctory and dismissive fashion even though clearly quite important in the overall scheme of things. But then Fiennes does leave cavernous gaps in the history when it comes to past affairs, like the one with Dolph Lundgren circa **Conan the Destroyer** (1984), and barely fleshes out the grandmother Jones is today lurking behind her dazzling lifestyle façade either. After a Paris interview where she opines that going to a Disco in the music genre's heyday was like going to church, she mimes on a French TV show to the wonderfully rippling *La vie en rose* (1977) in an absolutely brilliant Philip Treacy designed hat, resembling the head of H.R. Giger's **Alien** (1979) creature.

Surrounded by a tacky troupe of scantily dressed female dancers, Jones explodes at the bewildered producer, "I look like the lesbian madam in a whorehouse. Are there any male dancers?" The cuts to the studio audience in this section are hilarious. Some oldsters are clearly with the Disco programme, other younger members completely flummoxed by this ancient vision in muted red glitter. It's supposed to make a point about Jones' Disco past being just that, in the past. Yet this, coupled with her trying to remember the words to her quintessential No.1 Gay Disco anthem *I Need a Man* (1975), photos of her dancing at Studio 54 and a quick mention of graphic artist Richard Bernstein's stunning paintings that graced her 12-inch single and album covers does a disservice to the massive audience and cultural phenomenon that made her an international superstar. There are many self-aware moments to cherish in what Fiennes calls "a multi-narrative unmasking, a thrill-ride of verité cinema" though: Jones getting studio stroppy with her favourite duo Sly & Robbie; showing her intensive make-up regime; eating too-fresh oysters and saying "I wish my pussy was this tight!"; a telephone meltdown over an unpaid hotel bill concluding with the **Dolores Claiborne** (1995) quote "Sometimes you have to be a high-flying bitch"; and talking openly about sex with one-time paramour and frequent creative collaborator Jean-Paul Goude, which resulted in their son Paolo. Such self-revelation is fascinating of course but it's on the stage where Amazing Grace's most extreme embodiments are realised and her theatrical imagination lets loose.

No insight is given to Jones' current relationships, home life, passions, politics or other artistic interests outside her own universe, regrets or *je ne regrette riens*. She struts and poses in Jasper Conran's corsets, glares and glowers, showing everything showbiz stunning but revealing nothing of any real note. The movie ends with her Roxy Music cover version *Love Is the Drug* (1980) as she sings beneath laser beams flashing off her mirrorball bowler hat. It's a bravura image in a semi-touching if missed opportunity documentary that fans will nevertheless lap up because there isn't anything else except the video snapshot 'A One Man Show' (1985). Until the planned feature adaptation of her 2015 autobiography 'I'll Never Write My Memoirs' materialises and she finally spills her closely guarded secrets?

Keeping up with the Jones

Chic man Nile Rodgers described her best: "Part Marlene Dietrich, part Bela Lugosi and part Bob Marley". But I will never forget the moment I heard *I Need a Man* (1975) blaring from a Disco's speakers for the first time. It was one of the most thrilling and powerful drop-dead Gay Disco Anthems of the era and it still packs a raw punch today.

We all knew Jones wasn't a good singer; she shouted and bellowed the flat lyrics more than actually sung them. But her delivery was inimitable, unique, and her choice of material and producers to disguise her vocal limitations impeccable. Nor was she a great actress. A bit part in **Gordon's War** (1973) was barely an auspicious start to her acting career, hardly surprising that after the key blockbusters it all started fizzling out with **Vamp** (1986) and **Boomerang** (1992). Jones couldn't control her image in movies and could only do that on stage, so that's where she gravitated and stayed, rooted in her own lifestyled limelight.

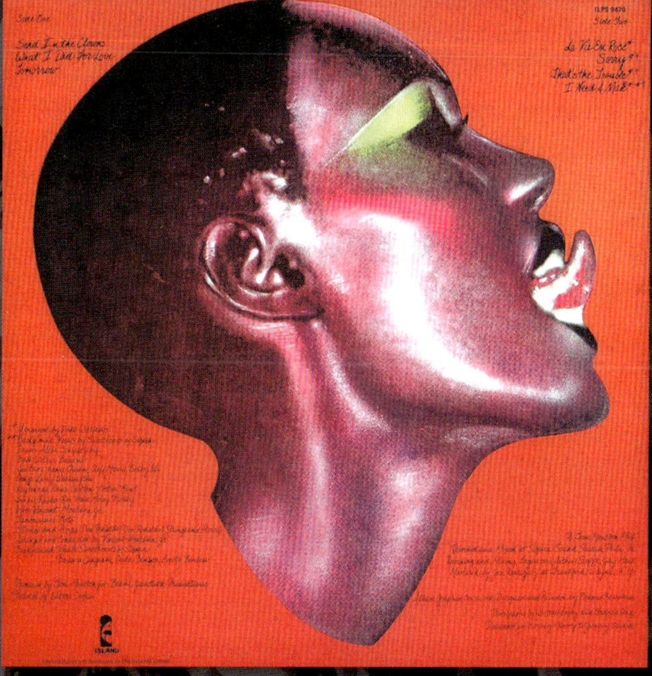

It was a demo of The Three Degrees hit *Dirty Ol' Man* (1973) and John Lennon's *Imagine* (1971), plus her massive celebutante reputation, that landed Jones her first record deal with the Orfeus label in Paris. It resulted in a Disco hit in France and Belgium for *I Need a Man*, written by French pianist Pierre Papadiamandis and Paul Slade, noted Italian composer Riz Ortolani's lyricist. She then co-wrote two more cuts, *Sorry* (1976) and *That's the Trouble* (1976), with Papadiamandis, which were recorded for Island Records in London and remixed by maestro DJ Tom Moulton. Thanks to Moulton's burgeoning reputation the double-sided 12-inch got vital exposure Stateside and became Jones' first U.S. Disco smash. *I Need a Man* was then released in America and shot all the way to the top of the 'Billboard' Disco Chart in April 1977.

Moulton then produced her first album *Portfolio* (1977) with the cream of Philadelphia's top talent including Salsoul arranger Vincent Montana Jr. and background vocals by the ubiquitous Sweethearts of Sigma. Cashing in on a formula that would become increasingly lucrative as the Disco genre evolved, the A-side of *Portfolio* was a medley of three popular Broadway showtunes of the era: Stephen Sondheim's classic *Send in the Clowns* from 'A Little Night Music', *What I Did for Love* from 'A Chorus Line' and *Tomorrow* from 'Annie'. Only the latter two cuts became Disco hits, *Send in the Clowns* being seen as more of a chill-out track for after hours winding down. The B-side featured the already released three hits plus a Disco version of Edith Piaf's signature torch song *La vie en rose*. That was Moulton's idea and set in stone Jones' trademark singing style – off-key, flamboyant, menacing but always entrancing and original. The album also featured a sleeve designed and painted by Richard Bernstein that singlehandedly created her quintessential otherworldly distinctive look. He would oversee all her Disco brand concepts from this point on.

Fame (1978) was the charismatic Jones' spectacular sophomore album. Once again produced by Tom Moulton, but this time arranged by John Davis of Monster Orchestra renown, the sumptuous grandiose A-side medley consisting of *Do or Die*, *Pride* and *Fame* portrayed the high-camp Disco Diva as a desperate supertrouper searching for lost love while suffering loneliness at the top and the increasingly emotional price of being so rich and famous. It's an epic, driving and tuneful drags-to-bitches assortment that transforms into a more mournfully soulful B-side with a soft Disco version of the evergreen ballad *Autumn Leaves, All on a Summer's Night, Am I Ever Gonna Fall in Love in New York City* and the fabulously pounding *Below the Belt.* Mostly penned by the songwriting team of James Bolden and Jack Robinson, the duo behind *I Love to Love (But My Baby Just Loves to Dance)* (1976) for Tina Charles, *Fame* is an exquisite Disco experience.

Jones' final album in her colossal Disco trilogy, *Muse* (1979) was an equally brilliant masterpiece but somehow got overlooked in the mushrooming Disco backlash. Moulton produced once more but the main arranger this time was Munich maestro Thor Baldursson (clients included Donna Summer, Roberta Kelly and Amanda Lear) who injected a Eurodisco energy into the A-side S&M suite of *Sinning, Suffer, Repentance (Forgive Me)* and *Saved*, relating the trials and tribulations of a woman brutalising and humiliating her lover who then takes romantic revenge. Complete with moans, sighs, sobbing, gospel wailing and whiplashes, it's an infectious panorama of sin, redemption, delicious pleasure and

pain floodlit with mirrorball excess. The B-side is a bright and summer breezy confection of *Atlantic City Gambler, I'll Find My Way to You, Don't Mess with the Messer* and the dominatrix Disco demand for atonement *On Your Knees*, written by *Cathedrals* (1976) D.C. LaRue and the only single to be released from the album, which reached No.28 on the Disco charts. *I'll Find My Way to You* was a re-recorded version of the Stelvio Cipriani composed song Jones originally sang in Massimo Dallamano's *poliziotteschi* thriller **Quelli della calibro 38/Colt 38 Special Squad** (1976) and reused again in Umberto Lenzi's radioactive zombie shocker **Incubo sulla città contaminata/Nightmare City** (1980).

With *Muse* hardly setting the dancefloors alight, Jones saw the writing on the Disco wall and within months of its release was already heading in the *Warm Leatherette* (1980) direction. She said at the time that through the Disco medium she had achieved everything she possibly could and now it was time to take her career to the next artistic level. Always uncategorisable and signifying the most outrageous side of the transgressive Disco oeuvre, Jones's legacy is a truly exceptional and timeless one. The one song she turned down she wished she hadn't? *Boogie Wonderland* (1979), which became a perennial Disco anthem for Earth, Wind & Fire. Can you imagine that brilliant track given the complete Grace Jones makeover? Only in our wildest Disco dreams!

Disco Memo

Maunkberry's

I met Grace Jones through a wealthy Italian playboy we both knew, Francesco Miani, first in a New York penthouse on the way to spend the night at Studio 54. And the next time we crossed paths was on a night I will never forget – the night I saw her perform *I Need a Man* at the tiny gay nightclub Maunkberry's in Jermyn Street, just off Piccadilly Circus. The venue was where Arlene Phillips' Hot Gossip dance troupe had a regular one-night-a-week booking, but on this occasion the singer 'New York' magazine once dubbed "The Secret Night Goddess" took their follow spot. Carried in Cleopatra-style by four musclemen wearing tight gold shorts and plonked on the postage stamp-sized stage, Jones immediately started puttin' on the Glitz with a bijou set I can still vividly remember. My plus one that night was an impressed Vivienne Westwood who I thought might just be tempted into the glamorous Disco Darkside by Jones's stellar set.

STUDIO 54 (2018)

For those who danced, gasped, stared, snorted and had sex there, Studio 54 was the epicentre of 1970s hedonism and a life-changing Disco experience. It redefined the idea of what a nightclub should be and came to symbolise an entire cultural era. So the proliferation of coffee table magazine articles, Sunday supplement features, books (Anthony Haden-Guest's 'The Last Party', Mark Fleischman's 'Inside Studio 54', etc.) and the movie **54** (1998) come as no real surprise because people are still completely besotted by its Disco fabulous urban legends.

But what director Matt Tyrnauer's feature documentary has that no one else got was the full co-operation of Ian

Diana Ross and Steve Rubell

Schrager who founded the Sing Sing bling emporium along with the late, attention-hogging master of ceremonies Steve Rubell. His perspective alone – although there are some moments of deliberate obfuscation and minimal frankness – does justice to both the after hours nightclub's historical importance and the resonance it still continues to have. Schrager makes this hustle through the Quaalude dreamland a more engaging glimpse than expected into the way Studio 54 mainstreamed alternative black, gay, lesbian and transgender communities and turned the media spotlight on celebrity in a way that has never been turned off since.

The perfect director to tackle the subject thanks to the gossipy bisexual procurer memo **Scotty and the Secret History of Hollywood** (2017), Tyrnauer's forensic account records all the expected bullet points: How Brooklyn boys Rubell and Schrager met in college, immediately became best friends and decided to seek their fortune by creating the perfect nightclub. After studying the emerging Disco scene and a test run with Enchanted Garden in Queens, they discovered a former CBS TV studio on West 54th Street, hired Tony Award-winning lighting designers and opened for business on a chilly April 26, 1977. With its fame spreading quickly (thanks to publicists paid for every

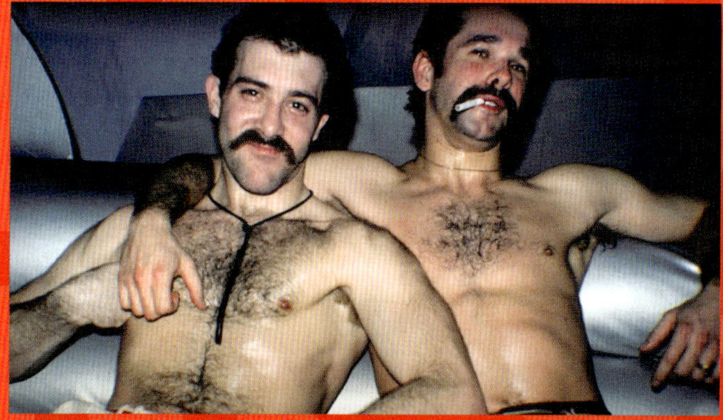

Grace Jones

Bianca Jagger, Liza Minnelli and Andy Warhol

Steve Rubell and Ian Schrager

Divine

famous face lured in and news story written), Liza Minnelli, Truman Capote, Bianca Jagger etc., management became infamous for instigating the choosy 'social experiment' velvet rope door policy. Then came the copious drug use, the balcony and basement sex shenanigans, the fact they didn't have a liquor license, just continual one-night-only catering permits, the money skimming, the Disco resentment, the arrogance and eventually the IRS tax evasion jail sentences.

Joining Schrager in the talking head sections are his lover, designer Norma Kamali, party promoter Carmen D'Alessio, silent business partner Jack Dushey, Chic genius Nile Rodgers, 'Andy Warhol's Interview' editor Bob Colacello, capricious doorman Marc Benecke (who even now still seems surprised his glitterati 'friends' deserted him when the club closed down!), Rubell's still distraught brother, and assorted DJs, Studio 54 staff, patrons and the police who raided the place in December 1978. Alongside a brilliant array of photos, film clips, archive footage and period newscasts Tyrnauer does the impossible and actually makes you feel like you are in the Hallowed Hall of High Life surrounded by blissed out dancers.

One great TV clip shows Michael Jackson interrupting Rubell being interviewed in his office, shyly kneeling by his chair and pronouncing the club's escapist vibe was unlike anywhere else in the world. All the archive footage involving Rubell, who died of AIDS complications in 1989, is fascinating because what comes across loud and clear is how untouchable he thought they all were. And the vintage material with the Disco duo's reptilian power-lawyer Roy Cohn, who once represented both Joseph McCarthy and Donald Trump, makes you realise exactly why they thought that.

Schrager claims Studio 54 was the first club that actually hired people to work the lights, something DJs were responsible for in other venues. We're also told it was Rubell who invented the 'Bridge and Tunnel' putdown to describe the polyester hordes from suburbia. Another juicy revelation refers to the apocryphal story that sacks of money were stashed in the club's ceiling. Apparently this was only a box of quarters for public telephone use. And was the raid prompted by Rubell's bragging about his financial success in the press or a disgruntled employee tipping off the law? All this and a lot more – even Rubell and Schrager's boutique hotel business is covered – comes under Tyrnauer's insightful gaze to provide the full slipped Disco facts and the hip and hypnotic myths.

The Disco music used to backdrop this definitive document couldn't be more battleaxe though. Heard at various junctures are Sylvester's *You Make Me Feel (Mighty Real)* (1978), Thelma Houston's *Don't Leave Me This Way* (1976), Candi Staton's *Young Hearts Run Free* (1976), Manu Dibango's *Soul Makossa* (1972), Silver Convention's *Fly, Robin, Fly* (1975), Bonnie Pointer's *Heaven Must Have Sent You* (1979), and Tasha Thomas' *Shoot Me (with Your Love)* (1978). Surely using cuts done and dusted from before the club even opened does show unfortunate sloppiness on the researchers' parts?

Got Tu Go Disco

What does a prominent Studio 54 doorman do when his work establishment is forced to close down? In Al Corley's case he became Steven Carrington in the long-running super-soap 'Dynasty' and released the terrific HiNRG Disco hit *Square Rooms* (1984). Maitre D' Marc Benecke took a different career trajectory by recreating his velvet-rope Nazi role in a notorious Broadway flop that became synonymous with Disco's darkest hour a mere two weeks later at the Comiskey Park Disco Demolition protest.

In 1979 rock promoter and producer Jerry Brandt, who owned the Electric Circus club, managed Carly Simon, discovered Patti LaBelle and tried to force Bowie clone Jobriath on the mass market (and I say that as his friend), thought the world was ready for the first Disco musical on the Great White Way just as the mainstream were beginning to tire of the genre. Conceived as a Disco 'Cinderella' concept, and originally titled 'Gotta Dance', 'Got Tu Go Disco' was the brainchild of famed costume designer Joe Eula, dresser of The Supremes, Marlene Dietrich and Liza Minnelli, and eventually directed by Larry Forde who had recently guided 'An Evening with Quentin Crisp'.

Officially costing $2 million, some say a lot more, the fiasco starred a pre-**Fame** (1980)/*Flashdance… What a Feeling* (1983) Irene Cara as Cassette, who hates being a clothes shop assistant in the Disco Rag store and loathes Disco music. That is until her boyfriend Billy (Patrick Jude from 'Jesus Christ Superstar') lures her to the local nightclub Dream Castle where she soon becomes Queen of the Dance Floor. Thirteenth down the cast list Marc Benecke played himself as the snotty Dream Castle doorman – his ironic showstopper was *In and Out* – and in interviews of the day explained his ill-advised career move thus, "Everything has been going well for you. You think, sure! Why not? There's a certain naivety…"

The behind-the-scenes problems in rehearsal became stuff of Shubert Alley legend. One major investor was arrested for drug smuggling. Brandt and Eula continually argued about copyright until the former finally cracked and banned the latter from entering the premises again. Original book writer Steven Gaines, author of 'Discotheque' and, with Robert Jon Cohen, 'The Club', a novel about a Studio 54-style venue, found out he'd been fired and replaced by former monk John Zodrow from a 'New York Times' story. Of the eleven billed composers only three had any Disco credibility – Monster Orchestra's John Davis and Motown marvels Ashford & Simpson – and it was the former who wrote the title song mainly as a vehicle for Pattie Brooks to create some form of recognition. Other passable songs

featured in the bland score include *Disco Shuffle*, *Pleasure Pusher*, *Chic to Cheap*, and *Dance Forever*.

Brandt had apparently changed the 'To' in the title to 'Tu' on the advice of his astrologist who swore it would mean boffo box-office. The more cynical thought it was just a shameless tie-in with the local Disco radio station WKTU who were tirelessly promoting it. Whatever, when the show opened on June 25th at the Minskoff Theatre after playing nine previews it got mauled by the Manhattan critics. "Will it catch on?" questioned one reviewer, "Well, German Measles periodically does!" The morning after the dismal premiere Brandt went on national television and told everyone that night's performance would be free to anyone who turned up at the theatre. He was convinced the critics were wrong and a papered audience would provide positive word of mouth. No such luck. And no one ever saw Irene Cara again as she was so devastated by the terrible reviews she went completely AWOL. And when her understudy accidentally fell into the orchestra pit, Brandt saw the writing on the wall and closed the show five days later.

Charging a then record $20 for the top price ticket, punters should have expected and got something more spectacular and tunefully thrilling. Apart from the opening number *Puttin' It On*, danced against a backdrop of film clips from such New York based movies as **On the Town** (1949), the show was unimaginatively staged, the book as bland as they come, and the choreography by Jo Jo Smith (John Travolta's dance consultant in **Saturday Night Fever**, 1977), Troy Garza (an 'A Chorus Line' understudy) and George Faison ('The Wiz' and Earth, Wind & Fire's dance moves man) nothing special that you couldn't see at any nearby local club. 'Got Tu Go Disco' was a missed opportunity with nothing going for it apart from the Studio 54 gimmick.

Dancing with Tiers in My Eyes

Was Studio 54 my favourite Manhattan Disco? No, those honours would be shared between 12 West and The Saint, based at the old Fillmore East theatre in the Bowery, where group sex in the balcony was *de rigueur*. I only walked through the Queen of Club's velvet ropes once, in May 1978 (my birthday month) – wearing Vivienne Westwood and with Angie Bowie, so no hassle – and loved it. Well we had just been at a drinks soiree with Grace Jones… An amazing place, from the astonishingly baroque entrance corridor and glittering inner sanctum to the anything goes balcony and everything snows basement. Did I see any movie stars or famous personalities – apart from the ones I was with – I can't remember in truth? And no, I wasn't on any drugs! It was all such an incandescent rush, a thrilling magic carpet ride, a blur of hustle and bustle.

What I do vividly recall is some of the music being played because those tracks became my all-time favourites; *How Much, How Much I Love You* by Love & Kisses, *Rough Diamond* by Madleen Kane, *At the Discotheque* by Lipstique and *Come Into My Heart/ Love's Coming* by USA-European Connection (all 1978). I find that quite a significant factor actually. I wanted to dance myself silly not pose around willy-nilly and although I can't recollect how long I stayed, I do remember walking along Broadway in the early hours of the morning thinking once was enough. Had I returned I do think it would have been a case of diminishing novelty value. Why go uptown when the downtown Discos satisfied all my dancer needs. I'm glad I made the effort to see what all the fuss was about, and it sure remains a party conversation piece, but I was happier amongst the dance maniacs not the celebrity watchers.

BOOGIE MAN (2018)

On the UK festival circuit for a while before getting a proper British release (it won two Flame awards at the UK Asian Film Festival for Best Music and Best Newcomer for Amy Jackson), co-writer and director Andy Morahan's sincere, sweet and determinedly old-fashioned coming-of-ager puts the culture clash back in comedy romance. Co-produced by rock video legend Scott Millaney for MGMM Studios, the leading outfit for edgy music promos when that format was in its 1980s infancy, Morahan's work with some of pop's biggest names – Paul McCartney, Elton John, Michael Jackson – would lead one to expect something sparkier than this safe kitchen sink fantasy. Nevertheless, it happily hits the Disco spot, provides oodles of fun nostalgia while everyone emerges with a tear in their eye despite the rose-coloured scrappiness.

Paavan (Kush Khanna) is a British-Indian teenager whose grandfather Rupesh (Roshan Seth) wants him to seriously consider going to University. All Paavan can think about is girls and having a good time, especially the one he sees making a celebrity appearance at a 'Seeking Out the 70s' Roller Disco event in South Kensington. But the older – and white – actress/model Stephanie (Jerry-Jane Pears) is firmly under the thumb of her ambitious manager Gerry (Nick Moran) and looks completely unapproachable.

Bemused by his obsession, best friend Danny (Aston Merrygold) and sister Nimisha (Jackson) look on in astonishment as Paavan wholly embraces the clothes, music and lifestyle of the Disco era while trying to keep

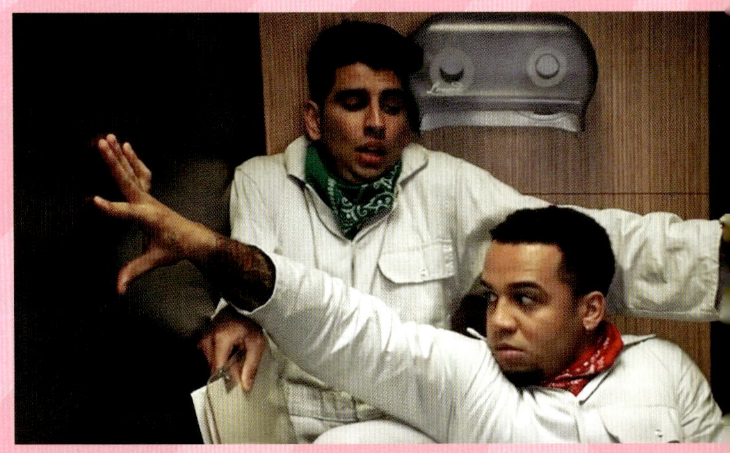

his family's Indian traditionalism and the impending responsibilities of adulthood at bay. Finding out his late father was an ace Disco mover (a terrific dream sequence showing both guys dancing in slow-motion), when he finally does meet Stephanie, she can't understand why he's ignoring his cultural roots.

Then his grandfather falls dangerously ill and Paavan is forced to face up to reality. At the Club Shiva he begins to understand clearly that the stylish Disco world he has created with Stephanie at its glamorously hollow epicentre is just a temporary means of escape from mundane existence. It's time to face up to life, get to know his inner personality and, yes, finally make that trip back to India to see the birthplace of his beloved father.

Wearing its timid heart firmly on its impeccably ironed sleeve and erring on the bland side quite often, lead Kush Khanna is too laid back in his attitude and delivery to be entirely convincing. It's the actors around him who carry the lightweight load and mainly punch the core self-discovery message across. And throughout the movie iconic tracks from the Disco era are relayed in their pristine original form or given a punchy new lease of life with re-recorded elements added for a modern twist. *Heaven Must Be Missing an Angel* (1976) by Tavares underscores the Roller Disco opening sequence and the finale gives *Right Back Where We Started From* (1975) by Maxine Nightingale the full Bollywood group dancing experience. Elsewhere KC and The Sunshine Band provides *Boogie Shoes* (1975) and *I'm Your Boogie Man* (1976), Jimmy 'Bo' Horne *Dance Across the Floor* (1978), George McCrae *Rock Your Baby* (1974) and Space Cadetz *Disco Wonderland*. The version of *Theme from S.W.A.T.* (1975) is by Rhythm Heritage.

The THP Orchestra

What was the first Canadian Disco album ever? *Early Riser* (1976) by The THP Orchestra is the surprising answer. The best-known studio project of prolific producers Willi Morrison and Ian Guenther, The THP Orchestra would dominate the Canadian Disco landscape and the US dance charts through three subsequent album releases and 12-inch single off-shoots prior to the rise of such soon-to-be-established Canuck artists as Lime, France Joli and Gino Soccio. "I was 12 years old and living in Glasgow, Scotland", co-producer Willi Morrison told me about how he got interested in music. "It was a rainy Wednesday in 1962 and I was having my supper at five o'clock in the afternoon. My family was watching television when suddenly I heard these strange sounds emanating from the screen and I became transfixed. My mother thought I was ill but I was simply glued to the band that just appeared to play the songs *Love Me Do* and *Please Please Me* (both 1963). From that moment on I knew whatever I was going to do I had to be involved with music. So The Beatles literally changed my life".

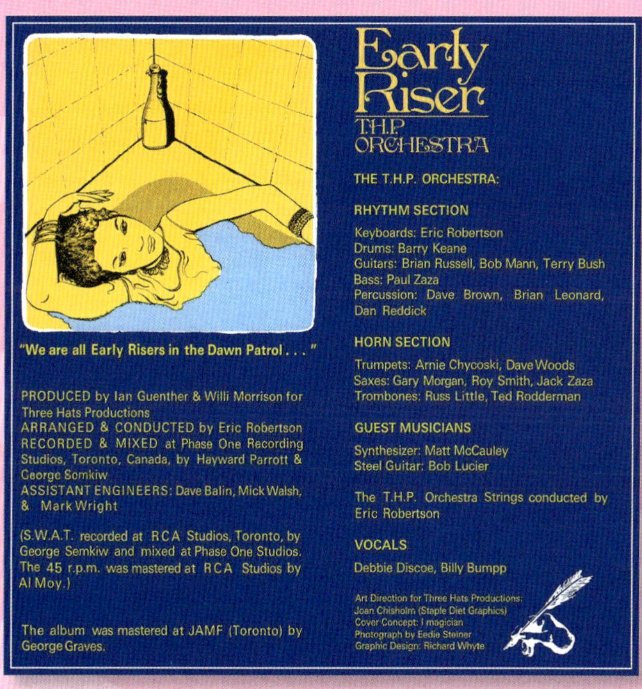

"The following day I started to write songs in maths class at school. Soon after I bought a guitar and learnt how to play. Then I teamed up with a schoolmate and formed a group. That was the most fantastic thing about the 1960s – there was just so much amazing music happening that we could pretend to be whoever we wanted every single day of our lives. I really enjoyed the fact there was no technology to hide behind, not like today. It was you, your instrument and your talent. The first band I formed that made a record was called Bundle".

Keen to become more involved in the music industry, Morrison teamed up with a friend (future pop star B.A. Robertson) to take a course in marketing and business studies to get a handle on how Tin Pan Alley actually worked. "You know how sometimes doors seem to open almost mystically? That's what happened to me. After studying the industry I got into writing, recording and publishing until one of my bosses decided I was becoming too much of an insistent pain and assisted my exit from Great Britain. He sent me off to meet record executive Neil Bogart who, before founding the pivotal Disco label Casablanca, ran the very successful Buddah, which at that time was having numerous Bubblegum pop hits with the likes of Lemon Pipers, 1910 Fruitgum Company and The Archies. En route to New York for the meeting I stopped off in Toronto because I had a sister living there. Being very young and foolish I decided the Canadian music business needed me more so I ended up staying".

Morrison did any and every job in Toronto; delivering pizza, pop journalism, sales promotion and finally got a job in the company that published music for the EMI label. "It was then I met Ian Guenther. Ian's wife's sister was a good friend of my sister and they suggested we meet up. Ian was a classically trained, absolutely phenomenal violinist whose accuracy on the musical side of things was just amazing. I followed what my ears told me, did everything instinctively and only played the guitar. It was a perfect partnership in the long run through the Disco era because Ian did all the technical chores like book the studio time and the musicians, while I tended to be more on the creative side. We named our company Three Hats Productions, the initials of which named the best known of our studio projects, The THP Orchestra".

How The THP Orchestra came into being is one of those fascinating music biz anecdotes. "We had a production deal at RCA Records and had our small offices there. I got on very well with the president of the company and one day in early 1976 he called me into a meeting to explain a tricky situation they were going through. Up to this point RCA were distributing the very famous US label ABC Dunhill in Canada but the contract was just about to expire. One particular track zooming up the US charts to the top was on that label and he was concerned they would miss out on its financial success because of their deal running out".

That track was *Theme from S.W.A.T.* (1975) by Rhythm Heritage, a fast tempo version of composer Barry De Vorzon's instrumental title music from the top-rated ABC TV cop drama. "So I was given the record on a Friday afternoon and told he needed a cover version by Monday morning! That weekend we put together the musicians, recorded it, mixed it, mastered it, gave it to the pressing plant on Monday and by Friday the same week we had sold 60,000 copies of the single. It was an incredible exercise to do and one that set Three Hats Productions in good stead for the subsequent Disco years. Once our *Theme from S.W.A.T.* (1976) had become a huge hit in Canada, RCA said they wanted an album to cash in on its success. We did some research and realised the average buyer for our crime drama theme was a 14-year-old male. Not exactly the demographic we could rely on for massive album sales. That's when Disco came into the equation. There was this fabulous music coming from Europe being sung by Donna Summer and it was the hottest sound around. We also recognised the biggest proportion of most Disco tracks was instrumental so that's why we decided to arrange The THP Orchestra's debut album *Early Riser* in the contemporary musical language of the day".

The album mainly comprised of Disco versions of a broad range of music Morrison and Guenther both loved. "It was a chance to take our favourite pieces of amazing music and making them work in Disco terms for a new audience. Through Disco we could maximise exposure to a mix of evergreen songs, wonderful film music and unsung classics. Again it was more a technical experiment. Take standards, cover them and open them up musically through clever arrangement and with all the new marketing possibilities the club environment offered".

Hence the reasoning behind the inclusion of *More*, the title theme from the Italian shockumentary **Mondo Cane** (1962), the Bubblegum anthem *Sugar, Sugar*, a massive hit for The Archies in 1969, *Manha de carnival*, the principal theme from the 1959 Brazilian art-house hit movie **Black Orpheus**, *Shadow of Your Smile*, the love theme from the 1965 Elizabeth Taylor/Richard Burton melodrama **The Sandpiper** and *Sleepwalk*, originally a chart-topping 1959 hit by Santo and Johnny (Farina). Morrison added in two compositions, *Dawn Patrol* and *Crazy, Crazy* and his favoured arranger/conductor Eric Robertson the title track because, "I thought about the overall concept of the album, what was required and what would fit in amongst the more well-known tracks. In tonal and augmentative terms those three tracks cemented the album together as a whole".

Early Riser was never released in America or the UK but it attracted the attention of the Los Angeles-based Butterfly Records. The founder of that signature label, responsible for launching Destination's *Move On Up* (1979) and Saint Tropez's *One More Minute* (1979), was Alfonso Juan Cervantes and he asked Morrison and Guenther to craft something squarely aimed at the burgeoning US Disco market. The result was the cleverly titled, 15-minute plus

Wayne St. John

Two Hot for Love (1977) moaner-and-groaner inspired by Donna Summer's *Love to Love You Baby* (1975) that was divided into five key segments – "Four Play", two parts "Excitement", a major "Climax" and then "Resolution". Very much in the orgasmic Eurodisco mould of Cerrone and Love and Kisses, *Two Hot for Love* is a richly textured, power-driven instrumental peppered with multi-faceted breaks, waves of sparkling strings, popping electronics and sexy girlie vocals by Barbara Fry.

In much the same way RCA demanded an immediate album follow-up to *Theme from S.W.A.T.*, once *Two Hot for Love* became a massive club hit Cervantes wanted a THP Orchestra product in record stores within 24 hours. And that could happen in this fast and furious instance because of the *Early Riser* limited release situation. So the flipside of the *Two Hot for Love* album was constructed from slightly elongated versions of four cuts from the first album, *Early Riser, Manha de carnival, Dawn Patrol* and *Crazy, Crazy*.

"Once we started using vocalists in The THP Orchestra we needed to give them different things to do. Wayne St. John was the first and only male vocalist we worked with and when we found these great Dominic Bugatti and Frank Musker songs, *Fightin' on the Side of Love*

(1976) and *Something's Up (Love Me Like the First Time)* (1977), we gave them to him as a reward. Morrison had met Bruce Ley while the latter was working with the Canadian band Brass Union and together they wrote three of the four songs on the third THP Orchestra album *Tender Is the Night* (1978), released on milk-white vinyl.

Bearing little resemblance to the second album, the sound was smoother, snappier, not quite as frenetic with Helen and Phyllis Duncan's velvety vocals replacing Barbara Fry's raucous sensuality from the prior record (the Duncan Sisters would eventually be rewarded for their sterling work with two fine albums under their own names in 1979 and 1981). After their experience in Los Angeles at the Producers Workshop Studio for their monumental masterpiece *On Such a Winter's Day* (1978) by Grand Tour, Morrison and Guenther clearly were leaning towards the silky and slick pop artistry of in-house Butterfly hotshot producers Rinder and Lewis whose reputations were branding a new standard of Disco excellence.

From the opening *Weekend Two Step* with its super-bouncy, super-cute texture, rammed full of daring changes executed with dazzling flair, a sense of Disco fun remains front and centre throughout the entire album. Within its deliciously stretched out length Thoroughly Modern Morrison recalls the Charleston dance craze counterpointed with synth-scat vocals that make the most of the chorus breaks and sharp delivery. *Music Is All You Need* accents vocals within its Eurodisco ambience and *Tender Is the Night* has a complex arrangement that cuts through its high romantic illusion with a fast hustle beat and crisp breaks. *Half As Nice* adheres to Morrison and Guenther's delightful habit of doing sensationally slinky Disco cover versions of past pop successes. In this instance the UK Number 1 hit in 1969 for Amen Corner, originally written by Italian superstar Lucio Battisti for spaghetti pop diva Patty Pravo. The dynamic producing duo's refreshment of their studio session project was not only a pleasant surprise to the Discognoscenti, and a perfect example of the Canadian Disco sound, being a unique hybrid of American and European styles, it also resulted in a 13-week tenure in the 'Billboard' Disco Chart Top Twenty.

"We went to whatever studio our favourite engineers were working in. Our recorder/mixer of choice was George Semkiw (responsible for Tapps) so wherever he went we did too. We started out at RCA Studios in Toronto then moved to Phase One Studios when he became staff engineer there. Once he founded Amber Studios in the centre of town we shifted our productions accordingly. Getting a great engineer is key in the music business. George got to the point where he knew what I liked and didn't like instinctively and we had a shorthand understanding that needed no explanation. He got into my headspace over a period of time so when my fascination with the work of Giorgio Moroder required his type of Munich Machine isolationist atmosphere, George knew exactly what I meant".

Bowled over by the chart and sales success they were having on the Butterfly label with The THP Orchestra and Grand Tour, the harsh economic realities of the times soon set in when Morrison and Guenther turned up at the LA office to collect their royalties. "We arrived the day before they declared Chapter 11 bankruptcy. It was a serious amount of money too. Our biggest record ever was *Two Hot for Love* but in the end it represented our biggest loss. I always remember going to MIDEM (the yearly business event dedicated to the music industry that takes place in Cannes over five days) when we had been involved in Disco for a while and people started talking to us about what massive mansions we must be living in! In Disco at the time, most people got £125,000 to make an album and they'd put a hundred grand in their pocket and produce it for the rest. We did completely the reverse –

make the album for £100,000. What was important was, if an album had our names on it, we wanted to stand by it as a quality product. Our mindset was completely different to practically everyone else because we went out of our way to make our records as good as they could possibly be. Butterfly folding was a disaster for us and a memory that still pains me greatly".

Because of that grim situation, the next album by The THP Orchestra was released by Atlantic Records, and to distance themselves further from the defunct label the act bore the moniker of just THP. "The Orchestra trend was over, Disco was moving on and everyone was making subtle changes to their musical output. We had to be conscious of that too. We still had calls from US labels to make dance music, but we constantly strived to find different flavours and interpretations to separate them from the pack. It was very much a case of here's the transforming Disco genre, how do we shake it up while still remaining true to the four-to-the-floor origins?"

The answers to all those questions were contained in the fabulous *Good to Me* album, written by Morrison and Ley, and conducted and orchestrated by favoured arranger, Pete Pedersen. The first track is a freaky romp that, against a dense backdrop of superb instrumentation and insistent brass, broadcasts the collective mantra that *Dancin' Is Alright*. This philosophy is taken even further in *Dancin' Forever*, positing the notion that "Dancing's no craze, Dancin' forever is all we need". Combined with the gripping groove of *Two Hearts, One Love* and the lyrically mature *Who Do You Love*, *Good to Me* is a fitting swansong for the hugely directional THP project that accents the soul in its neo Salsoul feel, one that can clearly be seen as moving towards early HiNRG tropes.

Best seen as an extension of their work with The THP Orchestra, the feel of the *Headin' South* (1979) album by Southern Exposure is lighter in touch yet melodically larger-than-life with an instrumental dynamism that intensifies its sensual melodrama. With their preferred arranger/conductor Pete Pedersen back on board (he also co-wrote the songs with Duncan Sisters' maven Jaine Rodack), the album only contained four tracks. However each grooved between the seductively louche and the lush orchestral, never afraid to skirt mild titillation or sleaze.

One glimpse at the softcore album cover, complete with underwear clad model and peeping Tom, clearly sets the naughty but nice tone from the very beginning. And then there's the suggestive song titles themselves – *Headin' South*, of the border or the body? *On Our Way*, to ecstasy? *Love Is*, anything goes? As for *Tight Pants*, well, say no more!

With succinctly delivered vocals by Jimmie Jamison and one-time Elvin Bishop backup singer Debbie Cathey, who effortlessly meld in with the velvety vibes of the musical backing, *Headin' South* is the perfect *après* Disco pick-me-up. "Bodies can say so much… Language lies in a touch… Dancing uncovers two lovers by chance… Wanna dance?" Sure you do! Still involved in the industry he adores, Morrison is a music consultant for writers/producers Carl Sturken and Evan Rogers who scored hits for Christina Aguilera and produced Rihanna's debut album *Music of the Sun* (2005). Ian Guenther retired in the early 1990s having had more than enough of the false side of the business that he saw increasing over the years. "Disco still lives because people like to dance and will always like to dance".

Den Harrow

DONS OF DISCO (2018)

In 1989, during a live MTV performance by the European pop act Milli Vanilli, the backing track to their current hit *Girl You Know It's True* jammed and skipped. Within months the pretty boy duo Fab Morvan and Rob Pilatus were fired by their Boney M. producer Frank Farian, had no other recourse than admit to lip-synching to performances by less visually marketable singers and had to give their Grammy Award back. But three years before this scandal broke there was Den Harrow, an Italo Disco artist who sold over 20 million records without singing a note. It's this riveting story that trailer cutter king turned documentary director Jonathan Sutak tells in his sharply observed, exquisitely balanced portrait of borrowed fame, desperate public image and belated recognition.

Den Harrow consistently beat the likes of Michael Jackson, Madonna, George Michael and Duran Duran to the top of the European charts with his biggest hits *Future Brain* (1985), *Bad Boy* (1985), *Don't Break My Heart* (1987), and *Catch the Fox* (1987). Each a perfectly formed melange of Giorgio Moroder, Patrick Cowley and Mediterranean Disco produced by Roberto Turatti and Miki Chieregato. Virtually unknown in Great Britain or America, Italo Disco cut a swathe through Europe and far beyond with its mix of super-catchy synthpop performed by interchangeable session singers and musicians. It was a simpler time and many didn't care whether or not their favourite stars were not actually singing their own songs. As long as they looked good in the accompanying rock videos.

Enter hungry American-born singer/songwriter Thomas Beecher Hooker who lived in Italy and, after releasing the very *Pop Muzik* (1979) influenced gimmick Roller Disco single *Flip Over*, entered the country's banner music event, the Sanremo Song Festival in 1981 with the eliminated *Toccami*. Just after starring in **Jocks** (1984), he met Turatti and Chieregato who were looking for songs for their Den Harrow studio project. The name was chosen because it sounded like the Spanish for money, 'dinero'.

Hooker ended up singing most of the songs on the debut album *Overpower* (1985).

But the decision was made to have an Italian male model become the face of their music. They chose Stefano Zandri, who couldn't speak English but looked like the classic blond all-American sex symbol. It worked, Den Harrow became an Italo-Disco powerhouse and Hooker wrote and sang all the songs for the second album *Day By Day* (1987). By the time of the third release, the cheekily titled *Lies* (1988), Hooker's own album *Bad Reputation* (1988) and the single *Feeling Okay* had flopped, allegedly buried by his label Baby Records, worried people would connect the vocal similarity dots. Throughout this time Hooker also wrote songs for other artists, like *U.S.S.R.* (1986) for Eddy Huntington, and *Boom Boom, Let's Go Back to My Room* (1986) for Paul Lekakis, and formed the cover-version electronica combo Elastic Band with Euro-house producer brothers Paolo and Gianni Visnadi.

Hooker eventually went back to the States to become more widely known as the American photographer Thomas Barbèy. But then the rumour mill started and the online spats began. Zandri's fans became outraged by Hooker's claims he sang the Den Harrow vocals, while Hooker wanted his proper artistic due – and missing royalties. It was these internet arguments that Sutak came across on YouTube under the title 'Tom Hooker responds to Den Harrow's threats' and felt there was a compelling story to be told about the music industry and its manufactured pop. And indeed there was. Sutak brilliantly puts together a fascinating Disco discourse about the dispute but strikes an exact equilibrium between the warring ego halves who were fused into the superstar brand name. Weaving archival footage, rock videos and newly shot interviews, a well-considered portrayal emerges of two artists shafted by the showbiz system.

Naturally Hooker remains bitter about the deception and says he wants to put the record straight. Zandri doesn't ever deny Hooker's involvement but essentially says it doesn't matter because he's the face everyone knows and the personality that still sells out Disco live appearances, albeit to backing tracks. Will they ever come to terms with the whole controversy and gossip? It seems doubtful due to Zandri claiming he can actually sing and slagging off Hooker's lack of charisma forcing him into the studio shadows. In retaliation Hooker wrote the song *Incredible Idiot* (2014) for his Las Vegas parody act 'Tam Harrow'. Why can Hooker forgive Chieregato for cheating him out of cash, but not the self-aware Zandri? It's a knotty, twisty, bitchy, juicy saga about creative satisfaction with no real resolution but a superior glimpse into the *macchiato* mirrorball for all ardent Italo Disco lovers.

Patrick Adams

Patrick Adams

During his prolific and influential Disco career, producer Patrick Adams recorded over 300 of his songs and worked with everyone from Sister Sledge, Loleatta Holloway, Main Ingredient, Shannon, The Spinners, Gladys Knight, Candi Staton, Eddie Kendricks, Narada Michael Walden, Rick James, Chatelaine and Cloud One. He got his musical start in Harlem where he grew up four blocks from the famed Apollo theatre, first playing with The Sparks, then managing Black Ivory featuring Leroy Burgess, and producing their first record *Don't Turn Around* (1972). When it became a hit, Adams' studio days began in earnest and he became known as "The Prince of R&B", working with artists like JJ Barnes, Debbie Taylor and Astrud Gilberto.

Adams' main dance chance came when Marvin Schlachter from Prelude Records told him he wanted a Disco record fast to compete with other labels. The lightning quick album result was *Keep on Jumpin'* (1978) by Musique that reached No.1 on the Disco charts with *In the Bush*. He built on that success with Inner Life's *I'm Caught Up (In a One Night Love Affair)* (1979) and Wish featuring Fonda Rae's *Touch Me (All Night Long)* (1984), which has been sampled dozens of times along with Cathy Dennis' hit 1991 remake. While most traditional Disco used eight beats to a rhythmic sequence, Adams' brand was earthy and spontaneous, introducing weird time changes, adding and dropping bars to extraordinary effect, a technique he termed 'stop-breaking'. Other notable tracks include Bumble Bee Unlimited's *Love Bug* (1976), Universal Robot Band's *Dance and Shake Your Tambourine* (1976), Four Below's *My Baby's Got E.S.P.* (1976), Sine's *Just Let Me Do My Thing* (1978), Herbie Mann's *Super Mann* (1978) album, and Venus Dodson's ageless Disco classic *Night Rider* (1979).

My Italo Disco Top Ten

1) *Tonight* (1987) by Ken Laszlo
2) *Midnight Girl* (1988) by Italian Boys
3) *I Want an Illusion* (1986) by Squash Gang
4) *I'm Losing You* (1988) by Savage
5) *My World* (1989) by Sophie
6) *Do You Really Need Me* (1986) by K.B. Caps
7) *What My Heart Wanna Say* (1986) by Roger Meno
8) *Secrets* (1986) by Albert One
9) *More Than a Kiss* (1986) by Michael Bedford
10) *Whenever You Go* (1989) by Danuta

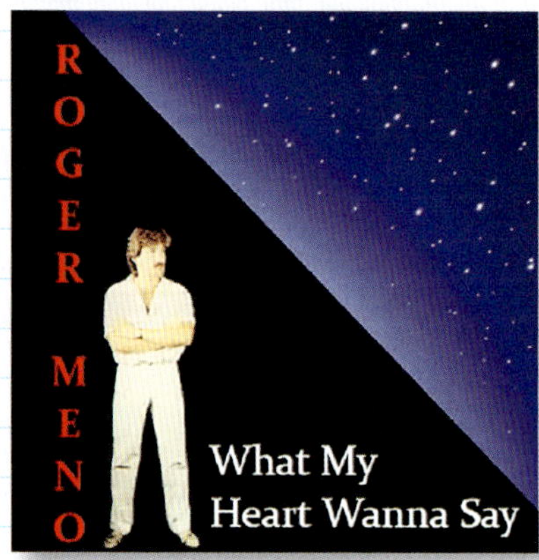

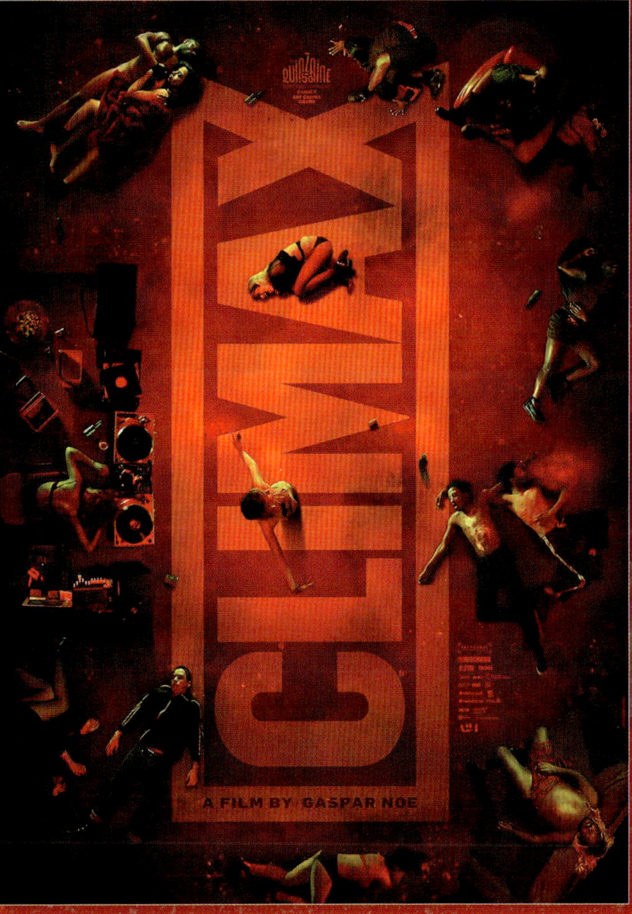

CLIMAX (2018)

Disco heaven and hell brilliantly epitomised by that incorrigible bad boy of French extreme cinema, Gaspar Noé, the director of **Seul contre tous/I Stand Alone** (1998), **Irreversible** (2002), **Enter the Void** (2009) and **Love** (2015). Set in 1996 and based on a supposedly true story/urban legend, this "**Fame** directed by the Marquis de Sade with a Steadicam" as one brilliant review put it after its showcase in the Cannes 2018 Director's Fortnight strand, is essentially a series of increasingly demented dance sequences depicting the glorious highs of musical frenzy and then the drug-fuelled destructive comedown. Basically a bad night out at your local club – or could it be the breakdown of harmony in multicultural France as hinted at by the tricolour flag Disco dressing? Whatever, a joyous celebration, social critique or pretentious commentary, Disconnoisseurs will adore the thrilling, intense and hypnotic gyrations to the classic full-length instrumental versions of Cerrone's *Supernature* (1977), Patrick Hernandez' *Born to Be Alive* (1979), and Giorgio Moroder's *Utopia – Me Giorgio* (1977).

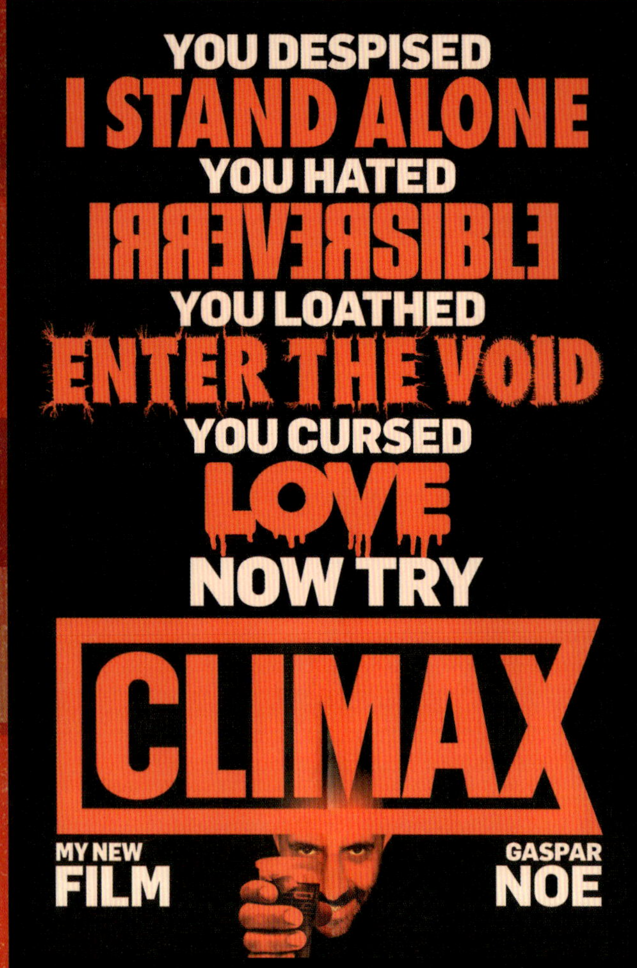

Beginning with the end credits over a bloodied body crawling through snow, **Climax** focuses on a dance troupe in training for an upcoming French and American tour. First we are privy to snippets of their taped auditions, played on a vintage television set surrounded by shelves of books, videos and DVDs. A perusal of the stacked titles reveals everything you need to know about the people interviewed, the trajectory of their planned 3-day practice session and hints of the horrors to come. Dario Argento's **Suspiria** (1977), Pier Paolo Pasolini's **Salò, or the 120 Days of Sodom** (1975), Masaki Kobayashi's **Harakiri** (1962), Andrzej Zulawski's **Possession** (1981), Luis Buñuel's **Un chien Andalou** (1929) and Rainer Werner Fassbinder's **Querelle** (1982) are among the movies, while the books include Franz Kafka's 'Metamorphosis', several studies of cinema auteurs like Fritz Lang and F.W. Murnau, Pierre Petit's sex-obsessed biography 'Molinier, une vie d'enfer' (1992), Romanian philosopher Emil Cioran's pessimistic views on humanity, and suicide manuals.

Once past these 'A Chorus Line' hopes/dreams/ambitions confessions, Noé shifts to the dingy closed-down boarding school assembly hall environs on the edge of a forest. There choreographer Selva (Sofia Boutella, the only professional actor in the cast) puts her ethnic and sexually diverse troupe through myriad dance styles

including, posing, strutting, hip-hop, voguing and sundry contortions as they rehearse a scorching performance to the Cerrone and Hernandez tracks. The spell-bindingly galvanising effect of this 30 minutes of solid sensuous ritual Disco is incredible as maestro Benoît Debie's continuous and fluid camerawork adds extra peripatetic flair to the stunningly rhythmic routines.

After all this turbo-charged exuberance, some of the spotlighted dancers get their characters nailed by Noé's forensic improvisation method. There's STD-ridden stud David (Romain Guillermic), Gazelle (Giselle Palmer) whose brother Taylor (Taylor Kastle) is perhaps a little too jealously protective of her date choices, Emmanuelle (Claude Gajan Maull) who unwisely brought her small son Tito along with her, zonked-out Daddy (DJ Kiddy Smile), virgin homosexual Rocket (Kendall Mugler) and German lesbian Psyche (Thea Carla Schøtt), who left Berlin's drug scene behind before she became another **Christiane F** (1981) casualty.

Then come the opening credits flashed in full Disco style as the 20 dancers descend on the buffet snack table and drink sangria. But someone has spiked the booze with LSD and what was supposed to be the carefree wind-down After Party becomes a fetishistic freak-out, a bacchanalian rave, an orgy of sex, violence, death and recrimination. Beginning in overhead jam-circle Busby Berkeley whirling dervish fashion and ending in dancing on the ceiling Sodom and Gomorrah style, thanks to genius Debie's upside down aesthetic, accompanied by the perfectly synched Moroder track and intercut, massive font proclamations like 'Life is a collective impossibility' and 'Existence is a fleeting illusion'.

Phew! Even though the ending hints at a possible **28 Days Later** (2002) scenario with the arrival of the authorities, Noé's throbbing musical is a Disco Paradise Lost going from thrilling delight to chilling debauchery. Electrifying throughout its entire visually arresting chaos, **Climax** also includes tracks by Soft Cell, Daft Punk, Thomas Bangalter, Gary Numan, M/A/R/R/S and The Rolling Stones. But it's the classic Disco trio that gets the longest airing and makes this brutal dance to the death an absolute must-see. Truly, an electrifying Disco Inferno.

Disco Top Twenty

Disco sparkles with melody, oozes emotion and screams extroverted fun. Both broad and multi-faceted, its dancefloor edges are defined by the artists who dared to dream bigger, better and brighter. This is my all-time Disco Top Twenty.

1) *Evita* (1979) by Festival, the magic combo of stage musical excellence and producer Boris Midney's craftsmanship.

4) *Love in C Minor* (1976) by Cerrone, a cascading symphony of mind-blowing orchestral delight.

2) *How Much, How Much I Love You* (1978) by Love and Kisses, producer Alec R. Costandinos' masterpiece of emotional melody, orchestration and arrangement.

5) *Forbidden Love Suite* (1979) by Madleen Kane, one of the best Disco lead-ins ever with a swirling sex and violins powerhouse finale.

3) *Follow Me* (1978) by Amanda Lear, the Queen of Eurodisco's magnum opus, a haunting and mesmerising Faustian fable.

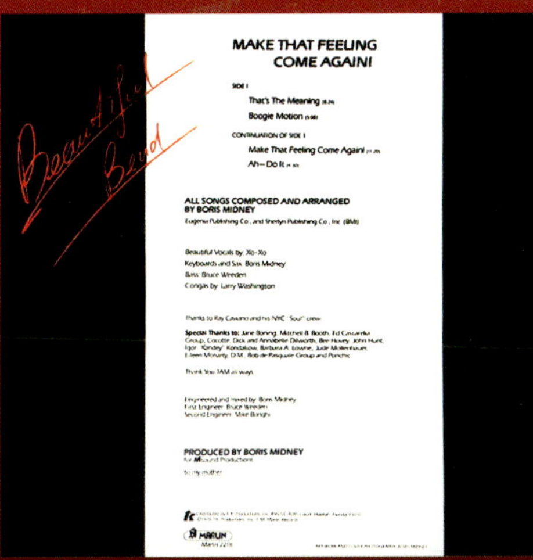

6) *Make That Feeling Come Again!* (1978) by Beautiful Bend, the classiest mind-altering Boris Midney production ever.

7) *Love Love Love/Still Not Over/On and On/Using You Suite* (1978) by the Michael Zager Band, dancing Disco soap opera perfection.

8) *Yes Sir, I Can Boogie* (1977) by Baccara, the quintessential, most haunting summer hit Eurodisco single ever.

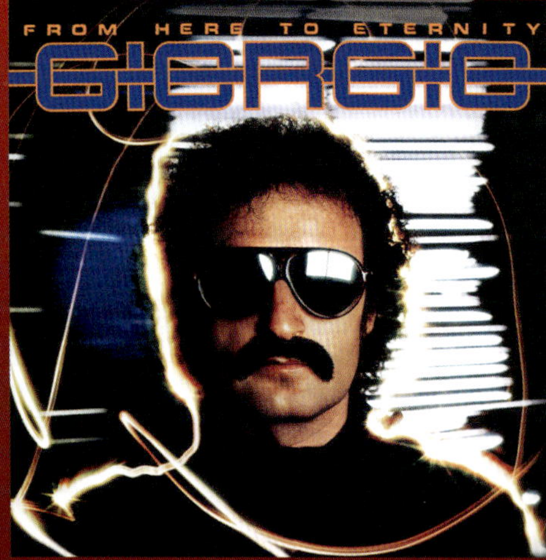

9) *From Here to Eternity* (1977) by Giorgio Moroder, the Munich Machine maven's seminal electronic venture.

10) *I Feel Love* (1977) by Donna Summer, the groundbreaking Giorgio Moroder production that changed Disco and music forever.

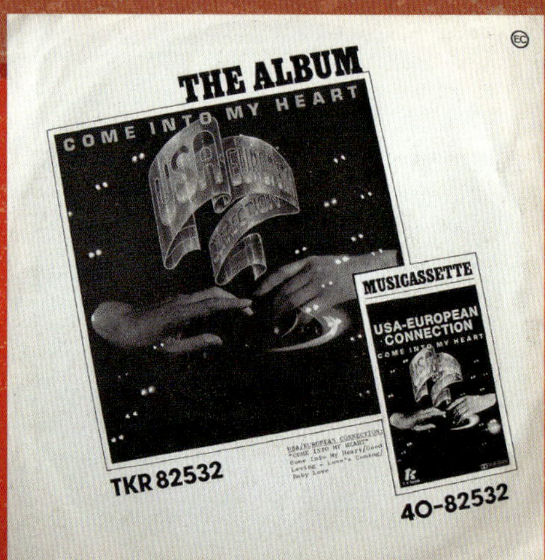

11) *Come Into My Heart* (1978) by USA-European Connection, another gold standard Boris Midney produced sensation.

12) *Midnight Love Affair Suite* (1976) by Carol Douglas, gentle, romantic loveliness in a spectacular dance package.

13) *Suite Seventeen* (1979) by Marlena Shaw, a soulful punch in the emotional gut.

14) *The Wizard of Oz* (1978) by Meco, a Hollywood chorus line extravaganza of the campest kind.

15) *Dance a Little Bit Closer* (1977) by Charo and The Salsoul Orchestra, the best example of the Salsoul sound and its sophisticated production.

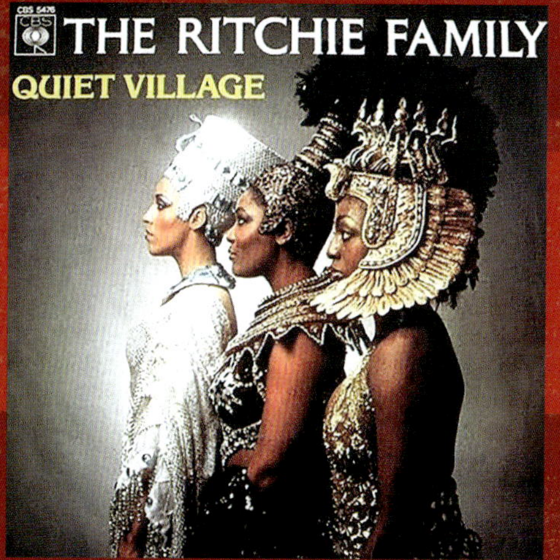

16) *Quiet Village* (1977) by The Ritchie Family, vintage Easy Listening meets gorgeous Disco arrangement.

17) *Romeo & Juliet* (1978) by Alec R. Costandinos and The Syncophonic Orchestra, the classic Shakespeare experience in 4/4 melodic complexity.

18) *Voyage* (1977) by Voyage, the ultimate Eurodisco world tour.

19) ***Cosmic Wind*** **(1977) by The Mike Theodore Orchestra, mind-blowing essential Disco cool.**

20) ***I Need a Man*** **(1975) by Grace Jones, the melodically precise crucial Gay Disco mantra.**

Disco Memo

Anarchy in the U.K., again!

I can never eradicate my Punk past and I honestly don't want to, but it never ceases to amaze me how it keeps reverberating back when least expected. If it isn't the infamous 'Forum' photo shoot, it's another ill-informed researcher wanting to put me in yet another documentary on how the Sex Pistols changed the world. They rocked mine that's for sure and I've carried that Punk attitude forward in everything I've ever done. Vivienne and Malcolm's son Joe Corré never forgot me being a constant on the scene but I was still surprised to be invited to join his unusual November 2016 protest against the capitalist establishment, which made a brand name out of Punk Britannia. I got it. I hated those merchandised Sid Vicious dolls too!

So just prior to him burning Punk memorabilia worth £5 million on a barge on the River Thames to de-celebrate the 40th Anniversary release of the *Anarchy in the U.K.* he asked me to join a number of his friends for afternoon Anarch-tea at the W Hotel in Leicester Square. We were filmed eating cupcakes iced with Mohican hairdos and safety pinned scones while discussing our memories. On my table was my **The Great Rock 'n' Roll Swindle** (1980) co-star Edward Tudor-Pole, my old Adam and the Ants mate Marco Pirroni and Joe, who made his own retail mark co-founding the upmarket lingerie brand Agent Provocateur in 1994.

Joe used to pop into SEX all the time when he was growing up, his younger half-brother Ben not so much. It was a terrific trip down memory lane for us all and I was surprised at how much flooded back as he set the stage to incinerate mannequins dressed in vintage Punkery, their faces masks of prominent British politicians. The bonds from that time are still so strong but although I haven't kept hold of too many Westwood designs, I still thought Joe's actions were pretty radical. And if he needed to clear his issue decks then all power to him, he plainly is indeed his mother and father's son as the socio-politico documentary record **Wake Up Punk** (2021) reveals in bondage spades.

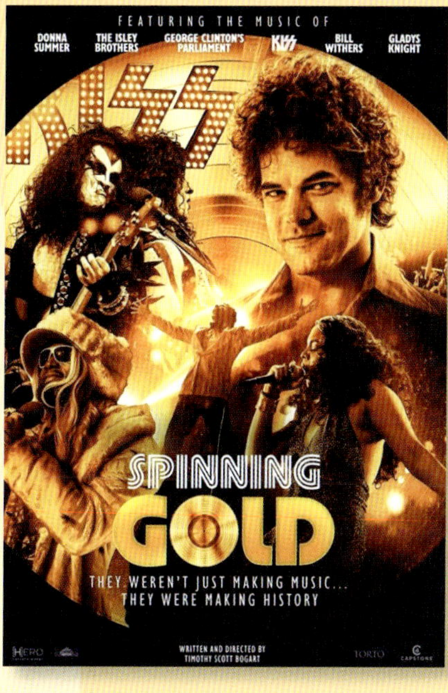

SPINNING GOLD (2023)

Although conceived in 1990, Timothy Scott Bogart first officially announced this biopic love letter to his late father Neil Bogart, the groundbreaking head of Casablanca Records, in 2011. It was to star Justin Timberlake as Bogart, and would also be the former NSYNC vocalist's first foray into feature producing alongside Boardwalk Films, the company owned by Timothy and his songwriting brother Evan 'Kidd' Bogart (he won a Grammy award for penning Beyonce's *Halo*, 2010). Samuel L. Jackson was down to play Parliament's George Clinton, Steven Strait as KISS frontman Gene Simmons, Neil Patrick Harris as KISS co-manager Bill Aucoin, Jazmine Sullivan as Gladys Knight and Jason Derulo as Ron Isley of The Isley Brothers.

Only the latter remained in the final movie produced by 29 people that Timothy dubbed "A saga about a young dreamer who started with nothing and came of age in the '60s and '70s, believing anything was possible and every risk was worth taking". Timberlake's excuse for backing out was that his music career became too busy and his schedule impossible to work around. By that time Bogart, after a long search for the right director that ultimately led to himself, said he wanted to go in a different direction anyway.

Adopting the 'breaking the fourth wall' technique so deathly dialogue of the "You're Donna Summer, singer of that massive Disco hit *I Feel Love*" variety is eschewed in favour of first person reportage, Bogart Jr.'s 142-minute agreeable hurtle through his dad's incredible life begins with him signing The Edwin Hawkins Singers for their 1967 song *Oh Happy Day* in a California church. It ends there too with him heading towards the bright white light behind the church doors as he dies of cancer in 1982. In between, and in no particular order, until the final 30 minutes when the Disco decade starts proper, we see Bogart (Jeremy Jordan), the Jewish dirt-poor son of Al Bogatz (Jason Isaacs), a gambling Brooklyn postal worker, continually reinventing himself via New York's School of the Performing Arts. After taxi-dancing, becoming a 'one-hit-wonder' teen idol as Neil Scott with *Cherry on Top* and serving an apprenticeship in payola as an MGM promotion man (Sam the Sham & the Pharaohs' 1964 hit *Wooly Bully* is the example given), he eventually found success with Buddah Records as the king of 1960s bubblegum pop.

Leaving Buddah to start Casablanca Records, its offices on Sunset Boulevard decorated like Rick's Café in the motion picture from which the label took its name, Bogart lurches from one disastrous launch to another in hock to

the Las Vegas mob. Despite Glam Rockers KISS clearly being arena crowdpleasers, no one buys their records. Parliament/Funkadelic is just too far out and refusing to go beyond its niche audience. And Giorgio Moroder's (Sebastian Maniscalco) protégée Donna Summer (Tayla Parx, Little Inez in **Hairspray**, 2007) can't get her single *Love to Love You Baby* (1975) heard on American radio. Until Bogart plays it continuously at a party and realises an extended 17-minute mix is what's needed. This last throw of the dice sparks instant chart and Disco success, followed by the triumphant KISS Army promotion, Parliament taking off too and Casablanca beginning its meteoric rise into music legend as a non-stop hit factory.

Engaging throughout, even if sometimes in a TV movie kind of way, **Spinning Gold** makes as many bold choices as it does bland and mawkish ones. Bogart's romantic life with wife Joyce (Lyndsy Fonseca) and lover Beth (Michelle Monaghan) is messily explained as it must have been in real life, although the "Sex before it was deadly" line tries papering over the puzzlement. The matter-of-fact cocaine use without any moralising is an interesting facet too. Kudos to Bogart for not whitewashing his father's clear flaws, making them the most interesting component of his character and the film itself. Did Tamla Motown head honcho Berry Gordy really hire goons to beat Bogart up after he put Gladys Knight (Ledisi) together with the mega-hit song *Midnight Train to Georgia* (1973), location changed from Houston? And the whole life/vinyl record is one long bumpy groove allegory does get a bit overused.

But the ace on the deck is Jeremy Jordan who is never less than incandescent as the Disco pioneer. With his Tony nominee acting chops, Broadway smarts, Grammy nominee know-how and 'Smash' TV series experience, he nails Bogart's addictive *joie de vivre*, enormous fiscal irresponsibility and high-wire risk-taking. Which all snaps into focus during the end credits roll where he thunderously performs the original theme song *Spinning Gold* on a stage with all the other actors chiming in with snippets of their featured tunes. Bogart opted for new versions of the famous hits that are meant to demonstrate how the most iconic songs went from demo phase to top of the 'Billboard' charts. So the Donna Summer Disco hits, all sung in live versions by Parx, are *Love to Love You Baby*, *Dim All the Lights* (1979), and *Bad Girls* (1979). The Village People are glimpsed rehearsing the choreography for *Y.M.C.A.* (1978), but the song is never heard due to the licensing issues rights holder Henri Belolo has always been so controlling over.

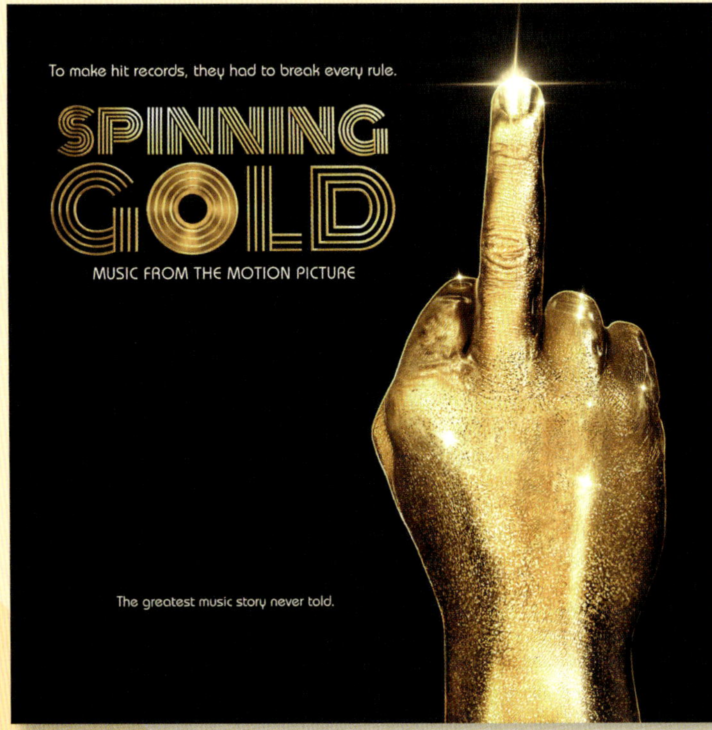

Is this the way it was: the crazy Swinging Sixties job-hopping through the Brill Building, the wild promotional excesses and the 1970s bacchanalian nights in Hollywood? Timothy Scott Bogart says he lived through it all so yes indeedy I suppose. Casablanca's ascent to the Disco stratosphere was relatively short, swift, substantial and hugely influential and that is well reflected in the tarnished gold spun here. He clearly loved his father and his visionary shrewdness because that adoration shines through with wonky precision in a project born out of many script drafts, multiple castings, colossal delays and distribution problems. So until someone else comes up with a more balanced view (unlikely!) of those decadent Casablanca Disco years, this will have to suffice as the Bogart record of first choice. And you know something, that's absolutely fine.

Queen of Fools

She was the Darlene Love of Disco. For just like that iconic Phil Spector muse, Jessica Williams was surprised to find her voice featured on numerous studio projects and barely got paid for any of them. One of the most accomplished artists in the history of Disco, Williams was signed to Motown records in 1973, where she learned microphone technique, and sang back-up vocals on Diana Ross' *Love Hangover* (1976) and Thelma Houston's *Don't Leave Me This Way* (1977). After Motown, Williams went to Polydor Records, Pattie Brooks was there, and she introduced her to her producer Simon Soussan. Soon Soussan started using her on a range of projects where her powerhouse vocalisations became an integral part of each.

The *Mr. Big Shot* (1979) album by The Simon Orchestra featured Williams on all cuts, the standout track being a cover version of the 1968 classic Dusty Springfield torch song *I Close My Eyes and Count to Ten. Dance My Way to Your Heart* (1979) by Romance and *Love and Desire* (1978) by Arpeggio put her instantly recognisable sound front and centre, so Soussan produced the *Queen of Fools* (1979) album for her to shine. And shine she did on the storming title track, a massive Gay Disco hit (twice, in a remixed 1983 version too) and the cover versions of *Love Masterpiece* and *Save the Last Dance for Me*.

But when it came to being paid royalties, it was alleged by Williams in her autobiography that creative accounting meant she was short changed; despite singing on every release under the Simon Soussan banner, she never got what she considered satisfactory compensation for her work. Putting it down to experience Williams let her resentment go and ended up providing background vocals for a host of artists like Engelbert Humperdinck, Connie Stevens, Ringo Starr, Lonnie Gordon and Martha Wash, and was a regular feature on 'The Arsenio Hall Show' (1989-94). In 1992 she released an unusual version of Donna Summer's *Sunset People* remixed by Rick Gianatos.

THE BEAST IN THE JUNGLE / LA BÊTE DANS LA JUNGLE (2023)

"Dance, no one can take that away from us" says one besotted clubber in Austrian director Patric Chiha's terrific adaptation of Henry James' classic 1903 novella 'The Beast in the Jungle'. By transporting the doomed existential love story from an upper class London house to the dizzying Disco environment, Chiha's fifth feature not only charts a cruel romance but also the progression of Disco through Italo Disco, Electro, Techno, Acid and Rave culture. It's an ambitious concept, one Chiha pulls off with acerbic aplomb as a catalogue of musical genres booms from the speakers practically non-stop on the superb soundtrack. Okay, director Ettore Scola's **Le Bal** (1983) got there first by depicting the passage of fifty years inside a Paris dance hall through moves, music and modes. And a few months after the French release of Chiha's stunner, director Bertrand Bonello also entered the flurry of concurrent James adaptations with **La bête/The Beast** (2023) starring Léa Seydoux and George MacKay in a futuristic Artificial Intelligence reading of the plot. Here, the time scale is between 1979 and 2004, which encompasses one of the best Disco years to DJ Sammy's *The Boys of Summer.*

At an unnamed Paris Disco (that is until the finale when 'The Beast in the Jungle' flashes in neon above the entrance), incurable Disco dancer May Bartram (Anaïs Demoustier) spies out-of-place wallflower John Marcher (Tom Mercier) whom she met years before at a Sardinade beach party. Back then John had confessed to May he was destined to do something extraordinary with his life. And he's still waiting for that major happening. Catastrophic, wonderful or both, he doesn't know what form it will take, but May decides to join him in his endless vigil. As the years pass by within the club interior – one particular 360 degree pan captures time fleeting impressively – May moves from a bisexual relationship with graphic designer Alice (Sophie Demeyer) to marriage with Pierre (Martin Vischer), who loves her unconditionally, as monumental events continue to unfold on the world stage.

From President François Mitterand's social-changing election in 1981, the onset of the AIDS epidemic heralded by Klaus Nomi's death in 1983, and May's 25th and 40th birthdays to the fall of the Berlin Wall in 1989, New Year's Eve 1999 and the 9/11 terrorists attacks in 2001, everything changes dance and fashion-wise. Except, that is, John idly waiting for his personal prophecy to materialise.

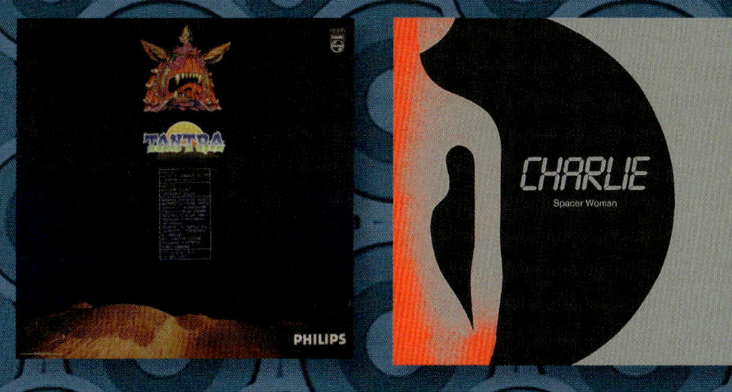

It never does of course – until May suddenly dies and John finally realises the cataclysmic experience should have been their grand love affair, now forever sadly unrequited. John's remote indifference to anything but his vain self-glorification and emotional obsession has meant he missed out on everything true human existence has to offer.

Narrated by La Physionomiste (a glowering and incomparable Béatrice Dalle, star of Chiha's **Domaine**, 2009) in charge of the club's velvet ropes and deciding those worthy of entrance every Saturday night, **The Beast in the Jungle** is an affecting remastered parable on the meaning of life. With Chiha's focus on busy feet walking, inquisitive hands clutching banisters and dancers cavorting in ecstasy, the best years of John's life evaporate as his preposterous sense of foreboding obliterates all the good surrounding him until it's too late. Mercier is perfect as the bland, bereft fatalist of James' creation where internal states of mind and social dynamics rule. Demoustier gives her hedonistic demimonde character the right dose of enigmatic power to convince she's under John's philosophical spell to the detriment of her own needs and the disbelief of her friends. Time and time again the movie hits a raw nerve that forms into a bizarre jigsaw of mood, atmosphere and melancholy, especially when the star-crossed couple only touch each other just before the end when they attempt to dance for the first time.

There is nowhere else but the Disco in **The Beast in the Jungle** where the lights and décor may alter but Monsieur Pipi (Pedro Cabanas) is always on hand in the unisex toilets to eavesdrop on the secrets and lies. Beginning with a huge amount of narrative told while Tantra's epic Disco track *Hills of Katmandu* booms out for a lengthy needle drop, segueing into a super swathe of Charlie's Italo Disco cut *Spacer Woman* (1983), the soundtrack then becomes the domain of French musicians Yelli Yelli (who composed **Domaine** under the alias Milkymee) and Florent Charissoux (Milkymee guitarist and vocalist) until a Tantra reprise at a nostalgic birthday party. *Dancing in Water, First Floor, The Drive, Moon Group, Night, The Race, Come to Blows, Got to Have, Reunion, You, The Beast, Warehouse War, Flutter, Have You Forgotten* and a Disco *Jingle Bells* are all clever cuts from Yelli Yelli and Charissoux encompassing every dance style of the latter part of the 20th Century.

"I love it when life is like a novel", says May at one particular meta point in **The Beast in the Jungle**. Most will love this art-house Berlin Film Festival attraction because life is shown as a perpetual Disco experience where everyone just continues to sway under swirling lights as the fashions change from glitter, moustaches and drag to macho, topless and stark. Dreams maybe unrealised as the world continually moves on, but the Disco community always survives inside this full-throttle musical ride, brilliantly choreographed by Chiha.

West End Records

Their offices had the same address as Studio 54 and for a while their output hit the Disco heights with an eclectic mix of Italian movie soundtracks and best-selling 12-inch releases. West End Records was formed in 1976 by Mel Cheren and Ed Kushins, both colleagues at Scepter Records, the original home of Dionne Warwick, The Shirelles and Tammi Terrell. Scepter closed down in 1975 after putting their toes in the Disco waters with B.T. Express (*Express* was their No.1 'Billboard' Disco Chart hit in 1974) and Cheren's pioneering idea of putting instrumental versions of a song on the B-side of singles earned the label the 'Trendsetter of the Year' Award from 'Billboard' in 1974.

The duo's first West End release in 1976 was the Italian soundtrack album for the Dino Risi directed **Sessomatto/ How Funny Can Sex Be?** (1973) composed by Armando Trovajoli, a master of the spaghetti erotic comedy genre. Two cuts from the cult movie, the title track *Sessomatto* and *Kinky Peanuts*, actually became the first ports of call for early hip-hop DJs to scratch from with their Manu Dibango influences and groovy Moog electronics. West End would also release the **Black Emanuelle** (1975) soundtrack by Nico Fidenco in the hope the infectious sambas would also hit Disco paydirt.

ORIGINAL MOTION PICTURE SOUNDTRACK

how funny can sex be?

STARRING

GIANCARLO GIANNINI · LAURA ANTONELLI

Mel Cheren and Grace Jones

Because his partner was Michael Brody, owner of the landmark Paradise Garage club, which he financially backed, Cheren had his finger mainly on the pulse of what was hot in Disco terms. Taana Gardner was a case in point as Paradise Garage DJ Larry Levan loved her voice, relentlessly played her records and literally made her a Disco star with *Work That Body, When You Touch Me* (both 1979) and especially the slower tempo *Heartbeat* (1981), all Top Ten 'Billboard' Chart Disco hits. *Heartbeat* is the song sampled the most from the West End catalogue, for example by Jamaican dance hall artist Ini Kamoze for *Here Comes the Hot Stepper* (1994), used on the soundtrack of Robert Altman's **Prêt-à-Porter** (1994).

West End's biggest Disco hit though was the 'Billboard' chart topper *Hot Shot* (1978) by Karen Young, which sold close to a record-busting million 12-inch singles. Other West End hits included Loose Joints' *Is It All Over My Face?* (1980) comprising of a female vocal A-side remixed

by Larry Levan and a male vocal B-side, NYC Peech Boys' *Don't Make Me Wait* (1982), Mahogany featuring Bernice Watkins' *Ride on the Rhythm* (1982), Bombers' *(Everybody) Get Dancin'* (1979), Michele's *Magic Love* (1977) album and ex-Ritchie Family member Ednah Holt's *Serious, Sirius Space Party* (1981).

West End as an independent New York label always remained on the cutting edge because being so close to the Manhattan action and vital words on the streets meant the excitement could transfer quickly from dance floor to studio project. Add in the unknown factor of undying love for the music and that's why Cheren and Kushins' label thrived through the darker days of Disco. An activist and a leading light in the fight against AIDS, Cheren wrote the autobiography 'My Life and the Paradise Garage: Keep on Dancin' (2000), which was turned into the acceptable Gene Graham directed documentary **The Godfather of Disco** (2007).

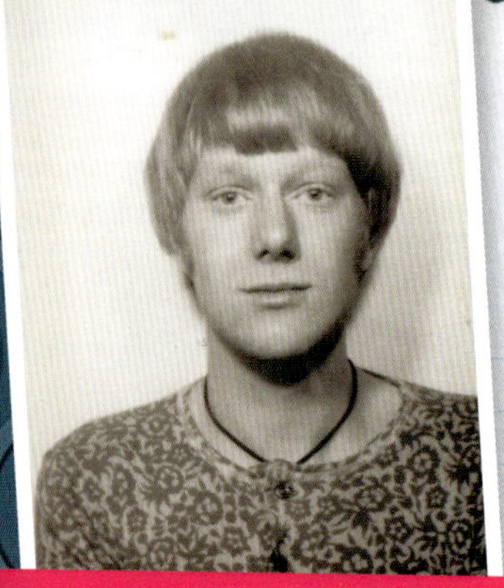

Alan Jones at 16, wearing the latest in mid-1960s high fashion – a purple 'Grandad' shirt bought at one of the first boutiques in Portsmouth market.

Disco Memo

This Is It

What have I learnt being in the film business now for nearly five decades? That novelist, playwright, and screenwriter William Goldman said it best in the opening sentence of his 1983 memoir 'Adventures in the Screen Trade' – "Nobody knows anything"! Aside from that all-encompassing pearl of wisdom there are a few lessons I feel I ought to pass down. Everyone told me when I first became a genre journalist that "It's not what you know, it's who you know". Not entirely true. I've found it's who knows you and what they feel you can do for them. I can honestly say I've never had to ask for a job in my life. I've either drifted accidentally into opportunities, fallen on my feet or simply taken advantage of every chance given to me – the harder you work the luckier you really do get. I made sure I could say yes to every job instantly. Can you go to Zagreb tomorrow to cover **Transylvania 6-5000** (1985) and interview up-and-coming actor Jeff Goldblum? Sure. A plane is leaving tonight for Dublin as Clive Barker wants you on the set of **Rawhead Rex** (1986) tomorrow, do you want to be on it? Of course. That's how I got so well known by everyone in the business because despite what anyone says it's a very small world.

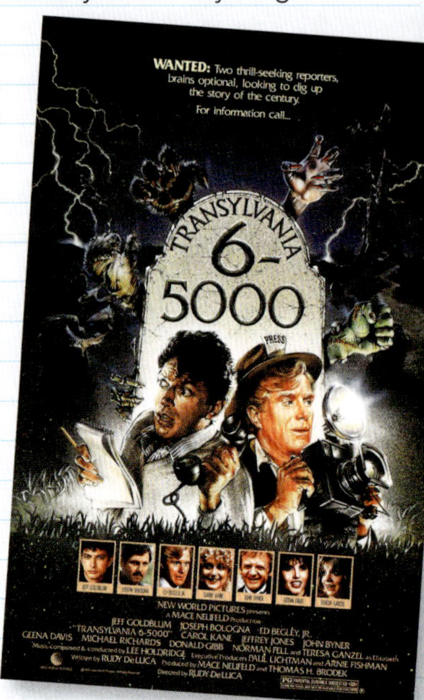

– People who work in the film industry rarely see any films. The times I've interviewed really prominent creatives who say they never go to the cinema. And while I have become close friends to many directors and stars you must always remember that they are an entirely different breed and liable to overreact to the silliest things. It always used to make me laugh when fellow journalists on locations or junkets would say to the talent, "I met you two/three/four (delete where applicable) years ago on (insert title here)…" and honestly expect them to remember even if they do say "Of course". Because they really don't. I spent every hour of every day with Christopher Lambert on **Highlander II: The Quickening** (1991) for a month talking about everything. A few weeks after shooting wrapped, he barely remembered me from Adam. Treat celebrities like strangers and you will never be disappointed because I've had so many of my contemporaries make the mistake of thinking they actually are friends.

– Everything is a drama in publicity, until it isn't. I can recall so many instances where a lowly PR person has gone off the deep end over absolutely nothing. OMG, Christopher Walken has lost a suitcase at Venice Airport. It's a disaster of monumental proportions! Lady Lee, Christopher's wife, has misplaced her hatbox and is beside herself. My first question there was, whoever still uses hatboxes? Then there was the time a huge comedy star asked if I'd mind a 24-hour delay for a TV interview that lasted 5 minutes! Because I was being paid quite a lot of money to do it, I agreed, but when his personal assistant told me how grateful I should be, I lost it, shouted at her remorselessly, and almost caused an international incident for being so 'difficult'. The arrant stupidity of the movie business really is something to behold and now with so much more at stake it's even worse.

– When writing bad reviews it's probably best to start on a positive note no matter how much you hate a movie. I've found that always works as the talent does then have something tenuous to cling to. My worst reviewing error?

I saw a preview of a 1984 A.I. romance and called up an interested friend to tell him all about it. He wasn't in, so I read my entire 'Starburst' review down the phone to his answering machine. Unbeknownst to me, the reason why my friend wanted to know what it was like was because he was just about to work with the director. And that director was with him when he later played his recorded messages back. Needless to say he didn't get the job and I got an awful call from the press office in question.

– Never be literal in reviews. When I saw **Friday the 13th Part VIII: Jason Takes Manhattan** (1989) actually in Manhattan, in a Times Square fleapit three months before its UK release, at one key shock, part of the theatre ceiling fell on top of me and I leapt out of my seat. I put that in my critique saying I had a heart attack at that moment. For ages afterwards readers actually thought I'd been hospitalised with a heart condition. And that was in the days before social media. I can't imagine how that would play out now.

– Everyone's view is valid. Just because I don't like a movie doesn't mean to say others won't. My analysis is my observation alone. If you agree with me, great, if you don't, fine. I won't quarrel with anyone over the merits of any film, except Mark Kermode because that's more like a sport! I can't tell you how many times I've argued with distributors over a bad review I gave their latest release, ending up telling them that because I went to see everything no matter what, that's what all genre fans do. It's the checklist mentality in action. FrightFest has really brought that ethos more to the fore than ever too.

– You always have to be honest in your reviews even if it goes against the grain. Today's default position for the multitude of online critics is over praising something just because they saw it first at a preview and were thrilled by that fact alone. It's the "No, really this Marvel movie is the best one ever!" effect, especially now film critics are being sidelined for 'fan' or 'influencer' screenings where everyone has made up their positive minds anyway. You will only have a long career by being truthful; if it gets known you are a PR whore, it's over. Future film reviewers, you have been warned!

Alan Jones with the book before this one: 30 years of my reviewing life condensed into the hefty volume 'Starburst: The Complete Alan Jones Film Reviews 1977-2008'.

– Have I made a difference to people's lives? Seems like it. If one person went to see – pick any movie – based on what I said rather than ignore it, then job done. Many over the years have told me how much they appreciated my 'Starburst' review column because it set their lives on an invaluable genre trajectory. When I interviewed Eric Valette, the director of **Maléfique**, at Cannes in 2002, the first thing he said to me was it was an honour to be interviewed by the person whose features he'd read in the French magazine 'L'Ecran Fantastique' when he was eight years old. I felt both thrilled and ancient at the same time, but happy I clearly played an important part in his eventual career choice.

THE ALAN JONES HALL OF FAME

Albin Grau

AJ with Christian Bale in Sitges 1996.

AJ with Udo Kier on the *Shadow of the Vampire* set in Luxembourg.

AJ with Spanish director Narciso Ibáñez Serrador.

AJ with Richard Lynch.

AJ with Molly Parker, star of *Kissed*.

AJ with Piper Laurie in Sitges, 1997.

AJ with Lance Henriksen.

AJ with Fay Wray.

Nigel Floyd, AJ and John Carpenter at our Fantasm 1994 event at the NFT.

Michael Ironside and AJ on the *Highlander II* set.

AJ with Alex Winter.

AJ with Kevin Sorbo on the Bratislava set of *Kull the Conqueror*.

Index of Films and TV

Titles highlighted in **bold** are reviewed in depth

Index of Songs and Album Titles

Index of People and Groups

Page numbers highlighted in **bold** refer to photographs